STRE [ ]

Shropshire

Bridgnorth, Ludlow, Oswestry, Shrewsbury, Telford, Wrexham

First published in 2003 by

Philip's, a division of
Octopus Publishing Group Ltd
www.octopusbooks.co.uk
2–4 Heron Quays, London E14 4JP
An Hachette Livre UK Company
www.hachettelivre.co.uk

Second edition 2008
First impression 2008
SHRBA

ISBN 978-0-540-09053-2 (pocket)

© Philip's 2008

Ordnance Survey®

This product includes mapping data licensed from Ordnance Survey®, with the permission of the Controller of Her Majesty's Stationery Office.

© Crown copyright 2008. All rights reserved. Licence number 100011710

Data for the speed cameras provided by PocketGPSWorld.com Ltd.

Ordnance Survey and the OS symbol are registered trademarks of Ordnance Survey, the national mapping agency of Great Britain

Printed and bound in China by Toppan

Contents

II **List of mobile speed cameras**

III **Key to map symbols**

IV **Key to map pages**

VI **Route planning**

X **Administrative and Postcode boundaries**

1 **Street maps** at 2⅔ inches to 1 mile

167 **Street maps** at 1⅓ inches to 1 mile

216 **Street maps** at 2⅔ inches to 1 mile

221 **Town map** of Wrexham

222 **Index** of towns, villages, streets, hospitals, industrial estates, railway stations, schools, shopping centres universities and places of interest

Digital Data

The exceptionally high-quality mapping found in this atlas is available as digital data in TIFF format, which is easily convertible to other bitmapped (raster) image formats.

The index is also available in digital form as a standard database table. It contains all the details found in the printed index together with the National Grid reference for the map square in which each entry is named.

For further information and to discuss your requirements, please contact james.mann@philips-maps.co.uk

On-line route planner

For detailed driving directions and estimated driving times visit our free route planner at www.philips-maps.co.uk

Mobile speed cameras

The vast majority of speed cameras used on Britain's roads are operated by safety camera partnerships. These comprise local authorities, the police, Her Majesty's Court Service (HMCS) and the Highways Agency.

This table lists the sites where each safety camera partnership may enforce speed limits

through the use of mobile cameras or detectors. These are usually set up on the roadside or a bridge spanning the road and operated by a police or civilian enforcement officer. The speed limit at each site (if available) is shown in red type, followed by the approximate location in black type.

A5
NSL Aston
NSL Gobowen, Moreton Bridge
60 Montford Bridge
NSL West Felton

A41
40,NSL Albrighton Bypass
NSL Chetwynd nr Newport
40 Tern Hill
NSL Whitchurch Bypass

A49
30 Dorrington

A442
40 Crudgington

A456
30 Newnham Bridge

A458
40 Morville
30 Much Wenlock

A528
30 Shrewsbury, Ellesmere Rd

A5064
30 Shrewsbury, London Rd

B4368
40 Hungerford

B4373
40 Telford, Castlefields Way
40 Telford, Wrockwardine Wood Way

B5060
40 Telford, Castle Farm Way

B5062
60 Newport, Edgmond Rd
30 Shrewsbury, Sundorne Rd

UNCLASSIFIED
30 Newport, Wellington Rd
30 Shrewsbury, Monkmoor Rd
30 Shrewsbury, Longden Rd (Rural)
30 Telford, Britannia Way
40 Telford, Stafford Park 1

Key to map symbols

III

Motorway with junction number	
Primary route – dual/single carriageway	
A road – dual/single carriageway	
B road – dual/single carriageway	
Minor road – dual/single carriageway	
Other minor road – dual/single carriageway	
Road under construction	
Tunnel, covered road	
Speed cameras - single, multiple	
Rural track, private road or narrow road in urban area	
Gate or obstruction to traffic (restrictions may not apply at all times or to all vehicles)	
Path, bridleway, byway open to all traffic, road used as a public path	
Pedestrianised area	
DY7 Postcode boundaries	
County and unitary authority boundaries	
Railway, tunnel, railway under construction	
Tramway, tramway under construction	
Miniature railway	
Railway station	
Walsall Private railway station	
South Shields Metro station	
Tram stop, tram stop under construction	
Bus, coach station	

Acad	Academy	Inst	Institute	Recn Gd	Recreation Ground
Allot Gdns	Allotments	Ct	Law Court		
Cemy	Cemetery	L Ctr	Leisure Centre	Resr	Reservoir
C Ctr	Civic Centre	LC	Level Crossing	Ret Pk	Retail Park
CH	Club House	Liby	Library	Sch	School
Coll	College	Mkt	Market	Sh Ctr	Shopping Centre
Crem	Crematorium	Meml	Memorial	TH	Town Hall/House
Ent	Enterprise	Mon	Monument	Trad Est	Trading Estate
Ex H	Exhibition Hall	Mus	Museum	Univ	University
Ind Est	Industrial Estate	Obsy	Observatory	W Twr	Water Tower
IRB Sta	Inshore Rescue Boat Station	Pal	Royal Palace	Wks	Works
		PH	Public House	YH	Youth Hostel

Ambulance station	
Coastguard station	
Fire station	
Police station	
Accident and Emergency entrance to hospital	
H Hospital	
+ Place of worship	
Information Centre (open all year)	
Shopping Centre	
P Parking	
P&R Park and Ride	
PO Post Office	
Camping site	
Caravan site	
Golf course	
Picnic site	
Prim Sch Important buildings, schools, colleges, universities and hospitals	
Built up area	
Woods	
River Ouse Tidal water, water name	
Non-tidal water – lake, river, canal or stream	
Lock, weir, tunnel	
Church Non-Roman antiquity	
ROMAN FORT Roman antiquity	
94 / 164 Adjoining page indicators and overlap bands The colour of the arrow and the band indicates the scale of the adjoining or overlapping page (see scales below)	

■ The small numbers around the edges of the maps identify the 1 kilometre National Grid lines ■ The dark grey border on the inside edge of some pages indicates that the mapping does not continue onto the adjacent page

The scale of the maps on the pages numbered in blue is 4.2 cm to 1 km • 2⅔ inches to 1 mile • 1: 23810

0	¼	½	¾	1 mile
0	250m	500m	750m	1 kilometre

The scale of the maps on pages numbered in green is 2.1 cm to 1 km • 1⅓ inches to 1 mile • 1: 47620

0	¼	½	¾	1 mile
0	250m	500m 750m	1 kilometre	

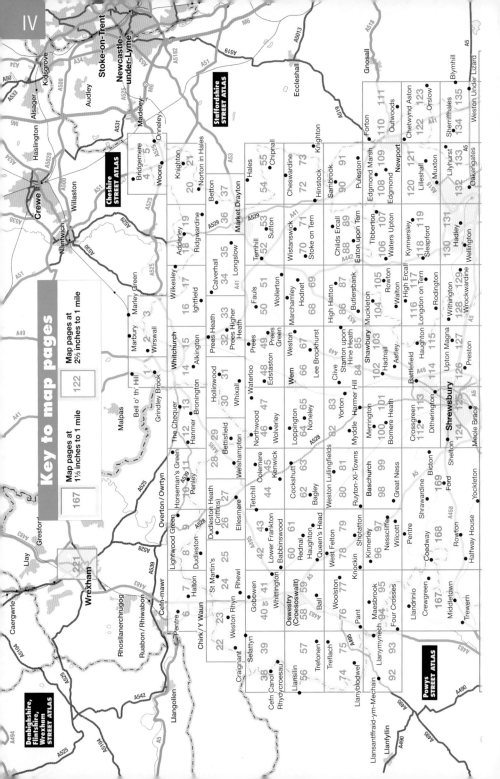

Key to map pages

Map pages at 1½ inches to 1 mile
167

Map pages at 2⅓ inches to 1 mile
122

Cheshire STREET ATLAS

Staffordshire STREET ATLAS

Denbighshire, Flintshire, Wrexham STREET ATLAS

Powys STREET ATLAS

Stoke-on-Trent
Newcastle-under-Lyme
Kidsgrove
Alsager
Audley
Haslington
Willaston
Crewe
Nantwich
Eccleshall
Gnosall
Blymhill
Weston Under Lizard
Chetwynd Aston
Orslow
Outwoods
Sherriffhales
Forton
Newport
Edgmond Marsh
Edgmond
Knighton
Chipnall
Cheswardine
Hinstock
Sambrook
Puleston
Muxton
Lilleshall
Lilyhurst
Oakengates
Hadley
Wellington
Wrockwardine
Admaston
Rodington
Waters Upton
Childs Ercall
Stoke on Tern
Eaton upon Tern
Tibberton
Kynnersley
Sleapford
High Ercall
Walton
Longdon on Tern
Haughton
Withington
Upton Magna
Preston
Rowton
High Hatton
Buttersbank
Muckleton
Shawbury
Hadnall
Astley
Stanton upon Hine Heath
Clive
Harmer Hill
Myddle
Yorton
Merrington
Battlefield
Crossgreen
Ditherington
Shelton
Meole Brace
Shrewsbury
Bicton
Shrawardine
Ford
Montford
Yockleton
Coedway
Rowton
Halfway House
Pentre
Llandrinio
Crewgreen
Middletown
Trewern
Llanymynech
Four Crosses
Llanyblodwel
Llansantffraid-ym-Mechain
Llanfyllin
Maesbrook
Kinnerley
Nesscliffe
Wilcott
Knockin
Woolston
Pant
Ball
Treflach
Trefonen
Llanforda
Oswestry (Croesoswallt)
Gobowen
Whittington
St Martin's
Weston Rhyn
Rhewl
Selattyn
Craignant
Cefn Canol
Rhydycroesau
Llansilin
Llanblodwel
Hengoed
Welshampton
Bettisfield
Hanmer
Bronington
Alkington
Whixall
Waterloo
Edstaston
Prees
Prees Green
Fauls
Wollerton
Hodnet
Marchamley
Weston
Lee Brockhurst
Noneley
Loppington
Wem
Higher Heath
Prees Heath
Whitchurch
Ightfield
Calverhall
Longslow
A41
Market Drayton
Ternhill
Sutton
Wistanswick
Hales
Betton
Norton in Hales
Knighton
Adderley
Ridgwardine
Wilkesley
Onneley
Woore
Madeley
Bridgemere
Marley Green
Marbury
Wirswall
Bell o' th' Hill
Grindley Brook
The Chequer
Malpas
Tetchill
Ellesmere
Dudleston Heath (Criftins)
Dudleston
Overton/Owrtyn
Horseman's Green
Penley
Lightwood Green
Halton
Cefn-mawr
Ruabon/Rhiwabon
Rhosllanerchrugog
Chirk/Y Waun
Llangollen
Wrexham
Gresford
Llay
Caergwrle

1
2
3
4
5
6
7
8
9
10
11
12
13
14
15
16
17
18
19
20
21
22
23
24
25
26
27
28
29
30
31
32
33
34
35
36
37
38
39
40
41
42
43
44
45
46
47
48
49
50
51
52
53
54
55
56
57
58
59
60
61
62
63
64
65
66
67
68
69
70
71
72
73
74
75
76
77
78
79
80
81
82
83
84
85
86
87
88
89
90
91
92
93
94
95
96
97
98
99
100
101
102
103
104
105
106
107
108
109
110
111
112
113
114
115
116
117
118
119
120
121
122
123
124
125
126
127
128
129
130
131
132
133
134
135
167
168
169
221

M54

Codsall
Bishops Wood 148
M6
A41

Nurton 166
Pattingham
Swindon
Wombourne
Wombourne
Seisdon 190

Kidderminster
A449
A451
A442
A442
A458
M5

Albrighton
Tong 147
Boningale 157
56
166
Pattingham

Beckbury
Albrighton 56 157
Burnhill Green 165
Ackleton 164
Worfield
Claverley
Bobbington
189
Stanmore
Claverley

Shifnal 145
146
Kemberton 155
Ryton 163
Grindle
Norton 162
Crowgreaves
Astley Abbotts 188
Stanmore 219
Eardington
Quatt
Hampton 200
Alveley
Romsley
Shatterford
Trimpley 211
Bewdley
Stourport on Severn

Worcestershire STREET ATLAS

A442
A451
A443
A443

Telford
Madeley 144
53
Strichley 154
Ironbridge 152
Wyke 151
Broseley 161
Willey
Acton Round 187
Morville
Chetton
Neenton 199
Sidbury
Stottesdon
Oreton
Cleobury Mortimer 209
Lem Hill
Buttonoak
Kinlet 210
Woodhill
Chelmarsh 200

Lawley 142 143
Little Wenlock
Shelnton 150
Wyke 151 160
Harley 159
Bourton
Brockton
Stanton Long
Ditton Priors
Cockshutford
Burwarton 198
Lindridge
Newnham Bridge
Boraston
Tenbury Wells 220
215
A4117

Uppington 140 141
Donnington
Buildwas 150
Much Wenlock 158
149
Cressage
Harley 159
186
Nash
Cleehill
Cleeton St Mary 208
Doddington
Cleehill 214
Bromdon
213

Atcham 138 139
Cross Houses
Pitchford 179
Ruckley
Plaish
Holdgate
Munslow 197
Clee St Margaret
Bitterley
Caynham
213
Brimfield
A456
A49

Bayston Hill 136 137
Annscroft
Stapleton
Dorrington 178
Longnor
Acton Burnell 179
Leebotwood
Cardington 185
Wall under Heywood
Shipton
Alcaston
Diddlebury
Selton
Stanton Lacy 207
Onibury
Ludlow 217
Ludford
Ashford Bowdler 212
Batchott
Richards Castle
Orleton

Hanwood
Longden 173
Pontesbury
Habberley
Pickiescott
177
Ratlinghope
Wentnor
Minton 183
Marshbrook
Craven Arms 195
Broome
Clungunford
Sheiderton
Leintwardine 205
Adforton
A4110

Westbury
Rowley 171
Aston Rogers 172
Minsterley
Snailbeach
Hope
Stiperstones
176
Lydham 182
Totterton
Lydbury North
Hopesay
Kempton 194
Clunbury
Clunton
Hoptonheath
Bucknell 204
Brampton Bryan
A4113

Welshpool (Trallwng) 170
Kingswood
Marton
Worthen
Rorrington
The Marsh 175
Priest Weston
Snead
Bishop's Castle
Acton
Whitcott Keysett
Clun 193
Churchbank
Purlogue
Knucklas 203
Stowe
Knighton/ Tref-y-Clawdd

Forden/Ffodun
Chirbury 174
Montgomery
Pentre
181
Mardu
Newcastle 192
Llanfair Waterdine
Llangunllo
202

Pentrehyling
City 180

Anchor
191
Felindre
Beguildy

Presteigne
A488

Scale
0 | 5 | 10 | 15 km
0 | 5 | 10 miles

Herefordshire, Monmouthshire STREET ATLAS

Route planning

Scale

| 0 | | | | | 5 | | | | | 10 km |
| 0 | 1 | 2 | 3 | 4 | 5 | | 6 miles |

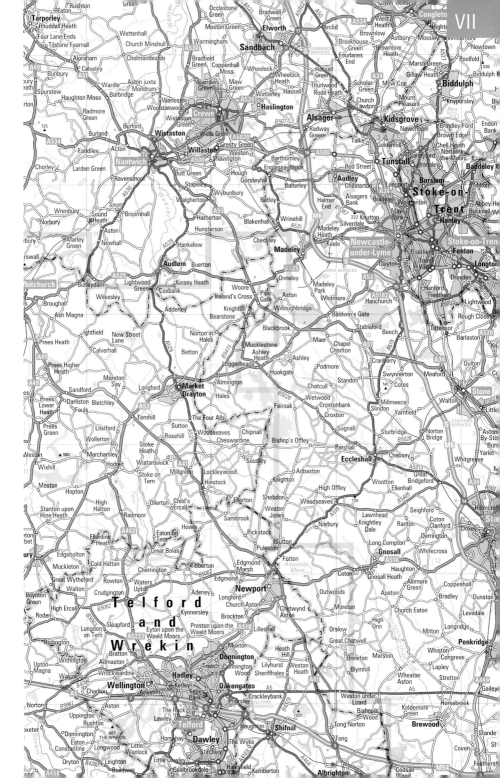

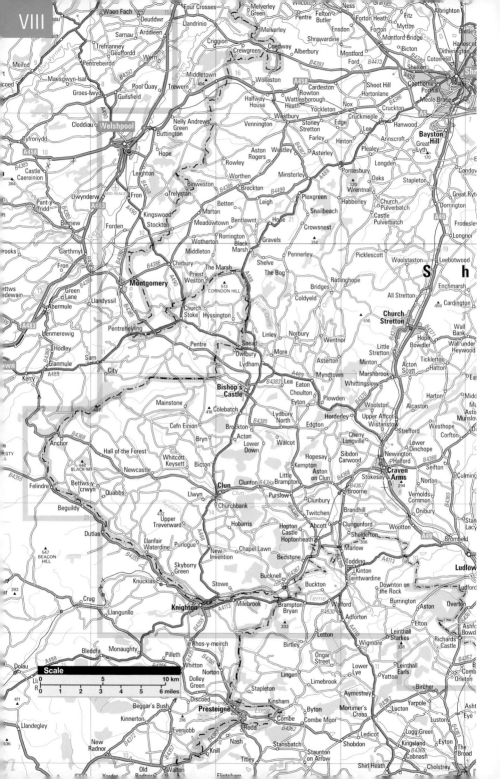

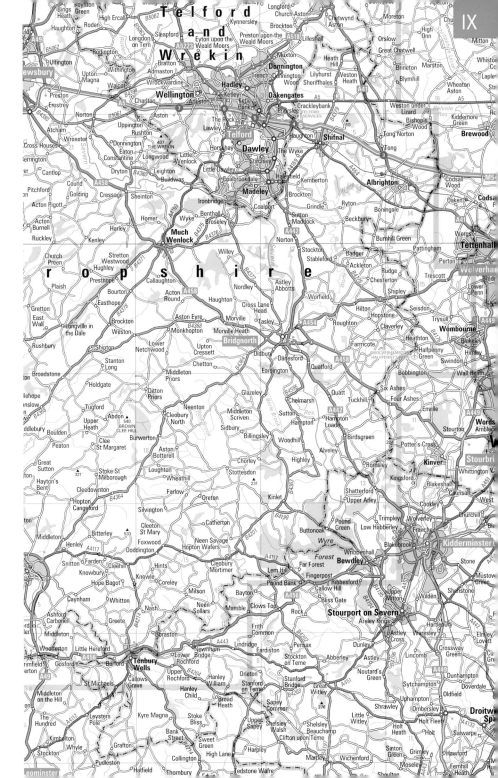

Administrative and
Postcode boundaries

County and unitary
authority boundaries

District boundaries

Postcode boundaries

Area covered by this atlas

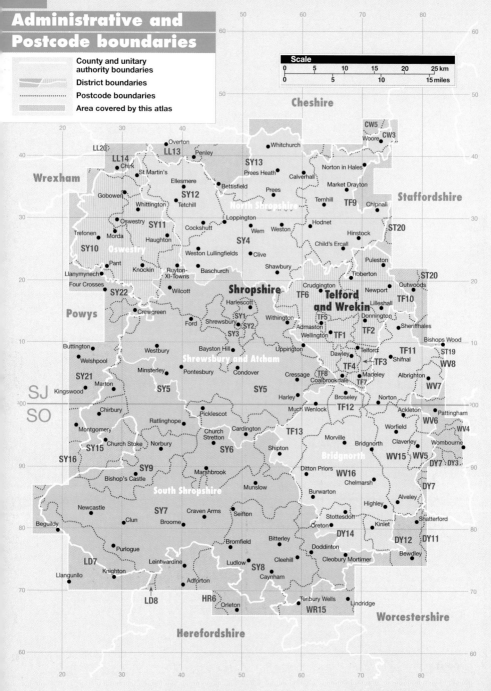

Scale

0	5	10	15	20	25 km
0		5		10	15 miles

Cheshire

CW5

Woore CW3

LL20

Overton

Whitchurch

LL13

Penley

Wrexham

LL14

Chirk

St Martin's

SY13

Prees Heath

Calverhall

Norton in Hales

Ellesmere

Bettisfield

Prees

Market Drayton

Staffordshire

Gobowen

SY12

Tetchill

Ternhill

TF9

Chipnall

Whittington

North Shropshire

Loppington

Hodnet

ST20

Trefonen

Oswestry

SY11

Cockshutt

Wem

Weston

Hinstock

Morda

Haughton

SY4

Child's Ercall

SY10

Oswestry

Weston Lullingfields

Clive

Puleston

Pant

Knockin

Ruyton-

Baschurch

Shawbury

Tibberton

ST20

Llanymynech

XI-Towns

Crudgington

Newport

Outwoods

Four Crosses

SY22

Wilcott

Shropshire

TF6

Telford

TF10

Powys

Crewgreen

Harlescott

SY1

Withington

and Wrekin

TF5

Donnington

Sheriffhales

Ford

Shrewsbury

SY2

Admaston

TF2

Buttington

SY3

Wellington

TF1

Bishops Wood

Welshpool

Westbury

Bayston Hill

Uppington

Dawley

Telford

TF11

ST19

SY21

Minsterley

Shrewsbury and Atcham

Shifnal

WV8

Marton

Pontesbury

Condover

Cressage

TF8

Madeley

Albrighton

Kingswood

SY5

SY5

Harley

Coalbrookdale

TF7

Broseley

Norton

WV7

SJ

Harley

Much Wenlock

TF12

Ackleton

Pattingham

SO

Chirbury

Picklescot

Worfield

WV6

WV4

Montgomery

Ratlinghope

Church

Cardington

TF13

Morville

Bridgnorth

Claverley

Wombourne

Church Stoke

Norbury

Stretton

SY6

Shipton

Bridgnorth

WV15

WV5

DY7

DY3

SY15

SY9

Marshbrook

Ditton Priors

WV16

DY7

Bishop's Castle

Munslow

Chelmarsh

SY16

South Shropshire

Burwarton

Alveley

Newcastle

SY7

Craven Arms

Seifton

Highley

Stottesdon

DY11

Beguildy

Clun

Broome

Creton

Kinlet

Shatterford

Purlogue

Bromfield

Bitterley

DY14

DY12

LD7

Leintwardine

Ludlow

Cleehill

Cleobury Mortimer

Bewdley

Llangunllo

Knighton

SY8

Doddinton

Adforton

Caynham

LD8

HR6

Orleton

Tenbury Wells

Lindridge

WR15

Worcestershire

Herefordshire

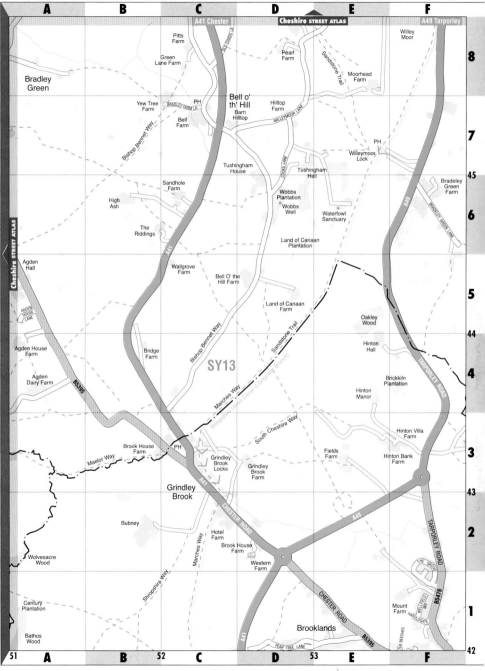

2
1

A41 Chester   A49 Tarporley

A   **B**   **C**   **D**   **E**   **F**

8

Bradley
Green

Pitts
Farm

Green
Lane Farm

Pearl
Farm

Sandstone Trail

Willey
Moor

Moorhead
Farm

Yew Tree
Farm

BRADLEY FARM LA

Bell o'
th' Hill

Hilltop
Farm

7

PH

Bell
Farm

Barn
Hilltop

WILLEYMOOR LANE

PH

Willeymoor
Lock

Bishop Bennet Way

COOKS LANE

45

Tushingham
House

Tushingham
Hall

Sandhole
Farm

Wobbs
Plantation

Bradeley
Green
Farm

BRADELEY GREEN LANE

High
Ash

Wobbs
Well

Waterfowl
Sanctuary

6

The
Riddings

Land of Canaan
Plantation

Agden
Hall

Wallgrove
Farm

Bell O' the
Hill Farm

5

A41

AGDEN HOUSE LANE

Land of Canaan
Farm

Oakley
Wood

Agden House
Farm

Bishop Bennet Way

SY13

Sandstone Trail

Hinton
Hall

44

TARPORLEY ROAD

Agden
Dairy Farm

B5395

Bridge
Farm

Brickkiln
Plantation

4

Marches Way

Hinton
Manor

Shropshire Union Canal (Llangollen Branch)

South Cheshire Way

Brook House
Farm

PH

Fields
Farm

Hinton Villa
Farm

3

Maelor Way

Grindley
Brook
Locks

Grindley
Brook
Farm

Hinton Bank
Farm

Grindley
Brook

A41

43

Bubney

Marches Way

CHESTER ROAD

Hotel
Farm

A49

2

Brook House
Farm

Shropshire Way

Western
Farm

THE GROVE

TARPORLEY ROAD

Mount
Farm

B5476

WELLFIELD

HARDGATE

Century
Plantation

CHESTER ROAD

1

Wolvesacre
Wood

A41

Brooklands

B5395

THE BEECHES

Bathos
Wood

PEAR TREE LANE

42

51   **A**   **B**   52   **C**   **D**   53   **E**   **F**

14
2

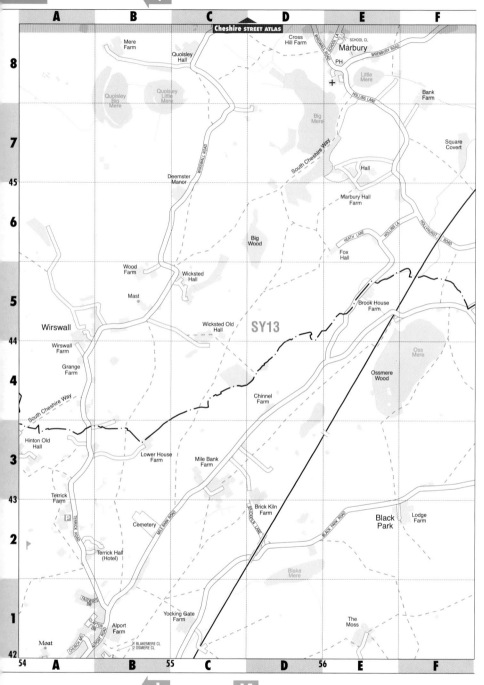
8

7

45

6

5

44

4

3

43

2

1

42

Mere
Farm

Quoisley
Hall

Quoisley
Big
Mere

Quoisley
Little
Mere

Cross
Hill Farm

SCHOOL CL

Marbury

PH

Little
Mere

Bank
Farm

WRENBURY ROAD

HOLLINS LANE

Square
Covert

Deemster
Manor

WIRSWALL ROAD

South Cheshire Way

Hall

Marbury Hall
Farm

Big
Mere

Big
Wood

HEATH LANE

HOLLINS LA

HOLLYHURST ROAD

Fox
Hall

Wood
Farm

Wicksted
Hall

Mast

Brook House
Farm

Wirswall

Wicksted Old
Hall

SY13

Oss
Mere

Wirswall
Farm

Grange
Farm

Ossmere
Wood

South Cheshire Way

Chinnel
Farm

Hinton Old
Hall

Lower House
Farm

Mile Bank
Farm

Tetrick
Farm

P

TERRICK ROAD

Cemetery

MILE BANK ROAD

Brick Kiln
Farm

BRICK KILN LANE

BLACK PARK ROAD

Black
Park

Lodge
Farm

Terrick Hall
(Hotel)

Blake
Mere

FAIRWAYS DR

CLIFTON DR

Alport
Farm

Yocking Gate
Farm

The
Moss

Moat

CHURCH LK

ALPORT ROAD

1 BLAKEMERE CL
2 OSMERE CL

54   **A**   **B**   55   **C**   **D**   56   **E**   **F**

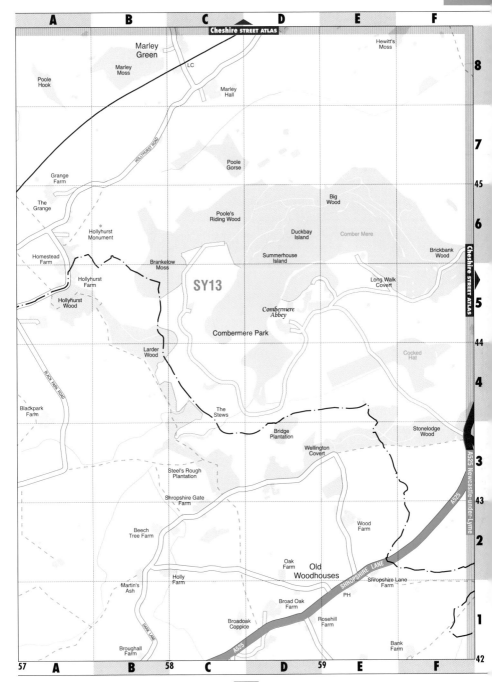

Marley
Green

Hewitt's
Moss

Marley
Moss

LC

Poole
Hook

Marley
Hall

8

Poole
Gorse

7

HOLLYHURST ROAD

45

Grange
Farm

Big
Wood

The
Grange

Poole's
Riding Wood

6

Hollyhurst
Monument

Duckbay
Island

Comber Mere

Homestead
Farm

Brankelow
Moss

Summerhouse
Island

Brickbank
Wood

SY13

Hollyhurst
Farm

Long Walk
Covert

5

Hollyhurst
Wood

Combermere
Abbey

BLACK PARK ROAD

Larder
Wood

Combermere Park

44

Cocked
Hat

4

Blackpark
Farm

The
Stews

Bridge
Plantation

Stonelodge
Wood

A525

Wellington
Covert

3

Steel's Rough
Plantation

43

Shropshire Gate
Farm

Wood
Farm

2

Beech
Tree Farm

Oak
Farm

Old
Woodhouses

SHROPSHIRE LANE

A525 Newcastle-under-Lyme

Martin's
Ash

Holly
Farm

Shropshire Lane
Farm

PH

PARK LANE

Broad Oak
Farm

Rosehill
Farm

1

Broadoak
Coppice

Bank
Farm

Broughall
Farm

A525

42

57   **A**   **B**   58   **C**   **D**   59   **E**   **F**

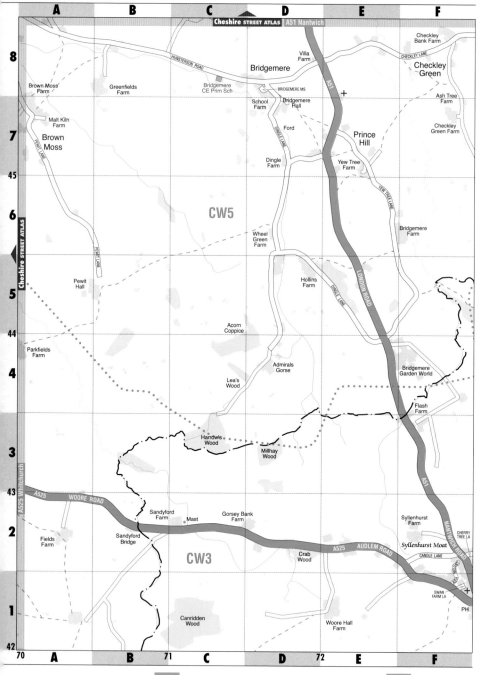

Checkley
Bank Farm

Villa
Farm

CHECKLEY LANE

Brown Moss
Farm

HUNSTERSON ROAD

Bridgemere

Checkley
Green

Greenfields
Farm

Bridgemere
CE Prim Sch

BRIDGEMERE MS

Ash Tree
Farm

Malt Kiln
Farm

School
Farm

Bridgemere
Hall

Brown
Moss

Ford

Checkley
Green Farm

DINGLE LANE

Prince
Hill

Dingle
Farm

Yew Tree
Farm

CW5

YEW TREE LANE

PEWIT LANE

Bridgemere
Farm

Wheel
Green
Farm

Pewit
Hall

Hollins
Farm

LONDON ROAD

DINGLE LANE

Acorn
Coppice

Parkfields
Farm

Admirals
Gorse

Bridgemere
Garden World

Lea's
Wood

Flash
Farm

Harrow's
Wood

Millhay
Wood

WOORE ROAD

A51

Sandyford
Farm

Mast

Gorsey Bank
Farm

Syllenhurst
Farm

NANTWICH ROAD

CHERRY
TREE LA

Fields
Farm

Sandyford
Bridge

A525 AUDLEM ROAD

Syllenhurst Moat

CANDLE LANE

CW3

Crab
Wood

SWAN
FARM LA

Canridden
Wood

Woore Hall
Farm

PH

A525

70   A   71   B   C   71   D   72   E   F

8

7

45

6

5

44

4

3

43

2

1

42

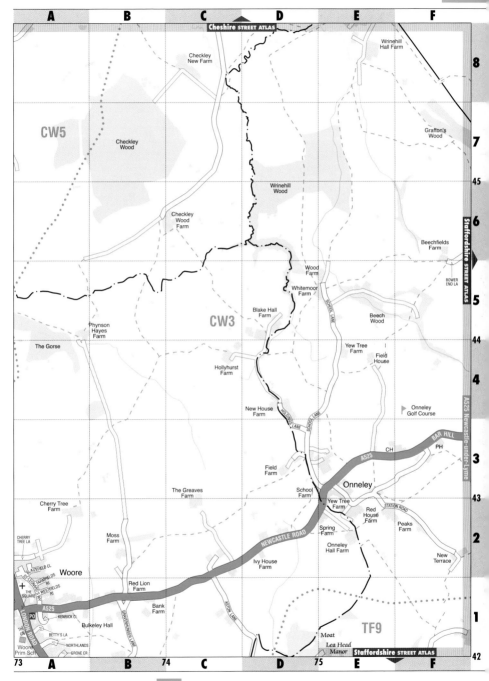

Staffordshire STREET ATLAS

A525 Newcastle-under-Lyme

CW5

Checkley New Farm

Wrinehill Hall Farm

8

Grafton's Wood

7

CW3

Checkley Wood

45

Checkley Wood Farm

Wrinehill Wood

6

Beechfields Farm

BOWER END LA

Phynson Hayes Farm

Wood Farm

Whitemoor Farm

SCHOOL LANE

Beech Wood

5

The Gorse

Blake Hall Farm

Yew Tree Farm

Field House

44

Hollyhurst Farm

4

New House Farm

HOLLOW LANE

SCHOOL LANE

Onneley Golf Course

BAR HILL

PH

3

A525

CH

Field Farm

The Greaves Farm

School Farm

Onneley

STATION ROAD

43

Cherry Tree Farm

Yew Tree Farm

Red House Farm

Peaks Farm

CHERRY TREE LA

Moss Farm

NEWCASTLE ROAD

Spring Farm

New Terrace

2

BLAZEFIELD CL

FARMFIELDS RI

WESTFIELDS RI

Woore

Red Lion Farm

Ivy House Farm

Onneley Hall Farm

THE SQUARE

KENRICK CL

Bank Farm

ASTON LANE

GARDENHOUSE LANE

LONDON ROAD

A525

PO

Bulkeley Hall

1

BETTY'S LA

NORTHLANDS

GROVE CR

Woore Prim Sch

Moat

Lea Head Manor

TF9

42

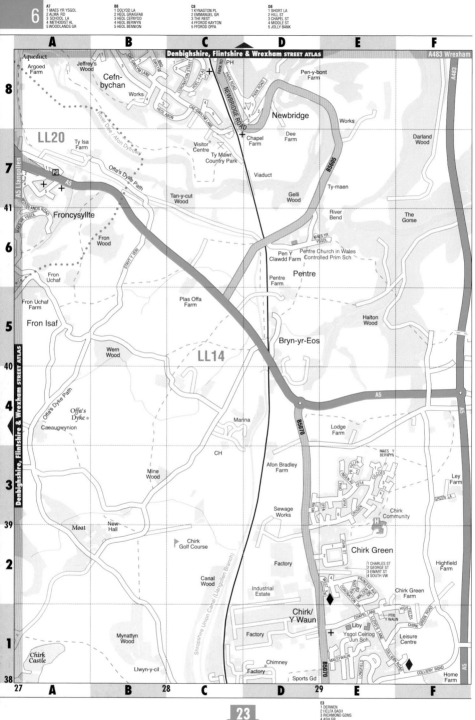

A7
1 MAES YR YSGOL
2 ALMA RD
3 SCHOOL LA
4 METHODIST HL
5 WOODLANDS GR

B8
1 DOLYDD LA
2 HEOL GRAIGFAB
3 HEOL CEFNYDD
4 HEOL BERWYN
5 HEOL BENNION

C8
1 KYNASTON PL
2 EMMANUEL GR
3 THE REST
4 FFORDD KAYTON
5 FFORDD OFFA

D8
1 SHORT LA
2 HILL ST
3 CHAPEL ST
4 MIDDLE ST
5 JOLLY BANK

A483 Wrexham

Aqueduct
Argoed Farm
Jeffrey's Wood
Cefn-bychan
Works
Pen-y-bont Farm
Newbridge
Works
Darland Wood

LL20
Ty Isa Farm
Visitor Centre
Chapel Farm
Dee Farm
Ty Mawr Country Park
Viaduct
Ty-maen
River Dee Afon Dyfrdwy
Offa's Dyke Path
Tan-y-cut Wood
Gelli Wood
A5 Llangollen
PO
River Bend
The Gorse
Froncysyllte
Fron Wood
Pen Y Clawdd Farm
Pentre Church in Wales Controlled Prim Sch
Maes yr Ysgol
Fron Uchaf
Pentre
Pentre Farm
Fron Uchaf Farm
Plas Offa Farm
Halton Wood
Fron Isaf
Wern Wood
LL14
Bryn-yr-Eos
Offa's Dyke Path
Offa's Dyke
Caeaugwynion
Marina
Lodge Farm
Maes Y Berwyn
Mine Wood
CH
Afon Bradley Farm
Chirk Community
Ley Farm
GREEN LA
Moat
New Hall
Chirk Golf Course
Sewage Works
Chirk Green
Chirk Green Farm
Highfield Farm
1 CHARLES ST
2 GEORGE ST
3 EWART ST
4 SOUTH VW
Factory
Canal Wood
Factory
Chirk Green Farm
Industrial Estate
Chirk/ Y Waun
Mynattyn Wood
Liby
Ysgol Ceiriog Jun Sch
Leisure Centre
Chirk Castle
Chimney
Factory
Factory
Llwyn-y-cil
Sports Gd
COLLIERY ROAD
Home Farm
Shropshire Union Canal (Llangollen Branch)

E3
1 DERWEN
2 HELIA BAGH
3 RICHMOND GDNS
4 ASH GR
5 SYCAMORE DR
6 CROGEN

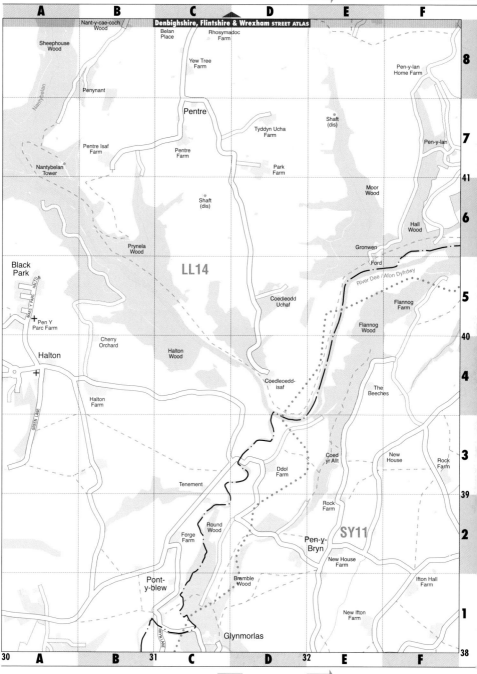

8

7

A B C D E F

8
7
41
6
5
40
4
3
39
2
1
38

30 31 32

24 8

Nant-y-cae-coch Wood

Belan Place

Rhosymadoc Farm

Sheephouse Wood

Pen-y-lan Home Farm

Yew Tree Farm

Penynant

Namybelan

Pentre

Shaft (dis)

Pen-y-lan

Tyddyn Ucha Farm

Pentre Isaf Farm

Pentre Farm

Park Farm

Nantybelan Tower

Moor Wood

Hall Wood

Prynela Wood

Gronwen

Ford

LL14

River Dee / Afon Dyfrdwy

Flannog Farm

Black Park

Coedleodd Uchaf

Flannog Wood

Pen Y Parc Farm

Cherry Orchard

Halton Wood

Halton

Coedleoedd-isaf

The Beeches

Halton Farm

Coed yr Allt

New House

Rock Farm

GREEN LANE

Ddol Farm

Rock Farm

Tenement

SY11

Forge Farm

Round Wood

Pen-y-Bryn

New House Farm

Pont-y-blew

Bramble Wood

Ifton Hall Farm

RHYN LANE

New Ifton Farm

Glynmorlas

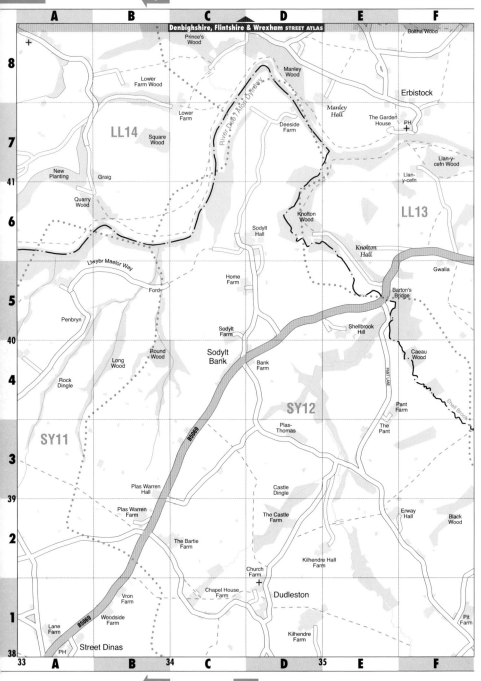

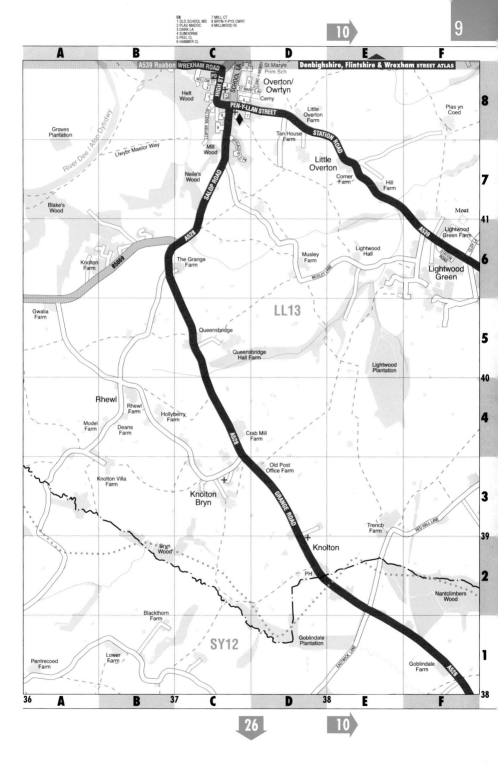

C8
1 OLD SCHOOL MS
2 PLAS MADOC
3 DARK LA
4 SUNDORNE
5 PEEL CL
6 HAMMER CL
7 MILL CT
8 BRYN-Y-PYS CWRT
9 MILLWOOD RI

| A | B | C | D | E | F |

A539 Ruabon **WREXHAM ROAD**

Denbighshire, Flintshire & Wrexham STREET ATLAS

St Mary's Prim Sch

Overton/
Owrtyn

Cemy

Helt
Wood

PEN-Y-LLAN STREET

Little Overton Farm

STATION ROAD

Groves Plantation

Little Overton

Plas yn Coed

River Dee / Afon Dyfrdwy

Llwybr Maelor Way

Mill Wood

Tan House Farm

Corner Farm

Hill Farm

Neile's Wood

Moat

Lightwood Green Farm

SALOP ROAD

Blake's Wood

A528

STATION ROAD

Knolton Farm

B5069

The Grange Farm

Musley Farm

Lightwood Hall

Lightwood Green

Gwalia Farm

MUSLEY LANE

LL13

Queensbridge

Queensbridge Hall Farm

Lightwood Plantation

Rhewl

Rhewl Farm

Hollyberry Farm

Model Farm

Deans Farm

A528

Crab Mill Farm

Knolton Villa Farm

Old Post Office Farm

Knolton Bryn

GRANGE ROAD

Trench Farm

RED HALL LANE

Bryn Wood

Knolton

39

PH

Nantclimbers Wood

Blackthorn Farm

SY12

Goblindale Plantation

EASTWICK LANE

Pentrecoed Farm

Lower Farm

Goblindale Farm

A528

| 36 | A | B | 37 | C | D | 38 | E | F | 38 |

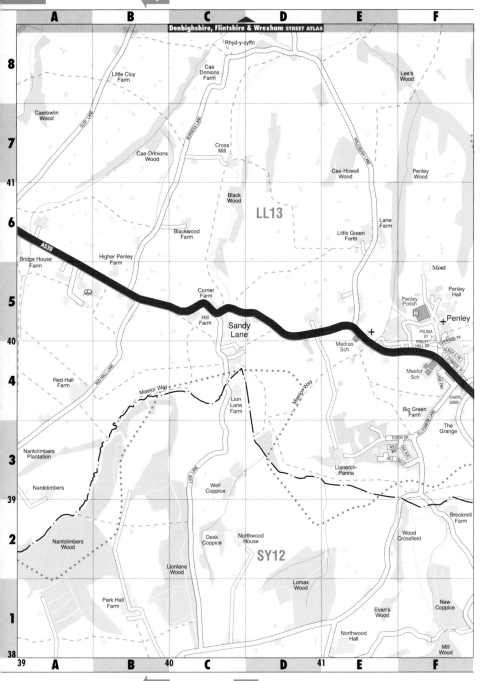

Rhyd-y-cyffn

Little Cloy Farm

Cae Drinions Farm

Lee's Wood

Caerowlin Wood

OLOY LANE

BIRCHES LANE

Cross Mill

Cae-Drinions Wood

Cae-Howell Wood

Penley Wood

Black Wood

HALFORD'S LANE

LL13

Lane Farm

Blackwood Farm

A539

Higher Penley Farm

Little Green Farm

Moat

Bridge House Farm

Penley Hall

Corner Farm

Penley Polish

H

Penley

Hill Farm

Sandy Lane

Madras Sch

POLSKA ST

PENLEY HALL DR

OAKWOOD PK

PENBA S PK

DYMOCK PL

Red Hall Farm

RED HALL LANE

Maelor Way

Maelor Way

Maelor Sch

LANE END

Lion Lane Farm

Big Green Farm

CHAPEL GDNS

The Grange

Nantclimbers Plantation

LION LANE

ELLESMERE LANE

TUDOR DR

WEST WY

OAK AVE

HILL CREST

Nantclimbers

Llanerch-Panna

Well Coppice

Nantclimbers Wood

Desk Coppice

Northwood House

Wood Crossfield

Brookmill Farm

SY12

Lionlane Wood

Lomax Wood

Evan's Wood

New Coppice

Park Hall Farm

Northwood Hall

Mill Wood

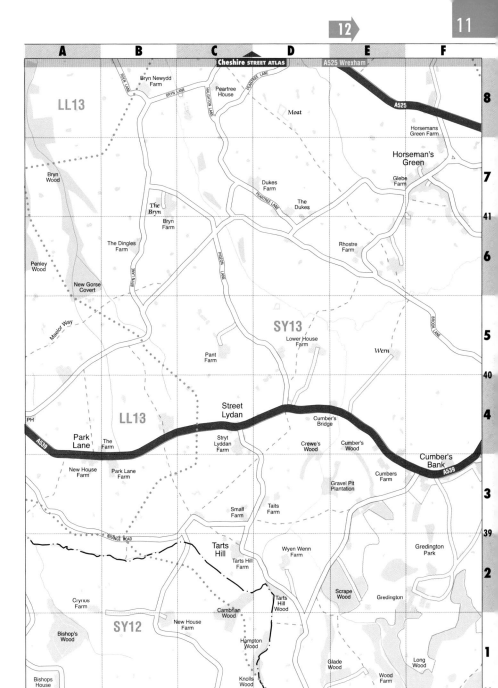

Cheshire STREET ATLAS

A525 Wrexham

A **B** **C** **D** **E** **F**

LL13

8

Bryn Newydd
Farm

ROCK LANE

BRYN LANE

HALGHTON LANE

Peartree
House

PEARTREE LANE

Moat

A525

Horsemans
Green Farm

Horseman's
Green

7

Bryn
Wood

Dukes
Farm

PEARTREE LANE

The
Dukes

Glebe
Farm

41

The
Bryn

Bryn
Farm

Rhostre
Farm

The Dingles
Farm

PIGEON LANE

BRYN LANE

6

Penley
Wood

New Gorse
Covert

Maelor Way

Pant
Farm

Lower House
Farm

SY13

Wern

BROOK LANE

5

40

PH

A539

LL13

Park
Lane

The
Farm

Street
Lydan

Stryt
Lyddan
Farm

Cumber's
Bridge

Crewe's
Wood

Cumber's
Wood

Cumber's
Bank

A539

4

New House
Farm

Park Lane
Farm

Cumbers
Farm

Gravel Pit
Plantation

3

Small
Farm

Taits
Farm

BRIDGE ROAD

39

Tarts
Hill

Tarts Hill
Farm

Wyen Wenn
Farm

Gredington
Park

2

Crynos
Farm

Cambrian
Wood

New House
Farm

Tarts
Hill
Wood

Scrape
Wood

Gredington

Bishop's
Wood

SY12

Hampton
Wood

Glade
Wood

Wood
Farm

Long
Wood

1

Bishops
House

Knolls
Wood

38

42 **A** **B** 43 **C** **D** 44 **E** **F**

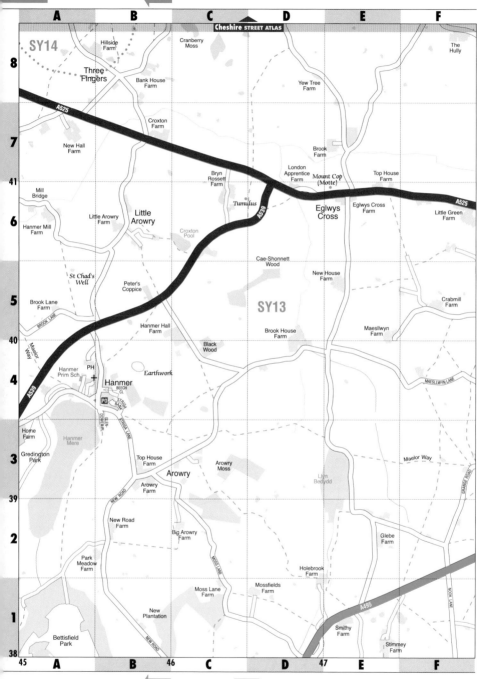

SY14

8

Three Fingers

Hillside Farm

Cranberry Moss

Yew Tree Farm

The Hully

A525

Bank House Farm

7

New Hall Farm

Croxton Farm

Brook Farm

41

Mill Bridge

Bryn Rossett Farm

London Apprentice Farm

Mount Cop (Motte)

Top House Farm

A525

6

Hanmer Mill Farm

Little Arowry Farm

Little Arowry

Tumulus

A539

Eglwys Cross

Eglwys Cross Farm

Little Green Farm

Croxton Pool

St Chad's Well

Peter's Coppice

Cae-Shonnett Wood

New House Farm

Crabmill Farm

5

Brook Lane Farm

SY13

BROOK LANE

Hanmer Hall Farm

Brook House Farm

Maesllwyn Farm

40

Maelor Way

Black Wood

A539

Earthwork

PH

Hanmer Prim Sch

MAESLLWYN LANE

4

Hanmer

BEECH CL.

STRIGA BANK

A539

GLEB RD.

DOWER DR.

STRIGA LANE

3

Home Farm

Gredington Park

Hanmer Mere

Top House Farm

Arowry

Arowry Moss

Llyn Bedydd

Maelor Way

GRANGE ROAD

NEW ROAD

Arowry Farm

39

New Road Farm

Big Arowry Farm

Glebe Farm

2

MOSS LANE

Park Meadow Farm

Holebrook Farm

NOOK LANE

Moss Lane Farm

Mossfields Farm

A495

1

New Plantation

NEW ROAD

Smithy Farm

Stimmey Farm

Bettisfield Park

38

45   A   B   46   C   D   47   E   F

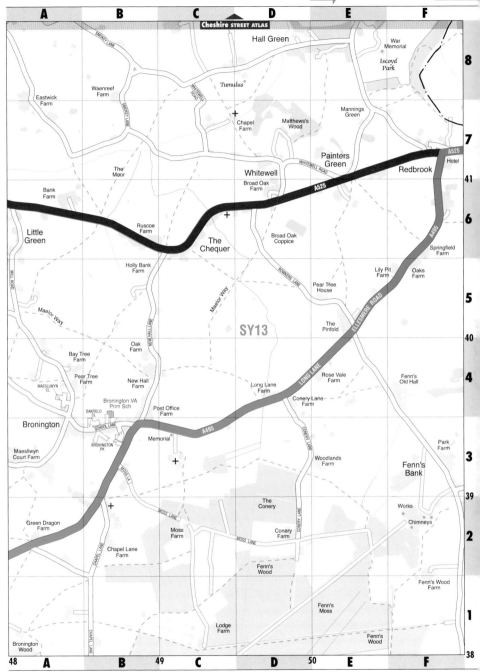

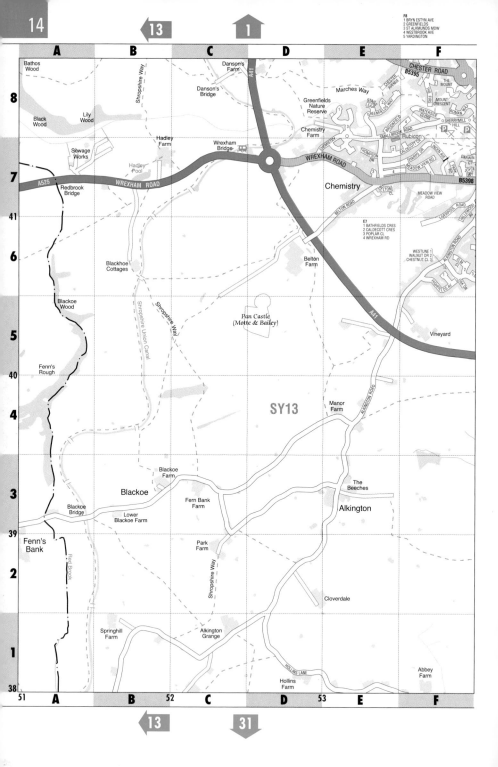

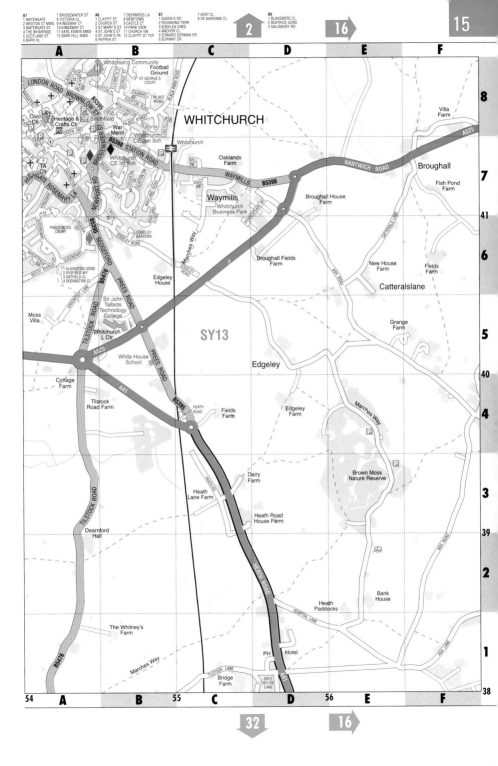

A7
1 WATERGATE
2 WESTON CT MWS
3 WATERGATE ST
4 THE WHARFAGE
5 SCOTLAND ST
6 BARK HL

7 BRIDGEWATER ST
8 VICTORIA CL
9 KINGSWAY CT
10 KINGSWAY CT
11 EARL EDWIN MWS
12 BARK HILL MWS

A8
1 CLAYPIT ST
2 CHURCH ST
3 ST MARY'S ST
4 ST JOHN'S ST
5 ST JOHN'S PK
6 PEPPER ST

7 DEERMOSS LA
8 CASTLE CT
9 CASTLE CT
10 PARK VIEW
11 CHURCH VW
12 CLAYPIT ST TER

B7
1 QUEEN'S RD
2 RICHMOND TERR
3 EDGELEA CRES
4 ANCHOR CL
5 EDWARD GERMAN DR
6 BURWAY DR

7 KENT CL
8 DE WARENNE CL

B8
1 BLAKEMERE CL
2 BEATRICE GDNS
3 SALISBURY RD

15

2

16

A	B	C	D	E	F

8

DARK LA

A525

White House Farm

Broughall Farm

Ivy Farm

The Green

New Woodhouses

FOXES LANE

Fir Tree Farm

Long Wood

7

Foxes Lane Farm

Springs Wood

The Springs

Longwood Hall

Meadows Farm

41

Abbey Farm

P Melverley Farm Nature Reserve

Melverley Farm

Ashwood Covert

6

Church Farm

5

Ashwood

SY13

+

CHURCH LANE

Greenfields

40

MAGNA DR

ASHWOOD LA

Ash Hall

Ashwood Cottages

Ashwood Farm

4

PH

Ash Magna

ASHWOOD LANE

CHURCH LANE

Wood Farm

Ash Parva

3

Grove Farm

Ashfields

Moat

39

ASH LANE

2

Lea Hall Lodge

Kennels Farm

PEMBERTON

+

Cross

Lanes Farm

Lea Hall

CHURCH STREET

1

New House Farm

Recreation Gd

Ightfield

Gables Farm

BIRCHEVHAM RD

ASHFIELD COURT

38

57	A	B	58	C	D	59	E	F

CALVERHALL ROAD

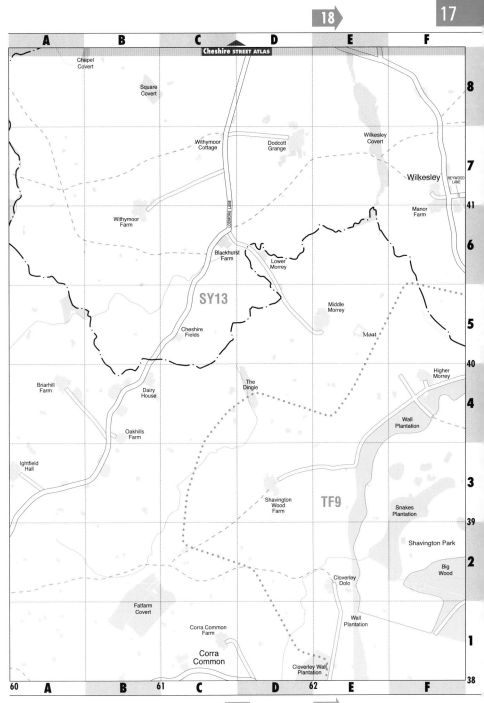

A B C D E F

8

Chapel
Covert

Square
Covert

Withymoor
Cottage

Dodcott
Grange

Wilkesley
Covert

7

Wilkesley

HEYWOOD
LANE

41

Manor
Farm

Withymoor
Farm

LONGMORE LANE

Blackhurst
Farm

Lower
Morrey

6

SY13

Middle
Morrey

Moat

5

Cheshire
Fields

40

Briarhill
Farm

Dairy
House

The
Dingle

Higher
Morrey

4

Wall
Plantation

Oakhills
Farm

Ightfield
Hall

Shavington
Wood
Farm

TF9

3

Snakes
Plantation

39

Shavington Park

Cloverley
Dolo

Big
Wood

2

Fatfarm
Covert

Wall
Plantation

Corra Common
Farm

Corra
Common

Cloverley Wall
Plantation

1

38

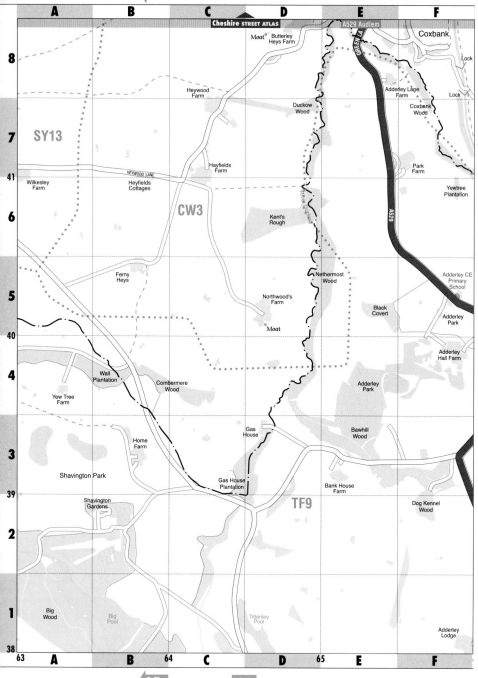

Cheshire STREET ATLAS

A529 Audlem

Coxbank

Lock

Moat Butterley
Heys Farm

Adderley Lane
Farm

Coxbank
Wodd

Heywood
Farm

Duckow
Wood

Lock

SY13

Park
Farm

Hayfields
Farm

Wilkesley
Farm

HEYWOOD LANE

Heyfields
Cottages

Yewtree
Plantation

CW3

Kent's
Rough

Ferny
Heys

Nethermost
Wood

Adderley CE
Primary
School

Northwood's
Farm

Black
Covert

Adderley
Park

Moat

Adderley
Hall Farm

Wall
Plantation

Yew Tree
Farm

Combermere
Wood

Adderley
Park

Home
Farm

Gas
House

Bawhill
Wood

Shavington Park

Gas House
Plantation

Bank House
Farm

Dog Kennel
Wood

Shavington
Gardens

TF9

Big
Wood

Big
Pool

Tittenley
Pool

Adderley
Lodge

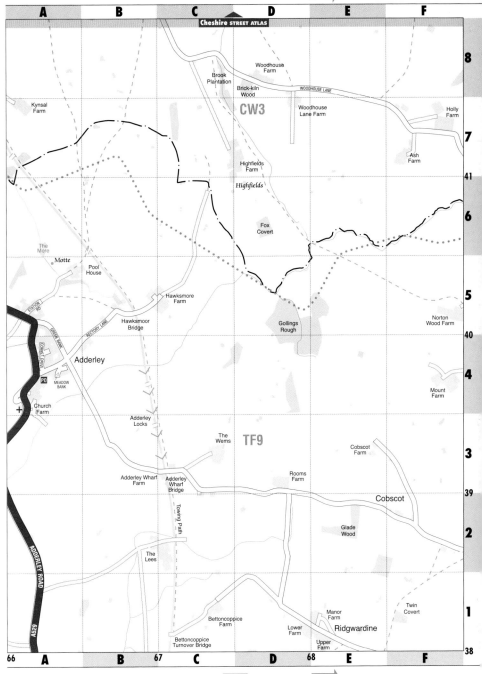

A	B	C	D	E	F

Woodhouse Farm

Brook Plantation

Brick-kiln Wood

WOODHOUSE LANE

8

Kynsal Farm

CW3

Woodhouse Lane Farm

Holly Farm

7

Highfields Farm

Ash Farm

41

Highfields

Fox Covert

6

The Mere

Motte

Pool House

Norton Wood Farm

5

Hawksmore Farm

Gollings Rough

STATION RD

GREEN BANK

Hawksmoor Bridge

RECTORY LANE

40

COBELANE

Adderley

Mount Farm

4

PO

MEADOW BANK

Church Farm

Adderley Locks

The Wems

TF9

Cobscot Farm

3

Adderley Wharf Farm

Adderley Wharf Bridge

Rooms Farm

Cobscot

39

Towing Path

Glade Wood

2

ADDERLEY ROAD

A529

The Lees

Twin Covert

1

Bettoncoppice Farm

Manor Farm

Lower Farm

Ridgwardine

Bettoncoppice Turnover Bridge

Upper Farm

38

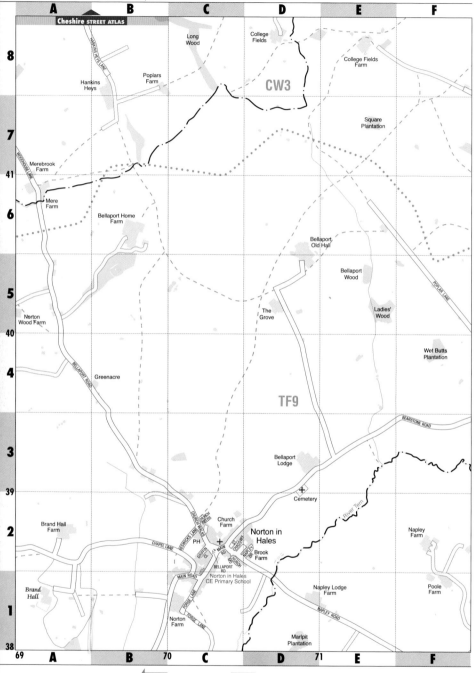

Cheshire STREET ATLAS

8

Long
Wood

College
Fields

College Fields
Farm

Hankins
Heys

Poplars
Farm

CW3

Square
Plantation

7

Merebrook
Farm

41

Mere
Farm

6

Bellaport Home
Farm

Bellaport
Old Hall

Bellaport
Wood

5

Norton
Wood Farm

The
Grove

Ladies'
Wood

40

Wet Butts
Plantation

4

Greenacre

BELLAPORT ROAD

POPLAR LANE

TF9

BEARSTONE ROAD

3

Bellaport
Lodge

39

Cemetery

River Tern

2

Brand Hall
Farm

Church
Farm

Norton in
Hales

Napley
Farm

CHAPEL LANE

PH

Brook
Farm

BELLAPORT
RD

Norton in Hales
CE Primary School

Napley Lodge
Farm

Poole
Farm

1

Brand
Hall

MAIN ROAD

Norton
Farm

FORGE LANE

NAPLEY ROAD

Marlpit
Plantation

38

69

70

71

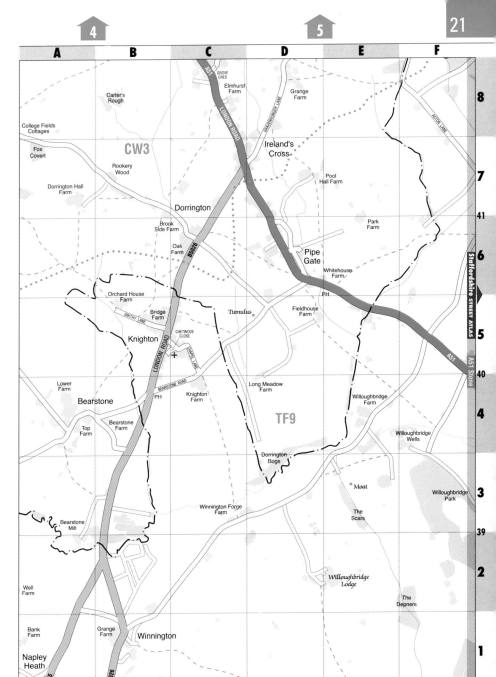

A B C D E F

Staffordshire STREET ATLAS

4 5

8
7
41
6
5
40
4
3
39
2
1
38

GROVE CRES
Elmhurst Farm
Grange Farm
Carter's Rough
College Fields Cottages
Fox Covert
Ireland's Cross
CW3
LONDON ROAD
BADDILEY GREEN LANE
Rookery Wood
Pool Hall Farm
ASTON LANE
Dorrington Hall Farm
Dorrington
Brook Side Farm
Park Farm
Oak Farm
B5026
Pipe Gate
Whitehouse Farm
Orchard House Farm
PH
SMITHY LANE
Bridge Farm
Tumulus
Fieldhouse Farm
Knighton
CHETWODE CLOSE
LONDON ROAD
CHAPEL LANE
Lower Farm
BEARSTONE ROAD
PH
Knighton Farm
Long Meadow Farm
Willoughbridge Farm
Bearstone
TF9
Willoughbridge Wells
Top Farm
Bearstone Farm
Willoughbridge Park
Dorrington Bogs
Moat
The Scars
Willoughbridge Park
Bearstone Mill
Winnington Forge Farm
Willoughbridge Lodge
Well Farm
The Depners
Bank Farm
Grange Farm
Winnington
Napley Heath
B5415
B5026

Staffordshire STREET ATLAS

A B C D E F

A51
A51 Stone

Staffordshire STREET ATLAS

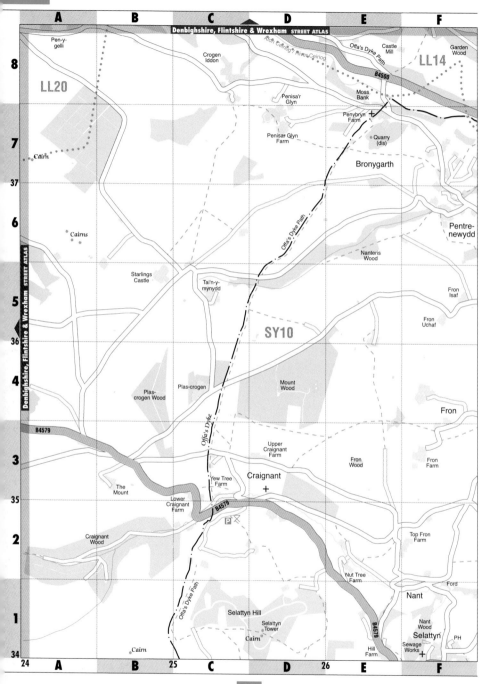

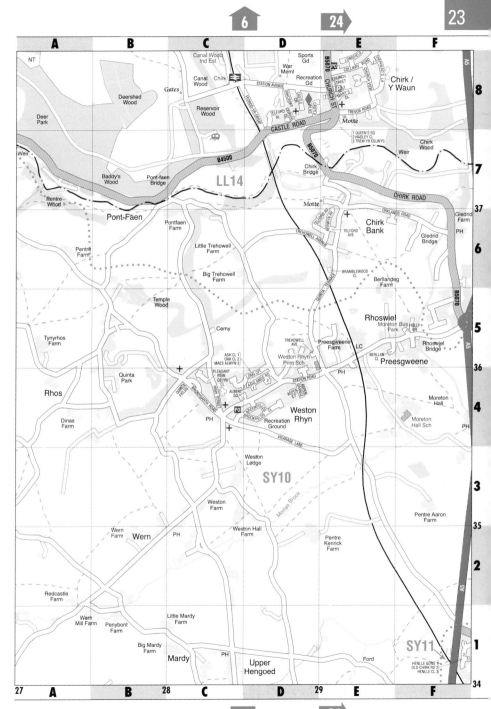

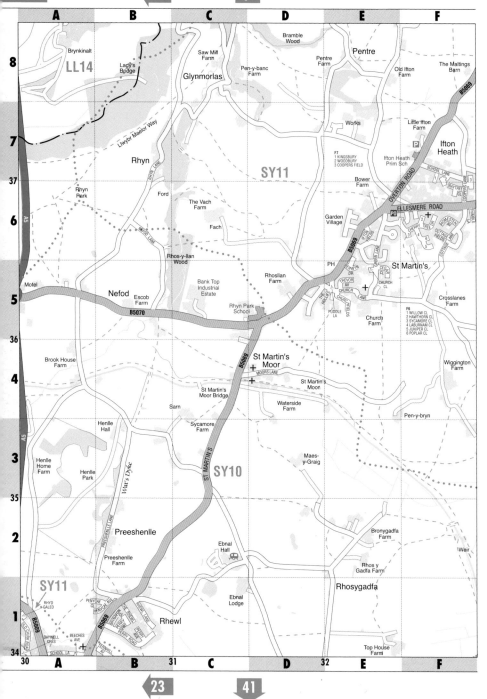

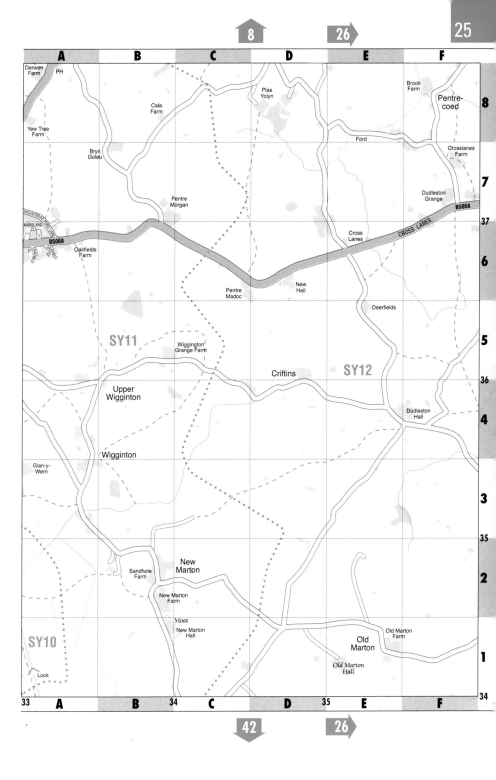

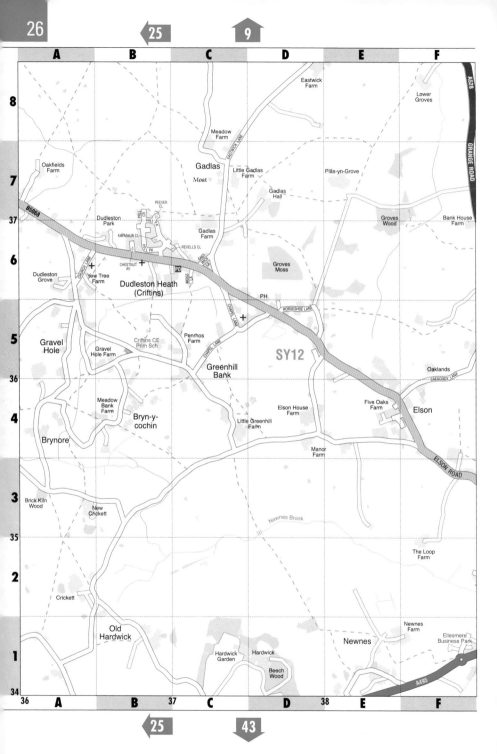

8

7

37

6

5

36

4

3

35

2

1

34

A B C D E F

Eastwick
Farm

A528

GRANGE ROAD

Lower
Groves

Meadow
Farm

Gadlas
Moat

Little Gadlas
Farm

Plâs-yn-Grove

Oakfields
Farm

Gadlas
Hall

PEEVER
CL

Dudleston
Park

Groves
Wood

Bank House
Farm

B5068

HILL CR

HILL AV

KAYMAUR CL

HY PK

CHESTNUT
AV

REVELLS CL

Gadlas
Farm

EASTWICK LN

CHURCH LANE

Yew Tree
Farm

MOSS
CL

PO

Groves
Moss

Dudleston
Grove

Dudleston Heath
(Criftins)

PH

HORSESHOE LANE

Gravel
Hole

Gravel
Hole Farm

Criftins CE
Prim Sch

Penrhos
Farm

CHAPEL LANE

Greenhill
Bank

SY12

Oaklands

CAEGOODY LANE

Meadow
Bank
Farm

Bryn-y-
cochin

Little Greenhill
Farm

Elson House
Farm

Five Oaks
Farm

Elson

Brynore

Manor
Farm

ELSON ROAD

Brick Kiln
Wood

New
Crickett

Newnes Brook

The Loop
Farm

Crickett

Old
Hardwick

Hardwick
Garden

Hardwick

Newnes

Newnes
Farm

Ellesmere
Business Park

Beech
Wood

A495

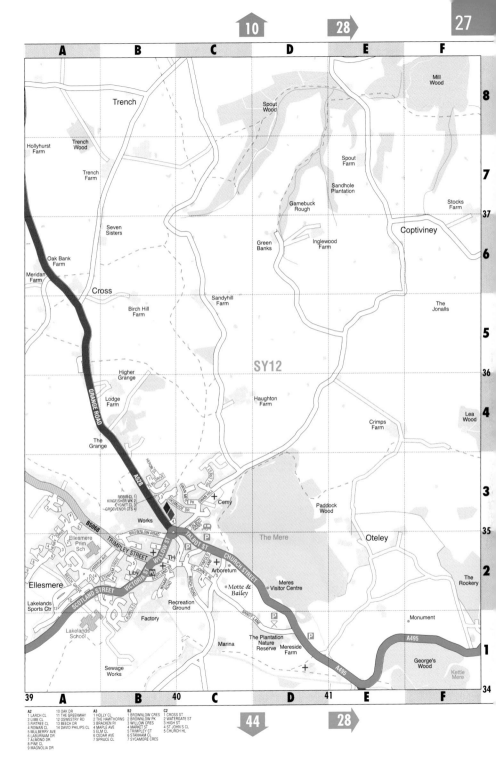

8
7
37
6
5
36
4
3
35
2
1
34

A B C D E F

Mill Wood

Trench

Spout Wood

Hollyhurst Farm

Trench Wood

Spout Farm

Trench Farm

Sandhole Plantation

Stocks Farm

Seven Sisters

Gamebuck Rough

Coptiviney

Oak Bank Farm

Green Banks

Inglewood Farm

Meridan Farm

Cross

The Jonalls

Birch Hill Farm

Sandyhill Farm

SY12

Higher Grange

Lodge Farm

Haughton Farm

Lea Wood

The Grange

Crimps Farm

GRANGE ROAD

A528

ROBIN CL 1
KINGFISHER WK 2
CYGNET CL 3
GROSVENOR CTS 4

Works

BROWNLOW ROAD

B5068

Ellesmere Prim Sch

TRIMPLEY STREET

Cemy

TALBOT ST

The Mere

Paddock Wood

Oteley

CHURCH STREET

VICTORIA ST

WILLOW S

TH

Lib'y

PO

SCOTLAND STREET

Arboretum

Meres Visitor Centre

The Rookery

Ellesmere

Motte & Bailey

Lakelands Sports Ctr

Recreation Ground

Factory

Sewage Works

Lakelands School

SANDY LANE

Marina

The Plantation Nature Reserve

Mereside Farm

Monument

A495

A495

George's Wood

Kettle Mere

39 A 40 B C 41 D E F 34

A2
1 LARCH CL
2 LIME CL
3 FIRTREE CL
4 ROWAN CL
5 MULBERRY AVE
6 LABURNAM DR
7 ALMOND DR
8 PINE CL
9 MAGNOLIA DR

10 OAK DR
11 THE GREENWAY
12 OSWESTRY RD
13 BEECH DR
14 DAVID PHILIPS CL

A3
1 HOLLY CL
2 THE HAWTHORNS
3 BRACKEN RI
4 MAPLE AVE
5 ELM CL
6 CEDAR AVE
7 SPRUCE CL

B2
1 BROWNLOW CRES
2 BROWNLOW PK
3 WILLOW CRES
4 MARKET ST
5 TRIMPLEY CT
6 STANHAM CL
7 SYCAMORE CRES

C2
1 CROSS ST
2 WATERGATE ST
3 HIGH ST
4 ST JOHN'S CL
5 CHURCH HL

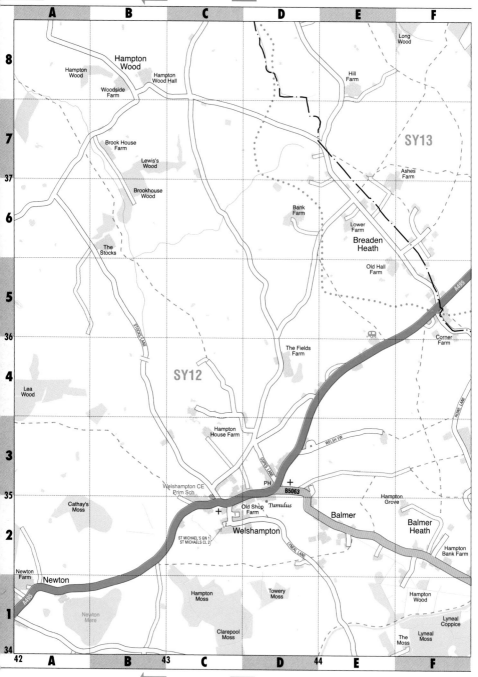

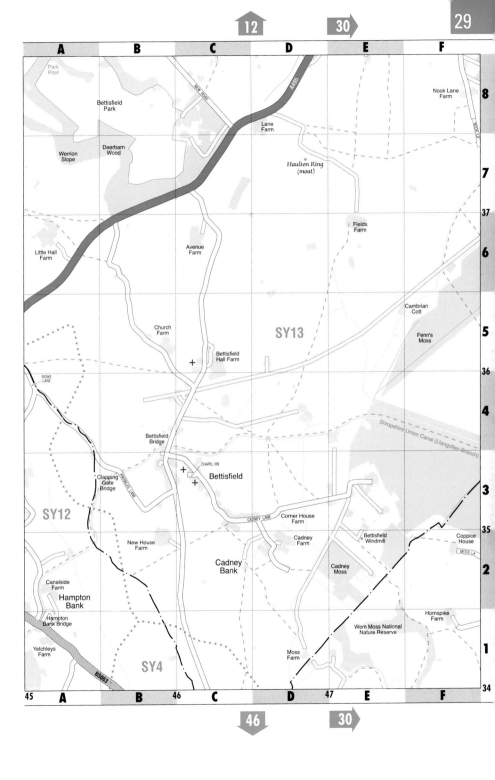

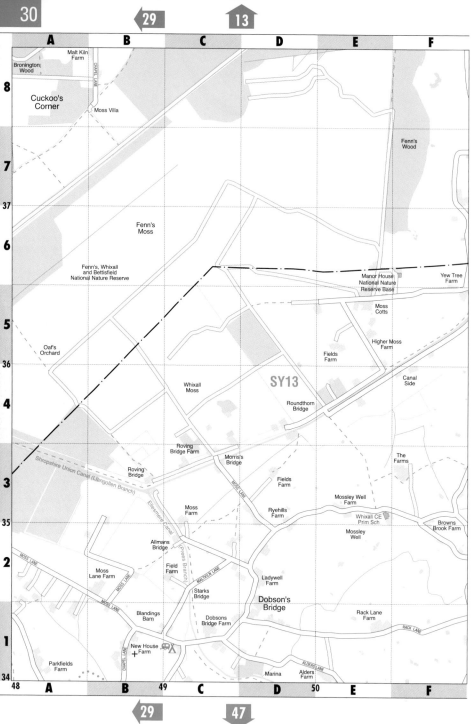

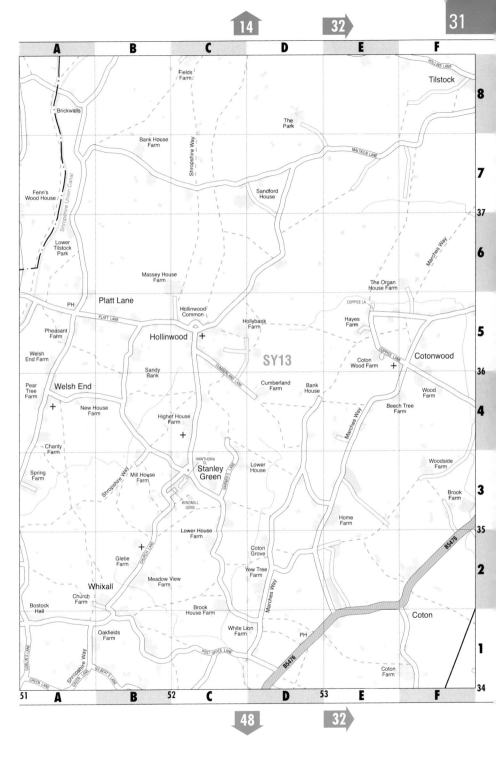

Tilstock

Hollins Lane

Brickwalls

Fields Farm

Shropshire Way

Bank House Farm

The Park

MALTKILN LANE

Marches Way

8

7

37

6

Fenn's Wood House

Shropshire Union Canal

Lower Tilstock Park

Sandford House

Massey House Farm

The Organ House Farm

PH

Platt Lane

PLATT LANE

Hollinwood Common

Hollinwood

Hollybank Farm

COPPICE LA

Hayes Farm

5

Pheasant Farm

SY13

Coton Wood Farm

Cotonwood

36

Welsh End Farm

Sandy Bank

CUMBERLAND LANE

Cumberland Farm

Bank House

COTON LANE

Wood Farm

Pear Tree Farm

Welsh End

New House Farm

Higher House Farm

Marches Way

Beech Tree Farm

4

Charity Farm

Shropshire Way

Mill House Farm

HAWTHORN CL

Stanley Green

GARNER'S LANE

Lower House

Woodside Farm

Brook Farm

3

Spring Farm

WINDMILL GDNS

Home Farm

35

B5476

Glebe Farm

CHURCH LANE

Lower House Farm

Coton Grove

Yew Tree Farm

2

Whixall

Church Farm

Meadow View Farm

Marches Way

Coton

Bostock Hall

Brook House Farm

White Lion Farm

PH

GOBLIN'S LANE

Oakfields Farm

POST OFFICE LANE

B5476

Coton Farm

1

GREEN LANE

Shropshire Way

GREEN LANE

GILBERT'S LANE

34

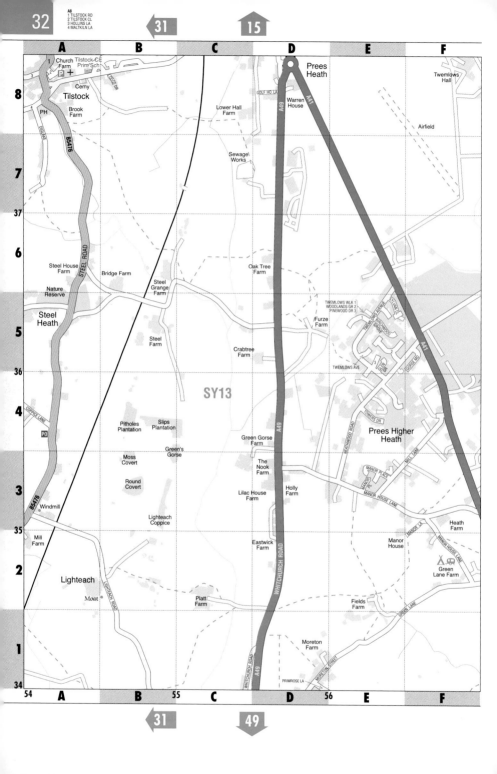

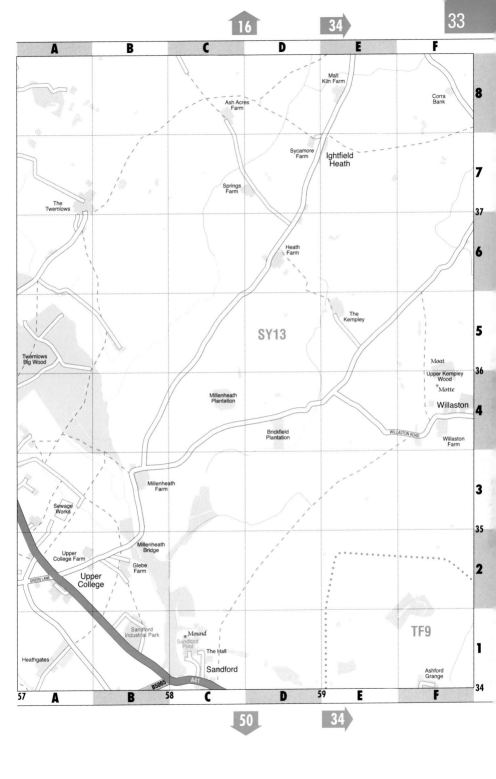

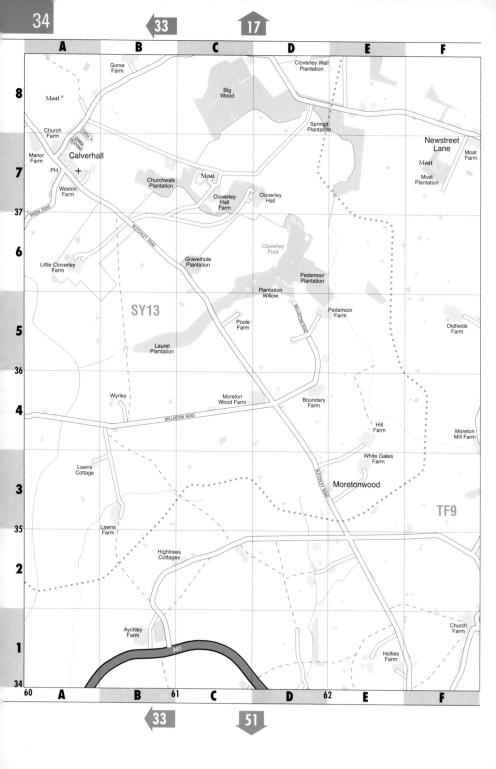

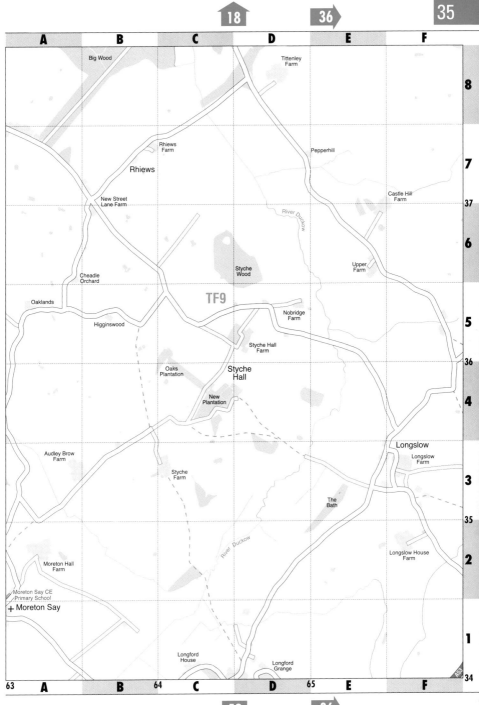

Big Wood

Tittenley
Farm

Rhiews
Farm

Pepperhill

Rhiews

Castle Hill
Farm

New Street
Lane Farm

River Duckow

Cheadle
Orchard

Styche
Wood

Upper
Farm

Oaklands

TF9

Nobridge
Farm

Higginswood

Styche Hall
Farm

Oaks
Plantation

Styche
Hall

New
Plantation

Longslow

Audley Brow
Farm

Longslow
Farm

Styche
Farm

The
Bath

Moreton Hall
Farm

Longslow House
Farm

Moreton Say CE
Primary School

River Duckow

+ Moreton Say

Longford
House

Longford
Grange

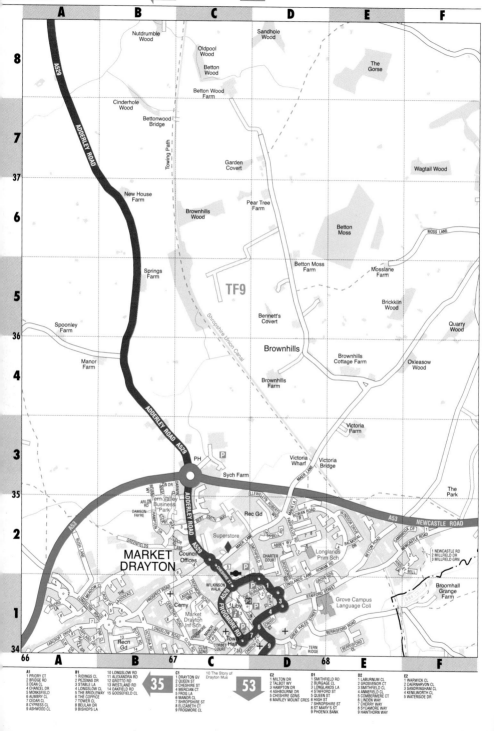

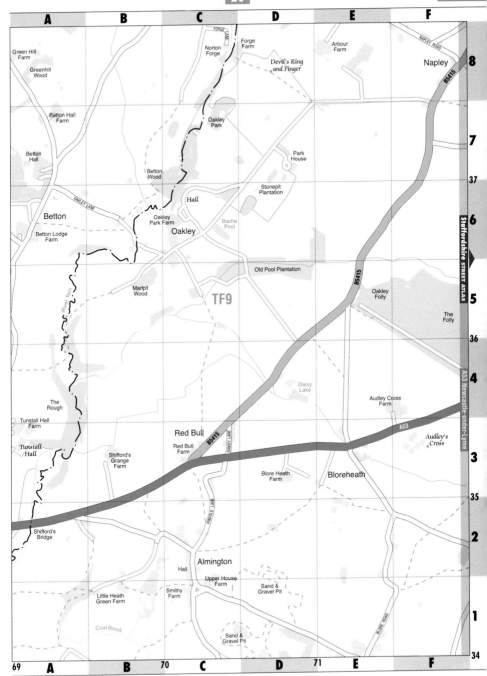

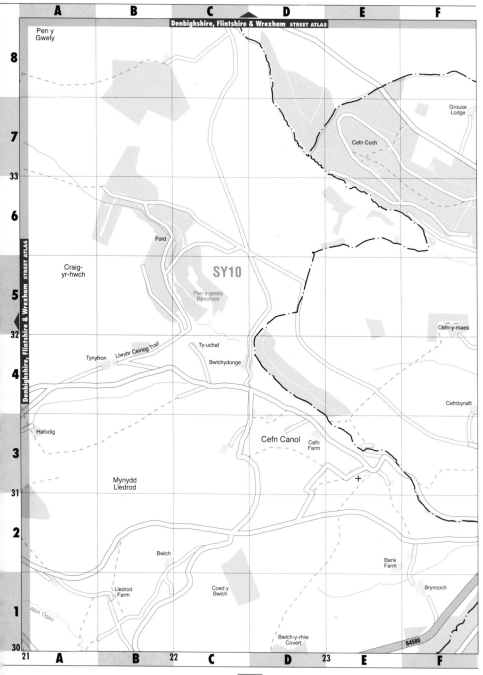

Pen y Gwely

Grouse Lodge

Cefn Coch

Ford

Craig-yr-hwch

SY10

Pen-y-gwely Reservoir

Cefn-y-maes

Tynyfron

Llwybr Ceiriog Trail

Ty-uchaf

Bwlchydonge

Cefnbyrallt

Hafodig

Cefn Canol

Cefn Farm

Mynydd Lledrod

Bwlch

Bank Farm

Bryncoch

Lledrod Farm

Coed y Bwlch

Afon Ogau

Bwlch-y-rhiw Covert

B4580

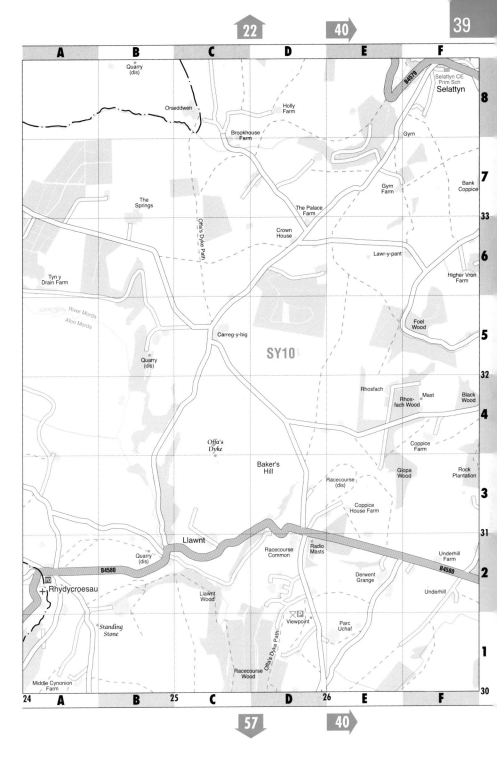

A   B   C   D   E   F

8

Quarry
(dis)

Orseddwen

Holly
Farm

Selattyn CE
Prim Sch
Selattyn

B4579

Brookhouse
Farm

Gyrn

7

The
Springs

Gyrn
Farm

Bank
Coppice

33

Offa's Dyke Path

The Palace
Farm

Crown
House

Lawr-y-pant

6

Tyn y
Drain Farm

Higher Vron
Farm

River Morda

Afon Morda

Foel
Wood

5

Carreg-y-big

SY10

Quarry
(dis)

32

Rhosfach

Rhos-
fach Wood

Mast

Black
Wood

4

Offa's
Dyke

Coppice
Farm

Baker's
Hill

Racecourse
(dis)

Glopa
Wood

Rock
Plantation

3

Coppice
House Farm

31

Llawnt

Racecourse
Common

Radio
Masts

Underhill
Farm

B4580

Quarry
(dis)

Derwent
Grange

Underhill

B4580

2

Rhydycroesau

Llawnt
Wood

Viewpoint

Parc
Uchaf

*Standing
Stone*

1

Middle Cynonion
Farm

Racecourse
Wood

Offa's Dyke Path

30

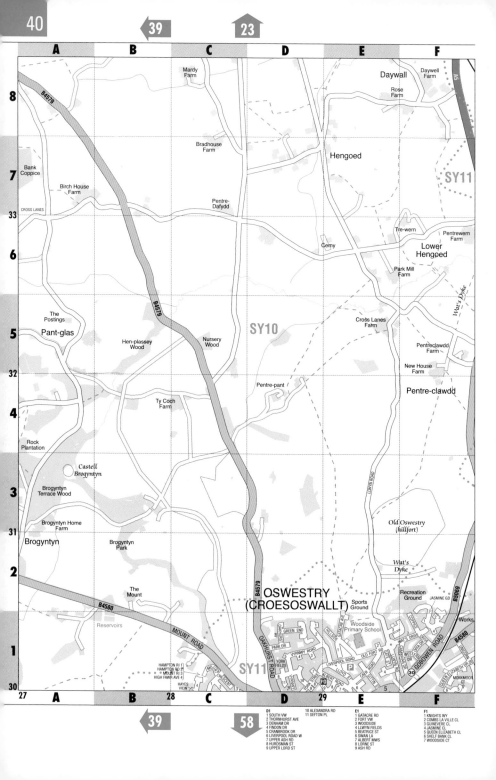

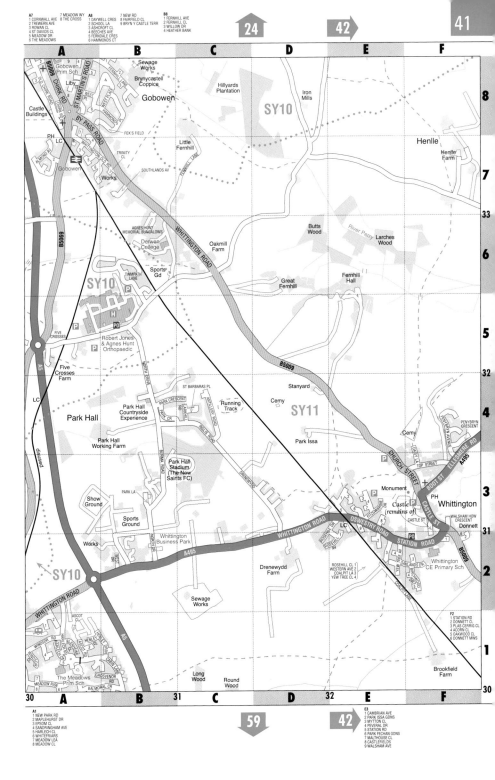

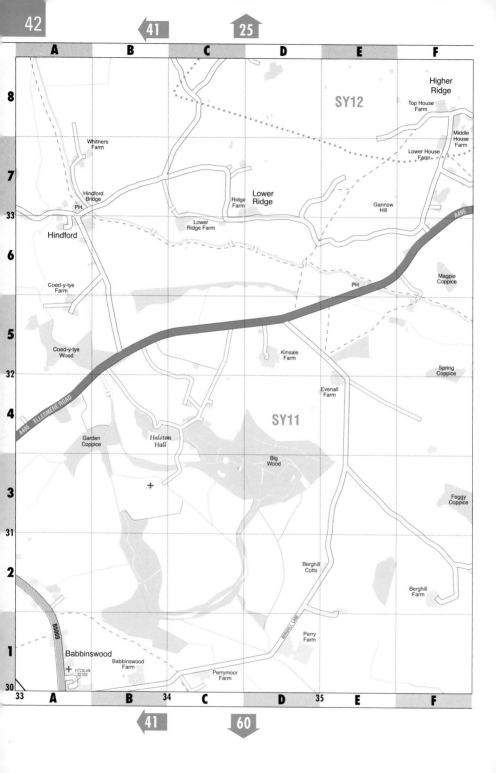

8

SY12

Higher
Ridge

Top House
Farm

Middle
House
Farm

Whitners
Farm

7

Lower House
Farm

Hindford
Bridge

Ridge
Farm

Lower
Ridge

Gannow
Hill

4495

33

PH

Lower
Ridge Farm

Hindford

6

Magpie
Coppice

Coed-y-tye
Farm

PH

5

Coed-y-tye
Wood

Kinsale
Farm

Spring
Coppice

32

4495 ELLESMERE ROAD

Evenall
Farm

4

SY11

Garden
Coppice

Halston
Hall

Big
Wood

Feggy
Coppice

3

+

31

Berghill
Cotts

Berghill
Farm

2

BERGHILL LANE

Perry
Farm

1

B5009

Babbinswood

Babbinswood
Farm

Perrymoor
Farm

+ FITZALAN
CLOSE

30

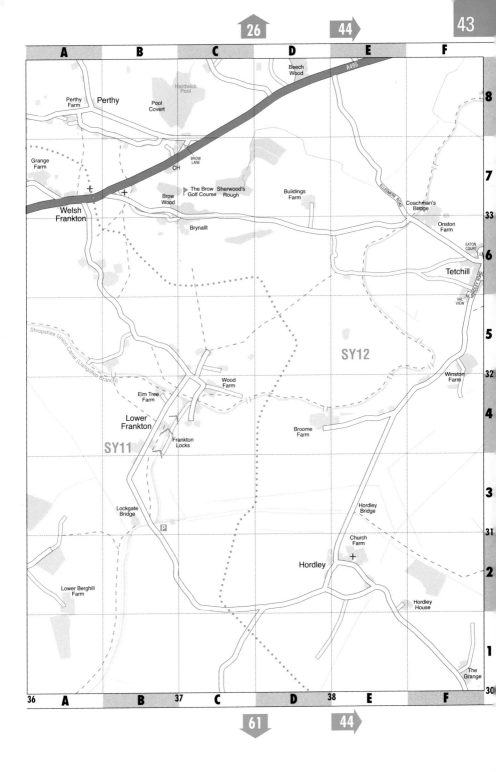

A   B   C   D   E   F

8

Perthy
Farm
Perthy

Pool
Covert

Hardwick
Pool

Beech
Wood

A495

Grange
Farm

BROW
LANE

CH

Brow
Wood

The Brow
Golf Course

Sherwood's
Rough

Buildings
Farm

7

ELLESMERE ROAD

Coachman's
Bridge

33

Welsh
Frankton

Brynallt

Onston
Farm

EATON
COURT

6

Tetchill

VAL
VIEW

MONDLEY ROAD

Shropshire Union Canal (Llangollen Branch)

SY12

5

32

Wood
Farm

Elm Tree
Farm

Winston
Farm

Lower
Frankton

SY11

Frankton
Locks

Broome
Farm

4

3

Lockgate
Bridge

Hordley
Bridge

31

P

Church
Farm

Hordley

2

Lower Berghill
Farm

Hordley
House

1

The
Grange

30

A   B   C   D   E   F

8

7

33

6

KENWICK VW

ELLESMERE ROAD

FARM LANE

Tetchill

5

32

4

Oak House Farm

3

Sycamore Farm

31

Tetchill Moor

2

Manor Farm

Outcast

1

Kenwick Grange Farm

30

39   A   B   40   C   D   41   E   F

Sewage Works

Ellesmere College

Birch Hall Farm

The Lyth

Spunhill

Mere Wood

White Mere

Lee

Lee Old Hall

Lee Hall Farm

Lee Wood

Yarnest Wood

Wood Lane

Pole Wood

Woodlane Farm

SY12

New Farm

Lee Bridges

Smithy Moor

Springs Farm

Brick Kiln Farm

Blake Mere

George's Wood

A528

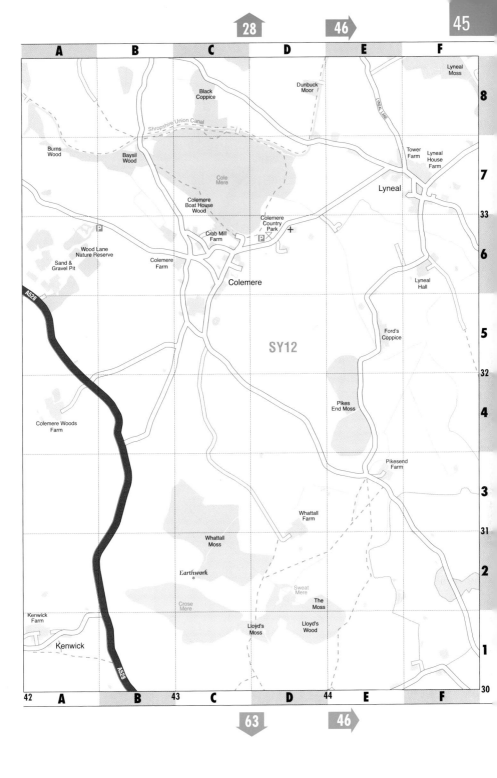

8

Lyneal
Moss

Black
Coppice

Dunbuck
Moor

LYNEAL LANE

Shropshire Union Canal

Burns
Wood

Baysil
Wood

Tower
Farm

Lyneal
House
Farm

7

Cole
Mere

Lyneal

33

Colemere
Boat House
Wood

Colemere
Country
Park

P

Crab Mill
Farm

Wood Lane
Nature Reserve

Colemere
Farm

6

Colemere

Sand &
Gravel Pit

Lyneal
Hall

SY12

Ford's
Coppice

5

32

A528

Pikes
End Moss

4

Colemere Woods
Farm

Pikesend
Farm

3

31

Whattall
Farm

Whattall
Moss

2

Earthwork

Sweat
Mere

The
Moss

Crose
Mere

Kenwick
Farm

Lloyd's
Moss

Lloyd's
Wood

1

Kenwick

A528

30

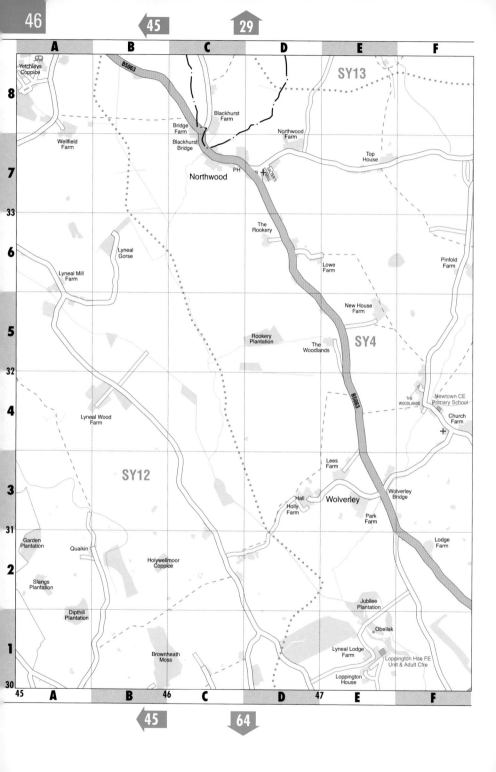

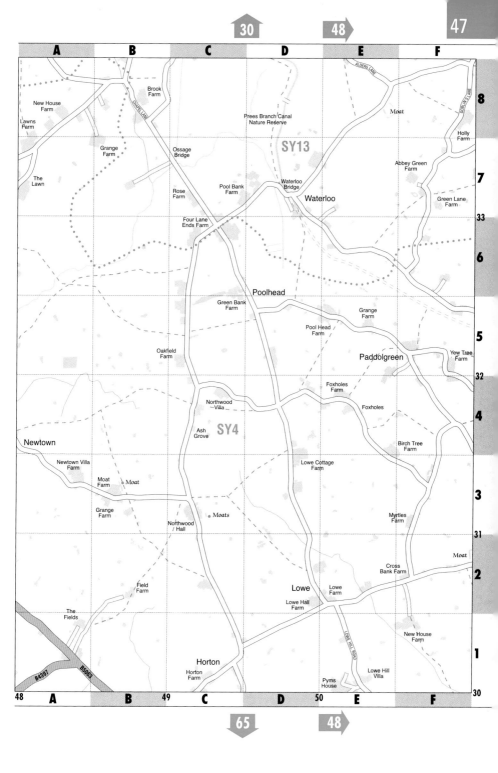

47
31

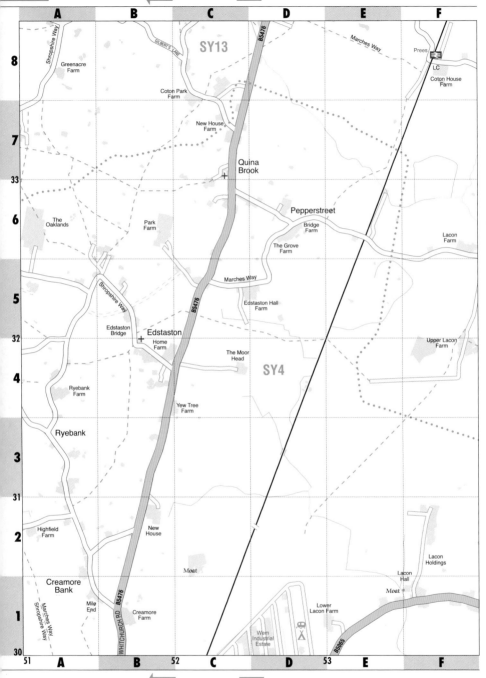

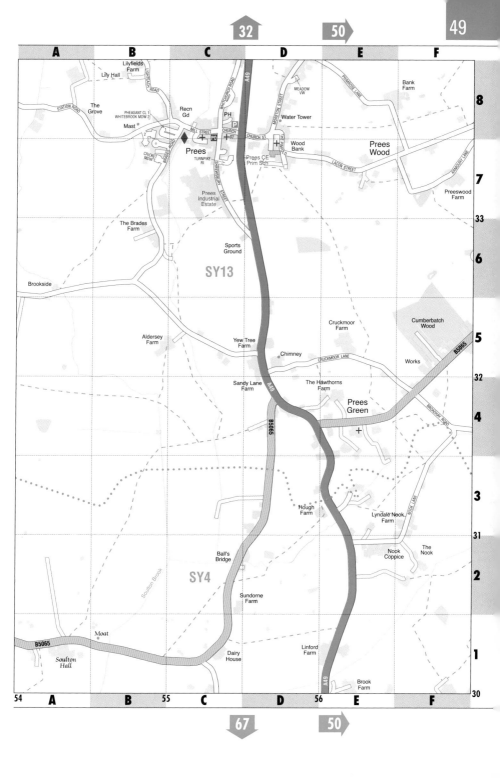

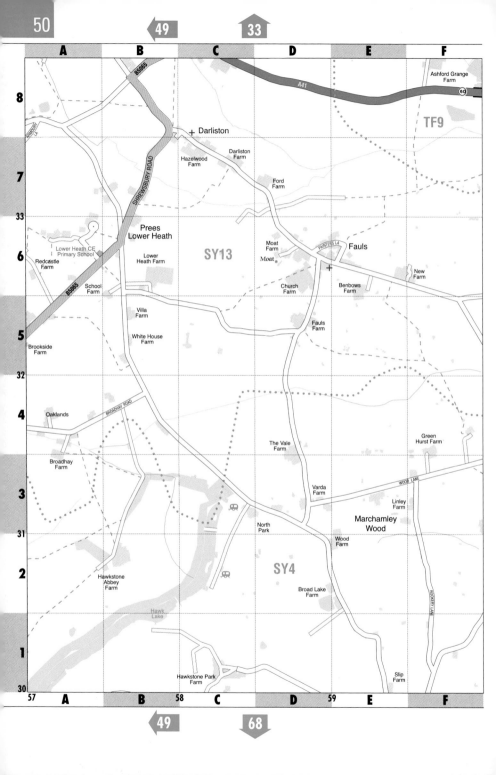

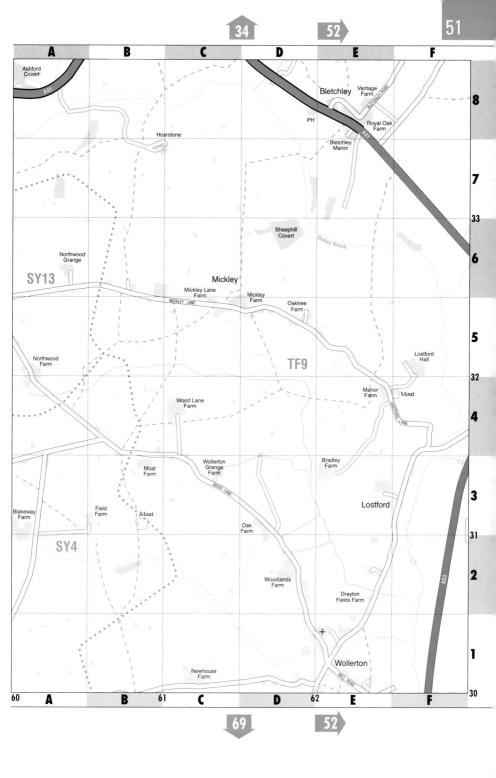

A B C D E F

Ashford
Covert

A41

Bletchley

Vantage
Farm

BLETCHLEY ROAD

8

PH

Royal Oak
Farm

A41

Hoarstone

Bletchley
Manor

7

33

Sheephill
Covert

Bailey Brook

6

Northwood
Grange

SY13

Mickley

Mickley Lane
Farm

Mickley
Farm

Oaktree
Farm

MICKLEY LANE

5

Northwood
Farm

TF9

Lostford
Hall

32

Manor
Farm

Moat

LOSTFORD LANE

4

Wood Lane
Farm

Moat
Farm

Wollerton
Grange
Farm

Bradley
Farm

3

Blakeway
Farm

Field
Farm

Moat

WOOD LANE

Lostford

31

SY4

Oak
Farm

A53

2

Woodlands
Farm

Drayton
Fields Farm

+

Wollerton

1

Newhouse
Farm

MILL ROAD

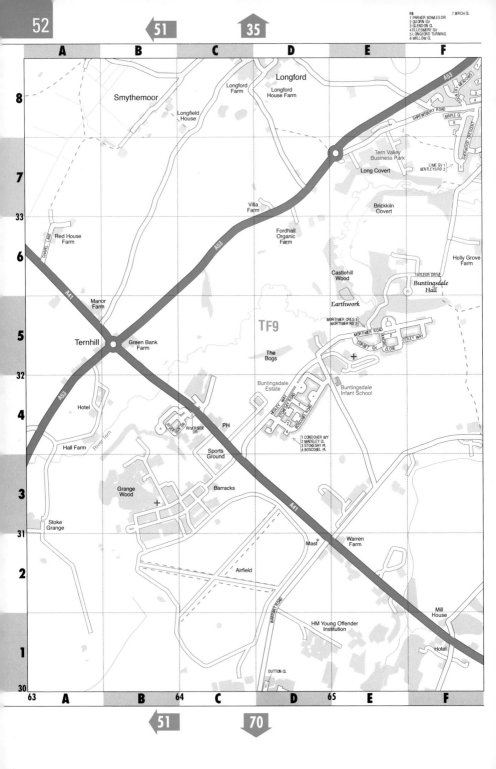

51
35

F8
1 PARKER BOWLES DR
2 QUORN GV
3 GLENDON CL
4 ELLESMERE GV
5 LONGFORD TURNING
6 WILLOW CL

7 BIRCH CL

8

33

7

6

5

32

4

3

31

2

1

30

A   B   C   D   E   F

Smythemoor

Longford

Longford
Farm

Longford
House Farm

Longfield
House

A53

Tern Valley
Business Park

Long Covert

SHREWSBURY ROAD

MAPLE CL

LIME GV 1
BENTLEYS RD 2

Villa
Farm

Red House
Farm

CHAPEL LANE

Fordhall
Organic
Farm

Brickkiln
Covert

Holly Grove
Farm

A41

Manor
Farm

Castlehill
Wood

TAYLEUR DRIVE

Buntingsdale
Hall

Earthwork

TF9

MORTIMER CRES 1
MORTIMER RD 2

MORTIMER ROAD

CORBET GV

OTLEY WAY

PREMO

CLOSE

Ternhill

Green Bank
Farm

The
Bogs

Buntingsdale
Estate

Buntingsdale
Infant School

A53

Hotel

River Tern

RIVERSIDE DR

RIVERSIDE
DR

PH

HEDLEY WAY

FOSCOTE ROAD

ROSCOBE ROAD

1 CONDOVER WY
2 MADELEY CL
3 STONESAY PL
4 BOSCOBEL PL

Hall Farm

Sports
Ground

Grange
Wood

Barracks

Stoke
Grange

Mast

Warren
Farm

A41

Airfield

WARREN ROAD

HM Young Offender
Institution

Mill
House

Hotel

DUTTON CL

63   A   B   64   C   D   65   E   F

51
70

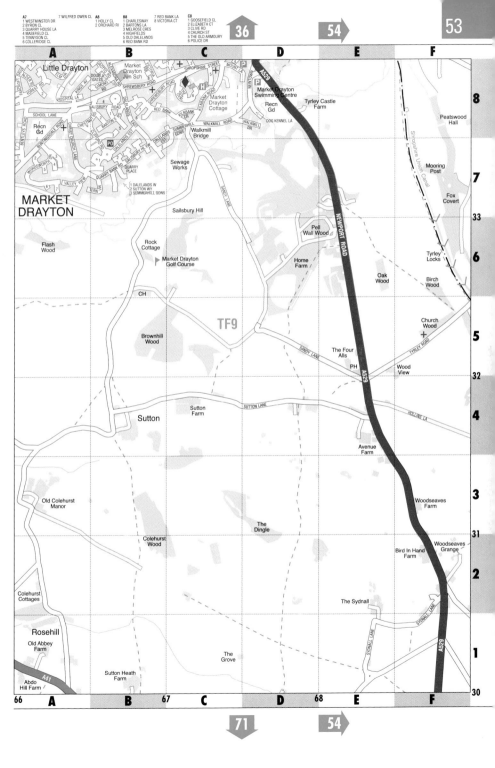

A7
1 WESTMINSTER DR
2 BYRON CL
3 QUARRY HOUSE LA
4 MASEFIELD CL
5 TENNYSON CL
6 COLLERIDGE CL

7 WILFRED OWEN CL

A8
1 HOLLY CL
2 ORCHARD RI

B8
1 CHARLESWAY
2 BARTONS LA
3 MELROSE CRES
4 HIGHFIELDS
5 OLD DALELANDS
6 RED BANK RD

7 RED BANK LA
8 VICTORIA CT

C8
1 GOOSEFIELD CL
2 ELIZABETH CT
3 CLIVE RD
4 CHURCH ST
5 THE OLD ARMOURY
6 POLICE DR

36
54
53

A   B   C   D   E   F

Little Drayton

Market Drayton Jun Sch

Shropshire Street

Market Drayton Swimming Centre

Tyrley Castle Farm

Peatswood Hall

8

Recn Gd

Market Drayton Cottage

Shropshire Union Canal

Mooring Post

7

Red Bank

Walkmill Road

Walkmill Bridge

DOG KENNEL LA

Fox Covert

33

Sewage Works

Sailsbury Hill

Rock Cottage

Pell Wall Wood

NEWPORT ROAD

Tyrley Locks

6

Flash Wood

1 DALELANDS W
2 SUTTON WY
3 SUMMERHILL GDNS

Market Drayton Golf Course

Home Farm

Oak Wood

Birch Wood

Church Wood

CH

TF9

Brownhill Wood

SANDY LANE

The Four Alls

PH

TYRLEY ROAD

5

Wood View

32

Sutton

Sutton Farm

SUTTON LANE

SANDY LANE

A529

HOLLINS LA

4

Avenue Farm

Old Colehurst Manor

The Dingle

Woodseaves Farm

3

Colehurst Wood

Bird In Hand Farm

Woodseaves Grange

31

Colehurst Cottages

2

The Sydnall

Rosehill

SYDNALL LANE

Old Abbey Farm

A41

The Grove

A529

1

Abdo Hill Farm

Sutton Heath Farm

30

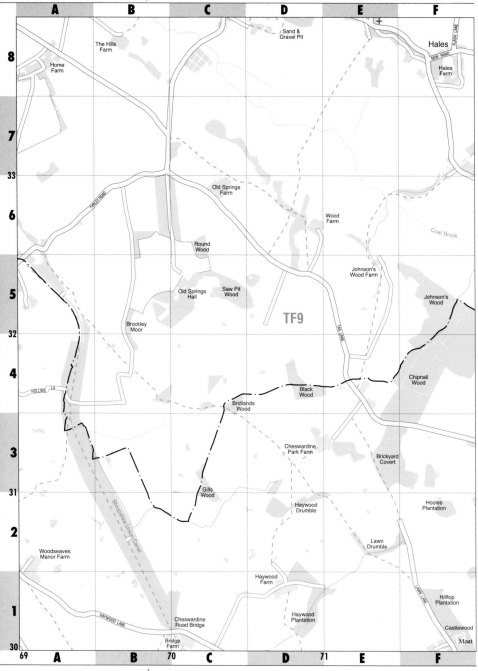

TF9

Hales

Hales Farm

Home Farm

The Hills Farm

Sand & Gravel Pit

Coal Brook

Old Springs Farm

Wood Farm

Round Wood

Old Springs Hall

Saw Pit Wood

Johnson's Wood Farm

Johnson's Wood

Brockley Moor

Chipnall Wood

Bridlands Wood

Black Wood

Cheswardine Park Farm

Brickyard Covert

Gills Wood

Haywood Drumble

Hooles Plantation

Shropshire Union Canal

Lawn Drumble

Woodseaves Manor Farm

Haywood Farm

Haywood Plantation

Hilltop Plantation

Cheswardine Road Bridge

Castlewood

Moat

Bridge Farm

HAYWOOD LANE

HOLLINS LA

TYRLEY ROAD

THE LANE

FLASH LANE

NEW ROAD

LAWN LANE

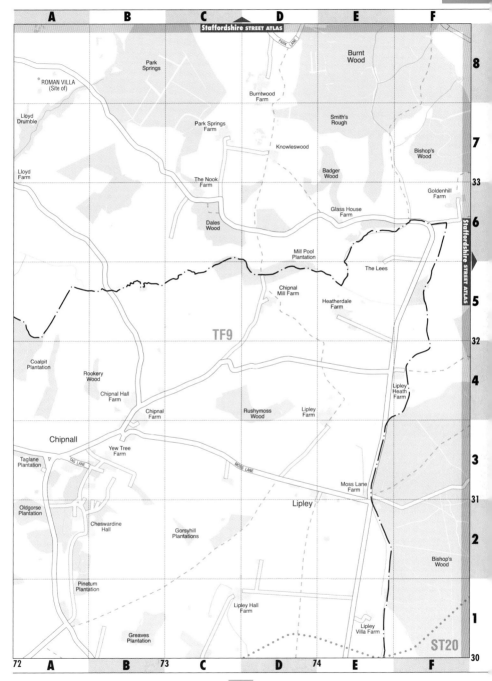

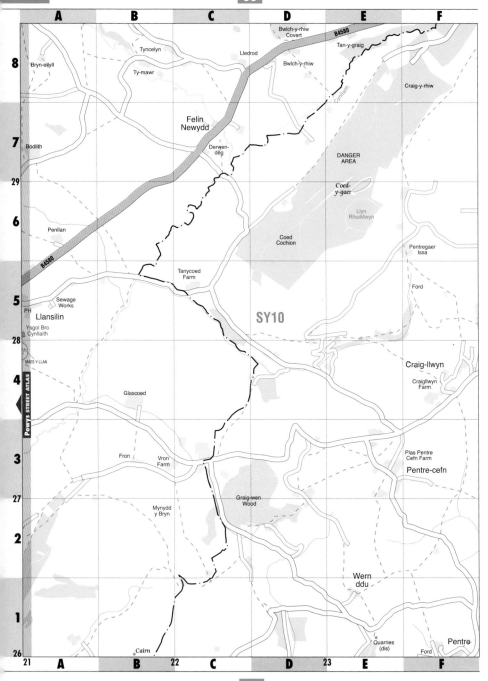

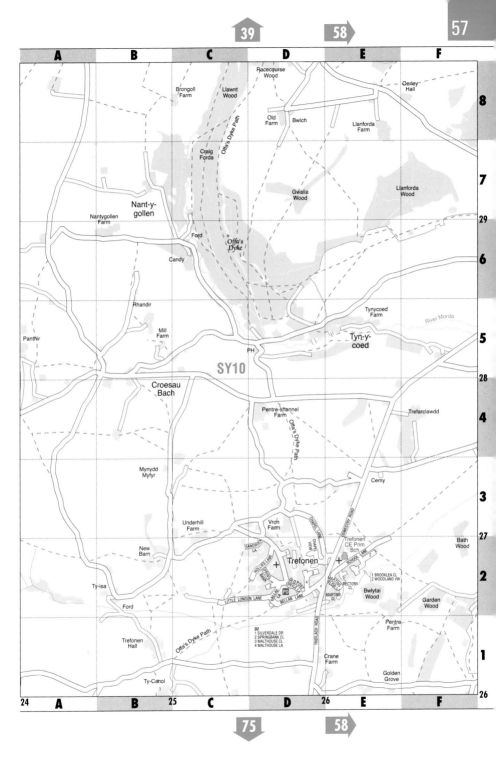

A B C D E F

8

Oerley
Hall

Brongoll
Farm

Llawnt
Wood

Racecourse
Wood

Old
Farm

Bwlch

Llanforda
Farm

7

Craig
Forda

Gwalia
Wood

Llanforda
Wood

Nant-y-
gollen

29

Nantygollen
Farm

Ford

Offa's
Dyke

River Morda

Candy

6

Rhandir

Tynycoed
Farm

Tyn-y-
coed

5

Mill
Farm

Panthir

PH

SY10

28

Croesau
Bach

Pentre-shannel
Farm

Trefarclawdd

4

Mynydd
Myfyr

Offa's Dyke Path

Cefny

3

Underhill
Farm

Vroh
Farm

Trefonen
CE Prim
Sch

Bath
Wood

27

New
Barn

SANDROCK
LA

CHAPEL
VIEW

HOLLIES LINK

CHAPEL LANE

OSWESTRY ROAD

SCHOOL LANE

1 BROOKLEA CL
2 WOODLAND VW

2

Ty-isa

Trefonen

MARTINS
FIELD

RECTORY
CL

Bwlytai
Wood

Garden
Wood

Ford

LITTLE LONDON LANE

BELLAN LANE

MARTINS
CL

TRELIBOR ROAD

Pentre
Farm

1

Trefonen
Hall

Offa's Dyke Path

D2
1 SILVERDALE DR
2 SPRINGBANK CL
3 MALTHOUSE CL
4 MALTHOUSE LA

Crane
Farm

Ty-Canol

Golden
Grove

26

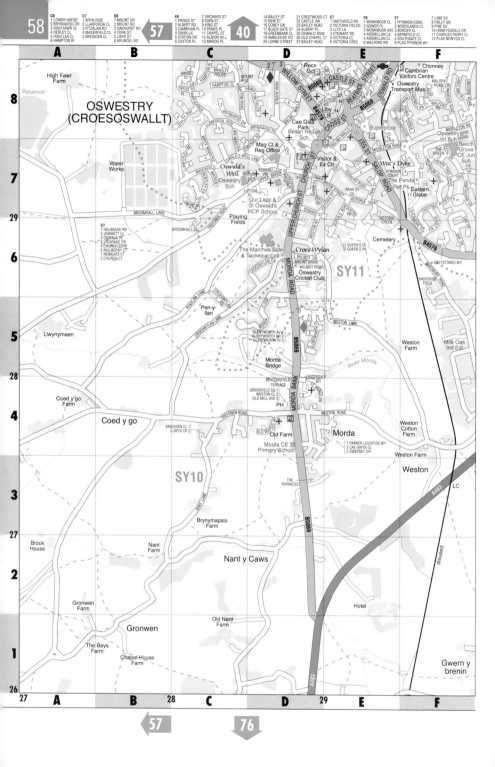

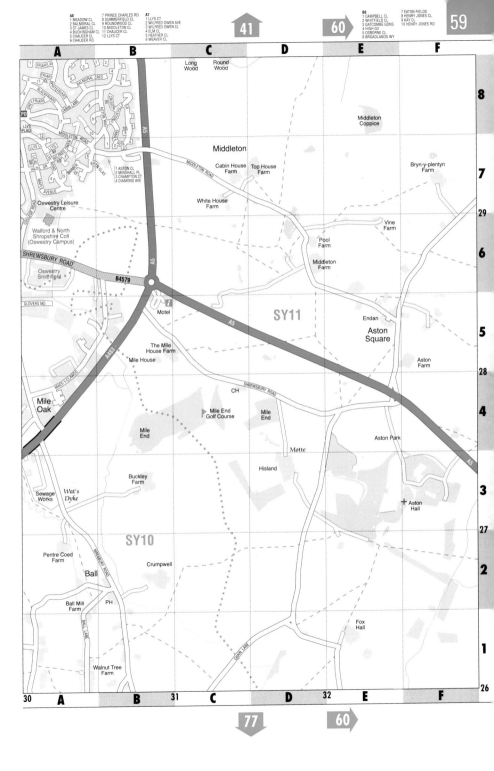

A8
1 MEADOW CL
2 BALMORAL CL
3 ST JAMES CL
4 BUCKINGHAM CL
5 CHAUCER CL
6 CHAUCER RD

7 PRINCE CHARLES RD
8 SUMMERFIELD CL
9 ROUNDWOOD CL
10 MIDDLETON CL
11 CHAUCER CL
12 LLYS CT

A7
1 LLYS CT
2 WILFRED OWEN AVE
3 WILFRED OWEN AVE
4 ELM CL
5 HEATHER CL
6 WEAVER CL

B8
1 CAMPBELL CL
2 WHITFIELD CL
3 GATCOMBE GDNS
4 HIGH GV
5 OSBORNE CL
6 BROADLANDS WY

7 EATON FIELDS
8 HENRY JONES CL
9 KAY CL
10 HENRY JONES RD

41 60

Long Wood
Round Wood
Middleton Coppice
Middleton
Bryn-y-plentyn Farm
Cabin House Farm
Top House Farm
White House Farm
Vine Farm
29
Pool Farm
Middleton Farm
Oswestry Leisure Centre
Walford & North Shropshire Coll (Oswestry Campus)
SHREWSBURY ROAD
B4579
Oswestry Smithfield
Endan
Aston Square
SY11
GLOVERS MD
Motel
The Mile House Farm
Mile House
CH
SHREWSBURY ROAD
Aston Farm
28
Mile Oak
Mile End Golf Course
Mile End
Mile End
Aston Park
Motte
Hisland
Aston Hall
Buckley Farm
Sewage Works
Wat's Dyke
27
Pentre Coed Farm
SY10
Crumpwell
Ball
Ball Mill Farm
PH
Fox Hall
Walnut Tree Farm

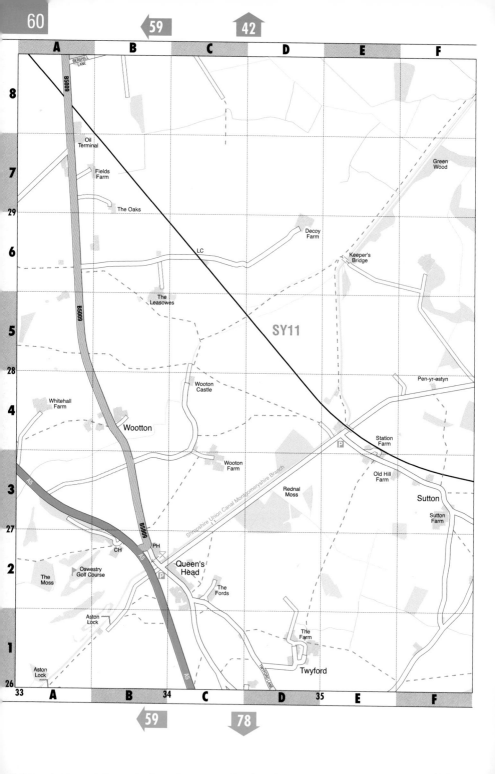

59
42

A B C D E F

8

7

29

6

5

28

4

3

27

2

1

26

BERGHILL LANE

B5009

Oil Terminal

Fields Farm

The Oaks

Decoy Farm

LC

Keeper's Bridge

Green Wood

The Leasowes

SY11

Pen-yr-estyn

Wooton Castle

Whitehall Farm

Wootton

Station Farm

Old Hill Farm

Sutton

Wooton Farm

Rednal Moss

Shropshire Union Canal Montgomeryshire Branch

Sutton Farm

B5009

A5

PH

CH

Queen's Head

Oswestry Golf Course

The Moss

The Fords

Aston Lock

The Farm

Aston Lock

Twyford

WYKORD LANE

A5

33 A B 34 C D 35 E F

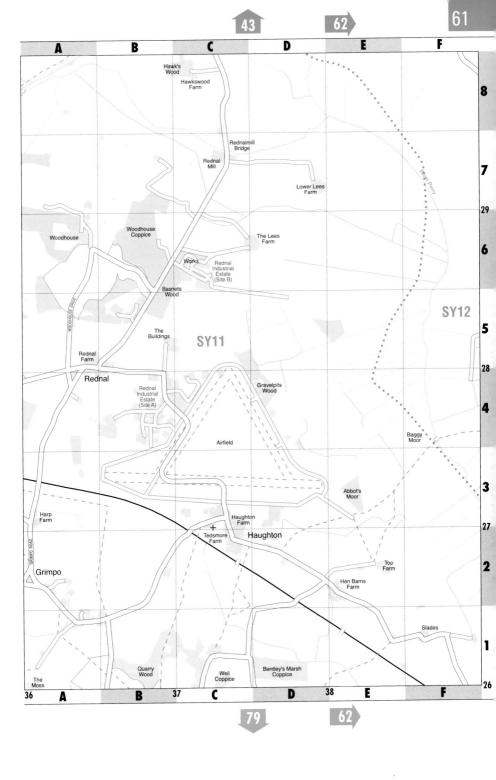

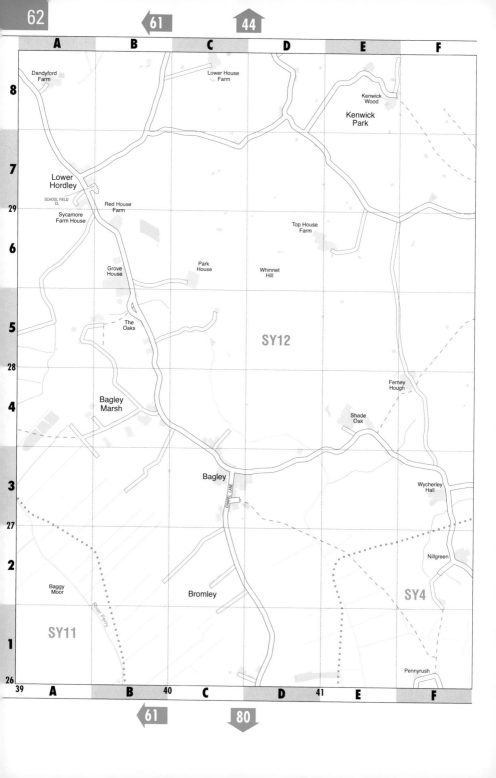

A   B   C   D   E   F

8

Dandyford
Farm

Lower House
Farm

Kenwick
Wood

Kenwick
Park

7

Lower
Hordley

29

SCHOOL FIELD
CL

Red House
Farm

Sycamore
Farm House

Top House
Farm

6

Grove
House

Park
House

Whinnet
Hill

5

The
Oaks

SY12

28

Ferney
Hough

4

Bagley
Marsh

Shade
Oak

3

Bagley

Wycherley
Hall

27

CHAPEL LANE

2

Nillgreen

Baggy
Moor

Bromley

SY4

1

SY11

River Perry

Pennyrush

26

39   A   B   40   C   D   41   E   F

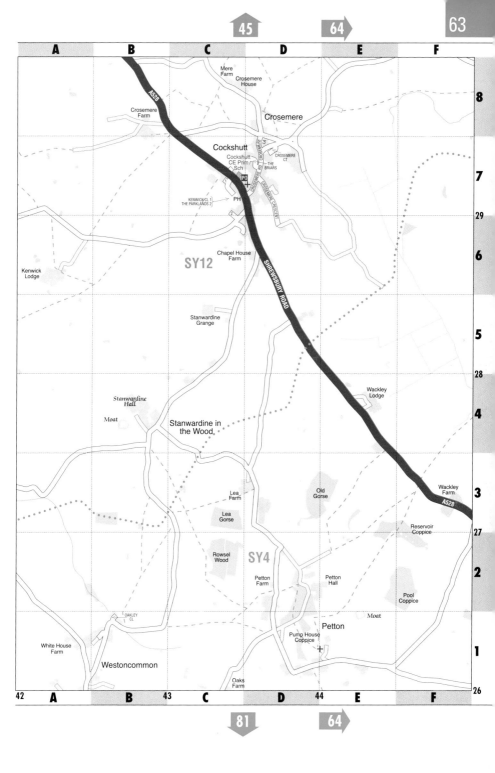

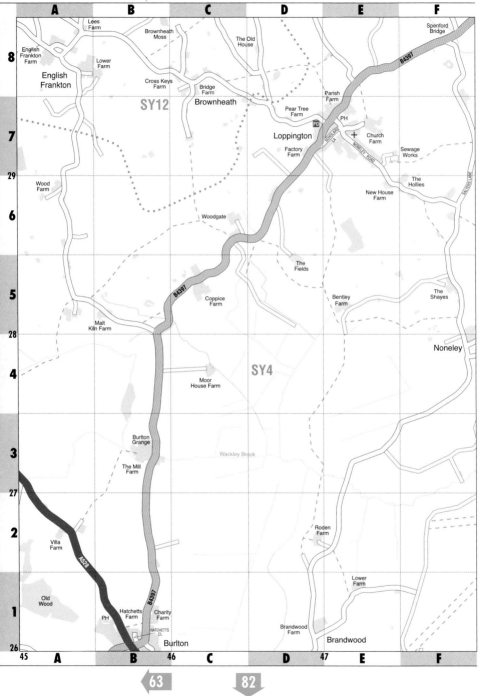

Horton

Yew Tree
Farm

Horton
House Farm

Horton
Hall Farm

LOWE HILL ROAD

TRENTHAM
RD

B5063

SOMERSET RD

BAILEY ROAD

PYMS ROAD

Chy

The Thomas
Adams School

7

Factory

Ditches
Farm

The Ditches
Hall

ELLESMERE ROAD

Wem

B5063

LOWE HILL RD

Thomas
Adams
Sports Ctr

29

Slangs
Plantation

River Roden

The Pools
Farm

HIGH ST

Green
Hill

6

BRIDGEWATER LA

COTTERILL WY

THE GROVE

GROVE CT

BARNARD
ST

SWAN CL

Marches Way

5

Manor
Farm

Commonwood
Farm

Pearl Farm

SY4

Ruewood Meadow
Nature Reserve

Tilley
Bridge

Brook
Farm

BROOK DR 1
RODEN GR 2
ALVIN CL 3

28

Grafton
Farm

Forrester
Farm

PH

Tilley

TILLEY ROAD

LC

Tilley
Farm

4

B5476

Sleap Brook

Sleap
Bridge

Rue Wood
Farm

3

27

Airfield

Sleap
House Farm

New House
Farm

Tilley
Park Farm

2

Sleap

Sleap
Gorse

LC

The
Drumble

B5476

WEM ROAD

1

LC

26

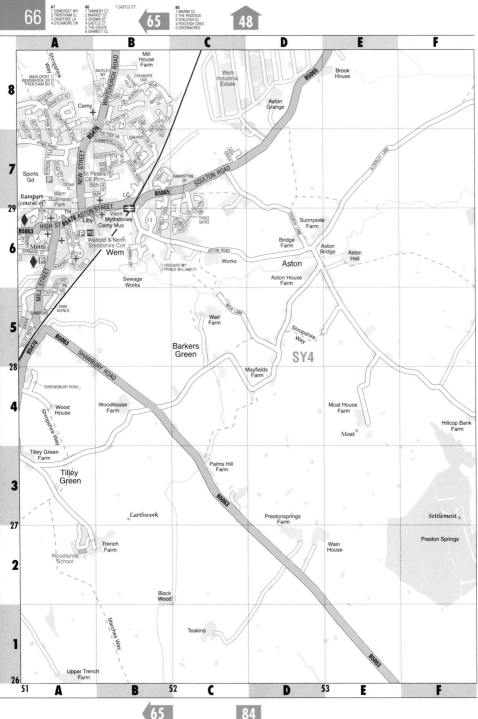

A7
1 SOMERSET WY
2 TRENTHAM CL
3 CRABTREE LA
4 SYCAMORE DR

A6
1 TANNERY CT
2 MARKET ST
3 CROWN ST
4 CASTLE CT
5 THE GROVE
6 GARBETT CL

7 CASTLE CT

B8
1 MARNE CL
2 THE PADDOCK
3 FOXLEIGH CL
4 FOXLEIGH CRES
5 GREENACRES

65   48

Mill House Farm

Wem Industrial Estate

Brook House

B5065

Aston Grange

Shropshire Way

Cemy

MARLCROFT 1
WEMSBROOK DR 2
TRENTHAM RD 3

Sports Gd

Rampart (course of)

Wem Business Park

St Peters CE Prim. Sch

SOULTON ROAD

Hawkstone Dr

B5065

Sunnyside Farm

B5063

Wem Mythstories Cemy Mus

THREE GATES

Bridge Farm

Aston Bridge

Aston Hall

Motte

Walford & North Shropshire Coll

Wem

1 ORCHARD WY
2 PRINCE WILLIAM CT

Aston Road

Works

Aston

Aston House Farm

Sewage Works

Park Avenue

ASTON STREET

HIGH ST

MILL STREET

Sungrove

SHAWBURY ROAD

B5063

B5476

Weir Farm

WEIR LANE

Shropshire Way

Barkers Green

SY4

Mayfields Farm

SHREWSBURY ROAD

Wood House

Woodhouse Farm

Moat House Farm

Moat

Hillcop Bank Farm

Shropshire Way

Tilley Green Farm

Tilley Green

Palms Hill Farm

B5063

Earthwork

Prestonsprings Farm

Settlement

Preston Springs

Trench Farm

Woodlands School

Wain House

Black Wood

Teakins

B5063

Upper Trench Farm

Marches Way

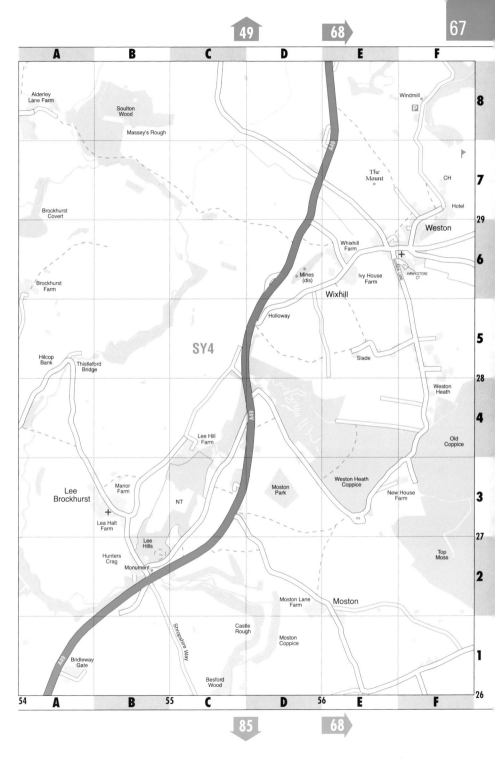

A B C D E F

8

Alderley
Lane Farm

Soulton
Wood

Massey's Rough

Windmill
P

CH

Hotel

The
Mount

7

Brockhurst
Covert

29

Whixhill
Farm

Weston

6

Brockhurst
Farm

Mines
(dis)

Ivy House
Farm

HAWKSTONE
CT

Wixhill

SY4

Holloway

5

Hilcop
Bank

Thistleford
Bridge

Slade

28

Weston
Heath

4

Lee Hill
Farm

Old
Coppice

Lee
Brockhurst

Manor
Farm

NT

Moston
Park

Weston Heath
Coppice

New House
Farm

3

Lea Halt
Farm

27

Lee
Hills

Top
Moss

2

Hunters
Crag

Monument

Moston Lane
Farm

Moston

Shropshire Way

Castle
Rough

Moston
Coppice

1

Bridleway
Gate

Besford
Wood

26

54
A
B
55
C
D
56
E
F

A B C D E F

8

7

29

6

5

28

4

3

27

2

1

26

Hawk
Lake

Grotto
Hill

Red
Castle

The
Terrace

Elysian
Hill

Visitor
Centre

The
Citadel

Bury
Park

Bury
Wood

Top
Moss

Hawkstone
Park

Obelisk

Hawkstone
Park

Rake
Park

Menagerie
Pool

Bury
Farm

SY4

Moat
Bank

Bury Walls
(fort)

Hermitage
Farm

Quarry
Farm

Quarry
Coppice

Old Shop
Farm

Hawkstone Hall
(Pastoral Centre)

Tower

Terrace
Plantation

Rakepark
Lodge

Spinnel
Wood

Chirbury
Wood

Morgan's
Coppice

Shaft
(dis)

Daneswell
Farm

Morgans
Coppice
Farm

School Lane

Chirbury
Farm

Hawkstone
Farm

Terrace
Plantation

Bank
Farm

Kenstone

Danes
Well

DAYS LANE

Hopley
Coppice

Stone House
Farm

Hopton

CHAPEL LANE

Well House
Farm

Marchamley

BARNS LA.

Marchamley
Hill

Hopley
Farm

TF9

ROOKERY LANE

A53

57 A

58 B

C

58 C

D

59 D

E

F

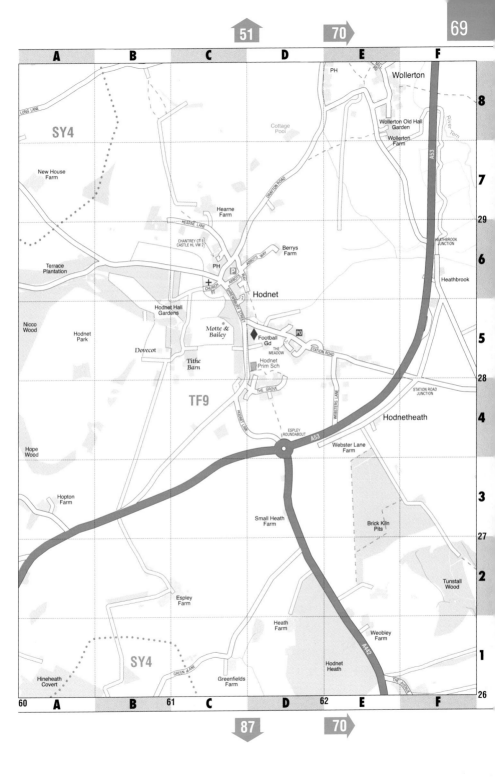

A B C D E F

8

Wollerton

7

29

6

5

28

4

3

27

2

1

26

LONG LANE

SY4

New House Farm

Hearne Farm

HEARNE LANE

CHANTREY CT 1
CASTLE HL VW 2

PH

Terrace Plantation

CHURCH ST

P

ABBOTS WAY

SHREWSBURY STREET

Berrys Farm

Hodnet

Hodnet Hall Gardens

Nicco Wood

Hodnet Park

Dovecot

Motte & Bailey

Tithe Barn

Football Gd

THE MEADOW

PO

STATION ROAD

Hodnet Prim Sch

TF9

THE GROVE

HODNET TRK

WEBSTERS LANE

STATION ROAD JUNCTION

Hodnetheath

Hope Wood

ESPLEY ROUNDABOUT

A53

Webster Lane Farm

Hopton Farm

Small Heath Farm

Brick Kiln Pits

Espley Farm

Heath Farm

Tunstall Wood

SY4

GREEN LANE

Greenfields Farm

A442

Weobley Farm

Hodnet Heath

Hinehealth Covert

THE AVENUE

PH

DRAYTON ROAD

Cottage Pool

Wollerton Old Hall Garden

Wollerton Farm

River Tern

A53

HEATHBROOK JUNCTION

Heathbrook

69 52

	A	B	C	D	E	F

8

Maurice Chandler
Sports Centre

Honeyspot
Farm

Stoke
Heath

Yew Tree
Farm

Helshaw
Grange

Spring Hill
Farm

Chapel Lane

North Moor
Farm

Sutton Camp
Farm

7

Hill House
Farm

ROSE HILL LA

Gallantry
Hill

Loxday
Farm

29

SANDY LANE

ROSE HILL ROAD

MOUNT LANE

Mount
Farm

6

WARRANT ROAD

Lythe-beck
Farm

Stoke on Tern
Primary School

Salters
Hill Farm

Heathcote

5

Cemy

TF9

Stoke on
Tern

Ivy House
Farm

LANGLEY
DL

Stoke Hall
Farm

Heathcote
Farm

28

Stoke
Bridge

Stoke
Farm

Stoke
Manor

Whitehall
Farm

4

Cotton
Farm

Petsey
Farm

Moat

3

River Tern

Stoke Park
Farm

The
Sytchpits

27

2

Tunstall
Wood

1

Tunstall
Farm

Woodhouse
Farm

Stoke Park
Farm

Firs
Farm

OLLERTON LANE

DODE LANE

26

The
Bendles

63	A	B	64	C	D	65	E	F

69 88

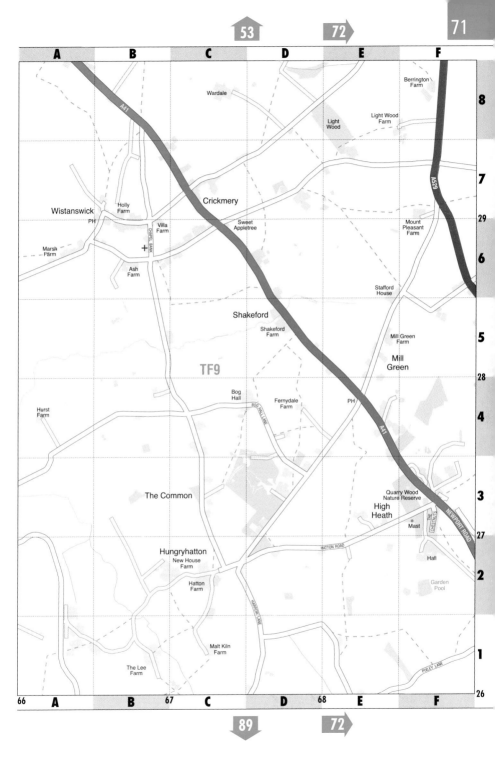

A   B   C   D   E   F

8

Berrington
Farm

Wardale

Light Wood
Farm

Light
Wood

7

A529

Holly
Farm

Crickmery

Wistanswick

29

PH

Sweet
Appletree

Mount
Pleasant
Farm

Villa
Farm

CHAPEL BANK

+

Marsh
Farm

6

Ash
Farm

Stafford
House

Shakeford

5

Shakeford
Farm

Mill Green
Farm

TF9

Mill
Green

28

Bog
Hall

Fernydale
Farm

PH

Hurst
Farm

BOG HILL LANE

A41

4

The Common

Quarry Wood
Nature Reserve

3

High
Heath

Hungryhatton

NEWPORT ROAD

THE CHESTNUTS

Mast

27

New House
Farm

HATTON ROAD

Hall

Hatton
Farm

2

Garden
Pool

HARROW LANE

Malt Kiln
Farm

1

The Lee
Farm

PIXLEY LANE

26

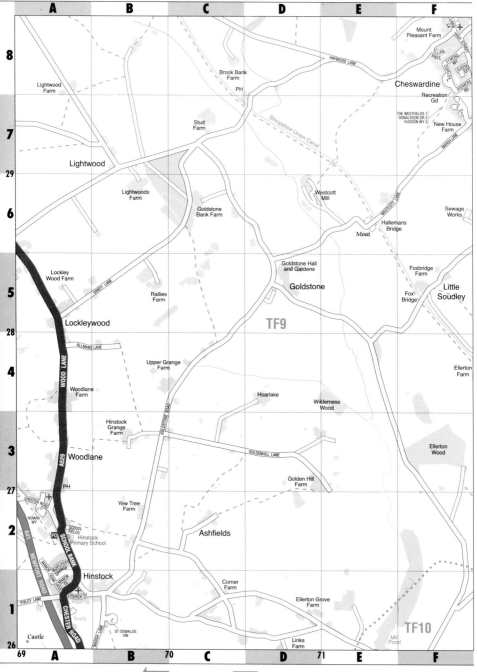

A **B** **C** **D** **E** **F**

8

Mount Pleasant Farm

Lightwood Farm

Brook Bank Farm

PH

Cheswardine

Recreation Gd

7

Stud Farm

Shropshire Union Canal

THE WESTFIELDS 1
DONALDSON DR 2
HUDSON WY 3

New House Farm

Lightwood

29

Lightwoods Farm

Westcott Mill

Sewage Works

6

Goldstone Bank Farm

Hallemans Bridge

Moat

Goldstone Hall and Gardens

Foxbridge Farm

Little Soudley

Lockley Wood Farm

SANDY LANE

Rallies Farm

Goldstone

Fox Bridge

5

Lockleywood

TF9

Ellerton Farm

28

ALLMANS LANE

Upper Grange Farm

4

WOOD LANE

Woodlane Farm

Hoarlake

Wilderness Wood

Ellerton Wood

Hinstock Grange Farm

GOLDSTONE ROAD

GOLDENHILL LANE

Woodlane

3

A529

PH

Golden Hill Farm

27

CHESTER ROAD

ROMAN WY

Yew Tree Farm

Ashfields

2

A41

NEWPORT ROAD

SCHOOL BANK

PO

SCHOOL FIELDS

Hinstock Primary School

Hinstock

Corner Farm

Ellerton Grove Farm

1

PIKLEY LANE

CHURCH ST

MARSH LANE

TF10

Castle

St OSWALDS VW

Links Farm

Mill Pond

26

69 **A** 70 **B** **C** 71 **D** **E** **F**

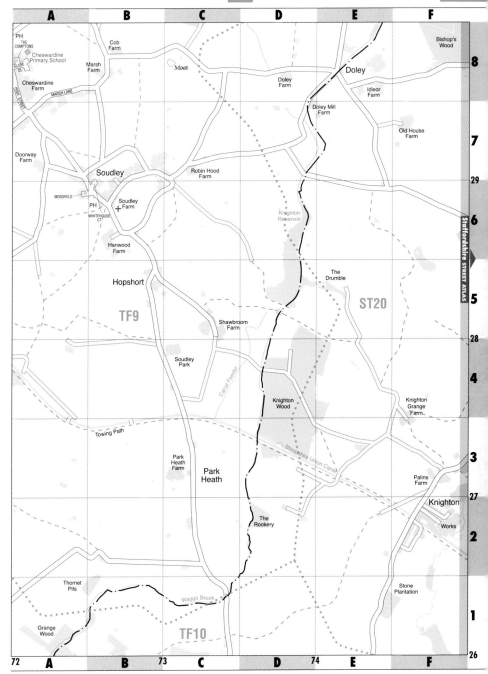

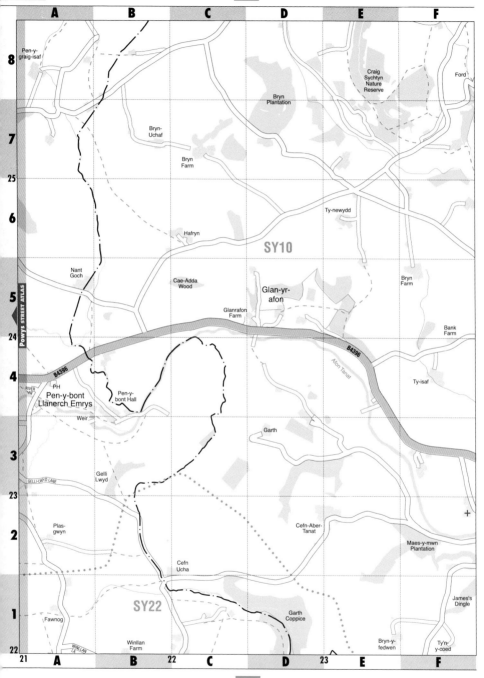

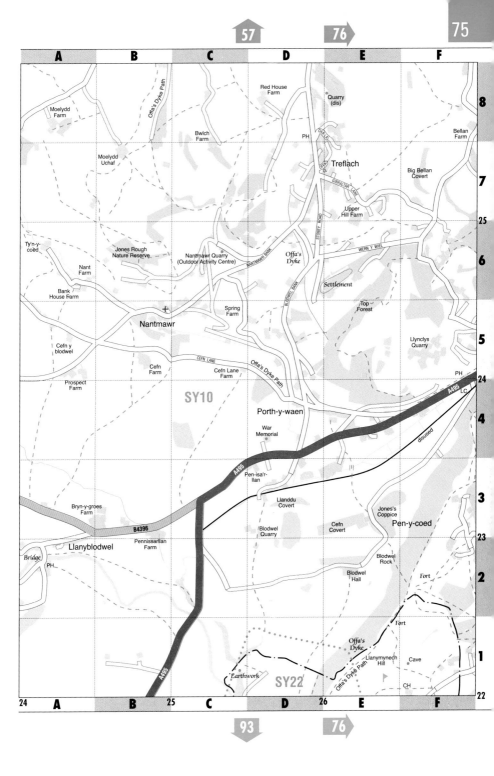

Moelydd
Farm

Red House
Farm

Quarry
(dis)

Bellan
Farm

Bwlch
Farm

PH

Moelydd
Uchaf

Treflach

Big Bellan
Covert

Ty'n-y-
coed

Upper
Hill Farm

WERN Y WIEL

Jones Rough
Nature Reserve

Nantmawr Quarry
(Outdoor Activity Centre)

Offa's
Dyke

Nant
Farm

NANTMAWR LANE

Settlement

Bank
House Farm

Top
Forest

Spring
Farm

BLODWEL LANE

Llynclys
Quarry

Cefn y
blodwel

Nantmawr

PH

CEFN LANE

Offa's Dyke Path

Cefn
Farm

Cefn Lane
Farm

A495

LC

Prospect
Farm

SY10

Porth-y-waen

disused

War
Memorial

A495

Pen-isa'r-
llan

Llanddu
Covert

Jones's
Coppice

Pen-y-coed

Bryn-y-groes
Farm

Cefn
Covert

B4396

Blodwel
Quarry

Llanyblodwel

Pennissarllan
Farm

Blodwel
Rock

Bridge

PH

Blodwel
Hall

Fort

Fort

Offa's
Dyke

Fort

Llanymynech
Hill

Cave

A495

Earthwork

SY22

Offa's Dyke Path

CH

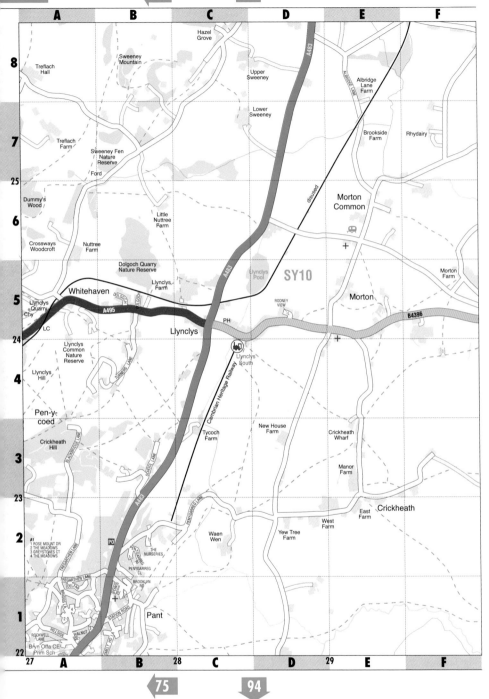

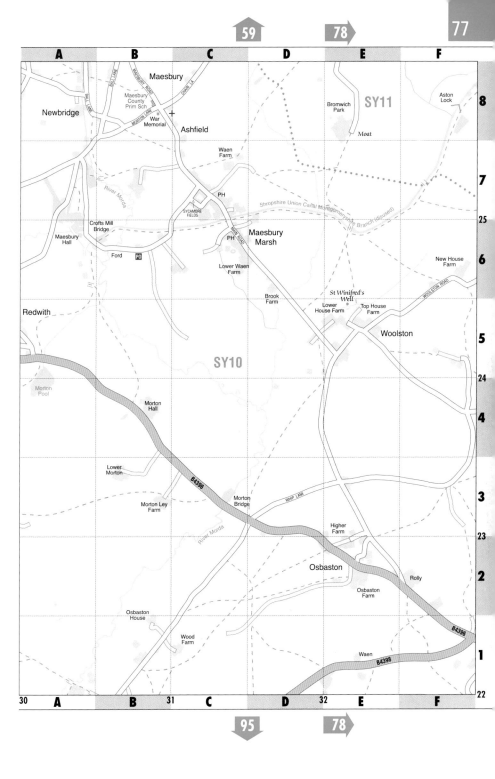

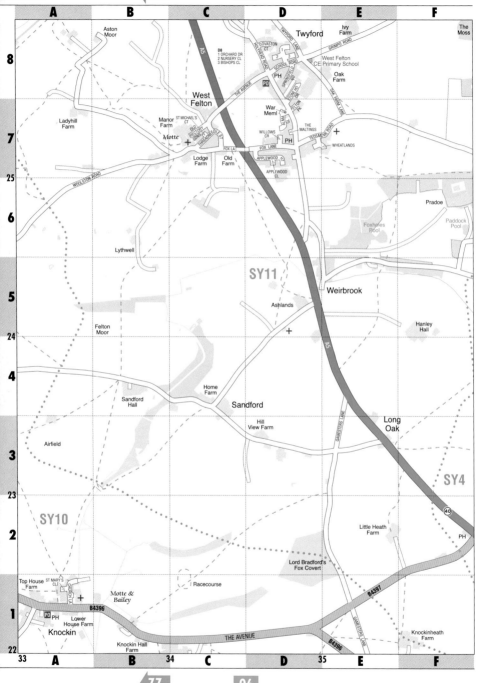

8

Aston Moor

Twyford

Ivy Farm

The Moss

D8
1 ORCHARD DR
2 NURSERY CL
3 BISHOPS CL

West Felton CE Primary School

DOVASTON CT

PH

PO

West Felton

Oak Farm

Ladyhill Farm

Manor Farm

ST MICHAEL'S CT

7

Motte

War Meml

THE MALTINGS

WILLOWS CR

PH

Wheatlands

Lodge Farm

Old Farm

FOX LA

FOX LANE

APPLEWOOD

APPLEWOOD CL

25

WOOLSTON ROAD

Pradoe

6

Foxholes Pool

Paddock Pool

Lythwell

SY11

5

Weirbrook

Ashlands

Hanley Hall

Felton Moor

24

4

Home Farm

Sandford Hall

Sandford

Long Oak

Hill View Farm

GAMESTERS LANE

A5

3

Airfield

23

SY4

SY10

2

Little Heath Farm

40

PH

Lord Bradford's Fox Covert

Top House Farm

ST MARY'S CL

CHURCH LA

B4597

Motte & Bailey

Racecourse

Knockinheath Farm

1

PO

PH

B4396

Lower House Farm

THE AVENUE

B4396

Knockin

22

Knockin Hall Farm

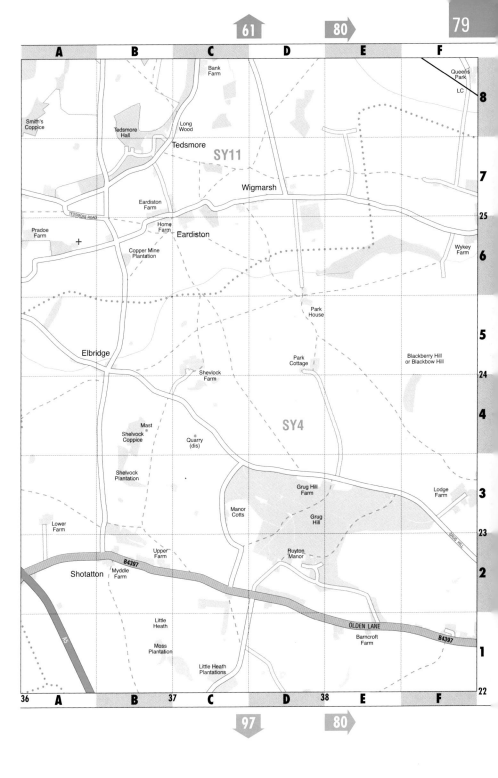

A   B   C   D   E   F

8

Queens
Park
LC

Smith's
Coppice

Long
Wood

Bank
Farm

Tedsmore
Hall

Tedsmore

SY11

7

Wigmarsh

Eardiston
Farm

TEDSMORE ROAD

25

Pradoe
Farm

Home
Farm

Eardiston

Wykey
Farm

6

Copper Mine
Plantation

Park
House

5

Elbridge

Park
Cottage

Blackberry Hill
or Blackbow Hill

24

Shevlock
Farm

SY4

4

Mast
Shelvock
Coppice

Quarry
(dis)

Shelvock
Plantation

Grug Hill
Farm

Lodge
Farm

3

Manor
Cotts

Grug
Hill

GRUG HILL

23

Lower
Farm

Upper
Farm

Ruyton
Manor

B4397

Shotatton

Myddle
Farm

OLDEN LANE

B4397

2

Little
Heath

Barncroft
Farm

1

Moss
Plantation

A5

Little Heath
Plantations

36   A   B   37   C   D   38   E   F   22

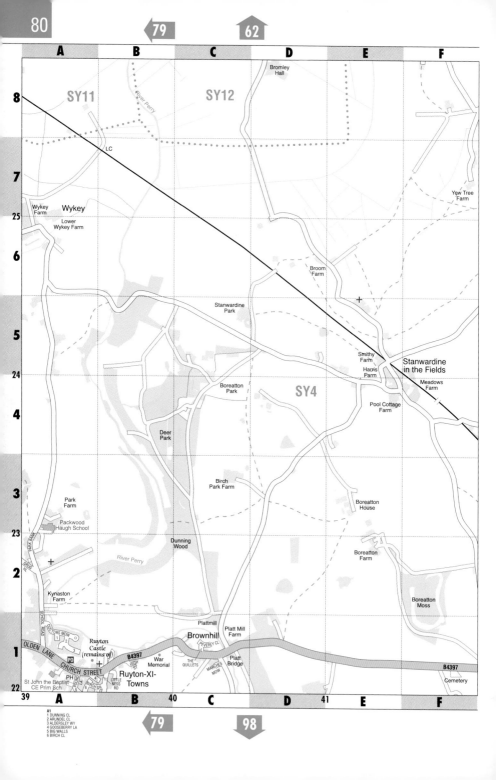

SY11

SY12

SY4

Bromley
Hall

Yew Tree
Farm

Wykey
Farm

Wykey

Lower
Wykey Farm

Broom
Farm

Stanwardine
Park

Smithy
Farm

Harris
Farm

Stanwardine
in the Fields

Meadows
Farm

Boreatton
Park

Pool Cottage
Farm

Deer
Park

Birch
Park Farm

Boreatton
House

Park
Farm

Packwood
Haugh School

Boreatton
Farm

Dunning
Wood

River Perry

Boreatton
Moss

Kynaston
Farm

Plattmill

Platt Mill
Farm

Brownhill

Ruyton
Castle
(remains of)

B4397

War
Memorial

THE
QUILLETS

Platt
Bridge

B4397

Cemetery

OLDEN LANE

CHURCH STREET

PH

St John the Baptist
CE Prim Sch

Ruyton-XI-
Towns

SCHOOL ROAD

LITTLE NESS RD

HIGH ST

VEREY CL

MARCHES MOW

LC

River Perry

A1
1 DUNNING CL
2 ARUNDEL CL
3 ALDERSLEY WY
4 GOOSEBERRY LA
5 BIG WALLS
6 BIRCH CL

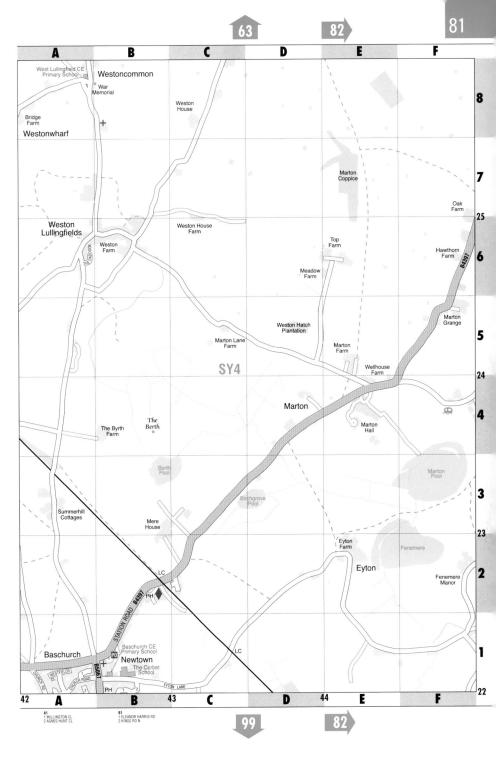

A   B   C   D   E   F

West Lullingfield CE Primary School

Westoncommon

War Memorial

Weston House

8

Bridge Farm

Westonwharf

Marton Coppice

7

Weston Lullingfields

Weston Farm

THE PADDOCK

Weston House Farm

Oak Farm

25

Top Farm

Meadow Farm

Hawthorn Farm

B4397

6

Weston Hatch Plantation

Marton Grange

5

Marton Lane Farm

SY4

Marton Farm

Wellhouse Farm

24

Marton

The Byrth Farm

The Berth

Marton Hall

Marton Pool

4

Berth Pool

Birchgrove Pool

Marton Pool

3

Summerhill Cottages

23

Mere House

Eyton Farm

Fenemere

Eyton

2

LC

STATION ROAD B4397

PH

Fenemere Manor

LC

Baschurch

B5067

PO

Newtown

Baschurch CE Primary School

1

CHURCH RD

WESTFIELDS CL

CHURCH ROAD

PH

The Corbet School

EYTON LANE

22

42   A   B   43   C   D   44   E   F

A1
1 MILLINGTON CL
2 AGNES HUNT CL

B1
1 ELEANOR HARRIS RD
2 KINGS RD N

A   **B**   **C**   **D**   **E**   **F**

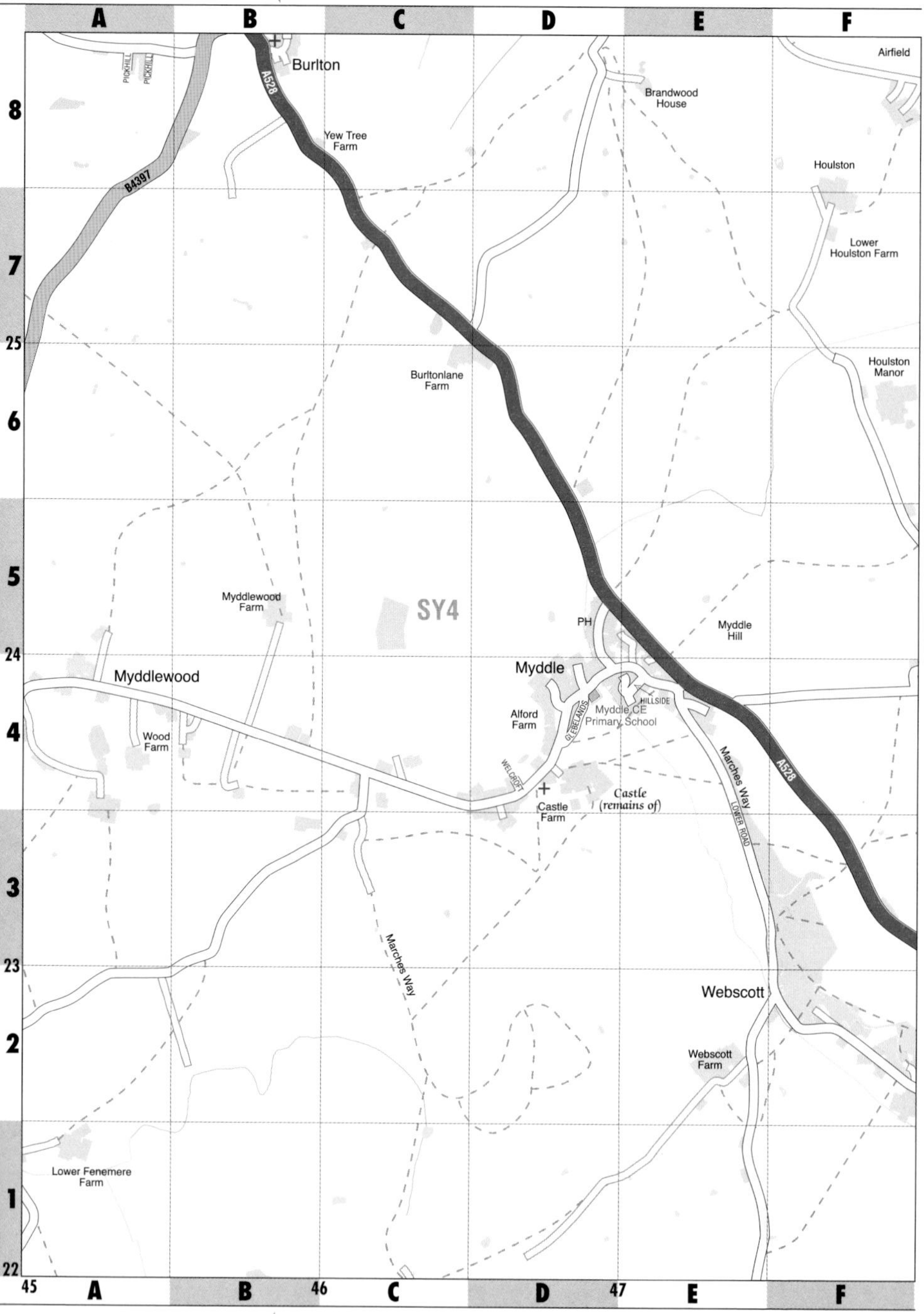

Airfield

8

PICKHILL

PICKHILL

Burlton

Brandwood
House

B4397

A528

Yew Tree
Farm

Houlston

7

Lower
Houlston Farm

25

Houlston
Manor

Burltonlane
Farm

6

SY4

5

Myddlewood
Farm

PH

Myddle
Hill

24

Myddlewood

Myddle

Wood
Farm

Alford
Farm

HILLSIDE

Myddle CE
Primary School

4

THE MOUND

WELSHCROFT

Marches Way

A528

LOWER ROAD

Castle
Farm

Castle
(remains of)

3

Marches Way

Webscott

23

Webscott
Farm

2

Lower Fenemere
Farm

1

22

45   **A**   **B**   46   **C**   **D**   47   **E**   **F**

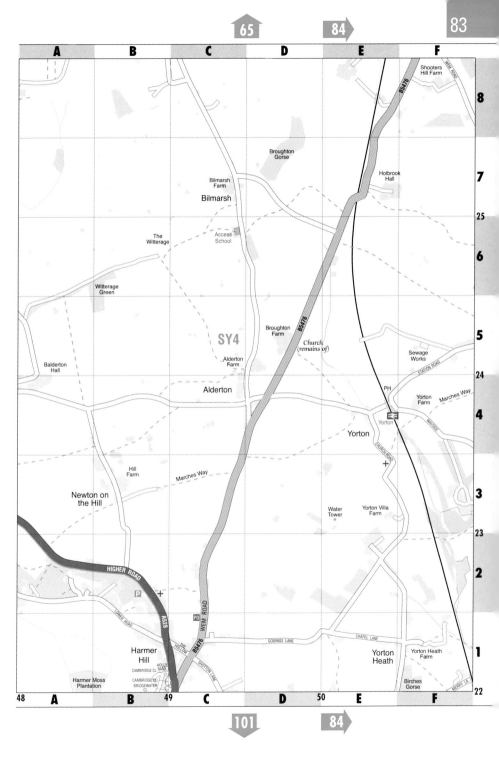

A B C D E F

8
7
25
6
24
5
4
23
3
2
1
22

Shooters Hill Farm
WEM ROAD
B5476

Broughton Gorse

Bilmarsh Farm
Bilmarsh

Holbrook Hall

The Witterage

Access School

Witterage Green

SY4

Broughton Farm

B5476

Church (remains of)

Sewage Works

STATION ROAD

Balderton Hall

Alderton Farm

Alderton

PH

Yorton Farm

Marches Way

WATERSIDE

Yorton

Yorton

Hill Farm

Marches Way

CHURCH ROAD

Newton on the Hill

Water Tower

Yorton Villa Farm

HIGHER ROAD

P

LOWER ROAD

A528

PIE HOLLOW

WEM ROAD

B5476

P

GODINGS LANE

CHAPEL LANE

Yorton Heath

Yorton Heath Farm

Harmer Hill

HOLLYBANK

CAMBRIDGE CL

CAMBRIDGE CL

BRIDGEWATER CL

SHOTTON LANE

Birches Gorse

MERRY LA

Harmer Moss Plantation

A **B** **C** **D** **E** **F**

8

83

7

25

Clivewood
Farm

Marches Way

Shropshire Way

Grove
Farm

Preston
Brockhurst

6

Preston
Hall

Sherwood
Bank

B5063

A49

Meadowfield
Farm

NEW ST
PO
STATION ROAD
FIELD DR
HIGH STREET
JUBILEE DR
HILL
DR FIELDS
HEATON HILL

Clive

Blaze
Coppice

5

JACK LANE
NOBOLD
GRANGE

Clive CE
Primary School

SY4

Birch
Coppice

24

Marches Way

Cliff
Plantation

Corbet
Wood

P

4

The
Cliff

Grinshill
Hill

GLOSSERLY LA

HIGH STREET

GROVE LANE
JONE LANE

Acton
Reynald

WAYSIDE

Hope
Farm

PH

Minor
Farm

Grinshill

Obelisk

3

Woodstyle
Farm

23

SANDY LANE

Shropshire Way

The Round
Clump

The
Slips

2

MERRY LANE
SANSAW ROAD

Boarpit
Rough

Sansaw
Heath

New
Plantation

Shropshire Way

Old
Plantation

A49

Acton Bank
Farm

1

22

51 **A** **B** 52 **C** **D** 53 **E** **F**

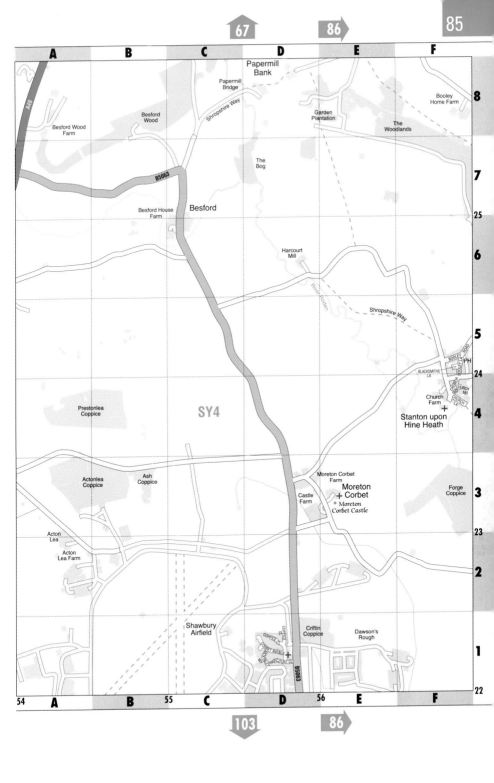

A B C D E F

8

Booley
Home Farm

Papermill
Bank

Papermill
Bridge

Besford
Wood

Shropshire Way

Garden
Plantation

The
Woodlands

Besford Wood
Farm

A9

B5063

The
Bog

7

25

Besford House
Farm

Besford

Harcourt
Mill

6

River Roden

Shropshire Way

5

BOOLEY ROAD

PH

BLACKSMITHS
LA

24

SY4

Church
Farm

Stanton upon
Hine Heath

4

Prestonlea
Coppice

Forge
Coppice

3

Actonlea
Coppice

Ash
Coppice

Moreton Corbet
Farm

Moreton
Corbet

Castle
Farm

Moreton
Corbet Castle

23

Acton
Lea

Acton
Lea Farm

2

Shawbury
Airfield

COPPICE LA

CORBET AVENUE

CHARCOURT CL

Criftin
Coppice

Dawson's
Rough

1

B5063

22

54 A 55 B C 56 D E F

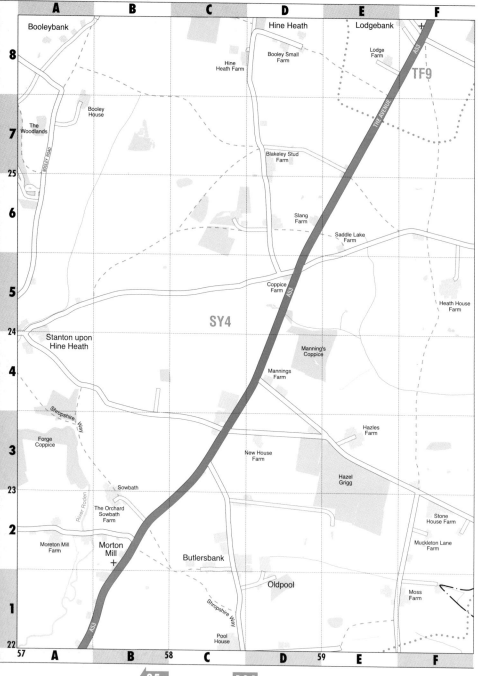

Booleybank

Hine Heath

Lodgebank

TF9

8

Hine Heath Farm

Booley Small Farm

Lodge Farm

Booley House

The Woodlands

7

BOOLEY ROAD

25

THE AVENUE

A53

Blakeley Stud Farm

6

Slang Farm

Saddle Lake Farm

5

Coppice Farm

A53

Heath House Farm

SY4

24

Stanton upon Hine Heath

Manning's Coppice

4

Mannings Farm

Shropshire Way

Forge Coppice

Hazles Farm

3

New House Farm

Hazel Grigg

23

Sowbath

River Roden

The Orchard Sowbath Farm

Stone House Farm

2

Moreton Mill Farm

Morton Mill
+

Butlersbank

Muckleton Lane Farm

Oldpool

Moss Farm

1

Shropshire Way

A53

22

Pool House

57

58

59

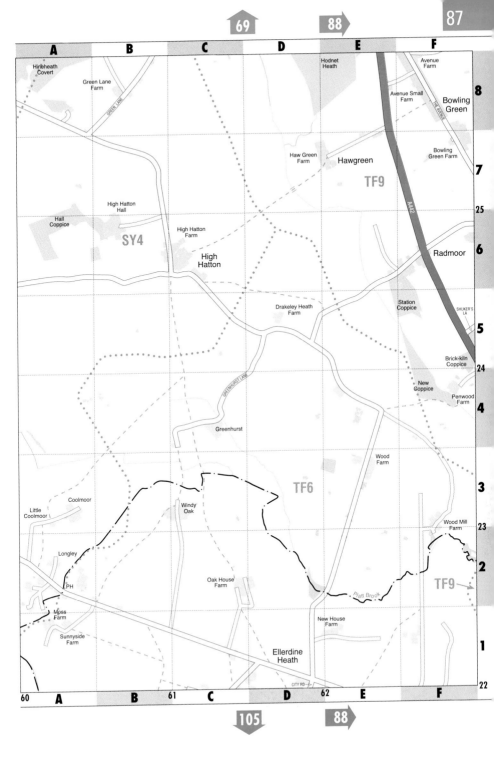

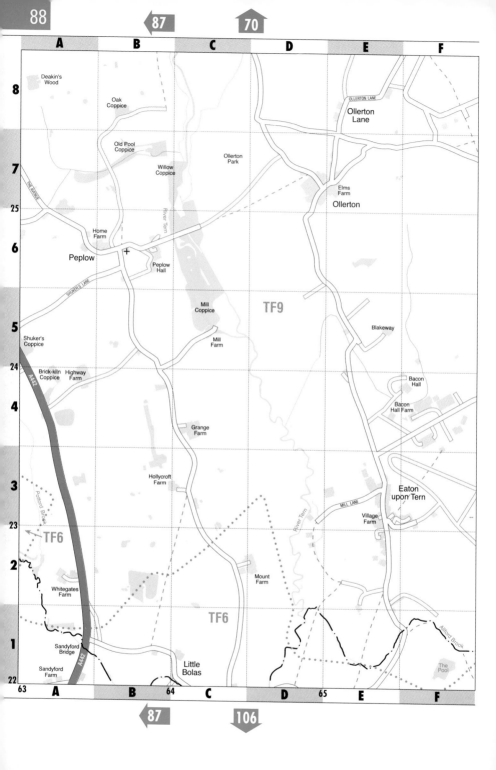

A B C D E F

8 Deakin's Wood

Oak Coppice

OLLERTON LANE

Ollerton Lane

Old Pool Coppice

7 THE AVENUE

Willow Coppice

Ollerton Park

Elms Farm

Ollerton

25

Home Farm

Peplow

+

Peplow Hall

6

SHUKER'S LANE

Mill Coppice

TF9

Blakeway

5 Shuker's Coppice

Mill Farm

A442

24 Brick-kiln Coppice Highway Farm

Bacon Hall

Bacon Hall Farm

4

Grange Farm

Eaton upon Tern

3 Potford Brook

Hollycroft Farm

MILL LANE

River Tern

Village Farm

23

TF6

2

Whitegates Farm

Mount Farm

TF6

Allford Brook

The Pool

1 Sandyford Bridge

A442

Little Bolas

Sandyford Farm

22

63 A B 64 C D 65 E F

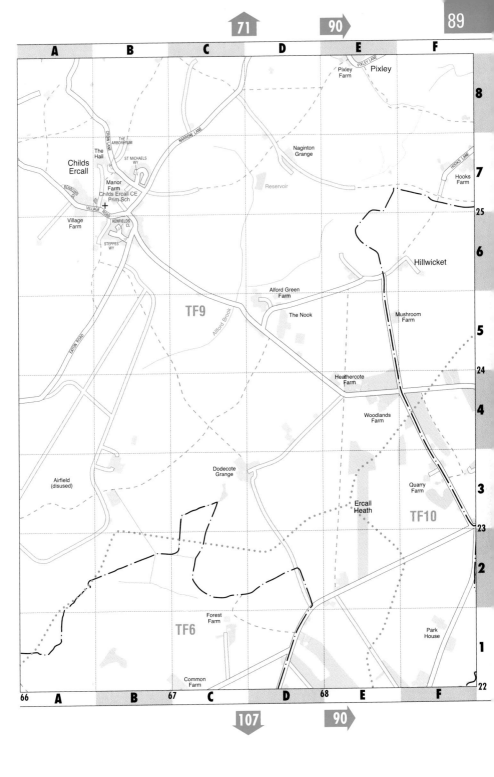

A   B   C   D   E   F

8

7

25

6

5

24

4

3

23

2

1

22

Pixley
Pixley
Farm   PIXLEY LANE

Naginton
Grange

Reservoir

Hooks
Farm   HOOKS LANE

The Hall   THE
ARBORETUM   MARROW LANE

Childs
Ercall   ST MICHAELS
WY

Manor
Farm
Childs Ercall CE
Prim Sch   CREWE LANE

BENBOWS RD   VILLAGE ROAD

Village
Farm   KEMFIELDS
CL

STEPPES
WY

TF9

Alford Green
Farm

The Nook

Hillwicket

Mushroom
Farm

Heathercote
Farm

Woodlands
Farm

Alford Brook

EATON ROAD

Airfield
(disused)

Dodecote
Grange

Ercall
Heath

TF10

Quarry
Farm

TF6

Forest
Farm

Park
House

Common
Farm

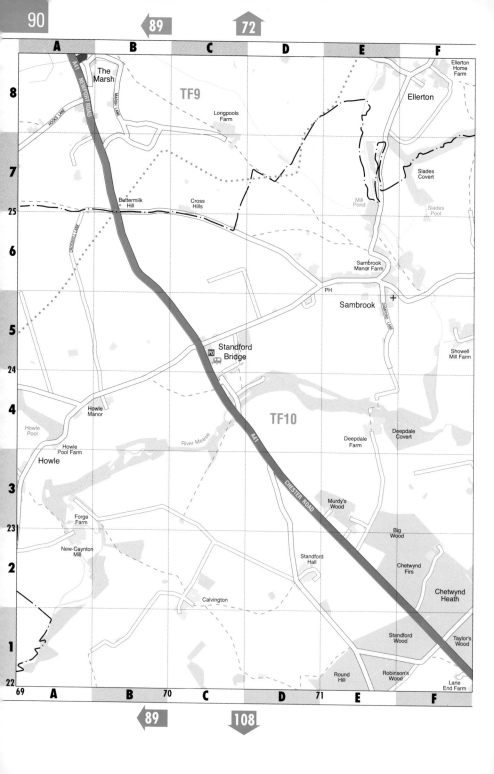

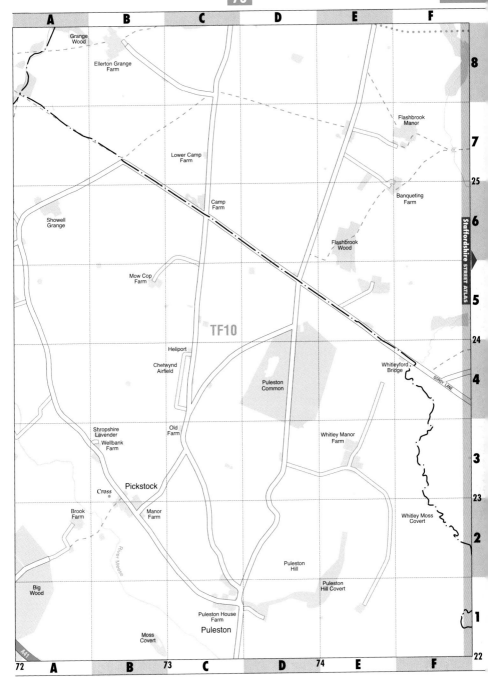

Grange Wood

Ellerton Grange Farm

Flashbrook Manor

Lower Camp Farm

Camp Farm

Banqueting Farm

Showell Grange

Flashbrook Wood

Mow Cop Farm

TF10

Heliport

Chetwynd Airfield

Puleston Common

Whitleyford Bridge

GORSY LANE

Shropshire Lavender
Wellbank Farm

Old Farm

Whitley Manor Farm

Pickstock

Cross

Brook Farm

Manor Farm

Whitley Moss Covert

River Meese

Puleston Hill

Big Wood

Puleston Hill Covert

Puleston House Farm

Puleston

Moss Covert

8
7
25
6
5
24
4
3
23
2
1
22

72
A
B
73
C
D
74
E
F

A441

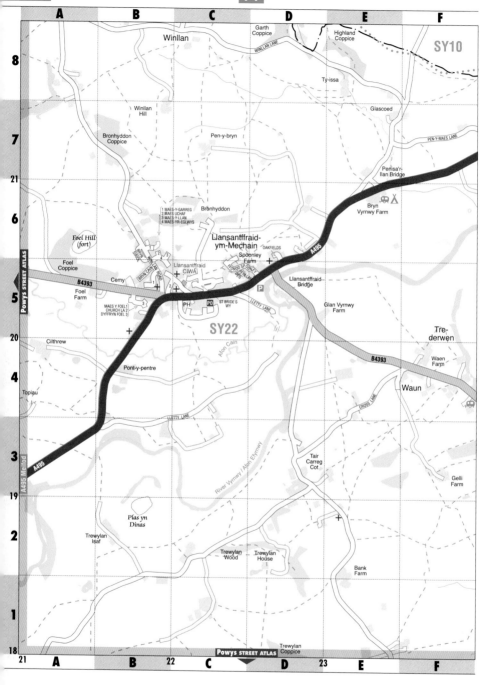

SY10

Winllan

Garth
Coppice

Highland
Coppice

WINLLAN LANE

Ty-issa

Winllan
Hill

Glascoed

PEN-Y-MAES LANE

Bronhyddon
Coppice

Pen-y-bryn

Penisa'r-
llan Bridge

1 MAES-Y-GARREG
2 MAES UCHAF
3 MAES-Y-LLAN
4 MAES-YR-EGLWYS

Bronhyddon

Bryn
Vyrnwy Farm

Foel Hill
(fort)

Llansantffraid-
ym-Mechain

A495

OAKFIELDS

Spoonley
Farm

Foel
Coppice

Cerny

Llansantffraid
CiWA

Llansantffraid
Bridge

B4393

Foel
Farm

PH

P0

ST BRIDE'S
WY

P

LLETTY LANE

Glan Vyrnwy
Farm

Tre-
derwen

MAES Y FOEL 1
CHURCH LA 2
DYFFRYN FOEL 3

SY22

Afon Cain

Cilthrew

B4393

Waen
Farm

Pont-y-pentre

Waun

Topiau

LLETTY LANE

A495

River Vyrnwy / Afon Efyrnwy

Tair
Carreg
Cot

Gelli
Farm

Plas yn
Dinas

CROSS LANE

Trewylan
Isaf

Trewylan
Wood

Trewylan
House

Bank
Farm

Trewylan
Coppice

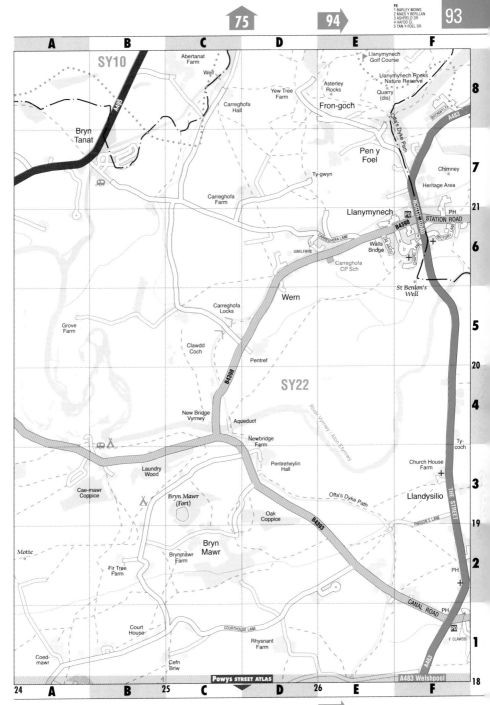

F6
1 BARLEY MDWS
2 MAES Y BERLLAN
3 ASHFIELD DR
4 HAFOD CL
5 TAN-Y-FOEL DR

SY10

Abertanat Farm

Weir

Bryn Tanat

Yew Tree Farm

Carreghofa Hall

Llanymynech Golf Course

Llanymynech Rocks Nature Reserve

Asterley Rocks

Quarry (dis)

Fron-goch

Chimney

Heritage Area

Carreghofa Farm

Ty-gwyn

Pen y Foel

Llanymynech

PO

STATION ROAD

PH

B4398

GWELFRYN

Walls Bridge

Carreghofa CP Sch

St Benion's Well

CARREGHOFA LANE

Wern

Grove Farm

Carreghofa Locks

Clawdd Coch

Pentref

SY22

B4398

New Bridge Vyrnwy

Aqueduct

River Vyrnwy / Afon Efyrnwy

Newbridge Farm

Pentreheylin Hall

Church House Farm

Ty-coch

Laundry Wood

Offa's Dyke Path

Llandysilio

Cae-mawr Coppice

Bryn Mawr (Fort)

Oak Coppice

B4398

PARSON'S LANE

Motte

Brynmawr Farm

Bryn Mawr

THE STREET

Fir Tree Farm

PH

Court House

COURTHOUSE LANE

CANAL ROAD

PH

Rhysnant Farm

PO

Y CLAWDD

Coed-mawr

Cefn Briw

A483 Welshpool

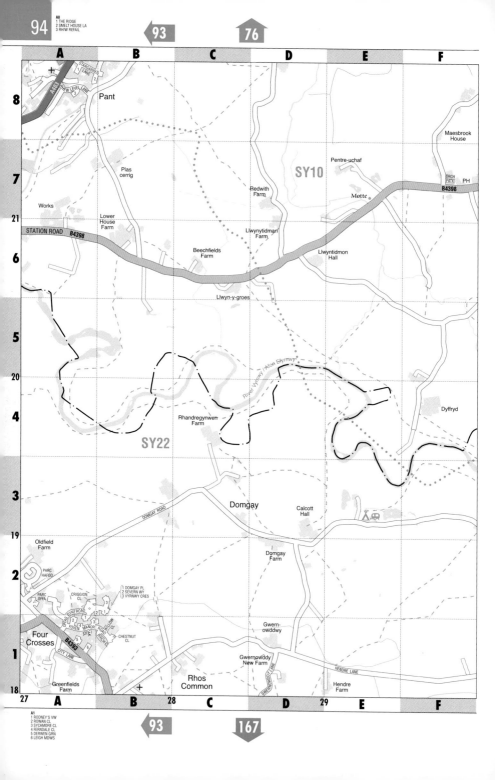

A | B | C | D | E | F

8

Pant

STARGATES
LANE

7

Plas cerrig

SY10

Pentre-uchaf

Maesbrook House

B4398

PH

21

Works

Lower House Farm

Redwith Farm

Motte

STATION ROAD   B4398

Llwynytidman Farm

6

Beechfields Farm

Llwyntidmon Hall

Llwyn-y-groes

5

20

River Vyrnwy / Afon Efyrnwy

Dyffryd

4

Rhandregynwen Farm

SY22

3

DOMGAY ROAD

Domgay

Calcott Hall

19

Oldfield Farm

Domgay Farm

2

PARC HAFOD

PARC OFFA

CRIGGION CL

1 DOMGAY PL
2 SEVERN WY
3 VYRNWY CRES

DIKE ROAD

CHESTNUT CL

Four Crosses

B4393

Gwern-owddwy

1

Gwernowddy New Farm

HENDRE LANE

Rhos Common

Greenfields Farm

Hendre Farm

18

27   A | B   28   C | D   29   E | F

A1
1 RODNEY'S VW
2 ROWAN CL
3 SYCAMORE CL
4 FERNDALE CL
5 DERWEN GRN
6 LEIGH MDWS

93

167

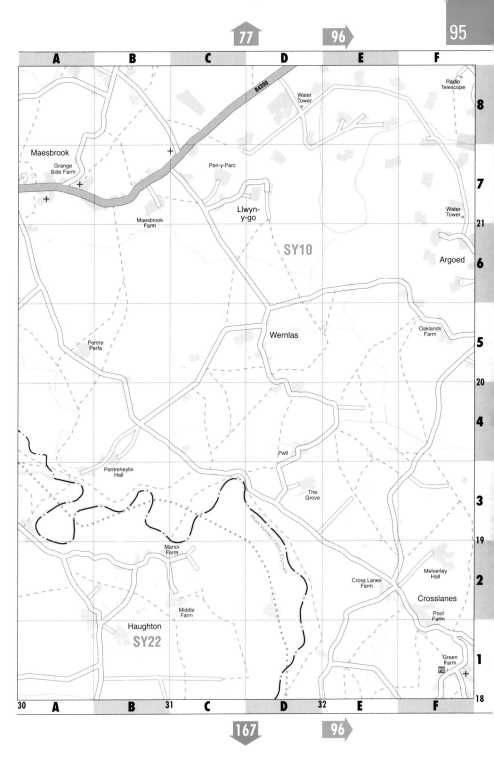

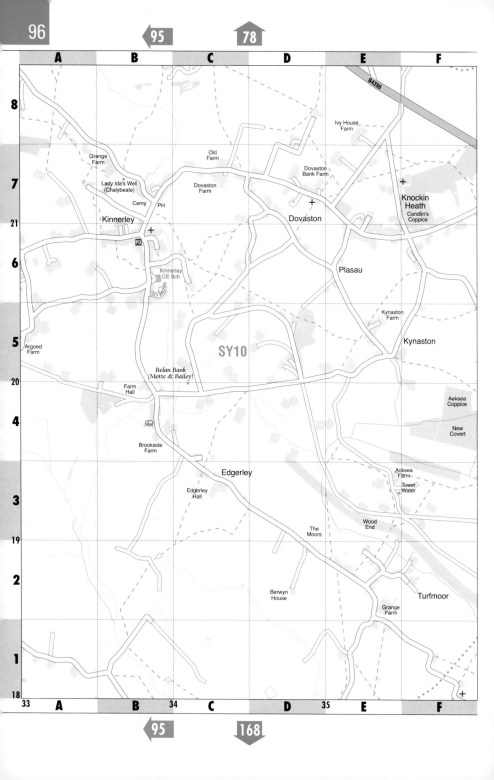

A **B** **C** **D** **E** **F**

8

B4396

Ivy House
Farm

Grange
Farm

Old
Farm

7

Lady Ida's Well
(Chalybeate)

Dovaston
Farm

Dovaston
Bank Farm

Knockin
Heath

Cemy

PH

Candlin's
Coppice

21

Kinnerley

PO

Dovaston

Plasau

6

Kinnerley
CE Sch

Kynaston
Farm

5

Argoed
Farm

SY10

Kynaston

Belan Bank
(Motte & Bailey)

20

Farm
Hall

Aeksea
Coppice

4

New
Covert

Brookside
Farm

Acksea
Farm

Edgerley

Tower
Water

3

Edgerley
Hall

Wood
End

19

The
Moors

2

Berwyn
House

Turfmoor

Grange
Farm

1

18

33 **A** **B** 34 **C** **D** 35 **E** **F**

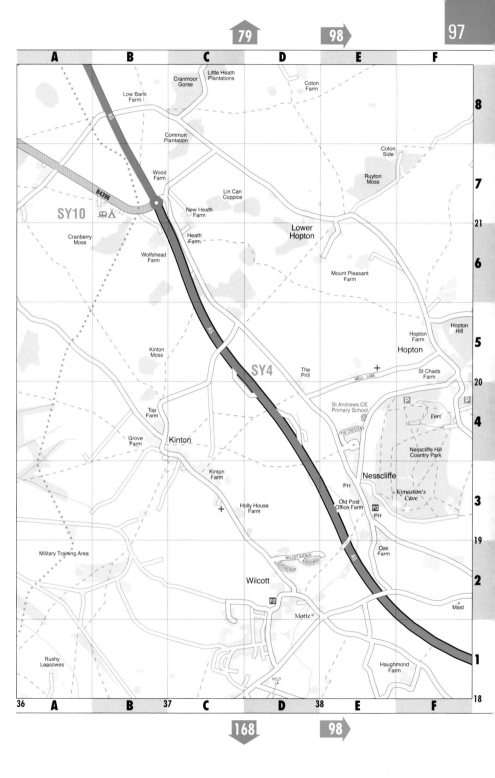

A B C D E F

8

7

21

6

5

20

4

3

19

2

1

18

Little Heath
Plantations
Cranmoor
Gorse
Low Bank
Farm
Coton
Farm
Common
Plantation
Wood
Farm
Coton
Side
Ruyton
Moss
SY10
Lin Can
Coppice
New Heath
Farm
Lower
Hopton
Cranberry
Moss
Heath
Farm
Wolfshead
Farm
Mount Pleasant
Farm
Hopton
Hill
Hopton
Farm
Hopton
Kinton
Moss
SY4
The
Prill
WELL LANE
St Chads
Farm
Top
Farm
St Andrews CE
Primary School
P
P
Fort
Kinton
Grove
Farm
THE CRESCENT
Nesscliffe Hill
Country Park
Kinton
Farm
Nesscliffe
PH
Kynaston's
Cave
Holly House
Farm
Old Post
Office Farm
PO
PH
Military Training Area
WILCOT AVENUE
KINGSWAY
GREENSWAY
Oak
Farm
Wilcott
PO
Mast
Motte
Rushy
Leasowes
HILLY
LA
Haughmond
Farm

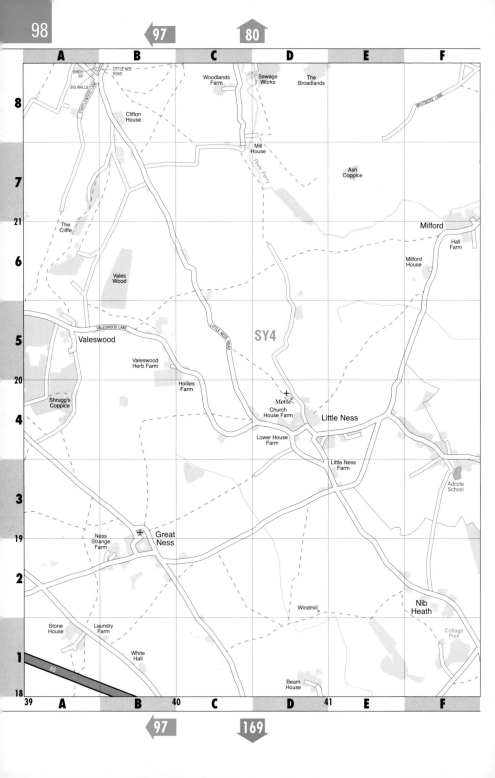

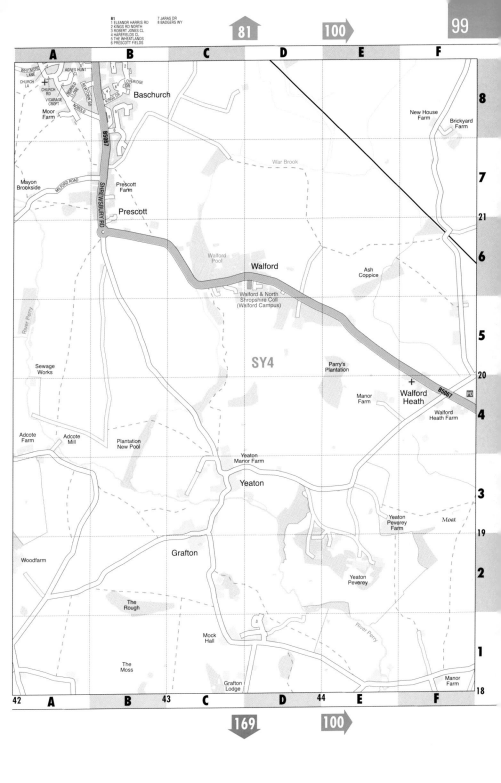

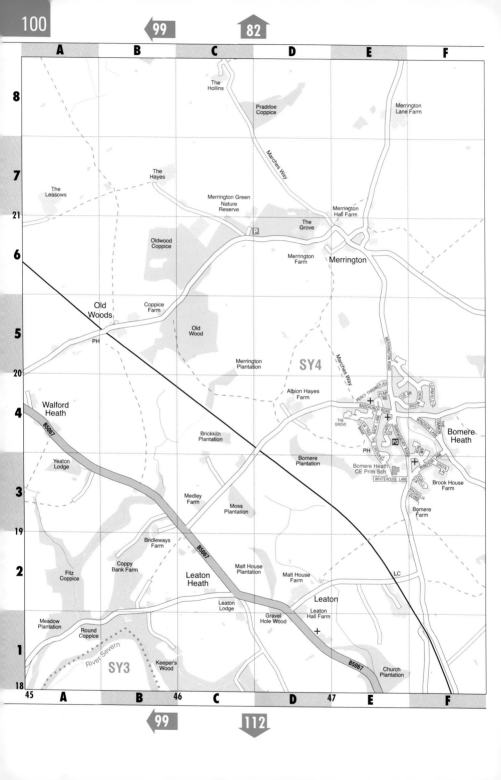

A B C D E F

8

The Hollins

Praddoe Coppice

Merrington Lane Farm

7

The Hayes

The Leasows

Marches Way

21

Merrington Green Nature Reserve

Merrington Hall Farm

The Grove

6

Oldwood Coppice

P

Merrington Farm

Merrington

Old Woods

Coppice Farm

Old Wood

5

PH

Merrington Plantation

SY4

Marches Way

20

MERRINGTON ROAD

Albion Hayes Farm

PERCY THROWER AVE

PUMP RD

CUE DR

CORNFIELD

4

Walford Heath

B5067

Brickkiln Plantation

BASCHURCH ROAD

BROAD

THE COMMON

THE GROVE

CHAD

Bomere Heath

Yeaton Lodge

Bomere Plantation

PH

PO

WINDSOR LANE

WINDSOR GREEN LA

Brook House Farm

3

Medley Farm

Moss Plantation

Bomere Heath CE Prim Sch

WHITEHOUSE LANE

Bomere Farm

19

Bridleways Farm

B5067

Coppy Bank Farm

Malt House Plantation

Malt House Farm

LC

2

Fitz Coppice

Leaton Heath

Leaton

Leaton Lodge

Gravel Hole Wood

Leaton Hall Farm

Meadow Plantation

Round Coppice

River Severn

SY3

Keeper's Wood

Church Plantation

B5067

1

18

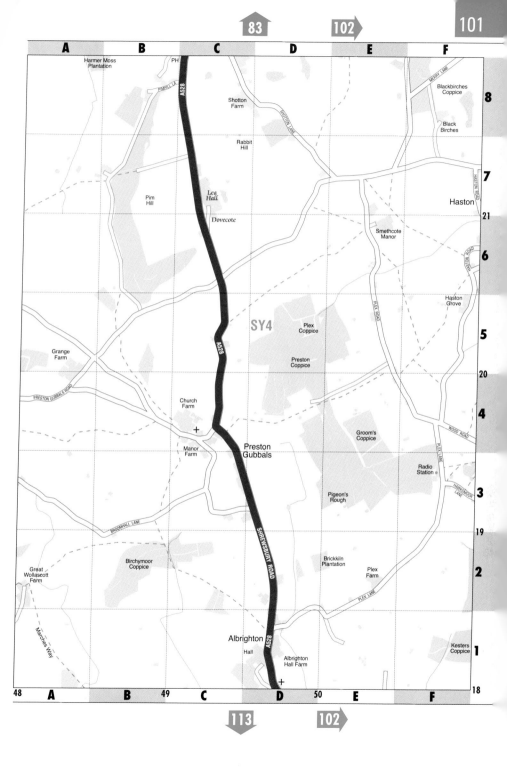

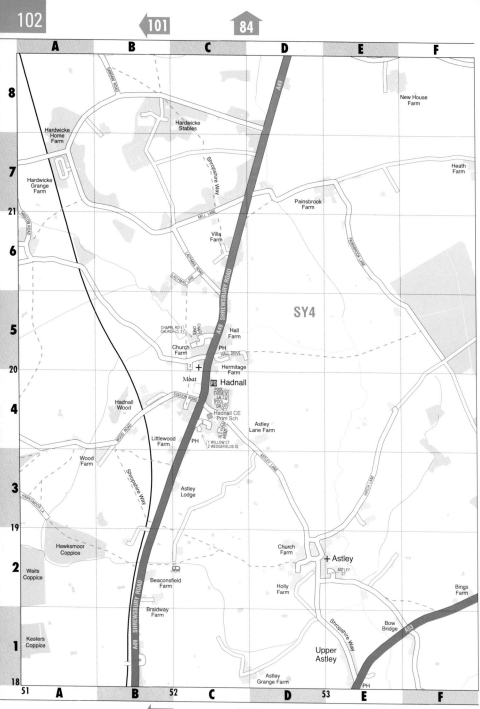

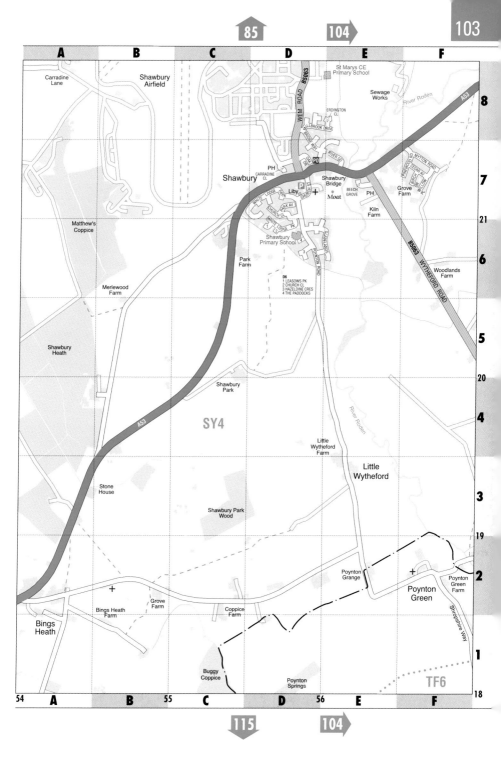

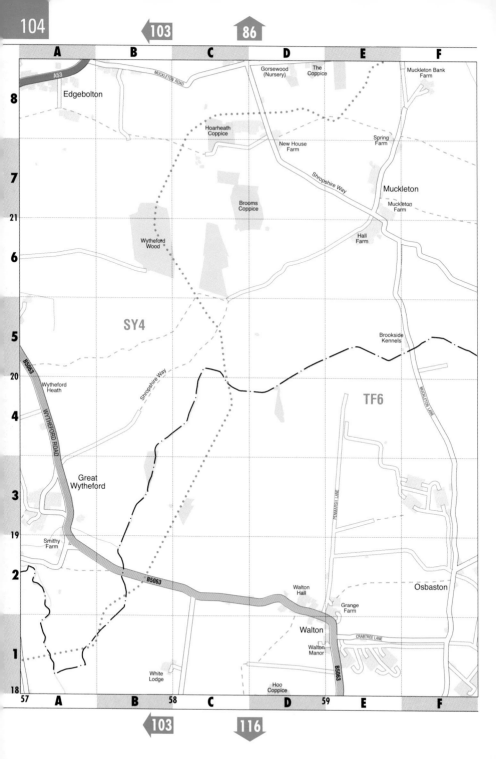

A B C D E F

8

A53

Edgebolton

MUCKLETON ROAD

Gorsewood
(Nursery)

The
Coppice

Muckleton Bank
Farm

7

Hoarheath
Coppice

New House
Farm

Spring
Farm

Shropshire Way

Muckleton

21

Brooms
Coppice

Muckleton
Farm

6

Wytheford
Wood

Hall
Farm

5

SY4

Brookside
Kennels

20

B5063

Wytheford
Heath

Shropshire Way

TF6

4

MICKLETON LANE

WYTHEFORD ROAD

3

Great
Wytheford

PEMBROKE LANE

19

Smithy
Farm

2

B5063

Walton
Hall

Osbaston

Grange
Farm

Walton

CRABTREE LANE

1

White
Lodge

Walton
Manor

B5063

18

Hoo
Coppice

57 A B 58 C D 59 E F

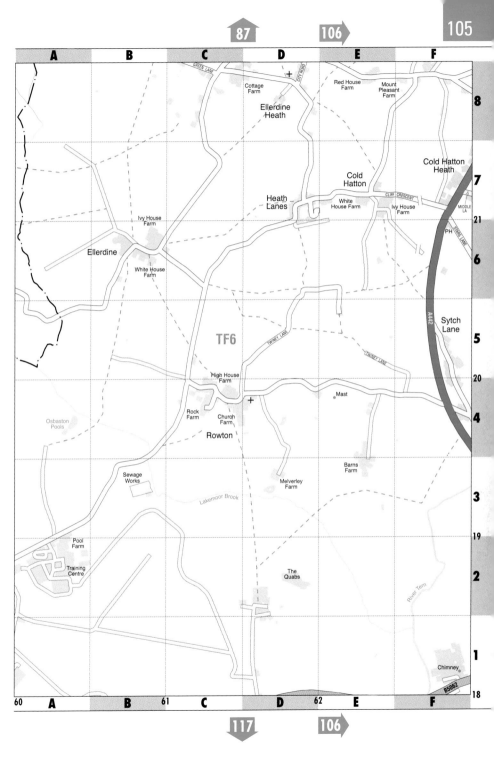

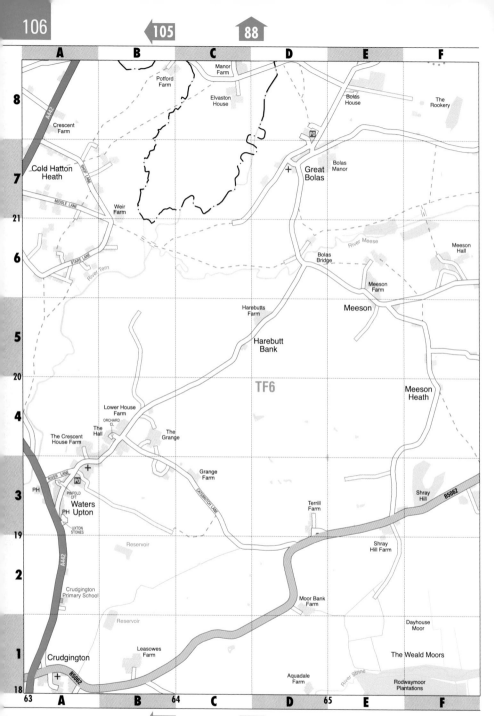

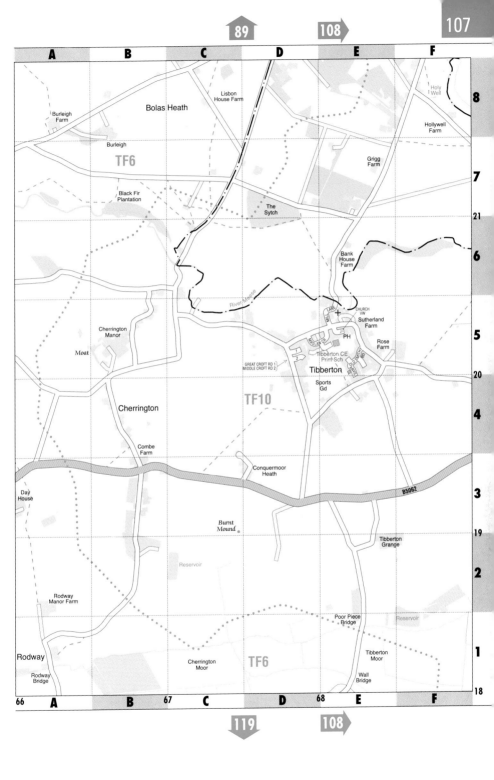

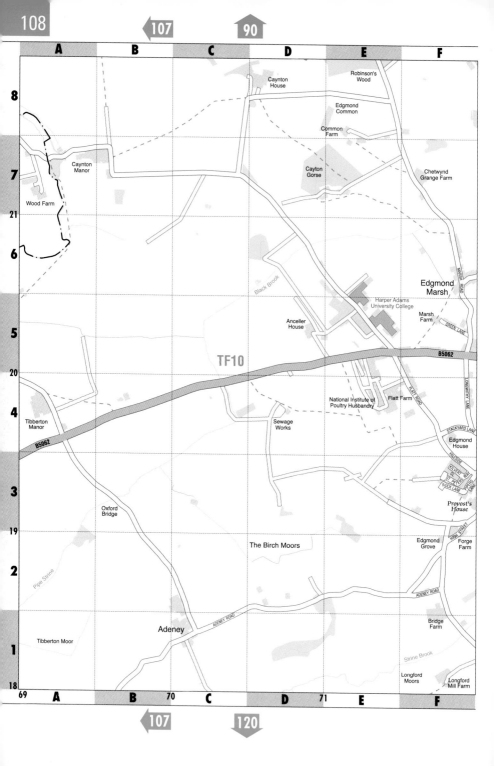

A   B   C   D   E   F

8

Robinson's
Wood

Caynton
House

Edgmond
Common

7

Caynton
Manor

Common
Farm

Chetwynd
Grange Farm

21

Wood Farm

Cayton
Gorse

6

Edgmond
Marsh

Black Brook

Harper Adams
University College

5

Marsh
Farm

Anceller
House

GREEN LANE

TF10

B5062

20

National Institute of
Poultry Husbandry

Flatt Farm

FLATT ROAD

LONGWITHY LANE

4

Tibberton
Manor

B5062

Sewage
Works

STACKYARD LANE

Edgmond
House

3

Oxford
Bridge

Provost's
House

19

The Birch Moors

Edgmond
Grove

Forge
Farm

2

Pipe Strine

ADENEY ROAD

Adeney

ADENEY ROAD

Bridge
Farm

1

Tibberton Moor

Strine Brook

Longford
Moors

Longford
Mill Farm

18

69   A   B   70   C   D   71   E   F

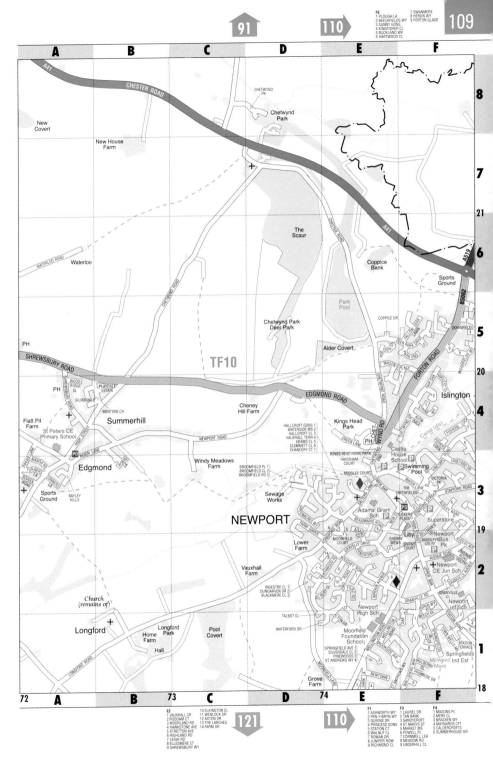

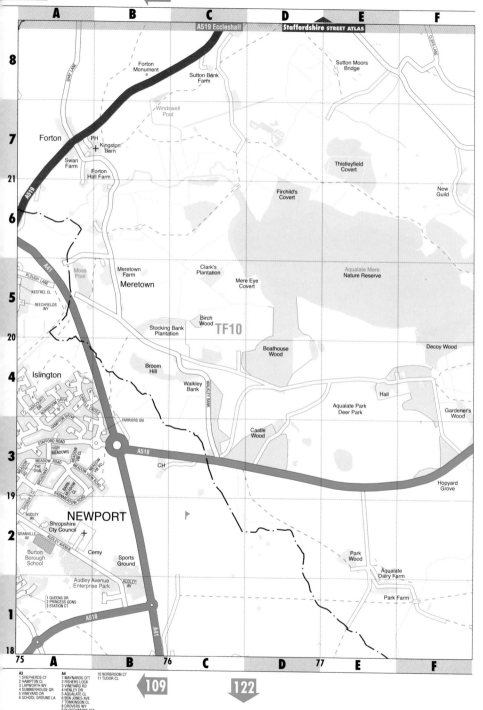

8

Forton
Monument

Sutton Moors
Bridge

Sutton Bank
Farm

Windswell
Pool

7

Forton

PH
Kingston
Barn

Thistlefield
Covert

Swan
Farm

21

Forton
Hall Farm

Firchild's
Covert

New
Guild

6

A519

Moss
Pool

Meretown
Farm

Clark's
Plantation

Aqualate Mere
Nature Reserve

A41

PLOUGH LANE

5

KESTREL CL

BEECHFIELDS
WY

Meretown

Mere Eye
Covert

Stocking Bank
Plantation

Birch
Wood

TF10

20

Broom
Hill

Boathouse
Wood

Decoy Wood

4

Islington

Walkley
Bank

WALKLEY BANK

Hall

Aqualate Park
Deer Park

Gardener's
Wood

NORBROOM DRIVE

DUNKIRK CROSS

HAMPTON DRIVE

FARRIERS GN

Castle
Wood

3

STAFFORD ROAD

HIGH
MEADOWS

MEADOW
ROAD

THE
OVAL

BROADWAY

MEADOW VIEW ROAD

MEADOW VW CL

BARN
MEADOW
CL

BARN MEADOW CL

A518

CH

Hopyard
Grove

19

AUDLEY
AV

SPIREA TCE

GRANVILLE
AV

2

NEWPORT

Shropshire
City Council

AUDLEY AVENUE

Cemy

Burton
Borough
School

Sports
Ground

Park
Wood

Aqualate
Dairy Farm

Audley Avenue
Enterprise Park

AUDLEY
AV

1 QUEENS DR
2 PRINCESS GDNS
3 STATION CT

Park Farm

1

A518

A41

18

A3
1 SHEPHERDS CT
2 HAMPTON CL
3 LAPWORTH WY
4 SUMMERHOUSE GR
5 VINEYARD DR
6 SCHOOL GROUND LA

A4
1 MAYNARDS CFT
2 FISHERS LOCK
3 VINEYARD RD
4 HENLEY DR
5 AQUALATE CL
6 BEN JONES AVE
7 TOMKINSON CL
8 DROVERS WY
9 PLOUGHMANS CFT

10 NORBROOM CT
11 TUDOR CL

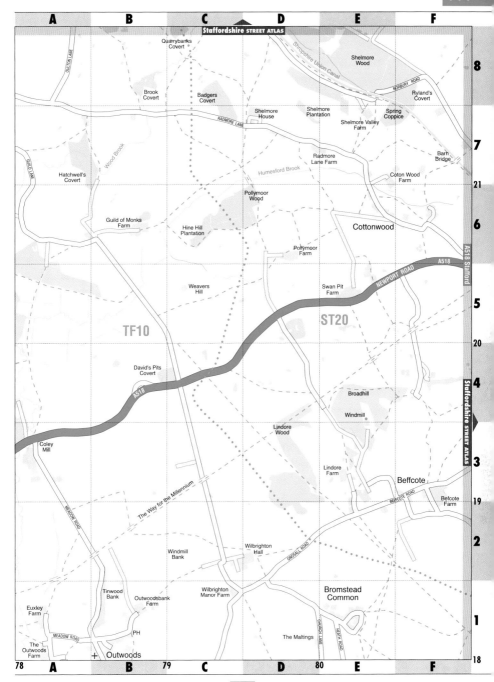

Staffordshire STREET ATLAS

Quarrybanks Covert

Shropshire Union Canal

Shelmore Wood

8

MORBURY ROAD

Brook Covert

Badgers Covert

Shelmore House

Shelmore Plantation

Shelmore Valley Farm

Spring Coppice

Ryland's Covert

RADMORE LANE

Radmore Lane Farm

Barn Bridge

7

Humesford Brook

Coton Wood Farm

Wood Brook

Hatchwell's Covert

21

Pollymoor Wood

Guild of Monks Farm

GUILD LANE

Hine Hill Plantation

Cottonwood

6

A518 Stafford

Pollymoor Farm

A518

NEWPORT ROAD

Weavers Hill

Swan Pit Farm

5

TF10

ST20

20

David's Pits Covert

A518

Broadhill

4

Windmill

Staffordshire STREET ATLAS

Lindore Wood

Coley Mill

3

Lindore Farm

Beffcote

The Way for the Millennium

BEFFCOTE ROAD

Befcote Farm

19

MEADOW ROAD

Windmill Bank

Wilbrighton Hall

GROSGALT ROAD

2

Tinwood Bank

Outwoodsbank Farm

Wilbrighton Manor Farm

Bromstead Common

Euxley Farm

MEADOW ROAD

PH

CHURCH LANE

HEATH ROAD

1

The Outwoods Farm

Outwoods

The Maltings

18

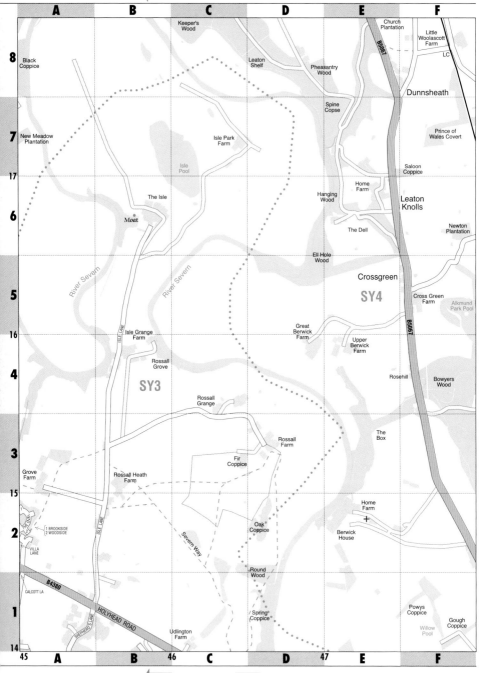

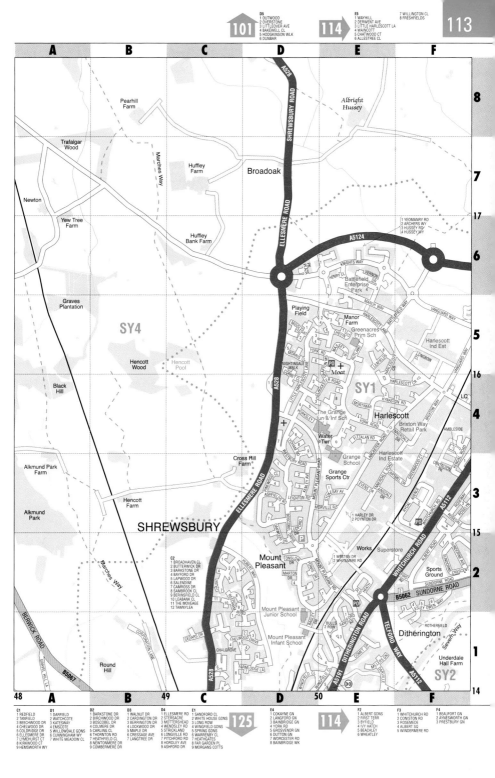

101
D5
1 OUTWOOD
2 OVERSTONE
3 LITTLEOVER AVE
4 BAKEWELL CL
5 HODGKINSON WLK
6 DUNBAR

114
E5
1 WAYHILL
2 DERWENT AVE
3 LITTLE HARLESCOTT LA
4 WAINCOTT
5 CHATWOOD CT
6 ALLESTREE CL

7 WILLINGTON CL
8 FRESHFIELDS

113

Pearhill
Farm

Trafalgar
Wood

Marches Way

Huffley
Farm

Broadoak

SHREWSBURY ROAD A528

ELLESMERE ROAD

Newton

Albright
Hussey

Yew Tree
Farm

Huffley
Bank Farm

A5124

1 YEOMANRY RD
2 ARCHERS WY
3 HUSSEY RD
4 HUSSEY WY

Graves
Plantation

SY4

Hencott
Wood

Hencott
Pool

Black
Hill

A528

Playing
Field

Manor
Farm

KNIGHTS WAY

HENRY CL

VERNON

Battlefield
Enterprise
Park

MARCH WAY

Greenacres
Prim Sch

Harlescott
Ind Est

Moat

SY1

Harlescott

The Grange
Jun & Inf Sch

MORTIMAR

KYNASTON RD

Brixton Way
Retail Park

Harlescott
Ind Estate

AMBLESIDE

LC

Alkmund Park
Farm

Cross Hill
Farm

Water
Twr

Grange
School

Grange
Sports Ctr

LEIGHTON WY

MORVILLE RD

1 HARLEY DR
2 POYNTON RD

Hencott
Farm

SHREWSBURY

ELLESMERE ROAD

MOUNT PLEASANT ROAD

WESTBURY ROAD

GREENWOOD

A5112

Alkmund
Park

Marches Way

CORPORATION LANE

C2
1 BROADHAVEN CL
2 BUTTERWICK DR
3 BARKSTONE DR
4 BAYFORD DR
5 LAPWOOD DR
6 SALENDINE
7 CAMROSS DR
8 SAMBROOK CL
9 BERINSFIELD CL
10 LEABANK CL
11 THE MOVEAGE
12 TAWNYLEA

Mount
Pleasant

ONSLOW

MARTON

Works

1 WESTON DR
2 WHITEMORE RD

Superstore

WHITCHURCH ROAD

Sports
Ground

B5062 SUNDORNE ROAD

LESLEY OWEN WAY

BENWICK ROAD

B5067

Round
Hill

CEDARS DR

CHELWOOD DRIVE

CHALGROVE

FARMLODGE LA

Mount Pleasant
Junior School

Mount Pleasant
Infant School

BULLS
ROW

A5191

DITHERINGTON ROAD

TELFORD WAY

A5112

Ditherington

ROTHERFIELD

Sevorn Way

Underdale
Hall Farm

SY2

30

C1
1 REDFIELD
2 TANFIELD
3 BEECHWOOD AV
4 CHELWOOD DR
5 COLDRIDGE DR
6 ELLESMERE DR
7 LYMEHURST CT
8 KIRKWOOD CT
9 HEMSWORTH WY

D1
1 DARFIELD
2 WATCHCOTE
3 KATESWAY
4 EMSCOTE
5 WILLOWDALE GDNS
6 CUNNINGHAM WY
7 WHITE MEADOW CL

D2
1 BARKSTONE DR
2 BIRCHWOOD DR
3 BOSCOBEL DR
4 COLMERE DR
5 CARLING CL
6 THORNTON RD
7 HEATHFIELD CL
8 NEWTONMERE DR
9 COMBERMERE DR

D3
1 WALNUT DR
2 CARDINGTON DR
3 BERRINGTON DR
4 LOCKWOOD DR
5 MAPLE DR
6 CRESSAGE AVE
7 LANGTREE DR

D4
1 ELLESMERE RD
2 STERSACRE
3 MOTTERSHEAD
4 WENDSLEY RD
5 STRICKLAND
6 LONGVILLE RD
7 PITCHFORD RD
8 HORDLEY AVE
9 ASHFORD DR

E1
1 SANDFORD CL
2 WHITE HOUSE GDNS
3 LONG ROW
4 WINGFIELD GDNS
5 SPRING GDNS
6 WARRENBY CL
7 HEATHGATES
8 FAR GARDEN PL
9 MORGANS COTTS

125

E4
1 COKAYNE GN
2 LANGFORD GN
3 BAINBRIDGE GN
4 YORK RD
5 GROSVENOR GN
6 DUTTON GN
7 WORCESTER RD
8 BAINBRIDGE WK

114

F2
1 ALBERT GDNS
2 FIRST TERR
3 BYFIELD
4 IVY HATCH
5 BEACHLEY
6 WHEATLEY

F3
1 WHITCHURCH RD
2 CONISTON RD
3 ROSEMEDE
4 ALBERT SQ
5 WINDERMERE RD

F4
1 BEAUFORT GN
2 AYNESWORTH GN
3 PRESTBURY GN

Upper Battlefield

SHREWSBURY ROAD

Battlefield
Farm

Ball's
Coppice

A49

ROBERT JONES WY

17

A53

Albrightlee Villa
Farm

Wheatley
Farm

Shropshire Way

6

A5124

A5112

Kendricks
Rough

Sunderton
Farm

PH

Battlefield

VANGUARD WY

BATTLEFIELD ROAD

Sunderton
Pool

SY4

Colins
Rough

Chy

5

BATTLEFIELD CT

SHILLINGTONE DRIVE

Albrightlee Hall
Farm

HOLT END

P&R

16

Superstore

Sundorne
Retail Park

ARLINGTON WY

ARLINGTON WY

HAM CAM DR

FARRAM GR

GLACKFORD LANE

B4
1 GREATFORD CL
2 LAWSON GDNS
3 TALLAM DR
4 PEACEHAVEN
5 GOWAN CT
6 RAMSEY MDWS
7 MALLARD CL
8 SWALLOW DR
9 WOODPECKER CL
10 KESTREL DR

The Dell
Farm

New

4

HARLESCOTT LANE

A5112

A49

HARTSFORD CL

Works

Harlescott

SY1

Superstore

FEATHERBED LANE

ROBIN CL

Sundorne
Farm

BROCKTON DRIVE

3

PIGEON

MEADOW FARM ROAD

STATION

FELLY CRESCENT

Harlescott
Junior School

BAY DRIVE

ALLERTON ROAD

C3
1 WREN CL
2 KESTREL DR
3 CURLEW CL
4 CHAFFINCH WY
5 WOODLARK CL
6 KINGFISHER CL
7 QUATFORD CL
8 NORTHSIDE CL

Sundorne
Castle Farm

Abbey
Farm

15

JOHNSON CRESCENT

Sundorne
Sec Sch

Sundorne
Inf Sch

Liby

ALLERTON ROAD

CONYBEE RD

AXELL CL

1 WHITTINGTON CL
2 HOLDGATE DR
3 OVERTON CL
4 FARMOOR

Hillside
Farm

Meadows
Farm

B5062

EAST CRESCENT

EBURY AVENUE

2

SUNDORNE ROAD

B5062

SUNDORNE ROAD

Sports
Ground

P P

FERNDALE RD 1
HOPTON DR 2

TA
Centre

Sports
Pitches

Sundorne Road
Education Centre

Welti
Tennis
Club

Sundorne
Pool

Shrewsbury
Sports Village

SHREWSBURY

Pimley
Manor

1

Severn Way

Shropshire Way

Gables
Farm

Shropshire Way

The
Hollies

14

SY2

CHURCH RD

A49

51   A   B   52   C   D   53   E   F

A2
1 SUNDORNE CR
2 CORNDON CL
3 CORNDON ROAD
4 MEADOW CL
5 MONTGOMERY WY
6 WELLINGTON CL
7 MARLBOROUGH CT

A3
1 DOUNTON CL
2 HARLESCOTT CL
3 HAUGHMOND AVE
4 ROSEWAY
5 CORNDON DR
6 MOSTON GN
7 ROSEDALE

A4
1 WHITCHURCH RD
2 HAWKESTONE RD

B3
1 THE BRADLEYS
2 THE SPRINGS
3 THE HIG
4 THE HASSACKS
5 CRAIG CL
6 ALLERTON RD

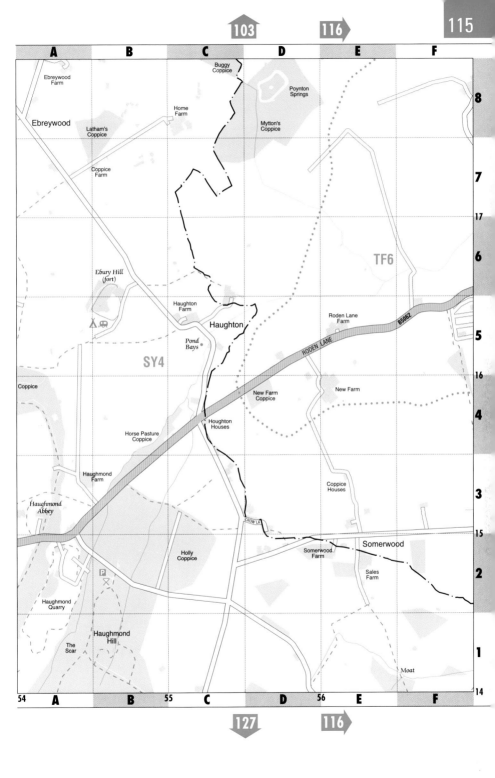

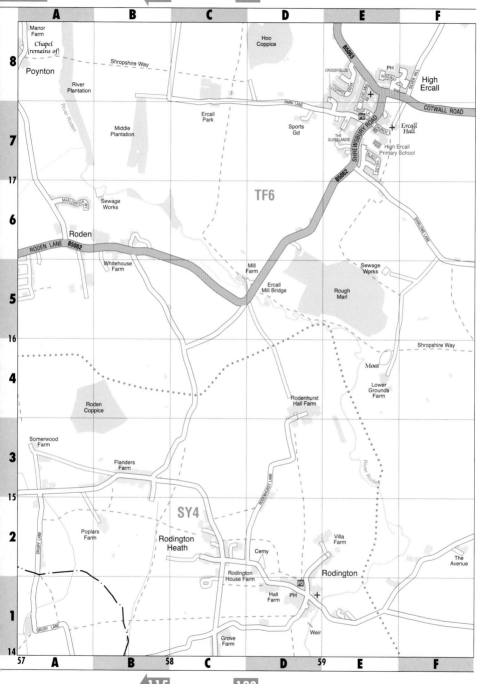

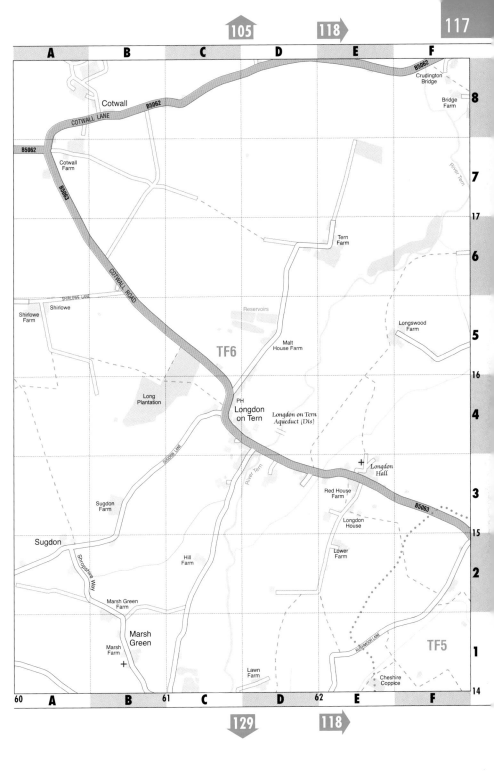

117 106

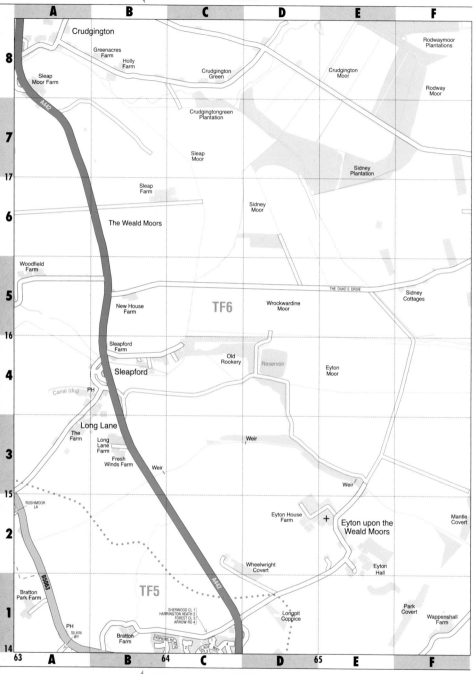

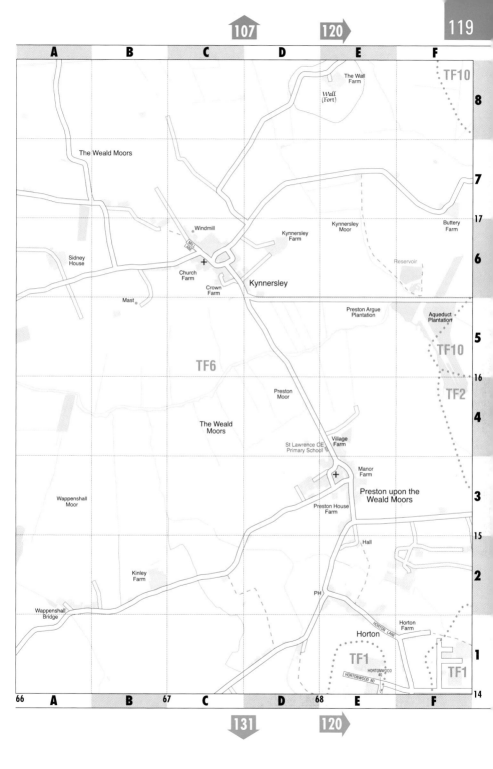

TF10

The Wall Farm

Wall (Fort)

8

The Weald Moors

7

17

Windmill

Kynnersley Farm

Kynnersley Moor

Buttery Farm

Sidney House

MILL LANE

Church Farm

Reservoir

6

Crown Farm

Kynnersley

Mast

Preston Argue Plantation

Aqueduct Plantation

TF10

5

TF6

16

Preston Moor

TF2

The Weald Moors

4

Village Farm

St Lawrence CE Primary School

Manor Farm

Wappenshall Moor

Preston upon the Weald Moors

3

Preston House Farm

15

Kinley Farm

Hall

2

PH

Wappenshall Bridge

HORTON LANE

Horton Farm

Horton

TF1

1

HORTONWOOD 40

HORTONWOOD 60

TF1

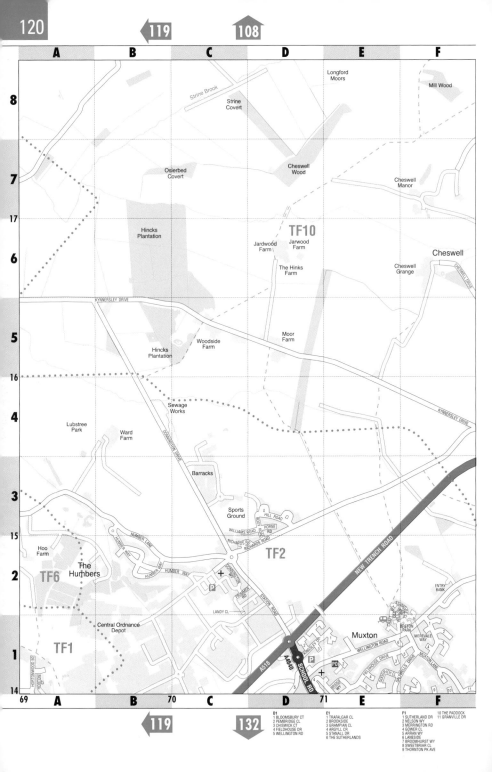

119   108

	A	B	C	D	E	F

8

Strine Brook

Longford
Moors

Mill Wood

Strine
Covert

7

Osierbed
Covert

Cheswell
Wood

Cheswell
Manor

17

Hincks
Plantation

TF10

Cheswell

6

Jardwood
Farm

Jarwood
Farm

Cheswell
Grange

The Hinks
Farm

CHESWELL DRIVE

KYNNERSLEY DRIVE

5

Hincks
Plantation

Woodside
Farm

Moor
Farm

16

Sewage
Works

KYNNERSLEY DRIVE

4

Lubstree
Park

Ward
Farm

DONNINGTON DRIVE

3

Barracks

Sports
Ground

HILL ROAD

HORNE RD

WILLIAMS ROAD

15

HUMBER LANE

RICHARDS RD

RICHARDS ROAD

Hoo
Farm

HUMBER WAY

TF2

NEW TRENCH ROAD

ENTRY
BANK

2

TF6

The
Humbers

HUMBER WK

HUMBER WAY

DONNINGTON RD

P

PENNANT RD

STATION ROAD

BRETON
PARK

MEREVALE
WAY

LANDY CL

Muxton

WELLINGTON ROAD

1

TF1

Central Ordnance
Depot

HORTONWOOD RD

A518

A4640

SCHOOL RD

P

PO

BRIDGE WY

GOUGH CL

SYWELL DRIVE

MUXTON LANE

FLEETHOUSE DRIVE

WELLINGTON DRIVE

14

119   132

D1
1 BLOOMSBURY CT
2 PEMBRIDGE CL
3 CHISWICK CT
4 FIELDHOUSE DR
5 WELLINGTON RD

E1
1 TRAFALGAR CL
2 BROOKSIDE
3 GRAMPIAN CL
4 ARGYLL CR
5 STANALL DR
6 THE SUTHERLANDS

F1
1 SUTHERLAND DR
2 NELSON WY
3 MERRINGTON RD
4 GOWER CL
5 ARRAN WY
6 LANESIDE
7 BROOMHURST WY
8 SWEETBRIAR CL
9 THORNTON PK AVE

10 THE PADDOCK
11 GRANVILLE DR

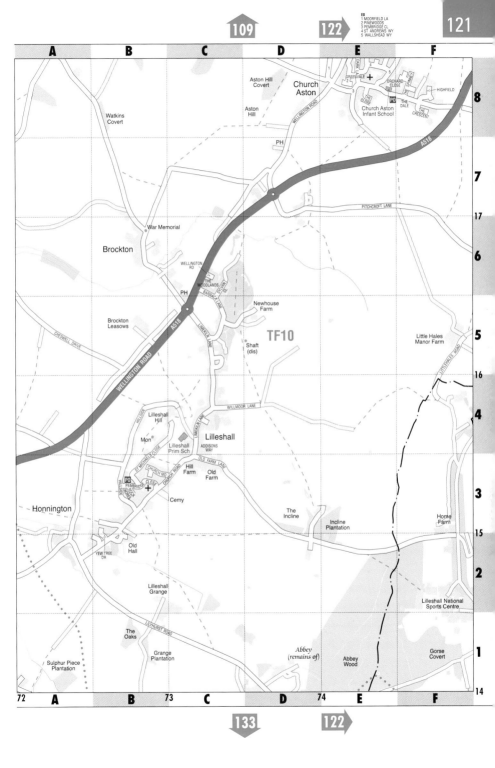

121
110

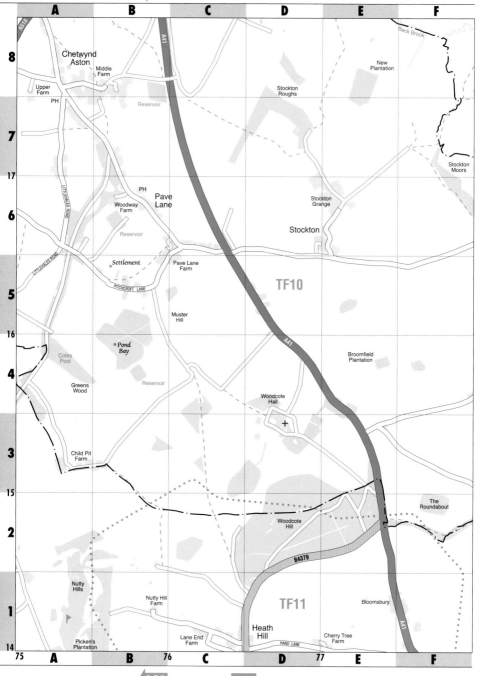

121
134

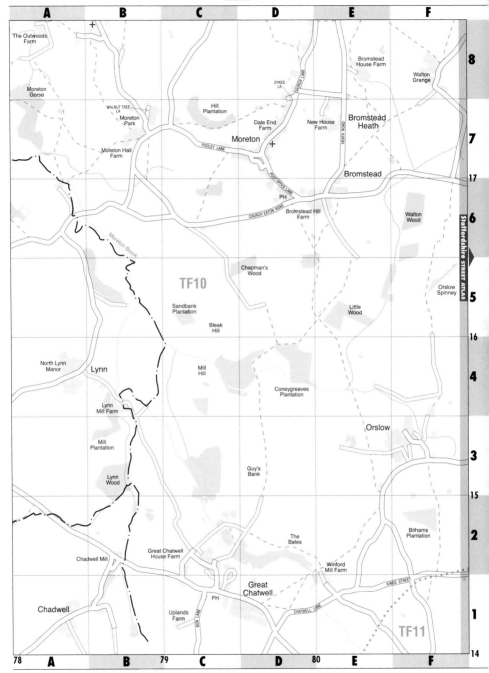

A B C D E F

8

The Outwoods Farm

Moreton Gorse

Bromstead House Farm

Walton Grange

WALNUT TREE LA

DYKES LA

CHURCH LANE

Hill Plantation

Moreton Park

Dale End Farm

New House Farm

Bromstead Heath

7

Moreton

POOLEY LANE

HEATH ROAD

Moreton Hall Farm

POST OFFICE LANE

Bromstead

17

PH

CHURCH EATON ROAD

Bromstead Hill Farm

Walton Wood

6

Moreton Brook

TF10

Chapman's Wood

Orslow Spinney

5

Sandbank Plantation

Little Wood

Bleak Hill

16

North Lynn Manor

Lynn

Mill Hill

4

Lynn Mill Farm

Coneygreaves Plantation

Orslow

3

Mill Plantation

Lynn Wood

Guy's Bank

15

Bithams Plantation

2

The Bates

Chadwell Mill

Great Chatwell House Farm

Winford Mill Farm

KINGS STREET

Chadwell

Uplands Farm

BILN LANE

PH

Great Chatwell

CHATWELL LANE

TF11

1

78 A B 79 C D 80 E F 14

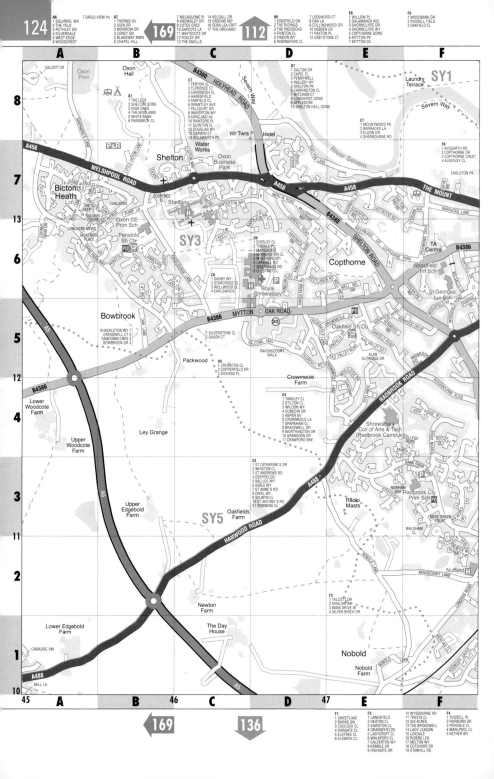

A6
1 SQUIRREL WK
2 THE YELD
3 ROTHLEY DR
4 SILVERDALE
5 WEST EDGE
6 WOODCREST

7 EARLS VIEW HL

A7
1 THORNS GV
2 SION DR
3 WORROW DR
4 CONEY GN
5 BLAKEWAY MWS
6 CHAPEL HILL

169

7 MELBOURNE RI
8 KNOWSLEY DR
9 COTES CRES
10 ORSONS MD
11 WHITECOTE DR
12 FOXLEY GR
13 THE KNOLLS

14 KELSALL DR
15 ORSONS MD
16 FERN LEA CRFT
17 THE ORCHARD

112

B6
1 EDGEFIELD GN
2 THE RIDINGS
3 THE PADDOCKS
4 FRINTON CL
5 FINDON WY
6 ROBINSFORD CL

7 LEESWOOD CT
8 OAK LA
9 COLLINGWOOD DR
10 HEBDEN GV
11 PAXTON PL
12 GREYSTONE CT

E6
1 WILLOW PL
2 SALAMANCA AVE
3 SHORNCLIFFE CL
4 SHORNCLIFFE WY
5 COPTHORNE GDNS
6 MYTTON PK
7 MYTTON GV

F5
1 WOODBANK DR
2 RUSSELL FIELD
3 OAKFIELD CL

SY1

Laundry Terrace

Severn Way

A458

Oxon Pool

Calcott Cr

Oxon Hall

B7
1 THE LEES
2 SHELTON GDNS
3 HIGH OAKS
4 THE WOODLANDS
5 WHITE BANK
6 PAINSWICK CL

Shelton

P&R

Water Works

Oxon Business Park

Wr Twrs Hotel

D7
1 DALTON DR
2 CAPEL CL
3 PENNYWELL
4 INGLEBY WY
5 SHELTON PK
6 CARRINGTON CL
7 MITCHAM CT
8 LONGHIRST GDNS
9 SHELTON PL
10 SHELTON HALL GDNS

E7
1 MOUNTWOOD PK
2 BARRACKS LA
3 ELDON DR
4 SHERBOURNE RD

River Severn

EARLSTON PK

THE MOUNT

BARRACKS LANE

F6
1 AYSGARTH RD
2 COPTHORNE DR
3 COPTHORNE CREST
4 ALVERLEY CL

Bicton Heath

WELSHPOOL ROAD

Shelton

C7
1 FENTON CL
2 FLORENCE CT
3 CAVENDISH CL
4 HARESFIELD
5 FARFIELD CL
6 GRANTLEY AVE
7 FELCOURT DR
8 SILVERTON WY
9 KIRKLAND AV
10 PAINTERS PL
11 QUINTON CL
12 DOUGLAS WY
13 DARWIN CT
14 HOLSWORTH PK

Oxon CE Prim Sch

Pensfold Sh Ctr

PO

C6
1 DADBY WY
2 STARCROSS CL
3 WELLWOOD CL
4 EARLSWOOD

SY3

H

Royal Shrewsbury

D6
1 EVERLEY CL
2 TINDALE PL
3 MARSHGATE
4 DONNINGTON CL
5 WESTHEAD
6 LARKHILL RD
7 WESTLANDS RD
8 CHESTNUT CL

Copthorne

SHELTON ROAD

TA Centre

B4386

Woodfield Inf Sch

St Georges Jun Sch

Bowbrook

B4386 MYTTON OAK ROAD

SHACKLETON WY 1
CRESSWELL CT 2
SANDOWN CRES 3
BOWBROOK GR 4

Packwood

1 SILVERSTONE CL
2 SAXON CT

D5
1 CRUCKTON CL
2 COPPERFIELD DR
3 DICKENS PL

Oakfield Sh Ctr

RAD VALLEY RD

Ravenscourt Walk

ALAN GUTRIDGE DR

RADBROOK ROAD

A5

B4386

Lower Woodcote Farm

Upper Woodcote Farm

Ley Grange

Crowmeole Farm

E4
1 TANSLEY CL
2 STILTON CL
3 WILDON WY
4 DUNEDIN DR
5 ASPEN GV
6 CROWMEOLE LA
7 SPARKHAM CL
8 WORTHINGTON DR
9 WORTHINGTON DR
10 GRANSDEN DR
11 CRAWFORD MW

Shrewsbury Coll of Arts & Tech (Radbrook Campus)

COLLEGE

Bank Farm Rd

E3
1 ST CATHERINE'S DR
2 WHISTON CL
3 ST ANDREWS RD
4 DEEPFIELDS
5 BALLIOL WY
6 KEBLE WY
7 ST ANNE'S RD
8 ORIEL WY
9 SELWYN CL
10 ST ANTONY'S RD
11 DOWNING CL

Upper Edgebold Farm

SY5

Oakfields Farm

HANWOOD ROAD

A488

Radio Masts

NEWHAM WAY

Radbrook Cty Prim Sch

WALSHAM CL

MERE GREEN COURT

Nuffield H

F2
1 TALCOTT DR
2 HENLOW PK
3 BANK DRIVE W
4 SILVER BIRCH DR

Lower Edgebold Farm

CARADOC VW

Newton Farm

The Day House

Nobold

Nobold Farm

MILL LA **A488**

A5

F1
1 SWEETLAKE
2 BARNS GN
3 CODLOCK CL
4 DARGATE CL
5 ELSTREE CL
6 ELSWICK CL

F3
1 LANESFIELD
2 HEATON CL
3 SAWSTON CL
4 GRANGEFIELDS
5 LADYCROFT CL
6 WALKFORD CL
7 CALVERTON WY
8 KEMBLE CL
9 HIGHGATE DR

10 WYEBOURNE RD
11 TRESTA CL
12 SIX ACRES
13 THE BROADWELL
14 LADY LEASOW
15 LOXDALE
16 RIDERS LEA
17 MELTON WY
18 COTSHIRE DR
19 STANHILL RD

F4
1 RUSSELL RI
2 FAIRBURN DR
3 PERIVALE CL
4 MARLPOOL CL
5 NETHER WY

8
13
7
6
5
12
4
3
11
2
1
10

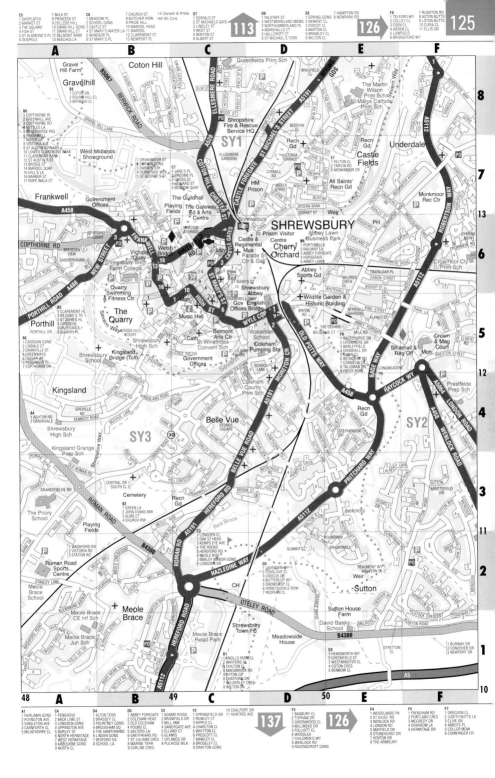

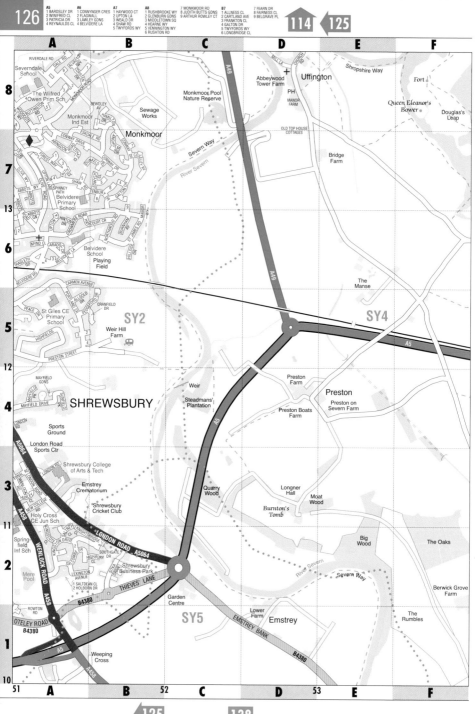

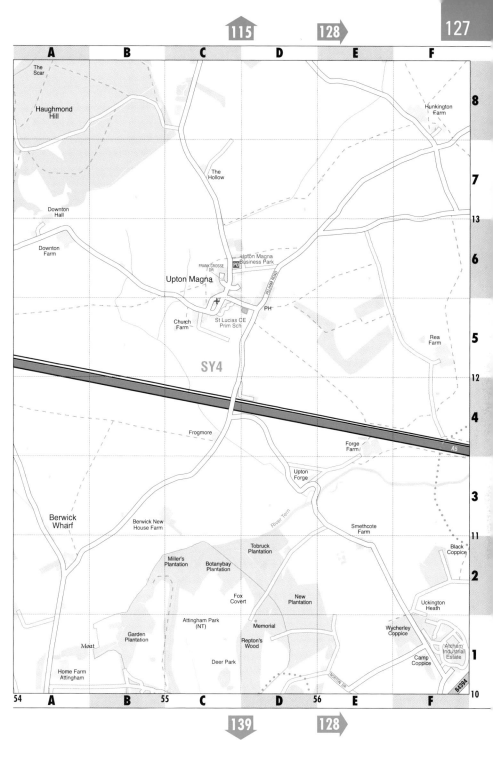

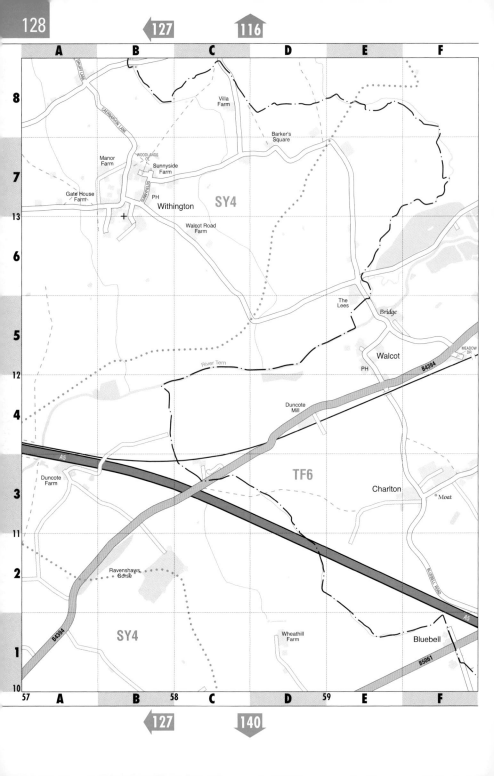

127

116

A B C D E F

8

7

13

6

5

12

4

3

11

2

1

10

57 A B 58 C D 59 E F

Villa Farm

Barker's Square

Manor Farm

WOODLANDS CE

Sunnyside Farm

Gate House Farm

PH

Withington

SY4

Walcot Road Farm

The Lees

Bridge

MEADOW DR

Walcot

PH

B4394

River Tern

Duncote Mill

A5

Duncote Farm

TF6

Charlton

Moat

BLUEBELL ROAD

Ravenshaws Gorse

SY4

Wheathill Farm

Bluebell

B4394

B5061

A5

PRIORY LANE

CAERNARVON LANE

SUNNYFIELDS

+

127

140

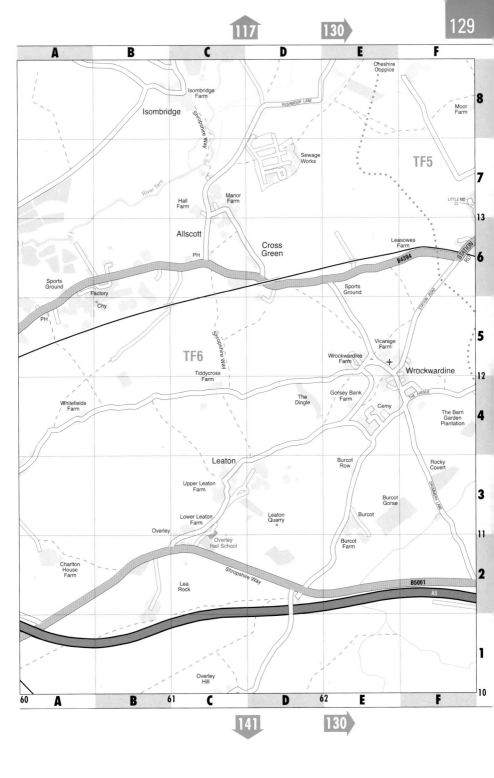

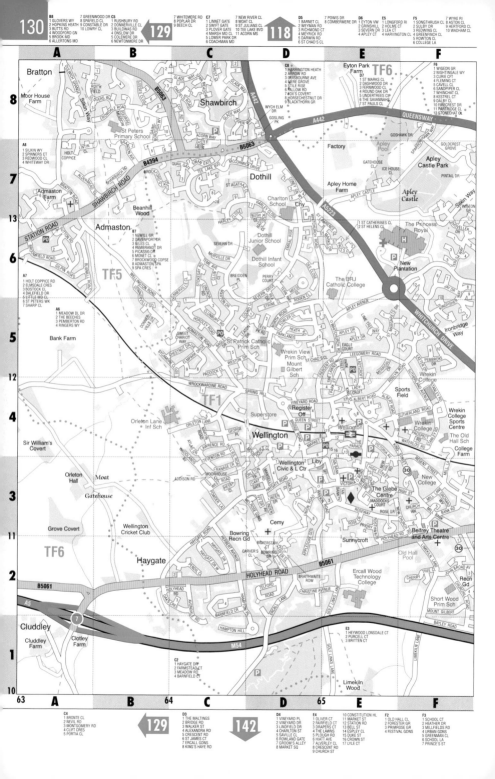

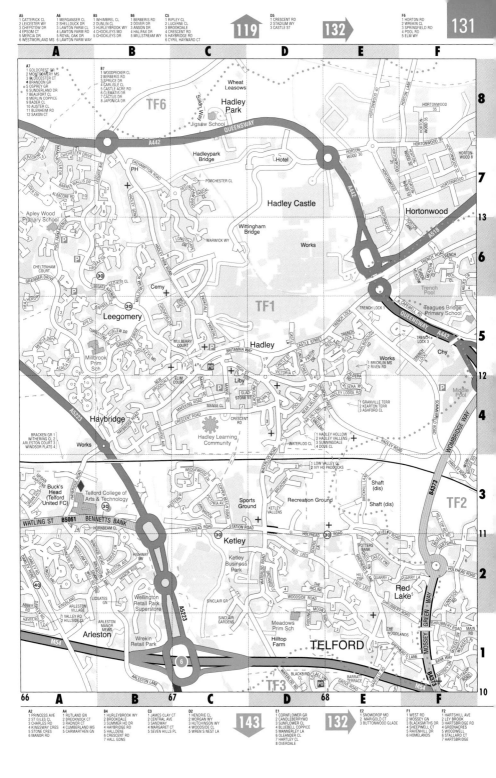

A5
1 CATTERICK CL
2 LEICESTER WY
3 CHEPSTOW DR
4 EPSOM CT
5 MERCIA WY
6 WESTMORLAND MS

A6
1 MERGANSER CL
2 SHELLDUCK DR
3 LAWTON FARM CL
4 LAWTON FARM RD
5 ROYAL OAK AV
6 LAWTON FARM WAY

B5
1 WHIMBREL CL
2 DUNLIN CL
3 HURLEYBROOK WY
4 CHOCKLEYS MD
5 CHOCKLEYS DR

B6
1 BERBERIS RD
2 DOVER DR
3 ANSON DR
4 HALIFAX DR
5 MILLSTREAM WY

C5
1 RIPLEY CL
2 LUCKING CL
3 BROOKDALE
4 CRESCENT RD
5 HAYBRIDGE RD
6 CYRIL HAYWARD CT

D5
1 CRESCENT RD
2 STADIUM WY
3 CASTLE ST

F6
1 HORTON RD
2 WREKIN CL
3 SPRINGFIELD RD
4 POOL RD
5 ELM WY

A7
1 GOLDCREST GR
2 MONTGOMERY MS
3 LEICESTER CT
4 BRANDON GR
5 OSPREY GR
6 SUNDERLAND DR
7 BEAUFORT CL
8 MERLIN COPPICE
9 BADER CL
10 AUSTER CL
11 BLENHEIM RD
12 SAXON CT

B7
1 WOODPECKER CL
2 BERBERIS RD
3 SPRUCE CL
4 CASTLE ACRE RD
5 CLEMATIS DR
6 CLEMATIS DR
7 CACTUS DR
8 JAPONICA DR

A2
1 PRINCESS AVE
2 ST GILES CL
3 CHARLES RD
4 KINGSWAY CRES
5 STONE CRES
6 MANOR RD

A4
1 RUTLAND GN
2 BRECKNOCK CT
3 RADNOR CT
4 CUMBERLAND MS
5 CARMARTHEN GN

B4
1 HURLEYBROOK WY
2 BROOKDALE
3 SUMMER HO DR
4 HAYBRIDGE RD
5 HALLDENE
6 CRESCENT RD
7 HALL GDNS

C3
1 JAMES CLAY CT
2 CENTRAL AVE
3 SANDWAY
4 MARGARET CT
5 SEVEN HILLS PL

D2
1 MENORIE CL
2 MORGAN WY
3 HUTCHINSON WY
4 WOODSIDE CL
5 WREN S NEST LA

E1
1 CORNFLOWER GR
2 CANDLEBERRYMD
3 SUNFLOWER CL
4 BLUEBELL COPPICE
5 MANNERLEY LA
6 OLEANDER CL
7 HARTLEY CL
8 OVERDALE

E2
1 SNOWDROP MD
2 MARIGOLD CT
3 BUTTONWOOD GLADE

F1
1 WEST RD
2 MOSSEY GN
3 BLACKSMITHS DR
4 SHEEPWELL CT
5 RAVENHILL DR
6 HOMELANDS

F2
1 HARTSHILL AVE
2 LEY BROOK
3 HARTSBRIDGE RD
4 GREENACRES
5 WOODWELL
6 STALLARD CT
7 HARTSBRIDGE

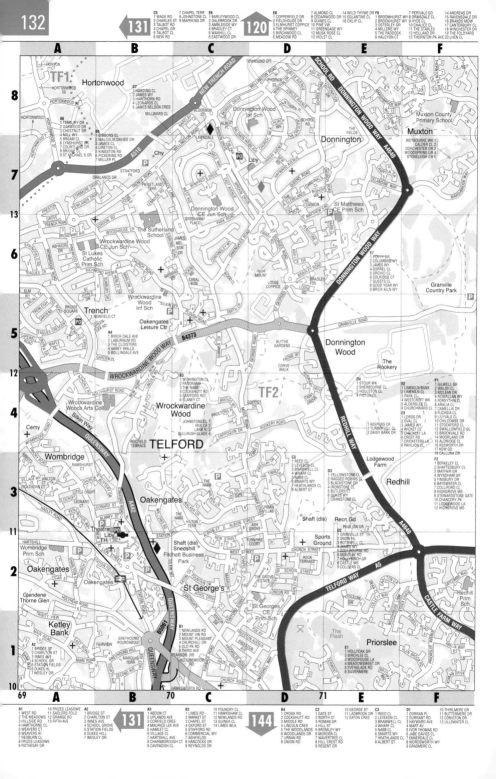

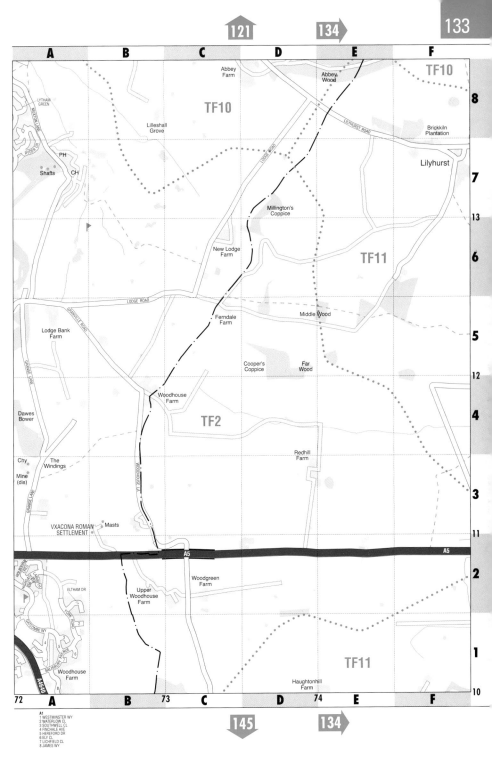

TF10

Abbey
Farm

Abbey
Wood

TF10

Lilleshall
Grove

LILYHURST ROAD

Brickkiln
Plantation

LYTHAM
GREEN

MAXTON LANE

PH

RYDES GR

Shafts

CH

Lilyhurst

8

7

13

Millington's
Coppice

New Lodge
Farm

TF11

6

LODGE ROAD

LODGE ROAD

GRANVILLE ROAD

Ferndale
Farm

Middle Wood

Lodge Bank
Farm

5

GRANGE LANE

Dawes
Bower

Cooper's
Coppice

Far
Wood

12

Woodhouse
Farm

TF2

4

Chy

The
Windings

Redhill
Farm

Mine
(dis)

GRANGE LANE

WOODHOUSE LA

3

11

VXACONA ROMAN
SETTLEMENT

Masts

A5

A5

2

MORBORN
HIGHT MEAD
DUNE CL

ELTHAM DR

Woodgreen
Farm

LODGE
ROAD

2

SEACOMBE WY

Upper
Woodhouse
Farm

SALISBURY AVENUE

4

5

6

Woodhouse
Farm

TF11

1

A5040

Haughtonhill
Farm

72

A

B

73

C

D

74

E

F

10

A1
1 WESTMINSTER WY
2 WATERLOW CL
3 SOUTHWELL CL
4 FINCHALE AVE
5 HEREFORD DR
6 ELY CL
7 LICHFIELD CL
8 JAMES WY

133
122

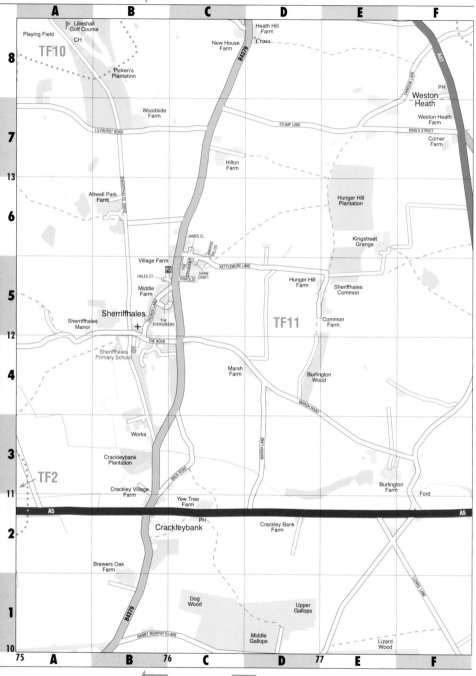

133
146

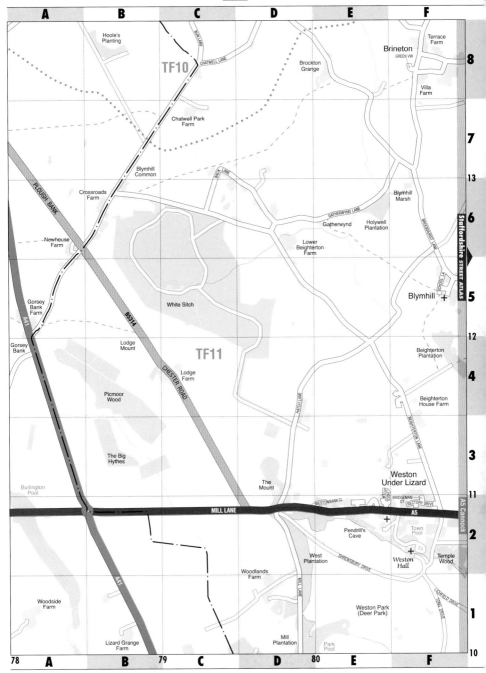

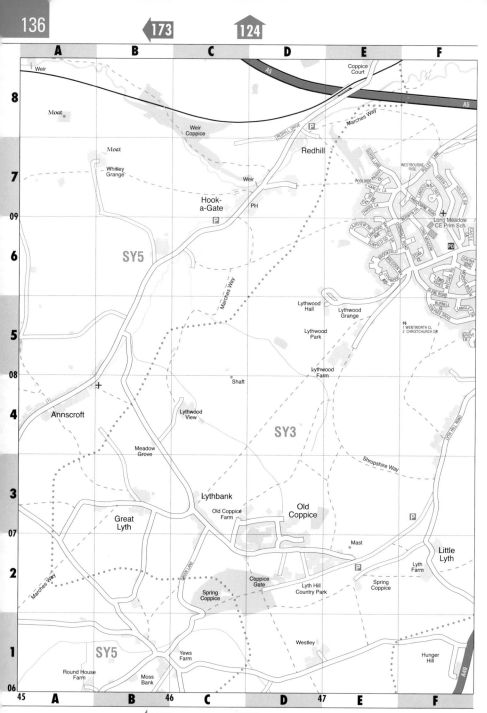

173
124

A **B** **C** **D** **E** **F**

8

Weir

Coppice
Court

A5

Moat

Weir
Coppice

REDHILL DRIVE

Marches Way

A5

Redhill

7

Moat

Whitley
Grange

Weir

Hook-
a-Gate

PH

09

GORSE LANE
POOLSIDE

WESTBOURNE
RISE

PULLEY LANE

GREEN LANE

HANLEY LA

LANSDOWNE DR

PARRS LA

LANSDOWNE ROAD

OAK DR

BENWAY DR

Long Meadow
CE Prim Sch

CASTLE

6

SY5

Marches Way

FAIRVIEW DR
HADFORD
SHEFFIELD DR

BOWNELL ROAD

LONG MEADOW

CEDAR CL

PO

DAVINA RISE

Lythwood
Hall

Lythwood
Grange

BROOKFIELD

BELGRAVE DR

LYTHWOOD

TWO ELMS RD
JAMES RD

BROOKSIDE WALK

GLEBE ROAD

GROVE
LA

5

Lythwood
Park

F6
1 WENTWORTH CL
2 CHRISTCHURCH DR

BURNELL
RD

THREE DRIVE

LANGLEY RD

08

Lythwood
Farm

Shaft

SY3

4

Annscroft

Lythwood
View

LYTH HILL ROAD

Meadow
Grove

Shropshire Way

3

Lythbank

Old Coppice
Farm

Old
Coppice

07

Great
Lyth

GREEN LANE

Mast

Little
Lyth

2

Marches Way

Coppice
Gate

Lyth Hill
Country Park

Lyth
Farm

Spring
Coppice

Spring
Coppice

1

Marches Way

SY5

Yews
Farm

Westley

Hunger
Hill

A49

06

Round House
Farm

Moss
Bank

45

A **B** 46 **C** **D** 47 **E** **F**

173
178

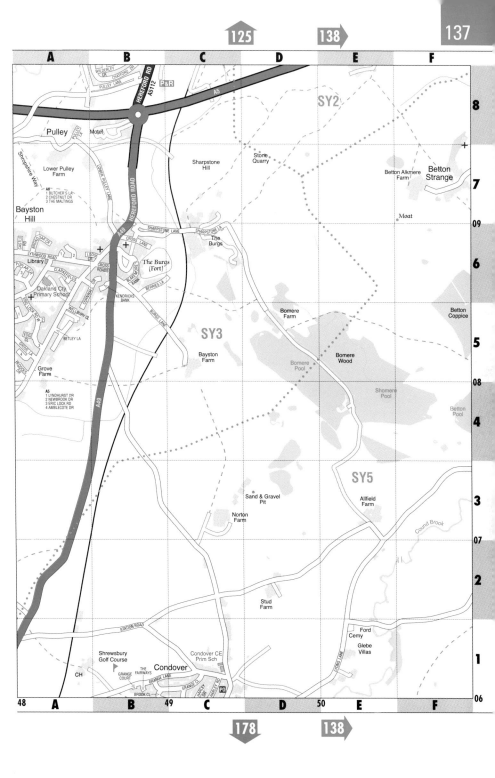

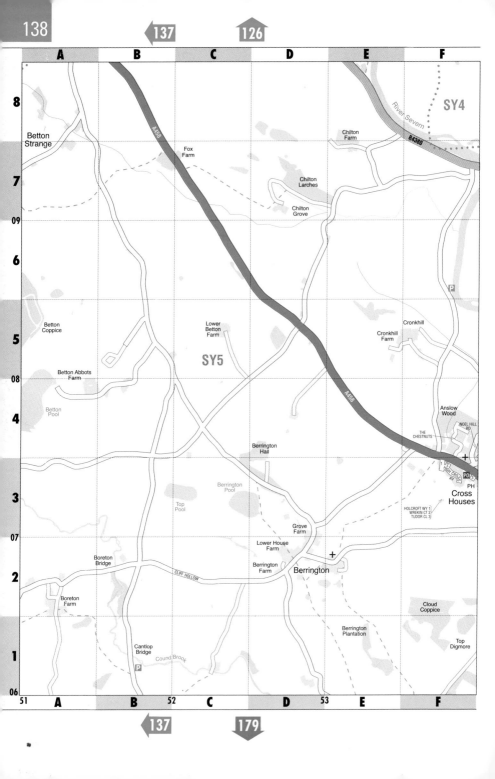

137 126

SY4

River Severn

B4380

Betton
Strange

Fox
Farm

Chilton
Farm

Chilton
Larches

Chilton
Grove

Betton
Coppice

Lower
Betton
Farm

SY5

Cronkhill

Cronkhill
Farm

Betton Abbots
Farm

Betton
Pool

Anslow
Wood

NOEL HILL
RD

THE
CHESTNUTS

A458

Berrington
Hall

HIGH CROSS
AV

PO

PH

Berrington
Pool

Cross
Houses

Top
Pool

HOLCROFT WY 1
WREKIN CT 2
TUDOR CL 3

Grove
Farm

Lower House
Farm

Boreton
Bridge

CLIFF HOLLOW

Berrington
Farm

Berrington

Cloud
Coppice

Boreton
Farm

Berrington
Plantation

Top
Digmore

Cantlop
Bridge

Cound Brook

51 52 53

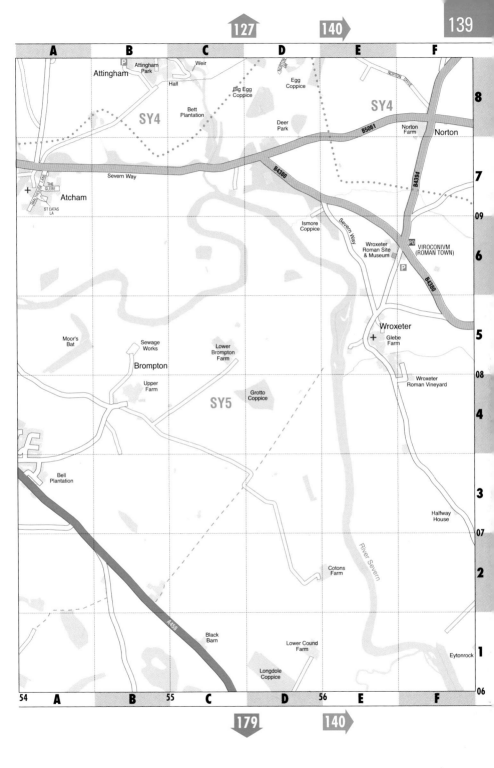

A B C D E F

8

Attingham Park
Attingham
Hall
Weir
Big Egg Coppice
Egg Coppice
Bett Plantation
Deer Park
SY4
SY4
B5061
Norton Farm
Norton
NORTON DRIVE

7

Severn Way
B4380
THE GLEBE
Atcham
St Eatas La
Ismore Coppice
Severn Way
B4394

09

Wroxeter Roman Site & Museum
PO
VIROCONIVM (ROMAN TOWN)
P
B4380

6

5

Moor's Bat
Sewage Works
Brompton
Upper Farm
Lower Brompton Farm
Grotto Coppice
SY5
Wroxeter
Glebe Farm
Wroxeter Roman Vineyard

08

4

Bell Plantation
A458

3

Halfway House

07

2

River Severn
Cotons Farm

Black Barn
Lower Cound Farm
Longdole Coppice
Eytonrock

1

06

54 A B 55 C D 56 E F

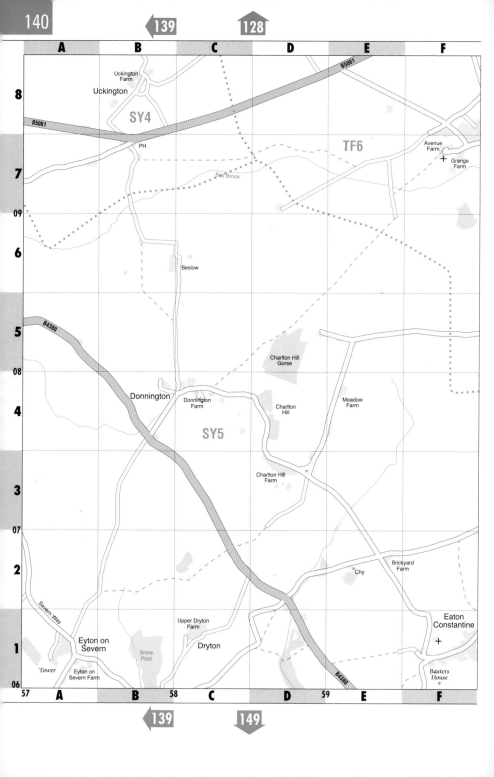

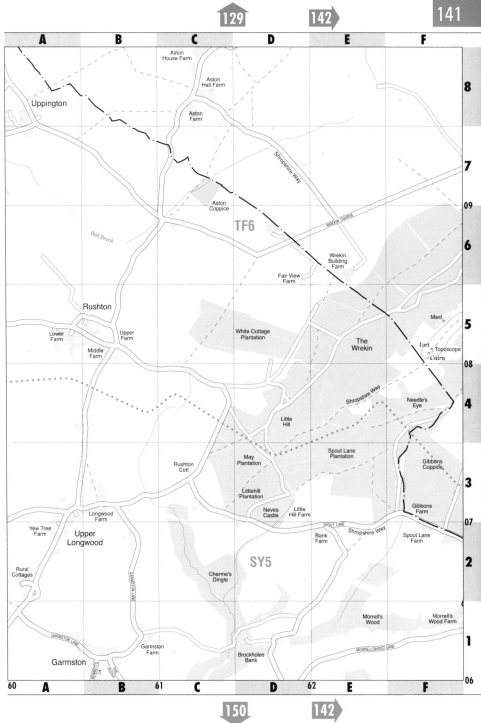

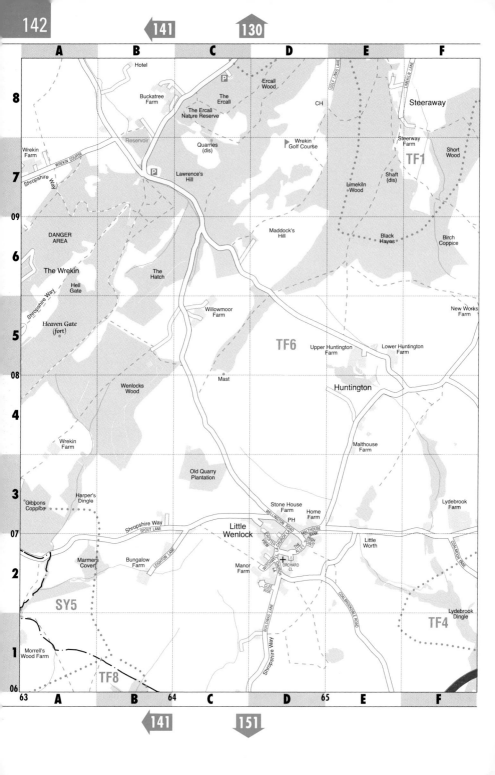

8

Hotel

Buckatree
Farm

The Ercall
Nature Reserve

The
Ercall

Ercall
Wood

CH

Steeraway

Reservoir

Wrekin
Farm

Quarries
(dis)

Wrekin
Golf Course

Steerway
Farm

TF1

Short
Wood

7

Shropshire Way

WREKIN COURSE

Lawrence's
Hill

Shaft
(dis)

Limekiln
Wood

09

DANGER
AREA

Maddock's
Hill

Black
Hayes

Birch
Coppice

6

The Wrekin

Hell
Gate

The
Hatch

Shropshire Way

Willowmoor
Farm

New Works
Farm

5

Heaven Gate
(fort)

TF6

Upper Huntington
Farm

Lower Huntington
Farm

08

Wenlocks
Wood

Mast

Huntington

4

Wrekin
Farm

Malthouse
Farm

3

Gibbons
Coppice

Harper's
Dingle

Old Quarry
Plantation

Stone House
Farm

Home
Farm

Lydebrook
Farm

07

Shropshire Way

SPOUT LANE

WELLINGTON ROAD

PH

MALTHOUSE
BANK

Little
Wenlock

Little
Worth

2

SY5

Marmer's
Covert

Bungalow
Farm

LEIGHTON LANE

Manor
Farm

WITCHWELL LANE

FOXES GLEN

LA CHURCH

ORCHARD
CL

THE ALLEY

HIGH ST

CLEE
RISE

COALMOOR LANE

Lydebrook
Dingle

TF4

1

Morrell's
Wood Farm

BULLHANGAR LANE

Shropshire Way

COALBROOKDALE ROAD

06

TF8

GOLF LINKS LANE

LIMEKILN LANE

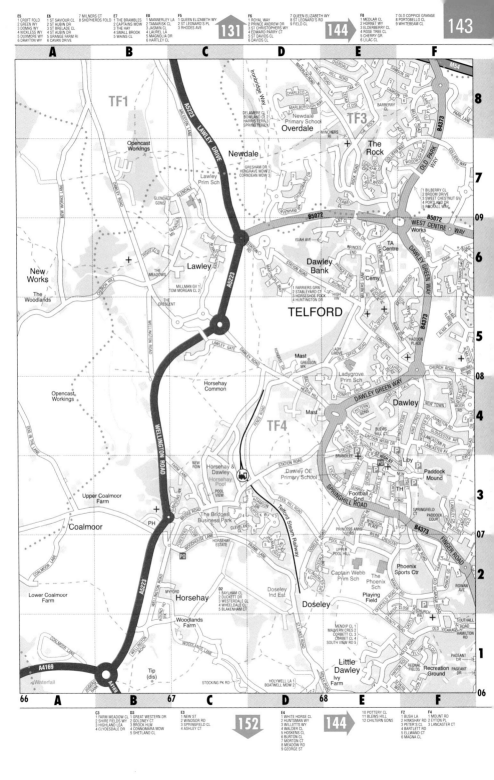

E5
1 CROFT FOLD
2 GREEN WY
3 DOMAS WY
4 NICKLESS WY
5 DUXMORE WY
6 DRAYTON WY

E6
1 ST SAVIOUR CL
2 ST AUBIN DR
3 ST BRELADE CL
4 ST AUBIN DR
5 GRANGE FARM RI
6 CAVAN DRIVE

7 MILNERS CT
8 SHEPHERDS FOLD

E7
1 THE BRAMBLES
2 CAPTAINS MDW
3 THE HAY
4 SMALL BROOK
5 WAINS CL

E8
1 MANNERLEY LA
2 TAMARISK CL
3 JASMIN CL
4 LAUREL LA
5 MAGNOLIA DR
6 HARTLEY CL

F5
1 QUEEN ELIZABETH WY
2 ST LEONARD S PL
3 RHODES AVE

131

F6
1 ROYAL WAY
2 PRINCE ANDREW DR
3 ST CHRISTOPHERS WY
4 EDWARD PARRY CT
5 ST DAVIDS CL
6 DAVIS CL

144

7 QUEEN ELIZABETH WY
8 ST LEONARD S RD
9 FIELD CL

F8
1 MEDLAR CL
2 HORNET WY
3 DERBERRY CL
4 ROSE TREE CL
5 CHERRY GR
6 LILAC CL

7 OLD COPPICE GRANGE
8 PORTOBELLO CL
9 WHITEBEAM CL

C3
1 FARM MEADOW CL
2 SHIRE FIELDS WY
3 HIGHLAND LEA
4 CLYDESDALE DR

D3
1 GREAT WESTERN DR
2 GOLONEY CT
3 BROCK HLW
4 CONNOMARA MDW
5 SHETLAND CL

E3
1 NEW ST
2 WINDSOR RD
3 SPRINGFIELD CL
4 ASHLEY CT

152

E4
1 WHITE HORSE CL
2 HUNTSMAN WY
3 WILLETTS WY
4 WALKER CL
5 HOSKENS CL
6 BURTON CL
7 MORTON CT
8 MEADOW ST
9 GEORGE ST

144

10 POTTERY CL
11 BLEWS HILL
12 CHILTERN GDNS

F2
1 BUSH LA
2 HINKSHAY RD
3 PETER'S CL
4 BARTLETT RD
5 ELLWANO CT
6 MAGNA CL

F4
1 MOUNT RD
2 EYTON PL
3 LANCASTER CT

D2
1 BAYLHAM CL
2 DUCKETT DR
3 WESTERDALE CL
4 WHEELDALE CT
5 BLAKENHAM CT

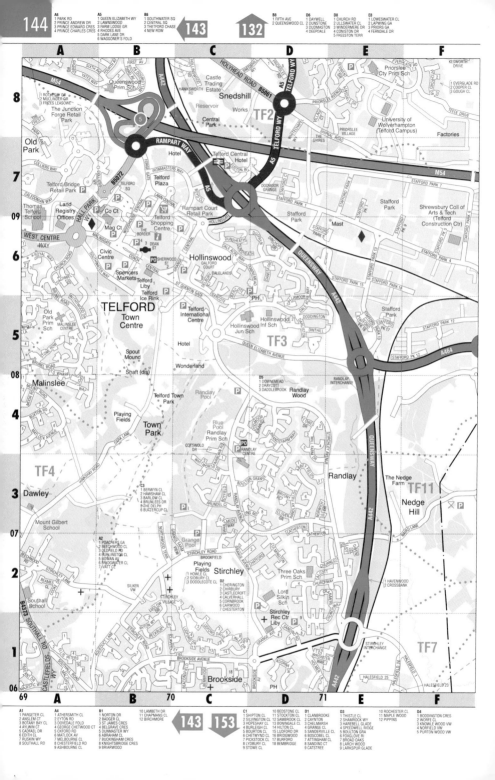

A6
1 PARK RD
2 PRINCE ANDREW DR
3 PRINCE EDWARD CRES
4 PRINCE CHARLES CRES

A5
1 QUEEN ELIZABETH WY
2 LAWNSWOOD
3 FARM LODGE GR
4 RHODES AVE
5 DARK LANE DR
6 WAGGONER'S FOLD

B6
1 SOUTHWATER SQ
2 CENTRAL SQ
3 THETFORD CHASE
4 NEW ROW

B8
1 FIFTH AVE
2 QUEENSWOOD CL

D6
1 DAYWELL
2 DUNSTONE
3 DUDMASTON
4 DEEPDALE

D6
1 CHURCH RD
2 ULLSWATER CL
3 WINDERMERE DR
4 CONISTON DR
5 FREESTON TERR

E8
1 LOWESWATER CL
2 LAPWING GA
3 PRIORS GA
4 FERNDALE DR

A1
1 PARGETER CL
2 ANSLEM CT
3 ROTARY BAY CL
4 ALYWIN CT
5 CADFAEL DR
6 EDITH CL
7 RUSKIN WY
8 SOUTHALL RD

A4
1 AYTHERSMITH CL
2 EYTON RD
3 DOVEDALE FOLD
4 GEORGE CHETWOOD CT
5 OXFORD RD
6 MATLOCK AV
7 MELBOURNE CL
8 CHESTERFIELD RD
9 ASHBOURNE CL

B1
1 NORTON DR
2 BADGER CL
3 ST JAMES CRES
4 BELGRAVE CRES
5 DURMASTER WY
6 ABRAHAM CL
7 BUCKINGHAM CRES
8 KNIGHTSBRIDGE CRES
9 BRIARWOOD
10 LAMBETH DR
11 CHAPMANS CL
12 BIRCHMORE

C1
1 SHIPTON CL
2 SILVINGTON CL
3 HOPESHAY CL
4 BURLEIGH CL
5 BOURTON CL
6 CHETWYND CL
7 PICKSTOCK CL
8 LYDBURY CL
9 STOWE CL
10 BEDSTONE CL
11 STOCKTON CL
12 SAMBROOK CL
13 BONINGALE CL
14 HILTON CL
15 LUDFORD CL
16 BRIDGEWOOD
17 BURFORD
18 BEMBRIDGE

D1
1 CLANBROOKE
2 CAYNTON
3 CHELMARSH
4 GRANGE CL
5 SANDERVILLE CL
6 BOSCOBEL CL
7 ATTINGHAM CL
8 SANDINO CT
9 CATSTREE

D3
1 THISTLE CL
2 SHAMROCK WY
3 HAREBELL GLADE
4 SPEEDWELL RIDGE
5 BOULTON GRA
6 FOXGLOVE RI
7 BROAD OAKS
8 LARCH WOOD
9 LARKSPUR GLADE
10 ROCHESTER CL
11 MAPLE WOOD
12 PIPPINS

D4
1 BODDINGTON CRES
2 WORFE CL
3 KNOWLE WOOD VW
4 NORFIELD VW
5 PURTON WOOD VW

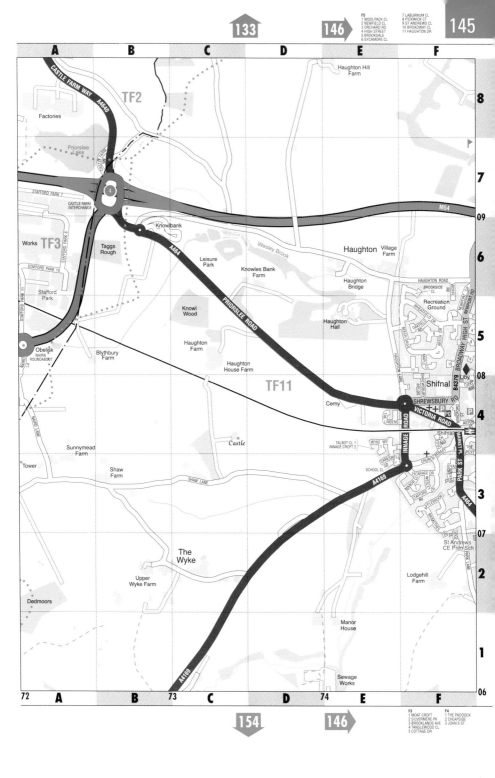

133
146

F5
1 WOOL PACK CL
2 NEWFIELD CL
3 ORCHARD RD
4 HIGH STREET
5 BROOKDALE
6 SYCAMORE CL

7 LABURNUM CL
8 PICKWICK CT
9 ST ANDREWS CL
10 BROADWAY CL
11 HAUGHTON DR

CASTLE FARM WAY A4640

TF2

Factories

Priorslee Lake

STAFFORD PARK 7

CASTLE FARM INTERCHANGE

4

M54

09

Knowlbank

Wesley Brook

Haughton

Village Farm

Works TF3

Taggs Rough

Leisure Park

Knowles Bank Farm

Haughton

HAUGHTON ROAD

BROOKSIDE CL

Recreation Ground

6

STAFFORD PARK 10

A464

Knowl Wood

Haughton Bridge

WHEATLEY DR

GARFIELD RD

BEECH DRIVE

MAPLE CL

BROADWAY HIGH ST

NEWPORT RD

STAFFORD PARK 11

Stafford Park

PRIORSLEE ROAD

Haughton Farm

Haughton Hall

HAUGHTON LANE

SHREWSBURY FIELDS

Shifnal

B4379

Lloy TUDO WA

08

Obelisk
NAIRN ROUNDABOUT

Blythbury Farm

Haughton House Farm

TF11

Cemy

SHREWSBURY RD

VICTORIA ROAD

P PO

P

ASTON

5

4

NUND LANE

Sunnymead Farm

Tower

Shaw Farm

SHAW LANE

Castle

THE LINDENS

INNAGE ROAD

TALBOT CL 1
INNAGE CROFT 2

WYKE WY

CAREGWELL GD

SCHOOL CL

Shifnal Sta

CHURCH STREET

VICARAGE DR

DYAS

MARKET PL

THE GROVE

PARK ST

3

07

The Wyke

A4169

STAFFORD

BRADFIEL

St Andrews
CE Prim Sch

A464

PARK LANE

Upper Wyke Farm

Lodgehill Farm

2

Dedmoors

Manor House

1

A4169

Sewage Works

06

154
146

F3
1 MOAT CROFT
2 SILVERMERE PK
3 BROOKLANDS AVE
4 TANGLEWOOD CL
5 COTTAGE DR

F4
1 THE PADDOCK
2 CHEAPSIDE
3 JOHN S ST

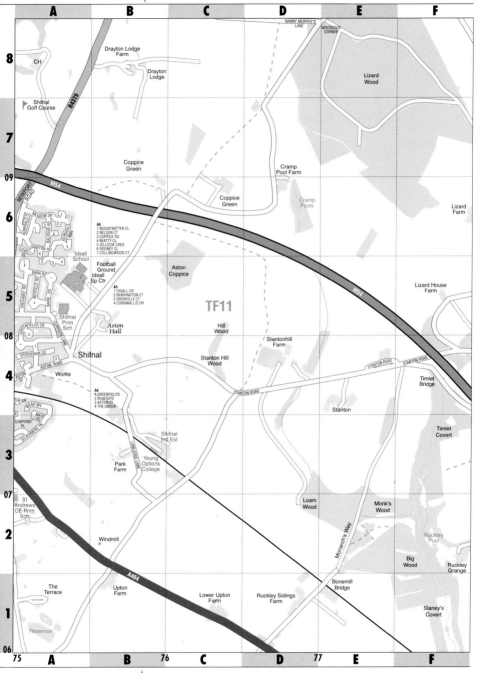

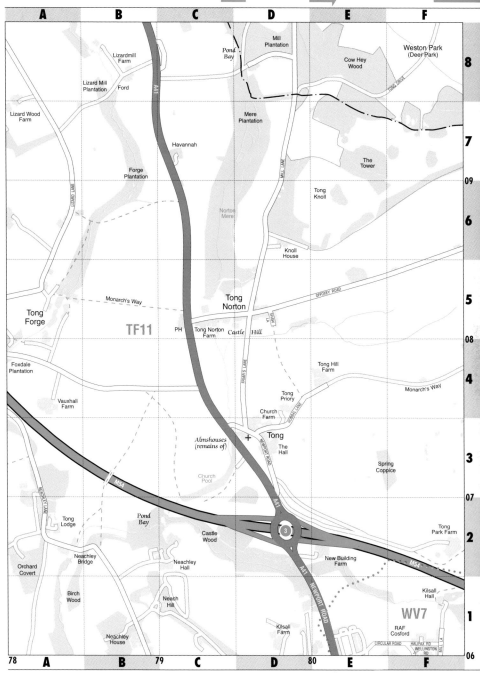

E8
1 THE FIRSWAY
2 BROOKSIDE GDNS
3 OAKAPPLE CL
4 ROYAL OAK DR
5 WESTON CL
6 SPRING LA

Staffordshire STREET ATLAS

Weston Park
(Deer Park)

Obelisk

Newport
Plantation

Moat

Bishops
Wood

Church
Farm

St Johns
CE First
Sch

BEACON
PK

Park Oak
Farm

Scilly
Grove

TONG ROAD

Offoxey
Plantation

White
Oak Farm

OFFOXEY ROAD

Tong
Rough

ST19

Hawkshead
Pool

The
Holt

Offoxey
Farm

Meashill
Farm

Boscobel
Dingle

Boscobel
House

TF11

Monarch's Way

Monarch's Way

Royal Oak
Wood

White Ladies
Priory
(rems of)

White Ladies
Plantation

Spring
Coppice

WV8

Monarch's Way

White Ladies
Farm

The
Wood
House

RENSHAW WOOD LANE

WV7

DONINGTON LANE

OLD SHACKERLEY LANE

SHACKERLEY LANE

Shackerley

M54

Wigmore
Wood

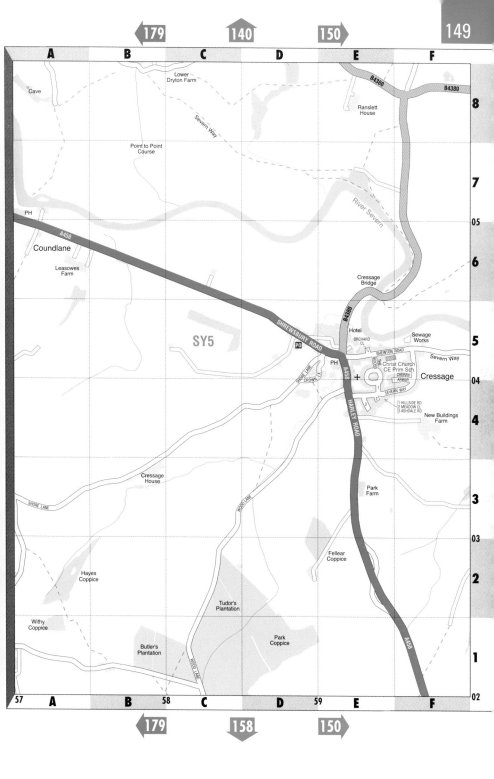

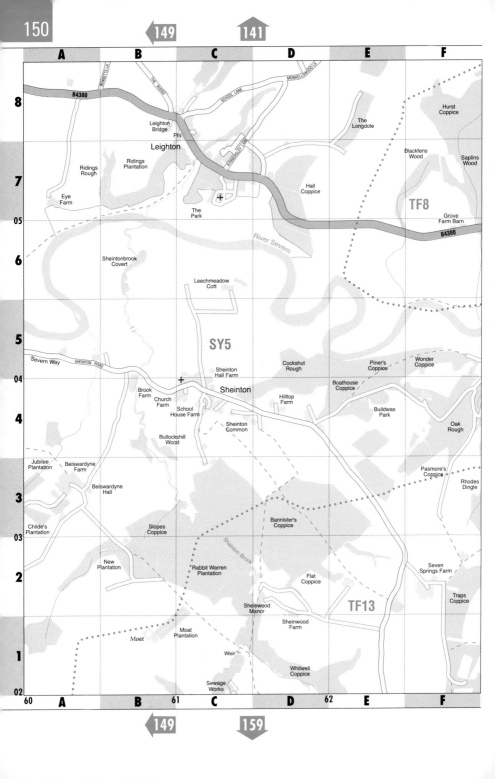

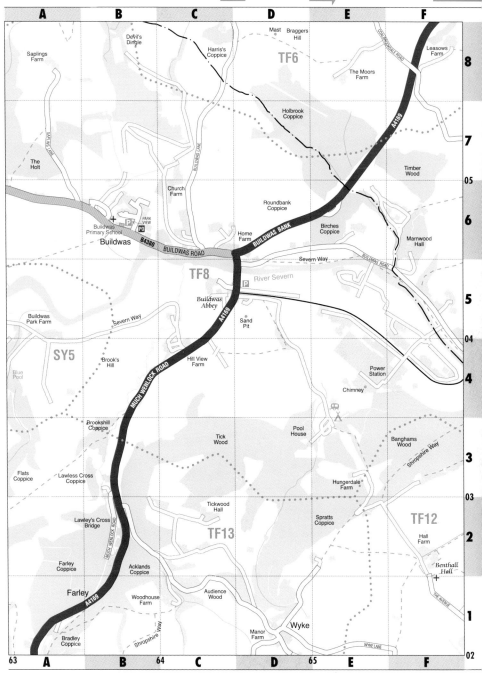

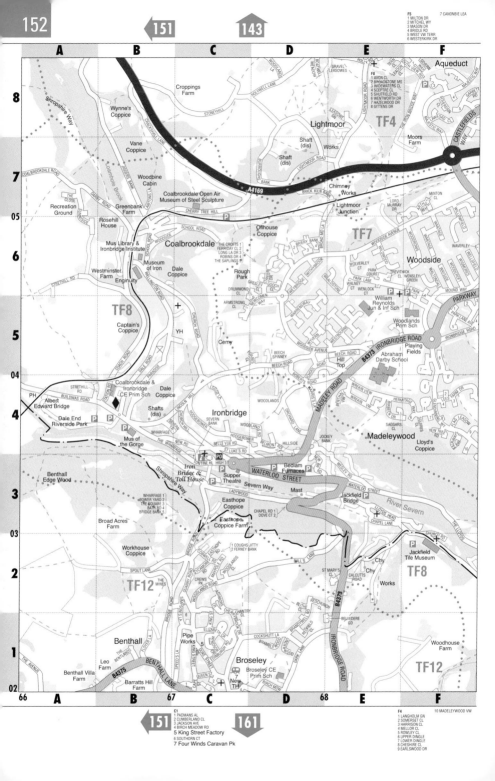

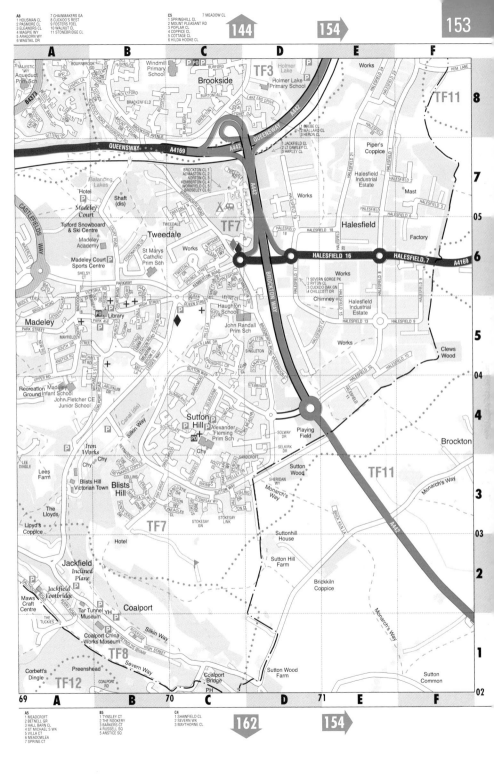

153
145

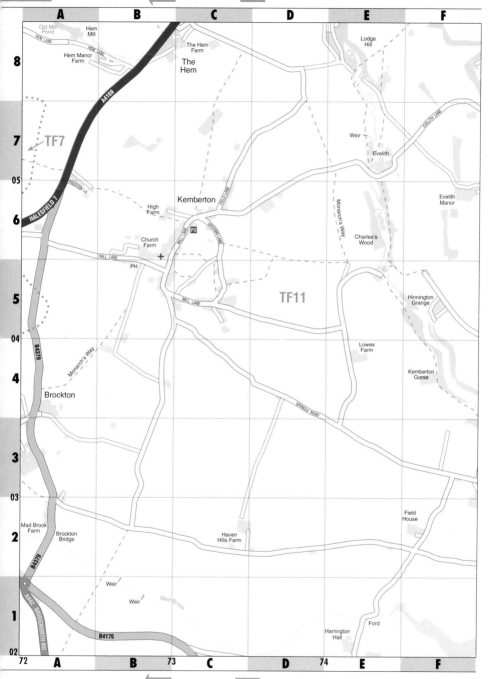

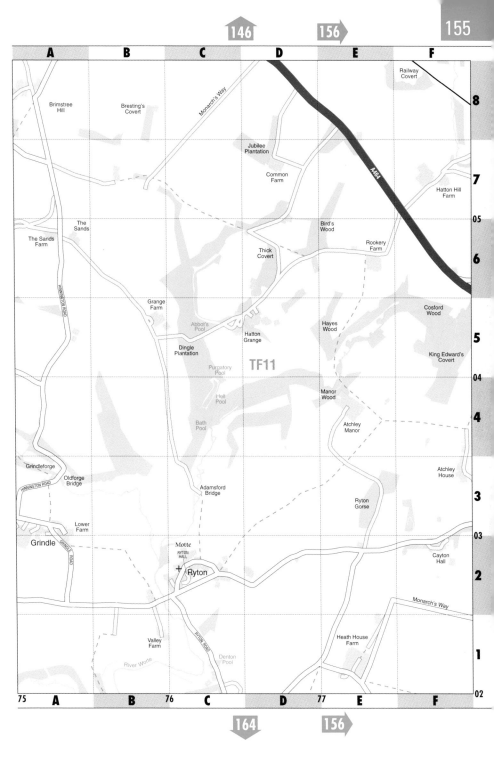

8

7

05

6

04

5

4

03

3

2

02

1

A B C D E F

Railway Covert

Brimstree Hill

Bresting's Covert

Monarch's Way

Jubilee Plantation

Common Farm

A464

Hatton Hill Farm

The Sands

Bird's Wood

Rookery Farm

The Sands Farm

Thick Covert

Cosford Wood

Grange Farm

Abbot's Pool

Hatton Grange

Hayes Wood

King Edward's Covert

HINNINGTON ROAD

Dingle Plantation

Purgatory Pool

TF11

Manor Wood

Hell Pool

Atchley Manor

Bath Pool

Grindleforge

Oldforge Bridge

Atchley House

HINNINGTON ROAD

Adamsford Bridge

Ryton Gorse

Lower Farm

Grindle

GRINDLE ROAD

Motte

RYTON HALL

Ryton

Cayton Hall

Monarch's Way

RYTON ROAD

Valley Farm

Denton Pool

Heath House Farm

River Worfe

75 76 77

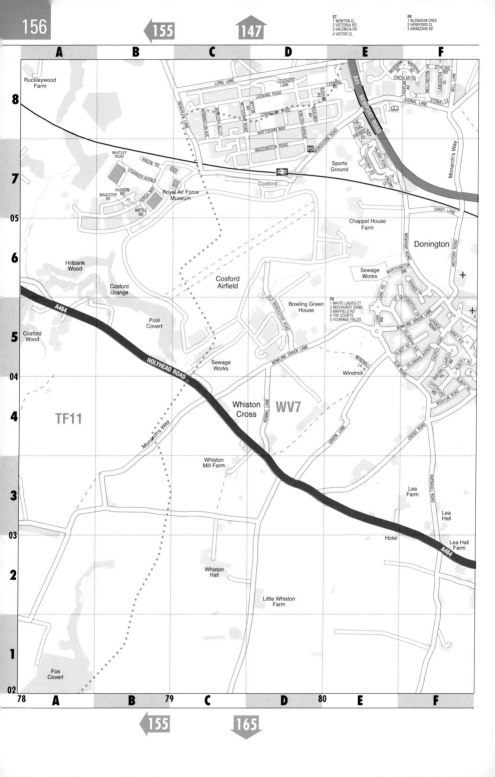

155
147

E7
1 NEWTON CL
2 VICTORIA RD
3 VALENCIA RD
4 VICTOR CL

F8
1 BLENHEIM CRES
2 HEREFORD CL
3 ABINGDON RD

A B C D E F

Ruckleywood
Farm

8

LONG LANE

ZEUCHERS
LANE

LEEMING ROAD

LEEMING
RD

WESTERN
CIRCULAR RD

EASTERN
CIRCULAR RD

STIRLING
AV

MILL LANE

LANCASTER
CL

SYDNAL LANE

SYDNAL LA

CONINGSBY ROAD

WATTISHAM WAY

WADDINGTON ROAD

POL

A41 NEWPORT ROAD

WHITLEY
ROAD

ANSON RD

LYSANDER AVENUE

HUDSON
RD

MAGISTER
RD

BATTLE
RD

PORSA WAY

Royal Air Force
Museum

Cosford

Sports
Ground

Monarch's Way

THE
OVAL
SWINGLEY

TALBOT
ROAD

WORCESTER ROAD

VALENCIA RD

SANDY LANE

7

05

Hillbank
Wood

Cosford
Grange

Pool
Covert

Chappel House
Farm

Sewage
Works

WORTHINGTON
DR

NEWPORT
ROAD

RECTORY
ROAD

Donington

6

A464

HOLYHEAD ROAD

Cosford
Wood

Sewage
Works

OLD WORCESTER ROAD

Bowling Green
House

F5
1 WHITE LADIES CT
2 BEECHURST GDNS
3 MAYFIELD RD
4 THE COURTS
5 VICARAGE FIELDS

OAK RD

ST CUTHBERTS LANE

BOWLING GREEN ROAD

GRANGE
ROAD

ABBEY RD

5

04

Monarch's Way

BOWLING GREEN LANE

Windmill

WINDMILL
LANE

TALBOT RD

DELAWARE AVENUE

ELM ROAD

CHARLES
RD

ABBEY RD

PITCHFORD
RD

BRIGHTON ROAD

TF11

Whiston
Cross

WV7

KENNEL LANE

GREEN LANE

CROSS ROAD

PATSHULL ROAD

4

3

03

Whiston
Mill Farm

Whiston
Hall

Lea
Farm

Lea
Hall

Hotel

Lea Hall
Farm

A464

2

Little Whiston
Farm

1

02

Fox
Covert

78 A 79 C D 80 E F

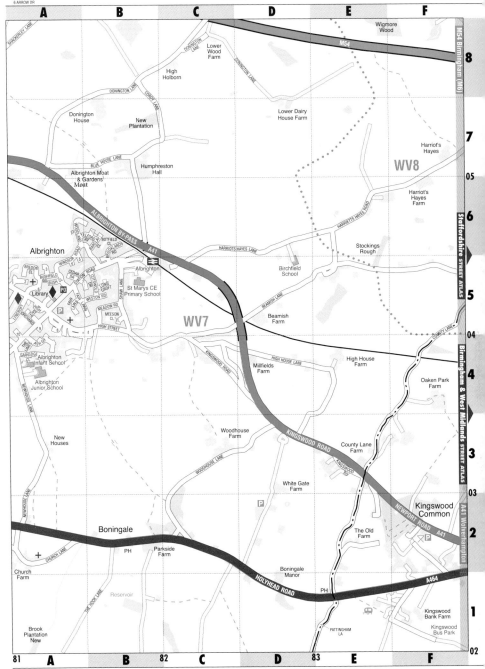

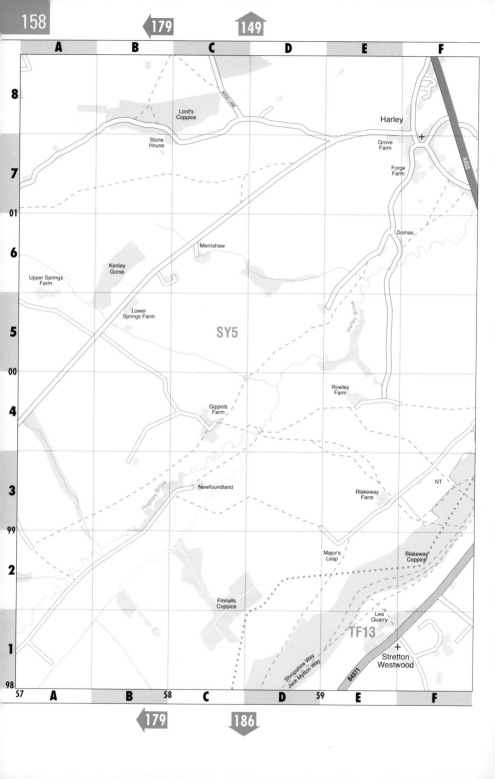

179
149

A   B   C   D   E   F

8

Lord's
Coppice

WOOD LANE

Harley

Stone
House

Grove
Farm

7

Forge
Farm

01

Domas

6

Merrishaw

Kenley
Gorse

Upper Springs
Farm

Harley Brook

Lower
Springs Farm

5

SY5

00

Rowley
Farm

4

Gippols
Farm

3

Hughley Brook

Newfoundland

Blakeway
Farm

NT

99

Major's
Leap

Blakeway
Coppice

2

Finnalls
Coppice

Lea
Quarry

TF13

1

Shropshire Way
Jack Mytton Way

Stretton
Westwood

B4371

98

57   A   B   58   C   D   59   E   F

A458

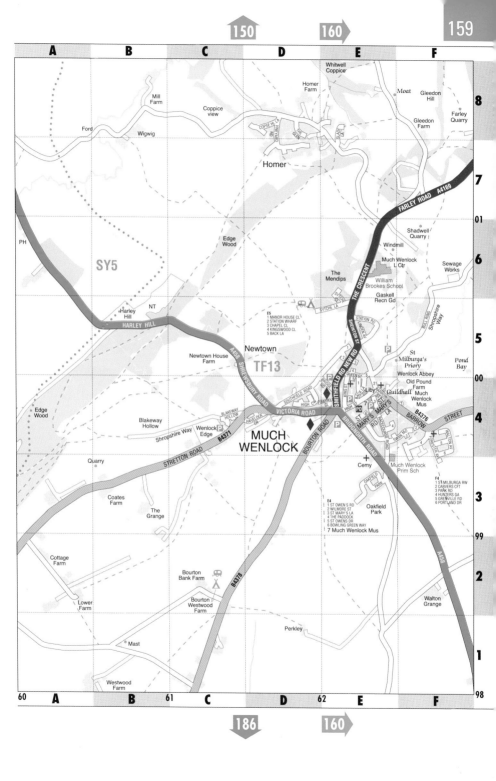

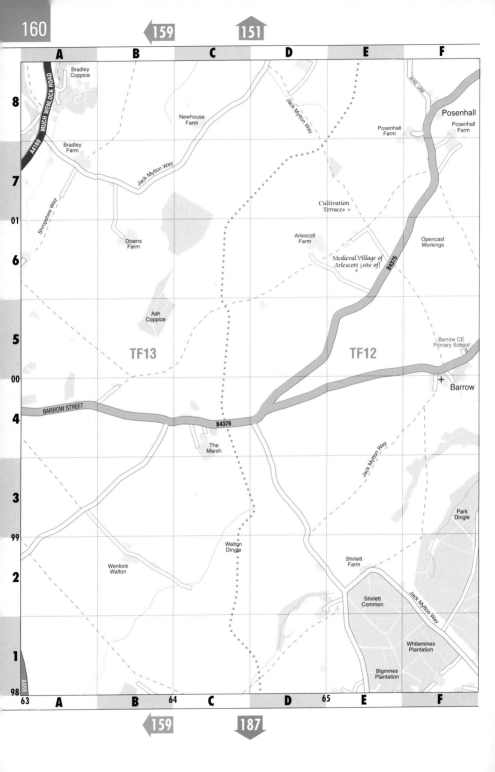

159

151

Bradley
Coppice

A4169 MUCH WENLOCK ROAD

Newhouse
Farm

Jack Mytton Way

Posenhall

Posenhall
Farm

Posenhall
Farm

WYKE LANE

8

Bradley
Farm

Jack Mytton Way

7

Shropshire Way

01

Downs
Farm

Cultivation
Terraces

Arlescott
Farm

Opencast
Workings

6

Medieval Village of
Arlescott (site of)

B4375

5

Ash
Coppice

TF13

TF12

Barrow CE
Primary School

00

Barrow

4

BARROW STREET

B4376

The
Marsh

Jack Mytton Way

3

Park
Dingle

99

Walton
Dingle

Shirlett
Farm

2

Wenlock
Walton

Shirlett
Common

Jack Mytton Way

Whitemines
Plantation

1

A458

Bigmines
Plantation

98

63

64

65

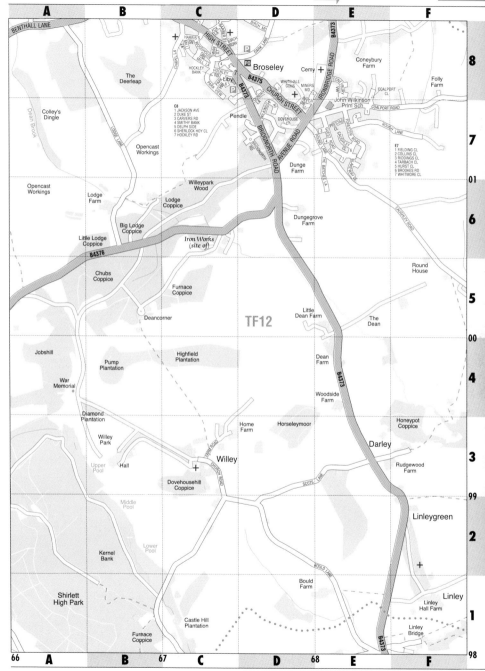

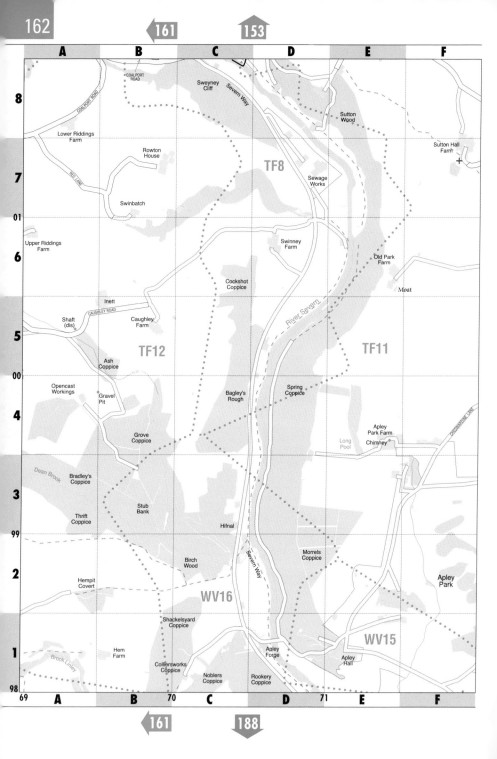

161
153

8

COALPORT ROAD

Sweyney Cliff

Severn Way

Sutton Wood

Lower Riddings Farm

Sutton Hall Farm

RED LANE

Rowton House

7

TF8

Sewage Works

Swinbatch

01

Upper Riddings Farm

Swinney Farm

Old Park Farm

6

Cockshot Coppice

Moat

Inett

CAUGHLEY ROAD

Shaft (dis)

Caughley Farm

River Severn

5

TF12

TF11

Ash Coppice

00

Opencast Workings

Gravel Pit

Bagley's Rough

Spring Coppice

Apley Park Farm

4

Grove Coppice

Long Pool

Chimney

CHESWARDINE LANE

Dean Brook

Bradley's Coppice

3

Stub Bank

Thrift Coppice

Hilfnal

Morrels Coppice

Apley Park

99

Severn Way

Birch Wood

2

Hempit Covert

WV16

Shackelsyard Coppice

WV15

1

Brook Linley

Hem Farm

Collersworks Coppice

Apley Forge

Apley Hall

Noblers Coppice

Rookery Coppice

98

69 A B 70 C D 71 E F

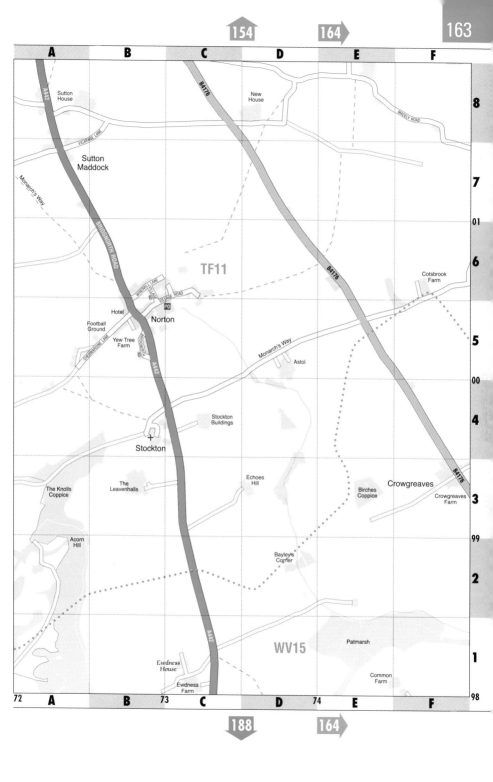

A   B   C   D   E   F

8
7
01
6
5
00
4
3
99
2
1
98

Sutton House
B4176
New House
MACKLEY ROAD

Monarch's Way

Sutton Maddock

VICARAGE LANE

BRIDGNORTH ROAD

TF11

B4176

Cotsbrook Farm

WINDMILL LANE
VILLAGE ROAD
PO

Hotel
Norton

Football Ground

OSBORNE LANE

A442
BRIDGNORTH RD

Yew Tree Farm

Monarch's Way
Astol

Stockton Buildings

Stockton

The Knolls Coppice

The Leavenhalls

Echoes Hill

Crowgreaves

Birches Coppice

B4176

Crowgreaves Farm

Acorn Hill

Bayley's Corner

WV15

Patmarsh

Ewdness House
Ewdness Farm

A442

Common Farm

72   A   73   B   C   74   D   E   F   98

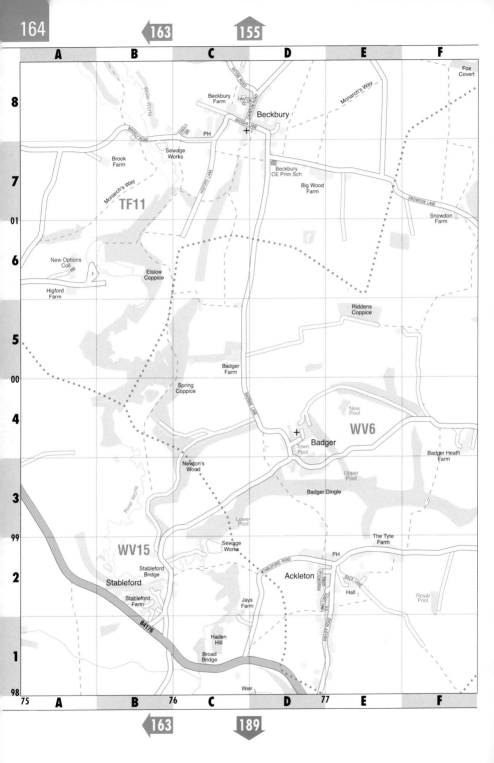

A B C D E F

8

Fox Covert

River Worfe

Beckbury Farm

PYTON ROAD

LAWTON RD

CAINTON ROAD

BADGER LANE

Beckbury

Monarch's Way

PH

MADELEY ROAD

DINGLE DR

Brook Farm

Sewage Works

Beckbury CE Prim Sch

7

Monarch's Way

HIGFORD LANE

Big Wood Farm

SNOWDON LANE

TF11

01

Snowdon Farm

6

New Options Coll

Elslow Coppice

Riddens Coppice

Higford Farm

5

Badger Farm

New Pool

00

Spring Coppice

BADGER LANE

4

Badger

Town Pool

WV6

Badger Heath Farm

Newton's Wood

Upper Pool

3

River Worfe

Badger Dingle

99

Lower Pool

The Tyte Farm

Sewage Works

PH

WV15

STABLEFORD ROAD

Ackleton

BACK LANE

2

Stableford Bridge

Stableford

ROSEHOLL

HALFPENNY GREEN

Hall

Royal Pool

Stableford Farm

Jays Farm

FINLEY ROAD

B4176

Haden Hill

1

Broad Bridge

Weir

98

75 A B 76 C D 77 E F

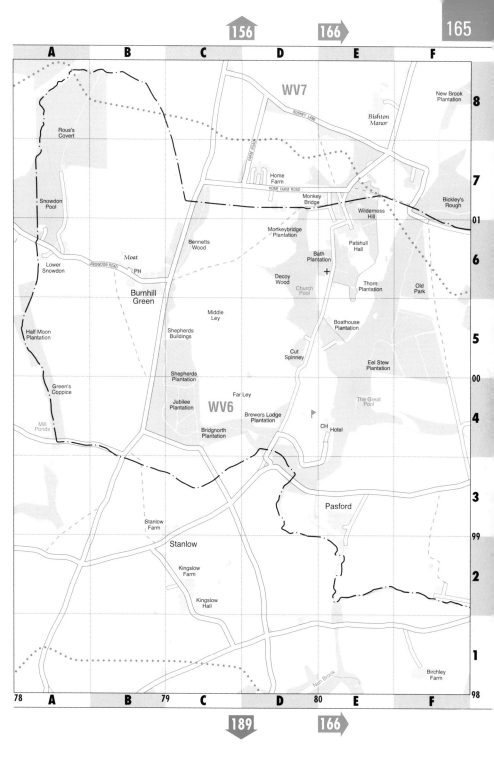

A B C D E F

8

WV7

New Brook
Plantation

RUSHEY LANE

Bishton
Manor

Rous's
Covert

7

Home
Farm

HOME FARM ROAD

Monkey
Bridge

Bickley's
Rough

Wilderness
Hill

01

Snowdon
Pool

Monkeybridge
Plantation

Patshull
Hall

6

Bennetts
Wood

Bath
Plantation

Moat

SNOWDON ROAD

Lower
Snowdon

PH

Decoy
Wood

Church
Pool

Thorn
Plantation

Old
Park

Burnhill
Green

Middle
Ley

Half Moon
Plantation

Shepherds
Buildings

Boathouse
Plantation

5

Cut
Spinney

Eel Stew
Plantation

00

Green's
Coppice

Shepherds
Plantation

Far Ley

The Great
Pool

Mill
Ponds

Jubilee
Plantation

WV6

Brewers Lodge
Plantation

4

Bridgnorth
Plantation

CH Hotel

Pasford

3

Stanlow
Farm

99

Stanlow

Kingslow
Farm

2

Kingslow
Hall

Nun Brook

Birchley
Farm

1

78

A B C D E F

79

80

98

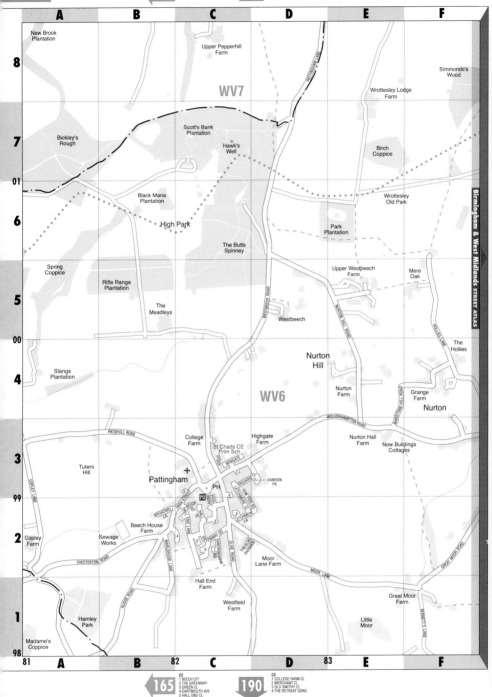

New Brook
Plantation

Upper Pepperhill
Farm

WV7

Simmonds's
Wood

Wrottesley Lodge
Farm

8

Bickley's
Rough

Scott's Bank
Plantation

Hawk's
Well

Birch
Coppice

7

01

Black Maria
Plantation

Wrottesley
Old Park

6

High Park

The Butts
Spinney

Park
Plantation

Spring
Coppice

Upper Westbeech
Farm

Mere
Oak

Rifle Range
Plantation

The
Meadleys

Westbeech

The
Hollies

5

00

Slangs
Plantation

Nurton
Hill

Grange
Farm

4

Nurton
Farm

Nurton

WV6

WOLVERHAMPTON ROAD

PATSHULL ROAD

College
Farm

St Chads CE
Prim Sch

Highgate
Farm

Nurton Hall
Farm

New Buildings
Cottages

3

Tuters
Hill

NEWGATE

DAMSON
PK

Pattingham

PH

PO

COPLEY LANE

99

Beech House
Farm

Sewage
Works

Moor
Lane Farm

2

Copley
Farm

CHESTERTON ROAD

MAIN BROOK LANE

RUDGE ROAD

Hall End
Farm

Westfield
Farm

MOOR LANE

Great Moor
Farm

BENNETT'S LANE

GREAT MOOR ROAD

1

Hamley
Park

Little
Moor

98

Madame's
Coppice

81

A

B

82

C

D

83

E

F

165

190

C2
1 BEECH CFT
2 THE GREENWAY
3 GREEN CL
4 DARTMOUTH AVE
5 HALL END CL
6 WINDSOR RD
7 BRAEMAR RD
8 ST CHADS CL

C3
1 COLLEGE FARM CL
2 MERCHANT CL
3 OLD SMITHY CL
4 THE RETREAT GDNS

Birmingham & West Midlands STREET ATLAS

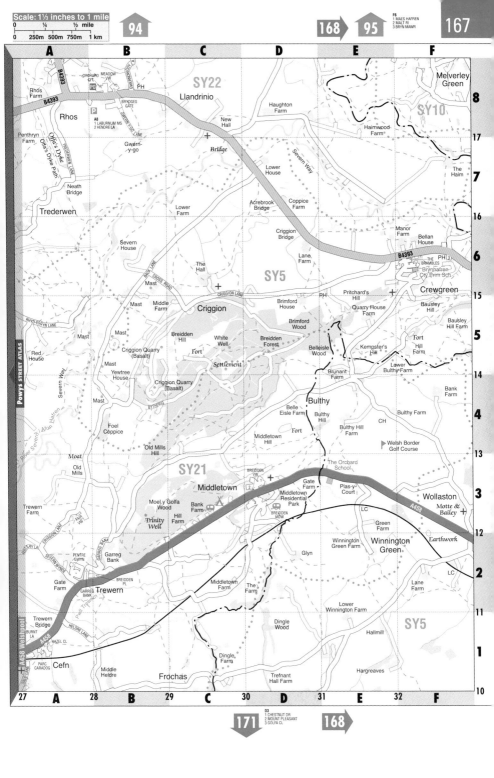

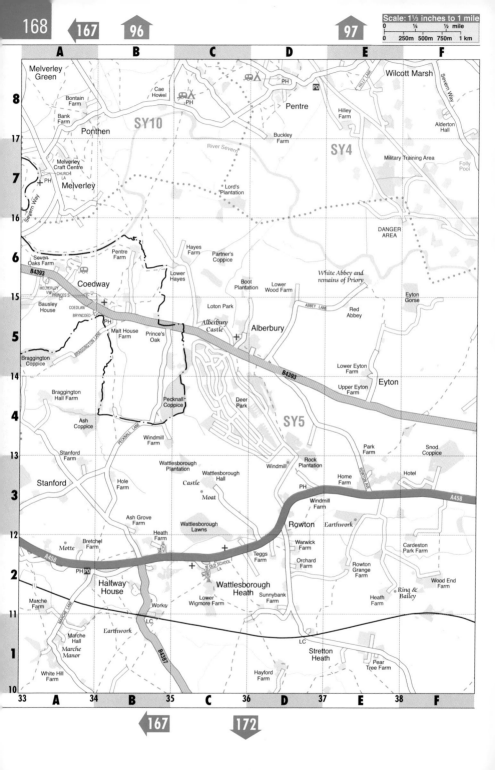

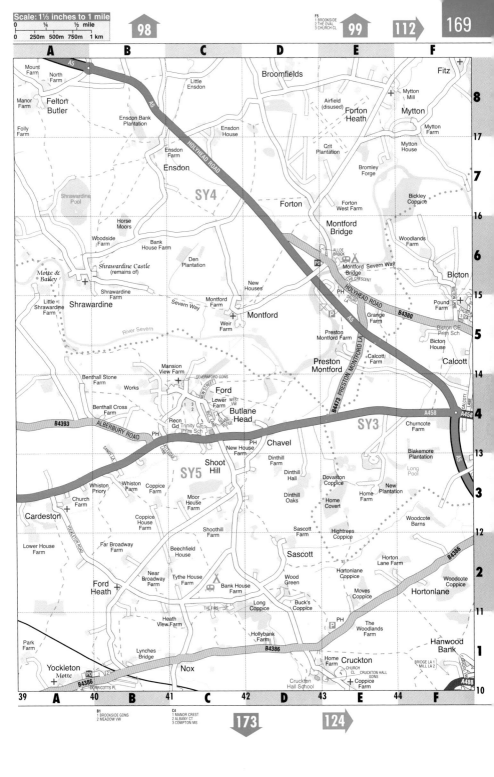

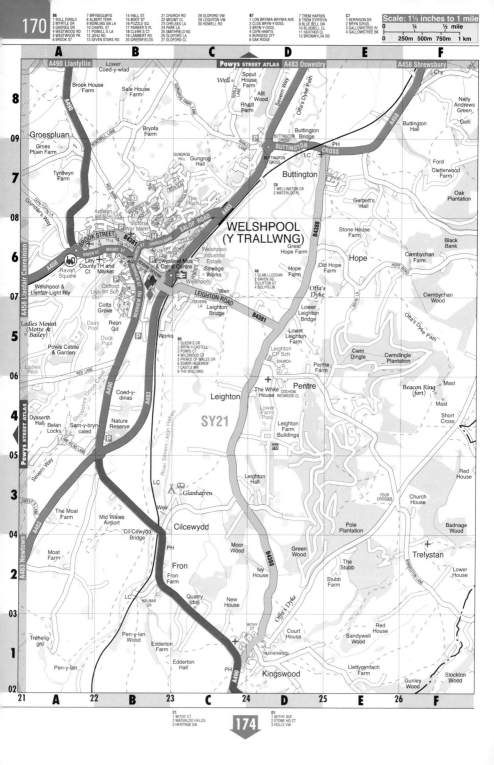

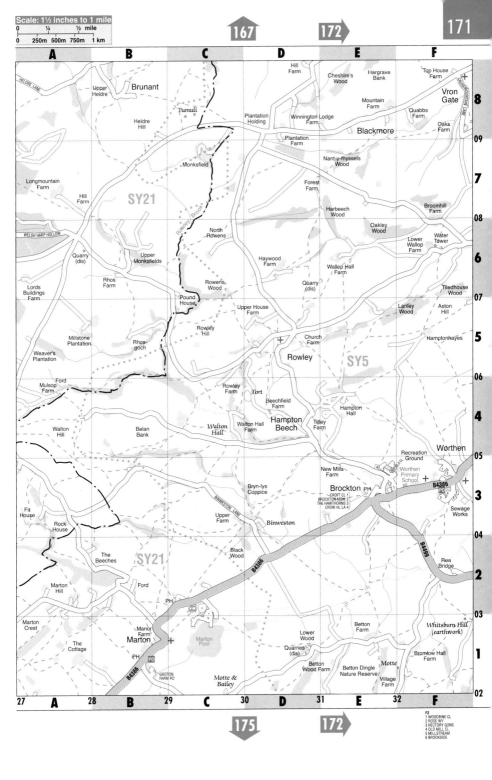

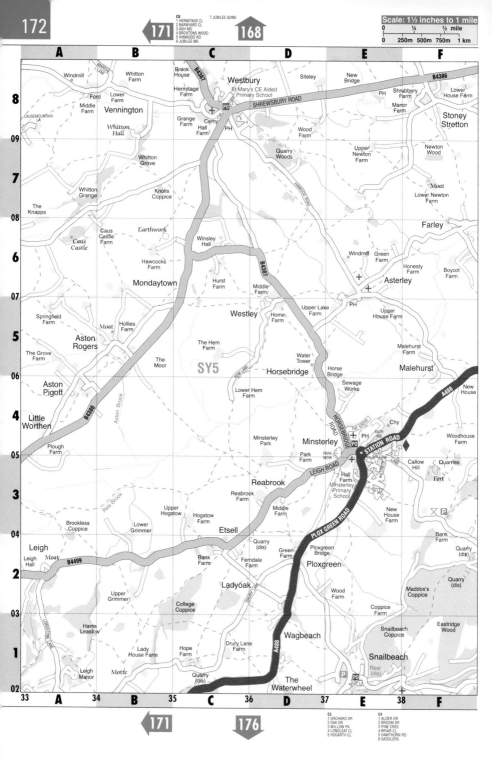

171

168

C8
1 HERMITAGE CL
2 BARNYARD CL
3 ASH MD
4 BROXTONS WOOD
5 HINWOOD RD
6 JUBILEE MS

7 JUBILEE GDNS

Scale: 1⅓ inches to 1 mile

0   ¼   ½ mile
0 250m 500m 750m 1 km

A   B   C   D   E   F

8

Windmill

Whitton
Farm

Brook
House

Westbury

Siteley

New
Bridge

PH

Shrubbery
Farm

Lower
House Farm

Ford

Lower
Farm

Hermitage
Farm

St Mary's CE Aided
Primary School

Manor
Farm

Middle
Farm

Vennington

Grange
Farm

SHREWSBURY ROAD

Stoney
Stretton

PO

Cemy

09

Whitton
Hall

Cemy

Grange
Hall
Farm

PH

Wood
Farm

Quarry
Woods

Upper
Newton
Farm

Newton
Wood

7

Whitton
Grove

Knolls
Coppice

Moat

08

Whitton
Grange

The
Knapps

Earthwork

Winsley
Hall

Lower Newton
Farm

Farley

Caus
Castle
Farm

6

Caus
Castle

Hawcocks
Farm

Mondaytown

Hurst
Farm

Middle
Farm

Windmill

Green
Farm

Honesty
Farm

Boycot
Farm

Asterley

07

Springfield
Farm

Moat

Hollies
Farm

Westley

Home
Farm

Upper Lake
Farm

PH

Upper
House Farm

5

Aston
Rogers

The
Moor

The Hem
Farm

Water
Tower

Malehurst
Farm

The Grove
Farm

SY5

Horsebridge

Horse
Bridge

Malehurst

06

Aston
Pigott

Lower Hem
Farm

Sewage
Works

New
House

4

Little
Worthen

Minsterley
Park

Minsterley

Woodhouse
Farm

05

Plough
Farm

Park
Farm

LEIGH ROAD

Hall
Farm

Callow
Hill

Quarries

Fort

3

Reabrook

Middle
Farm

Minsterley
Primary
School

New
House
Farm

Reabrook
Farm

P

Upper
Hogstow

Hogstow
Farm

Bank
Farm

04

Brookless
Coppice

Lower
Grimmer

Etsell

Quarry
(dis)

Green
Farm

Ploxgreen
Bridge

Quarry
(dis)

Leigh

Bank
Farm

Ferndale
Farm

Ploxgreen

Quarry
(dis)

2

Leigh
Hall

Moat

B4499

Upper
Grimmer

Ladyoak

Wood
Farm

Maddox's
Coppice

Quarry
(dis)

03

Hams
Leaslow

College
Coppice

Drury Lane
Farm

Wagbeach

Coppice
Farm

Snailbeach
Coppice

Eastridge
Wood

1

Leigh
Manor

Motte

Lady
House Farm

Hope
Farm

Snailbeach

Resr
(dis)

Quarry
(dis)

The
Waterwheel

02

33   A   34   B   35   C   36   D   37   E   38   F

171

176

E3
1 ORCHARD DR
2 OAK DR
3 WILLOW PK
4 LONGLEAT CL
5 HOGARTH CL

E4
1 ALDER DR
2 BROOM DR
3 PINE CRES
4 BRIAR CL
5 HAWTHORN RD
6 SADDLERS

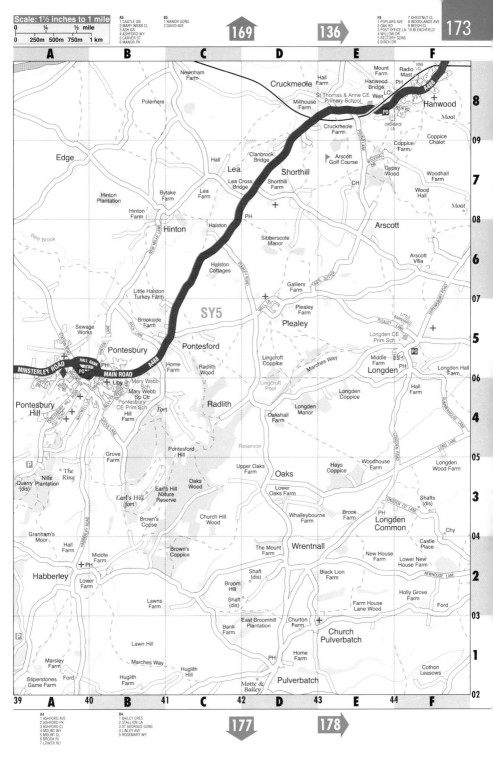

Scale: 1⅓ inches to 1 mile

0 ¼ ½ mile
0 250m 500m 750m 1 km

Columns: A B C D E F
Rows: 8 01 7 00 6 99 5 98 4 97 3 96 2 95 1 94

The Grove
Pen-y-lan
Gunley Wood
Lower Munlyn
Church Farm
Forden Cin W Prim Sch
Kingswood Farm
Ackley Farm
Stockton
Motte & Bailey
Nantcribbau Farm
Gunley Hall
Forden (Ffodun)
SY21
Rhyd-y-groes
LC
PH
Cwm Farm
Camlad
PO
Keith Davis Farm
Great Hem Farm
Upper Hem Farm
Lower Hem Farm
Pit (dis)
Quarry (dis)
CAMLAD DR 1
MAES-Y-FELIN 2
Hem Moor
Shiregrove Bridge
Salt Bridge
Walcot Farm
B4386
Stalloe
Earthwork
Chirbury CE Primary School
Quarry
Rownal
Crankwell Farm
Winsbury Farm
PH
PO
CAMLAD CTS
HORSESHOE RD
Hendomen
Motte & Bailey
Hendomen Farm
B4388
B4388
Chirbury
LC
B4385
Sewage Works
Dudston
Motte
Lower Lane
A490
STATION ROAD
FORDEN ROAD
Ffridd Wood
1 VERLON CL
2 ARTHURS GATE
NEW ROAD
County Boundary Bridge
Ffridd Faldwyn (fort)
Castle
CHIRBURY ROAD
Great Moat Farm
Moat
Timberth
The Old Bell Mus
POOL RD
PRINCES ST
Hendomen Dr
Upper Pool
Timberth Wood
SY15
Sidnal Farm
MONTGOMERY (TREFDLDWYN)
THE
BISHOP'S CASTLE STREET
Lymore Park
Broad Street Farm
KERRY GATE
P
Lower Pool
Boardyhall Wood
Whitley Wood
Rockley Wood
Caeprior
Hill Top Farm
War Memorial
New Covert
Motte
Rockley
Llwynobin
Gwarthlow
Rhiston
Pant-y-maen Wood
Weston Madoc
Pen-y-bryn Hall
Rockley Farm
Coed Farm
Upper Pentre
B4385
Little Brompton Farm
Churchstoke
COED LANE
A489

B3
1 GAOL RD
2 CHIRBURY GATE
3 SCHOOL BANK
4 ARTHUR ST
5 LYMORE VIEW
6 LIONS BANK
7 TAN Y MUR
8 CHURCH BANK
9 BROAD ST
10 KERRY ST
11 BACK LA
12 MALDWYN WY
13 CORNDON DR
14 WELL ST
15 KERRY RD
16 CASTLE WALK

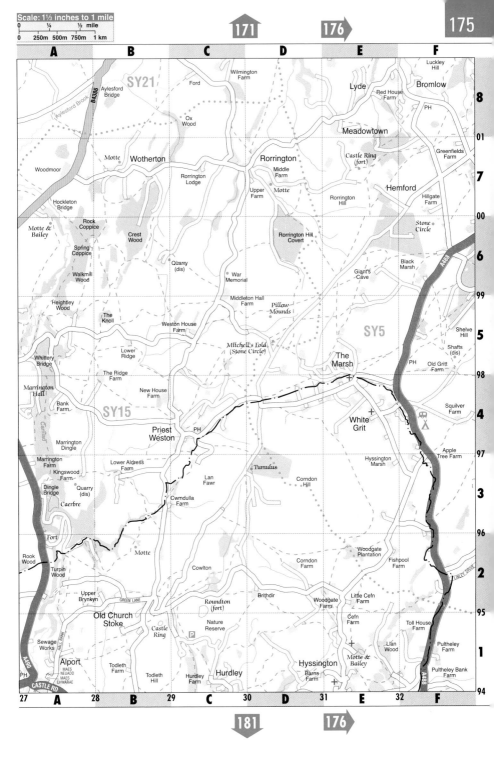

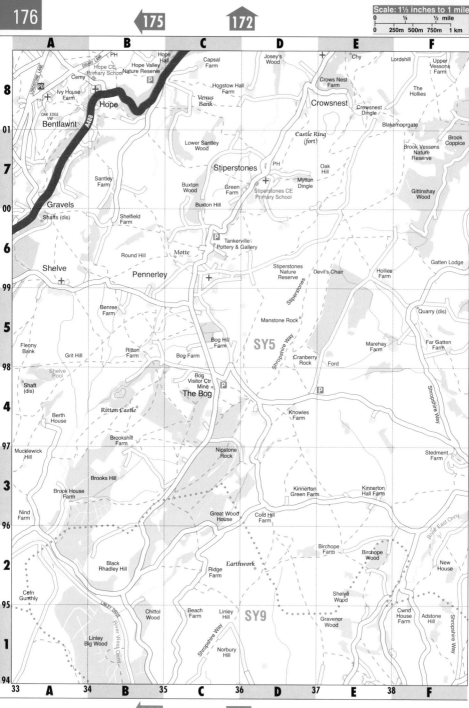

SY5

SY9

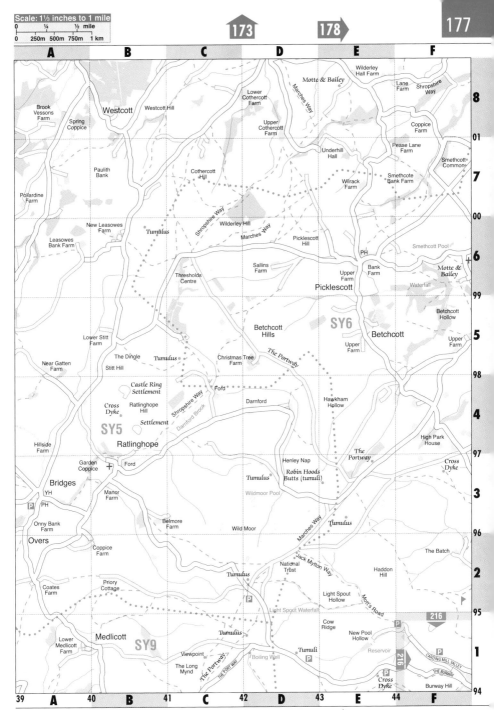

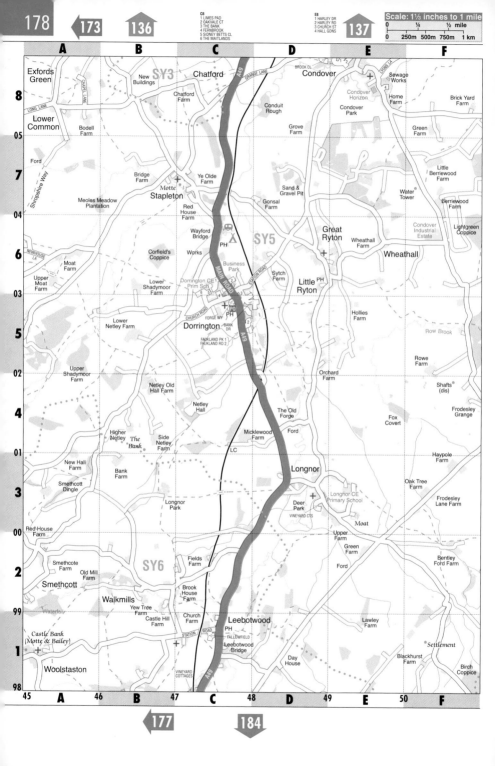

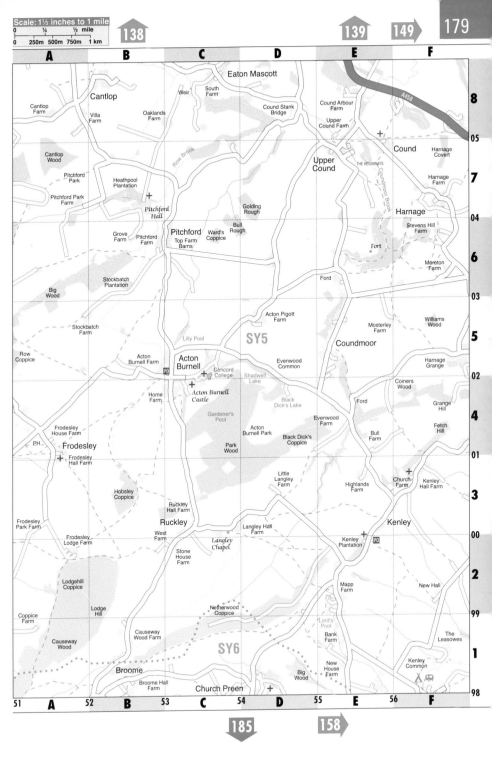

A   B   C   D   E   F

Cantlop Farm

Cantlop

Villa Farm

Oaklands Farm

Weir

South Farm

Eaton Mascott

Cound Stank Bridge

Cound Arbour Farm

Upper Cound Farm

A458

8

05

Cantlop Wood

Pitchford Park

Pitchford Park Farm

Heathpool Plantation

Row Brook

Upper Cound

THE HEIGHWAYS

Cound

Harnage Covert

Harnage Farm

7

04

Pitchford Hall

Grove Farm

Pitchford Farm

Pitchford

Top Farm Barns

Ward's Coppice

Golding Rough

Bull Rough

Coundmoor Brook

Harnage

Stevens Hill Farm

Fort

Moreton Farm

6

03

Big Wood

Stockbatch Plantation

Stockbatch Farm

Acton Pigott Farm

Lilly Pool

SY5

Ford

Coundmoor

Mosterley Farm

Williams Wood

Harnage Grange

5

02

Row Coppice

Acton Burnell Farm

PO

Acton Burnell

Concord College

Shadwell Lake

Evenwood Common

Coiners Wood

Grange Hill

Fetch Hill

4

01

Home Farm

Acton Burnell Castle

Gardener's Pool

Black Dick's Lake

Evenwood Farm

Ford

Bull Farm

Frodesley House Farm

PH

Frodesley

Frodesley Hall Farm

Acton Burnell Park

Park Wood

Black Dick's Coppice

Church Farm

Kenley Hall Farm

3

00

Hobsley Coppice

Ruckley Hall Farm

Little Langley Farm

Highlands Farm

Kenley

Frodesley Park Farm

Frodesley Lodge Farm

Ruckley

West Farm

Stone House Farm

Langley Chapel

Langley Hall Farm

Kenley Plantation

PO

2

99

Lodgehill Coppice

Lodge Hill

Mapp Farm

New Hall

Coppice Farm

Causeway Wood

Causeway Wood Farm

Netherwood Coppice

SY6

Lord's Pool

Bank Farm

New House Farm

The Leasowes

Kenley Common

1

98

Broome

Broome Hall Farm

Church Preen

Big Wood

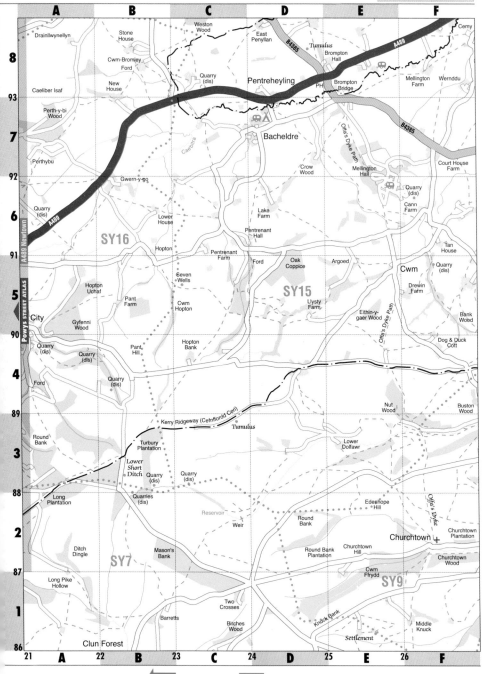

Scale: 1⅓ inches to 1 mile

0   ¼   ½   mile
0   250m 500m 750m   1 km

A   B   C   D   E   F

8

Drainllwynellyn

Stone House

Weston Wood

East Penyllan

Tumulus

Cemy

A489

B4385

Cwm-Bromley Ford

Brompton Hall

Quarry (dis)

Pentreheyling

Mellington Farm

Wernddu

New House

93

Caeliber Isaf

PH

Brompton Bridge

Perth-y-bi Wood

7

Perthybu

Bacheldre

B4385

Court House Farm

Caebitra

Offa's Dyke Path

Mellington Hall

92

Gwern-y-go

Crow Wood

6

Quarry (dis)

Lower House

Lake Farm

Argoed

Cwm

Quarry (dis)

A489 Newtown

A489

Hopton

Pentrenant Hall

Cann Farm

Quarry (dis)

SY16

Pentrenant Farm

Ford

Oak Coppice

Drewin Farm

Tan House

91

Seven Wells

SY15

Llysty Farm

Eithin-y-gaer Wood

Bank Wood

5

Hopton Uchaf

Pant Farm

Cwm Hopton

Dog & Duck Cott

Powys STREET ATLAS

City

Gyfenni Wood

90

Quarry (dis)

Pant Hill

Hopton Bank

Offa's Dyke Path

Quarry (dis)

Quarry (dis)

4

Ford

Quarry (dis)

Nut Wood

Buston Wood

89

Kerry Ridgeway (Cefnffordd Ceri)

Tumulus

Lower Dolfawr

Round Bank

Turbury Plantation

3

Lower Short Ditch

Quarry (dis)

Quarry (dis)

Offa's Dyke

Edenhope Hill

Long Plantation

88

Quarries (dis)

Reservoir

Churchtown

Churchtown Plantation

2

Ditch Dingle

Mason's Bank

Weir

Round Bank

Round Bank Plantation

Churchtown Hill

Churchtown Wood

SY7

Cwm Ffrydd

SY9

87

Long Pike Hollow

Knock Bank

Middle Knuck

1

Two Crosses

Barretts

Birches Wood

Settlement

86

Clun Forest

21   A   22   B   23   C   24   D   25   E   26   F

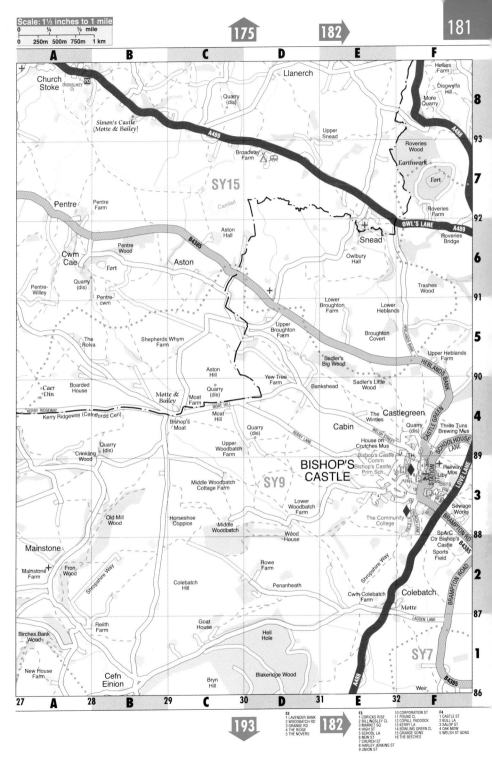

Church Stoke
CROSSLIKEY CL
Llanerch
Quarry (dis)
Hollies Farm
Disgwylfa Hill
Mote Quarry

8

Simon's Castle (Motte & Bailey)
A489
Upper Snead
Roveries Wood
Earthwork
93

Broadway Farm
Fort
7

Pentre
Pentre Farm
SY15
Camlad
Roveries Farm
92

Cwm Cae
Pentre Wood
B4385
Aston Hall
Snead
OWL'S LANE
A489
Roveries Bridge

Fort
Aston
Owlbury Hall
Trashes Wood
6

Pentre-Willey
Quarry (dis)
Pentre-cwm
Lower Broughton Farm
Lower Heblands

HEBLANDS BANK
91

The Rolva
Shepherds Whym Farm
Upper Broughton Farm
Broughton Covert
Upper Heblands Farm

Boarded House
Aston Hill
Sadler's Big Wood
HEBLANDS BANK
5

Caer Din
Motte & Bailey
Yew Tree Farm
Sadler's Little Wood

KERRY RIDGEWAY
Moat Farm
MOAT HILL
Bankshead
90

Kerry Ridgeway (Cefnffordd Ceri)
Bishop's Moat
Moat Hill
The Wintles
Castlegreen

CASTLE GREEN
Quarry (dis)
Three Tuns Brewing Mus
SCHOOLHOUSE LANE
4

Crinkling Wood
Quarry (dis)
Cabin
WELSH STREET
House on Crutches Mus
LOVE LANE

Upper Woodbatch Farm
Quarry (dis)
BISHOP'S CASTLE
Railway Mus
Liby
89

Middle Woodbatch Cottage Farm
Bishop's Castle Comm
Bishop's Castle Prim Sch.
TH
Bsns
3

Old Mill Wood
Horseshoe Coppice
Lower Woodbatch Farm
CHURCH LANE
Sewage Works

Mainstone
SY9
Middle Woodbatch
Wood House
The Community College
SpArC Ctr Bishop's Castle Sports Field
BRAMPTON RD
B4385

Malnstone Farm
Fron Wood
Rowe Farm
Shropshire Way
88

Shropshire Way
Colebatch Hill
Penanheath
Cwm Colebatch Farm
Colebatch
Motte
BRAMPTON ROAD
2

Birches Bank Wood
Reilth Farm
Goat House
Hell Hole
LAGDEN LANE
87

New House Farm
Cefn Einion
Bryn Hill
Blakeridge Wood
SY7
A488
Weir
B4385
1

27   A   28   B   29   C   30   D   31   E   32   F

E3
1 LAVENDER BANK
2 WOODBATCH RD
3 GRANGE RD
4 THE RIDGE
5 THE NOVERS

F3
1 CORICKS RISE
2 BILLINGSLEY CL
3 MARKET SQ
4 HIGH ST
5 SCHOOL LA
6 NEW ST
7 CHURCH ST
8 HARLEY JENKINS ST
9 UNION ST

10 CORPORATION ST
11 POUND CL
12 COPALL PADDOCK
13 KERRY LA
14 BOWLING GREEN CL
15 GRANGE GDNS
16 THE BEECHES

F4
1 CASTLE ST
2 BULL LA
3 SALOP ST
4 OAK MOW
5 WELSH ST GDNS

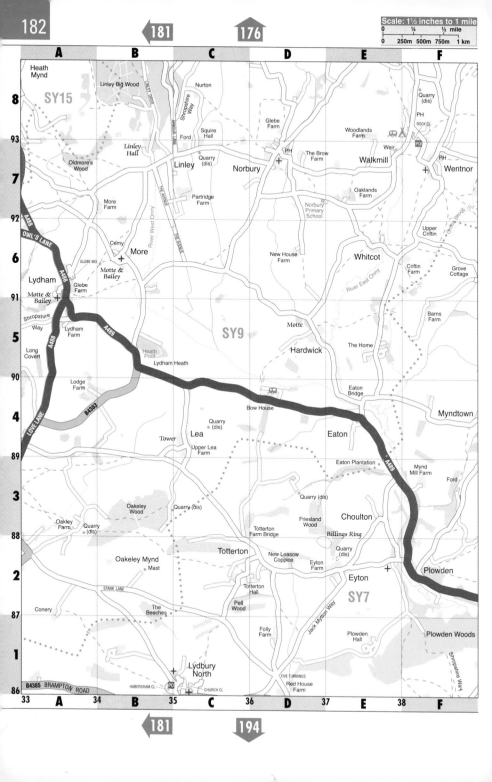

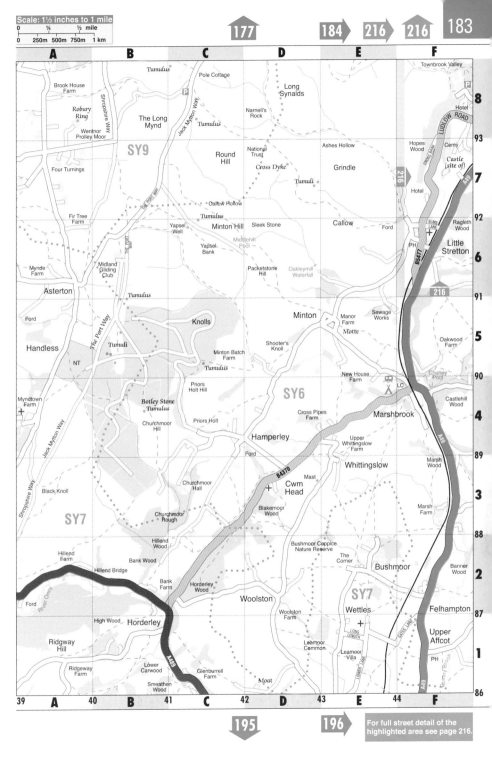

Townbrook Valley

Tumulus
Pole Cottage
Brook House Farm
Long Synalds
Robury Ring
The Long Mynd
Narnell's Rock
Shropshire Way
Wentnor Prolley Moor
Jack Mytton Way
Tumulus
Hotel

LUDLOW ROAD
8

Four Turnings
SY9
Round Hill
National Trust
Ashes Hollow
Hopes Wood
Castle (site of)
Cemy
GRINDLE BANK
216
A49
93

Cross Dyke
Grindle
Hotel
7

Fir Tree Farm
The Port Way
Callow Hollow
Tumuli
Tumulus
Minton Hill
Sleek Stone
Callow
Ford
ELMS LANE
PH
B5477
Ragleth Wood
Little Stretton
92

Mynde Farm
Midland Gliding Club
Yapsel Well
Yapsel Bank
Middlehill Pool
Packetstone Hill
Oakleymill Waterfall
216
6

Asterton
Tumulus
Knolls
Minton
Manor Farm
Sewage Works
91

Ford
Handless
The Port Way
Tumuli
NT
Minton Batch Farm
Tumulus
Shooter's Knoll
Motte
New House Farm
LC
Oakwood Farm
Chupey Pool
90

Myndtown Farm
Priors Holt Hill
Botley Stone Tumulus
Churchmoor Hill
Priors Holt
SY6
Cross Pipes Farm
Marshbrook
Castlehill Wood
A49
4

Shropshire Way
Jack Mytton Way
Black Knoll
Churchmoor Hall
Hamperley
Ford
Upper Whittingslow Farm
Whittingslow
Marsh Wood
89

SY7
Churchmoor Rough
B4370
Mast
Cwm Head
Blakemoor Wood
Marsh Farm
3

Hillend Wood
Bank Wood
Bushmoor Coppice Nature Reserve
The Corner
Bushmoor
Banner Wood
2

Hillend Farm
Hillend Bridge
Bank Farm
Horderley Wood
Woolston
SY7
Wettles
Felhampton
87

River Onny
Ford
High Wood
Horderley
Woolston Farm
Long Length
GATES LANE
Upper Affcot
PH
1

Ridgway Hill
Ridgway Farm
Lower Carwood
A49
Glenburrell Farm
Smeathen Wood
Moat
Leamoor Common
Leamoor Villa
LOWER LANE
Quinny Brook
A49
86

For full street detail of the highlighted area see page 216.

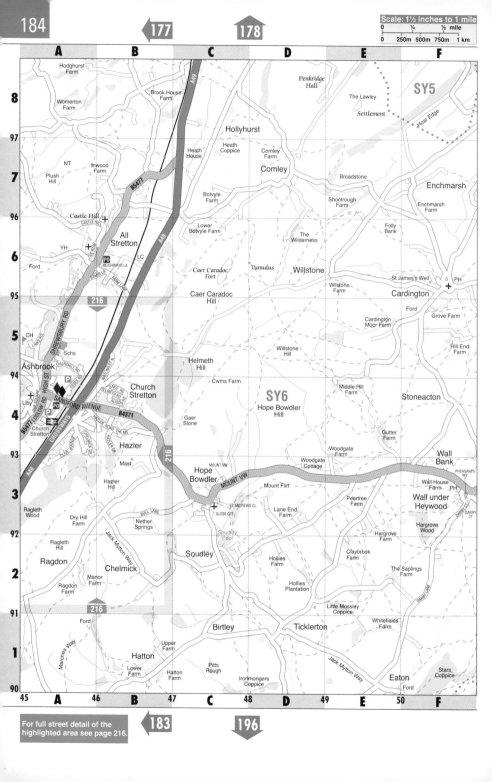

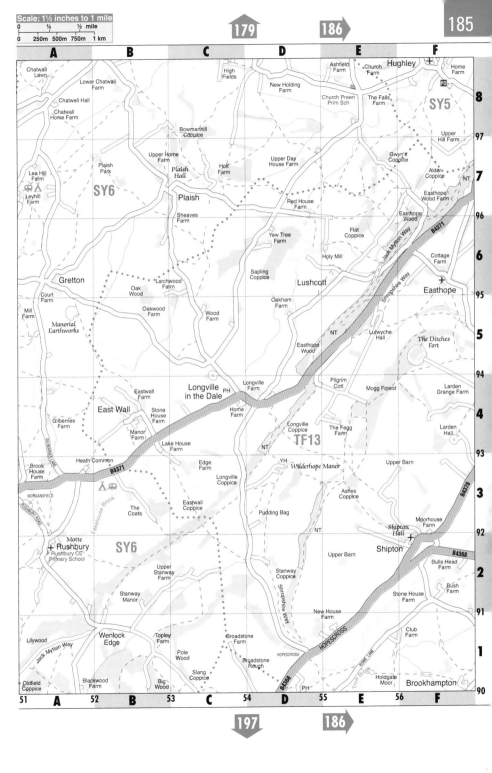

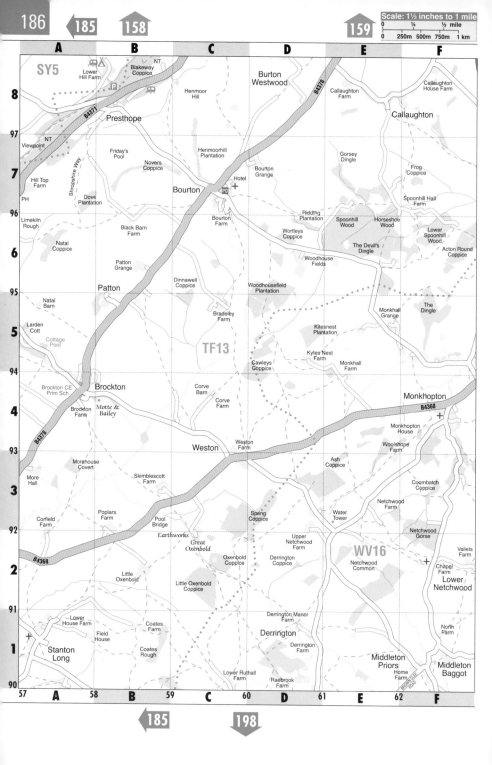

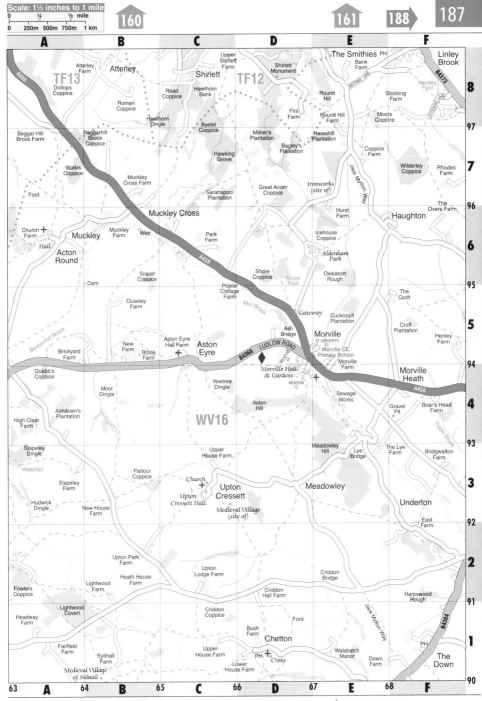

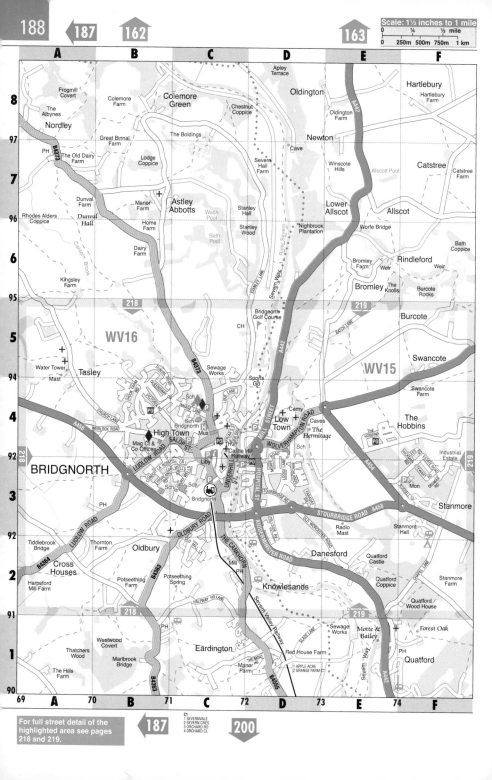

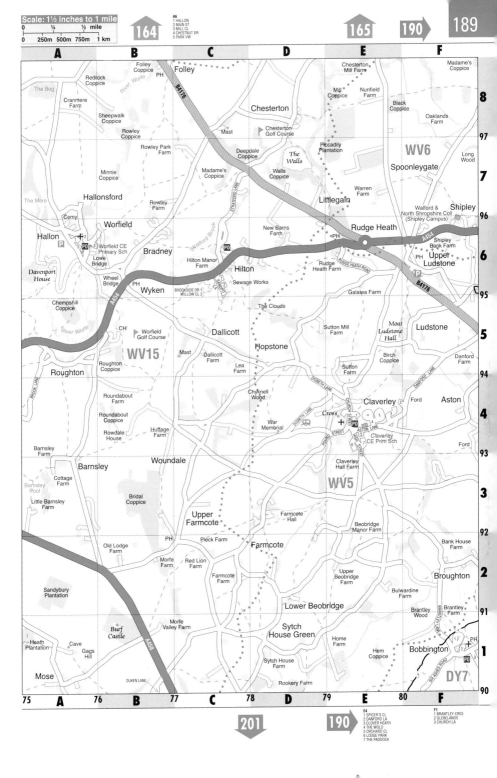

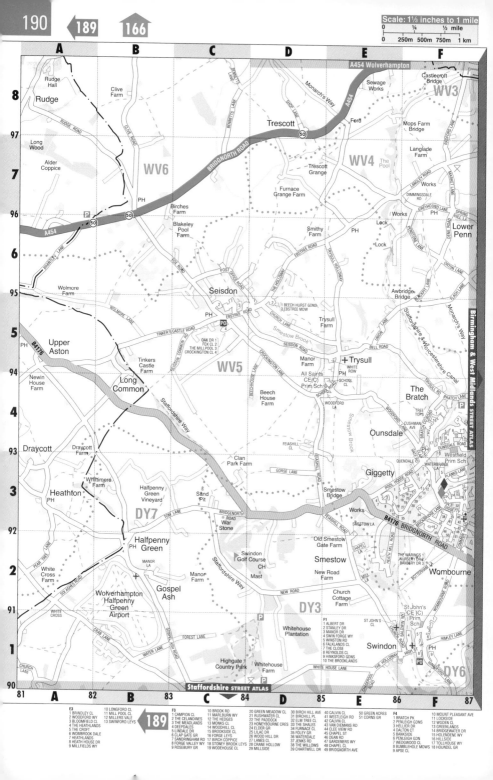

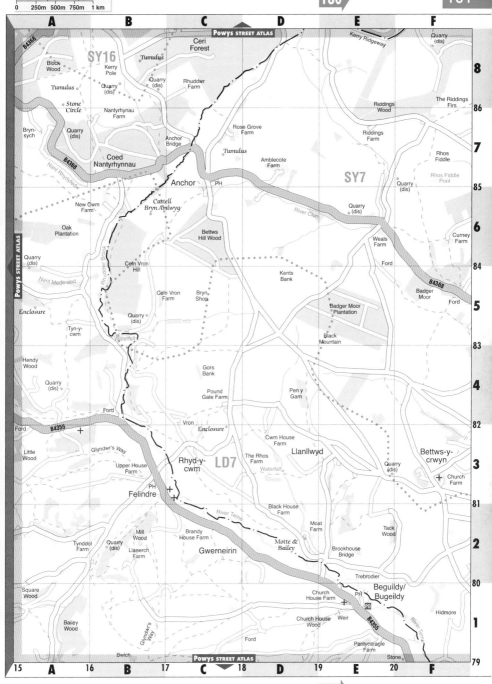

Scale: 1⅓ inches to 1 mile

0 ¼ ½ mile
0 250m 500m 750m 1 km

POWYS STREET ATLAS

SY16

Ceri
Forest

Block
Wood

Tumulus

Kerry Pole

Kerry Ridgeway

Quarry
(dis)

Rhuddwr
Farm

The Riddings
Firs

Tumulus

Quarry
(dis)

Riddings
Wood

Stone
Circle

Nantyrhynau
Farm

Rose Grove
Farm

Riddings
Farm

Rhos
Fiddle

Bryn-
sych

Quarry
(dis)

Anchor
Bridge

Tumulus

Amblecote
Farm

Rhos Fiddle
Pool

Coed
Nantyrhynau

SY7

Quarry
(dis)

Anchor

PH

Curney
Farm

New Cwm
Farm

Castell
Bryn Amlwyg

River Clun

Quarry
(dis)

Oak
Plantation

Bettws
Hill Wood

Weals
Farm

Cefn Vron
Hill

Ford

Quarry
(dis)

Kents
Bank

B4368

Badger
Moor

Enclosure

Cefn Vron
Farm

Bryn
Shop

Badger Moor
Plantation

Ford

Tyn-y-
cwm

Quarry
(dis)

Black
Mountain

Waterfall

Hendy
Wood

Gors
Bank

Quarry
(dis)

Pound
Gate Farm

Pen y
Garn

Ford

Ford

Vron

Enclosure

B4355

Cwm House
Farm

Llanllwyd

Bettws-y-
crwyn

Little
Wood

Glyndwr's Way

Upper House
Farm

Rhyd-y-
cwm

LD7

The Rhos
Farm

Waterfall

Quarry
(dis)

Church
Farm

PH

Felindre

River Teme

Black House
Farm

Tynddol
Farm

Quarry
(dis)

Mill
Wood

Brandy
House Farm

Moat
Farm

Tack
Wood

Llanerch
Farm

Gwerneirin

Motte &
Bailey

Brookhouse
Bridge

Square
Wood

Trebrodier

Beguildy/
Bugeildy

Church
House Farm

PH

Hidmore

Bailey
Wood

Glyndwr's Way

Church House
Wood

Weir

River Teme

Bwlch

Ford

Pantycaragle
Farm

Stone

POWYS STREET ATLAS

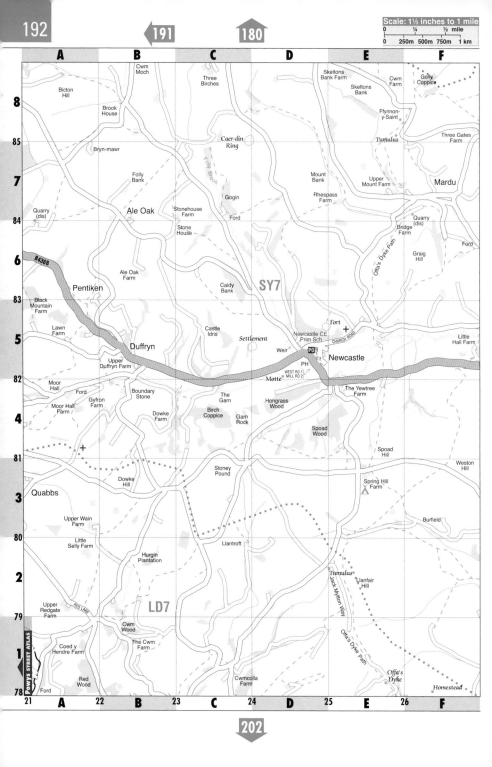

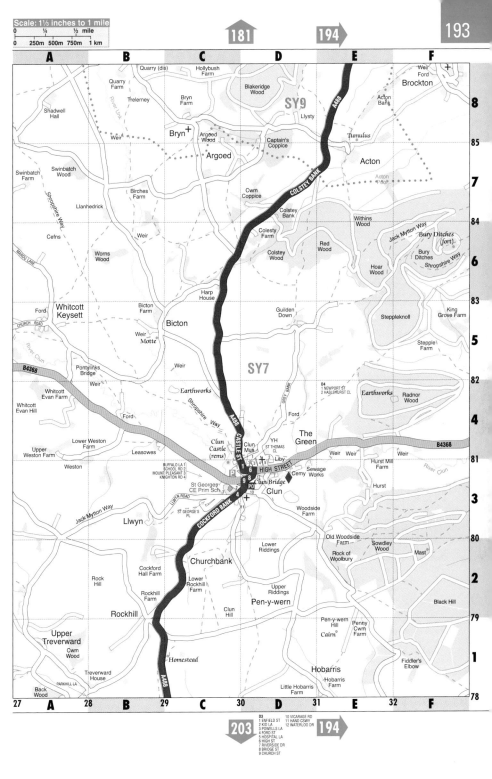

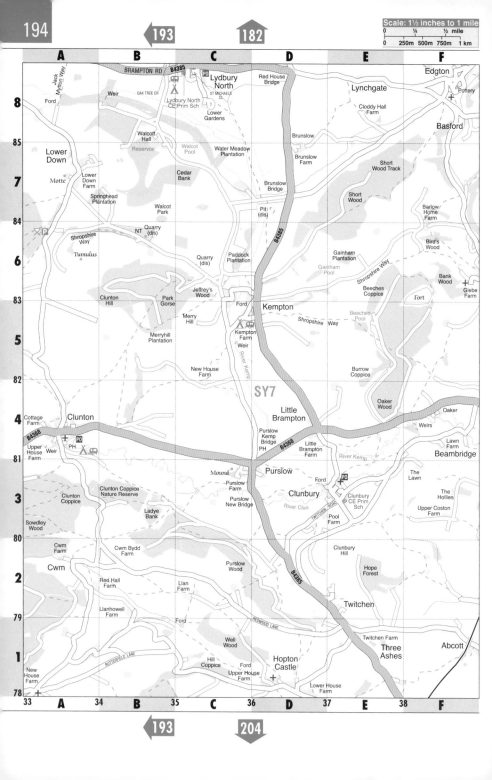

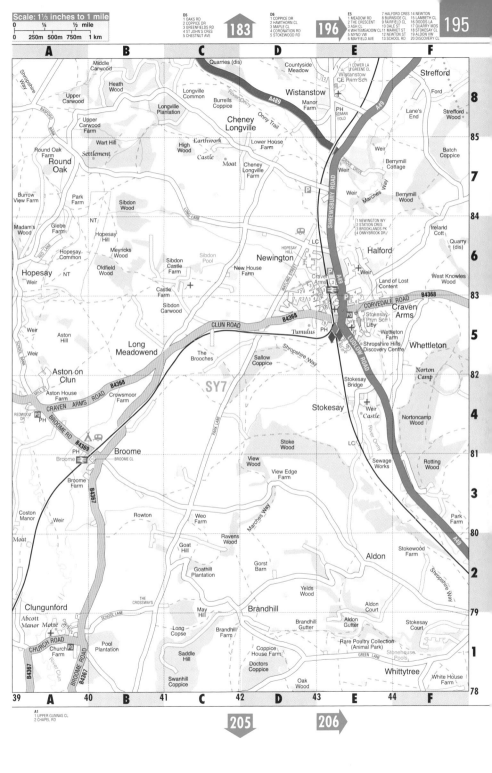

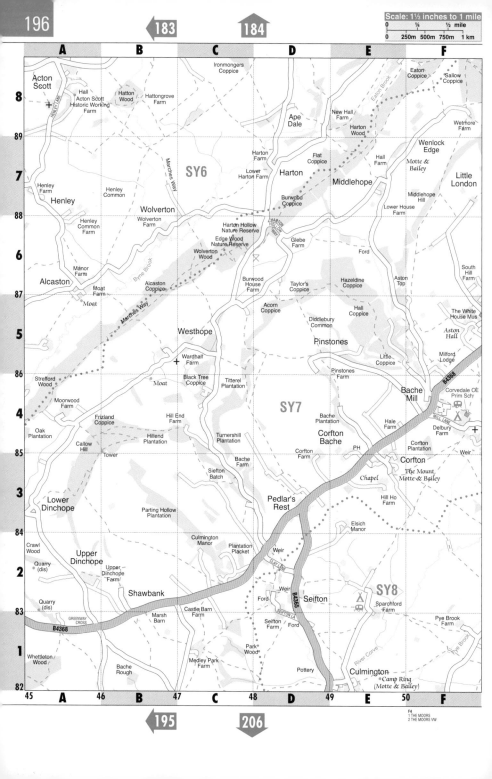

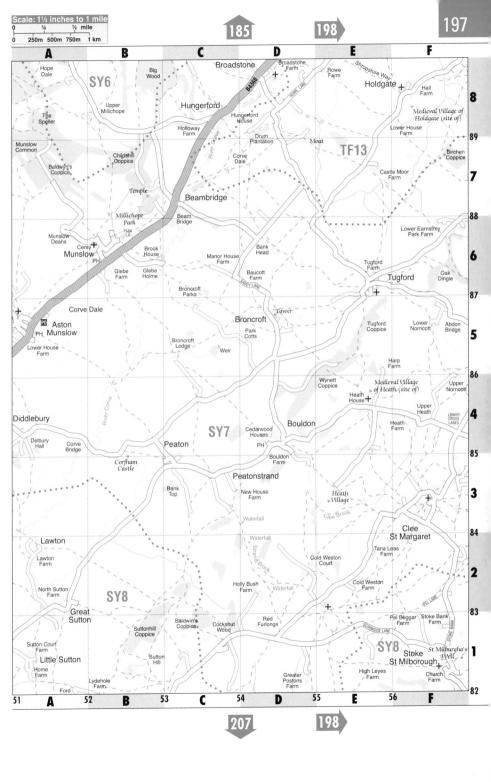

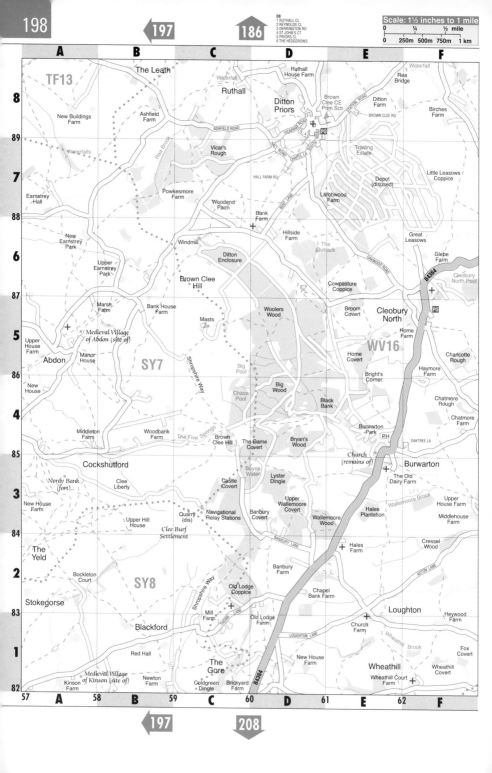

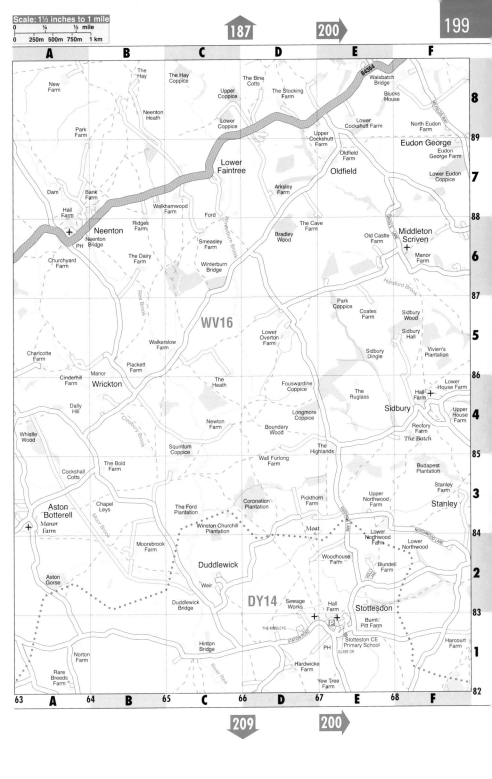

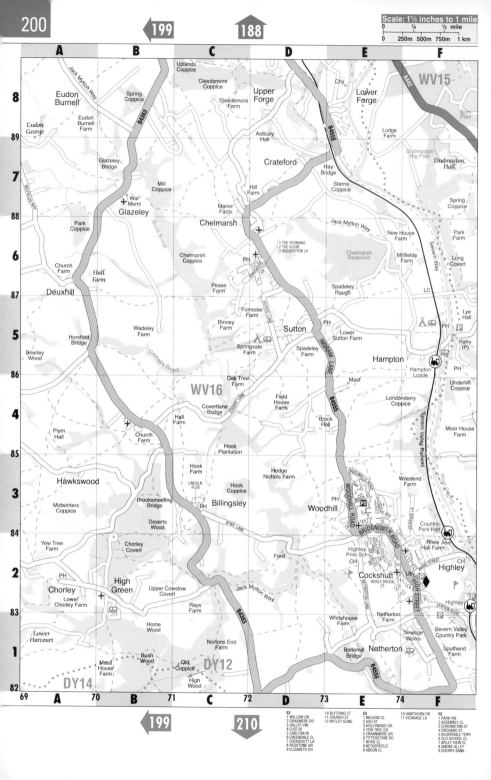

200

199

188

Scale: 1⅓ inches to 1 mile
0   ¼   ½   mile
0   250m   500m   750m   1 km

WV15

8

Eudon
Burnell

Spring
Coppice

Uplands
Coppice

Cleedsmore
Coppice

Cleedsmore
Farm

Upper
Forge

Chy

Lower
Forge

Brin
Pool

89

Eudon
George

Eudon
Burnell
Farm

Astbury
Hall

Lodge
Farm

Didmaston
Big Pool

Didmaston
Hall

Glazeley
Bridge

Crateford

Hay
Bridge

Sterns
Coppice

Spring
Coppice

7

Mill
Coppice

War
Meml

Hill
Farm

Jack Mytton Way

New House
Farm

Park
Coppice

88

Park
Coppice

Glazeley

Chelmarsh

Manor
Farm

Chelmarsh
Reservoir

Millfields
Farm

Long
Covert

6

Church
Farm

Hall
Farm

Chelmarsh
Coppice

1 THE YEOMANS
2 THE GLEBE
3 OCCUPATION LA

PH

Pease
Farm

Spadeley
Rough

LC

87

Deuxhill

Forrester
Farm

Sutton

PH

Lower
Sutton
Farm

Lye
Hall

Hampton

PH

5

Brierley
Wood

Horsford
Bridge

Wadeley
Farm

Dinney
Farm

Springvale
Farm

Spadeley
Farm

Ferry
(P)

86

Crutel's Brook

Oak Tree
Farm

Field
House
Farm

Masf

Hampton
Loade

Underhill
Coppice

WV16

Covertlane
Bridge

Londonderry
Coppice

Moor House
Farm

4

Plym
Hall

Hall
Farm

Church
Farm

Hook
Plantation

Brock
Hall

85

Hook
Farm

Hook
Coppice

Hodge
Nichols Farm

Woodend
Farm

Hawkswood

LINCOLN
FLDS

Billingsley

PH

Woodhill

3

Midwinters
Coppice

Brooksmeeting
Bridge

PH

Woodend
Farm

Country
Park Halt

Rhea
Hall Farm

84

Deserts
Wood

BYND LANE

Ford

Highley
Prim Sch

CH

Highley

Yew Tree
Farm

Chorley
Covert

CH

2

PH

Chorley

High
Green

Upper Cowslow
Covert

Jack Mytton Way

Cockshutt

Highley

83

Lower
Chorley Farm

Rays
Farm

Netherton
Farm

1

Lower
Harcourt

Home
Wood

Nortons End
Farm

Whitehouse
Farm

Sewage
Works

Netherton

Severn Valley
Country Park

Southend
Farm

Bush
Wood

Old
Coppice

DY12

Borlemill
Bridge

82

DY14

Mass
House
Farm

High
Wood

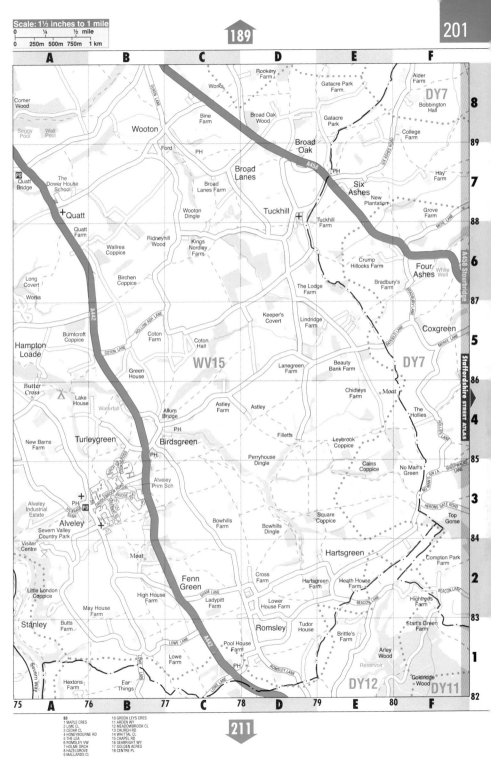

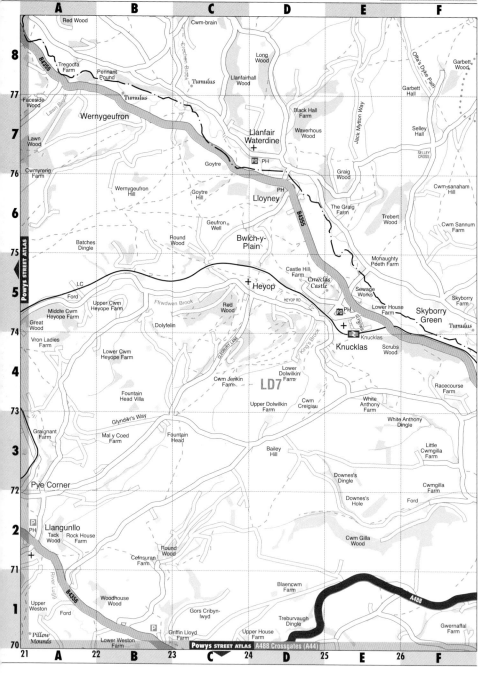

Powys STREET ATLAS

Red Wood

Cwm-brain

B4355

Tregodfa Farm

Pennant Pound

Pennant Pound

Long Wood

Llanfairhall Wood

Garbett Wood

Faceside Wood

Tumulus

Tumulus

Llanfair Waterdine

Black Hall Farm

Garbett Hall

Wernygeufron

Lawn Brook

Waverhous Wood

Jack Myton Way

Selley Hall

Lawn Wood

Goytre

PO PH

SELLEY CROSS

Cwmyrerig Farm

Wernygeufron Hill

Goytre Hill

PH

Lloyney

Graig Wood

Cwm-sanaham Hill

B4355

The Graig Farm

Trebert Wood

Cwm Sannum Farm

Geufron Well

Round Wood

Bwlch-y-Plain

Batches Dingle

LC

Monaughty Poeth Farm

Ford

Upper Cwm Heyope Farm

Ffrwdwen Brook

Heyop

Castle Hill Wood

Cnwclas Castle

HEYOP RD

Sewage Works

Lower House Farm

Skyborry Farm

Middle Cwm Heyope Farm

Red Wood

PO PH

Skyborry Green

Great Wood

Dolyfelin

Knucklas

Tumulus

Vron Ladies Farm

Knucklas

Scrubs Wood

Lower Cwm Heyope Farm

CLEBURY LANE

Cwm Jenkin Farm

King's Brook

Lower Dolwilkin Farm

LD7

Racecourse Farm

Fountain Head Villa

Upper Dolwilkin Farm

Cwm Creigiau

White Anthony Farm

Graignant Farm

Glyndwr's Way

White Anthony Dingle

Mal y Coed Farm

Fountain Head

Bailey Hill

Little Cwmgilla Farm

Pye Corner

Downes's Dingle

Cwmgilla Farm

Downes's Hole

Ford

P
PH

Llangunllo

Tack Wood

Rock House Farm

Round Wood

Cwm Gilla Wood

Cefnsuran Farm

River Lugg

B4355

Upper Weston

Woodhouse Wood

Blaencwm Farm

A488

Ford

P

Gors Cribyn-lwyd

Treburvaugh Dingle

Gwernaffal Farm

Pillow Mounds

Griffin Lloyd Farm

Upper House Farm

Lower Weston Farm

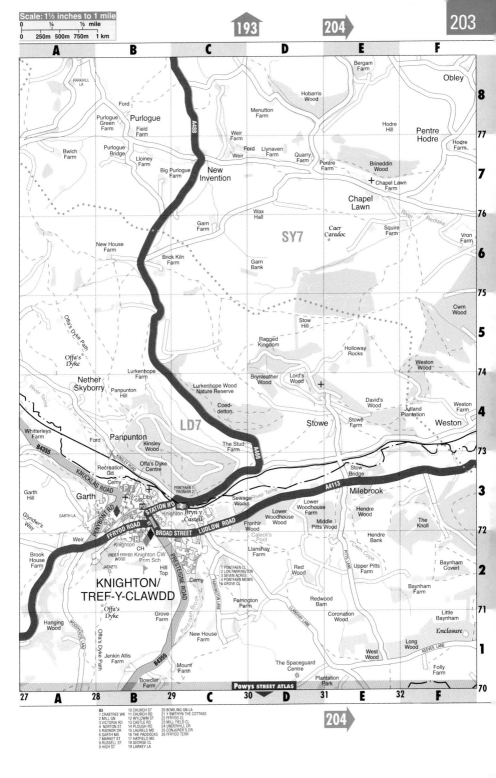

8

Bergam Farm

Obley

PARKHILL LA

Ford

Purlogue Green Farm

Field Farm

Purlogue

Hobarris Wood

Menutton Farm

Pentre Hodre

77

Bwlch Farm

Purlogue Bridge

Lloiney Farm

Weir Farm

Ford   Llynaven Farm

Quarry Farm

Pentre Farm

Hodre Hill

Hodre Farm.

Big Purlogue Farm

New Invention

Weir

Brineddin Wood

+ Chapel Lawn Farm

7

Garn Farm

Wax Hall

Chapel Lawn

Caer Caradoc

Squire Farm

Vron Farm

76

New House Farm

SY7

Brick Kiln Farm

Garn Bank

75

Offa's Dyke Path

Stow Hill

Cwm Wood

Offa's Dyke

Ragged Kingdom

Holloway Rocks

Weston Wood

5

Lurkenhope Farm

Lurkenhope Wood Nature Reserve

Brynleather Wood

Lord's Wood

David's Wood

Weston Wood

74

Nether Skyborry

Panpunton Hill

Coed-detton

Jutland Plantation

Weston Farm

Weston

River Teme

LD7

Stowe Farm

Stowe

4

Whitterleys Farm

Panpunton

Ford

Kinsley Wood

The Stud Farm

A488

Stowe Bridge

73

B4355

KNUCKLAS ROAD

Recreation Gd

Offa's Dyke Centre

A4113

Milebrook

3

Garth Hill

Cemy

PONTFAEN 1 FRONHIR 2

Sewage Works

River Teme

Lower Woodhouse Farm

Hendre Wood

The Knoll

Garth

Libr

STATION RD

Knighton Bryn y Castell

LUDLOW ROAD

Fronhir Wood

Lower Woodhouse Wood

Hendre Bank

72

Glyndwr's Way

GARTH LA.

FFRYDD ROAD

BROAD STREET

Caleck's Pool

Middle Pitts Wood

Baynham Covert

Weir

Knighton

CH

Llanshay Farm

Upper Pitts Farm

Brook House Farm

UNDER FFRYDD WOOD

Knighton CW Prim Sch

1 PONTFAEN CL
2 LON FARRINGTON
3 SEVEN ACRES
4 PONTFAEN MDWS
5 GROVE CL

Red Wood

Baynham Farm

2

JACKETS LA

Hill Top

Cemy

PRESTEIGNE ROAD

FARRINGTON LANE

Redwood Barn

Little Baynham

KNIGHTON/ TREF-Y-CLAWDD

Offa's Dyke

Grove Farm

Farrington Farm

LLANSHAY LANE

PITTS LANE

Coronation Wood

Enclosure

71

Hanging Wood

Offa's Dyke Path

New House Farm

Cwm Copa

Long Wood

REEVES LANE

Folly Farm

1

Jenkin Allis Farm

B4355

Mount Farm

The Spaceguard Centre

West Wood

Bowdler Farm

POWYS STREET ATLAS

Plantation Park

70

27   A   28   B   29   C   30   D   31   E   32   F

B3
1 CRABTREE WK
2 MILL GN
3 VICTORIA RD
4 NORTON ST
5 RADNOR DR
6 GARTH MS
7 MARKET ST
8 RUSSELL ST
9 HIGH ST
10 CHURCH ST
11 CHURCH RD
12 WYLCWM ST
13 CASTLE RD
14 PLOUGH RD
15 LAURELS MD
16 THE PADDOCKS
17 HATFIELD MS
18 GEORGE CL
19 LARKEY LA
20 BOWLING GN LA
21 Y BWTHYN THE COTTAGE
22 FFRYDD CL
23 MILL FIELD CL
24 UNDERHILL GR
25 CONJURER'S DR
26 FFRYDD TERR

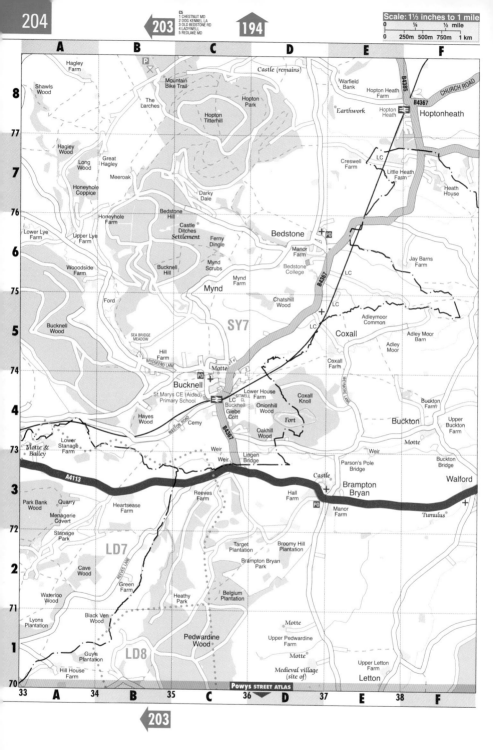

C5
1 CHESTNUT MD
2 DOG KENNEL LA
3 OLD BEDSTONE RD
4 LADYWELL
5 REDLAKE MD

Scale: 1⅓ inches to 1 mile
0   ¼   ½   mile
0   250m 500m 750m   1 km

CHURCH ROAD

Hagley
Farm

Shawls
Wood

P
Mountain
Bike Trail

The
Larches

Castle (remains)

Hopton
Park

Hopton
Titterhill

Hopton
Heath

Warfield
Bank

Hopton Heath
Farm

Earthwork

Hopton
Heath

B4367

Hoptonheath

Hagley
Wood

Long
Wood

Great
Hagley

Meeroak

Honeyhole
Coppice

Darky
Dale

Creswell
Farm

LC

Little Heath
Farm

Heath
House

Honeyhole
Farm

Upper Lye
Farm

Bedstone
Hill

Castle
Ditches
Settlement

Ferny
Dingle

Bedstone

PO

Manor
Farm

Jay Barns
Farm

Lower Lye
Farm

Wooodside
Farm

Bucknell
Hill

Mynd
Scrubs

Mynd
Farm

Bedstone
College

B4367

LC

Ford

Mynd

Chatshill
Wood

LC

Adleymoor
Common

Adley Moor
Barn

Bucknell
Wood

SEA BRIDGE
MEADOW

SY7

LC

Coxall

Adley
Moor

Adley Moor

Hill
Farm
BRIDGEMERE LANE

Motte

Coxall
Farm

HEYWOOD LANE

PO

Bucknell

Lower House
Farm

Coxall
Knoll

Buckton
Farm

Upper
Buckton
Farm

St Marys CE (Aided)
Primary School

Bucknell
Glebe
Cott

Onionhill
Wood

Fort

Buckton

Hayes
Wood

Cemy

Oakhill
Wood

Motte

Weir

Motte &
Bailey

Lower Stanage
Farm

B4367

Weir

Lingen
Bridge

Weir

Parson's Pole
Bridge

Buckton
Bridge

A4113

Weir

Castle

Brampton
Bryan

Walford

Park Bank
Wood

Quarry

Heartsease
Farm

Reeves
Farm

Hall
Farm

PO

Manor
Farm

Tumulus

Menagerie
Covert

Stanage
Park

LD7

REEVES LANE

Target
Plantation

Broomy Hill
Plantation

Cave
Wood

Green
Farm

Brampton Bryan
Park

Waterloo
Wood

Black Ven
Wood

Heathy
Park

Belgium
Plantation

Motte

Upper Pedwardine
Farm

Lyons
Plantation

LD8

Pedwardine
Wood

Motte

Upper Letton
Farm

Guyls
Plantation

Hill House
Farm

Medieval village
(site of)

Letton

Powys STREET ATLAS

33   A   34   B   35   C   36   D   37   E   38   F

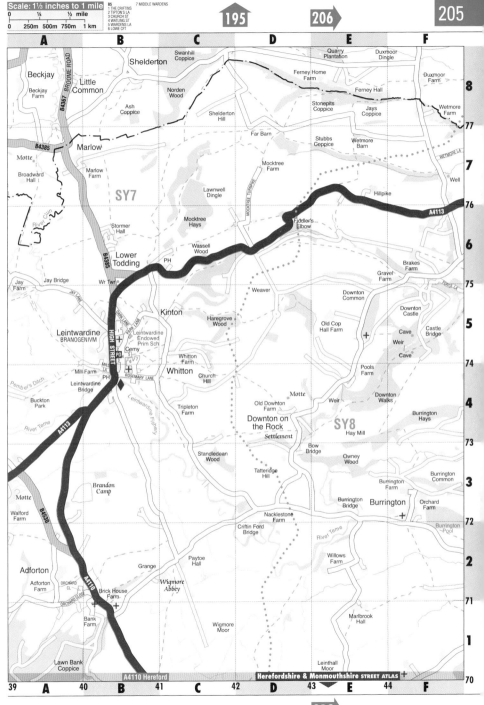

Scale: 1⅓ inches to 1 mile

0   ¼   ½   mile
0   250m 500m 750m 1 km

B5
1 THE CRIFTINS
2 TIPTON'S LA
3 CHURCH ST
4 WATLING ST
5 WARDENS LA
6 LOWE CFT

7 MIDDLE WARDENS

Beckjay

Beckjay
Farm

Motte

Broadward
Hall

Marlow

Marlow
Farm

SY7

Stormer
Hall

Lower
Todding

PH

Wr Twr

Jay
Farm

Jay Bridge

Leintwardine
BRANOGENIVM

Mill Farm

PH

Leintwardine
Bridge

Buckton
Park

Pember's Ditch

River Teme

Motte

Walford
Farm

Adforton

Adforton
Farm

Brick House
Farm

Bank
Farm

Lawn Bank
Coppice

Little
Common

Ash
Coppice

Shelderton

Swanhill
Coppice

Norden
Wood

Shelderton
Hill

Lawnwell
Dingle

Mocktree
Hays

Wassell
Wood

Kinton

Haregrove
Wood

Leintwardine
Endowed
Prim Sch

Cemy

PO

Whitton
Farm

Whitton

Church
Hill

Tripleton
Farm

Rosemary Lane

Leintwardine Fishery

Brandon
Camp

Grange

Paytoe
Hall

Wigmore
Abbey

Wigmore
Moor

Far Barn

Mocktree
Farm

Weaver

Standledean
Wood

Tatteridge
Hill

Nacklestone
Farm

Criftin Ford
Bridge

Quarry
Plantation

Ferney Home
Farm

Stonepits
Coppice

Stubbs
Coppice

Mocktree Turnpike

Fiddler's
Elbow

Downton
Common

Old Cop
Hall Farm

Motte

Old Downton
Farm

Weir

Downton on
the Rock

Settlement

Bow
Bridge

SY8

Hay Mill

Owney
Wood

Burrington
Bridge

Burrington

River Teme

Willows
Farm

Marlbrook
Hall

Leinthall
Moor

Duxmoor
Dingle

Ferney Hall

Jays
Coppice

Wetmore
Barn

Hillpike

Brakes
Farm

Gravel
Farm

A4113

Downton
Castle

Cave

Weir

Cave

Castle
Bridge

Pools
Farm

Downton
Walks

Burrington
Hays

Burrington
Farm

Burrington
Common

Orchard
Farm

Burrington
Pool

Duxmoor
Farm

Wetmore
Farm

Well

Wetmore La

A4113

A4110 Hereford

Herefordshire & Monmouthshire STREET ATLAS

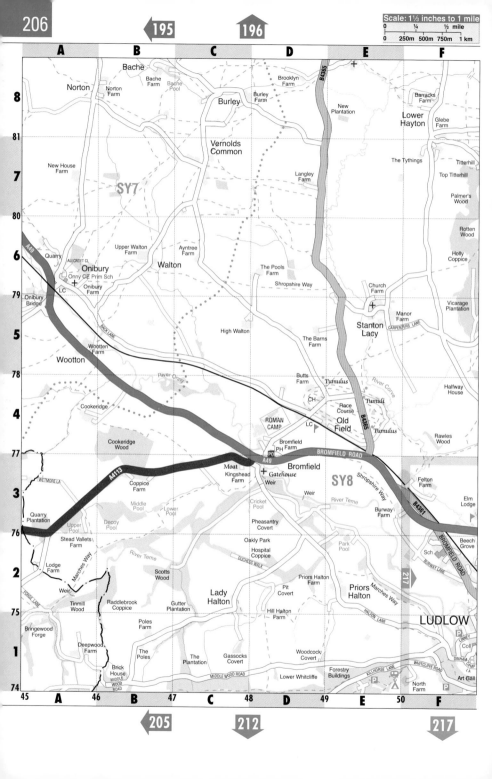

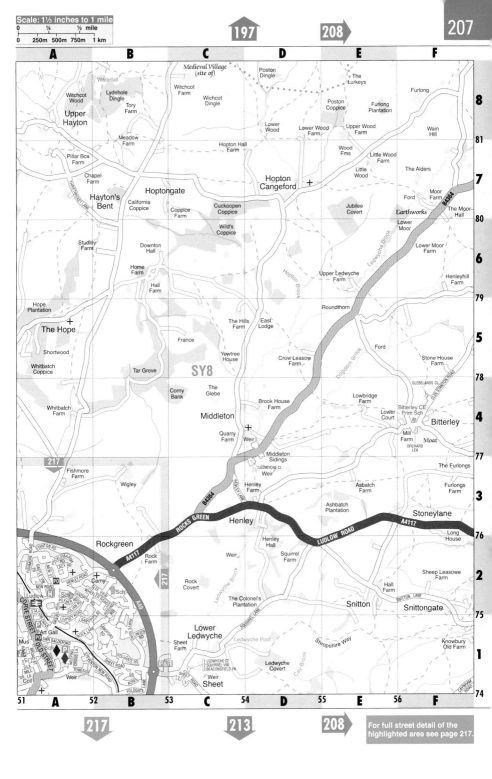

8
Medieval Village (site of)
Poston Dingle
The Turkeys
Furlong
Witchcot Wood
Lydehole Dingle
Tory Farm
Witchcot Farm
Wichcot Dingle
Poston Coppice
Furlong Plantation
Upper Hayton
Waterfall
Meadow Farm
Lower Wood
Lower Wood Farm
Upper Wood Farm
Wain Hill

81

7
Pillar Box Farm
Hopton Hall Farm
Wood Fms
Little Wood Farm
The Alders
Chapel Farm
Hayton's Bent
Hoptongate
Hopton Cangeford
Jubilee Covert
Little Wood
Ford
Moor Farm
Earthworks
The Moor Hall
California Coppice
Coppice Farm
Cuckoopen Coppice
Lower Moor
B4364

80

6
Studley Farm
Downton Hall
Wild's Coppice
Upper Ledwyche Farm
Lower Moor Farm
Henleyhill Farm
Home Farm
Hall Farm
Hopton Brook
Ledwyche Brook

79

5
Hope Plantation
The Hope
The Hills Farm
East Lodge
Roundthorn
Ford
Stone House Farm
Shortwood
France
Crow Leasow Farm
Dogditch Brook
Whitbatch Coppice
Tar Grove
Yewtree House

78
SY8
Corny Bank
The Glebe
Lowbridge Farm
GLEBELANDS CL
CLEE STANTON ROAD

4
Whitbatch Farm
Middleton
Brook House Farm
Lower Court
Bitterley CE Prim Sch
Bitterley
Quarry Farm
Weir
Mill Farm
Moat
ORCHARD LEA

77
Fishmore Farm
Middleton Sidings
LEDWYCHE CL
Weir
The Furlongs
217
Wigley
Henley Farm
Asbatch Farm
Furlongs Farm

3
B4364
ROCKS GREEN
Henley
Ashbatch Plantation
Stoneylane
A4117
Long House

76
Rockgreen
A4117
Rock Farm
Henley Hall
Squirrel Farm
LUDLOW ROAD
Ludlow
217
HENLEY ROAD
A49
Rock Covert
Weir
Hall Farm
SNITTON LANE
Sheep Leasowe Farm

2
Cemy
Sch
Art Gall
H
P
Mus
Sch
P&R
The Colonel's Plantation
Snitton
Snittongate

75
CORVE STREET
OLD STREET
Lower Ledwyche
Sheet Farm
Ledwyche Pool
Shropshire Way
Knowbury Old Farm
SILK MILL LA
Coll
Weir
1 LEDWYCHE CT
2 SQUIRREL VW
3 BEACONSFIELD PK
Ledwyche Covert
Cay Brook

1
TOLLGATE RD
FOLDGATE
SHEET RD
Weir
Sheet
CATTHAM ROAD

51 **A** 52 **B** 53 **C** 54 **D** 55 **E** 56 **F** 74

217   213   208
For full street detail of the highlighted area see page 217.

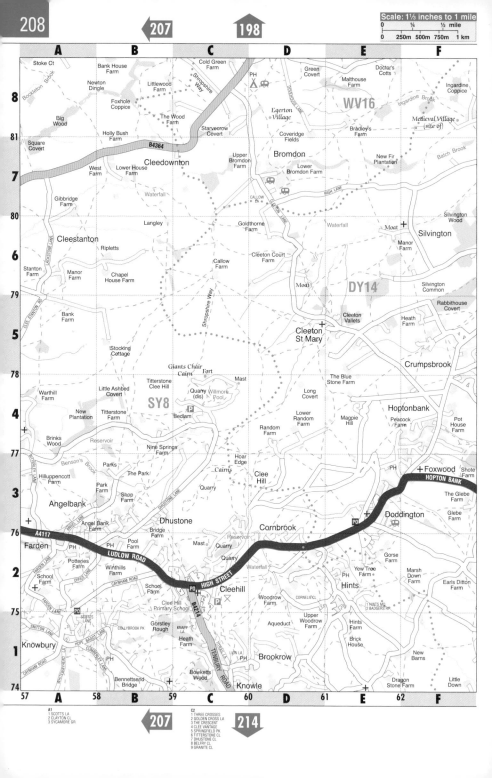

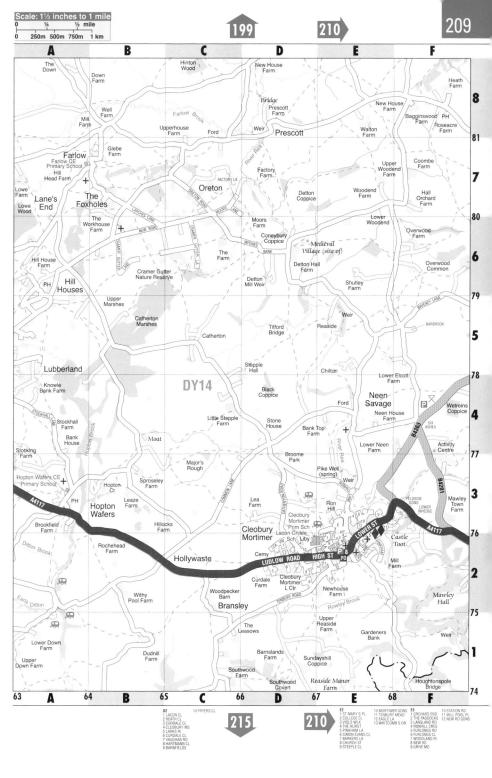

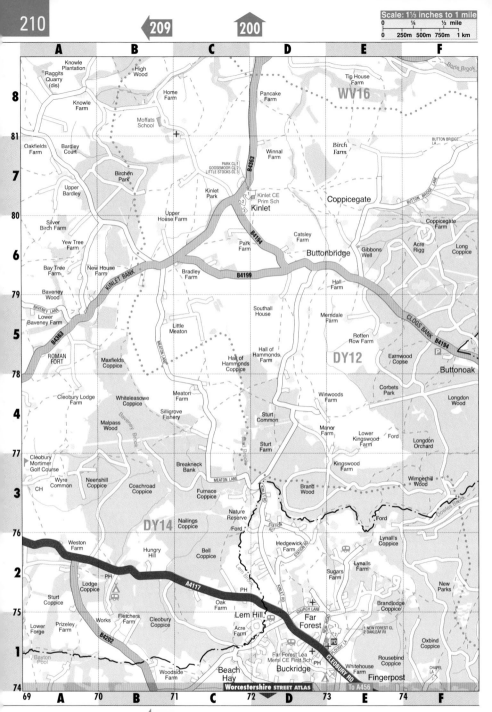

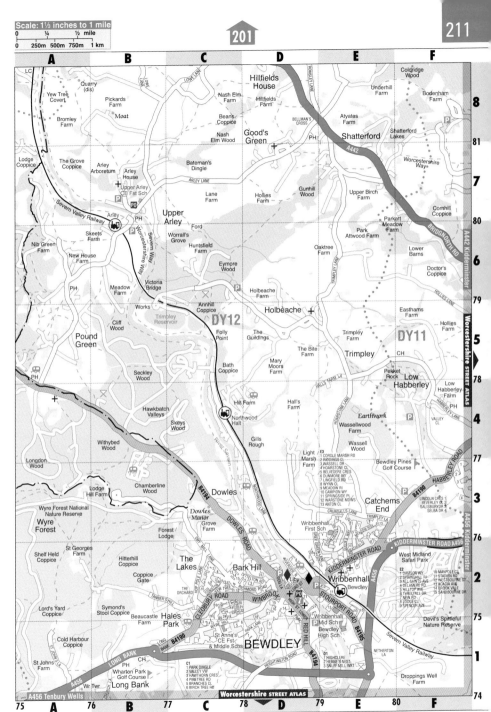

C2
1 RUSSETT WY
2 LAXTON DR
3 LAMBOURNE DR
4 NEWTON CL
5 DERWENT DR
6 MENTON CL
7 ELAN CL
8 LLESMERE DR
9 BRAMLEY WY

10 CONISTON WY
11 YEW TREE CL
12 MUSKOKA
13 THE LAKES RD
14 YORK RD
15 TUDOR RD
16 WATERLOO RD
17 ELTON RD
18 GROSVENOR WD
19 WHITE HEART CL

20 FORT-MAHON PL
21 OAKWOOD RD
22 FOREST CL
23 HALES PK
24 IRONSIDE CL
25 CHERRY CL
26 SEVERN WY
27 LAKES CT

C1
1 PARK DINGLE
2 VALLEY VW
3 HAWTHORN CRES
4 PINETREE RD
5 BRANCHES CL
6 BIRCH TREE LA

D2
1 WOODTHORPE DR
2 LANCASTER RD
3 COBHAM CRES
4 CHURCH VW
5 GREENACRES LA
6 SABRINA DR
7 NURSERY RD
8 RIVERWAY DR
9 DOG LA

D1
1 HIGHCLERE
2 HERNE'S NEST
3 SNUFF MILL WKT

10 SEVERN SIDE N
11 SEVERN SIDE S
12 PRITCHARD CT
13 GARDNERS MDW
14 PARK CL
15 ORCHARD RD
16 TELFORD DR
17 ROSENHURST DR
18 BARRATTS STILE LA
19 CLARENCE WY

20 GLOUCESTER WY
21 MARCH GR
22 MORTIMER GR
23 WOODTHORPE DR

For full street detail of Bewdley see Philip's
STREET ATLAS of Worcestershire

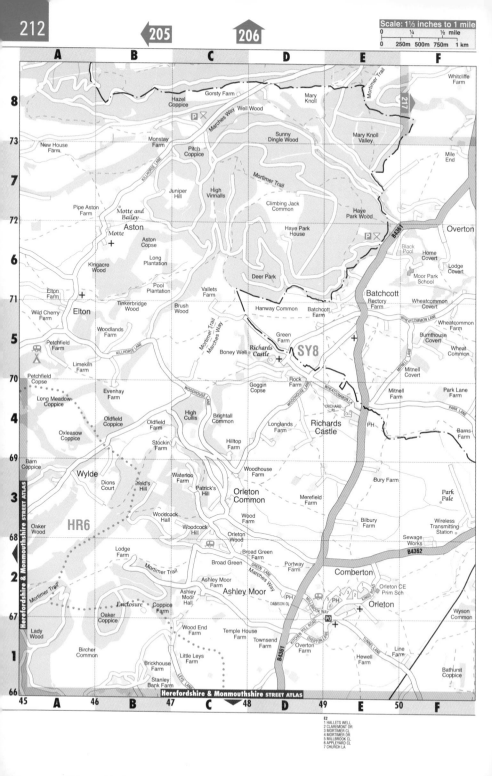

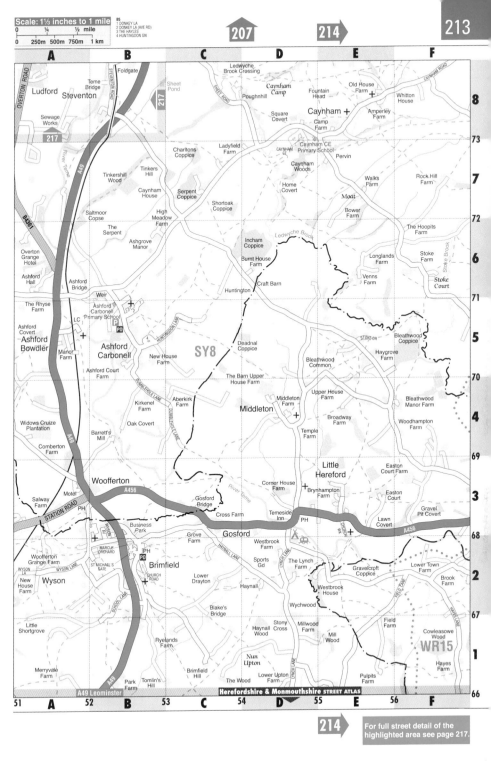

Scale: 1⅓ inches to 1 mile

0   ¼   ½ mile
0 250m 500m 750m 1 km

B5
1 DONKEY LA
2 DONKEY LA (AVE RD)
3 THE HAYLES
4 HUNTINGOON GN

207 214

8
73
7
72
6
71
5
70
4
69
3
68
2
67
1
66

OVERTON ROAD

Ludford   Steventon
Teme Bridge
Foldgate
Sheet Pond

Ledwyche Brook Crossing
Caynham Camp
Fountain Head
Old House Farm
Whitton House

Sewage Works

217

Poughnhill
Square Covert
Caynham
Amperley Farm

Camp Farm

Charltons Coppice
Ladyfield Farm
CAYNHAM CT.
Caynham CE Primary School
Pervin

Tinkershill Wood
Tinkers Hill
Caynham House
Serpent Coppice

Caynham Woods
Walks Farm
Rock Hill Farm

Saltmoor Copse
The Serpent
Ashgrove Manor
High Meadow Farm
Shortoak Coppice

Home Covert
Moat
Bower Farm

The Hoopits Farm

Ledwyche Brook
Incham Coppice
Burnt House Farm
Venns Farm
Longlands Farm
Stoke Farm

Stoke Brook

Overton Grange Hotel
Ashford Hall
Weir
Ashford Bridge
Huntington
Craft Barn
Stoke Court

The Rhyse Farm
Ashford Carbonell Primary School
LC
Ashford Covert
Ashford Bowdler
Manor Farm
Ashford Carbonell
New House Farm
Deadnal Coppice
SY8
STOKE DR
Bleathwood Coppice
Haygrove Farm
Bleathwood Common
Upper House Farm
Bleathwood Manor Farm

Ashford Court Farm
The Barn Upper House Farm
Middleton Farm
Woodhampton Farm

Kirkenel Farm
Aberkirk Farm
Middleton
Upper House Farm
Broadway Farm

Widows Cruize Plantation
Oak Covert
Temple Farm

Barrett's Mill
Comberton Farm

Wooferton
A456
Little Hereford
Easton Court Farm

Salway Farm
Motel
STATION ROAD
PH
Gosford Bridge
Cross Farm
Corner House Farm
Brynhampton Farm
Easton Court

River Teme
Temeside Inn
PH
Lawn Covert
A456
Gravel Pit Covert

Business Park
Grove Farm
Gosford
Westbrook Farm
The Lynch Farm
Gravelcroft Coppice
Lower Town Farm
Brook Farm

Wooferton Grange Farm
MARCLE ORCHARD
PH
PO
Brimfield
Lower Drayton
Sports Gd
Westbrook House
Wychwood

New House Farm
Wyson
WYSON LANE
ST MICHAEL'S GATE
CHURCH ROAD
Haynall
Blake's Bridge
Stony Cross
Millwood Farm
Mill Wood
Field Farm

Little Shortgrove
Ryelands Farm
Haynall Wood
Nun Upton
Cowleasowe Wood
WR15

Merryvale Farm
Park Farm
Tomlin's Hill
Brimfield Hill
The Wood
Lower Upton Farm
Pulpits Farm
Hayes Farm

A49 Leominster
Herefordshire & Monmouthshire STREET ATLAS

51 A 52 B 53 C 54 D 55 E 56 F

214

For full street detail of the highlighted area see page 217.

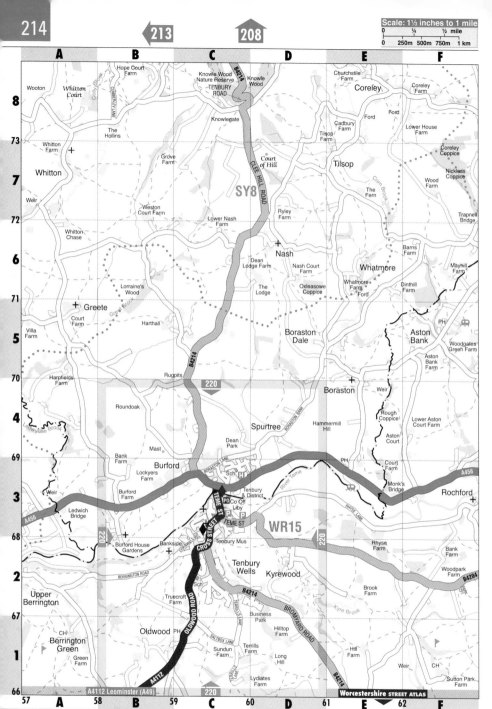

Scale: 1¼ inches to 1 mile

0   ¼   ½ mile
0 250m 500m 750m 1 km

A   B   C   D   E   F

8

Wooton
Whitton Court
Colly Brook
Hope Court Farm
CUMBERLEY LANE
Knowle Wood Nature Reserve
TENBURY ROAD
Knowle Wood
Churchstile Farm
Coreley
Coreley Farm

73

The Hollins
Knowlegate
Cadbury Farm
Ford
Ford
Lower House Farm
Coreley Coppice

Whitton Farm
Grove Farm
Court of Hill
Tilsop Farm
Tilsop
Nickless Coppice

7

Whitton
CLEE HILL ROAD
SY8
The Fern
Corn Brook
Wood Farm

Weir
Weston Court Farm
Trapnell Bridge

72

Lower Nash Farm
Ryley Farm
Barns Farm

Whitton Chase

6

Lorraine's Wood
Dean Lodge Farm
Nash
Nash Court Farm
Whatmore
Dinthill Farm
Mayhill Farm

Great Brook
The Lodge
Oxleasowe Coppice
Whatmore Farm
Ford

71

Greete
B4214
Harthall
Boraston Dale
Aston Bank
PH
Woodgates Green Farm

5

Court Farm
Aston Bank Farm

Villa Farm
Rugpits
Boraston
Weir
Rough Coppice
Lower Aston Court Farm

70

Harpfields Farm
220
Spurtree
Hammermill Hill
Aston Court
A456

4

Ledwyche Brook
Roundoak
BORASTON BANK
Dean Park
Court Farm
Monk's Bridge
Rochford

Mast
Bank Farm
River Teme
PH

69

Weir
Burford
Sch
H
PH
A456

3

Ledwich Bridge
Lockyers Farm
BORASTON LANE
Tenbury & District
PO Co Off Liby
P
P
RHYSE LANE
220

220
Burford Farm
TEME ST
Bankside
TEME ST
Tenbury Mus
WR15
Rhyse Farm
Bank Farm

68

Burford House Gardens
GRAVEL DR
CROSS STREET
Tenbury Wells
Kyrewood
Woodpark Farm
B4204

2

Upper Berrington
BERRINGTON ROAD
Sch
B4214
BROMYARD ROAD
Brook Farm
B4204

67

CH
Truecroft Farm
PH
Business Park
Hilltop Farm
Kyre Brook

Berrington Green
Oldwood
OLDWOOD ROAD
SALTBOX LANE
TERRILL'S LANE
Terrills Farm
Long Hill
Hill Farm
CH

1

Green Farm
Sundun Farm
Sutton Park Farm

A4112
A4112 Leominster (A49)
220
Lydiates Farm
B4214
Weir

66

57   A   58   B   59   C   60   D   61   E   62   F

Worcestershire STREET ATLAS

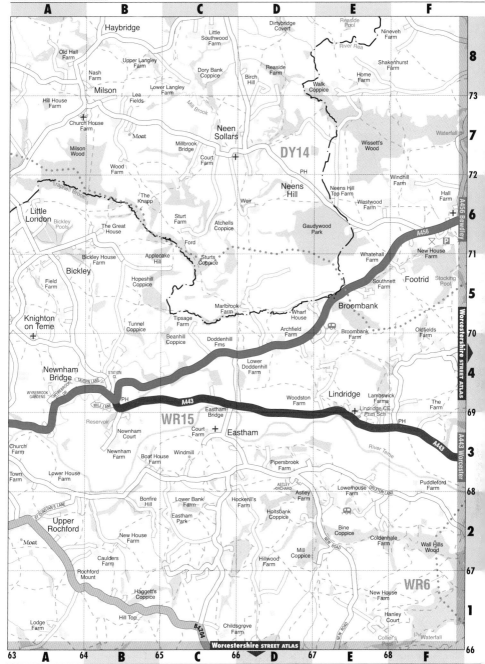

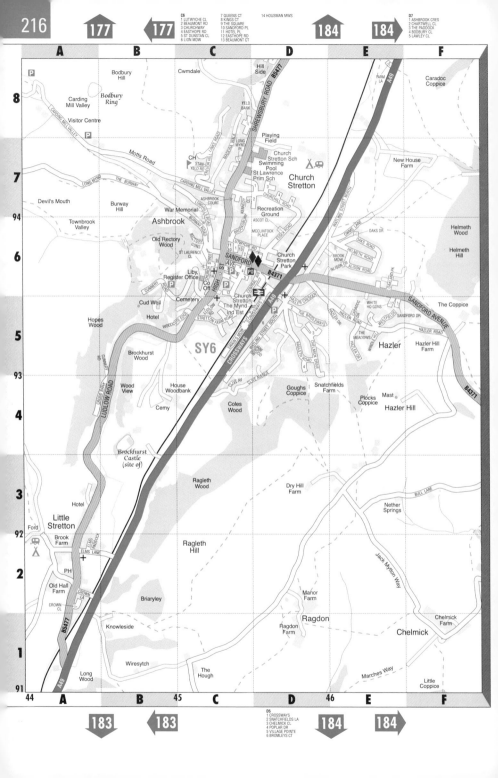

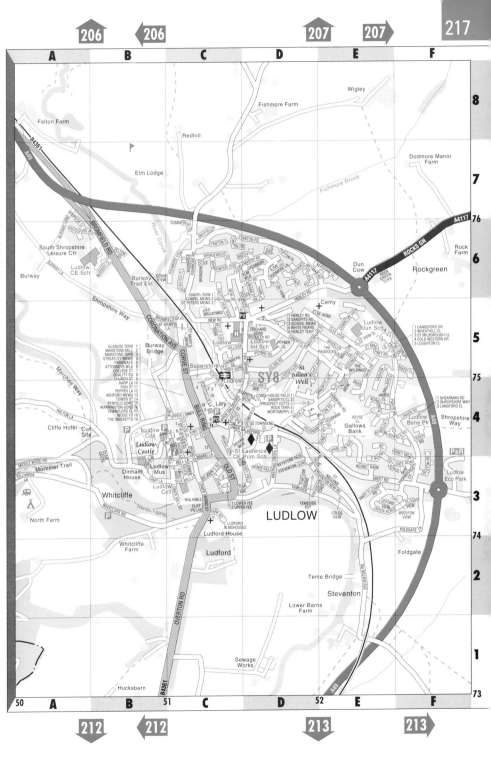

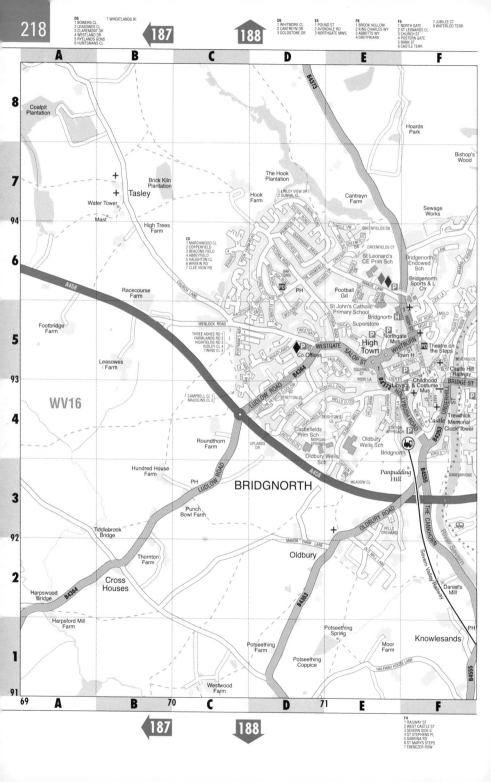

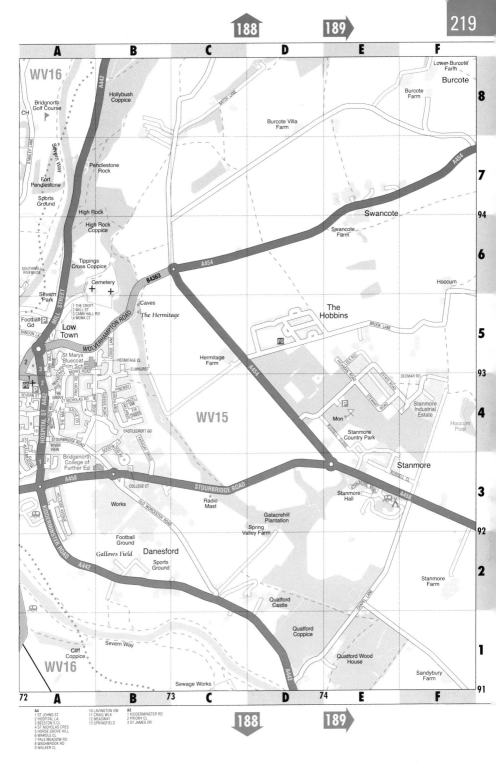

WV16

CH
Bridgnorth
Golf Course

STANLEY LANE
Severn Way

Hollybush
Coppice

A442

Burcote Villa
Farm

BATCH LANE

Lower Burcote
Farm

Burcote

Burcote
Farm

Burcote

8

Pendlestone
Rock

Fort
Pendlestone

Sports
Ground

A454

Swancote

7

High Rock

Swancote
Farm

94

High Rock
Coppice

6

SOUTHWELL
RIVERSIDE

Tippings
Cross Coppice

Cemetery

B4363

A454

The
Hobbins

Hoccum

Severn
Park

Caves

The Hermitage

MILL STREET
WOLVERHAMPTON ROAD

BROOK LANE

5

Football
Gd

BANDON LA

Low
Town

1 THE CROFT
2 MILL ST
3 CANN HALL RD
4 MONK CT

A454

P O

93

2

1

PO

SEVERN ST

St Marys
Bluecoat
Prim Sch

HERMITAGE CL

ELMHURST

Hermitage
Farm

TICKS RD

FESTEY ROAD

DECMAR RD

Hoccum
Pool

HOSPITAL ST

MORFE ROAD

ST NICHOLAS RD

PINEWAY

THE
GROVE

HAZEL
WK

TIR
TREES

HICKMAN ROAD

STEWART
ROAD

Stanmore
Industrial
Estate

4

A442

THE MALL

GROVE DR

LODGE LANE

BIRCH HSE

CASTLECROFT GD

PARKWAY DRIVE

P

Mon

RUSSELL CLOSE

Stanmore
Country Park

93

WV15

RIVER
VIEW

GOOD W

Stanmore
Hall

STANMORE MW

RUSSELL CL

Stanmore

WELLINGTON

Bridgenorth
College of
Further Ed

COLLEGE CT

STOURBRIDGE ROAD

A458

3

KIDDERMINSTER ROAD

HILLSIDE AVENUE

A458

A442

Works

OLD WORCESTER ROAD

Radio
Mast

Gatacrehill
Plantation

92

Football
Ground

Gallows Field

Danesford

Sports
Ground

Spring
Valley Farm

Stanmore
Farm

2

CHAPEL LANE

A442

Quatford
Castle

Quatford
Coppice

Quatford Wood
House

1

Severn Way

Cliff
Coppice

WV16

Sewage Works

Sandybury
Farm

91

A4
1 ST JOHNS ST
2 HOSPITAL LA
3 BEESTON S CL
4 ST NICHOLAS CRES
5 HORSE GROVE HILL
6 WARDLE CL
7 PALE MEADOW RD
8 WASHBROOK RD
9 WALKER CL

10 LAVINGTON VW
11 CRAIG WLK
12 MEADWAY
13 SPRINGFIELD

A3
1 KIDDERMINSTER RD
2 PRIORY CL
3 ST JAMES DR

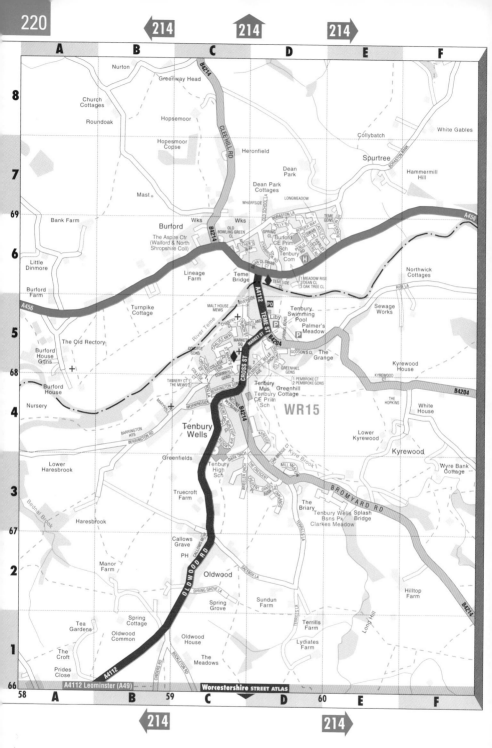

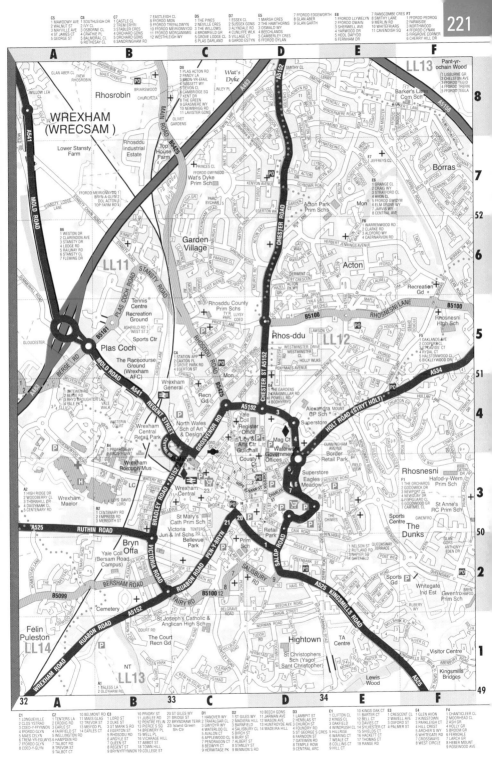

Index

Place name May be abbreviated on the map

Location number Present when a number indicates the place's position in a crowded area of mapping

Locality, town or village Shown when more than one place has the same name

Postcode district District for the indexed place

Page and grid square Page number and grid reference for the standard mapping

→ **Church Rd** **6** Beckenham BR2..........**53** C6

Cities, towns and villages are listed in CAPITAL LETTERS   Public and commercial buildings are highlighted in magenta
Places of interest are highlighted in blue with a star★

Abbreviations used in the index

Acad	Academy	Comm	Common	Gd	Ground	L	Leisure	Prom	Promenade
App	Approach	Cott	Cottage	Gdn	Garden	La	Lane	Rd	Road
Arc	Arcade	Cres	Crescent	Gn	Green	Liby	Library	Recn	Recreation
Ave	Avenue	Cswy	Causeway	Gr	Grove	Mdw	Meadow	Ret	Retail
Bglw	Bungalow	Ct	Court	H	Hall	Meml	Memorial	Sh	Shopping
Bldg	Building	Ctr	Centre	Ho	House	Mkt	Market	Sq	Square
Bsns, Bus	Business	Ctry	Country	Hospl	Hospital	Mus	Museum	St	Street
Bvd	Boulevard	Cty	County	HQ	Headquarters	Orch	Orchard	Sta	Station
Cath	Cathedral	Dr	Drive	Hts	Heights	Pal	Palace	Terr	Terrace
Cir	Circus	Dro	Drove	Ind	Industrial	Par	Parade	TH	Town Hall
Cl	Close	Ed	Education	Inst	Institute	Pas	Passage	Univ	University
Cnr	Corner	Emb	Embankment	Int	International	Pk	Park	Wk, Wlk	Walk
Coll	College	Est	Estate	Intc	Interchange	Pl	Place	Wr	Water
Com	Community	Ex	Exhibition	Junc	Junction	Prec	Precinct	Yd	Yard

Index of towns, villages, streets, hospitals, industrial estates, railway stations, schools, shopping centres, universities and places of interest

Abb–Ard

A

Abbeyfield **4** WV16. . . . . . 218 C6
Abbey Fields TF3 . . . . 144 D3
Abbey Foregate **1** SY2 . 125 D5
Abbey La SY5. . . . . 168 D5
Abbey Lawn Bsns Pk
SY2. . . . . 125 D6
Abbey Rd TF1. . . . . 131 A2
Abbey Walls **4** TF2 . . . . . 132 A4
Abbey Way TF9 . . . . 36 D2
Abbots Cl TF2 . . . . 132 A3
Abbotsfield Dr SY2 . . . . . 125 F3
Abbots Gn SY2 . . . . 126 A6
Abbots Pl **4** SY2 . . . . 125 F7
Abbots Rd SY2. . . . . 125 F7
Abbot St **17** LL11. . . . . . . 221 C3
Abbots Way
  Hodnet TF9 . . . . 69 C6
  Shrewsbury SY2 . . . . . . 126 A7
Abbotts Way **3** WV16. . . 218 F6
ABCOTT. 194 F1
ABDON. 198 A5
Abdon Cl **9** WV16. . . . . . 200 E3
Abdon Ct **1** TF2. . . . . . . 132 A3
Abelia Way TF2 . . . . 132 F1
Abenbury Rd LL13 . . . . . . 221 F1
Abingdon Rd
  3 Albrighton WV7 . . . . 156 F4
  Shrewsbury SY2 . . . . . . 126 A7
Abney Ave WV7 . . . . 156 F5
Abraham Cl **6** TF3. . . . . 144 B1
Abraham Darby Sch TF7 . 152 E5
Acacia Ave **13** DY12 . . . . 211 E2
Acacia Dr TF1. . . . . 131 A5
Access Sch SY4. . . . . 83 C6
Acer Cl TF3. . . . . 143 E8
ACKLETON. 164 D2
Acorn Cl **4** SY11. . . . . . . 41 F2
Acorn Mews **11** TF5. . . . 130 C7
Acorn Rise SY2 . . . . 170 B7
Acorn Way TF5 . . . . 130 C8
ACTON
  Lydbury North 193 E7
  Wrexham. 221 E6
ACTON BURNELL 179 C5
Acton Burnell Castle★
SY5. . . . . 179 C4

Acton Gate LL11 . . . . 221 D6
Acton Gdns LL11. . . . . . . 221 E7
Acton Hall Walks LL12 . . 221 E6
Acton Pk Prim Schools
LL11. . . . . 221 D7
Acton Pk Way LL12 . . . . . 221 D6
Acton Rd LL11 . . . . 221 C5
ACTON REYNALD. 84 F3
ACTON ROUND. 187 A6
ACTON SCOTT. 196 A8
Acton Scott Historic Working
Farm★ SY6. . . . . 196 A8
Adams Cl TF10. . . . . 109 E3
Adams Cres TF10 . . . . . . 109 E3
Adams' Gram Sch TF10. . 109 E3
Adamson Dr TF4. . . . . . . 143 D3
Adams Ridge **1** SY3. . . . 125 E3
Adcote Sch SY4 . . . . 98 F3
ADDERLEY. 19 A4
Adderley CE Prim Sch
TF9. . . . . 18 F5
Adderley Rd TF9. . . . . 19 A2
Addison Rd TF1. . . . . 130 C3
Addisons Way TF10 . . . . . 121 C4
Adelaide Dr SY21. . . . . . . 170 B7
ADENEY. 108 C1
Adeney Rd TF10 . . . . 108 C1
ADFORTON. 205 A2
ADMASTON 130 B6
Admaston Cl TF7 . . . . . . 153 C7
Admaston Rd TF1. . . . . . 130 C5
Admaston Spa **8** TF5. . 130 B7
Admirals Cl TF11. . . . . . . 146 A6
Admirals Way TF11. . . . . 146 A6
Adswood Gr SY3. . . . . . . 124 F1
Aelybryn LL11 . . . . 221 C7
Agden House La SY13. . . . . 1 A5
Agnes Hunt Cl **4** SY4. . . 81 A1
Agnes Hunt Orthopaedic
SY11. . . . . 41 B6
Ainsdale Dr
  Dawley TF4 . . . . 144 E8
  Shrewsbury SY1 . . . . . . 113 E3
Aintree La TF11. . . . . 131 A5
Alan Gutridge Dr SY3 . . . 124 E5
Albacore Rd TF1. . . . . . . 131 A7
Albany St **2** SY5. . . . . . . 169 C4
ALBERBURY 168 D5
Alberbury Dr SY1. . . . . . . 114 B3
Alberbury Rd SY5. . . . . . . 169 B4
Albert Dr **1** DY3. . . . . . . 190 F1
Albert Gdns **1** SY1. . . . . 113 F2
Albert Mews **7** SY11. . . . 40 E1

Albert Pl
  Donnington TF2 . . . . . . 132 C8
  24 Oswestry SY11. . . . . 58 E8
Albert Rd
  Albrighton WV7 . . . . . . 156 F4
  2 Oswestry SY11. . . . . 58 E8
  Shrewsbury SY1 . . . . . . 113 F2
  Wellington TF1 . . . . . . 130 E4
Albert Sq
  4 Shrewsbury SY1. . . . 113 F3
  Weston Rhyn SY10 . . . . . 23 C4
Albert St
  8 Oakengates/Donnington
  TF2. . . . . 132 C3
  6 Shrewsbury SY1 . . . 113 F2
  7 Wrexham LL13 . . . . 221 D2
Albert Terr **8** SY21 . . . . 170 B6
Albion Hill **12** SY21. . . . 58 E8
Albion St TF2. . . . . 132 C3
Albridge La SY10 . . . . 76 E8
ALBRIGHTON
  Donnington 157 A6
  Pimhill. 101 D1
Albrighton By-pass WV7 . 157 A4
Albrighton Inf Sch WV7 . 157 A4
Albrighton Jun Sch WV7 157 A4
Albrighton Moat & Gdns★
WV7. . . . . 157 B7
Albrighton Sta WV7. . . . . 157 B5
ALCASTON. 196 A6
Alder Dr **1** SY5. . . . . 172 E4
Alderley La SY4. . . . . 66 E7
Aldermead Cl TF5. . . . . . 130 A7
Alder Rd TF9 . . . . 53 A8
Alders La SY13 . . . . 30 C1
Alderslee Cl **5** TF2. . . . 132 E2
Aldersley Way **3** SY4. . . 80 A1
ALDERTON. 83 C4
Aldford Way **3** LL12 . . . 221 F6
ALDON 195 E2
Aldon View **19** SY7. . . . 195 E5
Aldridge Cl TF2 . . . . 132 F1
Aldwick Dr SY3 . . . . 124 F2
ALE OAK 192 B7
Alexander Fleming Prim Sch
TF7. . . . . 153 C4
Alexandra Ave SY3. . . . . 125 A2
Alexandra CP Sch LL12. . 221 D4
Alexandra Rd
  11 Market Drayton TF9. . 36 B1
  10 Oswestry SY11. . . . . 40 D1
  4 Wellington TF1 . . . 130 D3
  Wrexham LL13. . . . . 221 B2

Alfred St SY2. . . . . 125 E5
Algernon Ct TF2 . . . . 132 C8
Alison Dr SY6. . . . . 216 E6
Alison Rd SY6 . . . . 216 E6
ALKINGTON. 14 E3
Alkington Gdns **1** SY13. . 15 A6
Alkington Rd SY13. . . . . . 14 F6
Allcroft Cl SY7. . . . . 206 A6
Allerton Rd **6** SY1. . . . . 114 B3
Allertons Mdw **6** TF5. . 130 B8
Allestree Cl **8** SY1 . . . . 113 E5
Alley The TF6. . . . . 142 D2
Algold Dr SY2. . . . . 126 A5
Allmans La TF9. . . . . 72 A4
Allness Cl **1** SY2. . . . . . 126 B7
All Saints Ave **3** DY12 . 211 E3
All Saints CE (C) Prim Sch
WV5. . . . . 190 D4
ALLSCOTT. 188 E7
ALLSCOTT. 129 C6
ALL STRETTON. 184 B6
Alma Ave TF4. . . . . 143 F5
Alma Cl **1** SY11. . . . . 78 D7
Alma Fields TF4 . . . . 143 F5
Alma Rd **2** LL20. . . . . 6 A7
Alma St SY3 . . . . 125 B6
ALMINGTON. 37 C2
Almond Ave SY11. . . . . . . 41 A7
Almond Cl **7** TF2 . . . . . 132 E8
Almond Dr **7** SY12 . . . . . 27 A2
Almond Gr LL13 . . . . 221 F4
Almscliffe La TF1. . . . . . 144 B1
Alms Ct **3** SY3 . . . . 125 B2
ALPORT. 175 A1
Alport Rd SY13 . . . . 2 A1
Alton Gr TF10. . . . . 109 E1
Alton Terr **1** SY3 . . . . . 125 D4
Alvaston Way SY2. . . . . . 126 A8
ALVELEY. 201 A3
Aveley Dr SY13. . . . . 30 B8
Aveley End Est WV15. . . 201 A3
Aveley Prim Sch WV15 . 201 A3
Alverley Cl
  4 Shrewsbury SY3. . . 124 F6
  7 Wellington TF1 . . . 130 E4
Alvin Cl SY4. . . . . 65 F5
Alyndale Rd **3** LL12 . . . 221 D7
Amber Hill SY3 . . . . 124 E4
Ambleside Rd **10** SY8. . 58 E8
Ambleside Way **3** TF2. 132 E6
ANCHOR. 191 C7
Anchor Cl SY13. . . . . 15 B7

Andreas Dr **14** TF2. . . . 132 F8
ANGELBANK. 208 A3
Angel La SY8 . . . . 208 A3
Annefield Cl **4** TF9 . . . . . 36 D2
ANNSCROFT. 136 A4
Anslem Ct **2** TF3. . . . . . 144 A1
Anson Dr **3** TF1. . . . . . . 131 B6
Anson Rd WV7. . . . . 156 B7
Anstice Rd TF7 . . . . 153 A5
Anstice Sq **5** TF7. . . . . . 153 B5
Anthony Eden Dr **1** SY3 . 221 F2
Anton Cl **13** DY12 . . . . . 211 E3
Anvil Cl TF10 . . . . 107 E5
Apley Ave TF4 . . . . 130 E5
Apley Castle TF1. . . . . . . 130 A8
Apley Cl **4** TF1. . . . . 130 D6
Apley Dr TF1 . . . . 130 E5
Apley Wood Prim Sch
TF1. . . . . 131 A7
Apple Acre WV16 . . . . . . 188 D1
Applebrook TF11. . . . . . . 145 F3
Appledore **1** SY3. . . . . . 124 D7
Appledore Gdns TF1 . . . . 130 D2
Appleton TF9 . . . . 36 A1
Applewood Cl
  6 Offa LL13 . . . . 221 D1
  West Felton SY11 . . . . . 78 D7
Applewood Hts SY11. . . . 78 D7
Appleyard Cl **6** SY8 . . . 212 C5
Apse Cl **9** WV5. . . . . 190 F4
Aqualate Cl **5** TF10. . . . 110 A4
AQUEDUCT. 152 F8
Aqueduct La TF3 . . . . 144 B1
Aqueduct Prim Sch TF4 . 153 A8
Aqueduct Rd TF3 . . . . . . 153 A8
Aragorn Way **5** TF4 . . . 153 A8
Aralia Cl TF2. . . . . 132 F1
Aran Rd LL12 . . . . 221 E6
Arboretum The TF9 . . . . . 89 B7
Arbour La SY9. . . . . 182 B8
Arbourne Gdns **8** SY3 . 125 C4
Archer's Way
  Tenbury Wells WR15 . . 220 C6
  5 Wrexham LL13 . . . . 221 E4
Arden Cl
  4 Shrewsbury SY2. . . 125 F8
  Wem SY4. . . . . 66 B8
Arden Way **11** WV15. . . 201 B3
Ardern Ave TF4 . . . . 143 F4
Ardmillan Cl SY11 . . . . . . 58 F8
Ardmillan Ct SY11 . . . . . . 58 F8
Ardmillan La **4** SY11 . . . 58 F8

Ardwyn Infants Sch SY21 170 B6
ARGOED
  Clun 193 C7
  Kinnerley 95 F6
Argyle St 6 LL11 221 C3
Argyll Cres 4 TF2 120 E1
Argyll St SY1 125 D7
ARLESTON 131 B1
Arleston Ave TF1 131 B2
Arleston Ct TF1 131 D3
Arleston La TF1 131 B1
Arleston Manor Mews TF1 131 B1
Arleston Village TF1 131 A2
Arley La DY12 211 C7
Arley Sta DY12 211 B7
Arley View Cl 7 WV16 200 F2
Arlington Way SY1 114 A4
Arlon Rd TF9 36 B2
Armdale SY2 125 F8
Armoury Gdns SY2 125 F4
Armoury La SY13 49 F7
Armstrong Cl TF7 152 C5
AROWRY 12 C3
Arran Way 5 TF2 120 F1
Arrow Dr 6 WV7 157 A5
Arrow Rd 2 TF5 130 C8
ARSCOTT 173 E6
Arthur Rowley Cl 9 SY2 126 A8
Arthurs Gate SY15 174 B4
Arthur St
  4 Montgomery SY15 174 B3
  Oswestry SY11 58 D8
Arthur Way TF7 152 F7
Artillery Rd SY11 41 C4
Arundel Cl
  2 Ruyton SY4 80 A1
  Stirchley & Brookside TF3 144 C3
Arundel Rd 6 SY11 58 D8
Ascot Cl
  Church Stretton SY6 216 D6
  Oswestry SY11 41 A1
Ascot Rd SY11 41 A1
Ashbourne Cl 9 TF4 144 A4
Ashbourne Dr 4 TF9 36 C2
ASHBROOK 216 B6
Ashbrook Cres 1 SY6 216 D7
Ashbrook Ct SY6 216 C7
Ashburn Way LL13 221 F1
Ash Cl
  3 Craven Arms SY7 195 E5
  Ludlow SY8 217 E3
  Shrewsbury SY2 125 F2
  Weston Rhyn SY10 23 D4
Ashcroft 7 WV16 218 D5
Ashcroft Cl 3 SY11 41 A8
Ashdale Rd
  Cressage SY5 149 E4
  Telford TF2 132 A4
ASHFIELD 77 C8
Ashfield Dr 3 SY22 93 F6
Ashfield Rd
  Ditton Priors WV16 198 C8
  Rhosddu LL11 221 B5
ASHFIELDS 72 C2
Ashfields 7 TF2 132 B2
Ashfields Rd SY1 113 D3
Ashford Ave 1 SY5 173 A4
ASHFORD BOWDLER 213 A5
ASHFORD CARBONELL 213 B5
Ashford Carbonell Prim Sch SY8 213 B5
Ashford Cl
  Hadley TF1 131 E4
  3 Pontesbury SY5 173 A4
Ashford Dr
  Pontesbury SY5 173 A5
  9 Shrewsbury SY1 113 D4
Ashford Mews SY8 217 C4
Ashford Pk 2 SY5 173 A4
Ashford Way 4 SY5 173 A5
Ash Gr
  Albrighton WV7 157 A4
  4 Chirk LL14 6 E3
  3 Pontesbury SY5 173 A5
  Trench TF2 132 D3
  Wem Rural SY4 66 C7
  3 Wrexham LL13 221 F4
Ash La SY13 15 F1
Ashlands Rd SY10 23 D4
Ash Lea SY5 172 E3
Ashlea Dr TF2 132 D6
Ashley Ct 4 TF4 143 E3
ASHLEY MOOR 212 C2
Ashley Rd TF2 132 D2
Ashley St SY2 125 E7
Ashley View TF9 36 C1
ASH MAGNA 16 A4
Ash Mdw 3 SY5 172 C8
Ashmore Cl TF2 120 E2
Ashmore Cres TF12 152 C2
Ashmore Dr TF2 132 A6
Ash Mount CW3 4 F1
ASH PARVA 16 B3
Ash Rd
  Bridgnorth WV16 218 D6
  Oakengates/Donnington TF2 132 D8
  9 Oswestry SY11 40 E1
  Whitchurch Rural SY13 15 F2
Ash St 2 WV16 200 E3
Ashton Rd 1 SY3 125 A4
Ashwood Cl 9 TF9 36 A1
Ashwood La SY13 16 C4
Ashworth Way 1 TF10 109 F1
Aspen Ct SY10 23 D4
Aspen Gr 5 SY3 124 E4
Aspen Grange SY10 23 D4
Aspen Way
  Newport TF10 109 F2
  Wellington TF5 130 C8
Aspire Ctr The WR15 220 C6
Assembly Cl 2 WV16 200 F2
ASTERLEY 172 E6
ASTERTON 183 A6
ASTLEY 102 E2
ASTLEY ABBOTTS 188 C7
Astley Ct SY4 102 E2
Astley La SY4 102 D3
Astley Orch WR15 215 D3
ASTON
  Churchstoke 181 C6
  Claverley 189 F4
  Pipe Aston 212 B6
  Wem Rural 66 D6
ASTON BANK 214 F5
ASTON BOTTERELL 199 A3
Aston Butts 8 SY2 125 F8
Aston Cl
  Oswestry SY11 59 B7
  8 Wellington TF1 130 F5
Aston Dale 3 TF11 146 A4
Aston Dr 12 TF10 109 E2
ASTON EYRE 187 C5
Aston Gr LL12 221 E4
Aston La
  Claverley WV5 189 E4
  Maer TF9 21 F8
  Wheathill WV16 198 F2
  Woore CW3 5 C1
ASTON MUNSLOW 197 A5
ASTON ON CLUN 195 A5
ASTON PIGOTT 172 A4
Aston Rd
  Shifnal TF11 146 A4
  Wem Urban SY4 66 C6
ASTON ROGERS 172 A5
ASTON SQ 59 E5
Aston St
  Shifnal TF11 145 F4
  Wem SY4 66 A6
Aston Way SY11 59 B8
ATCHAM 139 A7
Atcham Ind Est SY4 127 F1
Athersmith Cl 1 TF4 144 A4
Athol Dr TF2 132 C2
Atlas Gr TF1 130 C4
ATTERLEY 187 B8
ATTINGHAM 139 B8
Attingham Cl 7 TF3 144 D1
Attingham Pk* SY4 127 C1
Attorneys Wlk SY8 217 C4
Attwood Terr TF4 143 F4
Audlem Rd CW3 4 E2
Audley Ave TF10 109 F2
Audley Ave Enterprise Pk TF10 110 A1
Audley Rd TF10 109 F3
Aumbry Cl 6 TF9 36 A1
Auster Cl 10 TF1 131 A7
Avalon Ct 5 LL13 221 D1
Avenue Rd
  Broseley TF12 161 D7
  Newport TF10 109 F2
Avenue Rd S TF10 109 F2
Avenue The
  Barrow TF12 151 F1
  Hodnet TF9 69 E1
  Knockin SY10 78 C1
  More SY9 182 B7
  Stanton upon Hine Heath SY4 86 E7
  West Felton SY11 78 C8
  Wrockwardine TF6 129 F4
Avon Cl
  1 Dawley TF4 152 F8
  4 Wrexham LL12 221 E6
Avondale TF4 143 E6
Avon Dale TF10 109 F4
Avondale Dr SY1 125 E7
Avondale Rd
  Bridgnorth WV16 218 E5
  Wellington TF1 130 C2
Aylwin Ct 4 TF3 144 A1
Aynesworth Gn 2 SY1 113 F4
Ayr Cl TF1 131 A5
Aysgarth Rd 1 SY3 124 F6

B

BABBINSWOOD 42 A1
BACHE 206 B8
BACHELDRE 180 D7
BACHE MILL 196 F4
Back La
  Bausley with Criggion SY5 167 B6
  Blymhill TF11 135 C7
  Bomere Heath SY4 100 E4
  Clive SY4 84 A5
  11 Montgomery SY15 174 B3
  5 Much Wenlock TF13 159 E5
  Onibury SY7 206 B5
  Pontesbury SY5 173 B5
  Worfield WV6 164 E2
Back Lime St 2 SY3 125 C4
Back Rd TF11 134 C3
Baddleys Ct TF10 109 F2
Bader Cl 9 TF1 131 A7
BADGER 164 D4
Badger Cl 2 TF3 144 B1
Badger La
  Badger WV6 164 C4
  Beckbury TF11 164 C8
Badgers Rise SY8 208 E2
Badgers Way 8 SY4 99 B1
Bage Way SY3 125 E4
BAGLEY 62 C3
Bagley Dr
  Shrewsbury SY1 113 D1
  Wellington TF1 130 C5
BAGLEY MARSH 62 B4
Bailey Cl SY4 65 F7
Bailey Cres 1 SY5 173 B4
Bailey Head
  23 Oswestry SY11 58 E8
  Whitchurch SY13 15 E8
Bailey St 14 SY11 58 E8
Bainbridge Gn 3 SY1 113 E4
Bainbridge Wlk 8 SY1 113 E4
Bakehouse La WV16 200 D6
Baker Cl SY8 217 F5
Bakewell Cl 4 SY1 113 D5
Baldwin Way DY3 190 F1
Baldwin Webb Ave TF2 132 C8
Balfour Rd TF11 146 A6
BALL 59 A2
Ballard Cl SY8 217 E4
Balliol Way 5 SY3 124 E3
Ball La SY10 59 A1
Balls Hill TF4 143 D4
Ball's La TF8 152 D2
BALMER 28 E2
BALMER HEATH 28 F2
Balmoral Cl
  2 Oswestry SY11 59 A8
  5 Wrexham LL11 221 C6
Balmoral Cres SY11 41 A1
Balmoral Dr TF9 36 E2
Balmoral Rd LL11 221 C6
Banbery Dr 3 WV5 190 F2
Banbury Cl 1 SY2 125 F3
Banbury La WV16 198 D2
Bandon La WV15 219 A5
Bank Dr
  Condover SY5 178 C5
  Shrewsbury SY3 125 A2
Bank Dr W 3 SY3 124 F2
Bank Farm Rd SY3 124 F3
Bankhouse La SY4 65 F6
Bank Rd
  Dawley TF4 143 E5
  Wellington TF1 130 F3
Bankside 5 WV5 190 F4
Bank St
  5 Bridgnorth WV16 218 F5
  Wrexham LL11 221 D3
Bank The 3 SY5 178 C6
Bank Top Ind Est SY11 24 C5
Bank Way TF2 131 F1
Baptist Ave TF4 143 F6
Barber Cl SY11 59 A7
Barberry Cl TF3 143 E8
Barber St TF12 161 C8
Barbrook DY14 209 F5
Barclay Cl WV7 157 B6
Barclay Ct TF2 132 C8
Bardsley Dr 1 SY2 126 A5
Bargates SY13 15 A8
Bar Hill CW3 5 F3
Barkers Ct 3 TF7 153 B5
BARKERS GREEN 66 C5
Barkers La 7 DY14 209 E2
Barker's La LL12 221 E8
Barker's La Com Sch LL12 221 F8
Barker St 16 SY1 125 B6
Barke St WV16 200 F2
BARK HILL 211 D2
Bark Hill 6 SY13 15 A7
Bark Hill Mews 12 SY13 15 A7
Barkstone Dr 1 SY1 113 D2
Barleyfield 3 SY2 125 F6
Barleyfields SY4 66 B7
Barley Mdws 1 SY22 93 F6
Barleywood Cl 1 TF2 132 E6
Barlow Cl 3 TF3 144 C3
Barnard St
  Wem SY4 66 A6
  Wem Urban SY4 65 F6
Barn Cl TF2 132 E6
Barnes Wallis Dr TF1 131 A7
Barnet Cl 1 TF1 130 D5
Barnfield 3 LL13 221 D2
Barnfield Ave SY4 66 A8
Barnfield Cl
  4 Oswestry SY11 58 F7
  2 Whitchurch SY13 14 E8
Barnfield Cres TF1 130 C1
Barnfield Ct 4 TF1 130 C2
Barnfields 9 DY14 209 D2
Barnmeadow Cl TF10 110 A3
Barnmeadow Rd TF10 110 A3
Barn Rd TF11 146 A5
Barns Gn 2 SY3 124 F1
Barns La SY4 68 F7
BARNSLEY 189 A3
Barnyard Cl 2 SY5 172 C8
Barons Rd LL13 221 E3
Barrack La TF10 121 C6
Barracks La SY3 124 E7
Barratts Stile La 18 DY12 211 D2
Barratt Terr TF3 131 E1
Barrington Cl 3 WV7 157 A5
Barrington Ct 2 TF11 146 A5
Barrington Hts WR15 220 B4
BARROW 160 F4
Barrow CE Prim Sch TF12 160 F5
Barrow St TF13 159 E4
Barter Ct 11 LL13 221 E1
Barter Rd LL13 221 E1
Bartholomew Rd TF4 143 C6
Bartlett Rd 4 TF4 143 F2
Barton Cl 4 SY1 125 E8
Bartons La 2 TF9 53 B8
Barton's Rd TF9 53 B8
BASCHURCH 81 A1
Baschurch CE Prim Sch SY4 81 B1
Baschurch Rd SY4 100 E4
BASFORD 194 F8
Basford Bank SY7 195 A8
BATCHCOTT 212 E6
Batches La The TF12 161 E7
Batch La WV15 219 C8
Batfield La DY7 201 E5
Bathfields Cres 1 SY13 14 E7
Bath Mews SY5 172 E4
Bath Rd
  Ironbridge TF8 152 C3
  Wrexham LL13 221 C2
Bath St SY13 15 B8
BATTLEFIELD 114 A5
Battlefield Ct SY1 114 B5
Battlefield Ent Pk SY1 113 E6
Battlefield Rd SY1 114 A5
Battlefield Way SY1 113 E5
Battle Rd WV7 156 B7
Baveney La DY14 209 F5
Bayford Dr 4 SY1 113 C2
Bayley Hills TF10 109 A3
Bayley Rd TF1 130 F1
Baylham Cl 1 TF4 143 D2
BAYSTON HILL 137 A7
Bayswater Cl 6 TF2 132 F2
Baytree Cl SY11 24 F6
Bazeley Way SY4 66 B8
Beacall's La SY1 125 D6
BEACH HAY 210 C1
Beachley 5 SY1 113 F2
Beacon La DY7 201 F2
Beacon Pk ST19 148 F7
Beaconsfield
  3 Bridgnorth WV16 218 C6
  Dawley TF3 144 C1
Beaconsfield Pk SY8 207 C1
Beaconsfield Terr SY10 58 D4
BEAMBRIDGE
  Abdon 197 C7
  Hopesay 194 F4
Beames Cl TF4 144 A2
Beamish La WV7 157 D5
Bearcroft Grange TF9 72 A1
BEARSTONE 21 A4
Bearstone Rd
  Loggerheads TF9 21 B4
  Woore TF9 20 F3
Beatrice Gdns 2 SY13 15 B8
Beatrice St 5 SY11 40 E1
Beatty Cl 4 TF11 146 A6
Beaufort Cl 7 TF1 131 A7
Beaufort Gn 1 SY1 113 F4
Beaumaris Rd TF10 109 E3
Beaumont Ct 13 SY6 216 C6
Beaumont Rd 2 SY6 216 C6
Beaumont Way SY2 125 E2
BECKBURY 164 D8
Beckbury CE Prim Sch TF11 164 D7
Beckbury Dr TF3 144 B1
BECKJAY 205 A8
Beddoes Dr SY3 137 A5
Beddon Cl SY1 125 D8
BEDSTONE 204 D6
Bedstone Cl 10 TF3 144 C1
Bedstone Coll SY7 204 D6
Bedwyr Ct 8 LL13 221 D1
Beech Ave SY13 15 A6
Beech Cl
  Hanmer SY13 12 B4
  9 Hanwood SY5 173 F8
  Ludlow SY8 217 D6
  Newport TF10 109 F1
  Pattingham WV6 166 C2
  9 Wellington TF1 130 C5
Beech Croft 1 WV6 166 C2
Beech Dr
  Broseley TF12 161 D8
  13 Ellesmere SY12 27 A2
  Shifnal TF11 145 F5
Beeches Ave 4 SY11 41 A8
Beeches La 13 SY1 125 C5
Beeches Rd SY3 136 F6
Beeches The
  2 Admaston TF5 130 A6
  16 Bishop's Castle SY9 181 F3
  Whitchurch Urban SY13 1 F1
  Wrexham LL12 221 D5
Beechfields Way 2 TF10 109 F5
Beech Gdns 10 LL13 221 D2
Beech Gr
  Ellesmere SY12 27 A2
  Oswestry SY11 58 F7
  Shawbury SY4 103 E7
Beech Gr CE Jun Sch SY11 58 F7
Beechhouse La WV5 190 D4
Beech Hurst Gdns WV5 190 D5
Beechlands 4 LL12 221 E5
Beechley Rd LL13 221 D2
Beech Rd
  Bridgnorth WV16 218 D6
  Madeley TF7 152 E5
Beech Spinney TF7 152 D5
Beech St WV16 200 E3
Beechurst Gdns 2 WV7 156 F5
Beechwood Cl 2 TF4 144 A2
Beechwood Dr 3 SY1 113 C1
Beechwood Rd TF4 144 A2
Beedles Cl TF4 153 A8
Beehive La SY3 125 B4
Beeston's Cl 3 WV15 219 A4
Beffcote Rd ST20 111 E2
BEGUILDY 191 E1
Beighterton La TF11 135 F3
Belfry Cl 8 SY8 208 C2
Belfry Theatre & Arts Ctr TF1 130 F3
Belgrave Cres 4 TF3 144 B1
Belgrave Ct SY1 125 E5
Belgrave Pl 9 SY2 126 B7
Belgrave Rd LL13 221 C2
Bellan House Sch SY11 58 D8
Bellan La SY10 57 D2
Bellaport Rd TF9 20 A4
Bell Ct 12 LL13 221 E1
Belle Orch WR15 220 D5
BELLE VUE 125 C4
Belle Vue Gdns SY3 125 C4
Bellevue Rd LL13 221 B3
Belle Vue Rd
  Ironbridge TF8 152 C4
  Shrewsbury SY3 125 C3
Belle Vue Terr SY8 217 C5
Bell La
  Ludlow SY8 217 C3
  Shrewsbury SY2 125 E5
Bellman's Cross DY12 211 D8
Bellman's Yd TF10 109 F2
BELL O' TH' HILL 1 C7
Bellpit Rd TF3 143 F8
Bell Rd WV5 190 E5
Bell St 13 TF1 130 E4
Belmont SY1 125 C5
Belmont Bank 12 SY1 125 C5
Belmont Rd
  Ironbridge TF8 152 D4
  10 Wrexham LL13 221 C2
Belton Cl SY13 14 E7
Belton Rd SY13 14 E7
Belvedere Cres 5 DY12 211 E3
Belvedere Dr LL11 221 A4
Belvedere Gdns TF12 152 E1
Belvidere Ave SY2 125 F5
Belvidere La 4 SY2 126 A6
Belvidere Prim Sch SY2 126 A7
Belvidere Rd 6 SY2 125 F6
Belvidere Sch SY2 126 A6
Belvidere Wlk SY2 125 F5
Bembridge TF3 144 C1
Benbow Cl 5 SY1 125 C8
Benbow Quay 5 SY1 125 C7
Benbows Cl TF9 89 A7
Benjamin Rd LL13 221 E2
Ben Jones Ave 6 TF10 110 A4
Bennett Rd TF7 153 C5
Bennetts Bank TF1 131 A3
Bennetts La
  Leighton & Eaton Constantine SY5 141 B1
  Pattingham & Patshull WV6 166 F1
Bennion's Rd 9 LL13 221 D2
BENTHALL 152 B1
Benthall Hall* TF12 151 F2
Benthall La
  Barrow TF12 161 A8
  Broseley TF12 152 B1
Benthall View TF7 152 E4
Bent La WV16 198 D7
Bentlands The TF12 152 B1
BENTLAWNT 176 A8
Bentley Dr SY11 58 C7
Bentleys Rd TF9 52 F7
Benyon St 5 SY1 125 D7
Berberis Rd 1 TF1 131 B6
Beresford Gdns SY11 58 D7
Berghill La SY11 42 D1
Berinsfield Cl 9 SY1 113 C2
Berkeley Cl 1 TF2 132 F2
Berllan Cl SY10 23 E5
Berllan Deg SY22 92 C5
Bernard Rd LL13 221 E3
Bernards Hill WV15 219 A4
Berries La SY3 137 B6
Berriew Rd SY21 170 B5
Berriew St SY21 170 B6
BERRINGTON 138 D2
Berrington Dr 3 SY1 113 D3
Berrington Gdns WR15 220 C4
BERRINGTON GREEN 214 A1
Berrington Rd WR15 220 B4
Berrisford Cl TF9 36 E1
Berrisford Rd TF9 36 E1
Berse Rd LL11 221 A4
Bersham Rd LL13 221 B2
Bertie Rd LL13 221 E3
Bert Smith Way TF9 36 C2
Berwick Ave SY1 125 B8
Berwick Cl SY1 125 B8
Berwick Rd
  Pimhill SY1 113 A1
  Shrewsbury SY1 125 B8
BERWICK WHARF 127 A3
Berwyn Ave LL14 23 E6
Berwyn Cl 1 TF3 144 C3
Berwyn Dr
  Bayston Hill SY3 136 F6
  St Martin's SY11 24 E5
BESFORD 85 C7
Besford Sq 7 SY3 125 D4
Beswicks La TF9 20 C2

BETCHCOTT.......177 E5
Betley La SY3.......137 A5
Betnell Gr 2 TF7.......153 A5
BETTISFIELD.......29 C3
BETTON.......37 A6
Betton Dingle Nature
  Reserve* SY5.......171 E1
Betton Rd TF9.......36 E2
Betton St SY3.......125 D4
BETTON STRANGE.......137 F7
BETTWS-Y-CRWYN.......191 F3
Betty's La CW3.......5 A1
Beulah Dr 8 TF9.......36 B6
Bevan Cl TF1.......131 D4
Bevan Way TF9.......36 B3
Beveley Rd TF2.......131 E2
Beverley Dr DY11.......211 F3
BEWDLEY.......211 D1
Bewdley High Sch DY12.......211 D1
Bewdley Sta DY12.......211 C2
Bewdley Wribbenhall Mid
  Sch DY12.......211 E2
Bickerstaff Ct TF1.......130 D2
BICKLEY.......215 A5
Bickleywood Dr 6 LL13.......221 F5
BICTON.......193 C5
Bicton CE Prim Sch SY3.......169 F5
BICTON HEATH.......124 A7
Bicton La SY3.......169 F6
Bieston Cl LL12.......221 F8
Big Walls SY4.......80 A1
Bilberry Cl TF3.......143 F7
BILLINGSLEY.......200 C3
Billingsley Ct 2 SY9.......181 F3
BILMARSH.......83 C7
BINGS HEATH.......103 A1
Binweston La
  Forden with Leighton &
  Trelystan SY21.......170 F2
  Worthen with Shelve SY5.......171 C3
Birbeck Dr TF7.......152 E4
Birch Cl
  Llandysilio SY22.......94 B1
  7 Market Drayton TF9.......52 F8
  6 Ruyton-XI-Towns SY4.......80 A1
Birch Coppice 17 WV5.......190 F3
Birch Dale Ave 1 TF2.......132 A4
Birch Dr
  6 Hanwood SY5.......173 F8
  Shawbury SY4.......103 F7
Birchfield Sch WV7.......157 D5
Birch Gr
  Alveley WV15.......201 B3
  Ruyton SY4.......80 A1
Birch Hill Ave 30 WV5.......190 F3
Birchill Pl 31 WV5.......190 F3
Birch La LL13.......10 D8
Birchlands WV15.......219 B4
Birchlee Cl 2 TF2.......132 E1
Birch Mdw TF12.......152 D1
Birch Mdw Rd 4 TF12.......152 C1
Birchmore 12 TF3.......144 B1
Birch Rd SY12.......27 C2
Birch Row TF12.......161 C8
Birch St SL13.......221 D2
Birchwood Cl 5 TF2.......132 E8
Birchwood Dr
  2 Shrewsbury SY1.......113 D2
  Whittington SY1.......41 F2
Birchwood Gr SY13.......32 E5
BIRDSGREEN.......201 C4
BIRTLEY.......184 C1
Bishopdale TF3.......153 B8
BISHOP'S CASTLE.......181 E3
Bishop's Castle Bsns Pk
  SY9.......181 F3
Bishop's Castle Com Hospl
  SY9.......181 F3
Bishop's Castle Prim Sch
  SY9.......181 F3
Bishop's Castle Rly Mus*
  SY9.......181 E3
Bishops Castle St SY15.......174 B3
Bishops Cl 3 SY11.......78 D8
Bishops La 8 TF9.......36 B1
Bishop St SY2.......125 E6
Bishops Wlk TF2.......132 D7
BISHOPS WOOD.......148 F8
Bishton Rd WV7.......156 F4
BITTERLEY.......207 F4
Bitterley CE Prim Sch
  SY8.......207 F4
Bitterley Cl SY8.......217 F5
Bitterley La SY8.......208 A3
Blackbird Cl TF3.......131 D1
Blackbridge La SY10.......76 A3
BLACKFORD.......198 B1
Blackfriars SY1.......59 A8
Black Gate St 17 SY11.......58 E8
Blackmere Cl TF10.......109 D2
BLACKMORE.......171 E8
Blackmore Gr SY13.......15 A8
BLACKOE.......14 B3
BLACK PARK
  Chirk.......7 A5
  Whitchurch Urban.......2 E2
Blackpit La WV5.......190 F5
Black Pk Rd
  Whitchurch SY13.......15 B8
  Whitchurch Urban SY13.......2 E2
Blacksmiths Dr 8 TF2.......131 F1
Blacksmiths La SY4.......85 F5
Blackstone Dr 3 TF2.......132 D3
Blackthorn Cl 9 TF5.......130 C8

Blaizefield Cl CW3.......5 A2
Blakemere Cl 2 SY13.......2 B1
Blakemore TF3.......144 B1
Blakemore's Bank SY3.......137 B6
Blakenham Ct 5 TF4.......143 D2
Blakeway Cl TF12.......161 E7
Blakeway Hollow TF13.......159 C4
Blakeway Mews 3 SY4.......124 A7
Blashfield Rd SY8.......217 F4
Bleachfield SY3.......173 F8
Blenheim Cl SY11.......41 A1
Blenheim Cres 1 WV7.......156 F8
Blenheim Rd 11 TF1.......131 A7
BLETCHLEY.......51 E8
Bletchley Rd SY13.......34 D3
Blews Hill 11 TF4.......143 E4
Blews Hill Ct TF4.......143 E4
BLISTS HILL.......163 B3
Blists Hill Victorian Town*
  TF7.......153 A3
Blithe Cl TF12.......152 D2
Blodwel Bank SY10.......75 D5
Bloomfield Cl 3 WV5.......190 E3
Bloomsbury Ct 1 TF2.......120 D1
BLOREHEATH.......37 E3
Blore Rd TF9.......37 E1
BLUEBELL.......128 F1
Bluebell Cl 10 SY21.......159 F1
Bluebell Coppice 4 TF1.......131 E1
Blue Bell Dr SY2.......170 B7
Bluebell Rd TF6.......128 F2
Bluegate 2 TF11.......146 A4
Blue House La WV7.......157 B7
BLYMHILL.......135 F5
Blythe Gdns TF2.......132 D5
Blything Ct 10 WV16.......200 E2
Boatwell Mdw
  Dawley Hamlets TF4.......152 D8
  Dawley TF4.......143 D1
BOBBINGTON.......189 F1
Bockleton Rd WR15.......220 C1
Bodbury Cl 4 SY4.......216 D7
Boddington Cres 1 TF3.......144 D4
Bodhyfryd 4 LL12.......221 D4
Body Rd TF2.......120 D3
Bogey La SY5.......173 B4
Bog Hall La TF9.......71 D4
Bog La WR15.......220 C4
BOG THE.......176 C4
BOLAS HEATH.......107 B8
Bollingale Ave 5 TF2.......132 A4
BOMERE HEATH.......108 C2
Bomere Heath CE Prim Sch
  SY4.......100 C3
BONINGALE.......157 B2
Boningale Cl 13 TF3.......144 C1
BOOLEYBANK.......86 A8
Booley La SY4.......85 F5
Booley Rd SY4.......85 E5
Boot St
  18 Welshpool SY21.......170 B6
  Whittington SY11.......41 F3
BORASTON.......214 E4
Boraston Bank WR15.......220 E7
Boraston La WR15.......220 D7
Border Cl 3 SY11.......58 F7
Border Ret Pk LL13.......221 E3
Border The TF3.......144 B6
Borderway WR15.......220 D6
Borfa Gn SY21.......170 B7
Borle Brook Ct WV16.......200 E2
BORRAS.......221 F7
Borras Pk Rd LL12.......221 F6
Borras Rd LL12.......221 F5
Boscobel Cl 8 TF3.......144 D1
Boscobel Dr 8 SY1.......113 D2
Boscobel House* ST19.......148 F5
Boscobel Pl TF9.......52 D4
Boscobel Rd TF9.......153 B8
Bostock Cl 3 TF5.......130 A7
Bostock Cres TF3.......153 B8
Botany Bay Cl 3 TF4.......144 A1
Botfield Cl
  Albrighton WV7.......157 B6
  Telford Dawley TF3.......144 C3
Botfield Rd TF11.......146 A5
Botterham La DY3.......190 F7
Boughey Rd TF10.......109 F2
Bould La TF12.......161 D2
BOULDON.......197 D4
Boulmer Ave WV7.......156 F8
Boulton Grange 5 TF3.......144 D3
Bournbrook Gdns TF3.......153 B8
Bournside Dr TF3.......153 B8
BOURTON.......186 C7
Bourton Cl 8 TF3.......144 C1
Bourton Rd TF13.......159 D4
BOWBROOK.......124 B5
Bowbrook Grange SY4.......124 B5
Bowdler Cl SY4.......217 E4
Bowens Field SY4.......66 A7
Bower End La SY7.......158 A6
Bowers Cl 1 WV16.......218 D5
Bower Yd TF8.......152 C3
Bowkers La SY13.......13 C5
Bowland Ct TF3.......143 D8
Bowlers Alley WV7.......156 C8
Bowling Gn Cl 14 SY4.......181 F3
Bowling Gn La
  Albrighton WV7.......156 D5
  20 Knighton LD7.......203 B3
  2 Welshpool SY21.......170 B6
BOWLING GREEN.......87 F8
Bowring Gr TF1.......159 C4
Bow Way SY4.......100 F4

Box La LL12.......221 E8
Boyd Cl TF3.......144 C7
Bracewell Dr 8 SY3.......124 E4
Brackenfield TF3.......153 B8
Bracken Cl SY3.......131 A3
Bracken Rise 3 SY12.......27 A3
Bracken Way 3 TF10.......109 F4
Brackley Dr SY3.......124 D7
Bradbury La DY7.......201 F6
Bradeley Gn La SY13.......1 F6
Bradele Rd SY13.......49 B7
Bradford St
  Shifnal TF11.......145 F4
  Shrewsbury SY2.......125 E6
Bradley Ct 4 TF2.......132 E6
Bradley Farm La SY14.......1 C7
Bradley Fields
  Donnington TF2.......132 D6
  Oswestry SY11.......58 C8
BRADLEY GREEN.......1 A8
Bradley Rd
  Oakengates/Donnington
  TF2.......132 D6
  Wrexham LL13.......221 B3
Bradleys The 1 SY1.......114 B3
BRADNEY.......189 B6
Braemar Rd SY3.......166 C2
Braggington La SY5.......168 A5
Braithwaite Row TF1.......132 D2
Bramble Ridge WV16.......218 F6
Brambles The
  Crewgreen SY5.......167 F6
  1 The Rock TF3.......143 E7
Bramblewood TF12.......152 D1
Bramblewood Cl LL14.......23 E6
Bramley Cl 3 SY1.......125 E8
Bramley Way 8 DY12.......211 C2
BRAMPTON BRYAN.......204 E3
Brampton Rd
  Bishop's Castle SY9.......181 F2
  Lydbury North SY7.......182 A1
Bramwell Ct 3 TF7.......132 C3
Branches Cl 5 DY12.......211 C1
BRANDHILL.......195 D2
Brandlee TF4.......143 E4
Brandon Ave TF5.......130 B7
Brandon Gr 4 TF1.......131 A7
Brands Farm Way TF3.......144 D4
Brands Mdw 16 TF12.......132 F8
BRANDWOOD.......64 E1
Brandywell Rd TF12.......152 D1
BRANSLEY.......209 C2
Brantley Cres 1 DY7.......189 F1
Brantley La
  Claverley WV5.......189 F2
  Trysull & Seisdon WV5.......190 A6
Brassey Cl 2 SY3.......125 D4
Bratch Comm Rd WV5.......190 A5
Bratch La WV5.......190 F4
Bratch Pk 1 WV5.......190 F4
BRATCH THE.......190 F4
BRATTON.......130 A3
Bratton Rd TF5.......130 A7
BREADEN HEATH.......28 E6
Bream Cl 3 TF2.......132 A6
Brecknock Ct 2 TF1.......131 A4
Bredon Cl WV7.......157 A5
Breidden Cl 5 SY10.......58 C7
Breidden Mdw SY21.......167 D3
Breidden Pl
  Trewern SY21.......167 B2
  Wellington TF1.......130 C6
Breidden View
  Frankwell SY3.......125 A6
  Middletown SY21.......167 D3
Breidden Way SY3.......136 E6
Brereton TF3.......153 C8
Brewery Pl 20 LL11.......221 C3
Briar Cl 8 SY5.......172 E4
Briars The SY21.......170 B6
Briarswood LL11.......221 B8
Briarwood 7 TF3.......144 B1
Brickbridge La WV5.......190 F3
Brickhill La TF1.......131 E3
Brick Kiln Bank TF7.......152 D7
Brick Kiln La TF7.......152 B2
Brick Kiln Way 8 TF12.......132 E7
Bricklin Mews TF1.......131 E5
Bridge Bank TF13.......152 C3
Bridge Cl 8 TF2.......132 A6
Bridgeend La SY7.......204 B5
Bridgeford Way 8 SY2.......125 F8
Bridge La SY5.......169 F1
Bridgeman Ct TF11.......135 F2
Bridgeman Rd SY11.......58 F8
BRIDGEMERE.......204 F7
Bridgemere CE Prim Sch
  CW5.......4 F8
Bridgemere Gdn World*
  CW5.......4 D8
Bridgemere Mews CW5.......4 D8
Bridgenorth Rd WV5.......190 C3
Bridgenorth Sports & Leisure
  Ctr WV16.......218 F6
Bridge Rd
  Alveley WV15.......201 B3
  Broseley TF12.......152 B1
  Dawley TF4.......143 C3
  2 Market Drayton TF9.......36 A1
  Much Wenlock TF13.......159 D4
  Wellington TF1.......130 D3
BRIDGES.......177 A3
Bridges Bsns Pk The
  TF4.......143 C3
Bridge Sea Mdw SY7.......204 B5
Bridge Sq TF2.......132 A5

Bridge St
  Bridgnorth WV16.......218 F4
  8 Clun SY7.......193 D3
  Knighton LD7.......203 B3
  1 Oakengates/Donnington
  TF2.......132 A2
  13 Shrewsbury SY1.......125 B6
  21 Wrexham LL13.......221 C3
Bridgewater St SY4.......83 B1
Bridgewater Dr 14 WV5.......190 F4
Bridgewater St 2 SY13.......15 A7
Bridge Way
  Oakengates/Donnington
  TF2.......132 B2
  Shawbury SY4.......103 D8
BRIDGNORTH.......218 D3
Bridgnorth Ave 40 WV5.......190 F3
Bridgnorth Castle*
  WV16.......218 E3
Bridgnorth Coll of Further Ed
  WV15.......219 A3
Bridgnorth Endowed Sch
  Tech Coll WV16.......218 F6
Bridgnorth Hospl WV16.......218 E5
Bridgnorth Rd
  Broseley TF8.......161 D7
  Dawley Hamlets TF3.......153 B8
  Highley WV16.......200 E2
  Madeley TF7.......153 C7
  Much Wenlock TF13.......159 E4
  Stockton TF11.......163 B5
  Sutton Maddock TF11.......154 A1
  Trysull & Seisdon WV6.......190 F3
  Wolverley & Cookley DY11.......211 F7
  Wombourne WV5.......190 F3
Bridgnorth Sta WV16.......218 D4
Bridgwater Cl 6 TF4.......144 A2
Bridgwood 7 TF3.......144 C1
Bridle Ct TF7.......153 A6
Bridle Rd 4 TF7.......152 F5
Bridle Terr TF7.......153 A5
Bridleways The SY6.......216 D5
Bridleway The 5 TF9.......36 B1
Briery Bank TF7.......152 D6
Briery La SY3.......124 A6
Briggs La SY10.......76 A1
Briggs Way TF2.......132 C4
Bright St LL13.......221 B3
Brightwell Cl SY3.......125 E2
BRIMFIELD.......213 B2
Brimstree Dr TF11.......145 F3
Brindley Cl
  5 Albrighton WV7.......157 A5
  1 Wombourne WV5.......190 E3
Brindleyford TF3.......153 B8
BRINETON.......135 F8
Bringewood Cl SY8.......217 C6
Bringewood Rd SY8.......217 C6
Bringewood Rise TF1.......130 D3
Britannia Way TF1.......131 C5
Britons La WV16.......187 E8
Britten Ct 8 TF1.......130 E3
Brixton Way SY3.......124 E4
Brixton Way Ret Pk SY1.......113 F4
BRJ Cath Coll The TF1.......130 E6
Broadhaven Cl 1 SY1.......113 C2
Broadhay Rd SY4.......49 F4
Broadlands Way 6 SY11.......59 B8
BROAD LANES.......201 D7
Broad Mdw La TF7.......152 D6
BROAD OAK.......113 D7
Broad Oaks 2 TF3.......144 D3
BROAD OAK.......201 D7
Broad Oak Cres SY3.......137 A6
Broad Oaks TF3.......144 D3
Broad St
  Knighton LD7.......203 B2
  Ludlow SY8.......217 C4
  9 Montgomery SY15.......174 B3
BROADSTONE.......197 C8
Broadstone Mews 2
  TF4.......152 F8
Broadway
  Hadley TF1.......131 D3
  Newport TF10.......110 A3
  Shifnal TF11.......145 F5
Broadway Ave TF2.......132 A6
Broadway Cl
  10 Shifnal TF1.......145 F5
  Shrewsbury SY2.......125 F1
Broadwell La WV6.......166 B2
Broadwell The 13 SY3.......124 F3
Brockford Glade TF5.......130 B7
Brock Hollow 3 TF4.......143 D3
BROCKTON
  Church Aston.......121 B6
  Lydbury North.......193 F8
  Stanton Long.......186 B4
  Sutton Maddock.......153 E4
  Worthen with Shelve.......171 B3
Brockton CE Prim Sch
  TF13.......186 A5
Brockton Cl TF7.......153 C7
Brockton Mdw SY5.......171 E3
Brockton Way TF7.......153 D6
Brockwood Copse 7
  TF1.......130 B7
Bro Gwilym LL14.......6 B8
BROGYNTYN.......40 A2
BROMDON.......208 D7
BROMFIELD.......206 D3
Bromfield Dr 2 SY3.......125 E3
Bromfield Gr 4 LL12.......221 D5
Bromfield Rd SY8.......217 B6
BROMLEY
  Hordley.......62 C2
  Worfield.......188 E6
Bromley Rd
  Ludlow SY8.......217 D5

Bromley Rd continued
  Shrewsbury SY3.......124 A7
Bromleys Cl 3 SY6.......216 D5
Bromley Way 5 TF2.......132 C2
BROMLOW.......175 F8
BROMPTON.......139 B5
BROMSTEAD.......123 E7
BROMSTEAD COMMON.......111 E1
BROMSTEAD HEATH.......123 E1
Bromyard Rd WR15.......220 E3
BRONCROFT.......197 D5
BRONINGTON.......13 A3
Bronington Pk SY13.......13 B3
Bronington VA Prim Sch
  SY13.......13 B4
Bronwylfa SY22.......93 F8
Bronwylfa Rd 12 SY21.......170 B7
Bronydre LL13.......221 B1
BRONYGARTH.......22 E7
Bronygarth Rd SY10.......23 C4
Bron-y-buckley SY21.......170 B7
Bron-y-nant 3 LL12.......221 D8
Bron-yr-efail 3 LL12.......221 D8
Brook Cl SY5.......137 B1
Brookdale
  2 Hadley TF1.......131 B4
  1 Hadley TF1.......131 C5
  5 Shifnal TF1.......145 F5
Brook Dr SY4.......65 F5
Brookes Rd 6 TF12.......161 E7
Brookfield
  Bayston Hill SY3.......136 E6
  Stirchley TF3.......144 C2
  Whitchurch SY13.......14 E8
Brookfield Cl SY10.......23 D4
Brookfield Rd SY21.......170 B7
Brookfields SY10.......23 C4
BROOKHAMPTON.......185 F1
Brook Hollow 1 WV16.......218 F6
Brookhouse Rd SY11.......58 E8
Brookhurst Way 2 TF2.......132 F8
Brook La
  Hanmer SY13.......11 F5
  Worfield WV15.......219 E5
BROOKLANDS.......1 E1
Brooklands Ave 3 TF11.......145 F3
Brooklands Pk SY7.......195 D6
Brooklands Rd WV7.......157 B5
Brooklands The 10 DY3.......190 F1
Brooklea Cl SY11.......57 E2
Brooklyn Rd SY10.......76 B1
Brook Mdw
  Church Stretton SY6.......216 E6
  5 Wellington TF5.......130 B8
Brook Rd
  Bomere Heath SY4.......100 F4
  Craven Arms SY7.......195 D6
  Madeley TF7.......153 C6
  Pontesbury SY5.......173 A4
  Shrewsbury SY3.......15 B7
  Whitchurch SY13.......15 B7
  10 Wombourne WV5.......190 F3
Brook Rise SY3.......173 A4
BROOKROW.......208 D1
Brooksbury SY6.......216 C6
BROOKSIDE.......144 C1
Brookside
  Bicton SY3.......112 A2
  2 Oakengates/Donnington
  TF2.......120 E1
  Pontesbury SY5.......173 A4
  6 Worthen with Shelve
  SY5.......171 E3
Brookside Ave
  Dawley TF3.......153 B8
  Newport TF10.......109 E3
  Stirchley & Brookside TF3.......144 D1
Brookside Cl
  Shifnal TF1.......145 F6
  10 Wombourne WV5.......190 F3
Brookside Dr WV15.......189 C6
Brookside Gdns
  2 Brewood ST19.......148 E8
  1 Westbury SY5.......169 B1
Brook St
  Shrewsbury SY3.......125 C3
  6 Welshpool SY21.......170 B6
  Wrexham LL13.......221 C3
Brook Vale 14 DY12.......211 E2
Brookvale Rd 2 TF1.......132 F1
Brook Vessons Nature
  Reserve* SY5.......176 F7
BROOMBANK.......215 E5
Broom Dr
  2 Minsterley SY5.......172 E4
  The Rock TF3.......143 F7
BROOME.......179 B1
  Cardington.......179 B1
  Hopesay.......195 B3
Broome Cl SY7.......195 B3
Broome Pl 2 SY21.......125 C2
Broome Rd
  Clungunford SY7.......195 A1
  Hopesay SY7.......195 A4
Broome Sta SY7.......195 A3
Broomfield Cl TF10.......109 D3
Broomfield Rd
  Admaston TF5.......130 A6
  Newport TF10.......109 D3
BROOMFIELDS.......169 D8
Broom Gr 8 LL13.......221 F4
Broomhall Gr SY3.......58 C6
Broomhall La
  Oswestry Rural SY10.......58 B7
  Pinhill SY4.......101 B2
Broomhurst Way 2 TF2.......120 F1
BROSELEY.......152 D1

Broseley CE Prim Sch
TF12. . . . . 152 D1
Broseley Cl
8 Shrewsbury SY2. . . . . . 125 F2
Tweedale TF7. . . . . 153 C7
Broseley Pipe Works*
TF12. . . . . 152 C1
BROUGHALL 15 F7
Brougham Sq 4 SY3. . . 125 D4
BROUGHTON. 189 F2
Broughton Rd SY1. . . . . 114 A3
Brow La SY12. . . . . 43 C7
Brown Clee CE Prim Sch
WV16. . . . . 198 E8
Brown Clee Rd WV16. . . 186 F1
BROWNHEATH 64 C7
BROWNHILL 80 C1
BROWNHILLS 36 D4
Brownlow Cres 1 SY2. . 27 B2
Brownlow Pk 2 SY2. . . . 27 B2
Brownlow Rd SY2. . . . . . 27 B2
Brownlow St SY13. . . . . . 15 A8
BROWN MOSS 4 A7
Brown Moss Nature
Reserve* SY13. . . . . . . 15 E3
Broxton Rd LL13. . . . . . 221 F4
Broxtons Wood 4 SY5. . 172 C8
BRUNANT 171 B8
Brunel Rd
Dawley TF4. . . . . 143 F5
Great Dawley TF3. . . . . . 144 A5
Brunel Way SY3. . . . . . . 125 D4
Brunlees Dr 4 TF3. . . . . 144 C3
Brydges Gate SY22. . . . . 167 B8
BRYN. 193 C8
Brynafon Cl SY10. . . . . . 26 A1
Bryn-a-glyn LL11. . . . . . 221 B7
Bryn Cain SY22. . . . . . . 92 B5
Bryncoed SY5. . . . . 168 A5
Bryndraw Terr 22 LL13. . 221 C3
Brynegiwys 2 SY5. . . . . 168 A5
Bryn Estyn Ave 1 SY13. . 14 F8
Bryn Glas
Oswestry SY11. . . . . 59 A7
Welshpool SY21. . . . . . . 170 B7
Bryn Gryffydd LL12. . . . . 221 F7
Bryn Hafod LL12. . . . . . . 221 F2
Brynhafod La 2 SY11. . . 58 C8
Brynhafod Rd SY11. . . . . 58 C8
Brynhafren Cty Prim Sch
SY5. . . . . 167 F6
Bryn La
Hanmer SY13. . . . . 11 B6
Trevern SY21. . . . . 170 E5
BRYN MAWR. 93 C2
Bryn Mawr SY3. . . . . . . 167 F6
BRYN OFFA 221 B2
Bryn Offa CE Prim Sch
SY10. . . . . 26 A1
BRYNORE 35 A5
Bryn Rd SY3. . . . . 124 F7
Bryn Rise 1 SY10. . . . . . 58 C7
Bryn Siriol
Llansantffraid SY22. . . . . 92 B6
2 Welshpool SY21. . . . . 170 C7
BRYN TANAT 93 A7
Bryncabanau Rd LL13. . . 221 D2
Bryn-y-castell 2 SY21. . 170 B5
Bryn y Castle Terr 9
SY11. . . . . 41 A8
BRYN-Y-COCHIN. 26 B4
Bryn-y-ddol SY21. . . . . . 170 B7
Brynyffynnon 9 LL11. . . 221 C3
Bryn-y-grog Hill LL13. . . 221 F1
Bryn-y-pys Cwrt 8 LL13. . 9 C8
BRYN-YR-EOS 6 D5
Bryony Rise TF3. . . . . . . 144 D3
Bryony Way TF2. . . . . . . 132 E1
Buchan Ave WV7. . . . . . 156 D8
Buckingham Cl 4 SY11. . 59 A8
Buckingham Cres 7
TF3. . . . . 144 B1
Buckingham Rd LL11. . . 221 C6
Buckland Wlk 5 TF10. . 109 F5
BUCKNELL. 204 C4
Bucknell Sta SY7. . . . . . 204 C4
BUCKRIDGE 210 D1
BUCKTON. 204 F4
Buffalo La 1 SY7. . . . . . 193 C3
BUILDWAS. 151 B6
Buildwas Bank TF8. . . . . 151 D6
Buildwas La
Buildwas TF8. . . . . 151 C7
Little Wenlock TF6. . . . . . 142 D1
Buildwas Prim Sch TF8. . 151 B6
Buildwas Rd
Buildwas TF8. . . . . 151 C6
Ironbridge TF8. . . . . 152 A4
3 Wellington TF1. . . . . . 130 C5
Bull Dingle 1 SY21. . . . 170 B6
Bull La
1 Bishop's Castle SY9. . 181 F4
Hope Bowdler SY6. . . . . 216 F3
Bull Ring
Ludlow SY8. . . . . 217 C4
Much Wenlock TF13. . . . 159 F5
Bullrush Glade TF2. . . . . 132 C4
Bulls Row SY11. . . . . . . 113 C1
BULTHY. 167 D4
Bumblehole Mdws 8
WV5. . . . . 190 F4
Bun La TF10. . . . . 123 C1
Buntingsdale Est TF9. . . 52 D4
Buntingsdale Inf Sch TF9. . 52 E4
Buntingsdale Rd TF9. . . 53 A7
BURCOTE. 219 F8

Burcot Row TF6. . . . . . . 129 E3
Burford 17 TF3. . . . . 144 C1
Burford CE Prim Sch
WR15. . . . . 220 D6
Burford House Gdns*
WR15. . . . . 220 A5
Burgage Cl 2 TF9. . . . . . 36 D1
Burgage The TF9. . . . . . 36 C1
Burgess Croft 5 SY21. . 170 B7
Burgess La LL13. . . . . . . 10 C7
Burgs La SY3. . . . . 137 B5
Burleigh Cl
4 Dawley TF3. . . . . 144 C1
Tenbury Wells WR15. . . . 220 C4
BURLEY 206 C8
Burleydam Rd SY13. . . . 16 E1
Burley St 5 SY3. . . . . . . 125 C4
Burlington Cl 4 TF4. . . 144 A2
BURLTON. 64 B1
Burma Rd SY11. . . . . . . 41 B4
Burnell Cl SY3. . . . . 136 F5
Burnell Rd TF5. . . . . 130 A6
Burnham Ave SY2. . . . . . 126 B6
BURNHILL GREEN. 165 B6
Burnside TF3. . . . . 153 B8
Burnside Cl 8 SY7. . . . . 195 E5
Burnside Gdns SY3. . . . 125 B1
Burnt La SY21. . . . . 167 A1
BURRINGTON. 205 F3
Burroughs Bank TF4. . . . 152 D7
Burton Borough Sch
TF10. . . . . 110 A2
Burton Cl 6 TF4. . . . . . . 143 E4
Burtondale TF3. . . . . 153 C8
Burton Dr LL12. . . . . 221 D8
Burton St
Dawley TF4. . . . . 143 E4
Shrewsbury SY1. . . . . . . 125 D7
BURTON WESTWOOD. . . 186 D8
BURWARTON. 198 F3
Bur Way SY6. . . . . 216 A7
Burway Cl SY8. . . . . 217 B6
Burway Dr
Shrewsbury SY2. . . . . . . 125 F1
6 Whitchurch SY13. . . . 15 B7
Burway La SY6. . . . . 217 A6
Burway Rd SY6. . . . . . . 216 C6
Burway The SY6. . . . . . . 216 B7
Burway Trad Est SY6. . . 217 B6
Bury St 6 LL13. . . . . 221 D2
Bury Walls (fort)* SY4. . 68 B4
Bush Cl
Albrighton WV7. . . . . . . 157 A5
Wellington TF1. . . . . 130 D7
Bushfield Rd WV7. . . . . . 157 A5
Bush La 1 TF4. . . . . 143 F2
BUSHMOOR. 183 E2
Bushmoor Coppice Nature
Reserve* SY6. . . . . 183 D2
Butcher Row SY1. . . . . . 125 C6
Butcher's La 1 SY3. . . . 137 A6
But La SY5. . . . . 169 C4
BUTLANE HEAD 94 B7
Butler Rd
Shrewsbury SY1. . . . . . . 125 B4
Wem SY4. . . . . 66 A8
BUTLERSBANK. 86 C2
Butlers Ct 5 TF2. . . . . . 132 D3
Buttercup Cl 6 TF1. . . . 144 C3
Buttercup Way 4 SY3. . 125 D3
Butterfield La SY7. . . . . . 194 B1
Buttermere Dr 2 TF2. . 132 D1
Butterwick Dr 2 SY1. . . 113 C2
Buttery Gr TF2. . . . . 132 B3
BUTTINGTON. 170 D7
Buttington Cross SY21. . 170 D7
Buttington Rd SY21. . . . 170 D7
BUTTONBRIDGE. 210 E6
Button Bridge La DY12. . 210 F7
BUTTONOAK. 210 F5
Buttonwood Glade 3
TF1. . . . . 131 D2
Butts Rd
Market Drayton TF9. . . . . 36 B1
3 Wellington TF5. . . . . . 130 B8
Buxton Rd TF4. . . . . 144 A4
BWLCH-Y-PLAIN. 202 D6
Byfield 3 SY1. . . . . 113 F2
Bynd La WV16. . . . . 220 C4
Bynner St SY3. . . . . 125 D4
By Pass Rd SY1. . . . . . . 41 A8
Byron Cl 2 TF9. . . . . . . 53 A7
Bytherig SY5. . . . . 167 B4

C

CABIN 181 E4
Cabin La SY11. . . . . 41 B1
Cactus Dr 7 TF1. . . . . . 131 B7
Cadfael Dr 5 TF3. . . . . . 144 A1
Cadman Dr TF2. . . . . . . 132 F1
Cadnant Gdns 1 SY3. . . 125 A6
Cadogan Gdns 1 SY3. . 125 A6
Cae Coed SY5. . . . . 174 F1
Caegoody La SY21. . . . . 26 F4
Cae-gwilym La LL14. . . . 6 B8
Cae Gwyn Cl SY10. . . . . 58 E4
Cae Haidd SY22. . . . . . . 93 E6
Caernarvon Ave SY2. . . . 126 B6
Caernarvon Rd LL12. . . . 221 F6
Caer Rd SY11. . . . . 40 E1
Caia Rd LL13. . . . . 221 D2
CALCOTT. 169 F5
Calcott TF3. . . . . 144 D2

Calcott Cres SY3. . . . . . 124 A8
Calcott La SY3. . . . . 112 A1
Calcutts Rd TF8. . . . . . . 152 E2
Caldecott Cres 2 SY13. . 14 E7
Caldera Rd TF1. . . . . 131 E5
Calder Cl
Lilleshall & Donnington
TF2. . . . . 132 F7
5 Shrewsbury SY2. . . . . 126 B7
Caldercrofts 5 TF10. . . 109 F4
Caledonian Way TF3. . . 144 A6
CALLAUGHTON. 186 F8
Callow Cres SY5. . . . . . . 172 E3
Callow La
Minsterley SY5. . . . . 172 E4
Wheathill DY14. . . . . . . 208 D7
Callows Mdw WR15. . . . 220 C2
Calluna Dr 10 TF2. . . . . 132 F1
CALVERHALL. 34 A7
Calverhall 4 TF3. . . . . . 144 D2
Calverhall Rd SY13. . . . . 16 F1
Calverton Way 7 SY3. . 124 F3
Calvin Cl 40 WV5. . . . . . 190 F2
Camberley Cres 5 LL12. . 221 E5
Camberley Dr LL12. . . . . 221 E5
Cambria Ave. 27 A2
Cambrian Ave 1 SY11. . 41 C1
Cambrian Dr SY11. . . . . 40 F1
Cambrian Heritage Railway*
SY10. . . . . 26 A1
Cambrian Pl 3 SY11. . . 58 E8
Cambrian Visitor Ctr*
SY11. . . . . 58 E8
Cambridge Cl SY4. . . . . 83 B1
Cambridge Sq 4 LL11. . 221 D8
Camellia Dr 7 TF2. . . . . 132 F1
Camlad Cotts SY15. . . . . 174 F5
Camlad Dr SY21. . . . . . . 174 A6
Campbell Cl
Bridgnorth WV16. . . . . . 218 C4
1 Oswestry SY11. . . . . . 59 B8
Campbell Rd TF9. . . . . . 36 D2
Campion Cl TF2. . . . . . . 132 E7
Campion Way 10 DY12. . 211 E3
Camp La SY9. . . . . 181 A4
Camross Dr 2 SY1. . . . . 113 C2
Canal Rd SY22. . . . . 93 F2
Canal Side TF2. . . . . 132 C6
Canal Wood Ind Est LL14. . 23 C8
Candleberry Mdw 2
TF1. . . . . 131 E1
Candle La CW3. . . . . 4 F7
Cangeford Dr SY8. . . . . . 217 F5
Cankhorn The WV16. . . . 218 F3
Cann Hall Dr WV15. . . . 219 A5
Cann Hall Rd WV15. . . . 219 A5
Canonbie Lea 7 TF7. . . 152 F5
Canonbury SY3. . . . . . . 125 A2
Canon St SY2. . . . . 125 E6
Canonvale 2 SY3. . . . . . 125 A2
Canterbury Dr 9 SY1. . . 113 C2
Canterbury Cl 17 TF2. . . 132 F8
CANTLOP. 139 B8
Cantreyn Dr 2 WV16. . . 218 D6
Capel Cl 2 SY3. . . . . . . 125 A2
Cape St TF12. . . . . 152 C1
Capewell Rd TF2. . . . . . 131 F5
Cappoquin Dr TF2. . . . . 132 C4
Captains Mdw 2 TF3. . . 143 E7
Captain Webb Dr SY1. . 218 E3
Captain Webb Prim Sch
TF4. . . . . 143 E2
Caradoc Cres SY3. . . . . . 126 A6
Caradoc Dr SY6. . . . . . . 216 E5
Caradoc View SY5. . . . . 169 F1
CARDESTON. 169 A3
Cardinals Cl TF2. . . . . . . 132 D7
Carding Mill Valley*
SY6. . . . . 216 A8
Carding Mill Valley SY6. . 216 C7
CARDINGTON. 184 F6
Cardington Dr 2 SY1. . . 113 D3
Careswell Gdns TF11. . . 145 E3
Carline Cres 9 SY3. . . . 125 D5
Carling Cl 5 SY1. . . . . . 113 D2
Carlisle Cl 3 TF1. . . . . . 131 B7
Carlson Dr LL11. . . . . . . 221 D8
Carlton Cl SY3. . . . . 124 B6
Carlton Dr TF7. . . . . 132 E2
Carlton Rise 5 WV16. . . 200 E4
Carmarthen Gn 5 TF1. . 131 A4
Carmen Ave SY21. . . . . . 126 A6
Carnforth Cl 4 SY3. . . . 125 A1
Carnoustie Dr TF7. . . . . 153 C3
Carpenters La SY8. . . . . 206 E5
Carradine Cl SY4. . . . . . 114 F8
Carreghofa Cty Prim Sch
SY22. . . . . 93 E6
Carreghofa La SY22. . . . 93 E6
Carrington Cl 6 SY3. . . 124 D7
Cart Gate TF1. . . . . 130 D3
Cartland Ave 2 SY2. . . . 126 B7
Cartmel Cl 8 LL13. . . . . 221 F1
Cartmel Dr SY1. . . . . . . 113 E3
Cartway SY11. . . . . 218 F5
Carver's Cl TF1. . . . . . . 130 D2
Carvers Croft 2 TF13. . . 159 F4
Carvers Rd 3 TF12. . . . 161 C8
Carver St 5 SY5. . . . . . . 173 A5
Carwood 6 TF3. . . . . . . 144 D2
Castilian Dr SY13. . . . . . 14 E7
Castle Acre Rd 5 TF1. . 131 B7
Castle Cl
Tenbury Wells WR15. . . . 220 D6
1 Wrexham LL11. . . . . . 221 C7
Castle Cres LL14. . . . . . . 23 D8

Castlecroft 3 TF3. . . . . 144 D2
Castlecroft Gdns WV15. . 219 B4
Castle Ct
4 Wem SY4. . . . . 66 A6
9 Whitchurch SY13. . . . 15 A8
Castle Farm Intc TF3. . . 145 A7
Castle Farm Way
Dawley TF2. . . . . 132 F7
St Georges & Priorslee
TF2. . . . . 145 A8
Castlefields
Bridgnorth WV16. . . . . . 218 D4
8 Whittington SY11. . . . 41 E3
CASTLE FIELDS. 125 E7
Castlefields Prim Sch
WV16. . . . . 218 D4
Castlefields Way
Dawley Hamlets TF4. . . . 152 F7
Dawley TF3. . . . . 144 A1
Hadley TF1. . . . . 153 A7
Castleford Rd SY8. . . . . 217 A6
Castle Foregate SY1. . . . 125 C7
Castle Gates SY1. . . . . . 125 C6
Castle Gn
1 Bishop's Castle SY9. . 181 F4
1 Pontesbury SY5. . . . . 173 A5
CASTLEGREEN. 181 F4
Castle Hill
Church Stretton SY6. . . . 184 A6
Whitchurch SY13. . . . . . 15 A7
Castle Hill View TF9. . . . 69 C6
Castle House Sch TF10. . 109 F4
Castle La
Bayston Hill SY3. . . . . . . 136 F6
Hadley TF1. . . . . 131 D5
Hadley TF4. . . . . 143 F1
13 Knighton LD7. . . . . . 203 B3
Castle Sq SY8. . . . . 217 C4
Castle St
Oswestry SY11. . . . . 193 C4
3 Hadley TF1. . . . . 131 D5
Ludlow SY8. . . . . 217 C4
Oswestry SY11. . . . . 58 E8
3 Shrewsbury SY1. . . . . 125 C6
Whittington SY11. . . . . . 41 F3
Castle Terr 6 WV16. . . . 218 F5
Castle Trad Est TF2. . . . 144 C8
Castle View
Hadley TF2. . . . . 131 E2
2 Oswestry SY11. . . . . . 58 E8
Castle View Terr SY8. . . 217 C5
Castlewalk SY11. . . . . . . 174 B3
Castle Wlk 7 SY21. . . . . 170 B5
CATCHEMS END. 211 E3
Catherton TF3. . . . . 144 D2
Catherton Rd DY14. . . . 209 D3
Catsbritch La TF6. . . . . . 142 A8
CATSTREE. 188 F7
Catstree 9 TF3. . . . . . . 144 D1
Catterals La SY13. . . . . . 15 E6
CATTERALSLANE. 15 E6
Catterick Cl 1 TF1. . . . 131 A5
Caughley Cl 2 TF7. . . . . 161 E7
Caughley Rd
Barrow TF12. . . . . 162 A5
Broseley TF12. . . . . 161 F6
Caus Castle* SY5. . . . . . 172 A6
Causemountain La SY5. . 171 F8
Cavan Dr 6 TF4. . . . . . . 143 E6
Cavell Cl 8 TF1. . . . . . . 130 F6
Cavendish Cl
3 Oakengates/Donnington
TF2. . . . . 132 A3
3 Shrewsbury SY1. . . . . 124 C7
Cavendish Sq 11 LL12. . 221 E8
Caxton Pl
6 Oswestry SY11. . . . . . 58 E8
2 Wrexham LL11. . . . . . 221 C4
CAYNHAM 213 E8
Caynham CE Prim Sch
SY8. . . . . 213 D7
Caynham Ct SY8. . . . . . 213 D7
Caynham Rd
Caynham SY8. . . . . 208 B2
Whitton SY8. . . . . 207 F1
Caynton 2 TF3. . . . . . . 144 D1
Caynton Rd TF1. . . . . . . 164 D8
Cecil Cl TF4. . . . . 143 E5
Cedar Ave
6 Ellesmere SY12. . . . . . 27 A3
Shrewsbury SY2. . . . . . . 103 F7
Cedar Cl
6 Alveley WV15. . . . . . . 201 B3
Bayston Hill SY3. . . . . . . 136 F6
7 Market Drayton TF9. . . 36 A1
St Martin's SY11. . . . . . . 24 E5
The Rock TF3. . . . . 143 E8
Wem SY4. . . . . 66 A7
Wrexham LL12. . . . . 221 D7
Cedar Dr WV7. . . . . 157 A5
Cedar Gr SY4. . . . . 66 A7
Cedars Cl SY1. . . . . 113 C1
Cedars Dr SY5. . . . . 125 E5
Cedarwood Dr 8 TF2. . . 132 E8
CEFN. 167 A1
CEFN-BYCHAN. 6 B8
CEFN CANOL. 38 C3
CEFN EINION. 181 B1
Cefn Hawys 4 SY21. . . . 170 B7
Cefn La SY10. . . . . 75 C5
Cefn-ysbin La SY21. . . . 170 A7
Ceiriog Cl LL14. . . . . 23 D8

Celandines The 2 WV5. . 190 F3
Celandine Way TF2. . . . 132 E7
Celyn Cl SY10. . . . . 23 C4
Cemetery Rd
Dawley TF4. . . . . 143 E6
Market Drayton TF9. . . . . 36 B1
Centenary Rd 1 LL13. . . 221 B2
Central Ct 3 SY13. . . . . 221 D3
Central Ave
Church Stretton SY6. . . . 216 C6
2 Hadley TF1. . . . . 131 C3
8 Wrexham LL12. . . . . . 221 E6
Central Dr SY3. . . . . 125 B3
Central Rd LL13. . . . . . . 221 B4
Central Sq 2 TF3. . . . . . 144 B6
Centre Pl WV16. . . . . . . 218 C4
Centruion Pk SY1. . . . . . 113 F3
Century La SY11. . . . . . . 59 C1
CHADWELL. 123 A1
Chaffinch Way 4 SY11. . 114 C3
Chain La SY11. . . . . 59 C1
Chainmakers Gate 7
TF3. . . . . 153 A8
Chalgrove SY1. . . . . 143 F8
Chalice Cl 10 TF2. . . . . 132 F8
Chancel Dr 4 TF3. . . . . 36 A1
Chancery Ct TF10. . . . . . 109 E3
Chancery Pk 10 TF2. . . 132 F2
Chandlers Cl SY8. . . . . . 217 C4
Chanticleer Cl 1 LL13. . 221 F4
Chantrey Ct TF9. . . . . . . 69 C6
Chantry Cl
Broseley TF12. . . . . 152 C1
Tenbury Wells WR15. . . . 220 C5
Chapel Bank TF9. . . . . . 71 B6
Chapel Cl
Bomere Heath SY4. . . . . 100 E4
3 Much Wenlock TF13. . 159 E5
48 Wombourne WV5. . . 190 F3
Chapel Cres SY4. . . . . . . 102 C5
Chapel Ct SY7. . . . . 195 A1
Chapel Gdns LL13. . . . . 10 F4
Chapel Gr 4 TF2. . . . . . 132 E1
Chapel Hill 6 SY3. . . . . 124 A7
Chapel La
Bridgnorth WV15. . . . . . 219 C2
Bronington SY13. . . . . . 13 B1
Broseley TF8. . . . . 152 E3
Chirk LL14. . . . . 6 E1
Dawley Hamlets TF3. . . . 153 A8
Ditton Priors WV16. . . . . 198 D7
Ellesmere Rural SY12. . . 26 C5
Hodnet TF9. . . . . 68 C2
Hordley SY12. . . . . 62 C3
Loggerheads TF9. . . . . . 21 C5
Longden SY5. . . . . 178 A8
Moreton Say TF9. . . . . . 52 A6
Myddle & Broughton SY4. . 83 E1
Norton in Hales TF9. . . . 20 B2
Oswestry Rural SY10. . . . 57 D3
Pant SY22. . . . . 92 F6
Rock DY14. . . . . 210 F1
Stoke upon Tern TF9. . . . 70 D7
Whixall SY4. . . . . 16 A5
Wombourne DY3. . . . . . 190 E2
CHAPEL LAWN. 203 E7
Chapel Mews SY4. . . . . . 217 C5
Chapel Rd
18 Ashley TF9. . . . . 201 B3
6 Clungunford SY7. . . . 195 A1
Hadnall SY4. . . . . 102 C5
Ironbridge TF8. . . . . 152 D3
Chapel Row SY8. . . . . . . 217 C5
Chapel St
3 Cefn-mawr LL14. . . . . 6 D8
Dawley TF4. . . . . 143 E3
3 Oakengates/Donnington
TF2. . . . . 132 B2
10 Oswestry SY11. . . . . 58 E8
Pontesbury SY5. . . . . . . 173 A4
10 Welshpool SY21. . . . 170 B6
Wem SY4. . . . . 66 A6
45 Wombourne WV5. . . 190 F3
Chapel Terr 7 TF2. . . . . 132 C5
Chapel View
Maelor South SY13. . . . . 29 C3
Trefonen SY10. . . . . 75 D8
Chapmans Cl 11 TF3. . . 144 B1
Charlecote Pk TF4. . . . . 143 E4
Charles Ave WV7. . . . . . 156 F5
Charles Parry Cl 11 SY11. . 58 F7
Charles Rd 3 TF1. . . . . 131 A4
Charles St
Chirk LL14. . . . . 6 E2
3 Oakengates/Donnington
TF2. . . . . 132 C5
Wrexham LL11. . . . . 221 D3
Charlesway 7 TF3. . . . . 53 B8
CHARLTON. 128 C3
Charlton Cl 3 SY21. . . . 170 C7
Charlton Rise SY8. . . . . . 217 E4
Charlton Sch TF1. . . . . . 130 D7
Charlton St
2 Oakengates/Donnington
TF2. . . . . 132 A2
4 Wellington TF1. . . . . . 130 D4
Charnborough Ct 8 TF2. . 132 A3
Charter Cl TF2. . . . . 132 C5
Chartwell Cl 2 TF5. . . . 130 B1
Chartwell Dr 50 WV5. . . 190 F3
Chasepool Rd DY3. . . . . 190 E1
CHATFORD. 178 C8
Chatford TF3. . . . . 144 D1
Chatford Dr 6 SY3. . . . . 125 B1
Chatwell La TF10. . . . . . 123 D1

Chatwood Ct 5 SY1 . . . . .113 E5
Chaucer Cl 5 SY11 . . . . .59 A8
Chaucer Rd 6 SY11 . . . . .59 A8
CHAVEL 169 D4
Cheapside 2 TF11 . . . . .145 F4
CHECKLEY GREEN 4 F8
Checkley La
  Checkley cum Wrinehill
   CW5 . . . . .4 F8
  5 Oakengates/Donnington
   TF2 . . . . .132 E3
CHELMARSH 200 C6
Chelmarsh 3 TF3 . . . .144 D1
CHELMICK 216 F1
Chelmick Cl 3 SY6 . . .216 D5
Chelmick Dr SY6 . . . . .216 D5
Chelsea La 22 SY21 . . .170 B6
Chelston Ave LL12 . . . .221 F8
Cheltenham Ct TF1 . . .131 A6
Chelwood Dr 4 SY1 . . .113 C1
CHEMISTRY 14 E7
Chemistry SY13 . . . . . .14 E7
CHENEY LONGVILLE 195 D8
Chepstow Dr 3 TF1 . . .131 A5
CHEQUER THE 13 C6
Cherington 1 TF3 . . . .144 D2
CHERRINGTON 107 B4
Cherry Arbor SY5 . . . . .149 E4
Cherry Bank 9 WV16 . .200 F2
Cherrybrook Dr TF12 . .152 C2
Cherry Cl
  2 Bewdley DY12 . . . .211 C2
  Wem SY4 . . . . .66 B7
Cherry Dr SY12 . . . . . .27 A2
Cherry Gr 5 TF2 . . . .143 F8
Cherry Hill Dr 6 LL12 . .221 F7
CHERRY ORCHARD 125 D6
Cherry Tree Cl TF1 . . .130 F2
Cherry Tree Dr
  Oswestry SY11 . . . . .58 F7
  St Martin's SY11 . . .24 F6
Cherry Tree Hill TF8 . .152 C7
Cherry Tree La CW3 . . . .5 A2
Cherry Way 7 TF9 . . . .36 D2
Cheshire Cl 8 TF7 . . .152 F4
Cheshire Gdns 5 TF9 . .36 C2
Cheshire St 3 TF9 . . .36 C1
Cheshire View LL13 . . .221 E4
Chester Ave SY13 . . . . .14 E8
Chesterfield Rd 8 TF4 . .144 A4
Chester Rd
  Chetwynd TF10 . . . . .109 B8
  Edgmond TF10 . . . . . .90 D3
  Hinstock TF9 . . . . . .72 A1
  Newport TF10 . . . . . .109 E6
  Weston under Lizard TF11 . . .135 C4
  Whitchurch SY13 . . . .1 E1
  Whitchurch Urban SY13 . . . .1 C2
  Wrexham LL11 . . . . . .221 D6
Chester St
  Shrewsbury SY1 . . . .125 C7
  Wrexham LL12 . . . . . .221 D3
CHESTERTON 189 D8
Chesterton 7 TF3 . . .144 D2
Chesterton Rd WV6 . . .166 A2
Chestnut Ave
  Ellesmere Rural SY12 . . .26 B6
  8 Newington SY7 . . .195 D5
  Oswestry SY11 . . . . .58 F7
  Wrexham LL12 . . . . . .221 D6
Chestnut Cl
  7 Hanwood SY5 . . . .173 F8
  Llandrinio SY22 . . . .94 B1
  8 Shrewsbury SY3 . .124 D6
  Whitchurch SY13 . . .14 F6
Chestnut Dr
  8 Bayston Hill SY3 . . .137 A6
  8 Oakengates/Donnington
   TF2 . . . . .132 A6
  11 Trewern SY21 . . .167 D3
  Wellington TF1 . . . .130 B5
  4 Worfield WV15 . . .189 A6
Chestnut Gr SY8 . . . .217 E4
Chestnut Mdw 1 SY7 . .204 C5
Chestnut Rd TF9 . . . . .53 A8
Chestnuts The
  Cross Houses SY5 . . .138 F4
  Hinstock TF9 . . . . . .71 F3
CHESWARDINE 72 F8
Cheswardine La TF11 . .162 F4
Cheswardine Prim Sch
  TF9 . . . . .73 A8
CHESWELL 120 F6
Cheswell Dr TF10 . . . .121 A5
CHETTON 187 D1
Chetwode Cl TF9 . . . . .21 C5
CHETWYND ASTON 122 A8
Chetwynd Cl 3 SY3 . . .144 C1
Chetwynd End TF10 . . .109 E3
Chetwynd Gr TF10 . . . .109 F4
Chetwynd Pk TF10 . . . .109 E8
Chetwynd Pk Deer Pk*
  TF10 . . . . .109 D5
Chetwynd Rd TF10 . . . .109 E4
Chevin Cl SY1 . . . . . .113 E5
Chichester Dr TF1 . . .131 A7
Chilcombe Dr 10 TF2 . .132 F1
Childe Rd DY14 . . . . . .209 F7
Childhood & Costume Mus*
  WV16 . . . . .218 F4
Children's Way 1 SY2 . .125 F3
CHILDS ERCALL 89 A7
Childs Ercall CE Prim Sch
  TF9 . . . . .89 B7
Chillcott Dr TF7 . . . .153 D6

Chiltern Gdns 12 TF4 . . . . .143 E4
Chilton Cl 3 SY3 . . . . .125 B1
Chimes The LL13 . . . . .221 E3
CHIPNALL 55 A3
CHIRBURY 174 E5
Chirbury 2 TF3 . . . . .144 D2
Chirbury CE Prim Sch
  SY15 . . . . .174 F5
Chirbury Gate 2 SY15 . .174 B3
Chirbury Rd SY15 . . . .174 B3
CHIRK BANK 23 E6
Chirk Castle* LL14 . . .6 A1
Chirk Com Hospl LL14 . .6 F3
Chirk Gn Rd LL14 . . . . .6 F1
CHIRK GREEN 6 E2
Chirk Rd
  Gobowen SY11 . . . . . .41 A8
  Weston Rhyn LL14 . . .23 E7
  Chirk Sta LL14 . . . .23 E8
CHIRK/Y WAUN 23 E8
Chiswick Ct 3 TF2 . . .120 D1
Chockleys Dr 5 TF2 . .131 B5
Chockleys Mdw 4 TF1 . .131 B5
CHORLEY 200 A2
CHOULTON 182 E3
Christ Church CE Prim Sch
  SY5 . . . . .149 F5
Christchurch Dr 2 SY3 . .136 F6
Christ Church La TF9 . . .53 A8
Christine Ave TF1 . . .130 D2
CHURCH ASTON 121 D8
Church Aston Inf Sch
  TF10 . . . . .121 E8
CHURCHBANK 193 C2
Church Bank
  8 Montgomery SY15 . .174 B3
  Welshpool SY21 . . . .170 B6
Church Cl
  3 Bicton SY3 . . . . .169 F5
  Forden with Leighton & Trelystan
   SY21 . . . . .170 D5
  Hadnall SY4 . . . . . .102 C5
  Lydbury North SY7 . .182 C1
  Madeley TF7 . . . . . .153 B5
  Pontesbury SY5 . . . .169 E1
  St Martin's SY11 . . .24 E5
Church Ct 8 SY11 . . . .58 D7
Church Eaton Rd TF10 . .123 D6
Churchfields SY21 . . .124 D6
Church Fields TF9 . . .20 C2
Church Hill
  5 Ellesmere SY12 . . .27 C2
  Ironbridge TF8 . . . . .152 C4
  Lawley TF4 . . . . . . .143 B6
Churchill Cl SY8 . . . .217 D3
Churchill Dr
  4 Oakengates/Donnington
   TF2 . . . . .132 B1
  Wem SY4 . . . . .66 C6
Churchill Rd
  Church Stretton SY6 . .216 D7
  Shrewsbury SY3 . . . .124 D5
  Wellington TF1 . . . .130 F2
Church La
  Baschurch SY4 . . . . .99 A8
  Bicton SY3 . . . . . . .169 F5
  Bishop's Castle SY9 . .181 F3
  3 Bobbington DY7 . .189 F1
  Boningale WV7 . . . . .157 A2
  Ellesmere Rural SY12 . .26 A6
  Gnosall TF10 . . . . . .111 D1
  Knockin SY10 . . . . . .78 A1
  Little Wenlock TF6 . .142 D2
  Llansantffraid SY22 . .92 B5
  Long Bank DY12 . . . .211 B1
  Melverley SY22 . . . .168 A7
  7 Orleton SY8 . . . .212 E2
  Rock DY14 . . . . . . .210 D2
  Sheriffhales TF11 . . .134 B5
  Shrewsbury SY3 . . . .125 B2
  Stanton upon Hine Heath
   SY4 . . . . .85 F4
  St Martin's SY11 . . .24 E5
  Tasley WV16 . . . . . .218 D6
  Trysull & Seisdon WV5 . .190 D5
  Wem Rural SY4 . . . . .66 D6
  Whitchurch Rural SY13 . .16 A4
  Whixall SY13 . . . . . .31 B2
Churchlea LL11 . . . . . .221 C8
Church Mdw
  Lilleshall TF10 . . . .121 B3
  Norton in Hales TF9 . .20 C2
  Shifnal TF11 . . . . . .145 F4
  Stanton upon Hine Heath
   SY4 . . . . .85 F4
Church Mdws SY13 . . . .2 A1
Church Par TF2 . . . . .132 A3
CHURCH PREEN 179 C1
Church Preen Prim Sch
  SY6 . . . . .185 E8
CHURCH
  PULVERBATCH 173 E1
Church Rd
  Albrighton WV7 . . . .156 F5
  8 Alveley WV15 . . .201 B3
  Barrow TF12 . . . . . .161 C3
  Baschurch SY4 . . . . .81 A1
  Brimfield SY8 . . . . .213 D2
  Broseley TF8 . . . . . .195 A1
  Clungunford SY7 . . .195 A1
  Condover SY5 . . . . .178 C5
  Dawley TF4 . . . . . . .143 F5
  High Ercall TF6 . . . .116 F7
  Ironbridge TF8 . . . .152 C5
  11 Knighton LD7 . . .203 B3
  Lilleshall TF10 . . . .121 B3
  Myddle & Broughton SY4 . .83 E4
  Newcastle on Clun SY7 . .193 A5

Church Rd continued
  1 Oakengates/Donnington
   TF2 . . . . .144 D8
  Shrewsbury SY3 . . . .125 A1
  Stanton upon Hine Heath
   SY4 . . . . .85 F4
St Georges & Priorslee
  TF2 . . . . .132 C1
  Shifnal TF11 . . . . . .190 E1
  Telford TF3 . . . . . . .144 A6
  Uffington SY4 . . . . .114 D1
  2 Welshpool SY21 . .170 B6
Church Row 4 SY3 . . .125 B2
Church St
  7 Bishop's Castle SY9 . .181 F3
  3 Bridgnorth WV16 . .218 F5
  Broseley TF12 . . . . .161 D8
  Chirk LL14 . . . . . . .23 E8
  Church Stretton SY6 . .216 C6
  Claverley WV5 . . . . .189 E4
  8 Cleobury Mortimer
   DY14 . . . . .209 E2
  9 Clun SY7 . . . . . .193 D3
  8 Condover SY5 . . .178 E8
  Ellesmere SY12 . . . .27 C2
  Hadley TF1 . . . . . . .131 D4
  11 Highley WV16 . . .200 E2
  Hinstock TF9 . . . . . .69 C6
  Hodnet TF9 . . . . . . .69 C6
  Ightfield SY13 . . . .16 E2
  10 Knighton LD7 . . .203 B3
  8 Leintwardine SY7 . .205 B5
  Ludlow SY8 . . . . . . .217 C4
  Madeley TF7 . . . . . .153 A5
  4 Market Drayton TF10 . .53 C8
  Oakengates/Donnington
   TF2 . . . . .132 A2
  Oswestry SY11 . . . . .58 D7
  Prees SY13 . . . . . . .49 D8
  Ruyton XI Towns SY4 . .80 A1
  Shawbury SY4 . . . . .103 D7
  Shifnal TF11 . . . . . .145 F3
  7 Shrewsbury SY1 . .125 A2
  Tenbury Wells WR15 . .220 C5
  9 Wellington TF1 . .130 E4
  Welshpool SY21 . . . .170 B6
  2 Whitchurch SY13 . .15 A8
  Whittington SY11 . . .41 E3
  3 Wrexham LL11 . . .221 D3
CHURCH STOKE 174 F1
CHURCH STRETTON 216 D7
Church Stretton Sch
  SY6 . . . . .216 D7
Church Stretton Sta SY6 . .216 C5
Church Terr 5 SY11 . .58 D7
CHURCHTOWN 180 F2
Church View
  4 Bewdley DY12 . . . .211 D2
  Chirk LL14 . . . . . . .23 E8
  Tibberton TF10 . . . .107 E5
  Whitchurch SY13 . . .15 A8
Church Walks TF9 . . . .20 C2
Churchward Cl 6 TF2 . .132 E2
Churchward Dr TF4 . . .143 D7
Churchway
  3 Church Stretton SY6 . .216 C6
  Telford Dawley TF3 . .144 D2
Church Wlk
  Dawley TF4 . . . . . . .143 F2
  Little Hereford SY8 . .213 E3
  Oakengates/Donnington
   TF2 . . . . .132 D7
  Wellington TF1 . . . .130 F3
Churncote SY3 . . . . . .144 D2
Churton Dr
  Whitchurch SY13 . . . .15 B7
  Wrexham LL12 . . . . . .221 E4
Cilcen Gr LL12 . . . . . .221 D5
CILCEWYDD 170 C3
Cilcoed LL14 . . . . . . .6 E3
Cinders Rd WR15 . . . .220 B1
Circular Rd WV7 . . . .147 E1
CITY 180 A5
City La SY22 . . . . . . .94 A1
City Rd TF6 . . . . .87 D1
Civic Gn SY13 . . . . . .15 C7
Clanbrooke 8 TF3 . . .144 D1
Clap Gate Gr 6 WV5 . .190 F3
Clap Gate Rd WV5 . . .190 F3
Claremont Bank 11 SY1 . .125 B6
Claremont Dr 3 WV16 . .218 D5
Claremont Hill 1 SY1 . .125 B6
Claremont Orch 2 SY8 . .218 D5
Claremont St 12 SY1 . .125 C6
Clarence Rd LL11 . . .221 C6
Clarence Way 10 DY12 . .211 D2
Clarendon Ave 8 LL11 . .221 B6
Clare's La Cl TF3 . . .143 F8
Clarkefields SY3 . . .137 A6
Clarke Rd 2 LL12 . . .221 F6
CLAVERLEY 189 E4
Claverley CE Prim Sch
  WV5 . . . . .189 E4
Claverley Dr TF3 . . .144 B1
Claverley Rd WV5 . . .189 E4
Claverly Cres SY1 . . .114 B2
Clay La SY8 . . . . .196 D2
Claypit St Terr 12 SY13 . .15 A8
Claypit St 1 SY13 . . .15 A8
Clays La TF9 . . . . . . .68 E5
Clayton Cl 2 SY8 . . .208 A1
Clayton Dr SY13 . . . .22 A1
Clayton Way SY13 . . .124 C7
CLEEDOWNTON 208 F5
Clee Gdns SY8 . . . . .217 D5
CLEEHILL 208 C2
Clee Hill Prim Sch SY8 . .208 C2

Clee Hill Rd
  Nash SY8 . . . . .214 C7
  Tenbury Wells WR15 . .220 C7
Clee Rise
  8 Highley WV16 . . . .200 D2
  Little Wenlock TF6 . .142 D2
CLEE ST MARGARET 197 F3
CLEESTANTON 208 A6
Clee Stanton Rd
  Bitterley SY8 . . . . .207 F4
  Stoke St Milborough SY8 . .208 A5
Cleeton La DY14 . . . . .208 D7
CLEETON ST MARY 208 D5
Clee Vantage 4 SY8 . .208 C2
Clee View SY8 . . . . . .217 E5
Clee View Cl SY8 . . .217 E5
Clee View Rd
  7 Bridgnorth WV16 . .218 C6
  44 Wombourne WV5 . .190 F3
Clematis Dr 8 TF1 . . .131 B7
Clemmett Cl TF10 . . . .109 E2
Cleobury La LD7 . . . .202 C4
Cleobury Mdws 4 DY14 . .209 D2
CLEOBURY MORTIMER . .209 D3
Cleobury Mortimer Leisure
  Ctr DY14 . . . . .209 D3
Cleobury Mortimer Prim Sch
  DY14 . . . . .209 D3
CLEOBURY NORTH 198 E5
Cleobury Rd DY12 . . . .211 C2
Clerc-y-mendy LL13 . . .9 D8
Clerk's Ct 18 SY21 . .170 B6
Cleveland Ave TF6 . . .116 E7
Cleveland Cl TF4 . . .143 C3
Cleveland St SY2 . . .125 E6
Cliff Cres TF6 . . . . .105 E7
Cliff Hollow SY5 . . .138 C2
Clifford Rd TF9 . . . . .53 A8
Clifford St SY2 . . . .125 E5
Cliff Rd WV16 . . . . . .218 F5
Cliffs La TF10 . . . . . .110 F8
Cliff Villas SY8 . . .217 C3
Cliff Cres 8 TF1 . . .143 C3
Clifton Cl 8 LL13 . .221 E1
Clifton St 3 SY21 . .170 A6
CLIVE 84 B5
Clive Ave SY6 . . . . . .216 C4
Clive CE Prim Sch SY4 . .84 B5
Clive Cotts SY8 . . . .217 B4
Clive Gdns SY6 . . . . .36 C1
Clive Gn 3 SY2 . . . . .125 F7
Clive Rd
  8 Market Drayton TF9 . .53 C8
  Pattingham & Patshull
   WV6 . . . . .190 B8
  Pattingham WV6 . . . .166 C2
  Shrewsbury SY2 . . . .126 A7
Clive Way SY2 . . . . . .126 A7
Clogs Bank DY12 . . . .210 F5
Cloisters The 3 TF2 . .132 A4
Clos Bryn y Ddol 2
  SY21 . . . . .170 B7
Close The
  Newport TF10 . . . . .121 E8
  7 Swindon DY3 . . . .190 F1
  The Gorge TF8 . . . .152 A7
Clos Ystrad 2 LL13 . .221 C1
Clover Gr 3 SY1 . . . .144 D3
Clover Heath 3 WV5 . .144 D3
Clowes Dr TF3 . . . . . .144 D4
Cloy La LL13 . . . . . . .9 F6
CLUDDLEY 130 A1
CLUN 193 D3
CLUNBURY 194 D3
Clunbury CE Prim Sch
  SY7 . . . . .194 E3
Clunbury Rd SY7 . . . .194 E3
Clun Castle* SY7 . . .193 C4
Clun Cl TF1 . . . . .130 C6
CLUNGUNFORD 195 A2
Clun Mus* SY7 . . . . .193 D4
Clun Rd SY7 . . . . . . .195 C5
CLUNTON 194 A4
Clunton Coppice Nature
  Reserve* SY7 . . . .194 B3
Clydesdale Dr 4 TF1 . .143 C3
Coach Central TF3 . .144 B6
Coach House Field SY8 . .217 D4
Coachman Mdw 6 TF1 . .130 C7
Coach Rd
  Shrewsbury SY3 . . . .124 A7
  The Gorge TF8 . . . .152 B5
Coachwell Cl TF3 . . .144 A6
COALBROOKDALE 152 C6
Coalbrookdale & Ironbridge
  CE Prim Sch TF8 . .152 B4
Coalbrookdale Mus of Iron*
  TF8 . . . . .152 D6
Coalbrookdale Open Air Mus
  of Steel Sculpture*
  TF8 . . . . .152 C2
Coalbrookdale Rd TF6 . .151 E8
COALMOOR 142 A3
Coalmoor La TF6 . . . .142 F2
Coalpit La SY11 . . . .41 E2
COALPORT 153 B3
Coalport China Works Mus*
  TF8 . . . . .153 B1
Coalport Cl TF12 . . .161 E8
Coalport Rd
  Broseley TF8 . . . . . .153 B1
  Madeley TF8 . . . . . .153 B4
Cobden Rd LL13 . . . .221 B3
Cob Gr SY4 . . . . .100 E4
Cobham Cres 3 DY12 . .211 D2
COBSCOT 19 F2

Cobwell Rd TF12 . . . . .152 C2
Cochion Redwood Cl
  SY21 . . . . .170 D4
Cockford Bank SY7 . . .193 C3
COCKSHUTFORD 198 B3
COCKSHUTT
  Crosemere 63 C7
  Highley 200 E2
Cockshutt CE Prim Sch
  SY12 . . . . .63 C7
Cockshutt La
  Broseley TF12 . . . . .152 D1
  7 Highley WV16 . . . .200 E2
Cockshutt Rd 2 TF2 . .132 B4
Coder Rd SY8 . . . . . .217 F4
Coed La SY15 . . . . . .174 F1
Coedlan SY5 . . . . . . .168 A5
COEDWAY 168 A6
Coed-y-ffynnon 3 LL13 . .221 C1
Coed-y-glyn 8 LL13 . .221 C1
COED Y GO 58 B4
Cokayne Gn 1 SY1 . . .113 C4
COLD HATTON 105 E7
COLD HATTON HEATH . .105 F7
Coldridge Dr 5 SY1 . .113 C1
Cold Western Dr SY8 . .217 E5
COLEBATCH 181 F2
Coleham Cty Prim Sch
  SY3 . . . . .125 D4
Coleham Head 2 SY3 . .125 D5
Coleham Pumping Sta*
  SY3 . . . . .125 C5
COLEMERE 45 C6
Colemere Dr 6 TF1 . .130 C5
COLEMORE GREEN 188 C8
College Cl 2 DY14 . .209 E2
College Ct
  Bridgnorth WV15 . . .219 B3
  Ludlow SY8 . . . . . . .217 C4
  Tenbury Wells WR15 . .220 C4
College Farm Cl 1 WV6 . .166 C3
College Gdns
  Copthorne SY3 . . . .124 F4
  Tenbury Wells WR15 . .220 C4
College Hill 9 SY1 . .125 C5
College La 6 TF1 . . .130 F5
College Rd 6 SY11 . .59 A6
College St
  Ludlow SY8 . . . . . . .217 C4
  10 Shrewsbury SY1 . .125 C3
College Terr WR15 . . .220 C5
College Yd 9 SY11 . .53 A7
Coller Mdw 8 SY2 . . .125 F7
Collett Way TF2 . . . .132 E2
Colley Cl 2 SY2 . . . .125 F8
Colliers Cl 9 TF2 . .132 D2
Colliers Way
  Dawley TF3 . . . . . . .144 A7
  Lawley & Overdale TF3 . .143 F7
Colliery Rd
  Chirk LL14 . . . . . . .6 E1
  Wrexham LL11 . . . . . .221 B6
Colliford Cl 7 TF2 . .132 F2
Collingwood Cl 7 TF11 . .146 A6
Collingwood Dr 9 SY3 . .124 B6
Collins Cl
  Blists Hill TF7 . . . .153 B3
  2 Broseley TF12 . . .161 E7
Collins Ct 8 LL13 . .221 E1
Collybrook Pk SY9 . . .208 B1
Colmere Dr 4 SY1 . . .113 D2
Colridge Ct TF2 . . . .132 E7
Colstey Bank SY7 . . .193 D7
Columbine Way 2 TF2 . .132 B4
Colwyn Rd LL13 . . . . .221 E3
Coly Anchor SY10 . . .96 B6
Combermere Abbey*
  SY13 . . . . .3 D5
Combermere Ct 5 TF9 . .36 D2
Combermere Dr
  9 Shrewsbury SY1 . .113 D2
  8 Wellington TF1 . .130 D5
COMBERTON 212 E2
Combsville La 2 SY11 . .40 F1
Com Coll The SY9 . . .181 F3
Comet Dr SY1 . . . . . .113 E1
COMLEY 184 D7
Commercial Way 6 TF2 . .132 B2
Common La DY14 . . . . .209 C3
Common Rd WV5 . . . . .190 F2
COMMON THE 71 B3
Common The
  Bomere Heath SY4 . .100 F4
  Oakengates/Donnington
   TF2 . . . . .132 D7
Compton Mews 8 SY5 . .169 C4
Comptons The TF9 . . . .73 A8
Concord Coll SY5 . . .179 C4
Concorde TF4 . . . . . .143 E5
CONDOVER 178 D8
Condover CE Prim Sch
  SY5 . . . . .137 C1
Condover Dr SY2 . . . .125 F1
Condover Horizon SY5 . .178 E8
Condover Ind Est SY5 . .178 F6
Condover Way TF2 . . .52 D4
Conduit La WV16 . . . .218 D4
Conery La SY13 . . . . .13 D2
Coneybury View TF12 . .161 E8
Coney Gn
  10 Oswestry SY11 . .58 E8
Coney Gn Way TF3 . . .130 D7
Coningsby Rd WV7 . . .156 D8
Coniston Dr 12 TF2 . .132 D1
Coniston Rd 5 SY11 . .113 F3
Coniston Way 10 DY12 . .211 C2
Conjurer's Dr 25 LD7 . .203 B3

Conners La TF10 . . . . 109 A3
Connomara Mdw 4 TF4 143 D3
Connor Cres LL13 . . . . .221 E2
Connynger Cres 6 SY2 .125 F7
Conroy Dr TF4 . . . . .143 E4
Constable Dr 9 TF5 . . . .130 B8
Constitution Hill 10 TF1 .130 E4
Conway Dr SY2 . . . . .126 A7
Cooke Dr TF4 . . . . .144 A2
Cookscross WV15 . . . . . . .201 B3
Cooks La SY13 . . . . .1 D6
Coolock Cl 3 SY3 . . . . . . .124 F1
Cooper Cl TF2 . . . . .144 F8
Coopers Cl 2 LL13 . . . . . .221 F5
Coopers Field 3 SY11 . . .24 F7
Coopers La SY11 . . . . .24 F6
Copall Paddock 12 SY9 .181 F3
Copelea TF9 . . . . .72 F8
Copes La SY12 . . . . .28 D3
Copley La WV6 . . . . .166 A3
Copper Beech Rd TF1 . .131 C3
Copperfield 2 WV16 . . .218 C6
Copperfield Dr
  1 Oakengates/Donnington
    TF2 . . . . .132 D8
  Shrewsbury SY3 . . . . . .124 D5
Coppice Cl
  4 Madeley TF7 . . . . .153 C5
  Shawbury SY4 . . . . .85 D1
Coppice Dr
  Chetwynd TF10 . . . . . . .109 E5
  1 Craven Arms SY7 . .195 D5
  High Ercall TF6 . . . . . . .116 E8
  Oakengates/Donnington
    TF2 . . . . .132 C4
  Oswestry SY11 . . . . .40 F1
COPPICEGATE 210 E7
Coppice Holt Rd 1 TF5 .130 A7
Coppice La SY13 . . . . .31 E5
Coppice Rd 3 TF11 . . . .146 A6
Coppice The 8 TF9 . . . . .36 B1
Copse Hill La TF13 . . . . . .159 D8
COPTHORNE 124 E6
Copthorne Crest 3 SY3 .124 C6
Copthorne Dr 2 SY3 . . .124 F6
Copthorne Gdns 5 SY3 .124 C6
Copthorne Pk SY3 . . . . . .124 C6
Copthorne Rd 3 SY3 . . .124 C6
Copthorne Rise 1 SY3 . .125 B6
COPTIVINEY 27 F6
Corbet Ave SY4 . . . . .85 D1
Corbet Cl
  Dawley TF4 . . . . .143 E1
  Shrewsbury SY1 . . . . . .113 D5
Corbet Ct TF9 . . . . .36 C1
Corbet Dr TF9 . . . . .19 A4
Corbet Gr TF9 . . . . .52 E5
Corbet Sch The SY4 . . . . .81 B1
Corbett Cl TF4 . . . . .143 E1
Cordingley Way TF2 . . . .132 C6
Cordle Marsh Rd 1
  DY12 . . . . .211 E3
Cordwell Pk SY4 . . . . .66 B6
Cordy La WV7 . . . . .157 B8
CORELEY 214 E8
Corfield Cres 3 TF2 . . . .132 A3
CORFTON 196 F3
CORFTON BACHE 196 E4
Coricks Rise 1 SY9 . . . .181 F3
Corinthian Dr SY2 . . . . . .125 F8
Cormill Sq SY1 . . . . .125 D7
CORNBROOK 208 D3
Cornbrook 5 TF3 . . . . . . .144 D2
Corndean Mdw TF3 . . . .143 D7
Corndon Cl 2 SY1 . . . . . .114 A2
Corndon Cres SY1 . . . . . .114 A3
Corndon Dr
  13 Montgomery SY15 . .174 B3
  3 Shrewsbury SY1 . . .114 A3
Corndon Rd 3 SY1 . . . . .114 A2
Cornelia Cres 7 SY2 . . .125 F6
Cornelie Cl SY8 . . . . .208 D2
Corner Farm Dr SY3 . . . .124 A6
Cornfield Cl SY4 . . . . .100 F4
Cornflower Gr 1 TF1 . . .131 E1
Cornmell La TF2 . . . . .132 A3
Corns Gr 55 WV5 . . . . . . .190 F2
Cornwall Ave 1 SY11 . . . .41 A7
Cornwall Dr SY3 . . . . .137 A5
Cornwall Gdns WR15 . . .220 C5
Cornwallis Dr 4 TF11 . . .146 A5
Coronation Ave SY8 . . . .217 B5
Coronation Cres TF7 . . .153 B6
Coronation Dr
  Chirk LL14 . . . . .6 E2
  Oakengates/Donnington
    TF2 . . . . .132 D8
Coronation Rd 4 SY7 . .195 D6
Coronation St
  Cefn-mawr LL14 . . . . .6 C8
  3 Highley WV16 . . . . .200 F2
Corporation La
  Pimhill SY1 . . . . .113 B1
  Shrewsbury SY1 . . . . . .125 B8
Corporation St 10 SY9 .181 F3
CORRA COMMON 17 C1
Corra Mdws SY13 . . . . . . .34 A7
Corra Pl SY13 . . . . .34 A8
Corsten Dr SY2 . . . . .126 A8
Corvedale CE Prim Sch
  SY7 . . . . .196 F4
Corvedale Rd SY7 . . . . . .195 E5
Corve St SY8 . . . . .217 C5
Corve View TF8 . . . . .217 B6
Corve Wlk TF2 . . . . .132 D5
Coseley Ave SY2 . . . . .126 B7
Cosford Airfield WV7 . . .156 C6

Cosford Sta WV7 . . . . . . .156 D7
Cote Rd TF5 . . . . .130 C8
Cotes Cres 9 SY3 . . . . . .124 A7
COTON 31 F1
Coton Cres 4 SY1 . . . . . .125 C8
Coton Gn SY1 . . . . .125 B8
Coton Hill SY1 . . . . .125 B8
COTON HILL. 125 B8
Coton Hill SY1. . . . . .125 C7
Coton La SY11 . . . . .201 B5
Coton Mount SY1 . . . . . .125 B8
COTONWOOD 31 F5
Cotshore Dr 18 SY3 . . . .124 F3
Cotswold Dr
  Albrighton WV7 . . . . . . .157 B5
  Teford TF3 . . . . .144 C4
Cottage Cl 5 TF7 . . . . . . .153 C5
Cottage Cl 9 TF11 . . . . .145 F3
Cottage Farm Cl TF7. . .153 B5
Cottage Fields SY1 . . . . . .24 F6
Cottage La SY11 . . . . .24 F6
COTTONWOOD 111 E6
COTWALL 117 B8
Cotwall La TF6 . . . . .117 A8
Cotwall Rd TF6 . . . . .116 F7
Coughs Jitty TF12 . . . . . .152 C2
COUND 131 C5
Cound Cl TF1 . . . . .130 C5
COUNDLANE 149 A6
COUNDMOOR 179 E5
Country Mdws TF9 . . . . . .52 F8
Country Pk Halt Sta
  WV16. . . . . .200 F3
County La WV7 . . . . .157 F4
Courthouse La SY3 . . . . . .93 C1
Courtland Dr 7 TF2 . . . .132 A6
Court Rd
  Madeley TF7 . . . . .153 B6
  Wrexham LL13 . . . . .221 B1
Court St TF7 . . . . .153 B5
Courts The 4 WV7 . . . . .156 F5
Court The TF7 . . . . .153 B3
Covert La WV16 . . . . .200 C4
COXALL 204 E5
COXBANK 18 F8
COXGREEN. 201 F5
Crab La DY7 . . . . .190 B1
Crabtree La
  Ercall Magna TF6 . . . . .104 E1
  3 Wem TF6 . . . . .66 A7
Crabtree Wlk 1 LD7 . . .203 B3
CRACKLEYBANK 134 C2
Crackshall La TF4. . . . . . .152 B8
Craft Way TF2 . . . . .120 E1
Craig Cl 5 SY1 . . . . .114 B3
CRAIG-LLWYN 56 F4
Craigmillar Rd 2 LL12 . .221 D4
CRAIGNANT. 22 D3
Craig Way 2 LL12 . . . . . .221 E6
Craig Wlk 11 WV15. . . . .219 A4
Cralves Mead WR15. . . . .220 C5
Cramer Gutter La DY14 .209 B6
Cramer Gutter Nature
  Reserve* DY14. . . . . . .209 B6
Crampton Ct SY11 . . . . . .59 B7
Cranage Cres TF1 . . . . . .130 C3
Cranbrook Dr 5 SY11 . . .40 D1
Crane Hollow 28 WV5 . .190 F3
Cranford Rd LL13 . . . . . . .221 F1
Cranmere TF3 . . . . .144 D2
Cranmore Dr 6 WV16 . .200 D7
CRATEFORD. 200 D7
Crathie Pl 4 LL11 . . . . . .221 C6
CRAVEN ARMS. 195 F5
Craven Arms Rd SY7 . . .195 A4
Craven Arms Sta SY7 . . .195 E6
Crawford Mdw 11 SY3 .124 E4
Crawstone Cl 7 TF2 . . . .132 D3
CREAMORE BANK 48 A1
Creamore Cnr SY4. . . . . . .66 B8
Crescent Cl 1 LL13 . . . . .221 E3
Crescent Fields SY1 . . . .125 B5
Crescent La SY1 . . . . .125 B5
Crescent Pl WR15. . . . . . .220 D3
Crescent The
  Hadley TF1. . . . . .131 C4
  Wellington TF1. . . . . . . .130 D5
  Wrexham LL13 . . . . .221 D1
Crescent The
  Bomere Heath SY4 . . . .100 E4
  3 Cleehill SY8 . . . . .208 C2
  2 Craven Arms SY7 . .195 E5
  Lawley TF4. . . . . .143 B5
  Montford Bridge SY4 . .169 E5
  Much Wenlock TF13. . . .159 E5
  Nesscliff SY4 . . . . .97 E4
  Newport TF10 . . . . .171 F8
  Oakengates/Donnington
    TF2 . . . . .132 D7
  Sheriffhales TF11 . . . . .134 C5
  Tenbury Wells WR15 . . .220 D3
CRESSAGE 149 F5
Cressage Ave 6 SY11 . .113 D3
Cresswell Ct SY5 . . . . . . .124 B5
Crest Rd 6 TF2 . . . . .132 E3
Crest The TF3 . . . . .144 A8
Crestwood Cl 21 SY11. . .58 E8
Crewe St SY1 . . . . .125 C8
CREWGREEN. 167 F6
Crews Pk TF12 . . . . .152 C2
Cricketers La 7 TF2 . . . .132 E3
Cricket Mdw WV16. . . . . .218 E6
CRICKHEATH. 57 A7
CRICKMERY. 71 C7
CRIFTINS 25 D5
Criftins CE Prim Sch SY12 .26 B5
Criftins The 1 SY12. . . . .205 B5
CRIGGION. 147 C5
Criggion Cl SY22. . . . . . . .94 A2

Criggion La SY5 . . . . .167 C5
Crispin La LL11. . . . . .221 B5
Crockington Cl WV5 . . . .190 C5
Crockington La WV5 . . . .190 D5
Crocus Dr 3 SY3 . . . . . . .125 D3
CROESAU BACH. 57 B4
Croesnewydd Rd LL11. . .221 A4
Croeswylan Cl SY10 . . . . .58 C6
Croeswylan Cres SY11 . .58 D6
Croeswylan La SY10. . . . . .58 C5
Croft Cl SY5 . . . . .171 E3
Crofters View TF6 . . . . . .142 D3
Croft Fold 1 TF4 . . . . . . .143 E5
Croft Rd SY21 . . . . .170 B6
Crofts The TF7 . . . . .152 D6
Croft The
  Bridgnorth WV15. . . . . . .219 A5
  5 Wombourne WV5 . . .190 E3
Croft Way TF9 . . . . .36 B1
Crogen 6 LL14 . . . . .6 E3
Cronk Hill SY4. . . . . .84 D4
CROSEMERE. 63 D8
Crosemere Cres SY12 . . .63 D7
Crosemere Ct SY12 . . . . .63 D7
Crosemere La SY12 . . . . .63 D7
Crosemere Rd SY12 . . . . .63 D7
CROSS. 27 A6
Crossbank TF3 . . . . .144 E2
Cross Bank SY6. . . . . .216 A4
Crossfields TF6 . . . . .116 E8
CROSSGREEN 112 E5
CROSS GREEN. 129 D6
Cross Hill 4 SY1 . . . . . . .125 B5
Cross Hill Cl SY1 . . . . . . .125 B5
Crosshill La TF9 . . . . .90 A6
CROSS HOUSES
  Berrington 138 F3
  Bridgnorth 218 B2
Cross La
  Bayston Hill SY3 . . . . . .137 B6
  Llansantffraid SY22. . . . .92 E4
CROSSLANES 95 F2
Cross Lanes
  Ellesmere Rural SY12 . . .25 E6
  Selattyn & Gobowen SY10. .40 A7
Crosslikey Cl SY15 . . . . .181 A8
Cross Rd
  Albrighton WV7 . . . . . . .156 F4
  Bausley with Criggion SY5. .167 B6
  1 Oakengates/Donnington
    TF2 . . . . .132 B4
Cross Roads SY3. . . . . . . .137 B6
Cross St
  1 Ellesmere SY12 . . . . . .27 C2
  Market Drayton TF9 . . . .36 D1
  Oswestry SY11 . . . . .58 E8
  3 Shrewsbury SY1 . . .125 C7
  Tenbury Wells WR15 . . .220 C4
  Wrexham LL11 . . . . .221 C5
Cross The 8 SY4 . . . . .41 A7
Crossways
  1 Church Stretton SY6. .216 D5
  7 Wrexham LL13 . . . . .221 E4
Crossways The 1 . . . . . .195 B2
Crowdale Rd TF5 . . . . . . .130 B8
CROWGREAVES 163 F3
Crow Hill La SY5. . . . . . . .171 E3
Crow La
  Childs Ercall TF9 . . . . . . .89 B8
  Ollerton Lane TF9 . . . . . .70 F2
  Upton Magna SY4 . . . . .115 C3
Crowmeole Dr SY3. . . . . .124 D5
Crowmeole La 6 SY3 . . .124 E4
Crowmere Gn 2 SY2 . . .125 F6
Crowmere Rd 2 SY2 . . .125 E6
Crown Cty Prim Sch
  SY2. . . . . .125 F6
Crown La SY8 . . . . .216 A2
Crown La
  Church Stretton SY6 . . .216 A2
  Cressage SY5 . . . . .149 D4
  Crown Mews TF10 . . . . .109 F3
Crown St
  Great Dawley TF4 . . . . .143 F3
  1 Wellington TF1. . . . .130 E4
  3 Wem SY4 . . . . .66 A6
CROWSNEST. 176 E8
Croxon Rise SY11. . . . . . . .59 B8
CRUCKMEOLE 173 D8
Cruckmoor La SY13. . . . . .49 D5
CRUCKTON 169 E1
Cruckton Cl SY3 . . . . .124 D5
Cruckton Hall Gdns SY5. .169 D1
Cruckton Hall Sch SY5. .169 D1
CRUDGINGTON 106 A1
Crudgington Prim Sch
  TF6. . . . . .106 A2
Crudgington Rd SY4. . . .120 E1
CRUMPSBROOK 208 F5
Crundalls La DY12 . . . . . .211 E3
Cuckoo Oak Gn TF7 . . . .153 D6
CUCKOO'S CORNER 30 A8
Cuckoo's Rest 8 TF4 . . .143 C4
CULMINGTON 196 E1
Culmington TF3 . . . . .144 D2
Cumberland Cl 2 TF11 .152 C1
Cumberland La SY13 . . . .41 A7
Cumberland Mews 4
  TF1 . . . . .131 A4
Cumberley La
  Caynham SY8. . . . . .208 A1
  Hope Bagot SY8. . . . . .214 B8
CUMBER'S BANK 11 F3
Cunliffe St LL11 . . . . .221 C5
Cunliffe Wlk 4 LL12 . . .221 D7
Cunnery Rd SY6 . . . . .216 A4
Cunningham Ave LL13. .221 E4
Cunningham Way 6
  SY1. . . . . .113 D1

Curdale Cl 3 DY14 . . . . .209 D2
Curia Cl 10 SY2 . . . . .125 F8
Curie Croft 3 TF1 . . . . . .130 F6
Curlew Cl 3 SY1 . . . . . . .114 C3
Curlew Dr TF1 . . . . .131 B5
Curriers La TF11 . . . . .146 A5
CWM
  Churchstoke. 180 F5
  Clunbury 194 A2
CWM CAE. 181 A6
CWM HEAD 183 D3
Cwms La SY6 . . . . .216 E6
Cygnet Cl SY12 . . . . .27 B3
Cygnet Dr TF3 . . . . .153 C8
Cypress Cl 8 TF9. . . . . . . .36 A1
Cyril Hayward Ct 6 TF1 .131 C5

D

Daddlebrook 3 TF3. . . . .144 D5
Daddlebrook Rd WV15. .201 B3
Dahn Cl SY3 . . . . .217 E4
Dahn La SY3 . . . . .217 E5
Dairy Cl TF9 . . . . .36 D1
Daisybank Cl 4 LL13 . . .221 A2
Daisy Bank Dr TF2 . . . . .132 E4
Daisy La SY11 . . . . .41 F4
Dalby Cl 3 TF1 . . . . .130 F6
Dale Acre Way SY3 . . . . .144 C6
Dalebrook Dr 2 TF2 . . . .132 E6
Dalefield Dr 4 TF5 . . . . .130 A7
Dalelands TF3 . . . . .144 C6
Dalelands Est TF9. . . . . . .53 B7
Dalelands W TF9 . . . . .53 B7
Dale Rd
  Ironbridge TF8. . . . . . . .152 B5
  Shrewsbury SY3 . . . . . .126 A8
Dale St
  10 Craven Arms SY7 . .195 E5
  Wrexham LL13 . . . . .221 E3
Dale The TF10 . . . . .121 F8
Dalford Ct TF3 . . . . .144 C6
Dallamoor TF3 . . . . .144 D5
Dallas La SY10. . . . . .57 D2
DALLICOTT 189 C5
Dalton Cl 4 WV5 . . . . . . .190 F4
Dalton Dr 1 SY7 . . . . . . .184 E2
Damford La TF10. . . . . . . .90 E5
Damson Cl SY8 . . . . .212 D2
Damson Dr 3 TF3 . . . . . .143 E8
Damson Fayre TF9 . . . . . .36 B2
Damson La TF11 . . . . .134 F8
Damson Pk WV6 . . . . . . .166 D3
Damson Way 1 DY12 . . .211 E2
Dana The SY1. . . . . .125 D6
Danesbridge WV15. . . . .218 F3
Danesbrook 2 WV5 . . . .189 A4
DANESFORD 219 B2
Danford La 2 WV5 . . . . .189 A4
Daniels Cross TF10. . . . .110 A4
Darby Cl SY6 . . . . .184 F3
Darby La SY6 . . . . .184 F2
Darby Rd TF8 . . . . .152 A7
Darfield 1 SY1 . . . . .113 D1
Dargate Cl 4 SY3 . . . . . .124 F1
Dark La
  Broseley TF12 . . . . .152 D1
  Great Dawley TF4 . . . . .144 B4
  Leintwardine SY7 . . . . .205 B5
  Newport TF10 . . . . .109 E1
  3 Overton LL13 . . . . .9 C8
  Shrewsbury SY2 . . . . . .125 F5
  Whitchurch Rural SY13 . . .3 B1
Dark La Dr 1 SY3 . . . . . .144 A5
Dark Orch WR15 . . . . . . .220 C3
DARLEY. 161 E3
DARLISTON 50 C8
Darliston TF1 . . . . .144 D5
Dartmouth Ave 4 WV6. .166 C2
Darville SY1 . . . . .113 E1
Darwin Cl TF9 . . . . .36 B3
Darwin Ct
  Whitchurch SY13 . . . . . .14 F7
  Darwin Gdns SY3 . . . . .125 A1
Darwin & Pride Hill Sh Ctr 13
  SY1. . . . . .125 C6
Darwin Rd 5 TF1 . . . . . .130 D5
Darwin St SY3 . . . . .125 B7
Dashwood Dr 2 TF1. . . .130 D7
Davenham Wlk TF3 . . . .143 D7
Davenport Dr 2 TF5 . . .130 B7
Davenport House*
  WV15. . . . . .189 A6
David Ave 2 SY5 . . . . . . .173 B5
David Banks Sch SY2 . . .125 E7
David Philips Cl 14 SY12 .27 A2
Davids Cl 6 TF4 . . . . . . .143 F6
Davies Cl 13 LL13 . . . . .221 B6
Davies Gr SY4 . . . . .66 A8
Davina Gdns SY3 . . . . . .136 F6
DAWLEY 143 F4
DAWLEY BANK 143 D6
Dawley CE Prim Sch TF4 143 E3
Dawley Gn Way TF4. . . .143 E4
Dawley Rd
  Lawley & Overdale TF1 . .143 B7
  Wellington TF1. . . . . . . .131 A2
DAWYALL. 40 E8
Daywall 1 LL11 . . . . .144 D6
Daywall Cres
  1 Gobowen SY11 . . . . . .41 A8
  Selattyn & Gobowen SY10. .24 A1
Dean Cl
  Dawley TF2 . . . . .132 E2
  3 Market Drayton TF9. .36 A1
  Tenbury Wells WR15 . . .220 D6

Dean Cl continued
  Wrexham LL12. . . . . .221 F6
Deane Cl SY3. . . . . .124 B7
Dean Rd
  4B Wombourne WV5 . . . .190 F3
  Wrexham LL12. . . . . .221 F6
Dean St TF3 . . . . .144 B6
Decmar Rd WV15 . . . . . .219 F4
Dee Ave LL12 . . . . .221 E6
Dec Cl TF1 . . . . .130 D6
Deedes Ave SY2 . . . . .125 F3
Deepdale 4 TF3 . . . . . . .144 D6
Deepdales 4 WV5 . . . . .190 F3
Deepfield Rd TF4 . . . . . . .143 E2
Deepfields 4 SY3 . . . . . .124 E3
Deercote TF3 . . . . .144 C5
Deermoss La 7 SY13 . . .15 A8
Deer Pk Dr TF10 . . . . . . .109 E5
Deer Pk Rd TF1. . . . . .130 D5
Deighton's Cl WV16. . . .218 E4
Delamere Cl TF3 . . . . . . .143 D8
Delamere Rd 4 DY12 . . .211 E2
Delaware Ave WV7. . . . . .156 F5
Delbury Ct TF3 . . . . .144 C6
Delfan SY10 . . . . .76 A1
Dell The SY3. . . . . .124 B6
Delph Side 5 TF12 . . . . .161 C8
Delph The 8 TF3 . . . . . . .144 C8
Delwood Dr SY21. . . . . . .170 B6
Dene Rd WV4. . . . . .190 F6
Denham Dr 3 SY11. . . . . .40 D1
Denning Rd LL12 . . . . . . .221 F2
Derby Rd LL13 . . . . .221 E2
Derfald St 1 SY1 . . . . . . .125 D7
DERRINGTON 14 E5
Derrington Rd 3 WV16 .198 D8
Derwen 1 LL14 . . . . .6 E3
Derwen Coll SY11. . . . . . .41 B6
Derwen Cl LL13. . . . . .221 C1
Derwen Gn 5 SY22 . . . . .94 A1
Derwent Cl LL12 . . . . . . .221 D6
Derwent Cl LL12 . . . . . . .221 D6
Derwent Cres LL12. . . . .221 D6
Derwent Dr
  8 Bewdley DY12 . . . . . .211 C2
  Dawley TF2 . . . . .132 E2
DEUXHILL 200 A6
Deuxhill Cl TF4 . . . . .143 E5
Deva Way LL13 . . . . .221 F3
Devil's Spittleful Nature
  Reserve* DY12. . . . . . .211 F1
Devon Cl 5 LL12 . . . . . . .221 D6
De Warenne Cl 8 SY13. .15 B7
DHUSTONE 208 C2
Dhustone La 9 SY8. . . . .208 C2
Diamond Ave SY11. . . . . .59 B7
Dickens Pl SY2 . . . . .132 C6
Dickens Rd TF2 . . . . .132 C6
Didcot Cl 3 SY1. . . . . . . .125 E5
DIDDLEBURY. 197 A4
Digbeth La WV5 . . . . .189 D4
Diglake SY13 . . . . .32 A8
Diksmuide Dr SY2 . . . . . .27 B3
Dimmingsdale Rd WV4. .190 F7
Dinchope Dr TF3 . . . . . . .144 D6
Dingle Dr TF11 . . . . .164 C8
Dingle La CW5. . . . . .4 D7
Dingle The LD7 . . . . .203 C2
Dingle View WV16. . . . . .218 E6
Dinham SY9 . . . . .217 B3
Dinham House* SY8 . . .217 B3
Dinthill TF3 . . . . .144 D5
Discovery Cl 20 SY9 . . .113 E5
DITHERINGTON 113 F5
Ditherington Rd SY1 . . .113 E1
DITTON PRIORS 198 D6
Dobell La SY4 . . . . .100 F3
DOBSON'S BRIDGE 30 D2
Doctors Mdw SY4. . . . . . .80 A1
DODDINGTON 208 F3
Doddington TF3 . . . . .144 D6
Doddlecote Cl TF3 . . . . . .144 E2
Dodds La 16 SY7 . . . . . . .195 E5
Dodington SY13 . . . . .15 A7
Dodmoor Grange TF1 . .144 D6
Dodmore La SY8 . . . . . . .217 D5
Dodson Cl 9 TF6 . . . . . .116 D6
Dog Kennel La
  2 Bucknell SY7. . . . . . .204 C5
  Market Drayton TF9 . . . .53 D8
Dog La 9 DY12. . . . . .211 D2
Dogpole 6 SY1 . . . . .125 C6
Dol Acton LL11 . . . . .221 B7
DOLEY. 73 E8
Dolgoch SY10 . . . . .76 B5
Dolgoch Quarry Nature
  Reserve* SY10. . . . . . . .76 B5
Dolydd La 1 LL14 . . . . . . .6 B8
Dolydd Rd LL13. . . . . .221 B3
Dolyfelin 4 SY21 . . . . . . .170 A3
Domas Way 3 TF4. . . . . .143 C5
DOMGAY 94 C3
Domgay Pl SY22. . . . . . . .94 B2
Domgay Rd SY22 . . . . . . .94 B3
Donaldson Dr 2 TF9. . . . .72 F7
DONINGTON 144 D5
Donington La WV8. . . . . .148 D2
Donkey La (Avenue Rd)
  SY8. . . . . .213 B5
Donnerville Cl TF1. . . . . .130 C5
Donnerville Dr TF1 . . . . .130 B5
Donnerville Gdns TF1. . .130 B6
Donnett Cl 2 SY11 . . . . . .41 F2

Donnett Mews SY11.......41 F2
DONNINGTON
Lilleshall and
  Donnington..........132 E7
Wroxeter and Uppington...140 B4
Donnington Dr TF2......120 B4
Donnington Way TF2.....120 C2
DONNINGTON WOOD.....132 E5
Donnington Wood CE Jun
  Sch TF2.............132 E5
Donnington Wood Inf Sch
  TF2................132 D8
Donnington Wood Way
  TF2................132 D5
Dorchester Dr TF2......132 F7
Dorran Pl ■ TF2........132 D1
Dorricotts Pl SY5......169 A1
DORRINGTON
  Condover............178 C5
  Woore...............21 C7
Dorrington CE Prim Sch
  SY5................178 C6
Dorset Dr LL12.........221 D8
Dorset St SY1..........125 D7
DOSELEY...............143 D2
Doseley Ind Est TF4....143 D2
Doseley Rd TF4.........143 D2
DOTHILL...............130 D7
Dothill Inf Sch TF1....130 D6
Dothill Jun Sch TF1....130 D6
Double Gates TF9.......53 B8
Douglas Way ■ SY3.....124 C7
Dounton Cl SY1........114 A3
DOVASTON.............96 D7
Dovaston Ct SY11.......78 D8
Dove Cl TF11..........131 D4
Dove Ct TF8...........152 D3
Dovedale Fold ■ TF4...144 A4
Dovehouse Ct TF2......161 D7
Dovehouse La WV16.....208 D8
Dover Dr ■ TF1........131 B6
Dower House Sch The
  WV15...............201 A7
DOWLES...............211 C3
Dowles Rd DY12........211 C3
Downemead ■ TF3.......144 D5
Downfield TF10........109 F5
Downfield Rd SY3......124 E7
Downing Cl ■ SY3......124 E7
DOWN THE.............187 F1
DOWNTON ON THE
  ROCK..............205 D4
Downton View SY8......217 E5
Drapers Ct ■ TF1......130 E4
Drawwell SY4..........84 A5
Drawwell La SY4........66 A6
Drawwell St SY3........125 C3
DRAYCOTT.............190 A4
Draycott Dr ■ TF3.....144 D5
Drayton Gdns ■ SY2....125 E7
Drayton Gr ■ TF9......36 C1
Drayton Rd
  Hodnet TF9..........69 D7
  Shifnal TF11........146 A6
Drayton Way TF4.......143 E5
Drenewydd SY11........41 C3
Drinkwater St SY3.....125 B7
Drovers Way ■ TF10....110 A4
Drummery La TF6.......129 F3
Drummond Cl TF7.......152 C6
Drury La
  Bicton SY4..........169 E5
  Minsterley SY5......172 C2
  Withington SY4......116 A1
  Worthen with Shelve SY5..176 A3
Dry Mill La DY12.......211 C3
DRYTON................140 C1
Duchess Dr WV16.......218 D6
Duchess Wlk SY8.......206 D2
Duckett Dr ■ TF4......143 D2
DUDDLEWICK...........199 C2
DUDLESTON............8 D1
DUDLESTON HEATH
  (CRIFTINS).........26 B6
Dudleston Pk SY12......26 B7
Dudmaston ■ TF3.......144 D6
Dudmaston Hall* WV15..200 F7
DUFFRYN..............192 B5
Duffryn TF3...........144 D6
Duken La WV15.........189 B1
Duke's Dr The TF6......118 E5
Dukes Hill ■ TF2......132 A2
Duke St
  Broseley TF12.......152 C1
  Oakengates/Donnington
  TF2................132 D2
  ■ Wellington TF1....130 E4
  ■ Wrexham LL11.....221 C3
Dukes Way ■ TF2......132 D2
Dulwich Grange TF5....130 A8
Dumblehole La SY8.....213 B5
Dunbar ■ SY1.........113 D5
Dunedin Dr ■ SY3......124 E4
Dungarven Dr TF10.....109 D2
Dunkeld Dr SY2........126 A7
DUNKS THE............221 C2
Dunlin Cl ■ TF1.......131 B5
Dunmaster Way ■ TF1..144 B1
Dunmore Rd ■ DY12....211 E3
Dunning Cl ■ SY4......80 A1
DUNNSHEATH..........112 F8
Dunsheath ■ TF3.......144 C6
Dunstone ■ TF3........144 C6
Dunval Cl WV16........218 D7
Dunval Rd WV16........218 D7

Durrant Rd ■ TF2......132 D1
Dutton Cl
  Clive Barracks TF9...70 D8
  Stoke upon Tern TF9..52 D1
Dutton Gn ■ SY1.......113 E4
Duxmore Way ■ TF4....143 E5
Dyas Cl TF11..........145 F3
Dyas Mews TF11........145 F3
Dyffryn Foel SY22.....92 B5
Dykes La TF10.........123 D8
Dymens Mew ■ SY2.....125 F6
Dymock Pl LL13........10 F4

E

Eagle Ct TF1..........130 E5
Eagle La ■ DY14.......209 E2
Eagles Meadow LL12....221 D3
EARDINGTON..........188 C1
EARDISTON...........79 C6
Earl Edwin Mews SY13..15 A7
Earles Ct ■ LL13......221 C2
Earle St ■ SY11......221 C2
Earls Dr TF4..........130 D7
Earlston Pk SY3.......124 F7
Earls View Hill ■ SY3..124 A6
Earlswood ■ SY3......124 C6
Earlswood Dr SY7......152 F4
East Ave
  Oakengates/Donnington
  TF2................132 C7
  Wrexham LL11.......221 C6
East Castle St WV16....218 F4
East Cres SY1.........114 A2
Eastern Ave WV7......156 F8
EASTHAM.............215 D3
EASTHOPE............185 F6
Easthope Rd
  ■ Ashbrook SY6.....216 C6
  Broseley TF12.......152 C2
  ■ Church Stretton SY6..216 C6
Eastleigh Cl ■ LL11...221 C7
East Rd TF2...........132 A1
EAST WALL...........185 B4
Eastwick La SY12.......9 E1
Eastwood Dr ■ TF2.....132 E6
Eastwood Rd SY3.......124 E7
EATON
  Easton-under-Heywood..184 C1
  Lydbury North.......182 E4
EATON CONSTANTINE....140 F1
Eaton Cres ■ TF2......132 C2
Eaton Ct SY12.........43 F6
Eaton Fields ■ SY11...50 F8
EATON MASCOTT.......179 D8
Eaton Rd TF9..........89 A5
Ebenezer Row ■ WV16..218 F4
Ebnal Rd SY2..........126 A3
EBREYWOOD..........115 A8
Ebstree Mdw WV5......190 D5
Ebstree Rd WV5.......190 C5
Ebury Ave SY1.........114 A2
Eckford Pk SY4........66 A5
Eden Cl ■ SY2.........125 F8
Eden St ■ SY11........58 E8
EDGE................173 A7
EDGEBOLTON.........104 A8
Edge Cl SY3...........137 A5
Edgefield Gn ■ SY3....124 B6
Edgeleia Cres ■ SY13..15 B7
EDGELEY.............15 D5
Edgeley Gdns SY13....15 B6
Edgeley Rd SY13.......15 B6
EDGERLEY...........96 C3
Edge Wood Nature Reserve*
  SY6................196 C6
EDGMOND............109 A3
EDGMOND MARSH......108 F6
Edgmond Rd TF10......109 D4
EDGTON.............194 F8
Edinburgh Rd
  Broseley TF12.......152 C1
  Wrexham LL11.......221 C6
Edith Cl ■ TF3........144 A1
EDSTASTON..........48 B5
Edward German Dr ■
  SY13...............15 B7
Edward Parry Ct ■ TF4..143 F6
Edward St
  Oswestry SY11......58 D7
  ■ Wrexham LL11....221 B2
Egerton Pl SY13.......15 A8
Egerton Rd SY13.......15 B8
Egerton St ■ LL11.....221 C4
Egerton Wlk LL11......221 D7
Eglantine Cl ■ TF2....144 B4
EGLWYS CROSS.......12 E6
Eider Dr TF1..........131 A7
Elan Cl ■ DY12........211 C2
ELBRIDGE............79 A5
Elderberry Cl ■ TF3...143 F8
Elder Gr ■ WV5.......190 F3
Eldon Dr SY3..........124 E7
Eleanor Harris Rd ■ SY4..81 E1
Eleanors Cl ■ TF4.....153 A8
Elgar Cl SY11.........58 C8
Elim Ct TF1...........131 C4
Eliot Cl TF3..........144 E2
Elizabeth Ave WV16....218 D5
Elizabeth Cres TF12...152 C1
Elizabeth Ct ■ SY9....59 C1
Elizabeth Gr ■ WV16...200 E2
Elizabeth St SY11.....15 B8
Elkington Cl ■ TF10...109 E2

Ellam Piece TF9.......72 F8
Ellan Ct ■ SY2........125 E3
ELLERDINE...........105 B6
ELLERDINE HEATH......87 D1
ELLERTON............90 F8
ELLESMERE...........A2
Ellesmere Bsns Pk SY12..26 F1
Ellesmere Coll SY12...26 E1
Ellesmere Ct ■ TF10...109 E2
Ellesmere Dr
  ■ Bewdley DY12.....211 C2
  ■ Shrewsbury SY11..113 C1
Ellesmere Gdns SY1....125 C7
Ellesmere Gr ■ TF9....52 F8
Ellesmere La LL13.....10 F3
Ellesmere Prim Sch SY12..27 A2
Ellesmere Rd
  Bronington SY13.....13 E5
  Ellesmere Rural SY12..43 E7
  ■ Shrewsbury SY4....113 D4
  St Martin's SY11....24 E6
  Wem Urban SY4......65 E7
  Whittington SY11....41 F3
Ellice Way LL13.......221 A4
Ellis Gn ■ SY2........125 F8
Ellis Peters Dr TF3....144 A1
Ellwand Ct ■ TF4......143 F2
Elm Cl
  ■ Shrewsbury SY12..27 A3
  Newport TF10........109 F1
  ■ Oswestry SY11.....59 A7
  Whittington SY13....15 C8
Elm Dr TF9............36 A1
Elmfield Rd SY2........125 F5
Elm Gr LL12...........221 E5
Elm Gr Way ■ LL12....221 E6
Elmhurst WV15.........219 B5
Empark Dr TF1.........130 C5
Elm Rd WV7...........156 E5
Elmsdale Cres ■ TF5...130 A7
Elms La SY6...........216 A2
Elms Paddock SY6......216 A2
Elms Paddock The WV6..166 C2
Elm St SY1............125 C8
Elm Tree Cl 32 WV5...190 F3
Elm Way ■ TF2........131 F6
Elm Wlk SY8..........217 D6
ELSON...............26 F4
Elson Rd SY12.........26 F3
Elstree Cl ■ SY3......124 F1
Elswick Cl ■ SY3......124 F1
Eltham Dr TF2.........133 A2
ELTON...............212 A5
Elton Rd ■ DY12......211 C2
Elvin Cl TF4..........143 D2
Ely Cl ■ TF2..........133 A1
Emmanuel Gr ■ LL14...6 C8
Empress Rd ■ LL13....221 B2
Emral Rise TF1........130 D6
Emscote ■ SY1........113 D1
EMSTREY.............126 D1
Emstrey Bank SY5......126 C1
ENCHMARSH..........184 F7
Eneurys Rd LL11.......221 D6
Enfield St ■ SY7......193 D3
Enginuity* TF8.......152 B6
English Bridge SY1....125 D2
ENGLISH FRANKTON....64 A8
English Walls SY11....58 E7
Ennerdale Cl ■ TF2....132 D1
Ennerdale Rd ■ TF2...113 E3
ENSDON.............169 C7
Entry Bank TF2.......120 F2
Epsom Cl ■ SY1.......41 A1
Epsom Ct ■ TF1.......131 A5
ERBISTOCK..........8 F8
Ercall Cl TF7.........132 A5
Ercall Gdns ■ TF1.....130 D3
Ercall La TF1.........130 D3
Ercall Nature Reserve The*
  TF6................142 C8
Ercall View TF3.......131 D1
Ercall Wood Tech Coll
  TF1................130 E2
Erddig Rd ■ LL13.....221 C2
Erdington Cl SY4......103 E8
Eric Lock Rd ■ SY3....137 A5
Eric Lock Rd W SY3....137 A6
Erw Las LL12..........221 E4
Escent TF9............52 E5
Eskdale Rd SY2........126 A7
Esless Rd ■ LL14......221 A1
Espley Cl ■ TF1.......130 E4
Espley Rdbt TF9.......69 D4
Essex Chase TF2.......132 F1
Essex Cl ■ LL12.......221 D7
Essex Rd SY6..........216 D6
Estate Rd WV5.........219 E4
ETSELL..............172 C3
EUDON BURNELL.......200 A8
EUDON GEORGE.......199 F6
Euston Way TF3.......144 C7
Evelith La TF11........154 F7
Everglade Rd
  ■ Dawley TF3.......132 E1
  Dawley TF3.........144 E8
Evergreens The TF11...134 B5
Everley Cl ■ SY3......124 D6
Ewart Rd TF2.........132 D6
Ewart St LL14.........6 C8
Exeter Dr TF1.........130 F5
EXFORDS GREEN......178 A8
EYTON
  Aldbury with Cardeston..168 A4
  Baschurch...........81 E2
  Lydbury North.......182 E2
Eyton La SY4..........81 B1
Eyton ON SEVERN......140 A1

Eyton Pl ■ TF4........143 F4
Eyton Rd ■ TF4.......144 A4
EYTON UPON THE WEALD
  MOORS.............110 B2
Eyton View ■ TF1......130 D6

F

Factory La DY14.......209 C7
Faintree Ave ■ SY12...125 F2
Fairburn Dr ■ SY3.....124 F4
Fairburn Rd TF3.......144 C3
Fairfield WV16........218 C6
Fairfield Cl
  ■ Craven Arms SY7..195 E5
  ■ Gobowen SY11....41 A8
Fairfield Ct ■ TF1.....130 E4
Fairfield St ■ LL13....221 C2
Fair Lawn WV7........157 A5
Fairlawn WV5.........125 A1
Fairlawn Gdns ■ SY1..125 A1
Fairness Cl ■ SY2.....126 B7
Fair Oak TF10.........109 F4
Fairview TF2..........132 B1
Fair View SY21........167 A3
Fairview Dr SY3.......136 E6
Fairways Dr
  Madeley TF7........152 F4
  Whitchurch SY13....2 A1
Fairways The SY5......137 B1
Fairy Rd LL13.........221 C2
Falcons Way SY5......124 C5
Falkland Pk SY5.......178 C5
Falkland Rd SY5.......178 C5
Falklands Cl ■ SY3....190 F1
Fallow Deer Lawn TF10..109 F5
Fallowfield SY6.......178 C1
Fallow Rd ■ TF5......130 C8
Falstaff St SY1.......125 D8
Faraday Dr WV15......219 B4
Farcroft Dr TF9.......36 A1
FARDEN.............208 A2
Farden La SY8........208 A2
Farfield Cl ■ SY3.....124 C7
FAR FOREST.........210 D1
Far Forest Lea Meml Fst CE
  Sch DY14...........210 D1
Far Gdn Pl ■ SY1.....113 C1
Farifields Rd TF9.....36 D2
FARLEY
  Much Wenlock......151 A1
  Pontesbury.........172 F6
Farley Rd TF13........159 F7
FARLOW.............209 A7
Farlow CE Prim Sch
  DY14...............209 A7
Farm Ct TF7..........153 C5
FARMCOTE...........189 D2
Farmfields Rise CW3....5 A1
Farm Gr TF10.........109 D3
Farm La
  All Stretton SY6....184 B6
  Church Stretton SY6..216 E8
  Dawley TF4.........143 C2
  Ellesmere Rural SY12..44 A6
Farmlands Rd WV16....218 C5
Farm Lodge Gr ■ TF3..144 A5
Farmlodge La SY1.....113 C1
Farm Mdw Cl ■ TF4...143 C3
Farmoor SY11.........114 C2
Farm Rd
  Barrow TF12........161 C3
  Boningale WV6......165 D7
Farnside ■ LL12.......221 F7
Farmstead Ct ■ TF1...130 C2
Farndon St ■ LL13....221 D3
Farran Gr ■ SY4......114 B4
Farriers Gn
  Dawley TF4.........143 D6
  Newport TF10.......110 B3
Farrington La LD7.....203 C1
Far Vallens TF1.......131 D4
FAULS..............50 E6
Fearn Dr ■ SY2.......132 D1
Featherbed La
  Bicton SY3.........112 C1
  Shrewsbury SY1.....114 B3
Feiashill Cl WV5......190 D4
Feiashill Rd WV5......190 E3
Felcourt Dr ■ TF2.....124 C7
FELHAMPTON........183 F2
FELINDRE...........191 B3
FELIN NEWYDD.......56 C7
FELIN PULESTON.....221 A1
Fellows Cl ■ TF4......143 F1
Fells Orch WV16......218 E3
FELTON BUTLER.....169 A8
Felton Cl
  Ludlow SY8.........217 B6
  ■ Shrewsbury SY4...125 E7
Feltons Pl TF3........70 D7
Fence Rd TF4.........143 D4
FENN GREEN........201 C2
FENN'S BANK........13 F3
Fenns Cres TF2.......132 D3
Fenton Cl ■ TF2......124 C7
Fenwick Dr LL13......221 F4
Fernbrook ■ SY5......178 C6
Ferndale Cl ■ SY2....92 A1
Ferndale Cres ■ SY11..41 A8
Ferndale Dr ■ TF7....114 D5
Ferndale Dr ■ TF1....114 B2
Ferney Bank TF11.....131 C4
Fernham Dr ■ LL12....221 D8
Fernhill Ave
  ■ Gobowen SY11....41 B8

Fernhill Ave continued
  Selattyn & Gobowen SY11..24 B1
Fernhill Cl ■ SY11.....41 B8
Fernhill Cl ■ SY1......41 B8
Fern Lea Croft 16 SY3..124 A7
Fernwood Cl ■ TF1....130 D7
Ferrers Rd SY1........58 E7
Ferriday Cl TF7.......152 D6
Ferry Rd TF8..........153 A2
Festival Gdns ■ TF1...130 F2
Ffordd Alafon LL12....221 F8
Ffordd Aled LL12......221 F8
Ffordd Alun LL12......221 F7
Ffordd Cynan ■ LL12..221 F7
Ffordd Dyfed LL12.....221 F7
Ffordd Dylan ■ LL12...221 F5
Ffordd Edgeworth ■
  LL12...............221 F5
Ffordd Elan LL12......221 F8
Ffordd Elfed LL12.....221 F8
Ffordd Elwy LL12......221 F8
Ffordd Estyn LL11.....221 C7
Ffordd Glyn ■ LL13....221 C1
Ffordd Gwilym ■ LL12..221 F7
Ffordd Gwynedd LL11..221 C7
Ffordd Hooson LL12...221 F5
Ffordd Jarvis LL12....221 F5
Ffordd Kayton ■ LL14..6 C8
Ffordd Lerry LL12.....221 F8
Ffordd Llywelyn ■ LL12..221 F8
Ffordd Madoc LL12....221 F7
Ffordd Maelor LL12....221 F8
Ffordd Meirionnydd 10
  LL11...............221 C7
Ffordd Mon ■ LL11....221 C7
Ffordd Morganwg 11
  LL11...............221 C7
Ffordd Offa ■ LL14....6 C8
Ffordd Owain ■ LL12..221 F7
Ffordd Pedrog ■ LL12..221 F7
Ffordd Spooney SY22..92 C5
Ffordd Tegid LL12.....221 F8
Ffordd Tegla LL12.....221 F8
Ffordd Trefaldwyn ■
  LL11...............221 C7
Ffordd Trefin LL12.....221 F8
Ffordd Tudno LL12.....221 F7
Ffordd-yr-orsaf LL14...23 D7
Ffrydd Cl 22 LD7......203 B3
Ffrydd Rd LD7........203 B2
Ffrydd Terr 23 LD7....203 B3
Ffynnon Cl SY1........58 E7
Ffynnon Gdns ■ SY1...58 F7
Field Cl
  ■ Dawley TF4.......143 F6
  Shrewsbury SY1.....114 A3
Field Cres SY1........114 A3
Field Dr SY4..........84 A5
Field House Dr ■ TF2..120 D1
Fielding Cl ■ TF12....161 E7
Field La
  Bishop's Castle SY9..181 F3
  Kemberton TF11.....154 C6
  Tenbury SY8........213 F2
Field Rd TF2..........132 E8
Fields The TF2........132 E8
Field View LL13.......221 E3
Fifth Ave 13 TF2......132 A1
Finchale Ave ■ TF2....133 A1
Findon Dr ■ SY3.......40 D1
Findon Way ■ SY3.....124 B6
FINGERPOST.........210 E1
Finger Rd TF4.........143 F2
Finney Cl LL11........221 B6
Finsbury Dr ■ TF2.....132 D3
Fireclay Dr TF2.......132 D3
Firecrest Dr 10 TF1...130 F6
Fir Gr SY11...........58 F6
Firgrove Cnr ■ SY7....221 F7
First Ave
  Oakengates/Donnington
  TF2................132 B1
  Shrewsbury SY1.....113 F2
Firs The
  Ford Heath SY5.....169 C2
  Whitchurch SY13....14 F8
First Terr ■ TF1......113 C2
Firsway The ■ ST19...148 E8
Firtree Cl ■ SY12.....27 A2
Fir Tree La SY4........66 B7
Fir Trees WV15........219 B4
Fisher Rd SY21........170 E7
Fishers Lock ■ TF10...110 A4
Fishguard Cl ■ SY13...221 F1
Fishmore Cl SY8......217 C6
Fishmore Rd SY8......217 C6
Fishmore View SY8....217 C6
Fish St
  Ludlow SY8.........217 C4
  ■ Shrewsbury SY1...125 C5
Fisnes Way 14 SY6....66 B8
Fitchett Bsns Pk TF2..132 C2
FITZ................169 F8
Fitzalan Cl SY11......42 A1
Fitzalan Rd
  ■ Oswestry SY11....58 C7
  Shrewsbury SY1.....113 C4
Fitzgwarine Dr SY11...41 E3
Five Crosses SY10....44 A7
Five Turnings SY7....182 D1
Flagg Leasow TF7.....152 F4
Flagwall ■ SY22......126 A6
Flash La
  Loggerheads TF9....54 F8
  Wombourne WV4....190 F5

Flatt Rd TF10 . . . . .108 F4
Fleming Ct **4** TF1 . . . . .130 F6
Fleming Dr **7** LI11 . . . . . . .221 B6
Florence Cl SY3 . . . . .124 C7
Florence Ct **2** SY3 . . . . . . .124 C7
Floyer La TF12 . . . . .152 B1
Foel Hill (Fort)* SY22 . . . .92 A6
Foldgate La DY8 . . . . .217 F3
Foldgate View SY8 . . . . .217 F3
Foldyard The **16** TF2 . . . . . .132 F8
Foley Gr **38** WV5 . . . . .190 F3
FOLLEY 189 C8
Folley Rd WV6 . . . . .164 E1
Folliott Cl **5** SY2 . . . . .125 F3
FOOTRID 215 F5
Forbes Cl TF7 . . . . .152 C5
FORD 169 C4
Forden CW Prim Sch
SY21 . . . . .174 B8
FORDEN/FFODUN 174 B7
Forden Rd SY15 . . . . .174 B4
FORD HEATH 169 B2
Ford Rd TF10 . . . . .109 E2
Ford St **4** SY7 . . . . .193 D3
Forest Cl
3 Bewdley DY12 . . . . .211 C2
3 Wellington TF5 . . . . . .118 C1
Wellington TF5 . . . . .130 C8
Forester Ave TF3 . . . . .159 F4
Forester Gr **2** TF1 . . . . .130 F2
Forester Rd TF12 . . . . .161 E7
Foresters Cl TF4 . . . . .144 C2
Forest La DY7 . . . . .190 C1
Forest Rd TF9 . . . . .53 A8
Forest Way SY7 . . . . .126 A7
Forge Gate TF3 . . . . .144 B7
Forge La
Leintwardine SY8 . . . . . . .205 F6
Norton in Hales TF9 . . . . . .20 C1
Forge Leys **16** WV5 . . . . . . .190 F3
Forge Valley Way **8**
WV5 . . . . .190 F3
Forge Way SY5 . . . . .178 C5
Foresters Rd WR15 . . . . .220 D6
Forsythia Cl **3** TF2 . . . . .132 F1
Fort-mahon Pl **20** DY12 . .211 C2
FORTON
Montford 169 D7
Newport 110 A7
Forton Glade **9** TF10 . . . .109 F5
FORTON HEATH 169 E8
Forton Rd TF10 . . . . .109 F4
Fort View **2** SY1 . . . . .40 E1
Foster Rd WR16 . . . . .218 D7
Foster Rd / Ffordd Foster
LL11 . . . . .221 C5
Fosters Foel **9** TF4 . . . . . . .153 A8
Fothergill Way SY4 . . . . .65 F6
Foundry Cl **10** TF2 . . . . .132 B2
Foundry La
Broseley TF12 . . . . .161 D7
Welshpool SY21 . . . . .170 B6
Foundry Rd **4** LL13 . . . . . . .221 D3
Fountain Dr TF2 . . . . .132 C2
FOUR ASHES 201 F6
Four Crosses 94 A1
Four Crosses SY21 . . . . .170 E5
Fourth Ave TF2 . . . . .132 B1
Fowler Cl TF1 . . . . .130 D5
Fox Ave TF2 . . . . .132 D1
Fox Cl WV5 . . . . .190 C5
Foxen Manor Rd SY22 . . . . .94 A1
Foxes La SY13 . . . . .16 B7
Foxes The TF7 . . . . .153 B3
Foxglove Cl **2** SY3 . . . . .125 D3
Fox Rd WV5 . . . . .190 B6
Fox's Covert **7** TF5 . . . . . .130 C8
Fox's Field SY1 . . . . .41 B8
FOXWOOD 208 F3
Foxwood Dr LL13 . . . . .221 A1
Frame La TF4 . . . . .143 D2
Frances Ave LL12 . . . . .221 D8
Frankton Cl **3** SY2 . . . . . . .126 B7
FRANKWELL 125 A2
Frankwell Quay SY3 . . . . . . .125 A3
Frankwell Quay TF1 . . . . . . .125 C5
Fraser Ct SY13 . . . . .15 A6
Freer Mdw **9** SY2 . . . . .125 E6
Freeston Ave TF2 . . . . .132 C1
Freeston Terr **5** TF2 . . . . . .144 D8
Frensham Rd **1** SY2 . . . . . .125 F5
Freshfields **8** SY1 . . . . .113 A5
Friars Ave SY11 . . . . .59 A8
Friars Cl
Oswestry SY11 . . . . .59 A8
Wrexham LL12 . . . . .221 B8
Friars Gdn SY8 . . . . .217 C4
Friar's La TF1 . . . . .147 D4
Friar's St WV16 . . . . .218 F5
Friars Wlk SY8 . . . . .217 D4
Frinton Cl **4** SY3 . . . . .124 B6
Frith Cl SY2 . . . . .126 A7
Frizes Leasowe **10** TF2 . . .132 A1
FROCHAS 167 C1
FRODESLEY 179 A4
Frog La **5** TF9 . . . . .36 C1
Frogmore Cl **9** TF9 . . . . . . .36 C1
Frome Way LI14 . . . . .132 D5

FRON
Forden with Leighton and
Trelystan. 170 C2
Weston Rhyn 22 F4
FRONCYSYLLTE 6 A6
FRON-GOCH 93 E8
Fronhir LD7 . . . . .203 C3
FRON ISAF 6 A5
Fryers Cl **8** TF2 . . . . .209 D2
Fuchsia Cl **8** TF2 . . . . .132 F1
Furlongs Cl **6** DY14 . . . . . . .209 E3
Furlongs Rd **5** DY14 . . . . . .209 E3
Furnace Cl **34** WV5 . . . . . . .190 F3
Furnace La TF2 . . . . .132 B7
Furnace Rd TF2 . . . . .132 C1
Fylingdales Dr TF4 . . . . .143 D2

G

GADLAS 26 C7
Gains Ave SY3 . . . . .124 A7
Gainsborough Way TF5 . . . . .130 B7
Gains Pk Way SY3 . . . . .124 A6
Gallowstree Bank **4**
SY21 . . . . .170 C7
Gallowstree Rise **3**
SY21 . . . . .170 C7
Galton Dr **4** SY2 . . . . .126 B7
Gambrell Ave SY13 . . . . .15 B8
Gamester's La SY10 . . . . .78 E1
Gaol Rd **1** SY15 . . . . .174 B3
Garbett Ave SY4 . . . . .66 A6
Garbett Rd TF4 . . . . .152 F8
Gardd Estyn **6** LL11 . . . . . . .221 D7
Garden Cl TF2 . . . . .132 B5
Garden Cl LL11 . . . . .221 D7
Gardeners Way **6** TF4 . . . . .143 D2
Garden Hs The* LL13 . . . . . .8 E7
Garden Rd LL11 . . . . .221 C6
Gardens The **11** LL12 . . . . .221 D4
GARDEN VILLAGE 221 C6
Garden Village SY11 . . . . . . .24 E6
Gardners Mdw **13** DY12 . . .211 D2
Garfield Rd TF3 . . . . .131 E1
GARMSTON 141 A1
Garmston La SY5 . . . . .141 A1
Garmston Rd TF2 . . . . .133 B2
Garner Rd LL13 . . . . .221 E4
Garner's La SY13 . . . . .31 C3
Garreg Bank SY21 . . . . .167 A2
Garreg Dr **3** SY21 . . . . .170 B6
Garridge Cl WV7 . . . . .157 A4
GARTH 203 A3
Garth La LD7 . . . . .203 A3
Garth Mdws **8** LD7 . . . . . . .203 B3
Gatacre Ave SY11 . . . . .40 E1
Gatacre Rd **4** SY11 . . . . . . .40 E1
Gatcombe Gdns **3** SY11 . . .59 B8
Gatcombe Way TF2 . . . . .132 F2
Gatefield LL13 . . . . .221 E2
Gatehouse Cl TF6 . . . . .130 E7
Gates La SY7 . . . . .183 F1
Gate St
1 Oakengates/Donnington
TF2 . . . . .132 C2
Gateway **1** LL12 . . . . .40 E1
Gateway Ed & Arts Ctr The*
SY3. . . . . .125 C7
Gatewen Rd **7** LL11 . . . . . .221 D3
Gatherwynd La TF11 . . . . . . .135 E6
Gelli-Iwyd La SY10. . . . . .74 A3
George Chetwood Ct **5**
TF4 .144 A4
George Cl **10** LD7 . . . . .203 B3
George Pl TF1 . . . . .130 C4
George Rd LD7 . . . . .203 B3
George St
Chirk LL14 . . . . .6 E2
9 Dawley TF4 . . . . .143 E4
Oakengates/Donnington
TF2 . . . . .132 D2
Whitchurch SY13 . . . . .15 B8
8 Wrexham LL11 . . . . . .221 C5
Gerald St LL11 . . . . .221 C4
Gibbons Cl **1** TF2 . . . . .132 B6
Gibbons Rd TF2 . . . . .132 B6
Gibraltar La SY10 . . . . .75 E7
Gibson St LL13 . . . . .221 B3
GIGGETTY 190 C3
Giggetty La WV5 . . . . .190 F3
Gilberries La SY6 . . . . .185 A4
Gilbert Cl TF10. . . . . .109 D2
Gilbert's La
Wem Rural SY13 . . . . .48 B8
Whixall SY13 . . . . .31 A1
Giles Cl **3** TF5 . . . . .130 B7
Gilpin Rd TF5 . . . . .130 A6
Gilwell Gr **1** TF2 . . . . .132 F1
Gittens Dr
8 Aqueduct TF4 . . . . . . .152 F8
Dawley TF4 . . . . .153 A8
Gittin St SY11 . . . . .40 E1
Glade Way TF5 . . . . .118 C1
Gladstone St TF1 . . . . .131 D4
Gladwyn Rd LL12 . . . . .221 D8
Glamis **8** LL13 . . . . .221 E5
Glan Aber **8** LL12 . . . . .221 E5
Glan Aber Cl LL12 . . . . .221 A8
Glan Garth **9** LL12 . . . . . . .221 E5
Glan Gors LL13 . . . . .221 F2
Glan Lleddan **1** SY21 . . . . .170 A6
GLAN-YR-AFON 74 D5
GLAZELEY 200 B7
Glebe Cl TF9 . . . . .73 A8
Glebe Croft SY6 . . . . .184 C3
Glebe Dr DY14. . . . . .199 E1

Glebelands
2 Bobbington DY7 . . . . . .189 F1
Myddle & Broughton SY4. . .82 D4
Shawbury SY4 . . . . .103 E6
Glebelands Cl SY8 . . . . .207 F4
Glebelands The
Ercall Magna TF6 . . . . .116 E7
Oakengates/Donnington
TF2 . . . . .132 D7
Glebe Mdw SY9. . . . . .182 A6
Glebe Rd SY3. . . . . .136 F6
Glebe St TF1. . . . . .130 E3
Glebe The
2 Albrighton WV7 . . . . . .157 A5
Atcham SY5 . . . . .139 A7
Chelmarsh WV16. . . . . .200 D6
Glen Avon **1** LL12 . . . . .221 E4
Glen Brook Rd TF2. . . . . .132 F1
Glenburn Gdns **2** SY2 . . . .126 A8
Glencoe Terr SY8 . . . . .217 C4
Glendale TF4 . . . . .143 C7
Glendale Gdns TF4. . . . . .143 C7
Glendale Mews TF4. . . . . . . .143 C6
Glendinning Way TF7 . . . . . .152 F4
Glendon Cl **3** TF9 . . . . .52 F8
Glendower Ct SY1 . . . . .125 D8
Glendower Pl SY13 . . . . .12 B3
Gleneagles Cl TF7 . . . . .153 B3
Glen Gr **1** SY3 . . . . .32 E5
Glen The TF13 . . . . .159 D8
Glentworth Ave SY11. . . . . . .58 D5
Glentworth Cl SY10. . . . . . . .58 D5
Glentworth Cl SY11. . . . . . . .58 D5
Glentworth Rise SY10. . . . . .58 D5
Gloucester Ave TF4 . . . . .143 F4
Gloucester Ct **3** TF1. . . . . .131 A7
Gloucester Dr LL11 . . . . .221 A5
Gloucester Rd SY1 . . . . .113 D4
Gloucester Way **20** DY12 . .147 F6
Glovers Mdw SY11 . . . . .58 D5
Glovers Way **1** TF5 . . . . . . .130 B8
Glyn Ave LL11 . . . . .221 E7
Glyndwr LD7. . . . . .202 E5
Glyndwr Rd LL12. . . . . .221 D7
GLYNMORLAS 7 D1
Gnosall Rd TF10 . . . . .111 D2
Goblin's La SY13. . . . . .31 A1
GOBOWEN 41 B8
Gobowen Prim Sch SY11. . . .41 A8
Gobowen Rd SY11 . . . . .40 F1
Gobowen Sta SY11 . . . . .41 A7
Goddwick Dr **2** LL13 . . . . . .221 F1
Godings La SY4 . . . . .83 D1
Godson's Cl WR15 . . . . .220 D5
Goldcrest Dr SY7 . . . . .114 B3
Goldcrest Gr **1** TF1. . . . . . .131 A7
Golden Acres **40** SY15 . . . .201 B3
Golden Cross La **2** SY8. . . .208 C2
Goldenhill La TF9 . . . . .72 D3
Goldney Ct **2** TF4 . . . . .143 D3
GOLDSTONE 72 D5
Goldstone Dr **3** WV16. . . . .218 D6
Goldstone Hall & Gdns*
TF9. . . . . .72 B3
Golfa Cl **3** SY21. . . . . .167 D3
Golf House La SY13 . . . . .15 D1
Golf Links La TF1 . . . . .130 E1
Gooch Cl TF7 . . . . .152 D6
Goodrich Cl TF2 . . . . .120 E1
GOOD'S GREEN 211 D8
Goodwood Ave WV15 . . . . . .219 B4
Goodwood Gr **8** LL13. . . . .221 F1
Goodwood Rd **3** TF2 . . . . .132 E7
Gooseberry La
Grinshill SY4 . . . . .84 C3
4 Ruyton SY4 . . . . .80 A1
Goosefield Cl **18** TF9. . . . . .36 E1
Goosemoor Cl DY12. . . . . . . .210 C7
Gordon Rd TF2 . . . . .132 B6
GORE THE 198 C1
Gorse La
Bayston Hill SY3 . . . . .136 E7
Trysull & Seisdon WV5. . . . .190 D3
Gorse Mdw SY3 . . . . .32 F5
Gorsy La TF10 . . . . .91 F4
GOSFORD 213 C3
Goshawk Dr TF6 . . . . .130 F8
Gosling Pk TF5 . . . . .130 D8
GOSPEL ASH. 190 B2
Gospel Ash Rd DY7 . . . . .190 B1
Gough Cl TF2 . . . . .144 F8
Goulbourne Rd **5** TF2 . . . . .132 D2
Gowan Ct **5** SY1 . . . . .114 B4
Gower Cl **4** TF2 . . . . .120 F1
Gower Pl **2** SY1 . . . . .58 F8
Gower St TF2 . . . . .132 D3
GRAFTON 99 C2
Grafton Mews SY1 . . . . .113 E4
Grainger Dr TF1 . . . . .131 B5
Grampian Cl **3** TF2. . . . . . .120 E1
Grange Ave
Stirchley & Brookside
TF3 . . . . .144 D1
Wrexham LL11 . . . . .221 C6
Grange Central TF3 . . . . .144 C6
Grange Cl
Condover SY5 . . . . .137 C1
4 Stirchley & Brookside
TF3 . . . . .144 D1
1 Wrexham LL11 . . . . . .221 C6
Grange Ct SY5 . . . . .137 B1
Grange Farm Ct TF9 . . . . . . .52 F8
Grange Farm SY10. . . . . .188 D1
Grange Farm Rise **5**
TF3. . . . . .143 E6
Grange Farm View TF3 . . . . .144 B3
Grangefields **4** SY3 . . . . . . .124 F3
Grangefields Rd SY3 . . . . . . .125 A3

Grange Gdns **15** SY9 . . . . .181 F3
Grange Jun & Inf Sch The
SY1. . . . . .113 E4
Grange La
Condover SY5 . . . . .137 B1
Lilleshall & Donnington
TF2 . . . . .133 A3
Grange Pk WV7 . . . . .156 F6
Grange Rd
Albrighton WV7 . . . . .156 F5
3 Bishop's Castle SY9 . . .181 E3
Bronington SY13 . . . . .12 F3
Ellesmere Urban SY22 . . . .27 A4
Knolton LL13 . . . . .9 D3
Maelor South LL13. . . . . . . .11 B2
12 Oakengates/Donnington
TF2 . . . . .132 A1
Shrewsbury SY3 . . . . .125 A6
Grange Sch The SY1 . . . . . . .113 E4
Grange Sports Ctr The
SY1. . . . . .113 E3
Gransden Dr **10** SY3 . . . . . .124 E4
Grantley Ave **8** SY3 . . . . . .124 C7
Granville Ave TF10 . . . . .109 F2
Granville Cl TF10. . . . . .109 F2
Granville Dr **11** TF2 . . . . . .120 F1
Granville Rd
Lilleshall & Donnington
TF2 . . . . .132 E5
Newport TF10 . . . . .109 F2
Granville St
1 Oakengates/Donnington
TF2 . . . . .132 E5
3 Shrewsbury SY3 . . . . .125 A6
Granville Terr TF1. . . . . .131 E4
Grasmere Cl **9** TF2. . . . . . . .132 D1
Grasmere Dr **2** WV16. . . . . .200 E2
Grasmere Way **8** LL12. . . . .221 D8
Grassy Bank WR15 . . . . .220 D3
GRAVELHILL 124 B6
GRAVELHILL 221 B5
Gravel Hill SY8 . . . . .217 D5
Gravel Hill La
Pimhill SY3 . . . . .113 A1
Shrewsbury SY3 . . . . .125 A8
GRAVEL HOLE. 26 A5
Gravel Leasowes TF4. . . . . . .152 E8
Gravelly Dr TF10 . . . . .109 E2
Gravels The WV5 . . . . .190 F3
GRAVELS 176 A7
Gravenhunger La CW3 . . . . .21 D8
GREAT BOLAS 106 D7
GREAT CHATWELL 123 D1
Great Croft **3** TF1. . . . . .143 E7
Great Croft Rd TF10. . . . . . . .107 D5
Greatford Gn **1** SY1. . . . . . .114 B4
Great Hales St TF9 . . . . .36 D1
Great Hay Dr TF7 . . . . .153 B3
GREAT LYTH 136 B3
Great Moor Rd WV6 . . . . . . .166 F2
GREAT NESS 98 B3
GREAT RYTON 158 C1
GREAT SUTTON 197 A2
Great Western Dr **1**
TF4 .143 D3
GREAT WYTHEFORD 104 A3
Grebe Cl TF3 . . . . .153 D8
Greenacre Rd SY3 . . . . .124 F6
Greenacres
4 Oakengates/Donnington
TF2 . . . . .131 F2
5 Wem SY4 . . . . .66 B8
Green Acres
Ludlow SY8 . . . . .217 E3
30 Wombourne WV5. . . . .190 F3
Greenacres La **5** DY12. . . . .211 D2
Greenacres Prim Sch
SY1. . . . . .113 C5
Greenacres Way TF10 . . . . . .109 D3
Greenaway Rd TF2 . . . . .132 A6
Green Bank TF9 . . . . .19 A5
Greenbank Cl **8** SY11. . . . . .58 E8
Greenbank St LL13. . . . . .221 D2
Green Cl **3** WV6. . . . . .166 C2
Greendale Cl **6** WV16. . . . . .200 E2
Greene Cl SY7 . . . . .195 E8
Green End SY11. . . . . .40 D1
Greenfield LL11 . . . . .221 C5
Greenfields
1 Shifnal TF11 . . . . .146 A4
20 Welshpool SY21 . . . . .170 B6
2 Whitchurch SY13 . . . .14 F8
Greenfields Cres
Bridgnorth WV16. . . . . .218 E6
Shifnal TF11 . . . . .146 A5
Greenfields Ct WV16 . . . . . . .218 E6
Greenfields Dr WV16. . . . . . .218 E6
Greenfields La TF9 . . . . .36 B2
Greenfields Prim Sch
SY1. . . . . .125 C8
Greenfield Sq SY10 . . . . .58 D4
Greenfields Rd
Bridgnorth WV16. . . . . .218 E6
3 Craven Arms SY7. . . . .195 D5
Greenfields Rise SY11. . . . . . .14 E8
Greenfield St **2** SY11 . . . . . .125 C8
Greenfinch Cl **4** TF1. . . . . . .130 F5
Greenfoot La TF11. . . . . .132 E8
Greenhall Ave **2** SY3 . . . . . .125 B6
GREENHILL BANK 26 C5
Greenhill Cl WR15 . . . . .220 D5
Greenhill Gdns WR15 . . . . . .220 D5
Greenhurst La TF9 . . . . .87 C4
Green La
Adderley CW3 . . . . .18 E8
Albrighton WV7 . . . . .156 A4
Bayston Hill SY3 . . . . .136 F7
Bomere Heath SY4 . . . . . . .100 F3

Green La continued
Chirk LL14 . . . . .6 F3
Churchstoke SY15 . . . . .175 B2
Edgmond Marsh TF10 . . . . .108 F5
Ercall Magna TF6 . . . . .105 C8
Longden SY3 . . . . .136 C2
Newport TF10 . . . . .109 E4
Onibury SY7 . . . . .195 E1
Orleton SY8 . . . . .212 D2
Prees SY13 . . . . .32 E1
1 Shrewsbury SY3 . . . . .125 B2
Stanton upon Hine Heath
TF9 . . . . .69 C1
St Martin's SY11 . . . . .24 D5
Whixall SY13 . . . . .31 A1
Greenlands **13** WV5 . . . . . . .190 F4
Greenlea Rd TF2. . . . . .132 A5
Green Leys Cres **10**
WV15 . . . . .201 B3
Greenman Cl **5** TF10 . . . . . .130 F3
Green Mdw Cl **20** WV5 . . . .190 F3
Green Pk LL13 . . . . .221 B1
GREEN THE 193 D4
Green The
Oswestry SY11 . . . . .58 F7
Woore SY3 . . . . .5 A1
8 Wrexham LL12 . . . . . .221 D8
Greenvale TF10 . . . . .121 E8
Green View TF11 . . . . .135 F8
Green Way **2** TF4 . . . . .143 E5
Greenway Ave WV5 . . . . .201 B3
Greenway Cross SY7 . . . . . . .196 A1
Greenway Gdns WV6 . . . . . . .166 C2
Greenways **4** SY3 . . . . .125 A6
Greenway The
11 Ellesmere SY12 . . . . .27 A2
2 Pattingham WV6. . . . . .166 C2
Greenwood Cl **3** SY2 . . . . . .125 F3
Greenwood Ct SY1 . . . . .113 F3
Greenwood Dr **7** TF5. . . . . .130 B8
GREETE 214 A5
Gregson Cl **1** SY2 . . . . .125 F7
Gregson Wlk TF4 . . . . .143 D5
Grenville Cl **3** TF11. . . . . . . .146 A5
Grenville Rd **6** TF13 . . . . . .159 F4
Gresford Way LL11 . . . . .221 D8
Gresham Dr TF3 . . . . .143 D7
Gresley Cl TF7 . . . . .152 D6
GRETTON 185 A6
Greville Rd SY3 . . . . .125 B4
Grey Bank SY7. . . . . .193 D4
Greyfriars
4 Bridgnorth WV16 . . . . .218 F6
Oswestry SY11 . . . . .59 A8
Greyfriars Rd **6** SY3 . . . . . .125 C5
Grey Gn La DY12. . . . . .211 D3
Greyhound Hill TF2 . . . . .132 B1
Greyhound La WV4. . . . . .190 F7
Greystone Ct **12** SY3 . . . . . .124 B6
Greystones Ct **3** SY3 . . . . . .125 A3
Greystones Way SY11 . . . . . .58 F6
Griffin Cl TF9 . . . . .20 C2
Grigg's La WV16 . . . . .199 E2
GRIMPO 61 A2
Grimpo Rd SY11 . . . . .78 E8
GRINDLE 155 A2
Grindle Rd
Grindle TF11 . . . . .155 A2
Kemberton TF11 . . . . .154 D4
GRINDLEY BROOK 1 C3
GRINSHILL 84 C3
Grinshill **2** TF1 . . . . .130 D6
Grinshill Dr **4** SY2 . . . . .125 F6
Grizedale Dr TF4. . . . . .143 D2
GROESPLUAN 170 A8
GRONWEN 58 B1
Groom's Alley TF1 . . . . .130 D4
Grooms La TF1 . . . . .154 C6
Grosvenor Cotts SY12 . . . . . .27 B3
Grosvenor Ct **2** TF9. . . . . . .36 D2
Grosvenor Gdns TF11 . . . . . .146 E4
Grosvenor Rd **5** SY1 . . . . . .113 E4
Grosvenor Rd
Market Drayton TF9. . . . . . .36 D1
Oswestry SY11 . . . . .41 A1
Wrexham LL11 . . . . .221 C4
Grosvenor Wood **8**
DY12. . . . . .211 C2
Groton Farm Rd SY21. . . . . .171 B1
Grotto Rd **2** TF9. . . . . .36 B1
Grove Campus Language Sch
TF9. . . . . .36 D2
Grove Cl LD7 . . . . .203 C2
Grove Cres
Bridgnorth WV15 . . . . .219 A4
Oswestry SY11 . . . . .5 A1
Grove Ct SY4 . . . . .65 F6
Grove Dr SY7 . . . . .195 E2
Grove Est The TF2 . . . . .132 D2
Grovefields TF1. . . . . .131 B5
Grove Gdns TF9 . . . . .36 D1
Grove La
Bayston Hill SY3 . . . . .137 A5
Grinshill SY4 . . . . .84 D4
Pontesbury SY5 . . . . .173 B4
Grove Lodge Cl **5** LL11. . . .221 C4
Grove Mdw **9** SY21. . . . . . .209 E3
Grove Pk Rd **3** LL11 . . . . . .221 C4
Grove Rd
Shrewsbury SY3 . . . . .125 E3
The Rock TF3 . . . . .131 E1
Whixall SY13 . . . . .31 A1
Grove St TF2 . . . . .132 D2
Grove The
Bridgnorth WV15. . . . . .219 A4

Grove The *continued*
Hadley TF1................131 C5
Hodnet TF9.................69 D4
Minsterley SY5............172 E4
Pimhill SY4...............100 E4
4 Shifnal TF11.........146 A4
5 Wem SY4...............66 A6
Whitchurch SY13............1 F2
Grug Hill SY4...........79 F2
Guest Rd TF12..........161 E7
Guests Cl 7 TF12.......132 E7
Guild La TF10..........111 A7
Guinea Cl 13 TF2.......132 B2
Guinea La SY4...........67 C6
Guinevere Cl 3 SY11.....40 F1
Guisbourne Ave 8 TF5...130 C8
Gungrog Fawr La SY21...170 C8
Gungrog Hill SY21......170 C7
Gungrog La SY21........170 B8
Guy Thornycroft Ct SY8.217 F3
Gwelfryn SY22...........93 D6
Gwenfro LL13...........221 F3
Gwenfro Prim Sch LL13..221 F2
GWERNEIRIN.............191 C2
Gwernodwddy La SY22.....94 D1
GWERN Y BRENIN..........58 F1
Gwern-y-go La SY22.....167 B8
Gwydyr Way 3 LL13.....221 D1
Gwyn Cl 5 SY25.........125 F6

H

HABBERLEY..............173 A2
Habberley La DY11......211 F4
Habberley Rd
Bewdley DY11..............211 F3
Pontesbury SY5...........173 A2
Habersham Cl SY7.......182 B1
Hackett Cl 16 LL13.....221 E1
Haddon Pl TF4..........143 F5
HADLEY.................131 D5
HADLEY CASTLE..........131 D7
Hadley Cl LL14..........23 E8
Hadley Gdns TF1........131 B7
Hadley Hollow TF1......131 D4
Hadley Learning Com
TF1......................131 C4
Hadley Lodge Rd TF1....131 E4
HADLEY PARK............131 C8
Hadley Pk Rd TF11......131 B6
Hadley Rd
Oakengates/Donnington
TF2......................132 A3
Hadley Vallens TF1.....131 D4
HADNALL................102 C4
Hadnall CE Prim Sch
SY4......................102 C4
Hafod Cl
Oswestry SY10.............58 C8
4 Pant SY22.............93 F6
Hafod-y-wern Prim Sch
LL13.....................221 F3
Hafren Cl SY3..........125 A6
Hafren Rd
Dawley TF4...............143 E1
Shrewsbury SY3...........125 A6
Haig Rd LL13...........221 D2
Halcyon Ct 6 TF2.......132 F8
HALES..................146 B6
Hales Ct TF11..........134 B5
HALESFIELD.............153 E6
Halesfield 1 TF7.......144 F1
Halesfield 2 TF7.......153 E7
Halesfield 3 TF7.......153 E7
Halesfield 4 TF7.......153 E7
Halesfield 5 TF7.......153 E7
Halesfield 7 TF7.......153 E6
Halesfield 8 TF7.......153 E6
Halesfield 9 TF7.......153 E5
Halesfield 10 TF7......153 E4
Halesfield 11 TF7......153 E4
Halesfield 13 TF7......153 E5
Halesfield 14 TF7......153 D5
Halesfield 15 TF7......153 E4
Halesfield 16 TF7......153 E6
Halesfield 17 TF7......153 D6
Halesfield 18 TF7......153 D6
Halesfield 19 TF7......153 D7
Halesfield 20 TF7......153 E4
Halesfield 21 TF7......153 E7
Halesfield 22 TF7......153 E8
Halesfield 23 TF7......153 E8
Halesfield 24 TF7......144 E1
Halesfield 25 TF7......144 E1
Halesfield Ind Est TF7..153 E5
Halesford Rd TF7.......153 C6
HALES PARK.............211 C2
Hales Pk 28 DY12.......211 C2
HALFORD................195 E6
Halford Cres 7 SY7.....195 E5
Halfpenny Gn Vineyard*
DY7......................195 B3
HALFPENNY GREEN........190 B3
HALFWAY HOUSE..........168 B2
Halfway House La WV16..218 E1
Halghton La SY13........11 C8
Halifax Dr 4 TF1.......131 B6
Halifax Rd WV7.........147 F1
Hallam Dr 3 SY1........114 B4
Hall Bank
Churchstoke SY15.........175 A1
Pontesbury SY5...........173 B5
Hall Barn Cl 3 TF7.....153 A5

Hall Cl WV6............166 C2
Hallcroft Cl TF10......109 E3
Hallcroft Ct 5 SY11....125 D8
Hallcroft Gdns TF10....109 E3
Halldene 5 TF1.........131 B4
Hall Dr SY4............102 C5
Hall End Cl 6 WV6......166 C2
Hall End La WV6........166 C2
Hallets Well 5 SY8.....212 E2
Hall Farm Rd WV16......198 D7
Hall Gdns
4 Condover SY5.........178 E8
7 Haybridge TF1........131 B4
HALL GREEN..............13 D8
Hall La TF11...........154 B6
HALLON.................189 A6
Hallon 1 WV15.........189 A6
HALLONSFORD............189 B7
Hall Pk Way TF3........144 A6
Hall Rd WV16...........198 D7
Halls Farm La DY12.....211 D4
Hall St 14 SY21........170 B6
Halmar Dr SY21........170 B2
Halston Cotts SY5......173 C6
Halstonwood Cl 6 LL13..221 F5
HALTON..................7 A4
Halton LL14.............7 A5
Halton La
Bromfield SY8............206 E2
Ludlow SY8...............217 A4
Hamilton Dr SY2........126 B8
Hamilton Rd TF4........143 F1
Hamlet Cl
Ludlow SY8...............217 D6
5 Oakengates/Donnington
TF2......................132 A3
Hamlet Rd SY8..........217 D6
Hammonds Ct 6 SY11.....41 A8
Hammonds Pl SY11.......41 B8
Hampden Rd 6 LL13.....221 C2
HAMPERLEY..............183 D4
Hampshire Dr LL11......221 C8
Hampson Ave LL13.......221 E2
HAMPTON................200 E5
HAMPTON BANK............29 A2
HAMPTON BEECH..........171 D4
Hampton Cl
3 Newport TF10........110 A3
Oswestry SY11.............41 A3
Hampton Dr
3 Market Drayton TF9....36 C2
Newport TF10.............110 A3
Hampton Fields SY11.....58 C8
Hampton Hill TF1.......130 C1
HAMPTON LOADE..........201 A5
Hampton Loade Sta
WV16.....................200 F5
Hampton Rd
Oswestry SY11.............40 C1
7 Shrewsbury SY1......125 E8
Hampton Rise 6 SY11....58 C8
HAMPTON WOOD............28 B8
Hancocks Dr 8 TF2......132 B2
Hand Cswy 11 SY7.......193 D3
Hand La TF11...........122 D1
HANDLESS...............183 A5
Hankins Heys La CW3.....20 A8
Hanley La SY3..........133 B6
HANMER..................12 B4
Hanmer Cl 6 LL13........9 C8
Hanmer Prim Sch SY13...12 A4
Hanover Ct TF7.........153 B6
Hanover Way 1 LL13.....221 D1
HANWOOD................173 F8
HANWOOD BANK...........169 F1
Hanwood Rd SY5.........124 C2
Harcourt Cl SY4.........85 D1
Harcourt Cres SY2......126 A6
Harcourt Dr TF10.......110 A4
Harding Cl 7 TF2.......132 C7
HARDWICK...............182 D5
Hardwick Dr SY3........124 D6
Harebell Glade 8 TF3...144 E3
HAREBUTT BANK..........106 D5
Harefields Cl 4 SY9.....99 B8
Haresfield 6 SY3.......124 C7
Harlech Cl 5 SY11.......41 A1
Harlech Ct SY11.........41 A1
Harlech Rd SY11.........41 A1
HARLESCOTT.............113 E4
Harlescott Cl 2 SY1....114 A3
Harlescott Cres SY1....113 E4
Harlescott Ind Est SY1.113 F5
Harlescott Jun Sch SY1.114 B3
Harlescott La SY1......113 E5
HARLEY.................158 E8
Harley Cl
Tweedale TF3.............153 D7
Wellington TF1...........130 C6
Harley Dr
8 Condover SY5........178 E8
Shrewsbury SY1...........113 E3
Harley Hill SY5........159 B5
Harley Jenkins St 8
SY9......................181 F3
Harley Rd
3 Condover SY5........178 E8
Cressage SY5.............149 E4
Harley Way WV16........218 C5
HARMER HILL.............83 B1
HARNAGE................159 E2
Haroldgate SY13.........1 F1
Harper Adams Univ Coll
TF10.....................108 E5
Harp La
Dawley TF4...............143 F2
Ludlow SY8...............217 D3
Harrietts Hayes Rd WV7.157 E6

Harrington Heath 2
TF5......................118 C1
Harrison Cl 3 TF7......152 F4
Harris's Gn TF12.......161 C8
Harris's La TF7........152 D4
Harrison Rd TF9........143 D8
Harrow La TF9...........71 D2
HARTLEBURY.............188 F8
Hartley Cl 7 TF1.......131 E1
Hartmann Cl 8 DY14....209 D2
HARTON.................196 D7
Harton Hollow Nature
Reserve*** SY6..........196 C6
Harton Hollow Way SY6..196 B6
Hartsbridge Rd 8 TF2...131 F2
Hartsbridge Rd 8 TF2...131 F2
HARTSGREEN.............201 E2
Hartshill TF2..........131 F2
Hartshill Ave 8 TF1....131 F2
Hartwood Cl 6 TF10.....109 F5
Harvest Cl TF10........109 F4
Harvey Cres TF1........131 B2
Harvington Cl 4 TF1....130 E5
Haslehurst Cl SY7......193 D4
Hassacks The SY4.......114 B3
HASTON.................101 F7
Haston Rd SY4..........101 F6
Hatchetts Cl SY4........64 B1
Hatch La
Astley SY4...............102 E3
Blymhill & Weston-under-Lizard
TF11.....................135 D4
Hatfield Mdws 17 LD7...203 B3
HATTON.................184 B1
Hatton Rd TF9...........71 D2
Haughmond Ave 3 SY1....114 A3
HAUGHTON
Llandysilio..............95 B1
Morville.................187 F6
Shifnal..................145 E6
Upton Magna.............115 C5
West Felton..............61 D2
Haughton Cl 5 WV16....218 C6
Haughton Dr 11 TF11....145 F5
Haughton La TF11.......145 E5
Haughton La TF11.......145 E6
Haughton Rd TF9........145 F5
Haughton Sch TF7.......153 C5
Havelock Rd TF13.......159 D4
Havelock Rd SY3.......125 D4
Havenwood TF3.........143 C8
Havisham Ct TF10.......109 E3
HAWGREEN................87 E7
Hawkestone Rd 2 SY1....114 A4
Hawkshaw Cl 11 TF2.....132 B2
Hawksmoor La SY4.......101 F3
Hawkstone Cl SY4.......109 E2
Hawkstone Ct SY4........67 F6
Hawkstone Dr SY4........66 C7
HAWKSWOOD..............200 A3
Hawksworth Rd
Oakengates TF2...........144 C8
St Georges TF2...........132 C1
Hawshaw Cl 7 TF3.......144 C3
Hawthorn Cl
2 Craven Arms SY7.....195 D6
Stanley Green SY13........31 C3
St Martin's SY11.......54 B6
Hawthorn Cres 8 DY12...211 C2
Hawthorn Dr 10 WV16....200 E3
Hawthorne Cl 4 TF2.....132 A1
Hawthorne Gr SY11.......58 F7
Hawthorn Pl TF2........132 D8
Hawthorn Rd
Minsterley SY5...........172 E4
2 Oakengates/Donnington
TF2......................132 C2
Hawthorns The
Bridgnorth WV16..........218 E4
2 Ellesmere Urban SY12..27 A3
5 Shrewsbury SY5......125 D4
Worthen with Shelve SY5..171 E3
2 Wrexham LL12.........221 E5
Hawthorn Way 9 TF9......36 C2
HAYBRIDGE
Hadley...................131 B4
Milson...................215 B8
Haybridge Ave TF1......131 B4
Haybridge Rd 6 TF1.....131 C5
Haycocks Cl TF1........130 D6
Haycock Way SY3........125 E4
Hayes Cl SY11...........58 C8
Hayes La WR15.........213 F2
Hayes Rd TF1...........131 A1
Hayes View SY11.........40 C1
HAYGATE................130 B2
Haygate Dr 1 TF1.......130 C2
Haygate Dr 8 TF1.......130 C2
Haygate Dr W TF1.......130 C2
Haygate Rd TF1.........130 C2
Hayes The SY8.........213 D8
Haynall La SY8.........213 C2
Hay The 3 SY3..........143 E7
HAYTON'S BENT..........207 B7
Hayton View SY8........217 D6
Haytor Rd LL11.........221 C6
Hayward Ave 3 TF2......132 D1
Haywood Cl 12 SY2......126 A7
Haywood La
Cheswardine TF9...........72 E8
Sutton upon Tern TF9......54 B1
Hazel Cl 3 SY21........167 A1
Hazeldine Cres 3 SY4...103 D6
Hazel Gr
Oswestry SY11.............58 F7
2 Wrexham LL12........221 D6
Hazelgrove 8 WV15......201 B3
Hazel View WV15........219 B4

Hazel Way TF2.........132 C1
Hazelwells Rd WV16.....200 E3
Hazelwood Dr 7 TF4.....152 F8
Hazledine Way SY3......125 C2
HAZLER.................216 E5
Hazler Cres SY6........216 D5
Hazler Dr SY6..........216 D5
Hazler Orch SY6........216 E5
Hazler Rd SY6..........216 E5
Hazlitt Pl SY4.........66 B7
Hearne La TF9...........69 C6
Hearne Way 4 SY22.....126 A8
Heathbrook Junc TF9.....69 F6
Heath Cl 2 DY14.......209 D2
HEATHCOTE...............70 F5
Heather Bank 4 SY11....41 B8
Heather Cl
5 Oswestry SY11........59 A7
11 Welshpool SY21.....170 B7
Heatherdale TF1........131 A5
Heather Dr 2 TF1.......130 F3
Heatherwood SY21.......170 D1
Heathfield Rd TF1......113 D2
Heathfield Rd DY12.....211 C2
Heathgates 7 SY1......113 E1
HEATH HILL.............122 D1
Heath Hill TF4.........143 D4
Heath House Dr 8 WV5...190 E3
Heath La SY13...........2 E6
Heathlands 7 WV5.......190 E3
Heathlands 7 TF5.......132 C3
Heathlands The 4 WV5...190 E3
HEATH LANES............105 D7
Heath Mill Rd DY3......190 E2
Heath Rd
Gnosall TF10.............111 E1
Wellington TF1...........130 D5
Whitchurch Rural SY13.....15 C3
HEATHTON...............190 A3
Heathwood Rd
Newport TF10.............109 D2
Prees Higher Heath SY13...32 E3
Heaton Cl 3 SY3........124 F3
Hebden Gr 10 SY3.......124 B6
Heber Mount 2 LL13.....221 F4
Heblands Bank SY9......181 F5
Hedgerows The 6
WV16.....................198 D8
Hedges The 12 WV5......190 F3
Hedingham Rd TF11......131 C8
Hedley Way TF9..........52 D4
Heightington Rd DY12...211 D1
Heighways La SY5.......184 B6
Heighways The SY5......179 E7
Heldre La SY21.........167 A1
Helfa Bach LL14.........6 E3
Hellier Dr 3 WV5.......190 F4
Helmeth Rd SY6.........216 E6
HEMFORD................175 F7
Hem La
Shifnal TF11.............153 F8
Westbury SY5.............172 C4
Hemsworth Way 9 SY1....113 C1
HEM THE................154 C8
Henblas St 2 LL11......221 D3
HENDOMEN...............174 A5
Hendomen Dr SY15......174 B3
Hendre La 2 SY22.......167 A8
Hendrie Cl 1 TF11......131 D2
Henfaes La SY22........170 C6
HENGOED.................40 E7
Hengrave Mdw TF3.......143 D7
HENLEY
Acton Scott.............196 A7
Ludford.................207 C3
Henley Cl SY11.........41 A1
Henley Dr
4 Newport TF10........110 A4
Oakengates/Donnington
TF2......................132 B6
Oswestry SY11.............41 A1
Henley La
Acton Scott SY6..........196 A8
Bitterley SY8............207 C3
Henley Orchards SY8....217 D6
Henley Rd SY8..........217 D6
Henley Terr SY8........217 C5
HENLLE..................41 F7
Henlle Cl SY11..........23 F1
Henlle Gdns SY11........23 F1
Henlow Rise 2 SY21.....124 F2
Henry Cl SY11..........113 E6
Henry Jones Cl 8 SY11...58 B8
Henry Jones Rd 10 SY11..59 B8
Heol Abon LL20..........6 B8
Heol Bennion 5 LL20.....6 B8
Heol Berwyn 4 LL20......6 B8
Heol Cefnydd 3 LL14.....6 B8
Heol Dinas LL11........221 C7
Heol Graigfab 2 LL14....6 B8
Herbert Ave TF1........130 C2
Herbert Jennings Ave
LL12.....................221 E6
Hereford Cl 2 WV7......156 F8
Hereford Dr 5 TF2......133 A1
Hereford Rd
Bayston Hill SY3.........137 B7
5 Shrewsbury SY3......125 C3
Heritage Gn 3 SY21....170 C1
Hermitage Cl
Bridgnorth WV15.........219 B5
1 Westbury SY5........172 C8
Hermitage Dr
5 Shrewsbury SY3......125 C8
Wrexham LL13............221 D1
Hermitage Hts SY4......219 A4
Hermitage Pk 9 LL13....221 D1

Hermitage Way TF7......152 E4
Hermitage Wlk SY3......125 B7
Herne's Nest 2 DY12....211 D1
Heronbrook 1 SY7.......14 E8
Heron Cl
Clive SY4.................84 B5
Dawley TF3...............153 D6
Ellesmere Urban SY12....27 B3
Heron Dr SY1...........114 B4
Herons Gate Rd DY7.....201 F3
Heron Way 8 TF10.......109 F5
Hertford Cl 9 TF1......130 F5
Hesba Cl TF1...........130 C3
Hexham Way SY22........125 C2
HEYOP..................202 D5
Heyop Rd LD7...........202 D5
Heywood Lonsdale Ct 1
TF1......................130 E3
Hiatt Ave 8 TF1........130 E4
Hickman Rd WV15........219 E4
Higford La TF11........164 B6
Highclere 1 DY12.......211 D1
High Cross Ave SY5.....138 F3
High Cswy TF13.........159 D4
High Ercall Prim Sch
TF6......................116 E7
Higher Rd SY4..........83 B2
HIGHER RIDGE............42 F8
High Fawr Ave SY10......58 C8
High Fawr Cl 3 SY10....58 C8
Highfield
Chetwynd Aston & Woodcote
TF10.....................121 F8
Lawley & Overdale TF4....143 B6
Highfields
Chirk Green LL14..........6 F1
4 Market Drayton TF9...53 B8
Shrewsbury SY2...........126 A5
Highfields Ave SY13.....14 F6
Highfields Rd WV16.....218 C5
Highgate SY13..........15 A7
Highgate Dr
Priorslee TF2............133 A2
9 Shrewsbury SY3......124 F3
High Gr 4 SY11..........59 B8
HIGH GREEN.............200 B2
Highgrove Mdws 8 TF2...132 F2
HIGH HATTON.............87 C6
High Hatch.............71 E3
High House La WV7......157 D4
Highland Lea 3 TF4.....143 C3
Highland Rd 6 TF10.....109 C2
Highlands Rd WV16......218 C4
High Lea Cl 5 SY11......58 C8
HIGHLEY................200 C2
Highley Prim Sch WV16..200 E2
Highley Sta WV16.......200 F2
High Mdws TF10.........110 A3
High Mount TF2.........132 D6
High Oaks 3 SY3........124 B7
High Path WV6..........166 C3
High Point TF6.........144 A2
High Ridge Dr 1 LL14...221 A2
High Ridge Way SY3.....124 F4
High St
Albrighton WV7...........157 A5
Bewdley DY12.............211 D2
4 Bishop's Castle SY9..181 F3
Bridgnorth WV16..........218 F5
Broseley TF12............161 C8
Cheswardine TF9..........72 F8
Church Stretton SY6......216 C6
Claverley WV5............189 E4
Cleehill SY8.............208 C2
Cleobury Mortimer DY14...209 F2
Clive SY4................84 A5
6 Clun SY7............193 D3
Coalport TF8.............153 B1
Dawley TF4...............143 E3
Edgmond TF10.............108 F2
3 Ellesmere SY12.......27 C2
Grinshill SY4............84 C3
Hadley TF1...............131 C5
Highley WV16.............200 F2
Ironbridge TF8...........152 C3
9 Knighton LD7........203 B3
Leintwardine SY7.........205 B5
Ludlow SY8...............217 C4
Madeley TF7..............153 B1
6 Market Drayton TF9...36 D1
Much Wenlock TF13........159 E4
Newport TF10.............109 F3
Overton LL13..............9 C8
Pattingham WV6...........166 C5
Ruyton-XI-Towns SY4......80 B1
4 Shifnal TF11........145 F5
Shrewsbury SY1...........125 C3
Swindon DY3..............190 F1
Wellington TF1...........130 E3
Wem SY4..................65 F6
Weston Rhyn SY10..........2 A3
Whitchurch SY13..........15 A8
Wrexham LL13.............221 D1
HIGHTOWN...............221 D1
HIGH TOWN..............218 E5
Hightown Rd LL13.......221 D3
High View TF4..........143 E6
Highway View TF1.......131 B2
Hilda Hooke Cl 6 TF7...153 C5
Hillbury Rd LL13.......221 E4
Hill Cres
Ellesmere Rural SY12......26 B7
Shrewsbury SY3...........125 B3

Hill Crest
Ellesmere Urban SY12.....27 C3
Penley LL13...........10 E3
4 Wrexham LL12.........221 E4
Hill Crest Rd 3 TF2....132 C2
Hill Ct 1 LL13.........221 E1
Hillewood Ave SY13.....14 F6
HILLFIELDS HOUSE......211 D8
Hill Fold TF4..........143 E6
HILL HOUSES..........209 A6
Hill Pk SY12..........26 B6
Hill Rd
Oakengates/Donnington
  TF2................120 D3
The Rock TF3..........143 E8
Hillrise 5 LL13.......221 E1
Hillside
Edgmond TF10.........108 F4
Ironbridge TF8........152 D4
Lilleshall TF10.......121 B4
Ludlow SY8............217 C5
Myddle & Broughton SY4..82 E4
Oswestry SY11.........40 E1
16 Dunsdale WV5.......190 F4
Pant SY10.............76 A1
Hillside Ave WV15.....219 A3
Hillside Cl TF1.......131 A1
Hillside Dr SY2.......126 B6
Hillside Rd
Cressage SY5..........149 E4
5 Oakengates/Donnington
  TF2................132 A1
Wrexham LL13..........221 C3
Hill Top TF1..........131 E2
Hilltop Ave 5 DY12....211 E3
Hill Top Rd TF7.......131 F3
Hilltop View Rd LL12...221 F7
HILLWICKET............89 F6
Hilly Bank WV16.......218 E4
Hilly La SY8..........168 E8
HILTON................189 C6
Hilton Cl 14 TF3......144 C1
Hilton Terr TF2.......132 C3
Himley La DY3.........190 F1
HINDFORD.............42 A6
HINE HEATH............86 D8
Hinksford Gdns 9 DY3..190 F1
Hinksford La DY12.....190 F1
Hinkshay Rd
2 Dawley TF4.........143 F2
Great Dawley TF4......144 A3
Hinnington Rd TF11....155 A3
Hinsley Mill La TF9....36 E2
HINSTOCK.............72 A1
Hinstock Prim Sch TF2..72 A2
HINTON...............173 C6
Hinton La SY5.........173 B5
HINTS................208 E2
Hints Mdw SY8.........208 E2
Hinwood Rd SY5........172 D2
Hoarstone Cl 4 DY12...211 E3
Hoarstone La DY12.....211 E4
HOBARRIS.............193 E1
HOBBINS THE..........219 E5
Hockley Bank TF11.....161 C8
Hockley Rd 4 TF12.....161 C8
Hodgebower TF8........152 C4
Hodginson Wlk 5 SY11..113 D5
HODNET...............69 D6
Hodnet Hall Gdns* TF9..69 E8
Hodnet Link TF7.......69 C4
Hodnet Prim Sch TF9....69 D5
Hoel-y-plas LL14......6 C8
Hogarth Cl SY5........172 E3
Holbache Rd SY11......211 D5
Holborn Dr 2 SY2......126 A2
Holbourn Cres TF12....133 A2
Holcroft Way SY5......138 F3
HOLDGATE.............197 E8
Holdgate Dr SY1.......114 C2
Holdings La CW3.......5 D8
Holendene Way 18 WV5..190 F4
Holland Dr 7 TF2......132 E8
Hollies Dr SY3........136 F7
Hollies La
Enville DY7...........201 F4
Kidderminster Foreign
  DY11...............211 F6
Pattingham & Patshull
  WV6...............166 F5
Trefonen SY10........57 D2
Hollies Rd TF1........130 C4
Hollies The SY11......24 E5
Hollingsgate TF3......144 C6
Hollins La
Marbury SY13.........2 E8
Market Drayton TF9....53 F4
Whitchurch Rural SY13..14 D1
HOLLINSWOOD.........144 C6
Hollinswood Inf & Jun Sch
  TF3................144 D5
Hollinswood Inf Sch TF4 144 D5
Hollinswood Rd TF2....132 C1
HOLLINWOOD..........31 C5
Hollow Ash La WV15....201 B5
Hollow Dr 22 WV5......190 F3
Holloway The DY3......190 E1
Holloway The SY4......83 C1
Holly Bank SY4........83 B1

Hollybirch Gr 7 TF2....132 D2
Hollybush La LL13.....10 E7
Hollybush Rd WV16.....218 E4
Holly Cl
Clive SY4.............84 B5
1 Ellesmere SY12......27 A3
1 Market Drayton TF9..53 A8
Holly Gn 8 SY11.......58 F7
Holly Gr 4 LL13.......221 F4
Holly Grange SY10.....23 F5
HOLLYHURST..........184 C8
Hollyhurst Rd
Marley Green SY13.....3 B7
Oakengates/Donnington
  TF2................132 A4
Holly La DY14.........199 E2
Hollyoak Gr 1 TF2.....132 E1
Holly Rd
Dawley Hamlets TF4....143 D1
Dawley TF4............143 E1
Tenbury Wells WR15....220 D6
Holly View 8 SY21.....170 D1
Holly Walks LL12......221 D5
HOLLYWASTE..........209 C2
Hollywood Dr 3 WV16...200 E3
Holme Ct 2 TF1........130 E5
Holmer La TF1.........143 A1
Holmer Lake Prim Sch
  TF3................153 D8
Holmes Orch 7 WV15....201 B3
Holm Lang Gn 1 TF7....152 F4
Holsworth Pk 14 SY3....124 C7
Holt Coppice TF5......130 A7
Holt End SY1..........114 B5
Holt Rd / Stryt Holt LI3 221 E4
Holt St LL12..........221 D3
Holy Cross CE Jun Sch
  SY2................126 A3
Holyhead Rd
Albrighton TF11.......156 B5
Bicton SY3...........112 B1
Hadley TF1...........131 D2
Montford SY4.........169 C7
Oakengates/Donnington
  TF2................131 F2
Wellington TF1........130 C2
West Felton SY11......78 D8
Holyrood Cres LL11....221 C6
Holywell La
Dawley Hamlets TF4....152 D8
Dawley TF4...........143 D1
Holywell St SY2.......125 E6
Home Farm Rd WV6......165 D7
Homelands 6 TF2.......131 F1
HOMER................159 D7
Homestead Ave SY11....24 F6
Homestead La LL12.....221 A2
Homestead The LL13....221 A2
Honeybourne Cres 23
  WV5................190 F3
Honeybourne Rd 4
  WV15...............201 B3
Honey Mdw SY8.........217 F4
Honeysuckle Dr 10 SY11..58 F7
Honeysuckle Row 6
  SY3................125 D7
Honington Ave WV7.....156 C8
HONNINGTON..........121 A3
Hoo Farm Animal Kingdom*
  TF6................119 F2
Hookacre Gr TF2.......132 E2
HOOK-A-GATE.........136 C7
Hook Farm Rd WV16.....218 D6
Hookfield The WV16....218 D6
Hook La The WV7.......157 A1
Hooks La SY4..........89 F7
HOPE
Trewern..............170 E6
Worthen with Shelve....176 B8
Hope Bagot La SY8.....208 A1
HOPE BOWDLER........184 C2
Hope CE Prim Sch SY5..176 B8
Hope Rd SY21.........170 E6
HOPESAY.............195 D6
Hopesay Hill Rd SY7...195 D6
Hopescross TF13.......185 D1
Hopeshay Cl TF3.......144 C1
Hope St LL11.........221 C3
HOPE THE............207 A5
Hope Valley Nature
  Reserve* SY5......176 B8
Hopkins Heath TF5.....130 A8
Hopkins The WR15......220 E4
Hop Pole La DY12......211 C2
HOPSHORT............73 B5
HOPSTONE............189 D5
HOPTON
Great Ness...........97 F5
Hodnet..............68 E2
HOPTONBANK.........208 F4
Hopton Bank DY14......208 F3
HOPTON CANGEFORD.....207 D7
HOPTON CASTLE.......194 D7
Hopton Cl SY8........217 D6
Hopton Dr SY1........114 B2
HOPTONGATE.........207 B7
HOPTONHEATH........204 F8
Hopton Heath Sta SY7..204 E8
HOPTON WAFERS......209 B3
Hopton Wafers CE Prim Sch
  DY14...............209 A3
HORDLEY.............43 D2
Hordley Ave 8 SY1.....113 D4
Hordley Rd
Ellesmere Rural SY12..43 F5
Wellington TF1........130 C5
Horksley SY1.........113 D4
Hornbeam Cl 1 TF1.....131 A3

Horne Rd TF2..........120 D3
Hornet Way 2 TF3......143 F8
Horsa Way WV7.........156 B7
HORSEBRIDGE.........172 C5
Horsebridge Rd SY5....172 E4
Horsechestnut Dr 8
  TF5................130 C8
Horsefair 4 SY2.......125 D6
Horse Gr Hill 5 WV15..219 A4
HORSEHAY............143 C2
Horsehay & Dawley Sta
Horsehay Est TF4......143 C3
HORSEMAN'S GREEN....11 F7
Horseshoe La SY12.....26 D5
Horseshoe Paddock TF4 143 D6
Horseshoe Rd SY15....174 F5
Horsley Dr LL12.......221 D8
HORTON
Hadley...............119 E1
Wem Rural............47 C1
Horton Cr
Hortonwood TF1........132 A8
Oakengates/Donnington
  TF2................120 A1
Horton La
Hadley TF6...........119 E1
Oakengates/Donnington
  TF2................131 F8
HORTONLANE.........169 F2
Horton Rd 1 TF2.......131 F6
HORTONWOOD.........131 F7
Hortonwood 1 TF1......131 E7
Hortonwood 2 TF1......131 F7
Hortonwood 7 TF1......131 F7
Hortonwood 8 TF1......131 F7
Hortonwood 10 TF1.....131 E7
Hortonwood 30 TF1.....131 E7
Hortonwood 31 TF1.....131 E7
Hortonwood 32 TF1.....131 F7
Hortonwood 33 TF1.....131 F7
Hortonwood 35 TF1.....131 F8
Hortonwood 37 TF2.....132 A8
Hortonwood 40 TF1.....119 E1
Hortonwood 50 TF2.....120 A1
Hortonwood 60 TF1.....119 E1
Hoskens Cl 8 TF4......143 E4
Hospital La
5 Clun SY7...........193 D3
Market Drayton TF9....53 A8
Whitchurch Rural SY13..15 D2
Hospital St SY1.......219 A4
Hotel Pl 11 SY6.......216 C6
Hotspur St SY1........114 B5
Houghton Houses TF6...115 C4
Houston Cl 8 TF2......132 D4
Houndel Gr TF1........130 E1
House on Crutches Mus*
  SY9................181 A4
Housman Cl
1 Dawley TF3.........153 A8
Ludlow SY8...........217 E4
Housman Mews SY6......216 C6
Howard St 4 SY1.......125 C7
Howell Rd 20 SY21.....170 B6
HOWLE...............90 A3
Howle Cl TF3..........144 C2
Hubbal La TF11........147 D3
Hubert Way SY1........113 D2
Hucklemarsh Rd SY8....217 D6
Hudson Rd WV7.........156 B7
Hudson Way 8 TF2......72 F7
HUGHLEY.............185 F8
Hullah La LL13........221 F4
Humber La TF2.........120 B3
HUMBERS THE.........120 A2
Humber Way TF2........120 B2
HUNGERFORD.........197 C8
HUNGRYHATTON.......71 C2
Hunsterson Rd CW5.....4 C8
Hunters Gate 4 TF13...159 F4
Hunter St SY3.........125 B7
Huntingdon Gn SY8.....213 B5
Huntingdon La SY8.....213 B5
HUNTINGTON.........142 E4
Huntington Dr TF4.....143 D6
Huntroyde Ave 12 LL11..221 E6
Huntsmans Cl 8 WV16...218 D6
Huntsman's Cnr LL12...221 F2
Huntsman Way 12 TF4...143 E4
HURDLEY............175 C1
Hurdsman St 8 SY1.....114 B4
Hurleybrook Way 1 TF1 131 B4
Hurst Cl 5 TF12.......161 E7
Hurst The 4 DY14......209 E2
Hussey Rd SY1.........113 E6
Hussey Way SY1........113 A6
Hutchinson Way 3 SY11 113 A6
Huxley Cl SY2.........126 A3
Hyde Cl 9 TF2.........132 F8
HYSSINGTON.........175 D1

I

Ice House Cl TF6......130 E7
Idsall Cres 1 TF11....146 A5
Idsall Sch TF11.......146 A6
Idsall Sports Ctr TF11..146 B5
Ifton Fields SY11.....24 E6
Ifton Heath Prim Sch
  SY11...............24 E7
IGHTFIELD...........16 E1
Ightfield Cl SY13.....16 F6
IGHTFIELD HEATH.....33 E7
Incline The TF8.......131 D2

Ingestre Cl TF10......109 D2
Ingleby Way 4 SY3.....124 D7
Inglis Rd TF1.........41 C4
Ingram La WV16........200 D5
Innage Cres WV10.....218 E6
Innage Croft TF11.....145 E4
Innage Gdns WV16......218 E5
Innage La WV16........218 E6
Innage Rd TF11........145 F4
Innes Ave 3 TF2.......132 A3
Institute of Iron TF8..152 B6
IRELAND'S CROSS.....21 D7
Iris Cres TF2.........132 C4
IRONBRIDGE.........152 C4
Ironbridge Rd TF12....152 E1
Iron Bridge & Toll House*
  TF8................152 C3
Iron Bridge Way The
  TF8................152 E8
Ironmasters Way 1 TF4..144 B7
Ironside Cl 3 DY12....211 C2
Ironstone Cl 4 TF7....132 D3
Isiah Ave TF4.........143 D6
Island Gn Sh Ctr LL11..221 C3
Isle La SY3...........112 B2
ISLINGTON...........109 F4
ISOMBRIDGE.........129 B8
Ivatt Cl 7 TF4........144 A2
Iverley Ct WR15.......220 D6
Ivetsey Bank Rd ST19...148 F8
Ivor Thomas Rd 5 TF2..132 D1
Ivy Cl 2 LL11.........221 C6
Ivy Gr TF1............130 D3
Ivy Hatch 4 SY1.......114 B2
Ivy House Paddocks TF1 131 D3

J

Jabe Davies Cl 6 TF2...132 D1
Jackets Cl LD7........203 B2
JACKFIELD..........153 A2
Jackfield Cl TF7......153 A2
Jackfield Tile Mus* TF8..152 F2
Jackson Ave 3 TF12....152 C1
James Cl
Ludlow SY8...........217 E4
3 Oakengates/Donnington
  TF2................132 B6
Sheriffhales TF11.....134 C6
James Clay Ct 1 TF1...131 C3
James Nelson Cres 5
  TF2................132 C7
James Way
3 Oakengates/Donnington
  TF2................132 E2
4 Oakengates/Donnington
  TF2................132 D7
3 Oakengates/Donnington
  TF2................132 E7
8 St Georges & Priorslee
  TF2................133 A1
Jane's Pl 1 SY1.......125 C7
Jane Wood Dr SY6......216 D5
Japonica Dr 8 TF1.....131 B7
Jaras Dr 2 SY4........99 B1
Jarman Ave 11 LL13....221 D2
Jarman Dr TF4.........143 D2
Jarvis Way 7 LL12.....221 E6
Jasmine Cl 4 SY11.....40 F1
Jasmine Dr SY11.......40 F1
Jasmine Gdns SY11.....40 F2
Jay Dr TF1............130 F6
Jay La SY7............205 A5
Jeffreys Cl LL12......221 E7
Jeffreys Rd LL12......221 F7
Jehu Rd 2 SY21........170 B6
Jellicoe Cres 3 TF11..146 A6
Jemmett Cl 2 SY11.....144 A8
Jenks Rd 8 WV5........190 F3
Jennings Rd SY11......58 C7
Jiggers Bank TF4......143 A1
Jigsaw Ave TF1........131 C8
Jockey Bank TF8.......152 D4
Jockey Field SY8......217 D3
John Broad Ave TF1....130 F2
John Evans Mews 2
  TF7................153 A4
John Fletcher CE Jun Sch
  TF7................153 C5
John Randall Prim Sch
  TF3................153 C5
John's St 8 TF11......145 F4
John St
Chirk LL14...........6 E2
Shrewsbury SY1........125 D7
Johnstone Cl 8 TF2....132 C5
Johnston Rd TF4.......143 F4
John Wilkinson Prim Sch
  TF12...............161 E7
Jolly Bank 5 LL14.....6 D8
Joseph Rich Ave TF7...153 A5
Joyce Way SY11.......14 F7
Jubilee Ave TF3.......153 A8
Jubilee Cl 6 TF11.....218 F5
Jubilee Ct WV16.......200 E3
Jubilee Gdns SY5......172 C8
Jubilee Mews SY5......172 C8
Jubilee Rd 9 LL13.....221 C3
Jubilee St SY4........84 A5
Judith Butts Gdns 8
  SY2................126 A8
Judith Butts La 2 SY2..125 F7
Julian Rd SY8.........217 D6
Junction Forge Ret Pk The
  TF3................144 A8

Juniper Cl
5 St Martin's SY11...24 F1
Wrexham LL12.........221 F1
Juniper Dr TF2........132 A5
Juniper Row 8 TF10....109 F7

K

Kateswas 3 SY1........113 D1
Kay Cl 9 SY11.........59 B8
Kaymaur Cl SY12.......26 B6
Kearton Terr TF1......131 E4
Keble Way 6 SY3.......124 D3
Keelton Cl SY3........124 C6
Keepers Cres TF2......132 E4
Keepside Cl SY8.......217 A6
Keep The SY3..........124 A7
Kelsall Dr 3 SY3......124 A7
Kelsalls La SY3.......124 F6
KEMBERTON..........154 C6
Kemberton Cl TF7......153 C7
Kemberton Dr TF7......153 C6
Kemberton Rd TF7......153 C6
Kemble Dr 6 SY3.......125 C3
KEMPTON............194 D5
Kendall Way LL12......221 E8
Kendal Rd SY1.........113 A3
Kendricks Bank SY3....137 B6
Kenfields TF19........89 B6
Kenilworth Cl 4 TF9....36 E2
KENLEY.............179 F3
Kenley Ave SY1........113 D3
Kennedy Cl SY6........216 C7
Kennedy Rd SY3........125 A4
Kennel La WV7.........156 D4
Kennet Bank SY8.......217 E3
Kenrick Cl CW3........5 A1
Kensington Llwyn LL12..221 D7
Kensington Way TF2....132 A3
KENSTONE..........68 D5
Kent Cl 2 TF13........15 B7
Kent Dr 7 LL12........221 D8
Kenton Dr 7 SY2.......125 F4
KENWICK............45 A1
Kenwick Cl SY12.......63 C7
KENWICK PARK.......62 E8
Kenwood Dr SY3.......124 E5
Kenwood Gdns SY3......124 E5
Kenwood Rd SY3........124 E5
Kenwray Dr TF2........132 D4
Kenyon Ave LL11.......221 D7
Kerrison Dr 1 SY21....170 C7
Kerry Gate SY15.......174 B3
Kerry La 13 SY9.......181 A5
Kerry Pl LL12.........221 E4
Kerry Ridgeway SY9....181 A4
Kerry St SY15........174 B3
Kershaw Cl SY8........217 F3
Kestrel Cl TF10.......110 A5
Kestrel Cl 8 TF1......130 F6
Kestrel Dr 2 SY11.....14 F7
Kesworth Dr 10 TF2....132 F1
KETLEY.............131 C2
KETLEY BANK........132 A1
Ketley Bsns Pk TF1....131 C2
Ketley Vallens TF1....131 D3
Kettlemore La TF1.....134 C5
Kew Gdns 11 TF2.......132 F1
Keyse Cl SY8..........217 E4
Keystone Gdns SY8.....217 D6
Kidderminster Rd
Bewdley DY12.........211 E2
1 Bridgnorth WV15....219 A3
Kid La 2 SY7..........190 F1
Kilhorse La
Kilton SY8...........212 B5
Whitcliff SY8........217 A3
Kilnbank Cres TF9.....53 C8
Kilnbank Rd TF4.......53 C8
Kilvert Cl TF10.......108 F3
King Charles Way 2
  WV16...............218 F6
Kingfisher Cl
4 Newport TF10.......109 F5
6 Shrewsbury SY1.....114 C3
Kingfisher Way
Morola SY10..........58 D5
Wellington TF1........130 F5
Kingfisher Wlk 7 SY3...27 B3
Kings Ave TF9.........53 A8
Kingsbury 1 SY1.......124 F7
Kings Cl 2 LL13.......221 E1
Kingscote Cl SY2......126 A2
Kings Cl 6 SY6........216 C6
Kings Dr SY4..........99 B8
King's Haye Rd 8 TF1..130 E3
KINGSLAND..........125 A4
Kingsland TF1.........131 A2
Kingsland Grange Prep Sch
  SY3................125 A3
Kingsland Rd SY3......125 B4
Kingsley Dr TF2.......120 D1
King's Loade WV16.....218 F4
Kingsmills Rd LL13....221 E1
Kings Oak Ct 10 LL13..221 E1
Kings Rd SY8..........212 E2
Kings Rd N 2 SY4......81 B1
Kings Rd S 2 SY4......81 B1
King's St SY10........134 F7
King St
Broseley TF12........152 C1

King St continued
Dawley TF4 . . . . 143 F4
Ludlow SY8 . . . . 217 C4
Much Wenlock TF13. . . . .159 E4
9 Oswestry SY11. . . . . . .58 E8
Shrewsbury SY2 . . . . . . .125 E5
Wellington TF1 . . . . 221 C4
Wrexham LL11. . . . . 221 C4
Kingston Dr SY2 . . . . . . 126 A2
Kingston Rd 5 TF2 . . . . . 132 B6
Kingstown 2 LL12. . . . . . 221 E4
Kingsway
Whitchurch SY13 . . . . . . .15 A7
Wilcott SY4 . . . . .97 D2
Kingsway Cres 4 TF1. . . 131 A2
Kingsway Ct SY13. . . . . . .15 A7
KINGSWOOD 170 D1
Kingswood Bsns Pk WV7 . 157 C4
Kingswood Cl 4 TF13. . . .159 E5
KINGSWOOD COMMON ..157 F2
Kingswood Cres 3 . . . . 124 D6
Kingswood Rd
Albrighton WV7 . . . . 157 C4
Shrewsbury SY3 . . . . 124 D6
KINLET 210 D7
Kinlet Bank DY14 . . . . . . .210 B6
Kinlet CE Prim Sch
DY12. . . . . 210 D7
Kinlet Rd DY12 . . . . 210 D3
Kinloss Ave WV7 . . . . . . 156 D8
KINNERLEY 96 B7
Kinnerley CE Sch SY10. . . .96 B7
Kinsley Rd LD7 . . . . 203 B3
Kinsleys The DY14. . . . . . 199 D1
KINTON
Great Ness 97 C4
Leintwardine 205 C5
Kirkland Ave 9 SY3 . . . . 124 C7
Kirkwood Cl 2 SY1. . . . . 113 C1
Kitchen Hill Rd SY8 . . . . 212 D1
Kittyoak La SY5. . . . . .169 B4
Knapp La SY8 . . . . 208 C1
KNIGHTON
Adbaston. 73 F2
Loggerheads. 21 B5
Knighton CW Prim Sch
LD7. . . . . 203 B2
KNIGHTON ON TEME. . . .203 A2
Knighton Rd 4 SY7 . . . . 193 C3
Knighton Sta LD7 . . . . . . .203 B3
KNIGHTON/TREF'-V-
CLAWDD 203 B2
Knightsbridge Cl SY2 . . . 126 A2
Knightsbridge Cres 8
TF3. . . . . 144 B1
Knights Way
1 Oswestry SY11. . . . . . .40 F1
Shrewsbury SY4 . . . . 113 E6
KNOCKIN 78 A1
KNOCKIN HEATH 96 F7
Knolls Farm Cl 1 SY3 . . . 125 B1
Knolls The 13 SY3. . . . . . 124 A7
KNOLTON 9 D2
KNOLTON BRYN 9 C3
KNOWBURY 208 A1
KNOWLE. 208 C1
KNOWLESANDS 218 F1
Knowles La SY12 . . . . . . .29 B3
Knowle Wood View 3
TF3. . . . . 144 D4
Knowsley Dr 8 SY3. . . . . 124 A7
KNUCKLAS. 202 E4
Knucklas Rd LD7 . . . . 203 A3
Knucklas Sta LD7 . . . . . . .202 E4
KYNASTON 96 F5
Kynaston Dr SY4. . . . . . . .66 B8
Kynaston Pl 1 LL14. . . . . .6 E8
Kynaston Rd SY1 . . . . . . 113 E4
Kynaston's Cave* SY4 . . . .97 F3
KYNNERSLEY 119 D6
Kynnersley Dr TF10 . . . . .120 B5
Kynnersley La SY5 . . . . . 150 C7
Kyreside WR15. . . . . 220 D4
Kyrewood Ct WR15. . . . . .220 E4

L

Laburnam Cl 4 SY11 . . . . .24 F6
Laburnam Dr 6 SY12. . . . .27 A1
Laburnum Cl
1 Market Drayton TF9. . . .36 D2
2 Shifnal TF11 . . . . .145 F5
Laburnum Dr
Madeley TF7. . . . . .153 B4
Oswestry SY11 . . . . .58 F7
Laburnum Mdws 1
SY2. . . . . 167 A8
Laburnum Rd 2 TF2. . . . 132 A4
Lackstone La SY4 . . . . . . .95 D8
Lacon Childe Sch DY14. . 209 D2
Lacon Cl 1 DY14 . . . . . . 209 D2
Lacon Dr SY4. . . . . .66 C6
Lacon St SY3 . . . . .49 E7
Lacy Rd SY8 . . . . 217 D6
Ladbrook Dr 11 TF2 . . . . 132 C2
Ladycroft 1 SY11. . . . . . 130 E4
Ladycroft Cl 5 SY1. . . . . 124 F3
Lady Gr TF4 . . . . 143 E5
Ladygrove Cty Prim Sch
TF4. . . . . 143 E5
LADY HALTON 206 C2
Lady Leasow 14 SY4 . . . . 124 F3
Ladymas La SY4. . . . . . . .102 B6

Ladymas Rd SY4. . . . . . . 102 C6
LADYOAK 172 C2
Ladywell 4 SY7 . . . . 204 C5
Ladywood TF8 . . . . 152 C3
Lagden La SY9. . . . . .181 F1
Lake End Dr TF3. . . . . . . 153 D8
Lakelands Sch SY12. . . . . .27 A1
Lakelands Sports Ctr
SY12. . . . . .27 A2
Lakes Ct 27 DY12 . . . . . . 211 C2
Lakes Rd The 16 DY12. . . 211 B7
LAKES THE. 211 C2
Lake View LL12 . . . . 221 F6
Lambert Rd 4 SY21 . . . . .170 B6
Lambeth Cl 16 SY7. . . . . 195 E5
Lambeth Dr
10 Dawley TF3. . . . . 144 B1
Priorslee TF2. . . . . 133 A2
Lambourn Dr SY3. . . . . . 124 B6
Lambourne Dr 8 DY12 . . 211 C2
Lambpit St 1 LL11 . . . . . 221 D3
Lamledge La TF11 . . . . . 146 B3
Lancaster Ave TF4 . . . . . 143 F4
Lancaster Cl WV7 . . . . . . 156 F8
Lancaster Ct 3 TF4 . . . . 143 F4
Lancaster Pl TF4. . . . . . . 143 F4
Lancaster Rd
2 Bewdley DY12. . . . . . . 211 D2
Shrewsbury SY1 . . . . 113 E3
Landy Cl TF2 . . . . 120 C2
Lane End LL13. . . . . .10 F4
Lanes Cl 27 WV5. . . . . . . .190 F3
LANE'S END 209 A7
Lanesfield 1 SY3 . . . . . . 124 F3
Laneside 6 TF2. . . . . 120 F1
Langford Ave SY3. . . . . . 136 E6
Langford Dr 9 TF4 . . . . . 217 F4
Langford Gn 2 SY1. . . . . 113 E4
Langland Rd
8 Cleobury Mortimer
DY14. . . . . 209 E3
Oswestry SY11 . . . . .58 F8
Langley Cres TF4 . . . . . . 143 F3
Langley Dale TF9 . . . . . . .70 C5
Langley Dr SY3 . . . . 136 F5
Langley Fold TF4 . . . . . . 143 F3
Langley Rd WV4 . . . . 190 F7
Langtree Dr 7 SY1 . . . . . 113 D3
Lansdowne Cres SY3 . . . 136 F7
Lansdowne Rd SY3 . . . . . 136 F7
Lapwing Gate 2 TF2. . . . 144 E8
Lapworth Cl SY1 . . . . . . 113 C2
Lapworth Way 3 TF10 . . 110 A3
Larch Cl 1 SY12. . . . . . . .27 A2
Larches La DY14 . . . . 209 B7
Larches The 13 TF10 . . . 109 E2
Larch Ct 2 LL13. . . . . . . 221 F4
Larch Wood 8 TF3 . . . . . 144 D3
Larchwood Rd LL12. . . . . 221 F7
Larkey 15 LD7 . . . . 203 B3
Larkhill Rd
Gobowen SY11. . . . . 41 C4
4 Shrewsbury SY3 . . . . . 124 D6
Lark Rise TF2. . . . . 132 C4
Larkrise Fields TF11 . . . . 134 C6
Larkspur Glade 9 TF3 . . 144 D3
Larks Rise 9 DY14. . . . . . 209 D2
Latchford La SY1 . . . . . . 114 B4
Laundry La SY1. . . . . 125 E3
Laurel Dr 1 TF10 . . . . . . 109 F3
Laurel La 4 TF13 . . . . . . 143 F8
Laurels Cl SY12 . . . . .27 B1
Laurels Mdws 16 LD7 . . . 203 B3
Laurels The LL12. . . . . . . 221 E6
Lavender Bank 1 SY9 . . . 181 E3
Lavender Way 1 SY3 . . . 125 D3
Lavington View WV15. . . . 219 A4
Lavister Gdns 11 LL12. . . 221 D8
Lawford Cl TF4 . . . . 152 F8
LAWLEY 143 C6
Lawley Cl 6 SY6. . . . . . . 216 D7
Lawley Dr TF3. . . . . 143 C8
Lawley Gate TF4. . . . . . . 143 C5
Lawley Gdns 8 SY3. . . . . 126 A6
Lawley Prim Sch TF4. . . . 143 C7
Lawn Central TF3. . . . . . . 144 B7
Lawn La TF9. . . . . .54 F1
Lawns The 4 TF1. . . . . . . 144 B8
Lawnswood 2 TF3. . . . . . 144 A5
Lawrence Rd TF1 . . . . . . 130 C4
Lawson Cl LL12 . . . . 221 D5
Lawson Gdns 2 SY1 . . . . 114 B4
LAWTON 197 A2
Lawton Cl TF1. . . . . 164 C8
Lawton Farm Cl 3 TF1. . . 131 A6
Lawton Farm Rd 4 TF1 . . 131 A6
Lawton Farm Way 6
TF1. . . . . 131 A6
Laxton La TF8 . . . . 152 B7
Laxton Dr 2 DY12 . . . . . 211 C2
LEA
Lydham 182 C4
Pontesbury 173 C7
Leabank Cl 10 SY1 . . . . . 113 C2
Lea Ct 3 TF1. . . . . 131 A6
Leadon Cl TF4 . . . . 132 E8
Leafields SY1. . . . . 113 E5
Leamore Cres SY3 . . . . . 125 E4
Lea Rd LL13 . . . . 221 C3
Leasowe Gn TF4 . . . . 152 E8
Leasowes Cl 2 WV16 . . . 218 D5
Leasows Pk 1 SY4 . . . . . 103 D6
Lea The 8 WV15. . . . . . . 201 B3
LEATH THE. 198 B8
LEATON
Pimhill 100 D2
Wrockwardine 129 C3

Leaton Dr TF1 . . . . 130 C5
LEATON HEATH 100 C2
LEATON KNOLLS 112 F6
Lea View DY14 . . . . 209 D2
Ledwyche Cl SY8 . . . . . . 207 D3
Ledwyche Ct SY8 . . . . . . 207 C1
LEE. 44 D6
LEEBOTWOOD. 178 C1
LEE BROCKHURST. 67 A3
Lee Dingle TF7 . . . . 153 A3
Leegate Ave TF1. . . . . . . 131 B7
LEEGOMERY 131 B5
Leegomery Rd TF1. . . . . . 130 C5
Leek St SY4 . . . . .66 A6
Leeming Rd WV7 . . . . . . 156 D8
Leeses Cl TF5. . . . . 130 B8
Lees Farm Dr TF7. . . . . . 152 F4
Lees Rd WV15 . . . . 219 E5
Lees The 1 SY3 . . . . 124 B7
Leeswood Ct 7 SY3 . . . . 124 B6
Legges Way TF7 . . . . 153 B5
Leg St SY11 . . . . .58 E8
Leicester Way 2 TF1 . . . 131 A5
LEIGH 172 A2
Leigh Mdws 6 SY22 . . . . .94 A1
Leigh Rd
Minsterley SY5. . . . . 172 D3
7 Newport TF10. . . . . . . 109 E2
LEIGHTON
Forden with Leighton and
Trelystan. 170 C4
Leighton and Eaton
Constantine 150 B7
Leighton CP Sch SY21 . . 170 D5
Leighton La TF6 . . . . 142 B2
Leighton Rd
Shrewsbury SY1 . . . . 113 D3
Welshpool SY21. . . . . . . 170 C6
Leighton View 26 SY21 . . 170 B6
LEINTWARDINE 205 A5
Leintwardine Endowed Prim
Sch SY7. . . . . 205 B5
LEM HILL 210 C1
Lennock Rd TF2. . . . . 132 B7
Leonard Ct TF2 . . . . 132 A3
Leonard's Cl 4 TF2. . . . . 132 C7
Leonard St TF2 . . . . 132 A3
Lesley Owen Way SY1. . . 113 F2
Lessar Ave 5 SY3 . . . . . . 125 A6
Letchmere Cl WV6 . . . . . 166 C3
Letchmere La WV6. . . . . 166 C2
LETTON. 204 E1
Leuchars La WV7 . . . . . . 156 D8
Levens Dr SY1 . . . . 113 E3
Levens Cl 2 TF2 . . . . 132 C3
Levins Ct TF7 . . . . 153 C5
Lexington Ave SY1 . . . . . 126 A2
Ley Brook 2 TF2 . . . . 131 F2
Leyburn Ave SY3 . . . . . . 124 F6
Leys La WR6. . . . . 212 C1
Lhen Cl 20 TF2 . . . . 132 F8
Lichfield Cl 7 TF2 . . . . . . 133 A1
Lichfield Dr TF11 . . . . . . 135 F1
Lidgates Gn TF1 . . . . 131 B2
LIGHTEACH. 32 A2
Lighteach Rd SY13 . . . . . .32 B2
LIGHTMOOR. 152 E8
Lightmoor Rd TF4. . . . . . 152 D7
LIGHTWOOD 72 B7
LIGHTWOOD GREEN 9 F6
Lilac Cl 8 TF3. . . . . 143 F8
Lilac Dr 22 WV5. . . . . . . 190 F3
Lilac Dro SY11. . . . . .59 A7
Lilac Way LL11. . . . . 221 B4
LILLESHALL 121 C4
Lilleshall National Sports Ctr
TF10. . . . . 121 F2
Lilleshall Prim Sch TF10. 121 C4
LILYHURST. 133 F7
Lilyhurst Rd
Lilleshall & Donnington
TF10. . . . . 121 B1
Sheriffhales TF10. . . . . . 133 E8
Lilyvale Cl 17 TF2 . . . . . 132 F1
Lime Cl
2 Alveley WV15. . . . . . . 201 B3
2 Ellesmere SY12 . . . . . .27 A2
Ludlow SY8 . . . . 217 D6
Lime Gr
Market Drayton TF9. . . . . .52 F7
7 Oswestry SY11. . . . . . .58 F7
Limekiln Bank 1 TF2 . . . 132 E2
Limekiln Ct 1 TF2 . . . . . 132 E2
Limekiln La
Lilleshall TF10 . . . . 121 C5
Little Wenlock TF1. . . . . . 130 F1
Lime Kilns La SY21 . . . . . 170 A4
Limes Paddock 1 SY5. . . 178 C6
Limes Rd 1 TF2 . . . . 132 B2
Limes The SY3 . . . . 125 C4
Lime St SY3 . . . . 125 C4
Limes Wlk TF7 . . . . 157 A4
Limes Wlk TF7. . . . . .132 B2
Lime Tree Way TF1 . . . . . 130 E5
Lincoln Cres
Kidderminster DY11. . . . .211 F3
4 Oakengates/Donnington
TF2. . . . . 132 B4
Lincoln Fields WV16 . . . . 200 C3
Lincoln Hill TF8 . . . . 152 C4
Lincoln Rd TF2 . . . . 132 B4
Lindale Ct 3 SY3 . . . . . . 125 A6
Lindale Dr 5 WV5 . . . . . . 190 F3
Linden Ave
Chirk LL14. . . . . .6 E3
Much Wenlock TF13. . . . .159 E5
Wellington TF1 . . . . 130 D3
Whitchurch SY13. . . . . . . .14 F7
Wrexham LL13. . . . . 221 E2

Linden Gdns 6 SY3. . . . . 125 D4
Linden Gr TF1 . . . . 130 D3
Lindens The TF1 . . . . 145 E4
Linden Way 3 TF9. . . . . . .36 D2
Lindfield Dr 8 TF1. . . . . . 130 D4
Lindley St 3 SY1 . . . . . . 125 D7
LINDRIDGE. 215 E4
Lindridge CE Prim Sch
WR15. . . . . 215 E4
Lineton Cl 4 TF2 . . . . . . 132 B6
Lingen Cl SY1 . . . . 125 E8
Lingen Rd SY8. . . . . 217 F4
Lingfield Rd 9 TF2 . . . . . 211 E3
Links Rd
Church Stretton SY6 . . . . 216 C7
Shrewsbury SY3 . . . . 125 A3
LINLEY
Barrow. 161 F1
More 182 C7
Linley Ave 4 SY5. . . . . . . 173 B4
LINLEY BROOK 187 F8
Linley Dr
Dawley TF3 . . . . 144 C1
More SY5. . . . . 175 F2
LINLEYGREEN. 161 F2
Linley Rd LL11 . . . . 221 C8
Linley Terr SY5 . . . . 173 B4
Linley View Dr WV16 . . . 218 D7
Linnet Cl 4 SY3. . . . . 124 B7
Linnet Gate 1 TF2 . . . . . 132 C7
Linney SY8 . . . . 217 C4
Lintin Cl TF5. . . . . 130 A7
Lion La
Cleobury Mortimer DY14. . 209 E2
Coreley SY8. . . . . 208 C1
Ellesmere Rural SY12 . . . .10 C3
Lion Mdw 6 SY4 . . . . 216 C6
Lions Bank 8 SY15 . . . . . 174 B3
Lion St TF2 . . . . 132 B2
LIPLEY. 55 D2
Lisburne Gr LL12 . . . . . . 221 F8
Listley St WV16 . . . . 218 E5
Little Acton Dr LL12. . . . 221 F7
LITTLE AROWRY. 12 B6
LITTLE BOLAS. 88 C1
LITTLE BRAMPTON 194 D4
LITTLE COMMON 205 B8
Little Croft TF2 . . . . 132 A3
LITTLE DAWLEY 143 E1
Little Dawley Cl TF7. . . . 153 D7
LITTLE DRAYTON 52 F5
Little Eyton Fold TF4. . . . 143 F4
LITTLEGAIN 189 E7
LITTLE GREEN. 13 A6
Littlehales Rd TF10 . . . . 121 E4
Little Harlescott La 3
SY1. . . . . 113 C5
Little Henfaes Dr SY21. . 170 C6
LITTLE HEREFORD. 213 E3
LITTLE LONDON
Knighton on Teme 215 A6
Munslow 196 F7
Little London La SY11 . . . .57 C2
LITTLE LYTH 136 F2
Little Mdw Cl 8 TF5. . . . 130 A7
LITTLE NESS. 98 E4
Little Ness Rd
Little Ness SY4 . . . . .98 C5
Ruyton-XI-Towns SY4 . . . .80 B1
Littleover Ave 5 SY1 . . . 113 D5
LITTLE OVERTON 9 D7
Little Oxton La SY3 . . . . 124 B7
LITTLE RYTON 178 D6
LITTLE SOUDLEY 72 F5
Littlestocks Cl DY12. . . . 210 C7
LITTLE STRETTON 216 A3
LITTLE SUTTON 197 A1
LITTLE WENLOCK 142 C3
LITTLE WORTHEN. 172 A4
LITTLE WYTHEFORD. . . . 130 E3
Liverpool Rd
Oswestry SY11. . . . . .40 E1
Whitchurch SY13 . . . . . . .14 F6
Liverpool Rd W 6 SY11. . .40 D1
Livesey Ave SY8 . . . . 217 D5
Livesey Rd SY8 . . . . 217 D5
Lizard La TF11 . . . . 134 F1
LLANDRINIO 167 C8
LLANDYSILIO. 93 F3
LLANERCH. 181 D8
LLANFAIR WATERDINE . . 202 D7
Llanforda Cl SY11. . . . . . .58 C7
Llanforda Mead SY10 . . . .58 C7
Llanforda Rise SY11. . . . .58 C8
LLANGUNLLO 202 A2
LLANLLWYD. 191 D3
Llansantffraid CIWA SY22 .92 C5
LLANSANTFFRAID-YM-
MECHAIN. 92 C5
Llanshay La LD7 . . . . 203 D2
LLANSILIN. 72 B5
LLANYBLODWEL. 75 A5
Llanymnech Rocks Nature
Reserve* SY22 . . . . .93 F8
LLANYMYNECH 93 E6
LLAWNT 39 C2
Lletty La
Llansantffraid SY22. . . . . .92 B3
Llansantffraid-ym-Mechain
SY22. . . . . .92 D5
Llewellyn Roberts Way
TF9. . . . . .36 D1
Lloyds Head TF8 . . . . 152 E3
Lloyds La LL14 . . . . .6 E2
Lloyd St SY11. . . . . .40 E1
Lloyds The TF8. . . . . 152 F3
LLOYNEY 202 D6

Llwybr Maelor LL13. . . . . .9 C8
LLWYN. 193 B3
Llwyn Cres SY10. . . . . . . .58 C4
Llwyn Fields 4 SY11. . . . .40 E1
Llwyn Rd
Clun SY7 . . . . 193 C3
Oswestry SY11 . . . . .40 E1
LLWYN-Y-GO. 95 D7
LLYNCLYS. 76 C5
Llynclys Comm Nature
Reserve* SY10 . . . . .76 A4
Llynclys Sta SY10 . . . . . . .76 C4
Llys Ave SY11. . . . . .59 A7
Llys Cl SY11 . . . . .59 A7
Llys Ct 1 SY11 . . . . .59 A7
Llys David Lord LL13 . . . 221 B3
Llys La SY11. . . . . .58 E7
Llys Pl SY11 . . . . .59 A8
Llys SY11. . . . . .59 A7
Llysy Coed LL11 . . . . 221 C5
Loak St SY11. . . . . 211 D2
Loak Rd WV7 . . . . 156 E5
LOCKLEYWOOD 72 A3
Lockside 11 WV5. . . . . . . 190 F4
Lockwood Dr 4 SY1 . . . . 113 D3
LODGEBANK. 86 D3
Lodge Cl
8 Bewdley DY12. . . . . . . 211 C2
Shifnal TF11. . . . . 145 F3
Lodge Coppice TF2 . . . . 132 D6
Lodge Cres SY3 . . . . 137 A6
Lodge Dr SY13. . . . . .32 B8
Lodge La
Barrow TF12 . . . . 161 B7
Bridgnorth WV15. . . . . . 219 A4
The Gorge TF8 . . . . 152 C4
Lodge Pk 6 WV5. . . . . . . 189 E4
Lodge Rd
Muxton TF2 . . . . 133 B5
Oakengates/Donnington
TF2. . . . . 132 D6
4 Wrexham LL11. . . . . . . 221 E6
Lodgewood La 11 TF2. . . 132 F2
Lodmore La LL13. . . . . . . .17 C6
Lon Brynfa-brynfa Ave 1
SY21. . . . . 170 B7
London Rd
Bridgemere CW5 . . . . .4 E5
Loggerheads TF9. . . . . . . .21 B5
Oakengates/Donnington
TF2. . . . . 132 D2
4 Shrewsbury SY2 . . . . . 125 F4
Shrewsbury SY2 . . . . 126 B2
Whitchurch Urban SY13. . .15 A8
Woore CW3. . . . . .21 C8
London Rd Sports Ctr
SY2. . . . . 126 A3
Longacre News SY3 . . . . 124 A6
LONG BANK. 211 B1
Long Bank DY12 . . . . 211 B1
Longbow Cl SY11 . . . . . . 113 F5
Longbridge Cl 6 SY2 . . . 126 B7
LONG COMMON 190 B4
Long Croft
Albrighton WV7 . . . . 157 B5
Weston Rhyn SY10 . . . . . .23 D4
LONGDEN. 173 E5
Longden Ave SY3 . . . . . . 125 C3
Longden CE Prim Sch
SY5. . . . . 173 E5
Longden Cl 1 SY3. . . . . . 173 E5
Longden Coleham SY3 . . 125 A3
Longden Common La SY5 . 173 E3
LONGDEN COMMON 173 E3
Longden Gdns 3 SY3 . . . 125 B3
Longden Gn 8 SY3 . . . . . 125 B3
Longden Gr 8 SY3 . . . . . 125 B3
Longden Rd
Longden SY5. . . . . 173 E4
Shrewsbury SY3 . . . . 124 F2
LONGDON ON TERN . . . 117 D4
Longfield LL14. . . . . .6 E1
LONGFORD
Church Aston. 109 A1
Moreton Say 52 D8
Longford Cl 10 WV5. . . . 190 E3
Longford Pk TF10. . . . . . 109 B1
Longford Rd TF10. . . . . . 109 A1
Longford Rise 1 TF1 . . . 130 E5
Longford Turning 5 TF7 . 152 F8
Longhills Rd SY6 . . . . . . 216 C2
Longhirst Gdns 8 SY3 . . 124 D7
Long La
Albrighton WV7 . . . . 156 C6
Bronington SY13 . . . . .13 D4
Hodnet TF9 . . . . .69 A8
Longden SY5 . . . . 173 F4
Sibdon Carwood SY7. . . . 195 C7
Longlands La 3 TF9. . . . . .36 D1
Longlands Prim Sch TF9 . .36 D2
LONG LANE. 118 B3
Longleat Cl 4 SY5. . . . . . 172 E3
Long Length SY7 . . . . . . 183 E1
Long Mdw
Bayston Hill SY3 . . . . 136 F6
Telford Dawley TF3 . . . . . 144 C3
Long Mdw CE Prim Sch
SY3. . . . . 136 F6
Long Mynd SY6. . . . . 216 A4
Longmynd Pl SY6. . . . . . 216 C7
Longner St SY3 . . . . 125 B6
LONGNOR. 178 D3

Longnor CE Prim Sch
SY5 . . . . .178 E3
Longnor Rd TF1 . . . . .130 C6
LONG OAK 78 E3
Long Pack SY1 . . . . .114 B4
Long Row **3** SY1 . . . . .113 E1
LONGSLOW 35 F3
Longslow Cl **4** TF9 . . . . . . .36 B1
Longslow Rd **10** TF9 . . . . . . .36 B1
Longthorpe Dr TF1 . . . . . .131 C6
Longueville **1** LL13 . . . . . .221 C1
Longueville Dr SY11 . . . . . .59 B8
LONGVILLE IN THE
DALE 185 C4
Longville Rd **6** SY11 . . . . .113 D4
Longwithy La TF10 . . . . . .108 F4
Lonsdale Dr SY3 . . . . .125 A1
LOPPINGTON 64 D7
Loppington Hse FE Unit &
Adult Ctre SY4 . . . . .46 E1
Lord Murray Dr TF7 . . . . . .152 E7
Lords Dr **1** TF2 . . . . .132 E3
Lord Silkin Sch TF3 . . . . . .144 D2
Lord St
5 Oswestry SY11 . . . . . . .58 D8
1 Wrexham LL11 . . . . . . .221 C3
Lordstone La SY5 . . . . . . .172 A1
Lorne St
8 Oswestry SY11 . . . . . . .40 E1
Wrexham LL11 . . . . .221 C4
LOSTFORD 19 C7
Lostford La TF9 . . . . .51 E4
Loton Butts **9** SY2 . . . . . .125 F8
LOUGHTON 198 F2
Loughton Cl SY8 . . . . .217 E5
Loughton La WV16 . . . . . .198 D1
Lovat Cl SY2 . . . . .126 A7
Love La
Bishop's Castle SY9 . . . . .181 F3
Bridgnorth WV16 . . . . . .218 F6
Cleobury Mortimer DY14 . .209 E2
Lydham SY9 . . . . .182 A4
Wem SY4 . . . . .66 B8
Lovell Cl TF11 . . . . .146 A6
Loveridge Dr SY4 . . . . .99 B7
LOWE 47 D2
Lowe Croft **8** SY7 . . . . . .205 B5
Lowe Hill Gdns SY4 . . . . . .65 F7
Lowe Hill Rd SY4 . . . . .65 F6
Lowe La
Alveley WV15 . . . . .201 B1
Upper Arley DY12 . . . . . .211 B8
LOWER ALLSCOT 188 E7
Lower Bar TF10 . . . . .109 E3
LOWER BEOBRIDGE 189 D2
Lower Broad St SY8 . . . . . .217 C3
Lower Brook St SY11 . . . . . .58 D7
Lower Claremont Bank **10**
SY1 . . . . .125 B6
LOWER COMMON 178 A8
Lower Cross Lanes SY7 . . .197 F4
LOWER DINCHOPE 196 A3
Lower Dingle **2** TF7 . . . . .152 F4
LOWER DOWN 194 A7
LOWER FAINTREE 199 C2
Lower Faw Terr SY8 . . . . .217 C3
LOWER FORGE 200 E8
LOWER FRANKTON 43 B4
Lower Galdeford SY8 . . . . .217 D4
Lower Hafod **1** SY11 . . . . . .58 C8
LOWER HAYTON 206 F8
Lower Heath CE Prim Sch
SY13 . . . . .50 A6
LOWER HENGOED 40 F6
LOWER HOPTON 97 D6
LOWER HORDLEY 62 A7
Lower Inhedge DY14 . . . . .209 F3
Lower La SY7 . . . . .183 E1
LOWER LEDWYCHE 207 C1
Lower Mill St SY8 . . . . .217 C3
Lower Minst
Oswestry SY11 . . . . .58 C8
Wrexham LL13 . . . . .221 E8
LOWER NETCHWOOD 186 F2
LOWER PENN 190 F6
Lower Pk DY12 . . . . .211 D2
Lower Pk Dr **5** TF1 . . . . . .130 C7
Lower Pulley La SY3 . . . . . .137 B7
Lower Raven La SY8 . . . . . .217 C3
Lower Rd
Middle & Broughton SY4 . .82 E4
Orleton SY8 . . . . .173 A4
LOWER RIDGE 42 D7
Lower St DY14 . . . . .209 E2
LOWER TODDING 205 B6
Lower Wood TF3 . . . . .143 E7
Loweswater Cl **1** TF2 . . . .144 E8
Lowfield **5** SY2 . . . . .125 F8
LOW HABBERLEY 211 F5
Lowry Cl **10** TF5 . . . . .130 B8
LOW TOWN 219 A5
Low Valley Cl TF1 . . . . . . .131 D3
Loxdale **15** SY3 . . . . .124 F3
LUBBERLAND 209 A5
Lucerne Cl **2** TF1 . . . . . . .131 C5
Luciefelde Rd SY3 . . . . . . .125 B4
Ludford Almshouses
SY8 . . . . .217 D3
Ludford Dr
6 Dawley TF3 . . . . .144 C1
Shrewsbury SY1 . . . . . . .113 D3
Ludford View SY7 . . . . . . .217 E3
LUDLOW 217 D3
Ludlow Castle* SY8 . . . . .217 B4
Ludlow CE Sch SY8 . . . . . .217 A6
Ludlow Coll
Ludlow SY8 . . . . .217 B4

Ludlow Coll _continued_
Ludlow SY8 . . . . .217 C3
Ludlow Dr TF3 . . . . .144 B2
Ludlow Eco Pk SY8 . . . . . .217 F3
Ludlow Hospl SY8 . . . . . . .217 C5
Ludlow Hts WV16 . . . . . . .218 D4
Ludlow Inf Sch SY8 . . . . . .217 E5
Ludlow Jun Sch SY8 . . . . .217 E5
Ludlow Mus* SY8 . . . . . .217 C4
Ludlow Rd
Aston Eyre WV16 . . . . . .187 D5
Bitterley SY8 . . . . .207 D2
Bridgnorth WV16 . . . . . .218 C3
Caynham SY8 . . . . .208 B2
Church Stretton SY6 . . . .216 A3
Cleobury Mortimer DY14 . .209 D7
Craven Arms SY7 . . . . . .195 E5
Knighton LD7 . . . . .203 C2
Ludlow Sta SY8 . . . . .217 C5
LUDSTONE 189 E5
Ludstone Hall* WV5 . . . .189 E5
Lurkenhope Wood Nature
Reserve* LD7 . . . . .203 C4
LUSHCOTT 185 D6
Lutton Cl SY1 . . . . .113 D7
Lutwyche Cl **1** SY6 . . . . . .216 C6
Lutwyche Rd TF6 . . . . .216 C6
Lydbury Cl **8** TF3 . . . . . . .144 C1
Lydbury N CE Prim Sch
SY7 . . . . .194 C8
LYDBURY NORTH 194 C8
LYDE 175 E8
LYDHAM 182 A6
Lydham Rd SY1 . . . . .113 D4
Lyle Cl **17** TF1 . . . . .130 E4
Lymehurst Ct **7** SY1 . . . . .113 C1
Lymore View **3** SY15 . . . . .174 B3
LYNCHGATE 194 E8
Lynch La SY8 . . . . .213 D2
Lyncroft WV7 . . . . .157 A5
Lyndale Gr LL12 . . . . .221 D7
Lyndhurst Dr
1 Bayston Hill SY3 . . . . .137 A5
6 Oakengates/Donnington
TF2 . . . . .132 A6
LYNEAL 45 E7
Lyneal La SY12 . . . . .28 D2
LYNN 118 B4
Lyons La SY5 . . . . .137 E1
Lysander Ave WV7 . . . . . . .156 B7
Lytham Gn TF2 . . . . .133 A8
LYTHBANK 136 C3
Lyth Hill Rd SY3 . . . . .136 F4
Lythwood Rd SY3 . . . . . . .136 E6
Lyttelton Rd DY12 . . . . . . .211 C2

M

McClintock Pl SY6 . . . . . . .216 D6
McCormick Dr TF1 . . . . . . .130 C5
McGredy Dr **3** SY2 . . . . . .125 C7
McKinley Way SY4 . . . . .85 D1
McLean Dr **3** TF2 . . . . . . .132 F1
Maddocks Cl SY7 . . . . .153 A5
Maddocks Ct TF1 . . . . .130 E3
Madebrook Cl TF7 . . . . . . .153 D5
Madeira Hill **2** LL13 . . . . .221 D2
Madeira Wlk SY6 . . . . .216 C2
MADELEY 153 A5
Madeley Acad TF7 . . . . . . .153 B6
Madeley Cl TF9 . . . . .152 B6
Madeley Ct Sports Ctr
TF7 . . . . .153 B6
Madeley Inf Sch TF7 . . . . .153 A4
Madeley Rd TF7 . . . . .152 D4
MADELEYWOOD 152 E4
Madeley Wood View **10**
TF7 . . . . .152 F4
Madely Rd TF11 . . . . .163 B8
Madog Pl **13** SY11 . . . . . . .58 E8
Madras Sch LL13 . . . . .10 E4
Madrid Ct SY11 . . . . .113 B6
Maer La TF9 . . . . .36 D3
Maes Alwyn SY10 . . . . .23 D4
MAESBROOK 95 A7
Maesbrook Rd **4** SY5 . . . .125 B1
MAESBURY 77 B8
Maesbury Cty Prim Sch
SY10 . . . . .77 B8
MAESBURY MARSH 77 D6
Maesbury Rd
Oswestry Rural SY10 . . . . .59 A2
Oswestry SY11 . . . . .58 F6
Maes Celyn **5** LL13 . . . . . .221 C1
Maes Chwarae SY15 . . . . .175 A1
Maes Glas LL13 . . . . .221 C2
Maesgwyn Rd LL13 . . . . . .221 B4
Maes Hafren **1** SY5 . . . . . .167 F6
Maes Hyfryd LL13 . . . . . . .221 B8
Maesllwyn Cl SY13 . . . . . . .13 A4
Maesllwyn La SY13 . . . . . . .12 F4
Maes Neuadd SY15 . . . . . .175 A1
Maes Uchaf SY22 . . . . .92 B6
Maes y Berwyn LL14 . . . . . .6 E3
Maes y Brilan **2** SY22 . . . .92 B6
Maesydre Rd LL12 . . . . . . .221 D5
Maes-y-felin SY11 . . . . . . .174 A6
Maes y Foel SY22 . . . . .92 B5
Maes-y-garreg SY22 . . . . . .92 B6
Maes-y-llan SY22 . . . . .92 B6
Maes y Llan SY10 . . . . .56 A4
Maes y Parc LL14 . . . . .7 A5
Maes-yr-eglwys SY22 . . . . .92 B6
Maesywaun LL14 . . . . .6 E1
Mafeking Dr **9** TF2 . . . . . .132 C5
Mafeking Rd TF1 . . . . .131 C4

Magister Rd WV7 . . . . .156 B7
Magna Cl
Dawley TF4 . . . . .143 F2
Whitchurch Rural SY13 . . .16 A4
Magnolia Dr SY4 . . . . .100 F3
Magnolia Dr
9 Ellesmere SY12 . . . . . .27 A2
5 The Rock TF3 . . . . . . .143 E8
Magpie Way **4** TF3 . . . . . .153 A8
Main Rd
Condover SY5 . . . . .178 C6
Maesbury Marsh SY10 . . .77 C6
Norton in Hales TF9 . . . . .20 C1
Oakengates/Donnington
TF2 . . . . .131 F1
Pontesbury SY5 . . . . . . .173 B5
Wrexham LL11 . . . . .221 B8
Main St **2** WV15 . . . . . . .189 A6
MAINSTONE 181 A2
Maitlands The **6** SY5 . . . .178 C6
Majestic Way
Aqueduct TF4 . . . . .153 D8
Dawley Hamlets TF4 . . . .152 F8
Dawley TF4 . . . . .144 A1
Malcolm Davies Dr 2
TF2 . . . . .132 B6
Maldwyn Way **12** SY15 . . .174 B3
MALEHURST 172 F5
Malinsgate TF3 . . . . .144 A6
MALINSLEE 144 A4
Malinslee Ctr TF3 . . . . . . .144 A5
Mallard Cl
Dawley TF3 . . . . .153 D8
2 Shrewsbury SY1 . . . . .114 B4
Mallards Cl **9** WV15 . . . . .201 B3
Mall The WV15 . . . . .219 A4
Malory Dr **3** TF2 . . . . .144 A1
Malory Rd SY11 . . . . .113 B6
Malthouse Bank TF6 . . . . .142 D2
Malthouse Cl
3 Trefonen SY10 . . . . . . .57 D2
7 Whittington SY11 . . . . .41 E3
Malthouse La
Atcham SY5 . . . . .139 A7
Trefonen SY10 . . . . .57 D2
Maltings Cl WV6 . . . . .164 D2
Maltings The
1 Bayston Hill SY3 . . . . .137 A6
1 Wellington TF1 . . . . . .130 D3
West Felton SY11 . . . . . . .78 D7
Maltkiln La
Whitchurch Rural SY13 . . .31 F7
Whixall SY13 . . . . .30 C2
Malt Rise **2** SY5 . . . . .167 F6
Malvern Cl SY2 . . . . .125 E2
Malvern Cres TF4 . . . . .143 E1
Manchester Dr TF1 . . . . . .131 A7
Manley Rd LL13 . . . . .221 D3
Mannerley La
5 Ketley TF1 . . . . .131 E1
1 The Rock TF3 . . . . . . .143 E8
Manor Cl
Hinstock TF9 . . . . .72 A1
6 Market Drayton TF9 . . .36 C1
Shifnal TF11 . . . . .145 F3
Manor Crest **1** SY5 . . . . .169 C4
Manor Dr
Oakengates/Donnington
TF2 . . . . .132 C1
3 Swindon DY3 . . . . . . .190 F1
Manor Farm SY4 . . . . .126 D8
Manor Farm Dr TF9 . . . . . .72 A1
Manor Farm La WV16 . . . .218 D2
Manor Gdns
8 Albrighton WV7 . . . . .157 A5
Dawley TF4 . . . . .143 F2
Market Drayton TF9 . . . . .36 C1
1 Pontesbury SY5 . . . . .173 B5
Manor House Cl **1** TF13 . .158 F5
Manor House La SY13 . . . . .32 E3
Manor La
Bobbington DY7 . . . . . . .190 B2
Prees SY13 . . . . .32 F2
Manor Pk **6** SY5 . . . . . . .173 A5
Manor Pl SY13 . . . . .32 E3
Manor Rd
Dawley TF4 . . . . .143 E2
Edgmond TF10 . . . . .109 A3
6 Wellington TF1 . . . . . .131 A2
Manor Rise TF1 . . . . .131 B2
Manor Way SY1 . . . . .126 B6
Manse Cl TF1 . . . . .131 C4
Mansell Rd TF1 . . . . .130 D3
Manse Rd TF1 . . . . .131 C4
Maple Ave
4 Ellesmere SY12 . . . . . .27 A3
Oswestry SY11 . . . . .59 A7
Wrexham LL12 . . . . .221 E6
Maple Cl
3 Craven Arms SY7 . . . .195 D6
Ludlow SY8 . . . . .217 D6
Market Drayton TF9 . . . . .52 F8
Oakengates/Donnington
TF2 . . . . .132 A5
Maple Cres **5** SY15 . . . . . .145 F5
Maple Dr **5** SY1 . . . . .113 D3
Maple Wood **11** TF13 . . . .144 D3
MARBURY 2 E8
MARCHAMLEY 68 F7
MARCHAMLEY WOOD 50 E3
Marche La SY4 . . . . .168 A1
Marches Mdw SY4 . . . . .80 C1

Marches Sch & Tech Coll
The SY11 . . . . .58 C6
March Gr **21** DY12 . . . . . .211 D2
March Way SY11 . . . . .113 E5
Marchwood Cl **1** WV16 . .218 D4
Marche Orch SY8 . . . . .213 B2
Mardol 11 SY1 . . . . .125 C6
Mardol Head **10** SY1 . . . .125 C6
Mardol Quay **14** SY1 . . . .125 B6
MARDU 192 F7
Mardu La SY7 . . . . .193 A6
MARDY 23 C1
Margaret Ct **4** TF1 . . . . . .131 C3
Marigold Cl **2** TF1 . . . . . .131 E2
Marine Terr **8** SY1 . . . . . .125 D5
MARKET DRAYTON 36 B2
Market Drayton Cottage
Hosp TF9 . . . . .53 C8
Market Drayton Inf Sch
TF9 . . . . .53 B8
Market Drayton Jun Sch
TF9 . . . . .53 B8
Market Drayton Swimming
Ctr TF9 . . . . .53 D8
Market La WV4 . . . . .190 F7
Market Mews **5** TF10 . . . .109 F3
Market Pl TF11 . . . . .145 F4
Market Sq
3 Bishop's Castle SY9 . . .181 F3
Tenbury Wells WR15 . . . .220 C5
1 Wellington TF1 . . . . . .130 D4
Market St
11 Craven Arms SY7 . . .195 E5
4 Ellesmere SY12 . . . . . .27 B2
7 Knighton LD7 . . . . . . .203 B3
Ludlow SY8 . . . . .217 C4
2 Oakengates/Donnington
TF2 . . . . .132 B2
2 Shrewsbury SY1 . . . . .125 C5
Tenbury Wells WR15 . . . .220 D5
1 Wellington TF1 . . . . . .130 E4
2 Wem SY4 . . . . .66 A6
Wrexham LL12 . . . . .221 E3
Marlborough Ct **7** SY1 . .114 A2
Marlborough Rd TF1 . . . . .131 E5
Marlborough Way **3** TF3 .143 D8
Marlbrook La WV6 . . . . . . .166 B2
Marlburn Way **10** WV5 . . .190 F3
Marlcroft **8** SY4 . . . . .66 A8
Marlebrook Way TF6 . . . . .116 A6
MARLEY GREEN 3 B8
Marley Mount Cres **6**
TF9 . . . . .36 C2
MARLOW 205 B7
Marlow Dr TF2 . . . . .132 B6
Marlpool Cl **3** SY2 . . . . . .124 F4
Marne Cl **3** SY4 . . . . .66 B8
Marquis Terr TF2 . . . . .132 B1
Marrion's Hill TF2 . . . . . . .132 C2
Marshalls Ct **4** SY1 . . . . .125 D8
MARSHBROOK 183 E4
Marshbrook Way TF2 . . . . .132 E8
Marsh Cres **1** LL12 . . . . . .221 E5
Marshgate **3** SY3 . . . . . . .124 D6
MARSH GREEN 117 B1
Marsh La
Cheswardine TF9 . . . . . . .73 A4
Hinstock TF9 . . . . .72 B1
Sheriffhales TF11 . . . . . .134 D3
Marsh Mdw Cl **4** TF1 . . . .130 C7
Marsh Rd
Edgmond TF10 . . . . .108 F6
Sheriffhales TF11 . . . . . .134 D4
MARSH THE
Chirbury with Brompton . .175 E5
Hinstock 90 B8
Marsland Cl SY11 . . . . .25 A6
Marstons Mill SY8 . . . . . . .217 C4
Marstons Terr SY8 . . . . . . .217 C4
Mart Ave **4** TF2 . . . . .132 D1
Martingale Way TF4 . . . . .143 D6
Martin Rd TF1 . . . . .130 C5
Martins Cl SY10 . . . . .57 E2
Martins Fields SY10 . . . . . .57 E2
Martin Wilson Prim Sch The
SY1 . . . . .125 E8
MARTON
Chirbury and Broughton . .171 B1
Myddle and Broughton . . .81 D4
Marton Dr
Shrewsbury SY1 . . . . . . .113 D2
Wellington SY1 . . . . .130 C6
Mary Elizabeth Rd SY8 . . .217 E3
Maryvale WR15 . . . . .220 B4
Mary Webb Cl **2** SY5 . . . .173 A5
Mary Webb Dr **3** SY5 . . . .125 B1
Mary Webb Sch SY5 . . . . .173 A4
Mary Webb Sports Ctr
SY5 . . . . .173 A4
Masefield Cl **4** TF9 . . . . . .53 A7
Maserfield SY11 . . . . .58 C7
Maserfield Cl SY11 . . . . . . .58 C7
Maslan Cres TF10 . . . . . . .107 D5
Mason Ave **12** LL13 . . . . .221 D2
Mason Dr **3** TF7 . . . . .152 F5
Mason's Pl TF10 . . . . .109 E5
Massey Cres SY1 . . . . .113 E5
Matthews Dr SY11 . . . . . . .58 F8
Maudlins Cl WV16 . . . . . . .218 D4
Maurice Chandler Sports Ctr
TF9 . . . . .70 C8
Maurice Lee Ave **4** TF2 . .132 A3
Mawddwy Ave **1** SY14 . . .14 F7
Mawley Cl **7** LL11 . . . . . . .221 C5
Maws Craft Ctr* TF8 . . . .153 A2
Mayfair Cl **2** WV7 . . . . . . .157 A5
Mayfair Dr **3** TF2 . . . . . . .132 F2
Mayfield TF7 . . . . .153 A5

Mayfield Ave **6** SY7 . . . . .195 E5
Mayfield Dr **5** SY2 . . . . . .125 F4
Mayfield Gdns SY2 . . . . . .126 A4
Mayfield Gr SY3 . . . . .136 E6
Mayfield Pk SY2 . . . . .125 F4
Mayfield Rd **3** WV7 . . . . .156 F5
Mayfields **8** 217 C6
Maynards Croft **4** TF10 . .109 F4
Maypole Cl **10** DY12 . . . . .211 E2
Maypole Rd TF12 . . . . .152 C2
Maythorne Cl TF7 . . . . . . .153 C4
Marville Ave **8** LL11 . . . . .221 C5
Meadcroft **1** TF7 . . . . . . .153 A5
Meadlands The 3 WV5 . .190 F3
Meadow Bank TF9 . . . . . . .19 A4
Meadow Brook SY3 . . . . . .136 F6
Meadowbrook Cl 12
WV15 . . . . .201 B3
Meadow Brook Cl TF7 . . . .153 B4
Meadow Cl
Aston Eyre WV16 . . . . . .187 D4
Bridgnorth WV16 . . . . . .218 E3
Cressage SY5 . . . . .149 E4
7 Madeley TF7 . . . . .153 C5
Market Drayton TF9 . . . . .36 A1
Morville WV16 . . . . .187 D5
Oakengates/Donnington
TF2 . . . . .131 F6
4 Oswestry SY11 . . . . . . .41 A1
4 Shrewsbury SY1 . . . . .114 A2
Wem SY4 . . . . .66 A8
Meadowcroft 3 SY13 . . . . .14 E8
Meadow Dale Dr **1** TF5 . .130 A6
Meadow Dr
5 Gobowen SY11 . . . . . .41 A7
Shifnal TF11 . . . . .146 A6
Meadow Farm Dr SY1 . . . .114 A3
Meadowlea **6** TF7 . . . . . . .153 A5
Meadow Lea
7 Oswestry SY11 . . . . . . .41 A1
Wrexham LL13 . . . . .221 E3
MEADOWLEY 187 C3
Meadow Pl **1** SY1 . . . . . .125 C6
Meadow Rd
Albrighton WV7 . . . . .157 B5
Clive SY4 . . . . .84 A5
1 Craven Arms SY7 . . . .195 E5
8 Dawley TF4 . . . . .143 E4
Gnosall TF10 . . . . .111 A2
8 Newport TF10 . . . . . .109 F3
Oakengates/Donnington
TF2 . . . . .132 E8
2 Pant SY10 . . . . .76 A1
Meadowsweet Dr 4 TF2 .132 E1
Meadow Terr SY1 . . . . . . .125 C6
Meadow The TF9 . . . . .69 D5
MEADOWTOWN 175 E8
Meadow View
Llandrinio SY22 . . . . . . .167 B8
Prees SY13 . . . . .49 D8
2 Westbury SY5 . . . . . .169 B1
Meadow View Cl TF10 . . . .110 A3
Meadow View
Newport TF10 . . . . .110 A3
Whitchurch SY13 . . . . . . .14 F7
4 Oswestry SY11 . . . . . . .41 A7
Meadway **12** WV15 . . . . . .219 A4
Mead Way TF11 . . . . .146 A4
Meaton La DY14 . . . . .210 B3
Medlar Cl **1** TF2 . . . . .143 F8
MEDLICOTT 177 B1
Meese Cl TF1 . . . . .130 D6
MEESON 106 E5
Meeson Cl WV7 . . . . .157 B5
MEESON HEATH 106 F4
Meifod Pl **13** LL13 . . . . . . .221 C2
Melbourne Cl **7** TF4 . . . . .144 A4
Melbourne Rise **2** SY3 . . .124 A7
Mellor Cl **4** TF7 . . . . .152 F4
Melrose Cres **3** TF9 . . . . . .53 B8
Melrose Dr SY2 . . . . .125 E1
Melrose Gdns TF1 . . . . . . .130 C3
Melton Way **17** SY3 . . . . .124 F3
MELVERLEY 94 A1
Melverley Craft Ctr*
SY22 . . . . .168 A7
MELVERLEY GREEN 167 F8
Melverley View SY11 . . . . .168 A6
Mendip Cl TF11 . . . . .143 E1
Mentone Cres TF10 . . . . . .109 B4
Meole Brace CE Prim Sch
SY3 . . . . .125 B2
Meole Brace Infants Sch
SY3 . . . . .125 A1
Meole Brace Jun Sch
SY3 . . . . .125 A1
Meole Brace Ret Pk SY2 . .125 C1
Meole Brace Sch SY3 . . . .125 B2
Meole Cres SY3 . . . . .125 B2
Meole Rise **6** SY3 . . . . . . .125 B2
Meole Wlk SY3 . . . . .125 A2
Merchant Cl **2** WV6 . . . . .166 C3

Mercia Dr **5** TF1 . . . . 131 A5
Mercian Cl SY3 . . . . .124 F1
Mercian Ct **4** TF9 . . . . . .36 C1
Mere Cl
2 Newport TF10. . . . . .109 F4
Shifnal TF11. . . . . .146 A3
Shrewsbury SY2 . . . . .125 E3
Mere Gn Ct SY3 . . . . .124 F3
Mere Gr **4** TF5 . . . . .130 C8
Mere La DY7. . . . . .201 F6
Mereside SY2. . . . . .125 F2
Meres Visitor Ctr* SY12. .27 D2
MERETOWN. 110 B5
Merevale Way TF2 . . . . . . .120 E1
Merganser Cl **1** TF1. . . .131 A6
Merlin Coppice **8** TF1 . .131 A7
Merlin Rd
Shrewsbury SY3 . . . . .124 D7
4 Wrexham LL12 . . . . .221 E8
Merricks La DY12 . . . . .211 C2
Merridale Cres TF1 . . . . . .130 E5
MERRINGTON 100 E6
Merrington Rd
3 Oakengates/Donnington
TF2. . . . . .120 F1
Pimhill SY4. . . . . .100 E5
Merry La
Grinshill SY4 . . . . .84 A1
Hadnall SY4 . . . . .83 F1
Merton Cl **6** DY12. . . . . .211 C2
Methodist Hill **4** LL20 . . . .6 A7
Mews The WR15 . . . . .220 C4
Meyrick Rd **4** TF1. . . . . .130 D5
MICKLEY. 51 C6
Mickley La TF9 . . . . .51 C5
Middle Croft Rd TF10 . . . .107 D5
Middlegate SY1. . . . . .113 D5
MIDDLEHOPE 196 E7
Middle La TF6 . . . . .105 F7
Middle Rd **3** TF2 . . . . . .132 B4
Middle St **4** LL14. . . . . .6 D8
MIDDLETON
Bitterley. 207 C4
Little Hereford. 213 D4
Oswestry Rural 59 C7
MIDDLETON BAGGOT 186 F1
Middleton Cl **10** SY11 . . .59 A8
MIDDLETON PRIORS 186 E1
Middleton Rd
Oswestry Rural SY11. . . . . . .59 C7
Oswestry SY11 . . . . .58 E7
MIDDLETON SCRIVEN. . . .199 F6
Middletown Residential Pk
SY21. . . . . .167 D3
Middletown Sq **3** SY21. .126 A8
Middle Wardens **7** SY7 .205 B5
Middle Wood Rd
Bromfield SY8. . . . . .206 E1
Ludlow SY8 . . . . .217 A3
Midgley Ct TF10 . . . . .109 E3
Mid Wales Airport SY21. .170 B3
Mile Bank Rd SY13. . . . . .2 B2
MILEBROOK. 203 E3
MILE OAK. 59 A4
Mile Oak Ind Est SY10. . . . .58 F5
Milfields Way WV16 . . . . . .199 F8
MILFORD 98 F6
Milford Rd SY4 . . . . .99 A7
Milk St **7** SY1. . . . . .125 C5
Mill Bank TF1 . . . . .130 F3
Millbank Rise LL13. . . . . . .221 E1
Millbrook Cl **5** SY8. . . . .212 E2
Millbrook Dr SY4 . . . . .103 D8
Millbrook Prim Sch TF1 . .131 A5
Millbrook Way SY4. . . . . . .212 D2
Mill Cl **3** WV15. . . . . . . .189 A6
Mill Ct **2** LL13. . . . . .9 C8
Miller PI **6** TF2. . . . . . . .132 B6
Millers Gn SY1. . . . . .113 E1
Millers Vale **12** WV5 . . .190 E3
Millers Way **4** TF2. . . . .132 F8
Mill Farm Dr TF11 . . . . . . .144 D4
Mill Field Cl **23** LD7. . . .203 B3
Millfield Dr TF9. . . . . .36 F2
Millfield Grange TF9. . . . . .36 F2
Millfields Rd **3** TF1. . . .130 F3
Millfields Way **8** WV5 . .190 E3
Mill Gn **8** LD7. . . . . .203 B3
MILL GREEN 71 E5
Millichope Pk* SY7. . . . . .197 B7
Millington Cl **1** SY4 . . . . .81 A1
Mill La
Blymhill & Weston-under-Lizard
TF11 . . . . .135 C2
Bronington SY13 . . . . .13 A4
Broseley TF12. . . . . .79 C4
Diddlebury SY7 . . . . .196 F4
Donington WV7 . . . . .147 F1
Hadnall SY4. . . . . .102 C6
Hanwood SY5 . . . . .169 F1
Kemberton TF11 . . . . .154 C6
Knighton on Teme WR15 . .215 B4
Kynnersley TF6. . . . . .119 C6
Leintwardine SY7. . . . . .205 B4
Madeley TF7. . . . . .153 B5
Prees Higher Heath SY13. . .32 F3
Smestow DY3. . . . . .190 E2
Stoke upon Tern TF9 . . . . . .88 E3
Tibberton TF10. . . . . .107 E5
Tong TF11. . . . . .147 D2
Uffington SY4. . . . . .126 D8
Wellington TF1. . . . . .130 F3
Welshpool SY21. . . . . .170 B6
Millman Gr TF4 . . . . .143 C6

Mill Mdw
3 Shrewsbury SY2. . . . . .125 E3
Tenbury Wells WR15 . . . . .220 D3
Millmead Dr **4** SY2. . . . .125 F3
Mill Pk SY13. . . . . .15 C7
Mill Pool Cl **11** WV5. . . .190 E3
Mill Pool PI **11** WV14 . .209 E3
Millpool The WV5 . . . . .190 C5
Mill Rd
Bronington SY13 . . . . .13 A5
Hodnet TF9 . . . . .51 E1
Knighton LD7. . . . . .203 B2
Newcastle on Clun SY7 . . .192 D5
Shrewsbury SY2 . . . . .125 B2
Millside **7** SY4. . . . . .190 F3
Mill St
Bridgnorth WV15. . . . . .219 A5
Hopesay SY7 . . . . .195 A4
Ludlow SY8 . . . . .217 C3
Prees SY13. . . . . .49 C8
Wem SY4 . . . . .66 A5
Millstream **5** SY5. . . . . .171 F3
Millstream Way **6** TF1. .131 B6
Millward Cl TF7 . . . . .132 B8
Mill Way **4** TF2. . . . . . . .132 A6
Millwood Rise **9** LL13. . . .9 C8
Milners Dr **4** TF4 . . . . . .143 E6
Milners La TF4 . . . . .143 E6
Milnthorpe Cl **5** SY3 . . .125 A1
Milson SY8 . . . . .215 B8
Milton Cl **6** SY1. . . . . . . .125 E8
Milton Dr
1 Madeley TF7 . . . . .152 F5
2 Market Drayton TF9 . . . .36 C2
Milton Rd SY8 . . . . .217 E4
Mimosa Cl TF7 . . . . .153 B3
Minchers Rise TF3 . . . . . . .143 E8
Miners Mdw TF12. . . . . . . .161 D8
Mines The TF12. . . . . .161 D8
Minshall PI SY11. . . . . .59 B7
MINSTERLEY 172 D4
Minsterley Prim Sch
SY5. . . . . .172 E3
Minsterley Rd SY5 . . . . . . .173 A5
MINTON. 183 D5
Minton Cl TF7 . . . . .152 F7
Mitcham Ct **2** SY3 . . . . .124 D7
Mitchel Way **2** TF7 . . . . .152 F5
Mitnell La SY13 . . . . .212 E5
Moat Cl **8** TF1. . . . . .130 C7
Moat Croft **4** TF11. . . . .145 F3
Moat Hall SY9. . . . . .181 C4
Moat House The WV16 . . .188 D1
Moat St SY16 . . . . .218 F5
Mocktree Turnpike SY7. . .205 D6
Modra Pk SY10. . . . . .88 B2
Moffats Sch DY12. . . . . . . .210 B8
Mold Ct WV10. . . . . .218 F5
Mold Rd LL11. . . . . .221 A7
Mole Way TF5 . . . . .130 C7
MONDAYTOWN. 172 B6
Monet Cl **5** TF5. . . . . . . .130 B7
Moneybrook Way SY21 . . .125 B1
Monger Rd LL13. . . . . .221 E1
MONKHOPTON 186 F4
MONKMOOR. 126 B7
Monkmoor Ave
3 Oswestry SY11. . . . . . . .58 F8
Shrewsbury SY2 . . . . .125 D3
Monkmoor Cl **1** SY11. . . .58 F8
Monkmoor Cres **3** SY2 .125 E7
Monkmoor Ct SY11 . . . . . . .40 F1
Monkmoor Ind Est SY2 . . .126 A8
Monkmoor Pool Nature
Reserve* SY2. . . . . .126 C8
Monkmoor Rd
Oswestry SY11. . . . . .58 F8
7 Shrewsbury SY2. . . . . .126 A8
Monkmoor Recn Ctr SY2 .125 F7
Monks Cl **18** WV5 . . . . . .190 F3
Monks Ct WV15. . . . . .219 A5
Monksfield **5** TF9 . . . . . .36 A1
Montague PI SY3 . . . . .125 D3
MONTFORD 169 D5
MONTFORD BRIDGE 169 E6
MONTGOMERY 174 A3
Montgomery Castle*
SY15. . . . . .174 B3
Montgomery Mews **2**
SY1. . . . . .131 A7
Montgomery Rd
3 Wellington TF1. . . . . . .130 C4
Wrexham LL13. . . . . .221 E4
Montgomery Way **5**
SY1. . . . . .114 A2
Montrose SY3. . . . . .124 A6
Moorfield Ct TF10. . . . . . . .109 E2
Moorfield Foundation Sch
TF10. . . . . .109 E1
Moorfield La TF10 . . . . . . .109 D1
Moorhead Cl **3** LL13. . .221 F4
Moorhouse Cl TF1. . . . . . . .130 C3
Moor La WV6. . . . . .166 D2
Moorland Ave LL13 . . . . . .221 F4
Moorland Dr **14** TF2. . .132 F1
Moorland Rd **3** TF10 . .109 E2
Moor Pk Sch SY8 . . . . .212 F6
Moor Rd TF4 . . . . .143 F4
Moors La
Farlow DY14 . . . . .209 C2
St Martin's SY11 . . . . .24 D4
Moors The
Cressage SY5 . . . . .149 E5
1 Ellesmere SY12. . . . . .217 A3
Moors View The **2** SY7. .196 F4
MORDA. 58 D4
Morda Bank SY10. . . . . .58 D4

Morda CE Prim Sch SY10. .58 D4
Morda Cl SY11. . . . . .58 D6
Morda Rd SY11. . . . . .58 D6
Morden Cl **6** TF2. . . . . . .132 C2
MORE. 182 B6
MORETON 123 D7
Moreton Bsns Pk SY10. . . .23 E5
MORETON CORBET. . . . .
SY4. .85 E3
Moreton Cres SY3 . . . . . . .125 D4
Moreton Hall Sch SY11. . . .23 F4
MORETON SAY 35 A1
Moreton Say CE Prim Sch
TF9. .34 A2
Moreton St SY11. . . . . .32 D1
MORETONWOOD 34 E3
Morfe La DY7. . . . . .201 F5
Morfe Rd WV15. . . . . .219 A5
Morgan Ave LL11 . . . . .221 C6
Morgan Cl SY1. . . . . .113 E1
Morgans Cotts **9** SY1. . .113 C1
Morgansfield SY6 . . . . .185 A3
Morgan Springs WV16 . . .218 E4
Morgan Way **2** TF1. . . . .130 C4
Morningside WV15. . . . . . .220 C4
Mornington Cl **4** SY3. . .124 D6
Morrellswood La
Leighton & Eaton Constantine
SY5. . . . . .141 E1
Little Wenlock SY5. . . . . . . .142 A1
Morris Cl SY1. . . . . .113 D5
Morris Dr TF2 . . . . .132 C8
Mortimer SY1. . . . . .113 E4
Mortimer Cl **3** SY8. . . . .212 E2
Mortimer Dr **4** SY8. . . . .212 E2
Mortimer Gdns **10** DY14.209 C2
Mortimer Gr **22** DY12. . .211 D2
Mortimer PI SY9. . . . . .217 D4
Mortimer Rd TF9 . . . . .52 E5
MORTON. 76 E5
MORTON COMMON. 76 E6
Morton Ct **7** TF4. . . . . . .143 E4
Morton La SY10. . . . . .77 B8
MORTON MILL 86 B2
MORVILLE. 187 E5
Morville CE Sch WV16 . . .187 E5
Morville Dr TF1. . . . . .130 D2
Morville Hall & Gdns*
WV16. . . . . .187 D4
MORVILLE HEATH 187 F4
Morville Rd TF1 . . . . .113 D3
Mosclay Rd **6** TF2. . . . . .132 D2
MOSE 189 A1
Mossbank Way SY3 . . . . . .124 D7
Mossey Gn **2** TF1 . . . . . .131 F1
Mossey Gn Way TF2. . . . . .131 F1
Mossfield TF9 . . . . .73 A6
Moss La
Bronington SY13 . . . . .13 B3
Cheswardine TF9. . . . . .55 C3
Ellesmere Rural SY12 . . . . . .26 C6
Hanmer SY13 . . . . .12 C2
Norton in Hales TF9. . . . . . . .36 F6
Moss Rd TF2 . . . . .132 C4
MOSTON. 67 E2
Moston Gn **3** SY11. . . . . .67 E2
Moston Rd SY11. . . . . .114 B3
Mottershead **3** SY11. . . .113 D4
Mound Way TF7 . . . . .152 F6
Mountbatten Cl **1** TF11. .146 A6
Mount Bradford La SY11 . .25 A7
Mount Cl
5 Pontesbury SY5 . . . . .173 A4
22 Welshpool SY21 . . . . .170 B6
Mount Cres
Shrewsbury SY1 . . . . .40 C1
Whitchurch SY13 . . . . .14 F8
Mount Dr **1** SY11 . . . . . . .58 D8
Mount Gilbert TF1. . . . . . . .130 F2
Mount Gilbert Sch
Dawley TF4 . . . . .144 A3
Wellington TF1. . . . . .130 D5
Mount La
Market Drayton TF9 . . . . . . .53 C8
Stoke upon Tern TF9 . . . . . .70 F6
Mount Orch WR15 . . . . . . .220 C4
MOUNT PLEASANT 113 D2
Mount Pleasant
3 Clun SY7 . . . . .193 C3
3 Oakengates/Donnington
TF2. . . . . .132 B1
Tenbury Wells WR15 . . . . .220 C4
2 Trewern SY21. . . . . . . .167 D3
Mount Pleasant Ave **10**
WV5 . . . . .190 F4
Mount Pleasant Dr TF3. . .153 B8
Mount Pleasant Inf Sch
SY1. . . . . .113 D1
Mount Pleasant Jun Sch
SY1. . . . . .113 D1
Mount Pleasant Rd
2 Madeley TF7. . . . . . . .153 C5
Shrewsbury SY1 . . . . .113 D2
Mount Rd
1 Dawley TF4. . . . . .143 F4
2 Oswestry SY11. . . . . . . .58 D8
Mount Rise SY11. . . . . .40 C1
Mounts Cl TF7 . . . . .153 C5
Mount Side TF1. . . . . .131 D2
Mount St
Shrewsbury SY3 . . . . .125 B7
Welshpool SY21. . . . . .170 B6
Wrexham LL11. . . . . .221 B3
Mount The
Rhosnesni LL12. . . . . .221 E4
Shrewsbury SY3 . . . . .124 F7
Whitchurch SY13 . . . . .14 F8
Mount View SY6 . . . . .184 C3

Mount View Rd **2** TF2 . .132 B1
Mount Way **4** SY5. . . . . .173 A4
Mountwood Pk SY3 . . . . . .124 E7
Mousecroft La SY3 . . . . . . .124 B8
Moveage The **11** SY1. . . .113 C2
MUCH WENLOCK 159 D4
Much Wenlock Leisure Ctr
TF13. . . . . .159 F6
Much Wenlock Mus* **7** . . . . . .
TF13. . . . . .159 E4
Much Wenlock Prim Sch
TF13. . . . . .159 F3
Much Wenlock Rd TF8 . . . .151 B4
MUCKLETON. 104 E7
Muckleton La TF6. . . . . . . .104 F4
Muckleton Rd SY4 . . . . . . .104 B8
MUCKLEY. 187 B6
MUCKLEY CROSS. 187 C6
Mulberry Ave **5** SY12. . .27 A2
Mulberry Cl TF10 . . . . .109 F5
Mulberry Ct
Hadley TF1. . . . . .131 C5
6 Oswestry SY11. . . . . . . .58 D7
Mullinder Dr TF2 . . . . .148 A8
Mulsow Cl **4** SY4. . . . . . .125 B5
Murivance **5** SY1. . . . . . .125 B5
Museum of the Gorge*
TF8. . . . . .152 B4
Muskoka SY13 . . . . .13 B4
Musk Rose Cl **2** TF12. . .132 E8
Musley La LL13 . . . . .9 D6
MUXTON. 120 E1
Muxton Cty Prim Sch
TF2. . . . . .132 F8
Muxton La
Lilleshall & Donnington
TF2. . . . . .133 A8
Oakengates/Donnington
TF2. . . . . .120 F1
MYDDLE 82 D4
Myddle CE Prim Sch SY4 .82 D4
MYDDLEWOOD 82 A4
Myford TF4 . . . . .143 B2
MYND. 204 C6
Mynd Cl SY2. . . . . .126 A6
Mynd Ind Est The SY6. . . .216 C5
MYNDTOWN 182 F4
Mynd View **7** SY1. . . . . .195 E5
Myndyke **6** SY7 . . . . . . .170 B6
Mythstores Mus* SY4. . . .166 B6
MYTTON. 169 F8
Mytton Cl **3** SY1. . . . . . . .41 E3
Mytton Gr **7** SY3. . . . . . .124 E6
Mytton Oak Rd SY3 . . . . . .124 C5
Mytton Pk **6** SY3. . . . . . .124 C5
Mytton Rd SY4. . . . . .103 F7

N

Nabb Cl **5** TF2 . . . . .132 C3
Nabb The **3** TF2. . . . . . . .132 B3
Naird La
Hollinswood & Randlay
TF11 . . . . .145 A5
Stirchley & Brookside TF11 144 F2
Nairn Rdbt TF11 . . . . .145 A5
Nanny Murphy's La TF11 .134 B1
NANT. 22 F1
Nant La SY10. . . . . .75 C3
NANTMAWR 75 B5
Nantmawr Bank TF12 . . . . .75 C6
Nantmawr Quarry (Outdoor
Activity Centre)* SY10 . .75 C6
Nantwich Rd
Whitchurch Urban SY13. . . .15 E7
Woore CW3 . . . . .4 D2
NANT Y CAWS. 58 D2
NANT-Y-GOLLEN 57 B7
Napier Sq LL13 . . . . .221 E2
NAPLEY. 37 F8
Napley Dr TF9 . . . . .20 D2
NAPLEY HEATH 21 A1
Napton Dr **9** SY11. . . . . .20 D1
Napoleon Dr SY3 . . . . .124 C6
Narrow La TF9 . . . . .71 D2
NASH. 214 D6
Neachley La TF11. . . . . . . .147 A3
Near Vallens TF1. . . . . .131 D4
NEDGE HILL. 144 F3
NEEN SAVAGE. 209 E4
NEEN SOLLARS. 215 C7
NEENTON. 199 B6
NEFOD. 24 B5
Nefod La SY11. . . . . .24 B6
Nelson Cl **2** TF11. . . . . . .146 A6
Nelson St LL13 . . . . .221 E2
Nelson Way **7** TF1. . . . . .120 F1
NESSCLIFFE 97 E3
Nesscliffe Hill Ctry Pk*
SY4. .97 F4
Netherfield **8** WV16 . . . .200 E3
NETHER SKYBORRY 203 A4
NETHERTON. 200 E3
Netherton La
Bewdley DY12 . . . . .211 E1
Highley WV16 . . . . .200 E2
Nether Way **5** SY3 . . . . .125 B1
Netley Rd SY3 . . . . .125 B1
Nettles La **8** SY3 . . . . . .125 B6
Neuchatel Cl SY13 . . . . . . .125 B7
Neville Cres **2** LL11 . . . .221 D6
Nevil Rd **2** TF1. . . . . .130 C4
NEWBRIDGE
Cefn 6 D8
Oswestry Rural 77 A8
Newbridge Rd LL14 . . . . .6 C8
New Bridge Rd TF8 . . . . . .152 D4

Newbrigg Rd **10** LL12 . .221 D8
New Brookdale TF1. . . . . . .131 B4
Newbrook Dr **2** SY3. . . .137 A5
NEWCASTLE 192 E5
Newcastle CE Prim Sch
SY7. . . . . .192 D5
Newcastle Rd
Market Drayton TF9. . . . . . .36 F2
Woore CW3 . . . . .5 D2
New Church Rd TF1 . . . . . .130 E3
New Coll TF1 . . . . .130 F3
Newcomen Way TF7 . . . . . .152 D5
NEWDALE. 143 C7
Newdale Prim Sch TF1 . . .143 D8
Newent Cl **2** SY11. . . . . .125 E8
Newfield Cl **2** TF11 . . . .145 F5
Newfield Dr **2** TF2 . . . . .132 A5
Newfield Dr
Oakengates/Donnington
TF2. . . . . .132 A5
Shrewsbury SY1 . . . . .125 D7
New Forest Cl DY14. . . . . .210 E1
New Guild SY8. . . . . .166 C3
Newgate Ct **7** SY11 . . . . .58 D7
Newhall Gdns SY2 . . . . . . .125 E5
New Hall La SY3 . . . . .113 B4
New Hall Rd TF1. . . . . .130 E3
Newham Way SY3 . . . . .124 E3
Newhouse La
Albrighton WV7 . . . . .157 A4
Church Pulverbatch SY5 . .173 F2
Condover SY5. . . . . .178 A6
New Houses SY4. . . . . .169 D6
Newill Gr **11** TF5 . . . . . . .30 B7
NEWINGTON 195 D6
Newington Way SY7 . . . . . .195 E6
NEW INVENTION 203 C7
Newlands Rd
12 Oakengates/Donnington
TF2. . . . . .132 B2
2 Oakengates TF2. . . . . .132 B1
NEW MARTON. 25 C2
New Mills La SY5 . . . . .173 B6
NEWNES. 26 E1
NEWNHAM BRIDGE. 215 A4
New Options Coll TF11. . . .164 A6
Newpark St SY1 . . . . .125 D7
New Pk Cl SY1. . . . . .125 D7
New Pk Rd SY1 . . . . .125 D7
New Pk St SY1 . . . . .125 D7
NEWPORT 109 F2
Newport Bsns Pk TF10 . . .109 F2
Newport CE Jun Sch
TF10. . . . . .109 F2
Newport Cl **3** LL13 . . . . .221 F1
Newport Cres TF11. . . . . . . .45 F4
Newport Dr SY2 . . . . .125 F1
Newport High Sch TF10 . .109 E2
Newport Inf Sch TF10 . . . .109 F2
Newport PI **9** SY1 . . . . . .125 C6
Newport Rd
Albrighton WV7 . . . . .156 E8
Donington TF11 . . . . .147 D1
Edgmond TF10. . . . . .109 C4
Gnosall ST20 . . . . .111 E5
Hinstock TF9 . . . . .71 F3
1 Oswestry SY11. . . . . . . .41 A1
Perton WV7 . . . . .157 F2
Shifnal TF11. . . . . .145 F5
Sutton upon Tern TF9. . . . . .53 E7
Tong TF11. . . . . .147 D3
Whitchurch SY13 . . . . .15 A7
Newport St SY7. . . . . .193 D4
Newport Swimming Pool
TF10. . . . . .109 F2
Newquay Dr **4** LL13 . . . .221 F1
New Rd
7 Bewdley DY12 . . . . . .211 E4
Bridgnorth WV16. . . . . .218 F4
8 Cleobury Mortimer
DY14. . . . . .209 E3
Dawley TF4 . . . . .143 F2
Farlow DY14 . . . . .209 B6
7 Gobowen SY11. . . . . . . .41 A8
Hanmer WR6. . . . . .215 E1
Ironbridge TF8. . . . . .152 C4
Loggerheads TF9. . . . . .54 F8
Ludlow SY8 . . . . .217 C5
Madeley TF7. . . . . .153 A5
Montgomery SY15. . . . . . . .174 B4
Much Wenlock TF13. . . . . .159 C5
8 Oakengates/Donnington
TF2. . . . . .132 C5
Rock DY14. . . . . .210 D1
Swindon DY3. . . . . .190 D2
New Rd Gdns **12** DY14. .209 E3
New Rhosrobin LL11. . . . . .221 A8
New River Cl **7** TF1. . . . .130 C7
New Row
4 Hollinswood TF3. . . . .144 B6
Hanwood SY4. . . . . .143 C3
New St
8 Bishop's Castle SY9 . .181 F3
Clive SY4 . . . . .84 A5
1 Dawley TF4. . . . . .143 E3
Ford SY5 . . . . .169 C4
Ludlow SY8 . . . . .217 C6
Newport TF10 . . . . .109 F3
Oakengates/Donnington
TF2. . . . . .132 A3
15 Oswestry SY11 . . . . . .58 E8
Shrewsbury SY1 . . . . .125 A6
Welshpool SY21. . . . . .170 B6
Wem SY4 . . . . .66 A7
NEWSTREET LANE. 34 F7
Newton **14** SY7 . . . . .195 E5

NEWTON
Welshampton and Lyneal....28 A1
Worfield..................188 D8
Newton Cl
1 Albrighton WV7.......156 E7
2 Bewdley DY12.........211 C2
Newtonmere Dr
8 Shrewsbury SY1......113 D2
6 Wellington TF1.......130 C5
NEWTON ON THE HILL...83 B3
Newton St
12 Craven Arms SY7.....195 E5
Wrexham LL13..........221 E2
NEWTOWN................81 B1
Newtown TF9............53 D8
NEWTOWN................159 D5
Newtown TF10...........109 E1
NEWTOWN................47 A4
Newtown 8 SY13.........15 A8
New Town TF4...........18 F5
Newtown CE Prim Sch
SY4....................46 F4
Newtown Gdns SY4.......99 A8
New Trench Rd
Lilleshall & Donnington
TF2...................120 E2
Oakengates/Donnington
TF2...................132 C8
NEW WOODHOUSES........16 E8
NEW WORKS.............143 A6
New Works La TF6.......143 A6
NIB HEATH..............98 F2
Nickless Way 4 TF4.....143 E5
Nightingale Way 2 TF1..130 F6
Nightingale Wlk SY1....113 D5
Noble St SY4............66 A6
NOBOLD................124 E1
Nobold SY4.............99 A8
Nobold Cl SY7...........99 A8
Nobold La SY5..........124 E1
Noel Hill Rd SY5........138 F4
No Man's Gn La DY7.....201 F3
NONELEY...............64 F4
Noneley Rd SY4..........64 E7
Nook La
Bronington SY13........12 F1
Cuckoo's Corner SY13...29 F8
Prees SY4..............49 F3
Norbroom Ct 10 TF10....110 A4
Norbroom Dr TF10.......110 A4
NORBURY...............182 D8
Norbury Prim Sch SY9..182 D7
Norbury Rd ST20........111 E8
NORDLEY...............188 A8
Norfield View 4 TF2....221 F7
Norfolk Rd LL12.........221 F7
Normandie Cl SY8.......217 E4
Norman Rd LL13.........221 D1
North Cl 9 SY3..........125 C4
North Dr SY10...........41 B5
North Gate 1 WV16......218 F5
Northgate Mews 3
WV16..................218 E5
Northgate Mus* WV16...218 E5
North Hermitage 6 SY3..125 C4
Northlands CW3..........5 A5
Northleigh Gr LL11......221 C7
North Rd
Pant SY22..............93 F7
Wellington TF1.........130 D5
Northside Cl 8 SY1......114 C3
North St
2 Oakengates/Donnington
TF2...................132 C2
Shrewsbury SY1.........125 D7
Northumberland Pl 3
SY1...................125 D8
North Wales Sch of Art &
Design LL11............221 B4
NORTHWOOD.............46 C7
Northwood 3 LL12.......221 F7
Northwood Halt Sta
DY12..................211 C4
Northwood La
Kidderminster Foreign
DY12..................211 D3
Stottesdon WV16........199 F3
Northwood Rd SY2.......126 B6
Northwood Terr TF3.....144 B3
NORTON................
Culmington............206 A8
Stockton..............163 B5
Wroxeter and Uppington...139 F8
Norton Cl TF7...........153 C7
Norton Dr
1 Dawley TF3...........144 B1
Wroxeter & Uppington SY4 127 C1
NORTON IN HALES.......20 D2
Norton in Hales CE Prim Sch
TF9....................20 C1
Norton St 5 LD7........203 B3
Norwich Dr TF3.........144 D3
Novers The 5 SY9.......181 E3
NOX...................169 C1
Nuffield Hospl SY3.....124 F2
Nurseries The SY10......76 B2
Nursery Cl 2 SY11.....78 D8
Nursery Dr 2 WV5.....190 F2
Nursery Mdws SY1......125 C8
Nursery Rd 7 DY12.....211 D2
NURTON................166 F4
NURTON HILL...........166 D4
Nurton Hill Rd WV6.....166 E5

O

Oadby Way 1 SY3......124 C6
Oakapple Cl 3 ST19....148 E8
Oak Ave
Newport TF10...........109 F1
Penley LL13............10 F3
Oak Bridge Ct WR15....220 D3
Oak Cl
Llandysilio SY22........94 A1
Madeley TF7............153 C6
Weston Rhyn SY10.......23 D4
Oakcroft LL14...........23 D8
Oak Dr
10 Ellesmere SY12......27 A2
2 Minsterley SY5.......172 E3
Oswestry SY11..........58 F6
Shawbury SY4...........103 D7
Trysull & Seisdon WV5..190 C5
Whitchurch SY13........14 F6
Wrexham LL12...........221 E6
Oak Edge View SY5.....176 A8
OAKENGATES............132 A2
Oakengates Leisure Ctr
TF2...................132 B5
Oakengates Rd 2 TF2...132 C6
Oakengates Sta TF2....132 C6
Oakengates Theatre*
TF2...................132 B3
Oak Farm La SY11......78 E8
Oakfield 3 LL13........221 E1
Oakfield Cl
Bronington LL13........13 B3
3 Shrewsbury SY3......124 F5
St Martin's SY11.......25 A6
Worthen with Shelve SY5..171 E3
Oakfield Dr SY3........124 E5
Oakfield Pk TF13.......159 E3
Oakfield Rd
14 Market Drayton TF9...36 B1
Shifnal TF11...........145 F5
Shrewsbury SY3.........124 F5
Wellington TF5.........130 C8
Oakfields SY22.........92 D6
Oak Gdns WV16.........218 D6
Oakhurst Ave SY11......40 D1
Oakhurst Rd SY11......40 D1
Oak La
Oswestry Rural SY10....75 D8
8 Shrewsbury SY3.....124 B6
Oakland Cty Prim Sch
SY3...................137 A6
Oakland Pk SY6........216 E6
Oaklands
Bicton Heath SY3.......124 B7
Bridgnorth WV15........219 B4
Oaklands Ave 1 LL12...221 F5
Oaklands Dr
Oakengates/Donnington
TF2...................132 A7
Whittington SY11.......41 E2
Oaklands Rd LL14.......23 E6
Oaklands The WR15.....220 D3
Oakleaf Rise DT10......210 E1
OAKLEY................37 C6
Oakley Ave SY3........125 C3
Oakley Cl SY4..........63 B1
Oakley La TF9..........37 A6
Oakley Manor Sch 7
SY3...................125 C3
Oakley St SY3..........125 C4
Oak Mdw 4 SY3.........181 F4
Oak Rd
2 Hanwood SY5........173 F8
The Rock TF3..........143 E8
Oak Ridge 6 SY21......170 B7
Oaks Cres TF1.........130 B2
Oaks Dr SY6...........216 E6
Oaks Rd
Church Stretton SY6....216 E6
1 Craven Arms SY7....195 D5
Oak St
Highley WV16...........200 E3
Oswestry SY11..........58 D8
Shrewsbury SY3........124 F5
Oak Tree Cl WR15.......220 D6
Oak Tree Cres SY7.....194 B8
Oak Tree Dr SY3........136 E7
Oaktree La WV16........198 F4
Oakvale Cl 2 SY5.......178 C6
Oakwood Cl 5 SY11.....41 F2
Oakwood Dr
2 Oakengates/Donnington
TF2...................132 A6
Shrewsbury SY3.........113 D3
Oakwood Pk LL13.......10 F4
Oakwood Rd
21 Bewdley DY12.......211 C2
Cleobury North WV16...198 E6
Oatfield Cl 3 SY13.....15 A6
OBLEY.................203 F8
Occupation La WV16....200 D6
Oerley Cl 4 SY10......58 C8
Oerley Way SY10........58 C8
Offa La................6 E3
Offa Dr SY11...........40 F1
Offas Cl SY10..........75 D7
Offas Dyke Rd SY22....94 A1
Office La SY8..........208 A2
Offoxey Rd TF11.......147 E5
Okehampton Rd TF11...131 E4
Old Armoury The 1 SY8..53 C8
Old Bedstone Rd 8 SY7..204 C5
Old Bell Mus The* SY15..174 B3
Old Bowling Gn Cl WR15 220 C6

Old Brickyard SY8......217 C5
OLDBURY...............218 D2
Oldbury Rd WV16.......218 E3
Oldbury Wells WV16....218 E4
Oldbury Wells Sch WV16 218 E4
Old Chads La SY11......1 C8
Old Chapel Ct 26 SY11..58 E8
Old Chirk Rd SY11......23 F1
OLD CHURCH STOKE.....175 B1
Old Coach Rd SY19.....148 F7
Old Coleham 8 SY3.....125 D5
OLD COPPICE...........136 D3
Old Coppice Grange 7
TF3...................143 F8
Oldcroft TF2...........132 A3
Old Dalelands 8 TF9....53 B8
Olden La
Ruyton SY4.............80 A1
Ruyton-XI-Towns SY4....79 E1
Old Farm La TF10.......121 C3
Old Farm Rd
2 Ecclusham LL14......221 A1
Hadnall SY4............102 C4
OLDFIELD..............199 E7
OLD FIELD.............206 E4
Oldfield Rd 8 TF4......144 A2
Oldford Inf Sch SY21...170 B6
Oldford Inf Sch SY21...170 B6
Oldford La 28 SY21.....170 B6
Oldford Rise SY21......170 B6
Oldford View 28 SY21...170 B6
Old Fort Rd SY11.......40 E1
Old Hall Cl
Albrighton WV7........156 F5
1 Wellington TF1......130 F2
Old Hall Sch The TF1...130 F4
OLD HARWICK...........26 B1
Old Heath SY11.........113 E2
OLDINGTON............188 C1
Old Mapsis Way SY10...58 D4
Old Marton..............25 E1
Old Mill Cl 4 SY5......171 F3
Old Mill La WV16.......218 E2
Old Nursery Cl TF7.....153 B6
Old Office Cl TF4......143 E5
Old Office Rd TF4......143 E5
Old Oswestry (Hillfort)*
SY10..................40 F3
OLD PARK..............144 A7
Old Pk Sch TF4.........144 A6
Old Pk Rd 5 TF2.......132 B1
Old Pk Way TF3........143 F7
OLDPOOL...............86 D1
Old Post Office La SY10.57 D2
Old Potts Way SY3......125 D4
Old Rectory Gdns SY11..78 C7
Old Roman Rd SY3......125 A3
Old Sch Cl 6 WV16.....200 F2
Old Sch La
Tenbury Wells WR11....220 D7
Westbury SY5..........168 C2
Old Sch Mews 1 SY11....9 C8
Old Shackerley La WV7..148 A1
Old Smithy Cl 3 WV6...166 C3
Old Smithy Rd TF10.....107 E5
Old St SY8.............217 C3
Old Toll Gate TF2......132 C3
Old Top House Cotts
SY4...................126 D8
Old Vicarage Rd TF4....143 F1
Old Weston Rd SY19.....148 E8
Old Wharf TF3..........144 A5
Old Willow Rd TF2......120 E1
OLDWOOD..............220 C2
OLD WOODHOUSES.......3 D2
Oldwood Rd WR15.......220 C2
OLD WOODS............100 B5
Old Worcester Rd
Albrighton WV7........156 D6
Bridgnorth WV15.......219 B3
Oleander Cl 6 TF3......131 E1
Oliver Ct 1 TF1........130 E4
Olivet Gdns LL11.......221 C8
OLLERTON..............88 E7
Ollerton La
Childs Ercall TF9......70 F1
Stoke upon Tern TF9....88 E8
OLLERTON LANE.........88 E8
ONBURY................206 A6
ONNELEY...............5 E3
Onnybrook Dr SY7......195 E6
Onny CE Prim Sch SY7..206 A6
Onny Gr TF2............132 D4
Onslow Dr
Shrewsbury SY3........113 D2
4 Wellington TF1......130 C5
Orchard Cl
Adforton SY7..........205 A1
Church Aston TF10......121 E8
5 Claverley WV5.......189 E4
Cressage SY5..........149 E5
4 Eardington WV16....188 C1
Hadley TF1............131 D2
Little Wenlock TF6.....144 A2
Pattingham WV6.......166 C3
Waters Upton TF6......111 A5
Orchard Croft SY22....167 B8
Stoke upon Tern TF9....88 E8
Orchard Ct WR15.......220 D5
Orchard Dr
Bridgnorth WV16........218 D6
1 Minsterley SY5......172 E3
1 West Felton SY11....170 E3
Orchard Fields LL14....221 D4
Orchard Fields SY4.....84 B5
Orchard Gdns
Ludlow SY8............217 D5
4 Wrexham LL11.......221 C4
Orchard Gn SY22.......93 E6

Orchard La
Great Hanwood SY5.....173 E8
The Gorge TF8.........152 D4
Orchard Lea SY8........207 F4
Orchard Pk SY10.......94 F7
Orchard Rd
1 Eardington WV16....188 C1
2 Shifnal TF11........145 F5
Orchard Rise
1 Bewdley DY12........211 D2
2 Market Drayton TF9...53 A8
Richards Castle (Hereford)
SY8...................212 F4
Orchard Sch The SY21..167 E3
Orchard St
4 Highley WV16........200 F2
1 Oswestry SY11......58 E8
Orchard The 1 LL13....221 F1
Orchard Way
Wellington TF1........130 F3
Wem Urban SY4........66 B6
Orchid Cl 8 TF7........132 E7
ORETON................209 C7
Oreton Rd DY14.......209 C7
Oriel Way 8 SY3.......124 E3
ORLETON...............212 E2
Orleton CE Prim Sch
SY8...................212 C2
ORLETON COMMON......212 C3
Orleton La
Eastham WR15.........215 E3
5 Wellington TF1......130 C4
Orleton La Inf Sch TF1..130 B4
Orleton Rd SY8........217 F3
Orleton Terr TF1.......130 C3
Ormsdale Cl 8 TF2......132 F8
ORSLOW................123 E3
Orsons Mdw 15 SY3....124 A7
Orton La WV4..........190 F6
OSBASTON
Ercall Magna..........104 F2
Kinnerley.............77 E2
Osborne Cl
5 Oswestry SY11......59 B8
3 Wrexham LL11.......221 C6
Osborne Rd LL11.......221 C6
Osmere Cl 1 SY13.....2 B1
Osprey Gr 8 TF1.......132 E8
Osterley Gr 8 TF2......132 F8
Oswald Pl 8 SY11......58 E7
Oswald Rd SY11........58 E8
Oswald Row 28 SY11....58 E8
Oswalds Cl SY11........58 D7
Oswald's Well La SY11..58 C7
Oswald Way 8 LL12....221 E5
Oswell Rd SY2.........125 F8
OSWESTRY
(CROESWALLT)..........58 B8
Oswestry Inf Sch SY11..58 F8
Oswestry Leisure Ctr
SY11..................59 A7
Oswestry Rd
12 Ellesmere SY12....27 A2
Oswestry Rural SY10....57 E2
Whittington SY11.......41 E3
Oswestry Sch SY11.....58 F7
Oswestry Transport Mus*
SY11..................58 F8
Oswestry Visitor & Ex Ctr*
SY11..................59 A7
OTELEY................27 E2
Oteley Rd
Atcham SY2............126 A1
Shrewsbury SY2........125 C2
Ottley Way TF9.........52 E5
Oulton La TF10.........111 A8
OUNSDALE.............190 E4
Ounsdale Rd WV5.......190 F4
Our Lady & St Oswald's Rcp
Sch SY11..............58 D7
OUTWOODS.............111 B1
Outwood 1 SY1.........113 D5
OUTWOODS.............111 B1
Oval The
Albrighton WV7........156 E8
Bicton SY3............112 A2
Market Drayton TF9.....53 C8
Newport TF10..........110 A3
Overcross SY3.........125 E3
OVERDALE.............143 D8
Overdale
8 The Rock TF3.......131 E1
The Rock TF3..........143 E8
Overdale Rd SY3.......136 E6
Overley Hall Sch TF6...129 C2
OVERS.................177 A2
Overstone St SY11......113 D5
OVERTON...............212 F6
Overton La SY8........212 D1
OVERTON/OWRTYN......9 C8
Overton Rd
Ludlow SY8............217 C2
St Martin's SY11.......24 E6
Overton View SY8......217 E3
Owen Cl TF3...........144 E2
Owl's La SY5..........181 F6
Oxford Rd
5 Dawley TF4.........144 A4
Great Dawley TF4......143 F1
Oxford St
2 Oakengates/Donnington
TF2...................132 B2

Oxford St continued
3 Whitchurch LL13.....221 E3
Oxlip Cl 18 TF2........132 E8
Oxon Bsns Pk SY3.......124 C7
Oxon CE Prim Sch SY3..124 B6

P

Packwood Haugh Sch
SY4....................80 A3
Paddock Cl 1 TF1.......130 C5
Paddock La TF4.........143 F3
Paddock La TF1.........154 A6
Paddocks The
Baschurch SY4..........81 A6
2 Cleobury Mortimer
DY14..................210 B3
16 Knighton LD7.......203 B3
Ludlow SY8............217 E5
Market Drayton TF9.....36 B1
4 Shawbury SY4.......103 D6
8 Wrexham SY13.......124 B6
Paddock The
3 Church Stretton SY6..216 D7
7 Claverley WV5.......189 E4
Much Wenlock TF13....159 E4
10 Oakengates/Donnington
TF2...................120 F1
1 Shifnal TF11........145 F4
4 Wem SY4............66 B8
22 Wombourne WV5....190 F3
PADDOLGREEN..........47 E5
Padmans Alley 1 TF12..152 C1
Pageant Dr
Dawley Hamlets TF4....143 F1
Dawley TF4............144 A1
Painsbrook La SY4......102 E6
Painswick Cl 8 SY3.....124 B7
PAINTERS GREEN........13 E7
Painters La SY13........50 D6
Pale Mdw Rd 7 WV15...219 A4
Palmer St 4 LL13.......221 E3
Pandy La 2 LL12.......221 D8
Panorama 2 SY21......203 B4
PANPUNTON............203 B4
Pant....................76 B1
PANT-GLAS.............40 A5
Pant La SY12...........8 E4
Pantulf Rd SY4.........66 B8
PAPERMILL BANK.......85 D8
Parade The
Donnington TF2.........132 C2
Wellington TF1.........130 C4
Paradise TF8...........152 B4
Parc Bychan LL11.......221 C7
Parc Caradog SY21.....167 A1
Parc Hafod SY22........94 A2
Parc Offa SY22.........94 A2
Pargeter Ct 1 TF3......144 A1
Parish Cl TF3..........143 E2
Parish Dr TF1..........131 D5
Park Ave
Madeley TF7...........153 B5
2 Oswestry SY11......58 D8
Shawbury SY4..........103 D7
Shrewsbury SY3........125 A6
Wem SY4..............66 A5
Whitchurch SY13.......15 A7
Wrexham LL12.........221 D4
Park Bank SY4.........80 A2
Park Cl
14 Bewdley DY12......211 D2
Kinlet DY12...........210 C7
3 Oakengates/Donnington
TF2...................132 C2
Park Cres SY11.........41 B4
Park Croft WR15........214 F2
Park Ct TF7............152 E6
Parkdale TF1...........131 C5
Park Dingle 1 DY12.....211 C1
Park Dr SY11...........40 D1
Park End TF10..........109 F5
Parker Bowles Dr 1 TF5 .52 F8
Parker Leighton Way
SY10..................58 E4
Parkers Cl LL11........221 C6
Parker's Pl 17 SY21....170 B6
Park Fechan Gdns 6
SY11..................41 E3
PARK HALL.............41 A4
Park Hall Countryside
Experience* SY11......41 A4
Park Hall Stadium (The New
Saints FC) SY11.......41 C3
PARK HEATH............73 C3
Parkhill La SY7........193 A1
Park Issa Gdns 2 SY11..41 E3
Park La
Bewdley DY12..........211 D1
Craven Arms SY7.......195 C4
Ercall Magna TF6.......116 D7
Leintwardine SY7......205 B5
Loggerheads TF9........55 D8
Madeley TF7...........152 E6
Munslow SY7...........197 B6
Richard's Castle (Shropshire)
SY8...................212 F4
Shifnal TF11...........145 F2
The Rock TF3..........143 F8
24 Welshpool SY21....170 B6
Whittington SY11.......41 B3
Park La Ave TF7........152 F5
Parklands TF1..........130 D5

Parklands The SY12........63 C7
PARK LANE..............11 A4
Parkleigh Ct **3** LL12....221 E4
Park Mdw SY5..........172 E4
Park Plaza SY1.........113 D6
Park Rd
  Cefn-mawr LL14..........6 C8
  Dawley TF4............143 F6
  Ludlow SY8............217 C3
  3 Much Wenlock TF13..159 F4
  Oakengates/Donnington
   TF2.................132 C6
  Wem SY4...............66 A7
  Whitchurch SY13.......14 F7
Park St Cl SY11.........58 E7
Park St
  Madeley TF7...........153 A5
  Oswestry SY11.........58 E7
  Shifnal TF11..........145 F3
  Wellington TF1........130 E4
  Wrexham LL11.........221 C5
Parks The SY1..........114 B3
Park View
  Broseley TF12.........161 C8
  Buildwas TF8.........151 B6
  1 Highley WV16......200 F2
  10 Whitchurch SY13...15 A8
  6 Worfield WV15....189 A6
Parkway TF7............152 F5
Parkways SY8..........217 C4
Parrs La SY3..........136 E7
Parrys Cl SY3.........136 E7
Parson's La SY22.......93 F2
Partridge Cl
  Shrewsbury SY1.......114 C4
  1 Wellington TF1...130 F6
Parys Rd SY8..........217 E4
PASFORD...............165 E3
Pasmore Cl **2** TF3...153 A8
Pasteur Dr **1** TF1...130 F6
Patricia Dr **3** SY2..126 A5
Patshull Rd
  Albrighton WV7.......156 F3
  Pattingham & Patshull
   WV6................166 B3
PATTINGHAM...........166 B3
Pattingham La WV7....157 E1
PATTON...............186 B6
Paulbrook Rd WV16....218 E5
Pauls Moss Ct SY13....15 A6
PAVE LANE.............122 B6
Pavilion Cl **3** TF2..132 E3
Pavilion Gr TF2.......132 E2
Paxton Pl **1** SY2....124 B6
Peace Dr SY2..........126 A5
Peacehaven **4** SY11.114 B4
Pearl Yd SY13..........15 A7
Pearson Rd TF2........132 C1
Peartree La SY13......11 D7
Pear Tree La
  Claverley WV5........190 A2
  Whitchurch Urban SY13.1 D1
PEATON...............197 C4
PEATONSTRAND.........197 D4
Pecknall La SY5.......168 B4
PEDLAR'S REST........196 D3
Peel Cl **5** LL13.......9 C8
Peel St LL13..........221 B3
Peever Cl SY12.........26 B7
Pelham Rd SY4.........127 D6
Pel La SY8............197 F2
Pemberton Cl SY13.....16 E2
Pemberton Rd **3** TF5.130 A6
Pemberton Way SY3....125 D4
Pembridge Cl
  3 Newport TF10....121 E8
  2 Oakengates/Donnington
   TF2.................120 D1
Pembroke Cl SY5.......220 D5
Pembroke Ct WR15.....220 D5
Pembroke Dr TF11.....130 F6
Penda Ret Pk The SY1..58 E7
Pembroke Way **2** SY13.58 E7
Pendil Cl TF1.........130 C2
Pendle Way SY3.......125 A1
Pendragon Ct **7** LL21.221 D1
Pendril Cl TF9.........52 E5
Pengrove **3** SY3.....125 C4
Pengwern Cl SY13.....125 A6
Pengwern Rd SY3......125 B6
Penistone Cl TF2......132 D6
Penleigh Gdns **2** WV5.190 F4
PENLEY................10 F5
Penley Hall Dr LL13...10 F4
Penley Polish Hospl LL13.10 F5
Penlu Rd WR15........220 D6
Penmarch La TF6......104 E3
PENNERLEY............174 D6
Pennywell **8** SY2....124 D7
Pensfold SY3..........124 B6
Penstone La WV4......190 F6
PENTIKEN.............192 A6
PENTRE
  Chirk...............6 D6
  Churchstoke.........181 A4
  Forden with Leighton and
   Trelystan..........170 D4
  Montford............168 D8
  Oswestry Rural......56 F1
  St Martin's.........24 E8
PENTRE-CEFN..........56 F3
PENTRE-CLAWDD.......40 F4
PENTRE-COED.........42 C5
Pentre CW Controlled Prim
  Sch LL14...........6 E6

Pentre Felin **12** LL11..221 C3
Pentre Gwyn SY21....167 A2
PENTREHEYLING........180 D8
PENTRE HODRE........203 F8
PENTRE-NEWYDD........22 F6
PEN-Y-BONT LLANERCH
  EMRYS...............74 A4
Penybont Rd LD7......203 B2
PEN-Y-BRYN...........7 E2
Pen-y-bryn LL13......221 C2
Penybryn Ave SY11....41 F4
Penybryn Cres SY11...41 F4
Pen-y-bryn Way **2** TF10.109 F1
Penycae Ave SY10......24 A1
Penycae Cl SY10.......24 A1
PEN-Y-COED..........75 F3
PEN Y FOEL...........93 E7
Penygarreg Cl SY10....76 B2
Penygarreg La SY10...76 C2
Penygarreg Rise SY10..76 B2
Penylan La SY10.......58 C5
Pen-y-llan St LL13.....9 C8
Penymaes Ave LL21...221 D5
Pen-y-maes La SY22...92 F7
Pen y Waun LL14.......41 F3
PEN-Y-WERN..........193 D2
PEPLOW...............88 A6
Pepper La SY8........217 C4
Pepper St **6** SY13...15 A8
PEPPERSTREET.........48 D6
Percy Rd LL13.........221 C1
Percy St N SY1........125 C8
Percy St SY1..........125 C8
Percy Thrower Ave SY4.100 E4
Peregrine Way TF1....131 A7
Perivale Cl **3** SY3...124 F4
Perivale Gdns **7** TF2.132 F8
Perry Ave SY10........24 B1
Perry Cl TF1..........130 D6
Perry Rd TF1..........130 D6
Perry View SY10.......24 B1
PERTHY...............43 B8
Peter's Cl **3** TF4...143 F2
PETTON...............63 E1
Peveral Dr **4** SY11..41 E3
Peverey Cl SY4........80 C1
Peveril Bank TF4.....143 F5
Pewit La CW5..........4 B6
Pezenas Dr **2** TF9...36 B1
Pheasant Cl SY11......49 B8
Pheasants Way SY6....184 F3
Philips Cl LL12.......221 F6
Phoenix Bank **9** TF9.36 D1
Phoenix Cl TF2........132 D8
Phoenix Sch The TF4..143 E2
Phoenix Sports Ctr TF4.143 F2
Picasso Dr **5** TF5...130 B7
Pickering Rd TF2.....132 B6
Pickhill SY4..........82 A8
PICKLESCOTT..........177 E6
Pickmere Cl **4** SY11..41 E3
Pickwick Ct **8** TF11..145 F5
Picton Cl **4** TF2....132 D4
Pierce's Sq **13** LL13.221 C3
Pigeon La SY11........11 C6
Pimhill La SY4........101 B8
Pine Cl
  6 Ellesmere SY12...27 A2
  Market Drayton TF9....36 B1
Pine Cres SY5.........172 E4
Pinefield Cl TF13.....159 E4
Pine Gr **9** SY1......58 F7
Pines The **1** LL12...221 D5
Pinetree Rd **4** DY12.211 C2
Pine View **10** TF2...120 D1
Pineway WV15.........219 B4
Pinewood Ave TF2....132 A6
Pinewood Cl SY11.....113 D3
Pinewood Dr SY3......32 E5
Pinewood Rd SY4.....103 F7
Pinewoods **2** TF10..121 E8
Pinfold Cl TF11.......134 C5
Pinfold Croft TF6....106 A3
Pinfold La
  Ellesmere SY12.......27 C2
  Loggerheads TF9......37 C2
  Pinfold The SY13.....49 D8
Pinkham DY14.........209 E2
Pinkham La SY4.......113 D4
Pinkham La **5** TF4...209 E2
PINSTONES...........196 E5
Pintail Dr TF1........130 F7
PIPE GATE.............41 D6
Pipers La SY8.........108 F3
Pippins **7** SY3.....144 D3
Pitchcroft La TF10...121 E7
PITCHFORD............179 C6
Pitchford Dr TF2.....144 F8
Pitchford Rd
  Albrighton WV7.......156 F4
  7 Shrewsbury SY1..113 D4
Pitts La LD7..........203 E2
PIXLEY...............89 E8
Pixley La TF9.........71 F1
PLAISH...............185 C7
Planks La WV5........190 F3
Plant Cl TF4.........143 E6
Plas Acton Rd **1** LL12.221 D8
PLASAU...............96 E6
Plas Cerrig Cl **3** SY11.41 F2
PLAS COCH............221 B5
Plas Coch Rd LL11....221 B5
Plas Darland LL11....221 D5
Plas Ffynnon Way **6**
  SY11...............58 F7
Plas Gwyn LL12.......221 C5
Plas Madoc **2** LL13...9 C8

Plas Newydd **12** SY11..58 F7
Platt La SY13.........31 B5
PLATT LANE...........31 B5
Playdale Est TF10....109 B4
PLEALEY..............173 D5
Plealey La SY5........173 E5
Plealey Rd SY5........173 C6
Pleasant View SY10...23 C4
Plex La SY4...........101 E2
Plex Rd SY4...........101 E5
Plough Bank TF1......135 A6
Plough La
  1 Newport TF10....109 F5
  Rock DY14............210 E1
Ploughmans Croft **9**
  TF10...............110 A4
Plough Rd
  8 Knighton LD7....203 B3
  Oakengates/Donnington
   TF2.................132 C5
  9 Wellington TF1..130 C7
Plover Gate **3** TF1..130 C7
PLOWDEN.............182 F2
Plox Gn Rd SY5.......172 D2
PLOXGREEN...........172 D2
Poachers Gate **1** TF4.144 A2
Podmore Rd TF7.......132 B7
Police Dr **6** TF9....53 C8
Polska St LL13........10 F5
PONTESBURY..........173 B5
Pontesbury CE Prim Sch
  SY5................173 B4
PONTESBURY HILL.....173 A4
Pontesbury Hill Rd SY5.173 A4
PONTESFORD.........173 C5
Pontfaen LD7.........203 C3
PONT-FAEN..........23 B6
Pontfaen Cl LD7......203 C2
Pontfaen Mdws LD7...203 C2
PONTHEN.............168 A8
Pont Wen LL13........221 E2
PONT-Y-BLEW........7 C1
Pont-Y-Blew Dr TF1..131 F6
Pool Dr
  Bridgnorth WV16......218 E5
  Hadnall SY4..........102 C4
Pooler Cl TF1.........130 D2
Pooley La TF10.......123 C7
Pool Farm Ave TF4....131 A6
Pool Farm La SY4.....102 C4
POOLHEAD.............47 D6
Pool Hill TF4........143 E2
Pool Hill Rd TF4.....143 D3
Pool House Rd WV5....190 E3
Pool Mdw TF1.........131 D4
Pool Rd
  Hadnall SY4..........102 C4
  Montgomery SY15......174 B3
  4 Oakengates/Donnington
   TF2.................131 F6
Pool Rise SY2.........125 F2
Poolside SY3..........136 E7
Pool View TF4........143 C3
Poor House La TF9.....70 D7
Poplar Ave WV7......156 F8
Poplar Cl
  3 Madeley TF7....153 C5
  3 St Martin's SY11..24 F7
  3 Whitchurch SY13..14 E7
Poplar Ct SY3.........137 A6
Poplar Dr
  4 Church Stretton...216 D5
  8 Wellington TF1..130 C5
Poplar La TF9.........20 F5
Poplar Rd LL13.......221 C2
Poplars Ave **1** SY5..173 E8
Poppy Dr **3** TF2.....132 E7
Porchester Cl TF1....113 C2
Porchfield SY2.......125 F7
Portal Ave LL13......221 E3
Portcullis La SY8....217 C4
Porthill Cl SY3......125 A5
Porthill Dr SY3......124 F5
Porthill Gdns SY3....125 A6
Porthill Rd SY3......125 A5
PORTH-Y-WAEN........75 D4
Portia Cl **3** TF1....130 C4
Portland Cres **2** SY2.125 F5
Portland Dr
  Market Drayton TF9....36 A1
  6 Much Wenlock TF13.159 F4
  The Rock TF3.........143 F7
Portley Rd TF4.......143 E3
Portman's Way WV16...218 D5
Portobello **1** TF2...132 C6
Portobello **8** TF3...143 F8
Port Way TF7.........153 C6
Port Way The SY6.....177 C1
POSENHALL...........160 F8
Postern **4** WV16....218 F5
Post Office La
  Gnosall TF10.........123 D7
  5 Longden SY5....173 F8
  Wem Rural SY13.......31 C1
Post Office Rd WV5...190 C6
Potter Cl SY8........217 D6
Potters Bank TF1....131 E2
Pottery Cl **10** TF4..143 E4
Pound Cl
  1 Bishop's Castle SY9.181 F3
  5 Shrewsbury SY3..125 D5
POUND GREEN........211 A5
Pound La
  Broseley TF12........161 C2
  Pontesbury SY5.......173 E8
  Ruyton SY4...........80 A1

Pound St
  Bridgnorth WV16......218 E5
  Claverley WV5........189 D4
Pountney Gdns **3** SY3.125 D4
Powder La TF1........130 C3
Powell Pl **6** TF10...109 F3
Powell Rd
  Dawley TF2...........132 F1
  3 Wrexham LL12....221 D4
Powells La **8** SY7...193 D3
Powell's La **1** SY21..170 B6
Powis Ave SY1........58 F8
Powis Castle & Gdn*
  SY21...............170 A5
Powis Cl SY10.........76 B1
Powis Ct **3** SY4.....170 B6
Powis Dr
  Shrewsbury SY1.......113 D2
  2 Wellington TF1..130 D5
Powis Pl
  Dawley TF4...........143 E5
  10 Oswestry SY11...58 E8
Poyner Cl SY8........217 D5
Poyner Rd SY8........217 D5
POYNTON.............116 A8
Poynton Dr SY11.....113 E3
POYNTON GREEN......103 F2
Poynton Rd SY4......103 D6
Poyser St **3** LL13...221 C2
PREES................49 C7
Prees CE Prim Sch SY13.49 D7
PREES GREEN.........49 E4
PREESGWENE.........23 F5
PREES HEATH.........32 D8
PREESHENLLE.........24 B2
Preeshenlle La SY11...24 B2
Prees Ind Est SY13....49 C7
PREES HIGHER HEATH...32 E4
PREES LOWER HEATH...50 B6
Prees Rd
  Ightfield SY13.......34 A6
  Whitchurch Urban SY13.15 B6
Prees Sta SY13........48 F8
PREES WOOD..........49 E7
PRESCOTT
  Baschurch...........99 B7
  Stottesdon..........209 D8
Prescott Cl **6** SY2..125 F2
Prescott Fields **3** SY9..99 B8
Prestage Cl TF12.....161 E7
Prestbury Gn **3** SY11.113 F4
Presteigne Rd LD7....203 B2
Prestfelde Prep Sch SY2.125 F4
PRESTHOPE...........186 B8
PRESTON.............172 A4
PRESTON BROCKHURST.84 E6
Preston Cl **2** TF2...132 A7
PRESTON GUBBALS....101 D4
Preston Gubbals Rd SY4.101 A4
Preston Montford*......84 F6
PRESTON MONTFORD...169 E5
Preston Montford La
  SY3................169 E4
Preston St SY2........125 F5
PRESTON UPON THE WEALD
  MOORS.............119 E3
Price's La LL11.......221 A6
Pride Hill **8** SY1...125 C6
Priestland Terr TF2..132 B7
PRIEST WESTON........175 B4
Primmer Rd TF2......120 C2
Primrose Dr
  Newport TF10.........109 F1
  Shrewsbury SY3.......125 D3
Primrose Gr **8** TF1..132 A2
Primrose La **3** SY2...49 E8
Primrose Way **1** LL13.221 B4
Prince Andrew Dr **2**
  TF4................143 F6
Prince Charles Cres **4**
  TF3................144 A6
Prince Charles Rd
  1 Oswestry SY11...59 A8
  Shrewsbury SY2.......126 A5
Prince Edward Cres **3**
  TF3................144 A6
PRINCE HILL..........4 E7
Prince of Wales Dr **5**
  SY21...............170 B5
Princes Cl SY11......221 C7
Princes End TF4......143 E6
Princess Anne Gdns TF4.143 E3
Princess Ave
  Chirk LL14...........6 E2
  1 Wellington TF1..131 A2
Prince's Ct SY5......168 A6
Princess Gdns TF10...109 F1
Princess Royal Hospl The
  TF1................130 F6
Princess St
  Shrewsbury SY1.......125 C5
  Wrexham LL13........221 B2
Princes St SY3.......174 B3
Prince's St **7** TF1..130 F3
Prince St
  Madeley TF7..........153 C6
  1 Oswestry SY11...58 E8
Prince William Ct SY4..66 B6
Priors Cl **3** WV16...198 D8
Priors Gate **3** TF3..144 E8
Priors Halton SY8....206 E2
Priors La **1** SY7....36 A1
PRIORSLEE...........132 E1

Priorslee Ave
  Dawley TF2...........132 F1
  St Georges & Priorslee
   TF2.................144 D8
Priorslee Cty Prim Sch
  TF2................144 E8
Priorslee Rd
  Oakengates/Donnington
   TF2.................144 D8
  Shifnal TF11.........145 C5
Priorslee Village TF2..144 E8
Priory Cl
  2 Bridgnorth WV15..219 A3
  Wellington TF1.......130 E3
Priory Ct **1** TF9....36 A1
Priory Dr SY3.........125 A3
Priory Rd
  Bridgnorth WV15......219 A4
  Oakengates/Donnington
   TF2.................132 A4
  Shrewsbury SY1.......125 B6
Priory Ridge SY3.....125 A2
Priory Sch The SY3...125 A3
Priory St **10** LL11..221 C3
Prison Visitor Ctr* SY1.125 D6
Pritchard Ct **12** DY12.211 D2
Pritchard Way TF2....125 E3
Proctors Pl TF2......132 C4
Prospect Cotts SY8...217 D4
Prospect Rd
  Market Drayton TF9....36 B1
  Wellington TF1.......130 F4
Puddle La SY11.......24 E5
PULESTON.............91 C1
PULLEY..............137 A8
Pulley La SY3........136 F7
Pulrose Wlk **8** SY3..125 E3
PULVERBATCH........143 C1
Pump La SY13.........124 B7
Pump Rd SY4.........100 E4
Punta Verde Dr TF7...153 B3
Purbeck Dale TF4....143 E4
Purcell Ct **2** TF1...130 C3
PURLOGUE...........203 B8
PURSLOW............194 D3
Purton Wood View **5**
  TF3................144 E8
Puzzle Sq **10** SY21..170 B6
PYE CORNER.........202 A3
Pyms Rd SY4..........65 F7
Pynfold Gdns SY8....217 C4

Q

QUABBS..............192 A3
Quail Gate TF1.......130 C7
Quail Ridge SY5......169 C4
Quality Sq SY8.......217 C4
Quarry Bank Rd TF9...53 E3
Quarry Gdns SY8.....217 C5
Quarry House La **3** TF9.53 A4
Quarry La **1** TF1....131 E2
Quarry Mdws **3** SY7..195 E5
Quarry Pl
  Great Dawley TF4.....143 E3
  Market Drayton TF9....53 B7
  6 Shrewsbury SY1..125 B5
Quarry Rd TF12.......152 C2
Quarry Swimming & Fitness
  Ctr TF11............146 B5
QUARRY THE.........125 B5
QUATFORD............157 A1
Quatford Cl **2** SY1..114 C3
QUATT...............201 A7
Queen Elizabeth Ave
  TF3................144 C5
Queen Elizabeth Cl **5**
  SY11...............40 F1
Queen Elizabeth Dr SY11..40 F1
Queen Elizabeth Way **1**
  TF3................143 F5
Queens Cl SY11.......58 E6
Queens Croft TF1.....72 F8
Queens Ct
  7 Ashbrook SY6...216 C6
  Madeley TF7..........153 C5
  Queens Dr **3** TF10..109 F1
  Queens Dr **1** SY21..170 B5
QUEEN'S HEAD........60 C2
Queen's Pk SY11......58 E6
Queens Rd
  Bridgnorth WV15......219 B4
  Oakengates/Donnington
   TF2.................132 D7
Queen's Rd
  Shrewsbury SY13.....58 E6
  Whitchurch SY13.....15 B7
Queen's Sq LL14......22 C3
Queen St
  Broseley TF12........152 C8
  Madeley TF7..........153 C5
  Market Drayton TF9....36 C1
  Much Wenlock TF13....159 E5
  Shrewsbury SY1.......125 E7
  Wellington TF1.......130 D4
  7 Wrexham LL11....221 C3
Queensway
  Dawley Hamlets TF7...153 B7
  Dawley TF3...........144 D6
  Hadley TF1...........131 C8
  Oakengates TF2......132 B1
  Stirchley & Brookside TF7.153 D7
  Wem SY4.............66 B7
  Wilcott SY4..........97 D2
  Wrexham LL13........221 C1
Queen's Way DY12....211 E2

Que–St J 237

Queensway Dr WV16 218 D6
Queensway Terr LL13 221 E2
Queenswood Cl 2 TF2 144 B8
Queenswood Prim Sch TF2 144 B8
Quendale WV5 190 F3
Quillets The SY4 80 C1
QUINA BROOK 48 C7
Quines Cl 9 TF2 132 E8
Quinta Fields SY10 23 C4
Quinta Terr LL14 23 D5
Quinton Cl 11 SY3 124 C7
Quorn Gr 2 TF9 52 F8

R

Raby Cres SY3 125 C4
Racecourse Ave SY2 125 E6
Racecourse Cres SY2 125 F6
Racecourse Dr WV16 218 C5
Racecourse Gn 1 SY2 125 F6
Racecourse La SY3 124 B6
Racecourse Rd TF13 159 E4
Rack La SY13 30 F1
Radbrook Cty Prim Sch SY3 124 F3
Radbrook Rd SY3 124 E4
Radford La WV4 190 F7
Radfords Field SY11 58 F6
RADLITH 173 C4
RADMOOR 87 F6
Radmore La ST20 111 C7
Radnor Ct 3 TF1 131 A4
Radnor Dr 5 LD7 203 B3
Rad Valley Gdns SY3 124 E5
Rad Valley Rd SY3 124 E5
RAF Tern Hill TF9 52 C2
RAGDON 216 D1
Ragged Robins Cl 2 TF2 132 D3
Ragleth Gdns SY2 126 A6
Ragleth Rd SY6 216 D5
Railway La 2 SY2 125 D6
Railway St 1 WV16 218 F4
Rampart Ct Ret Pk TF3 144 C7
Rampart Way TF3 144 B7
Ramsey Mdws 6 SY1 114 B4
Ramshurst Ct TF2 132 A3
RANDLAY 144 E3
Randlay Ave TF3 144 C3
Randlay Ctr TF3 144 C4
Randlay Fields TF3 144 D3
Randlay Intc TF3 144 E4
Randlay Prim Sch TF3 144 C3
Ranford Way SY4 66 B7
Range Rd 18 LL13 221 E1
Ranscombe Cres 7 LL12 221 E8
RATLINGHOPE 177 B4
Ravenhill Dr 5 TF2 131 F1
Raven La SY8 217 C4
Raven Mdws SY1 125 C6
Ravenscourt Wlk SY3 124 D5
Ravenscroft Gdns 9 SY2 125 F3
Ravensdale Dr 15 TF2 132 F8
Raven Sq 2 SY21 170 A6
Raven St SY21 170 A6
Rays Farm* WV16 200 C2
REABROOK 172 D3
Reabrook Ave SY3 125 E4
Rea Dr TF1 130 D6
Rea St SY3 125 E4
Rectory Cl SY10 57 E2
Rectory Dr TF11 135 F2
Rectory Gdns
Church Stretton SY6 216 C6
Hanwood SY5 173 F8
3 Worthen with Shelve SY5 171 F3
Rectory La
Adderley TF9 19 B4
Pant SY22 93 F6
Rectory Rd WV7 156 F6
Red Bank
Market Drayton TF9 53 B8
Welshpool SY21 170 B7
Red Bank La 7 TF9 53 B8
Red Bank Rd 6 TF9 53 B8
Red Barn La SY3 125 B4
REDBROOK 13 F7
RED BULL 37 C3
Redburn Cl 7 TF2 132 A1
Redchurch Cl TF12 152 D2
Redfern Cl 7 SY3 125 D3
Redfield 1 SY1 113 C1
Redfield Cl TF12 152 D1
Redford Dr 7 WV7 157 A5
Redgate Ave WR15 220 C4
Red Hall La LL13 9 F3
REDHILL
Bayston Hill 136 D7
Lilleshall and Donnington 132 E3
Red Hill DY12 211 D2
Redhill Dr SY5 136 D7
Redhill Prim Sch TF2 132 F2
Redhill Way TF2 132 E4
Red Kite Cl TF1 131 B6
Red La
Broseley TF12 162 A7
Hopesay SY7 195 A6
Llanfair Waterdine LD7 192 A2
Welshpool SY21 170 A5
RED LAKE 131 F2
Redlake Mdw 5 SY7 204 C5
Redlands Rd TF1 131 E5
Red Lees TF1 131 D2
REDNAL 61 A4
Rednal Fields TF4 143 F1
Rednal Ind Est (Site A) SY11 61 B4
Rednal Ind Est (Site B) SY11 61 C6
Redstone Dr 8 WV16 200 E2
Redwing Cl 3 TF1 130 F5
REDWITH 77 A5
Redwood Cl 3 TF5 130 A8
Redwood Dr SY7 195 A4
Redwood La SY7 194 D1
Reed Cl 1 TF2 132 C3
Reedham Rd SY1 113 C2
Reet 3 LL13 221 B2
Reeves La LD7 203 F1
Regent Dr 9 TF2 132 C2
Regents Dr SY1 125 E8
Regent St
Wellington TF1 130 F3
8 Wrexham LL11 221 C3
Rembrandt Dr 4 TF5 130 B7
Renshaw Wood La WV8 148 F2
Rest The 3 LL14 6 C8
Retreat Gdns The 4 WV6 166 C3
Revells Cl SY12 26 C6
Reynards Coppice TF7 153 B3
Reynards Mdw TF7 153 B4
Reynaulds Cl 4 SY2 126 A5
Reynolds Cl
2 Ditton Priors WV16 198 D8
8 Swindon DY3 190 F1
Reynolds Dr 9 TF2 132 B2
Reynolds Wharf TF8 153 B1
Rhallt La SY21 170 C8
RHEWL
Overton 9 B4
Selattyn and Gobowen 24 B1
Rhew Level La SY10 94 A8
Rhewl La SY10 24 B1
Rhewl The SY10 24 B1
RHIEWS 35 B7
Rhiw Refail 3 SY10 94 A8
Rhodes Ave 3 TF4 143 F5
RHOS
Llandrinio 167 A8
Weston Rhyn 23 A4
RHOS COMMON 94 C1
RHOS-DDU 221 D5
Rhosddu Cty Prim Schools LL11 221 C5
Rhosddu Ind Est LL11 221 B7
Rhosddu Rd LL11 221 C4
Rhos Ddu Rd 5 LL11 221 C3
RHOSNESNI 221 F3
Rhosnesni High Sch LL13 221 F5
Rhosnesni La LL12 221 E5
RHOSROBIN 221 B8
Rhosrobin Rd LL11 221 B8
RHOSWIEL 23 E5
RHOSYGADFA 24 E1
Rhyd Broughton La LL11 221 A4
Rhyd-esgyn La SY21 167 A5
Rhyd Galeo SY10 24 A1
RHYDYCROESAU 39 A2
RHYD-Y-CWM 191 C3
RHYN 24 B7
Rhyn La SY11 7 C1
Rhyn Pk Sch SY11 24 C5
RICHARDS CASTLE 212 E4
Richards Rd TF2 120 C2
Richmond Ave TF2 132 A6
Richmond Cl 9 TF10 109 F1
Richmond Ct 3 TF1 130 D5
Richmond Dr SY3 124 F6
Richmond Gdns
Bridgnorth WV16 218 E6
3 Chirk LL14 6 E3
Richmond Rd
Bewdley DY12 211 C2
Wrexham LL12 221 D8
Richmond Terr 2 SY13 15 B7
Riddings Cl
2 Bewdley DY12 211 E3
3 Broseley TF12 161 E7
Hadley TF1 131 D1
Riddings La WV16 199 E3
Riddings Mdw SY8 217 E4
Riddings Rd SY8 217 E5
Riders Lea 16 SY3 124 F3
Ridgebourne Rd SY3 124 F4
Ridge The
4 Bishop's Castle SY9 181 E3
1 Pant SY10 94 A8
RIDGWARDINE 19 E1
Ridgway TF6 116 E8
Ridings Cl 1 TF9 36 B1
Ridings The 2 SY3 124 B6
Ridley Cl WV16 218 C5
RINDLEFORD 188 F6
Ringers Way 4 TF5 130 A6
Ripley Cl 1 TF1 131 C5
Ripple Cl 3 SY2 125 F2
Rise La
Rochford WR15 214 E3
Tenbury Wells WR15 220 F6
Riven Rd TF1 131 E5
River Cl LL13 221 F1
River Gdns SY4 103 E7
River La TF6 106 A3
Riverside WR15 220 C5
River Side WV16 218 F5
Riverside Ave TF8 153 B1
Riverside Dr
7 Clun SY7 193 D3
Ternhill TF9 52 C4
Riverside N DY12 211 D2
River View
Bridgnorth WV15 219 A4
Pen-y-bont Llan Emrys SY10 74 A4
Riverway Dr 8 DY12 211 D2
Rivington Ave 2 SY3 125 A1
Rivulet Rd LL13 221 E2
Robert Jones & Agnes Hunt Orthopaedic Hospl SY10 41 B5
Robert Jones Cl 3 SY4 99 B8
Robert Jones Way SY4 114 B6
Roberts Dr TF4 143 D5
Robertson Way SY2 125 F6
Roberts Rd TF7 152 D5
Robin Cl
Ellesmere Urban SY12 27 B3
Shrewsbury SY1 114 C4
Robin La TF10 109 A3
Robins Dr TF7 152 D6
Robinsford Cl 6 SY3 124 B6
Rocfield Terr TF2 132 B4
Rochester Cl 10 TF3 144 D3
ROCHFORD 214 F3
Rock Acres TF10 121 B3
Rockall Way TF3 143 F7
Rock Cl SY9 182 F8
Rocke's Mdw LD7 203 C2
Rocke St SY3 125 E4
Rock Gn Terr SY8 217 E6
ROCKHILL 193 B2
Rock La
Edgmond TF10 108 F3
Hanmer LL13 11 B8
Ludlow SY8 217 D4
Rock Rd TF3 143 E7
Rocks Gn
Ludford SY8 207 C3
Ludlow SY8 217 F6
Rocks The 4 SY3 125 C3
Rock Terr
Ludlow SY8 217 D4
St Georges TF2 132 D2
ROCK THE 143 E7
Rock The
Sheriffhales TF11 134 B4
The Rock TF3 143 E8
Rockwell La SY10 76 A1
Roddam Ct 2 TF10 109 E2
RODEN 116 A6
Roden Cl TF1 130 D5
Roden Gr SY4 65 F5
Rodenhurst La SY4 116 D2
Roden La TF6 115 D5
RODINGTON 116 E2
RODINGTON HEATH 116 C2
Rodney Cl 6 TF11 146 A6
Rodney's View 1 SY22 94 A1
Rodney View SY10 76 D5
RODWAY 107 A1
Roe Deer Gn TF10 109 E5
Roft St SY11 58 E7
Roman Fold SY7 195 E8
Roman Gr 3 TF2 132 C2
Roman Rd SY3 125 A3
Roman Rd Sports Ctr SY3 125 A2
Roman Way
Hinstock TF9 72 A2
Whitchurch SY13 14 F8
ROMSLEY 201 D1
Romsley Dr SY2 125 E3
Romsley La DY12 201 D1
Romsley View 6 WV15 201 B3
Ronhill Cres 4 DY14 209 E3
Ronhill La DY14 209 E3
Rookery La SY4 50 F2
Rookery Rd TF2 132 D4
Rookery The 2 TF7 153 B5
Rope Wlk Ct 17 SY3 125 B6
RORRINGTON 175 D7
Rosebury Gr 9 WV5 190 F3
Rose Cres TF1 130 E3
Rosedale 7 SY1 114 A3
Rose Gr TF1 130 E3
ROSEHILL 53 A1
Rosehill Ave SY11 41 D2
Rosehill Cl SY11 41 E2
Rosehill Dr
Bridgnorth WV16 218 D4
Whittington SY11 41 D2
Rose Hill Rd TF9 70 F6
Rose La WV16 218 E5
Roselyn SY1 113 F3
Rosemary La
Leintwardine SY7 205 B4
Whitchurch SY13 15 A7
Rosemary Way 5 SY5 173 B4
Rosemede 3 SY1 113 F3
Rose Mount Dr 1 SY10 76 A1
Rosemount Gdns WV6 164 D2
Rosenhurst Dr 17 DY12 211 D2
Rose Tree Cl 4 TF3 143 F8
Roseway
Shrewsbury SY1 113 F3
Wellington TF1 130 E3
Rose Way 2 SY5 171 F3
Rosewood Ave 9 LL13 221 F4
Roslyn Rd TF1 130 E4
Rossett Way 4 LL12 221 D8
Rosthwaite TF1 130 E3
Rotherfield SY1 113 F1
Rothesay Cl 6 LL11 221 C6
Rothesay Gr 9 TF2 132 A1
Rothley Cl SY3 124 F4
Rothley Dr 3 SY3 124 A6
Rough La TF12 161 E7
ROUGHTON 189 A5
Round Hill Cl SY1 125 B8
Round Hill Gn SY1 125 B8
Round Hill La SY1 125 B8
Round House Pk TF4 143 B1
ROUND OAK 195 A7
Round Oak Dr 4 TF1 130 D7
Roundway SY3 125 E2
Roundwood Cl 9 SY11 59 A8
Roushill SY1 125 C6
Rowallan Way 4 TF2 132 F1
Rowan Ave
5 Dawley TF4 144 A2
Great Dawley TF4 143 F2
Rowan Cl
4 Ellesmere SY12 27 A2
3 Gobowen SY11 41 A7
2 Llandysilio SY22 94 A1
Rowan Dr 7 TF10 109 F1
Rowan Rd TF9 36 D2
Rowe La
Maelor South SY12 29 A4
Munslow TF13 185 E1
Welshampton & Lyneal SY12 28 F4
Rowland Gate 6 TF1 130 D4
ROWLEY 171 D5
Rowley Cl 5 TF7 152 F4
Rowley Ct 2 SY2 125 F2
Row The SY6 184 A6
ROWTON
Alderbury with Cardeston 168 D3
Ercall Magna 105 C4
Rowton Ave SY5 168 E3
Rowton Cl 5 TF1 130 F5
Rowton Rd SY2 125 F1
Royal Air Force Mus* WV7 156 C7
Royal Oak Dr
4 Brewood ST19 148 E8
5 Hadley TF1 131 A6
Royal Shrewsbury Hospl SY3 124 D6
Royal Way
Dawley TF3 144 A6
1 Great Dawley TF4 143 F6
Ruabon Rd LL13 221 A1
Rubery Way LL13 221 F2
Rubicon SY13 14 E7
RUCKLEY 179 C3
RUDGE 190 A8
RUDGE HEATH 189 E6
Rudge Heath Rd WV15 189 E6
Rudge Rd
Pattingham & Patshull WV6 166 B1
Rudge WV6 190 A8
Rudge The SY5 141 B1
Ruewood Mdw Nature Reserve* SY4 65 D4
Ruith Field TF5 130 B8
Rural Cotts SY5 141 A2
Rushbrooke Way 1 SY2 126 A8
RUSHBURY 185 A2
Rushbury CE Prim Sch SY6 185 A2
Rushbury Rd
Rushbury SY6 185 A3
1 Wellington TF1 130 C5
Rushey La WV7 165 D8
Rush La TF9 36 A2
Rushmoor La TF5 117 E1
RUSHTON 141 B5
Rushton Rd 7 SY2 125 F8
Rushwater Cl 21 WV5 190 F3
Ruskin Way 7 TF3 144 A1
Russell Cl WV15 219 E4
Russell Field 2 SY3 124 F5
Russell Gr LL12 221 E5
Russell Rd TF7 153 B5
Russell Ridge 1 SY3 124 F4
Russell Sq 4 TF7 153 B5
Russell St 8 LD7 203 B3
Russett Way 1 DY12 211 C2
RUTHALL 198 C8
Ruthall Cl 1 WV16 198 D8
Ruthin Rd LL13 221 A3
Rutland SY1 113 E5
Rutland Gn 1 TF1 131 A4
Rutland Rd LL13 221 E2
Ruyton Castle (remains of)* SY4 80 A1
RUYTON-XI-TOWNS 80 B1
Rydal Ave
Shrewsbury SY1 113 F3
Whitchurch SY13 15 B7
Rydal Ct 4 LL13 221 F5
Ryder Dr TF2 133 A7
RYEBANK 48 A3
Ryebank Rd TF2 131 F1
Ryefield Way 2 SY13 15 A6
Ryelands SY3 124 E4
Ryelands Gdns 5 WV16 218 D5
RYTON 155 C2
Ryton Cl
5 Shrewsbury SY3 125 B1
Tweedale TF7 153 D6
Ryton Hall TF11 155 C2
Ryton Rd
Beckbury TF11 164 C8
Ryton TF11 155 C1
Ryton Way TF3 144 B1

S

Sabrina Dr 6 DY12 211 D2
Sabrina Rd 5 WV15 218 F4
Saddlers SY5 172 E4
Sadlers Fold 11 TF2 132 A1
Saggars Cl TF7 152 E4
St Agathas Cl TF1 130 C7
St Alkmond Mdw 3 SY13 14 F8
St Alkmond's Pl 5 SY1 125 C5
St Andrews CE Prim Sch
Great Ness SY4 97 E4
Shifnal TF11 145 F2
St Andrews Cl
Hope Bowdler SY6 184 C3
9 Shifnal TF11 145 F5
St Andrews Rd 3 SY3 124 E3
St Andrews Way 4 TF10 121 E8
St Anne's CE Fst & Mid Schools DY12 211 C1
St Annes Dr SY10 58 D4
St Anne's RC Prim Sch LL13 221 F3
St Anne's Rd 7 SY3 124 E3
St Antony's Rd 10 SY3 124 E3
St Aubin Dr 2 TF4 143 E6
St Austin's Friars 9 SY1 125 B6
St Austin's St 12 SY1 125 B6
St Barbaras Pl SY11 41 C4
St Brelade Cl 3 TF4 143 E6
St Bride's Way SY22 92 C5
St Catherines Cl TF1 130 E6
St Catherine's Dr 1 SY3 124 E3
St Chads CE Prim Sch WV6 166 C3
St Chads Cl 8 WV6 166 C2
St Chad's Cl 6 TF1 130 D5
St Chad's Terr 2 SY1 125 B5
St Chads Way TF9 20 C2
St Christophers Sch / Ysgol Sant Christopher LL13 221 D1
St Christophers Way 3 TF4 143 F6
St Cuthberth's Cres WV7 156 E5
St Davids Cl
5 Dawley TF4 143 F6
4 Gobowen SY11 41 A7
St David's Cres LL13 221 E4
St Davids' Ct 3 LL13 221 F5
St Dunstan Cl 5 SY6 216 C6
St Dunstan's La WR15 215 A2
St Eatas La SY5 139 A7
ST GEORGE'S 132 C2
St Georges CE Prim Sch
Clun SY7 193 C3
Oakengates/Donnington TF2 132 D2
St George's Cres 5 LL12 221 D3
St Georges Ct SY3 125 B6
St George's Ct SY13 15 B8
St Georges Gdns 3 SY5 173 B4
St Georges Jun Sch SY3 124 F6
St George's Pl SY7 193 C3
St Georges Rd TF2 132 D5
St George's St SY3 125 B7
St Giles CE Prim Sch SY2 126 A5
St Giles Cl 2 TF1 131 A2
St Giles Cres LL13 221 E4
St Giles Prim Sch LL13 221 D2
St Giles' Rd 2 SY2 125 F4
St Giles Way 1 LL13 221 D2
St Giles Way / Ffordd San Silyn 20 LL13 221 C3
St Gregorys Cl WV16 187 E5
St Helens Cl TF1 130 E6
St Helier Dr TF4 143 E6
St James Cl 3 SY11 59 A8
St James Cres 3 TF3 144 B1
St James Ct
6 Wellington TF1 130 D3
4 Wrexham LL11 221 C5
St James Dr 3 WV15 219 A3
St James Rd SY2 126 B6
St John's Cath Prim Sch WV16 218 E5
St Johns CE Fst Sch ST19 148 E7
St John's CE Prim Sch DY3 190 F2
St John's Cl
4 Ellesmere SY12 27 C2
Swindon DY3 190 E1
St John's Cres 4 SY7 195 D5
St John's Ct 4 WV16 198 D8
St John's Dr TF2 132 A6
St John's Hill
Ellesmere SY12 27 C2
3 Shrewsbury SY1 125 B5
St John's La
Bewdley DY12 211 A1
Ludlow SY8 217 C3
St John's Pk 5 SY13 15 A8
St John's Rd SY8 217 C3
St Johns St 1 WV15 219 A4
St John's St
4 Whitchurch SY13 15 A8
Wrexham LL13 221 E2
St John St TF1 130 E3
St John the Baptist CE Prim Sch SY4 80 A1

St Joseph's RC High Sch
LL13 . . . . 221 C1
St Julian's Ave SY8 . . . . . . 217 D4
St Julian's Cl 9 TF1 . . . . . 130 C7
St Julian's Cres 7 SY1 . . . 125 C5
St Julian's Friars SY1 . . . 125 C5
St Julian's Well SY8 . . . . . 217 D4
St Kellens SY8 . . . . 217 E3
St Laurence CE Prim Sch
SY8 . . . . 217 D4
St Laurence Cl SY6 . . . . . . 216 C6
St Lawrence CE Prim Sch
TF6 . . . . 119 D4
St Lawrence Cl TF1 . . . . . 130 D7
St Lawrence Prim Sch
SY6 . . . . 216 D4
St Leonard's CE Prim Sch
WV16 . . . . 218 E6
St Leonard's Cl 2 WV16 . 218 F5
St Leonard's Pl 2 TF4 . . . 143 F5
St Leonard's Rd 8 TF4 . . 143 F6
St Leonard's Way CW3 . . . . 5 A2
St Lucias CE Prim Sch
SY4 . . . . 127 C5
St Lukes Cath Prim Sch
TF2 . . . . 132 A4
St Lukes Rd TF4 . . . . 143 D1
St Luke's Rd TF1 . . . . 152 C4
St Margaret Rd SY8 . . . . . 217 E5
St Margarets Dr TF1 . . . . 130 E5
St Margaret Way LL12 . . . 221 D6
St Marks Cl 1 TF1 . . . . . . 130 D7
St Marks Dr TF1 . . . . 130 D6
St Mark's Rd 3 LL11 . . . . 221 C3
ST MARTIN'S 24 F5
ST MARTIN'S MOOR 24 D4
St Martin's Rd
Gobowen SY11 . . . . 41 A8
Selattyn & Gobowen SY10 . 24 C3
St Mary's Ave LL13 . . . . . . 9 C8
St Marys Bluecoat Prim Sch
WV15 . . . . 219 A5
St Marys Cath LL11 . . . . . 221 C3
St Marys Cath Prim Sch
TF7 . . . . 153 B6
St Mary's Cath Prim Sch
LL13 . . . . 221 C3
St Mary's CE Aided Prim Sch
SY5 . . . . 172 C8
St Marys CE (Aided) Prim
Sch SY7 . . . . 204 C4
St Marys CE Prim Sch
SY4 . . . . 103 C8
St Mary's Cl
1 Albrighton WV7 . . . . . 157 A5
Broseley TF8 . . . . 152 E2
Chirk LL14 . . . . 23 E8
Knockin SY10 . . . . 78 A1
Tenbury Wells WR15 . . . . . 220 C5
St Mary's Ct SY1 . . . . 125 C6
St Mary's La
Ludlow SY8 . . . . 217 C5
3 Much Wenlock TF13 . . 159 E4
St Mary's Mews SY8 . . . . 217 C5
St Mary's Pl
1 Cleobury Mortimer
DY14 . . . . 209 E2
6 Shrewsbury SY1 . . . . . 125 C6
St Mary's Prim Sch
Albrighton WV7 . . . . 157 B5
Overton LL13 . . . . 9 D8
St Marys RC Prim Sch
SY1 . . . . 125 C6
St Mary's Rd TF13 . . . . . . 159 E4
St Marys St WV16 . . . . . . 218 E5
St Mary's St
1 Market Drayton TF9 . . . 36 D1
4 Newport TF10 . . . . 109 F3
Shrewsbury SY1 . . . . 125 C6
Whitchurch SY13 . . . . 15 A8
St Mary's Wr La SY1 . . . . 125 C6
St Matthews CE Prim Sch
TF2 . . . . 132 E7
St Matthew's Rd TF2 . . . . 132 D6
St Michaels Cl
Lydbury North SY7 . . . . . . 194 C8
Welshampton & Lyneal
SY12 . . . . 28 C2
St Michael's Cl
Lilleshall TF10 . . . . 121 B3
Madeley TF7 . . . . 153 B4
St Michael's Ct SY11 . . . . . 78 C7
St Michael's Dr 9 TF2 . . 132 A6
St Michaels Gate 2 SY1 125 D7
St Michael's Gate TF8 . . 213 B2
St Michael's Gn SY10 . . . . 22 E5
St Michael's St TF7 . . . . . 153 A5
St Michael's St SY1 . . . . . 125 D7
St Michael's Terr 6 SY1 . 125 D8
St Michaels Way TF4 . . . . . 89 B7
St Michael's Wlk 4 TF7 . 153 A5
St Milborough Cl SY8 . . . 217 E5
St Milburga Row 1
TF13 . . . . 159 E4
St Nicholas Cres 4
WV15 . . . . 219 A4
St Nicholas Rd WV15 . . . . 219 A4
St Oswalds View TF9 . . . . . 72 B1
St Owens Dr 5 TF13 . . . . 159 E4
St Owen's Rd TF13 . . . . . 159 E4
St Patrick Cath Prim Sch
TF1 . . . . 130 E6
St Pauls Cl 7 TF1 . . . . . . 130 D7
St Pauls Dr TF1 . . . . 130 E6

St Peters CE Prim Sch
Edgmond TF10 . . . . 109 A4
Wem SY4 . . . . 66 B7
St Peters Mews SY8 . . . . 217 C5
St Peters Prim Sch TF5 . 130 B8
St Peter's Way TF1 . . . . . 108 F3
St Peters Wlk 8 TF5 . . . . 130 B8
St Quentin Gate TF3 . . . . 144 C6
St Saviour Cl 1 TF4 . . . . . 143 E6
St Stephen's Cl SY8 . . . . 217 C4
St Stephens Pl 4 WV15 . 218 F4
St Thomas Cl SY7 . . . . . . 193 D4
**St Thomas & St Anne CE
Prim Sch** SY1 . . . . 173 E8
St Winefrides Convent Sch
SY1 . . . . 125 C5
Salamanca Ave SY3 . . . . . 124 E6
Salcombe Dr SY2 . . . . 126 A2
Sale La SY21 . . . . 167 A1
Salendine 6 SY1 . . . . 113 C2
Salisbury Ave TF2 . . . . . . 133 A1
Salisbury Cl 4 LL13 . . . . 221 D2
Salisbury Dr DY11 . . . . . . 211 F3
Salisbury Hill View TF1 . . 53 B7
Salisbury Rd
Market Drayton TF9 . . . . . . 53 A8
3 Whitchurch SY13 . . . . . 15 B8
Wrexham LL13 . . . . 221 C2
Salop Rd
Oswestry SY11 . . . . 58 E7
Overton LL13 . . . . 9 C7
Welshpool SY21 . . . . 170 C6
Wrexham LL13 . . . . 221 D2
Salop St
3 Bishop's Castle SY9 . . 181 F4
Bridgnorth WV16 . . . . 218 E5
Saltbox La WV15 . . . . 220 D2
Saltdean Cl 1 SY2 . . . . . 126 A2
Salters La
Loppington SY4 . . . . 64 F6
Newport TF10 . . . . 109 E3
5 Shrewsbury SY3 . . . . . 125 D5
Salter's Mill SY4 . . . . 46 D7
Salthouse Rd TF8 . . . . . . 153 A2
Saltney Cl SY2 . . . . 126 A2
Saltwells Dr TF2 . . . . 120 E1
SAMBROOK 90 E5
Sambrook Cl
12 Dawley TF3 . . . . 144 C1
8 Shrewsbury SY1 . . . . . 113 C2
Sambrook Cres TF9 . . . . . 36 E2
Sandal Cl TF1 . . . . 131 C7
Sandbourne Dr 18 DY12 211 E2
Sandbrook TF1 . . . . 131 C3
Sandcroft TF7 . . . . 153 D3
Sanderville Cl 5 TF4 . . . 144 D1
SANDFORD
Prees 33 C1
West Felton 78 C4
Sandford Ave
Church Stretton SY6 . . . . 216 F5
Shrewsbury SY1 . . . . 113 E1
Sandford Cl 1 SY1 . . . . . 113 E1
Sandford Dr SY6 . . . . 216 E5
Sandford Ind Pk SY1 . . . . 33 B1
Sandford Pl 10 SY6 . . . . 216 C6
Sandford Rd SY8 . . . . 217 C4
Sandiford Cres TF10 . . . . 109 E2
Sandino Ct 8 TF3 . . . . . . 144 D1
Sandino Rd TF3 . . . . 144 D1
Sandiway SY3 . . . . 124 E4
Sandown Cres SY5 . . . . . 124 B5
Sandpiper Cl 6 TF1 . . . . 130 F6
Sandpit La WV5 . . . . 189 C6
Sandpits Ave SY8 . . . . . . 217 E4
Sandpits Cl SY8 . . . . 217 D4
Sandpits Rd SY8 . . . . 217 D5
Sandringham Ave 4
SY11 . . . . 41 A1
Sandringham Cl 3 TF9 . . 36 E2
Sandringham Cl SY3 . . . . 125 A6
Sandringham Rd
Pattingham WV6 . . . . 166 C2
7 Wombourne WV5 . . . . 190 F3
5 Wrexham LL13 . . . . . . 221 C7
Sandrock La SY10 . . . . 57 C2
Sandway 3 TF1 . . . . 131 C3
Sandway Rd LL11 . . . . . . 221 C6
Sandycroft 3 TF10 . . . . . 109 F3
Sandygate Ave 4 SY5 . . 125 E3
Sandy La
Alberbury with Cardeston
SY5 . . . . 169 B4
Broncroft SY7 . . . . 197 D6
Donington WV7 . . . . 156 F7
Ellesmere Urban SY12 . . . . 27 C1
Grinshill SY4 . . . . 84 C2
Hinstock TF9 . . . . 72 B5
Loggerheads TF9 . . . . 37 C3
Stoke upon Tern TF9 . . . . . 70 E7
Sutton upon Tern TF9 . . . . 53 C7
SANDY LANE 37 C3
SANSAW HEATH 84 A1
Sansaw Rd
Grinshill SY4 . . . . 84 A1
Hadnall SY4 . . . . 102 B8
Sapcote La SY3 . . . . 124 A7
Saplings The TF7 . . . . 152 D6
Saplins La TF8 . . . . 151 A7
SASCOTT 102 E8
Saunders Cl SY8 . . . . 217 C5
Savannahs The 6 TF1 . . 130 D7
Saville Cl 9 TF1 . . . . 130 D4
Sawston Cl SY3 . . . . 124 F3
Saxon Ct
12 Hadley TF1 . . . . 131 A7
Shrewsbury SY3 . . . . 124 C5
Saxon St LL13 . . . . 221 D1

Sceptre Cl 4 TF4 . . . . . . 152 F8
Scholars La SY4 . . . . 64 E7
School Bank
Hinstock TF9 . . . . 72 A2
Hopesay SY7 . . . . 195 A5
3 Montgomery SY15 . . . 174 B3
School Cl
Marbury cum Quoisley SY13 . 2 E8
Shifnal TF11 . . . . 145 E3
Trysull & Seisdon WV5 . . . 190 E4
School Ct TF1 . . . . 130 D3
School Field Cl SY12 . . . . 62 A7
School Fields TF8 . . . . 72 A2
School Gd La 6 TF10 . . . 110 A3
School Gdns 2 SY3 . . . . 125 C6
School Gr 1 TF12 . . . . . . 121 A7
Schoolhouse La SY9 . . . . 181 F4
School La
5 Bishop's Castle SY9 . . 181 F3
Blymhill & Weston-under-Lizard
TF11 . . . . 135 F5
Brimfield SY8 . . . . 213 B2
Bronington SY13 . . . . 13 B3
Cherry Orchard SY3 . . . . . 125 B5
Clungunford SY7 . . . . 195 B1
Gobowen SY11 . . . . 24 A1
Hadley TF1 . . . . 131 D2
Leighton & Eaton Constantine
SY5 . . . . 150 C8
3 Llangollen Rural LL20 . . 6 A7
Madeley SY5 . . . . 5 E5
Marbury cum Quoisley SY13 . 2 A8
Market Drayton TF9 . . . . . . 53 A8
Overton LL13 . . . . 9 C8
Pant SY10 . . . . 76 B3
St Martin's SY11 . . . . 24 F7
Sutton WV16 . . . . 200 D5
Trefonen SY10 . . . . 57 E2
6 Wellington TF1 . . . . . . 130 F3
Wem SY4 . . . . 68 E8
Weston under Lizard TF11 . 135 E2
School Mews SY8 . . . . . . 217 D5
School Rd
2 Clun SY7 . . . . 193 C3
13 Craven Arms SY7 . . . 195 E5
Edgmond TF10 . . . . 109 A3
Ironbridge TF8 . . . . 152 B6
Oakengates/Donnington
TF2 . . . . 120 D1
Ruyton SY4 . . . . 90 D1
Trysull & Seisdon WV5 . . . 190 D4
Twyford SY11 . . . . 78 D8
School St TF2 . . . . 132 D2
School View TF1 . . . . 58 D7
Scirmiedge La SY8 . . . . . 197 E1
Scotland Pl WR15 . . . . . . 220 D5
Scotland St
Ellesmere SY12 . . . . 27 B2
5 Whitchurch SY13 . . . . . 15 A7
Scots La TF12 . . . . 161 D3
Scott Cl TF7 . . . . 153 C3
Scotts La 1 SY8 . . . . 208 A1
Scott St SY3 . . . . 125 D4
Seabright Way 10 WV15 . 201 B3
Seabury Cl SY1 . . . . 125 E4
Second Ave TF2 . . . . 132 B1
Sedgeford SY13 . . . . 15 A6
Sedgeford Dr SY2 . . . . . . 126 A5
Sefton Pl SY11 . . . . 40 D1
SEIFTON 196 D2
Seifton La SY8 . . . . 196 C2
SEISDON 190 C6
Seisdon Comm Rd WV5 . 190 C5
Seisdon Rd WV5 . . . . 190 D5
SELATTYN 39 F8
Selattyn CE Prim Sch
SY10 . . . . 39 F8
Selba Dr DY11 . . . . 211 F3
Selbourne TF7 . . . . 153 C4
Selkirk Dr TF7 . . . . 153 D4
Selley Cross LD7 . . . . 202 F7
Selwyn Cl 9 SY3 . . . . 124 E3
Seven Acres LD7 . . . . 203 C2
Seven Hills Pl 6 SY1 . . . 131 C3
Seven Stars Rd 13 SY21 . 170 B6
Severn Bank
Shrewsbury SY2 . . . . 125 D7
The Gorge TF8 . . . . 152 C4
Severndale Sch SY2 . . . . 126 A8
Severn Dr 3 TF1 . . . . 130 D6
Severn Dr SY21 . . . . 170 D6
Severn Gorge Pk TF7 . . . 153 D6
Severn La SY21 . . . . 170 C4
Severnmeade WV15 . . . . 218 F5
Severnside WV15 . . . . . . 218 F5
Severn Side N 10 DY12 . 211 D2
Severn Side S
11 Bewdley DY12 . . . . . 211 D2
2 Bridgnorth WV15 . . . . 218 F4
Severn St
Bridgnorth WV15 . . . . 219 A4
Shrewsbury SY1 . . . . 125 D7
Welshpool SY21 . . . . 170 B6
Severn Terr TF8 . . . . 152 B4
Severnvale 1 WV15 . . . . 218 F5
Severn Valley Ctry Pk*
WV16 . . . . 200 F1
Severn View Dr 2 WV16 188 C1
Severn Way
20 Bewdley DY12 . . . . . 211 C2
Cressage SY5 . . . . 149 E4
Dawley TF4 . . . . 143 E1
Llandysilio SY22 . . . . 94 A2
Severn Wlk 2 TF7 . . . . . . 153 C4
Severn Wynde SY21 . . . . 167 A2
Sgwir Heulwen 6 SY21 . 170 B5
SHACKERLEY 148 B1
Shackerley La WV7 . . . . . 148 B1

Shackleton Way SY3 . . . . 124 B5
Shaftesbury Cl 2 TF2 . . . 132 F2
SHAKEFORD 71 D5
Shakespeare Way
Madeley TF7 . . . . 153 C3
Whitchurch Urban SY13 . . . 15 C6
Shales The 33 WV5 . . . . 190 F3
Sham La WV15 . . . . 201 C2
Shamrock Way 2 TF3 . . 144 D3
Sharp Cl 7 TF5 . . . . 130 A7
Sharps Dr SY13 . . . . 14 F7
Sharpstone La SY3 . . . . . 137 B6
SHATTERFORD 211 E8
SHAWBANK 196 B2
SHAWBIRCH 130 C8
Shawbirch Rd TF5 . . . . . . 130 B7
SHAWBURY 103 C7
Shawbury Airfield SY4 . . . 85 C1
Shawbury Prim Sch SY4 103 D6
Shawbury Rd SY4 . . . . 66 A5
Shaw Croft TF11 . . . . 145 C4
Shawfield Cl 1 TF7 . . . . . 153 C4
Shaw Hedge Rd DY12 . . 211 E2
Shaw La
Albrighton WV7 . . . . 157 B5
Shifnal TF11 . . . . 145 C3
Tong TF11 . . . . 147 D5
Shaw Rd 4 SY2 . . . . 126 A7
Shay La TF10 . . . . 110 A8
Shearman Rd SY8 . . . . . . 217 E4
Sheepwalks La SY7 . . . . 201 F3
Sheepwell Ct 4 TF2 . . . . 131 F1
SHEET 207 C1
Sheet Rd
Ludford SY8 . . . . 213 C8
Ludlow SY8 . . . . 217 E3
SHEINTON 150 C4
Sheinton Rd SY5 . . . . 149 E5
Sheinton St TF13 . . . . . . 159 E5
SHELDERTON 205 B8
Shelf Bank Cl 6 SY11 . . . 40 F1
Shelbuck Dr 2 TF1 . . . . . 131 A6
Shelley Dr TF7 . . . . 153 C3
Shelsy Cl TF7 . . . . 153 A6
SHELTON 124 B7
Shelton Fields SY3 . . . . . 124 D7
Shelton Gdns 2 SY3 . . . 124 B7
Shelton Hall Gdns 10
SY3 . . . . 124 D7
Shelton Hosp SY3 . . . . . . 124 C6
Shelton La SY3 . . . . 124 C6
Shelton Rd 3 SY3 . . . . . 124 D7
Shelton Rd SY3 . . . . 124 B7
SHELVE 176 A6
Shepherds La SY8 . . . . . 110 A3
Shepherds Fold 8 TF4 . . 143 E5
Shepherd's La
Bicton SY3 . . . . 112 A1
Chirk LL14 . . . . 23 E8
Hadley TF1 . . . . 131 E2
Shrewsbury SY3 . . . . 124 A8
Sherbourne Cl 2 TF7 . . . 153 C3
Sherbourne Rd SY3 . . . . 124 E7
Sheridan Way TF7 . . . . . . 153 B2
Sheriffhales Dr TF11 . . . 134 B7
Sheriffhales Prim Sch
TF11 . . . . 134 B4
Sherlock Hoy Cl 7 TF12 146 C8
SHERRIFFHALES 134 B5
Sherrymill Hill SY13 . . . . . 14 F8
Sherwell Ave 3 LL12 . . . 221 E8
Sherwood La TF6 . . . . . . 116 F6
Sherwood Cl 1 TF5 . . . . 118 C1
Sherwood Cres TF9 . . . . . 52 F7
Sherwood St TF3 . . . . 144 B6
Shetland Cl 18 TF4 . . . . 143 D3
Shields Ct 15 LL13 . . . . . 221 E1
SHIFNAL 145 F4
Shifnal Ind Est TF11 . . . . 146 C3
Shifnal Prim Sch TF11 . . 146 A5
Shifnal Rd TF11 . . . . 144 D8
Shifnal Sta TF11 . . . . 145 F4
Shillingstone Dr SY1 . . . 118 B8
SHIPLEY 189 F7
SHIPTON 185 E2
Shipton Cl 8 TF1 . . . . . . 144 C1
Shipton Hall* TF13 . . . . 185 E3
Shire Fields Way 2 TF4 . 143 E5
Shires The TF2 . . . . 144 D8
SHIRLETT 187 C8
Shirlowe La TF6 . . . . 116 F6
Shomere Cres SY3 . . . . . 125 B1
SHOOT HILL 169 C3
Shop La
High Ercall TF6 . . . . 116 E7
Perton WV6 . . . . 190 D8
Waters Upton TF6 . . . . 86 D3
Worthen with Shelve SY5 . 172 E1
Shoplatch 1 SY1 . . . . . . 125 C5
Shore La SY5 . . . . 149 A3
Shorncliffe Dr 3 SY4 . . . . 94 A7
Shorncliffe Way 4 SY4 . 124 E6
SHORTHILL 169 C2
Short La 1 LL14 . . . . 6 C8
Short Wood Prim Sch
TF1 . . . . 130 D2
SHOTATTON 79 A2
Shotton La SY4 . . . . 83 C1
Shoveller Dr TF1 . . . . 130 F6
SHRAWARDINE 81 E2
Shrawardine Castle*
SY4 . . . . 81 E2
SHREWSBURY 125 D6
Shrewsbury Abbey*
SY2 . . . . 125 D6
Shrewsbury Castle*
SY1 . . . . 125 C6

**Shrewsbury Coll of Arts &
Tech** SY3 . . . . 126 A3
**Shrewsbury Coll of Arts &
Tech (Radbrook Campus)**
SY3 . . . . 124 E4
**Shrewsbury Coll of Arts &
Tech (Teford Construction
Centre)** TF3 . . . . 144 F6
Shrewsbury Dr TF11 . . . . 135 E2
Shrewsbury Fields TF1 . . 145 F5
Shrewsbury High Sch
SY3 . . . . 125 A4
Shrewsbury Rd
Bomere Heath SY4 . . . . . 100 E4
Church Stretton SY6 . . . . 216 C7
Cockshutt SY12 . . . . 63 D6
Cressage SY5 . . . . 149 D5
Darliston SY13 . . . . 50 B7
Edgmond TF10 . . . . 109 A5
Hadnall SY4 . . . . 102 C5
High Ercall TF6 . . . . 116 E7
Longden SY5 . . . . 173 F5
Market Drayton TF9 . . . . . . 52 F8
Much Wenlock TF13 . . . . 159 C5
Oswestry SY11 . . . . 59 A6
Pimhill SY4 . . . . 101 D3
Prescott SY4 . . . . 99 B7
Shifnal TF11 . . . . 145 F4
Wem SY4 . . . . 66 A4
Westbury SY5 . . . . 172 D8
Wistanstow SY7 . . . . 195 E6
Shrewsbury Sch 5 SY3 . 125 A3
Shrewsbury Sixth Form Coll
SY1 . . . . 125 B2
Shrewsbury Sports Village
SY1 . . . . 114 B2
Shrewsbury St
Hodnet TF9 . . . . 69 C5
Prees SY13 . . . . 49 C7
Shrewsbury Sta SY1 . . . . 125 C6
Shrewsbury Town FC
SY2 . . . . 125 C1
Shrewsbury Way 9
TF10 . . . . 109 E2
**Shropshire Hills Discovery
Ctr The*** SY7 . . . . 195 E5
Shropshire La SY13 . . . . . . 3 E1
Shropshire Lavender*
TF10 . . . . 91 B3
**Shropshire Nuffield Hospl
The** SY3 . . . . 124 F2
**Shropshire Regimental
Mus*** SY2 . . . . 125 C6
Shropshire St
7 Market Drayton TF9 . . . 36 D1
Market Drayton TF9 . . . . . . 53 C8
Shropshire Way SY8 . . . . 217 E4
Shrubbery Gdns SY3 . . . . 66 B7
Shrubbery Rd TF1 . . . . . . 131 E2
Shuker's La TF9 . . . . 87 F5
Shutfield Rd 8 TF4 . . . . 152 F8
SIDBURY 199 F4
Sidbury Cl TF3 . . . . 144 A4
Sidney Betts Cl 5 SY5 . . 178 C6
Sidney Cotts TF6 . . . . 118 F5
Sidney Rd SY8 . . . . 217 E4
Silken View TF3 . . . . 144 B2
Silkin Way
1 Wrockwardine TF5 . . . 130 A8
Wrockwardine Wood & Trench
TF2 . . . . 132 B5
Silk Mill La SY8 . . . . 217 C3
Silver Birch Dr 4 SY3 . . 124 F2
Silverdale
4 Shrewsbury SY3 . . . . . 124 A6
Summerhill TF10 . . . . 109 A4
Silverdale Cl TF10 . . . . . 109 C1
Silverdale Dr 3 SY10 . . . . 57 D2
Silverdale Terr 5 WV16 . 200 F2
Silver Hill TF6 . . . . 116 F8
Silvermere 6 TF2 . . . . . . 132 E1
Silvermere Pk 2 TF1 . . . 145 F3
Silverstone Cl SY5 . . . . . 124 C5
SILVINGTON 208 F6
Simon Cl TF3 . . . . 144 C1
Simon Cl TF11 . . . . 130 D3
Simon Evans Cl 6 DY14 . 209 E2
Simons Rd TF9 . . . . 53 B8
Simpson's La TF12 . . . . . 152 C2
Simpsons Wlk TF4 . . . . . 143 C3
Sinclair Gdns TF1 . . . . . . 131 C1
Sinclair Gr TF1 . . . . 131 C2
Singleton TF7 . . . . 153 D5
Singleton Ave 3 SY5 . . . 124 B5
Sir John Talbots Tech Coll
SY13 . . . . 15 B5
Sisters Field SY4 . . . . 66 B8
Sitka Dr SY2 . . . . 126 B2
Sitwell Cl SY7 . . . . 204 C4
Six Acres SY12 . . . . 124 F3
SIX ASHES 201 E7
Six Ashes Dr TF4 . . . . 144 B3
Six Ashes Rd DY7 . . . . . . 189 F1
Sixth Ave TF2 . . . . 144 A8
SKYBORRY GREEN 202 F5
Slade La
Eardington WV16 . . . . 188 D1
Much Wenlock TF13 . . . . 159 E8
Slaney Cl 6 TF2 . . . . 132 B3
Slaney St TF2 . . . . 132 B3
SLEAP 65 B1
SLEAPFORD 118 B4
Smale Rise SY11 . . . . 59 B8
Smallbrook 3 TF7 . . . . . 143 C7
Smallbrook Rd SY13 . . . . . 14 C1
Smallwood TF7 . . . . 153 B3

Smarts Way [6] TF2 ..... 132 C3
Smelt House La SY10 .... 76 B1
SMESTOW 190 E2
Smestow La WV5 ..... 190 E3
SMETHCOTT 178 A2
Smith Cres TF2 ....132 C5
Smithfield Cl [3] TF9 ....36 D2
Smithfield Rd
  [1] Market Drayton TF9 ....36 D1
  Much Wenlock TF13....159 E4
  [1] Oswestry SY11.........58 E7
  Shrewsbury SY1 ....125 C6
  [22] Welshpool SY21 ....170 B6
  Wrexham LL13..........221 D3
Smithfield Sh Ctr SY13....15 A8
Smithfields The TF10....109 F3
SMITHIES THE.........187 E8
Smithy Bank [4] TF12....161 C8
Smithy Cl LI12..........221 D8
Smithy La
  Hightown LL13...........221 F1
  Loggerheads TF9........21 B5
  Wrexham LL12..........221 D8
Smoke Alley [8] WV16....200 F2
Smokey La SY13 ....13 B7
SMYTHEMOOR 52 B8
SNAILBEACH 172 E1
Snatchfields La [2] SY6..216 D5
SNEAD 181 E6
SNEDSHILL 144 C8
Snedshill Way
  Oakengates/Donnington
  TF2...................132 D1
St Georges & Priorslee
  TF2...................144 C8
Snicketts The SY8........217 C4
SNITTON 207 E2
SNITTONGATE..........207 F2
Snitton La SY8..........207 E2
Snowdon La WV6........164 F7
Snowdon Rd WV6........165 B6
Snowdrop Cl [5] SY3 ....125 D3
Snowdrop Mdw [1] TF1...131 E2
Snow Hill 2 TF2.........132 D2
Snows Ct TF10...........109 F4
Snuff Mill Wlk [3] DY12..211 D1
SODYLT BANK..........B C4
Solva Cl LL11............221 A8
Solway Dr TF7...........153 D4
Somerby Dr SY3 ....124 C7
Somerset Cl 2 TF7.....152 F4
Somerset Way SY4........65 F8
SOMERWOOD 115 E2
Sommerfeld Rd TF2....184 E8
Songthrush Cl [1] TF1...130 F5
Sontley Rd LL13 ....221 C1
Sorrel Cl 4 TF2 ....132 E7
SOUDLEY
  Cheswardine 73 B7
  Hope Bowdler 184 C2
Soulton Cres SY4........66 C6
Soulton Hall* SY4........49 A1
Soulton Rd SY4...........66 C7
Southall Tf4.............143 F1
Southall Rd
  Dawley Hamlets TF3....153 B8
  [8] Dawley TF3.........144 A1
Southall Sch TF4........144 A2
South Cl SY3...........125 B3
South Dr TF7..........153 A5
Southfield TF7..........153 C3
Southfield Rd TF13....159 D4
Southgate TF7..........153 B4
Southgate Cl [3] SY11...58 F7
South Hermitage SY3...125 C4
Southlands Ave SY11....41 B7
Southleigh Dr [1] LL11 ...221 C6
Southorn Ct [6] TF12....152 C1
South Rd WV16.........198 D7
South Shropshire Leisure Ctr
  SY8...................217 A6
South View
  Chirk Green LL14.........6 E2
  [1] Oswestry SY11....40 D1
South View Rd TF4.....143 E1
Southville Cl SY3 ....124 B4
Southwater Sq [1] TF3..144 B6
Southwater Way TF3 ...144 A6
Southwell Cl [3] TF2....133 A1
Southwell Riverside
  WV16..................219 A3
Sovereign Cl 4 TF2....152 F8
Spaceguard Ctr The*
  LD7...................203 D1
Spa Cres [9] TF5.......130 B7
Spafield Cl [8] TF5......130 B8
Span Mdw TF10........130 C8
SpArC Ctr Bishop's Castle
  SY9...................181 F2
Sparkham Cl [7] SY3 ...124 E4
Sparrowhawk Way TF6...130 F7
Sparrow La 4 SY2......125 F5
Spa St SY3 ....125 C4
Speed's La TF12.........152 C1
Speedwell Ridge 4 TF3..144 D3
Spencer Ave [9] DY12...211 E7
Spencer Dr TF1..........153 C3
Spicer's Cl [4] SY5......189 E4
Spinners Ct [8] TF6.....145 D6
Spinney Path SY2........126 A7
Spinney The
  Newport TF10.........121 F8
  [4] Oakengates/Donnington
  TF2...................132 E8
SPOONLEYGATE.......189 F7
Spout La
  Barrow TF12...........152 B2
  Dawley TF3 ....144 A5

Spout La continued
  Leighton & Eaton Constantine
  SY5...................141 E2
  Little Wenlock TF6......142 B3
Spout Way TF13 ....144 A5
Spring Bank SY10.........57 D2
Springbank Cl 2 SY10 ..57 D2
Spring Cl WR15...........220 D6
Spring Ct [7] TF7........153 D5
Springfield 13 WV15 ....219 A4
Springfield Ave TF10....109 E1
Springfield Cl
  [1] Dawley TF4..........143 E3
  Ludlow SY8 ....217 D4
Springfield Ct TF4........143 F3
Springfield Gdns SY11 ...78 D8
Springfield Gn [1] SY2...125 F2
Springfield Infants Sch
  SY2...................126 A2
Springfield Pk
  [6] Clehill SY8........208 C2
  Overton LL13..............9 C7
Springfield Rd [3] TF2...131 F6
Springfields TF10........109 F1
Springfields Ind Est
  TF10..................109 F1
Springfield Way SY2....125 F3
Spring Gdns
  [5] Shrewsbury SY1.....113 E1
  Tenbury Wells WR15 ....220 D5
  Wrexham LL11..........221 C5
Spring Gr La WR15.......220 C2
Spring Hill
  Dawley TF4.............143 E3
  Wellington TF1.........130 C4
Springhill Cl [1] TF7....153 C5
Springhill Cres TF7 ....153 C5
Springhill La WV4.......190 F7
Springhill Rd TF4 ....143 E3
Springhill Rise 2 DY12..211 E2
Spring La [8] SY19 ......148 E8
Spring Mdw TF7 ....153 C4
Spring Rd LL11..........221 C5
Springside Pl [1] DY12..211 E3
Springs The 2 SY1......114 B3
Spring Terr TF3 ....143 D8
Spruce Cl [7] SY12.......27 A3
Spruce Dr [3] TF1.......131 B7
SPUNHILL...............44 E7
Square The
  [9] Ashbrook SY6......216 C6
  Ironbridge TF8.........152 C3
  [3] Shrewsbury SY1....125 C5
  Woore CW3...............5 A1
Squires Cl TF7..........152 F4
Squires Ct SY3 ....124 A7
Squirrel La [8] WV16....218 E5
Squirrel Ct WV16 ....218 E5
Squirrel Mdw TF5......130 B8
Squirrel View SY8........207 C1
Squirrel Wlk [1] SY3....124 A6
STABLEFORD...........164 B2
Stableford Rd WV6.....164 D2
Stable La 3 TF9..........36 B1
Stabler Cres [1] LL11...221 C7
Stables The [1] TF2.....132 F8
Stableyard Ct TF4......143 D6
Stackyard La TF10......108 F4
Stadium Way [2] TF1...131 D5
Stafford Ave TF11......145 F3
Stafford Cl TF3..........144 D7
Stafford Pk 1 TF3.......144 D6
Stafford Pk 2 TF3.......144 D6
Stafford Pk 3 TF3.......144 D6
Stafford Pk 4 TF3.......144 F6
Stafford Pk 5 TF3.......144 F6
Stafford Pk 6 TF3.......144 F6
Stafford Pk 7 TF3.......144 E6
Stafford Pk 8 TF3.......144 E6
Stafford Pk 9 TF3.......144 E6
Stafford Pk 10 TF3......145 A6
Stafford Pk 11 TF3......145 B6
Stafford Pk 12 TF3......144 E5
Stafford Pk 13 TF3......144 A6
Stafford Pk 15 TF3......144 C6
Stafford Pk 16 TF3......144 C6
Stafford Pk 17 TF3......144 C6
Stafford Pk 18 TF3......144 E5
Stafford Pl TF11.........146 A3
Stafford Rd
  Newport TF10.........109 F3
  4 Oakengates/Donnington
  TF2...................132 B3
Stafford St
  4 Market Drayton TF9...36 D1
  Newport TF10.........109 F3
  Oakengates/Donnington
  TF2...................132 C1
Stags Leap SY13........114 E8
Stallard Ct [8] TF12......131 F2
Stallion La 2 SY5.......173 B4
Stanall Dr [5] TF2.......120 E1
Stanbrook Rd WR15....220 D6
STANDFORD BRIDGE...90 C5
STANFORD..............168 A3
Stanham Cl [8] SY12.....27 B2
Stanham Dr SY12........27 B2
Stanhill Rd [8] SY3.....124 F3
Stanier Dr TF7..........152 D6
Stank La SY9............182 B2
STANLEY
  Alveley 201 A1
  Stottesdon...........199 F3
Stanley Dr 2 DY3.......190 F1
STANLEY GREEN......31 C3
Stanley La
  Astley Abbotts WV16....188 D6
  Shrewsbury SY3 ....125 A2

Stanley Rd TF1.........130 F4
Stanley St [8] LL13 ....221 D2
STANLOW................165 C2
STANMORE.............219 F3
Stanmore Dr TF2......132 A7
Stanmore Ind Est WV15..219 F4
Stanmore Mews WV15...219 E3
Stansty Chain Rd LL11..221 A7
Stansty Cl 3 LL11.......221 B6
Stansty Dr 3 LL11.......221 B6
Stansty Lodge La LL11..221 A7
Stansty Rd LL11.........221 B6
Stanton Cl SY8.........217 C6
Stanton Dr SY8.........217 C6
Stanton Gn SY5.........114 A3
STANTON LACY.........206 E5
STANTON LONG.........186 A1
Stanton Rd
  Ludlow SY8 ....217 D6
  Shifnal TF11............146 C4
STANTON UPON HINE
  HEATH 85 F4
STANWARDINE IN THE
  FIELDS 80 F5
STANWARDINE IN THE
  WOOD 63 C4
Stanwyck TF7...........153 D5
Stanyeld Rd SY6........216 C7
STAPLETON.............178 B7
Stapleton Rd SY11......221 C1
Starcross Cl 2 SY3......124 C6
Stargarreg La SY10 ....94 A8
Starr La SY6.............184 A6
Stars La TF8.............105 F6
Starstile Mdw SY8......217 D4
Startlewood La SY4......98 A8
Station App
  Bridgnorth WV16......218 E4
  [8] Wrexham LL11......221 C4
Station Ave LL14.........23 D8
Station Cl WR15.........215 B4
Station Cres SY7........195 E6
Station Ct [5] TF10.....109 F1
Station Ct [8] SY8......217 C5
Station Fields [5] TF2...132 A2
Station Hill TF2........132 B2
Station La LL10..........218 E4
Station Rd
  Adderley TF9............19 A5
  Admaston TF5.........130 A6
  Albrighton WV7........157 A5
  Baschurch SY4..........81 B1
  [1] Bewdley DY12......211 E2
  [8] Cleobury Mortimer
   DY14..................209 E3
  Clive SY4................83 F5
  Condover SY5..........137 B1
  Dawley TF4.............143 D3
  Ditton Priors WV16....198 E8
  Hadley TF1.............131 C3
  Hadnall SY4............102 C4
  Highley WV16..........200 F2
  Hodnet TF9..............69 D5
  Ironbridge TF8.........152 B4
  Lawley & Overdale TF4..143 D6
  Leebotwood SY6........178 C1
  Lightwood Green LL13...9 F6
  Madeley TF7............153 B5
  Minsterley SY5.........172 E4
  Montgomery SY15 ....174 A4
  Much Wenlock TF13....159 E5
  Newport TF10.........109 F2
  Oakengates/Donnington
   TF2...................120 D2
  Onneley CW3.............5 E2
  [5] Overton LL13........58 E8
  Overton LL13............9 D8
  Pant SY10...............76 B1
  Pontesbury SY5........173 A5
  Prees SY13...............49 A8
  Richard's Castle (Shropshire)
   SY8...................213 A3
  Rock DY14..............210 D2
  Shrewsbury SY3 ....125 A2
  Stottesdon DY14......199 D1
  [12] Wellington TF1....130 E4
  Wem SY4.................66 B7
  Weston Rhyn SY10.....23 D4
  Whitchurch SY13......15 B7
  [1] Whittington SY11..66 A7
  Wrockwardine TF6....129 F5
Station Rd Junc TF9.....69 F4
Station St SY9..........181 F3
Station Terr TF10.......109 F1
Station Wharf 2 TF13..159 E5
Stebbings TF7...........153 D4
STEEL HEATH...........32 A5
Steeple Cl [2] DY14.....209 E2
Steepside SY3 ....124 E3
STEERAWAY............142 F8
Stephenson Dr SY3 ...125 E4
Steppes Way TF9.........89 B6
Stersacre 2 SY1.......113 D4
Steventon Cres SY8....217 D3
Steventon Gdns SY8....217 D3
Steventon New Rd SY8..217 E3
Stevenson Rd
  Ludlow SY8 ....217 E2
  Shifnal TF11............130 C3
Stewardstone Gate [9]
  TF2...................132 F2
Stewart Rd
  4 Oswestry SY11.......58 E7
  Stanmore WV15........219 E4
Stile Rise [5] TF5.......130 C8
Stilton Cl 2 SY3.........124 E4

STIPERSTONES.........176 C7
Stiperstones CE Prim Sch
  SY5...................176 D7
Stiperstones Nature
  Reserve* SY5..........176 D6
STIRCHLEY.............144 C2
Stirchley Ave TF3......144 E4
Stirchley Intc TF7......144 E1
Stirchley La TF4........144 A2
Stirchley Rd TF3........144 B1
Stirchley Recn Ctr TF3..144 D1
Stirchley Village TF3....144 B2
Stirling Ave LL11........221 C7
Stirling Ave TF3........144 D1
Stirling Dr TF7..........153 C3
Stirling Rd WV7........156 F8
Stockford Cl [1] TF7....132 F1
Stockhall La DY14......209 A4
Stocking La WV16......187 F8
Stocking Pk Rd TF4....143 C1
Stocks La SY12...........28 B5
STOCKTON
  Chetwynd Aston and
  Woodcote 122 D6
  Chirbury with Brompton ..174 F8
  Madeley................163 B4
Stockton Cl [11] TF3....144 C1
Stockwell Gr LL13......221 D1
Stoke Bank SY8.........197 F1
Stoke Dr SY8...........213 E5
STOKE GORSE.........198 A2
Stoke Heath.............97 C1
STOKE ON TERN.......70 C5
Stoke on Tern Prim Sch
  TF9....................70 E6
STOKE ST
  MILBOROUGH 197 F1
STOKESAY.............195 E4
Stokesay Ave SY1.......113 E3
Stokesay Cl 18 SY7.....155 B5
Stokesay Fore TF7......153 C3
Stokesay Gn TF7........153 C3
Stokesay Link TF7.......153 C3
Stokesay Pl TF9.........153 C3
Stokesay Prim Sch SY7..195 E5
Stokesay Rd
  Clive Barracks TF9.......52 D4
  Wellington TF1.........130 C6
Stokesay Way TF7......153 C3
Stokewood Rd [5] SY7..195 D6
STONEACTON...........184 F4
Stonebridge Cl [1] TF4..153 A8
Stonechat Cl 3 TF1....130 F6
Stone Cres [5] TF1......131 A2
Stonedale TF7..........153 C4
Stone House Ct 2 SY21..170 D1
Stone House Dr SY11...76 D7
Stonehurst Dr [2] SY2..125 F4
Stoneleigh Gr TF2......132 F7
Stone Row TF3..........144 A5
Stones Sq SY3...........125 C4
Stoney Brook Leys [18]
  WV5...................190 F3
Stoneyhill TF4..........152 C8
STONEYLANE..........207 F3
STONEY STRETTON ...172 E8
Story of Drayton Mus The*
  [10] TF9...............36 D1
STOTTESDON..........199 E2
Stotteston CE Prim Sch
  DY14..................199 E2
Stourbridge Rd WV15...219 A4
Stourport Rd DY12......211 D2
Stour La 1 TF2..........132 D4
STOWE.................132 D4
Stowe Cl [9] TF3........144 C1
Stratford Cl 3 LL12.....221 E6
Stratford La WV15......189 C7
Stratford Rd TF7........153 C4
Streatley Mews SY8....217 C4
STREET DINAS 8 A1
STREET LYDAN.........11 C4
Street The SY22..........93 F3
STREFFORD.............195 F8
Strethill Rd TF8.........152 A4
Stretton Ave [5] TF10..109 E2
Stretton Cl
  Bridgnorth WV16......218 D4
  Madeley TF7...........153 C3
  Shrewsbury SY2 ....125 C6
Stretton Farm Rd SY6...216 C5
Stretton Rd TF3.........159 B3
STRETTON WESTWOOD..158 E1
Strickland [5] SY11....113 D4
Striga Bank SY13........12 B4
Striga La SY13..........12 B4
Strine Cl TF1............130 D5
Strine Way TF10........109 F4
Stryt y Wern LL20.......6 B6
Stuart St LL13..........221 D1
Stuart Way TF9..........36 E2
Stump La TF11..........144 D7
STYCHE HALL..........35 D4
Suffolk Way TF4........143 D3
SUGDON...............117 A2
Sugdon La TF6..........117 B3
Sulby Dr 2 TF6.........130 F5
Summer Ct TF1.........130 C5
Summer Cres TF2......132 C5
Summerfield Cl 8 SY11..59 A8
Summerfield Rd SY4....66 B7
Summerfields SY8......217 C5
SUMMERHILL..........153 C4
Summerhill TF7.........153 C4
Summerhill Gdns TF7...153 C4
Summerhill Rd LL11....221 B7
Summer House Dr [3]
  TF1...................131 B4

Summerhouse Gr [6]
  TF10..................109 F4
Summerhouse La SY5...173 F4
Summit Cl SY3 ....125 D2
Sunbury Dr TF2.........132 B6
Sunderland Dr [8] TF1...131 A4
Sundorne [4] LL13.......9 C8
Sundorne Ave SY1 .....113 F2
Sundorne Cres SY1....113 F2
Sundorne Inf Sch SY1...114 A2
Sundorne Rd SY1........113 F2
Sundorne Rd Ctr SY1...114 B2
Sundorne Ret Pk SY1...114 A3
Sundorne Sec Sch SY1..114 A3
Sunfield Gdns SY3......136 E6
Sunflower Cl [3] TF1...131 E1
Sungrove SY4............65 F5
Sunningdale TF1........131 D4
Sunniside TF8..........152 A7
Sunnybank Rd SY2......125 F2
Sunnycroft* TF1.........130 E2
Sunnyfields SY4........128 B7
Sunny Gdns [3] TF10..109 F5
Sunnymead TF7.........153 C4
Sunnyside Rd TF2.......131 F2
Sussex Dr SY3..........125 D3
Sussex Gdns [1] LL11...221 D7
Sutherland Ave TF1....130 F5
Sutherland Dr 1 TF7...120 F1
Sutherland Rd TF1......130 F4
Sutherland Sch The TF2..132 B6
Sutherlands The [6] TF2..120 E1
SUTTON
  Chelmarsh 200 D5
  Shrewsbury 125 E2
  Sutton upon Tern 53 B4
  West Felton............60 F3
Sutton Gr SY2..........125 E3
Sutton Grange Dr SY3..125 D2
SUTTON HILL..........153 C4
Sutton La
  Shrewsbury SY3 ....125 D4
  Sutton upon Tern TF9...53 D4
SUTTON MADDOCK....163 B7
Sutton Rd
  Admaston TF5.........130 A6
  Shrewsbury SY2 ....125 F3
Sutton Way
  Madeley TF7...........153 C5
  Market Drayton TF9....53 B7
  Shrewsbury SY2 ....125 F3
Swain's Mdw SY6.......216 C5
Swallow Dr [8] SY1.....114 B4
Swallowfield Cl [2] TF2..132 F1
Swan Cl
  Tenbury Wells WR15 ...220 D6
  Wem SY4.................65 F6
SWANCOTE.............219 E7
Swan Ct WR15..........220 D6
Swan Farm La CW3......4 F1
Swan Hill
  Ellesmere SY12.........27 C3
  Shrewsbury SY1........125 B5
Swan Hill Ct [11] SY1...125 C5
Swan Hill Gdns [10] SY1..125 C5
Swan La
  [6] Oswestry SY11......40 E1
  [4] Oswestry SY11......58 E8
  Wem SY4.................66 A7
Swanmere [7] TF10.....109 F5
Swan Mdw TF13........159 E4
Swannere 2 TF10.......109 F5
Swansmede Way TF3....144 C2
Swan St TF12...........161 C8
Sweeney Dr SY10........58 E4
Sweeney Fen Nature
  Reserve* SY10.........76 B7
Sweep's La SY21.......170 A3
Sweetbriar Cl [2] TF7...120 F1
Sweet Chariot Way TF1..130 C5
Sweet Chestnut Gr TF3..143 F7
Sweetlake [3] SY1......124 F1
Swift Cl SY1............114 B4
Swift Gate [2] TF1......130 C7
Swinburne Ct TF7......153 C3
Swinderby Cl WV7......156 E8
SWINDON...............190 E1
Swinford Leys [13] WV5..190 F3
Swin Forge Way TF4....190 F1
Swiss Farm Rd SY3 ....124 D5
Sycamore Cl
  [3] Llandysilio SY22....94 A1
  Ludlow SY8 ....217 D6
  [8] Shifnal TF11.......145 F5
  St Martin's SY11........24 F6
  Wellington TF1.........130 B5
Sycamore Cres [7] SY12..27 B2
Sycamore Dr
  Clark LL14 ....6 E3
  Oswestry SY11..........58 F7
  Wem SY4.................66 A7
Sycamore Fields SY10...77 C2
Sycamore Gr SY3........208 A1
Sycamore Rd [2] TF12..152 C2
Sycamore Way
  Highley WV16..........200 E3
  [2] Market Drayton TF9..36 D2
Sydnal La TF11.........156 F8
Sydnall La 1 TF1........53 E1
Sydney Ave SY2.........125 C1
Sydney Cottage Dr
  WV16..................218 D6

Sylvan Cl
Lilleshall TF10 . . . . 121 C6
Prees Higher Heath SY13 . . 32 E5
Sylvester Ct 🔟 LL13 . . . . . 221 E1
Symons Way TF9 . . . . 72 F8
Sytche Cl TF13 . . . . 159 E6
Sytche La TF13 . . . . 159 D5
SYTCH HOUSE GREEN . . . 189 D1
SYTCH LANE 105 F5

T

Tadorna Dr TF3 . . . . 144 D1
Tag La TF9 . . . . 55 A3
Tag's Gutter SY5 . . . . 173 D6
Talbot Cl
Church Aston TF10 . . . . . 109 D1
🔟 Oakengates/Donnington
TF2 . . . . 132 C5
Shifnal TF11 . . . . 145 E4
Talbot Cres SY11 . . . . 15 B8
Talbot Ct 🔟 LL13 . . . . 221 C2
Talbot Fields TF6 . . . . 116 E7
Talbot Gdns SY12 . . . . 27 C3
Talbot Mews SY13 . . . . 15 B8
Talbot Rd
Albrighton WV7 . . . . 156 A6
🔟 Oakengates/Donnington
TF2 . . . . 132 C5
🔟 Wrexham LL13 . . . . 221 C2
Talbot St
Ellesmere SY12 . . . . 27 C2
Whitchurch SY13 . . . . 15 B8
Talbot Way 🔟 TF9 . . . . 36 C2
Talcott Dr 🔟 SY1 . . . . 124 F2
Talisman Dr 🔟 SY2 . . . . . . 125 F6
Tamarisk Cl 🔟 TF3 . . . . . . 143 E8
Tan Bank
🔟 Newport TF10 . . . . 109 F3
Wellington TF1 . . . . 130 E3
Tanfield 🔟 SY1 . . . . 113 C1
Tanglewood Cl 🔟 TF11 . . . 145 F3
Tankerville Pottery & Gall* . .
SY5 . . . . 176 C6
Tankerville St SY2 . . . . 125 E6
Tanners Hill DY12 . . . . 211 B2
Tannery Ct
Tenbury Wells WR15 . . . . 220 C4
🔟 Wem SY4 . . . . 66 A6
Tansley Cl 🔟 SY3 . . . . 124 E4
Tan-y-foel Dr 🔟 SY22 . . . . 93 F6
Tan y Mur 🔟 SY15 . . . . . . 174 B3
Tapley Ave LL12 . . . . 221 F6
Tarbach Cl 🔟 TF2 . . . . 161 E7
Tarporley Rd SY13 . . . . 1 F2
TARTS HILL 11 C2
Tar Tunnel Mus* TF8. . . 153 A2
Tarvin Rd 🔟 SY1 . . . . 125 E7
TASLEY 218 B7
Tasley Cl WV16 . . . . 218 D5
Tavern La WR15 . . . . 215 A4
Tawnylea 🔟 SY1 . . . . 113 C2
Tayleur Dr TF9 . . . . 52 F6
Teagues Bridge Prim Sch
TF2 . . . . 131 F5
Teagues Cres TF2 . . . . 131 F6
Teal Cl TF3 . . . . 153 C8
Teal Dr SY12 . . . . 27 B3
Teaswell Cl TF3 . . . . 143 E7
TEDSMORE 79 C7
Tedsmore Rd SY11 . . . . 79 A7
Teece Dr TF2 . . . . 144 F8
Tee Lake Bvd 🔟 TF1 . . . . 130 C7
TELFORD 144 B5
Telford Ave
Albrighton WV7 . . . . 157 A6
Weston Rhyn LL14 . . . . . . 23 E6
Telford Bridge Ret Pk
TF3 . . . . 144 A7
Telford Central Sta TF3 . 144 C7
Telford Coll of Arts & Tech
TF1 . . . . 131 B3
Telford Dr 🔟 DY12 . . . . . . 211 D2
Telford Ice Rink* TF3 . . . 144 B6
Telford Int Ctr TF3 . . . . . 144 C5
Telford Rd TF1 . . . . 130 D2
Telford Rise LL14 . . . . 23 D8
Telford Sh Ctr TF3 . . . . . 144 B5
Telford Snowboard & Ski
Ctr* TF7 . . . . 153 B6
Telford Sq TF3 . . . . 144 B7
Telford Town Pk* TF3 . . . 144 B4
Telford Way
Priorslee TF2 . . . . 132 E2
Shrewsbury SY1 . . . . 113 E1
Teme Ave
Ludlow SY8 . . . . 217 D3
Wellington TF1 . . . . 130 C6
Temeside SY8 . . . . 217 D3
Temeside Cl WR15 . . . . . . 220 D6
Temeside Est SY8 . . . . 217 D3
Temeside Gdns SY8 . . . . . 217 D3
Teme St WR15 . . . . 220 D5
Temple Row 🔟 LL13 . . . . . 221 D3
Temple CE Prim Sch
WR15 . . . . 220 D4
Tenbury Com Hospl
WR15 . . . . 220 D6
Tenbury Dr
🔟 Oakengates/Donnington
TF2 . . . . 132 A4
Shrewsbury SY2 . . . . 126 A7
Tenbury High Sch WR15 . 220 C3
Tenbury Mead 🔟 DY14 . . 209 E2

Tenbury Rd
Caynham SY8 . . . . 208 C1
Cleobury Mortimer DY14 . 209 D2
Hope Bagot SY8 . . . . 214 C8
TENBURY WELLS 220 C4
Tenbury Wells Bsns Pk
Clarkes Mdws WR15 . . . 220 E3
Tenbury Wells Mus* . .
WR15 . . . . 220 D5
Tennyson Cl 🔟 TF9 . . . . . . 53 A7
Tenters La 🔟 LL13 . . . . . . 221 C2
Tenters Sq LL13 . . . . 221 C2
Teresa Way TF1 . . . . 130 F6
Tern Cl TF4 . . . . 152 E8
TERNHILL 52 A5
Tern Ridge TF9 . . . . 53 A7
Tern Valley Bsns Pk TF9 . . 36 B2
Tern View TF9 . . . . 53 A7
Tern Way TF1 . . . . 130 D6
Terraces The SY10 . . . . 58 D3
Terrick Rd SY13 . . . . 2 A2
Terrills La WR15 . . . . 220 D3
TETCHILL 43 F6
Theatre on the Steps*
WV16 . . . . 218 F5
Thetford Chase 🔟 TF3 . . 144 B6
Thieves' La SY1 . . . . 126 B2
Thimble La SY11 . . . . 24 F6
Third Ave 🔟 TF2 . . . . 132 B1
Thirlmere Gr 🔟 TF2 . . . . . 132 D1
Thistle Cl 🔟 TF3 . . . . 144 D3
Thomas Adams Sch SY13 . . 65 F7
Thomas Adams Sports Ctr
SY13 . . . . 15 B5
Thomas St 🔟 LL13 . . . . . . 221 E1
Thomas Telford Sch TF3 . 144 A6
Thompson Dr SY13 . . . . 14 E7
Thornhill Dr 🔟 LL13 . . . . 221 A2
Thornhill Rd SY3 . . . . 124 E7
Thornhurst Ave 🔟 SY11 . . 40 D1
Thorn La WV16 . . . . 198 C1
Thorns Gr 🔟 SY3 . . . . . . 124 A7
Thornton Pk Ave 🔟 TF2 . 120 F1
Thornton Rd 🔟 SY1 . . . . . 113 D2
Threadneedle St SY11 . . . . 78 C7
THREE ASHES 194 E1
Three Ashes Rd WV16 . . . 218 C5
Three Crosses 🔟 SY8 . . . 208 C2
THREE FINGERS 1 A8
Three Gates SY4 . . . . 66 C6
Three Oaks Prim Sch
TF3 . . . . 144 D2
Three Tuns Brewing Mus*
SY9 . . . . 181 F4
Threlfall Dr 🔟 DY12 . . . . . 211 E3
Thriftwicket La SY8 . . . . . 207 A7
TIBBERTON 107 E5
Tibberton CE Prim Sch
TF10 . . . . 107 E5
TICKLERTON 184 D1
Tilbrook Dr SY1 . . . . 125 E2
TILLEY 65 F4
TILLEY GREEN 66 A3
Tilley Rd
Wem Rural SY4 . . . . 65 F4
Wem SY4 . . . . 66 A5
TILSOP 214 E2
TILSTOCK 32 A8
Tilstock CE Prim Sch
SY13 . . . . 32 A8
Tilstock Cl 🔟 SY13 . . . . . . 32 A8
Tilstock Cres SY13 . . . . . . 125 F2
Tilstock La SY13 . . . . 15 C1
Tilstock Rd
Whitchurch Rural SY13 . . . 15 A3
Whitchurch Urban SY13 . . 15 A5
Timbers The TF2 . . . . 132 D3
Tindale Pl 🔟 SY3 . . . . . . 124 D6
Tining Cl 🔟 SY1 . . . . 218 C5
Tinker's Castle Rd WV5 . . 190 B5
Tipton's La 🔟 SY7 . . . . . . 205 B5
Titrail La SY8 . . . . 208 C1
Titterstone Cl 🔟 SY8 . . . 208 C2
Titterstone Rd 🔟 WV16 . 200 E3
Tollgate Rd SY8 . . . . 217 F3
Tollhouse Way 🔟 WV5 . . 190 F4
Toll Rd TF1 . . . . 131 A2
Tomkinson Cl 🔟 TF10 . . . 110 A4
Tom La DY7 . . . . 190 B3
Tom Morgan Cl TF4 . . . . . 143 C6
Tong Cl ST19 . . . . 148 E8
Tong Dr TF11 . . . . 135 F1
TONG 147 D3
TONG FORGE 147 A5
TONG NORTON 147 D5
Tong Rd ST19 . . . . 148 F7
Tontine Hill TF8 . . . . 152 C3
Top Farm Rd LL11 . . . . . . 221 B7
Topham Dr 🔟 SY2 . . . . . . 125 F3
Top Rd SY5 . . . . 173 A4
Top St SY11 . . . . 41 F3
Torrin Dr SY1 . . . . 124 F4
TOTTERTON 182 C2
Tower Cl 🔟 TF7 . . . . 36 B1
Towers Dr SY13 . . . . 32 E4
Tower St SY8 . . . . 217 C4
Tower View LL13 . . . . 217 C4
Town Hill 🔟 LL13 . . . . . . 221 C3
TOWN PARK 144 B4
Townsend Cl SY8 . . . . 217 D4
Townsend Croft TF2 . . . . 132 D8
Town Walls SY1 . . . . 125 B5
Town Wells Mews TF10 . . 109 F1
Trafalgar Cl
🔟 Oakengates/Donnington
TF2 . . . . 120 E1
🔟 Wrexham LL13 . . . . . . 221 D1
Trafalgar Pl SY12 . . . . 125 E6

TREDERWEN 167 A7
TRE-DERWEN 92 F5
Trederwen La SY22 . . . . . 167 A7
Tree Tops WV5 . . . . 190 F4
TREFLACH 75 E7
Treflach Rd SY10 . . . . 57 D1
TREFONEN 57 D2
Trefonen CE Prim Sch
SY10 . . . . 57 E2
Trefonen Rd SY11 . . . . 58 C6
Tregarthen La SY10 . . . . . . 76 A1
Trehowell Ave SY10 . . . . . . 23 D5
TRELYSTAN 170 F2
Trem Dyffryn 🔟 SY21 . . . 170 B7
Trem Eryri 🔟 LL11 . . . . . 221 C7
Trem Hafren 🔟 SY21 . . . 170 B7
Trem yr Eglwys LL14 . . . . . 23 E8
Trem-yr-eglwys 🔟 LL13 . 221 C1
TRENCH
Ellesmere Rural 27 B8
Oakengates 132 A5
Trench Cl TF2 . . . . 131 F6
Trench Lock 🔟 TF1 . . . . . 131 E5
Trench Lock 1 TF1 . . . . . . 131 E5
Trench Lock 2 TF1 . . . . . . 131 E5
Trench Lock 3 TF1 . . . . . . 131 E5
Trench Lock 4 TF1 . . . . . . 131 F5
Trench Rd TF2 . . . . 131 F6
Trenleigh Gdns TF2 . . . . . 132 A5
Trentham Cl 🔟 SY4 . . . . . 66 A7
Trentham Rd
Wem SY4 . . . . 66 A8
Wem Urban SY4 . . . . 65 F8
TRESCOTT 190 D8
Tresta Cl 🔟 SY3 . . . . 124 F3
Trevithick Cl TF7 . . . . 152 E6
Trevor Ave SY11 . . . . 24 E5
Trevor Rd SY11 . . . . 130 C8
Trevor Rd LL14 . . . . 23 E8
Trevor St / Stryt Trefor 🔟
LL13 . . . . 221 C2
Trevor St 🔟 LL13 . . . . . . 221 C2
TREWERN 167 B2
Trewern Ave 🔟 SY11 . . . . 41 A7
TRIMPLEY 211 E5
Trimpley Ct 🔟 SY12 . . . . . 27 B2
Trimpley La DY12 . . . . 211 E3
Trimpley St SY12 . . . . 27 B2
Trinity CE Prim Sch SY5 . 169 C4
Trinity Cl SY11 . . . . 41 B8
Trinity Rd TF4 . . . . 143 E1
Trinity St
Shrewsbury SY1 . . . . 125 D4
Wrexham LL11 . . . . 221 C3
Trinity View LL13 . . . . 221 A2
Troon Way TF7 . . . . 153 C3
TRYSULL 190 E5
Trysull Holloway WV5 . . . 190 E6
Trysull Rd WV5 . . . . 190 F4
Tuckers Pl TF10 . . . . 109 F3
TUCKHILL 201 D7
Tuckies The TF8 . . . . 153 A1
Tudor Cl
Berrington SY5 . . . . 138 F3
Market Drayton TF9 . . . . . 36 B2
🔟 Newport TF10 . . . . . . 110 A4
Tudor Dr LL13 . . . . 10 E3
Tudor Mdw TF2 . . . . 131 F6
Tudor Rd
🔟 Bewdley DY12 . . . . . . 211 C2
Shrewsbury SY2 . . . . 125 E3
Wrexham LL13 . . . . 221 D1
Tudor Way TF11 . . . . 145 F4
TUGFORD 197 F6
Tunnel La SY8 . . . . 212 E1
Turbervill Cl TF2 . . . . 132 E4
TURFMOOR 96 F2
TURLEYGREEN 201 B4
Turners La
Edgmond TF10 . . . . 109 A3
Llanyblodwel SY10 . . . . . . 76 B4
Turnpike Ct TF2 . . . . 132 B4
Turnpike Rise SY13 . . . . . . 49 C7
Turnstone Dr TF1 . . . . . . 131 A5
Turreff Ave TF1 . . . . 132 D7
Tuttle St LL13 . . . . 221 D2
TWEEDALE 153 B6
Tweedale Cres TF7 . . . . . 153 C6
Tweedale Cl TF7 . . . . 153 C6
Tweedale N TF7 . . . . 153 C7
Tweedale Rd TF7 . . . . 153 C6
Tweedale Wharf TF7 . . . . 153 C6
Twemlows Ave SY13 . . . . . 32 E5
Twemlows Wlk SY13 . . . . . 32 E5
Twiney La TF6 . . . . 105 D5
TWITCHEN 194 E2
Twitchen Rd SY7 . . . . 194 D3
Twmpath La SY11 . . . . 41 B6
Twn Ashes SY3 . . . . 136 F6
TWYFORD 60 D1
Twyford La SY11 . . . . 60 D1
Twyfords Way 🔟 SY2 . . . 126 A7
Ty Gwyn La LL11 . . . . 221 C8
Ty-maen SY11 . . . . 58 D7
Ty'r Parc LL11 . . . . 221 C5

U

UCKINGTON 140 B8
UFFINGTON 126 C8
Ullswater Cl 🔟 TF2 . . . . . 132 D1
UNDERDALE 125 F7

Underdale Ave SY2 . . . . . 125 E7
Underdale Rd SY2 . . . . . . 125 E7
Under Ffrydd Wood LD7 . 203 B2
Underhill Cres SY4 . . . . . . 109 E3
Underhill Cres 24 LD7 . . . 203 B3
Underhill St WV16 . . . . . . 218 F4
UNDERTON 187 F3
Undertrees Cl 🔟 TF1 . . . 130 D7
Underwood TF12 . . . . 152 D1
Unicorn Rd SY11 . . . . 40 F1
Union La WV5 . . . . 190 E5
Union Rd
🔟 Oakengates/Donnington
TF2 . . . . 132 B4
Wellington TF1 . . . . 130 D6
Union St
🔟 Bishop's Castle SY9 . . 181 F3
Hadley TF1 . . . . 131 D5
University of Wolverhampton
(Telford Campus) 🔟 TF2 . . 144 E8
Uplands Ave 🔟 TF2 . . . . . 132 A3
Uplands Dr
Bridgnorth WV16 . . . . . . 218 D4
🔟 Shrewsbury SY3 . . . . 125 E3
Upper Affcot SY6 . . . . . . 183 F1
Upper Arley 🔟 211 C7
Upper Arley CE Fst Sch
DY12 . . . . 211 B7
Upper Ashj Rd 🔟 SY11 . . 40 D1
UPPER ASTERLEY 102 E1
UPPER ASTON 190 A5
Upper Bar TF10 . . . . 109 F2
UPPER BATTLEFIELD 114 B8
UPPER BERRINGTON 214 A2
Upper Brook St SY11 . . . . 58 D7
UPPER CHURCH SY11 . . . . 58 D7
UPPER COLLEGE 33 A2
UPPER COUND 179 E7
UPPER DINCHOPE 196 A2
Upper Dingle 🔟 TF7 . . . . 152 F4
UPPER FARMCOTE 189 C3
Upper Fee SY8 . . . . 217 C3
UPPER FORGE 200 D8
Upper Galdeford SY8 . . . 217 C4
Upper Gunnas Cl 🔟 SY7 . 195 A1
UPPER HAYTON 207 B8
UPPER HENGOED 23 D1
Upper Linney SY8 . . . . . . 217 C4
UPPER LONGWOOD 141 A2
Upper Lord St 🔟 SY11 . . . 40 D1
UPPER LUDSTONE 189 F6
UPPER NETCHWOOD 186 D3
Upper Pool TF4 . . . . 143 E2
Upper Rd
Madeley TF7 . . . . 153 A4
Shrewsbury SY3 . . . . 125 B2
UPPER ROCHFORD 215 A2
UPPER TREVERWARD 193 A1
Upper Well SY11 . . . . 58 C7
UPPER WIGGINTON 25 B4
Upper Wood TF3 . . . . 143 E7
UPPINGTON 141 A8
Uppingtion Ave 🔟 SY3 . . 125 C4
UPTON CRESSETT 187 C3
UPTON MAGNA 127 C6
Upton Magna Bsns Pk
SY4 . . . . 127 D6
Urban Gdns 🔟 TF1 . . . . . 130 F3
Urban Rd TF2 . . . . 132 B4
Urban Villas TF2 . . . . 132 D3
Uxton Stones TF6 . . . . . . 106 A3

V

Valencia Rd 🔟 WV7 . . . . 156 E7
VALESWOOD 98 A5
Valeswood La SY4 . . . . 98 A5
Valiant Rd WV7 . . . . 156 E7
Valley Cl SY11 . . . . 211 F4
Valley Rd
The Rock TF3 . . . . 143 D8
Wellington TF1 . . . . 131 A1
Valley View
🔟 Bewdley DY12 . . . . . . 211 C1
🔟 Highley WV16 . . . . . . 200 E2
Market Drayton TF9 . . . . . 53 A7
Valley Way LL13 . . . . 221 D1
Val View SY12 . . . . 43 F5
Van Diemans Rd 🔟 WV5 . 190 F3
Vane Rd SY5 . . . . 125 B4
Vanguard Way SY11 . . . . . 113 F5
Vashon Cl SY8 . . . . 217 E5
Vaughan Rd 🔟 TF4 . . . . . 209 D2
Vauxhall Cres 🔟 TF10 . . . 109 E2
Vauxhall Terr TF10 . . . . . 109 E3
VENNINGTON 172 B8
Verbena Way 🔟 SY2 . . . . 126 B4
Verlon Cl SY15 . . . . 174 B4
VERNOLDS COMMON . . . 206 C2
Vernon Dr
Harlescott SY1 . . . . 113 C6
Market Drayton TF9 . . . . . 36 B3
Vernon St 🔟 LL11 . . . . . . 221 C4
Vicarage Bank WV15 . . . . 201 A3
Vicarage Croft SY4 . . . . . . 99 D8
Vicarage Dr
🔟 Oswestry SY11 . . . . . 58 D7
Shifnal TF11 . . . . 145 F3
Vicarage Fields 🔟 WV7 . 156 F5
Vicarage Gr TF4 . . . . 143 E3
Vicarage Hill 🔟 LL11 . . . 221 C3
Vicarage La
🔟 Highley WV16 . . . . . . 200 E3
Sutton Maddock TF11 . . . 163 A7
Weston Rhyn SY10 . . . . . . 23 D4

Vicarage Rd
🔟 Clun SY7 . . . . 193 D3
Ditton Priors WV16 . . . . . 198 D8
Shrewsbury SY3 . . . . 125 B2
Vicar St TF2 . . . . 132 A2
Victor Cl 🔟 WV7 . . . . 156 E7
Victoria Ave
Hadley TF1 . . . . 131 C3
🔟 Shrewsbury SY1 . . . . 125 B6
Wellington TF1 . . . . 130 E4
Victoria Cl
🔟 Oswestry SY11 . . . . . . 58 E7
Whitchurch SY13 . . . . 15 A7
Victoria Cres SY11 . . . . . . 58 E7
Victoria Ct
Hadley TF1 . . . . 131 C3
🔟 Market Drayton TF9 . . 53 B8
Victoria Fields 🔟 SY11 . . 58 E7
Victoria Gn SY11 . . . . 58 E7
Victoria Jun & Inf Schools
LL13 . . . . 221 C3
Victoria Pk TF10 . . . . 109 F3
Victoria Rd
🔟 Albrighton WV7 . . . . . 156 E7
Bridgnorth WV16 . . . . . . 218 D6
🔟 Knighton LD7 . . . . . . 203 B3
Madeley TF7 . . . . 153 A6
Market Drayton TF9 . . . . . 36 B1
Much Wenlock TF13 . . . . 159 D4
Oswestry SY11 . . . . 58 E7
Shrewsbury SY3 . . . . 125 A2
Wellington TF1 . . . . 130 E3
Wrexham LL13 . . . . 221 B1
Victoria St
Ellesmere SY12 . . . . 27 B2
Oswestry SY11 . . . . 58 D7
Shrewsbury SY1 . . . . 125 D6
🔟 Wellington TF1 . . . . . 130 E3
Victoria War Meml Hospl
SY21 . . . . 170 B6
Viewlands Dr TF2 . . . . . . 132 A3
Villa Cl 🔟 TF7 . . . . 153 A5
Village Cl 🔟 TF2 . . . . 132 A3
Village Ct
Dawley TF2 . . . . 144 D8
🔟 Wrexham LL11 . . . . . 221 D7
Village Pointe 🔟 SY6 . . . 216 D5
Village Rd
Childs Ercall TF9 . . . . 89 A7
Stockton TF11 . . . . 163 B5
Villa La SY13 . . . . 112 A2
Villiers St LL13 . . . . 221 B3
Vincent Cl WV7 . . . . 156 E7
Vine Cl SY5 . . . . 173 F8
Vineyard Cotts SY1 . . . . . 178 D3
Vineyard Dr
Newport TF10 . . . . 109 F3
🔟 Wellington TF1 . . . . . 130 D4
Vineyard Pl 🔟 TF1 . . . . . 130 D4
Vineyard Rd
Much Wenlock TF13 . . . . 159 D8
🔟 Newport TF10 . . . . . . 109 F3
Wellington TF1 . . . . 130 D4
Violet Cl 🔟 TF7 . . . . 152 E8
Viols Wlk 🔟 DY14 . . . . . . 209 E2
Virginia Rd WV7 . . . . 156 F5
Viscount Ave TF4 . . . . . . 153 A8
VRON GATE 171 F8
Vyrnwy Cres SY22 . . . . 94 B2
Vyrnwy Pl SY11 . . . . 40 D1
Vyrnwy Rd SY11 . . . . 40 D1

W

Waddington Rd WV7 . . . . 156 D7
Wade Rd 🔟 TF2 . . . . 132 C5
Wadham Cl 🔟 TF1 . . . . . . 130 F5
WAGBEACH 172 E2
Waggoner's Fold 🔟 TF3 . 144 A5
Wagtail Dr 🔟 TF4 . . . . . . 153 A8
Waincott 🔟 SY1 . . . . 113 E5
Wains Cl 🔟 TF3 . . . . 143 E7
Wakeman Sch SY2 . . . . . 125 D5
WALCOT 128 E5
Walden Cres LL11 . . . . 6 E2
Walder Cl 🔟 TF4 . . . . . . 143 E4
WALFORD
Baschurch 99 D6
Leintwardine 204 F3
WALFORD HEATH 99 F4
Walford & N Shropshire Coll
SY4 . . . . 66 B6
Walford & N Shropshire Coll
(Oswestry Campus)
SY11 . . . . 58 D7
Walford & N Shropshire Coll
(Shipley Campus) WV6 . 189 F7
Walford & N Shropshire Coll
(Walford Campus) SY4 . . 99 D6
Walford Rd 🔟 SY11 . . . . . 58 D7
Walker Cl 🔟 WV15 . . . . . 219 A4
Walker Cres 🔟 TF2 . . . . . 132 C3
Walker St 🔟 TF1 . . . . . . 130 D3
Walkmill Cl 🔟 SY3 . . . . . 124 F3
Walkmill Bank TF10 . . . . 110 C4
WALKMILL . . . .
Walkmill St 🔟 217 C3
Walkmill Dr TF9 . . . . 53 C8
Walkmill Rd TF9 . . . . 53 C8
WALKMILLS 178 B2
WALL BANK 184 F4
Wallshead Way TF11 . . . . 169 F3
**WALL UNDER
HEYWOOD** 184 F3
Walney Ct TF7 . . . . 152 E6

Walnut Cl
🔟 Dawley TF4. . . . . 153 A8
🔟 Newport TF10. . . . . . . 109 F1
Pant SY10 . . . . .76 A1
Walnut Dr
🔟 Shrewsbury SY1. . . . . . 113 D3
Whitchurch SY13. . . . . .14 F6
Walnut St 🔢 LL11. . . . . . . 221 C5
Walnut Tree La TF10. . . . . .123 B7
Walsham Ave SY4. . . . . . .41 E3
Walsham Cl SY3 . . . . .124 F3
Walsham How Cres SY11. .41 F3
Walsh Cl 🔢 TF2 . . . . .132 F1
WALTON
Ercall Magna 104 D1
Onibury 206 B6
Walton Ave TF13. . . . . . . .159 F4
Walton Cl TF2. . . . . .132 A3
Waltondale TF7 . . . . .152 F5
Walton Rd SY3 . . . . .125 D3
Wantage TF7 . . . . .152 F6
Wardens La 🔢 SY7 . . . . . .205 B5
Wardle Cl 🔢 WV15. . . . . . .219 A4
Waring Ct 🔢 LL13 . . . . . . .221 E1
Warings The 🔟 WV5 . . . . .190 F2
Warrant Rd TF9. . . . . .52 D1
Warrenby Cl 🔢 SY13 . . . . .113 E1
Warrensway TF7. . . . . . . .152 D5
Warrenwood Rd 🔢 LL12 .221 F6
Warrington Gdns SY8. . . .217 C4
Warstone Hill Rd WV6 . . .166 E3
Warstone Mdws 🔢 DY12 .211 E3
Warwick Ave LL13 . . . . . . .221 E2
Warwick Cl 🔢 TF9 . . . . . . .36 E2
Warwick Way TF1. . . . . . .131 C6
Washbrook Rd 🔢 WV15 . .219 A4
Washford Rd SY3 . . . . . . .125 A1
Wassell Dr 🔢 DY12 . . . . . .211 E3
Watchcote 🔢 SY1 . . . . . . .113 D1
Waterdale 🔢 WV5 . . . . . . .190 F3
Waterford Dr TF10 . . . . . .109 D1
Watergate 🔢 SY13. . . . . . .15 A7
Watergate St
🔢 Ellesmere SY12 . . . . . . .27 C2
🔢 Whitchurch SY13 . . . . . .15 A7
Water La
Enville DV7. . . . . .190 B1
Newport TF10 . . . . .109 F3
🔢 Shrewsbury SY1. . . . . .125 B6
WATERLOO 47 D7
Waterloo Cl
Hadley TF1. . . . . .131 D4
🔢 Wrexham LL12 . . . . . . .221 D1
Waterloo Dr 🔢 SY7 . . . . .193 D3
Waterloo Fields 🔢 SY21 .170 C1
Waterloo Pl 🔢 SY21 . . . . .170 C6
Waterloo Rd
🔟 Bewdley DY12 . . . . . . .211 C2
Edgmond TF10 . . . . .109 A6
Hadley TF1. . . . . .131 D2
Lawley & Overdale TF3 . .143 D8
Wellington TF1. . . . . .130 F4
Waterloo St TF8 . . . . .152 D3
Waterloo Terr 🔢 WV16. . .218 F5
Waterlow Cl 🔢 TF2 . . . . . .133 A1
Waterside Cl SY13 . . . . . . .14 F8
Waterside Dr 🔢 TF9 . . . . .36 E2
Waterside Mews TF10. . . .109 E3
Water St SY1 . . . . .125 D7
WATERS UPTON 106 A3
WATERWHEEL THE 172 D1
Watery La SY21. . . . . .167 A2
Watery Rd LL13. . . . . .221 B3
Watkin Dr SY11. . . . . .58 C7
Watling St N SY6 . . . . . . .216 E6
Watling St S SY6 . . . . . . .216 C5
Watling St
Craven Arms SY7. . . . . . .195 D6
🔢 Leintwardine SY7. . . . .205 B5
Wellington TF1. . . . . .131 A3
Wat's Dr SY11 . . . . .40 E1
Wat's Dyke Prim Sch
LL11 . . . . .221 C7
Wat's Dyke Way LL11 . . . .221 C7
Wattisham Way WV7 . . . .156 D8
WATTLESBOROUGH
HEATH 168 C2
WAUN 92 F4
Wavell Ave 🔢 LL13 . . . . . .221 E3
Waverley TF7 . . . . .152 F6
Waverton Way SY3 . . . . . .124 C7
Wavertree Cl 🔢 TF2 . . . . .132 C2
Waxhill Cl 🔢 SY7 . . . . . . .132 E6
Wayford Cl 🔢 SY21 . . . . .125 B1
Wayhill 🔢 SY1. . . . . .113 C5
Wayland Cl SY13. . . . . .15 B6
Wayland Rd SY13. . . . . . . .15 B7
WAYMILLS. 15 C7
Waymills SY13. . . . . .15 C7
Wayside
Clive SY4 . . . . .83 F4
Madeley TF7 . . . . .152 F6
Weald Dr 🔢 SY2. . . . . . . .126 A7
Wealdstone TF7. . . . . . . .152 D6
Wealstone Ct 🔢 LL13 . . . .221 E1
Weaver Cl 🔢 SY1. . . . . . . .59 A7
Weaver Ct 🔢 TF2 . . . . . . .132 A1
Weavers Rise TF11. . . . . .131 F1
Webb Cres TF4 . . . . .143 E2
WEBSCOTT 82 E2
Websters La TF4 . . . . .152 D6
Wedgefields Cl SY4. . . . . .102 C4
Wedgewood Cres TF1. . . .131 C3
Wedgwood Cl SY4. . . . . . .190 F4
Weeping Cross La SY8 . . .217 D3
WEIRBROOK 78 E5
Weir La SY4. . . . . .66 C5
Weir Rd SY5 . . . . .173 F8

Welcroft SY4 . . . . .82 D4
Wellbury Cl SY3 . . . . .137 A5
Wellfield Way SY13 . . . . . .1 F1
Wellgate SY4 . . . . .66 A6
WELLINGTON 130 D4
Wellington Cl 🔢 SY1. . . . .114 A2
Wellington Cres 🔢 SY21 .170 C6
Wellington Leisure Ctr
TF1. . . . . .130 D3
Wellington Rd
Albrighton WV7 . . . . .147 F1
Church Aston TF10. . . . . .121 D8
Dawley Hamlets TF4. . . . .143 B4
Ironbridge TF8. . . . . .152 B6
Lilleshall & Donnington
TF10. . . . . .121 B4
Little Wenlock TF6 . . . . . .142 D3
Newport TF10 . . . . .109 E1
🔢 Oakengates/Donnington
TF2 . . . . .120 D1
Oakengates/Donnington
TF2. . . . . .132 C7
The Gorge TF4 . . . . .143 B1
🔢 Wrexham LL13 . . . . . . .221 C2
Wrockwardine TF1. . . . . . .130 B6
Wellington Ret TF1 . . . . . .131 B2
Wellington Sta TF1. . . . . .130 E4
Well La
Great Ness SY4 . . . . .97 E5
Pontesbury SY5 . . . . .173 D5
Well Mdw Gdns SY3 . . . . .124 C6
Well Mdw Rd SY3 . . . . . . .124 C6
Well Mead La SY5 . . . . . . .173 F5
Wellmeadow WV15 . . . . . .219 A4
Well Pl 🔢 LL11 . . . . .221 C3
Wells Cl WV16 . . . . .218 E4
Wellsfield TF7 . . . . .152 F6
Well St 🔢 SY3. . . . . .174 B3
Wellswood Ave TF2 . . . . . .144 B8
Wellswood Rd 🔢 LL12 . . .221 D1
Wellwood Cl 🔢 SY3. . . . . .124 C6
WELSHAMPTON. 28 D2
Welshampton CE Prim Sch
SY12 . . . . .28 C3
WELSH END. 31 A4
WELSH FRANKTON. 43 A7
Welsh Harp Hollow
SY21. . . . . .171 A6
Welshpool Ind Est SY21. .170 C6
Welshpool Rd SY3 . . . . . .124 A7
Welshpool Sta SY21. . . . .170 C6
WELSHPOOL
(TRALLWNG). 170 D6
Welsh St Gdns 🔢 SY9 . . .181 F4
Welsh St SY9 . . . . .181 E4
Welsh View SY12. . . . . . . .28 E3
Welsh Walls SY11. . . . . . . .58 D8
WEM 66 B6
Wem Bsns Pk SY4 . . . . . . .66 A7
Wem Ind Est SY4 . . . . .48 D1
Wem Moss Nature National
Reserve* SY13. . . . . .29 C1
Wem Rd
Clive SY4 . . . . .84 A6
Myddle & Broughton SY4. .83 C1
Shawbury SY4 . . . . .103 D8
Wembrook Dr 🔢 SY4 . . . . .66 A8
Wembrook Rd SY4 . . . . . . .66 A8
Wem Sta SY4. . . . . .66 B6
Wendsley Rd 🔢 SY1 . . . . .113 D4
Wenlock Abbey TF13 . . . .159 F5
Wenlock Ct TF7 . . . . .152 E6
Wenlock Dr 🔟 TF10. . . . . .109 E2
Wenlock Edge* TF13 . . . .159 C4
Wenlock Rd
Bridgnorth WV16. . . . . . .218 C5
🔢 Shrewsbury SY3 . . . . .125 F4
Wensley Gn TF7. . . . . . . .152 F6
Wentworth Cl 🔢 SY3. . . . .136 F6
Wentworth Dr 🔢 TF1 . . . .130 E1
WERN 93 D5
Wern LL14. . . . . .6 D3
WERN 23 B2
WERN DDU 56 E1
WERNLAS 95 D5
WERNYGEUFRON. 202 B7
Wern y Wiel SY10. . . . . . .145 F3
Wesley Cres TF11. . . . . . . .14 F5
Wesley Dr 🔢 TF2 . . . . . . .132 A2
Wesley Rd TF8. . . . . .152 E3
West Ave TF2. . . . . .132 C7
Westbeech Rd WV6 . . . . .166 D5
Westbourne TF7 . . . . .152 E5
Westbourne Rise SY3 . . . .136 F7
Westbourne St 🔢 DY12 . .211 E2
Westbrook Ave 🔢 SY13 . . .14 F8
WESTBURY. 172 C8
Westbury Rd SY11. . . . . . .113 D4
West Castle St 🔢 WV16 . .218 F4
West Circ 🔢 LL13. . . . . . .221 E4
WESTCOTT. 177 B8
Westcott La TF9 . . . . .72 E6
Westcott Wlk 🔢 TF2 . . . . .132 E2
West Ctr Way TF4 . . . . . . .143 F6
West Dr SY11 . . . . .41 B2
West Edge 🔢 SY3 . . . . . . .124 A6
Westerdale Cl 🔢 TF4. . . . .143 D2
Westerkirk Dr 🔢 TF7 . . . .152 F5

Westfields SY6. . . . . .216 E5
Westfields Cl SY4. . . . . . . .81 A1
Westfields Rise CW3 . . . . .5 A1
Westfields The 🔢 TF9 . . . .72 F7
Westgate WV16 . . . . .218 D5
Westgate Dr WV16. . . . . .218 D5
West Hermitage 🔢 SY3 . .125 C4
Westhleigh Way 🔢 LL11. .221 C7
WESTHOPE 196 C5
Westhope Ave 🔢 SY4 . . . .124 D6
Whitbatch Cl SY8. . . . . . .217 C6
Westland Dr 🔢 TF9. . . . . . .36 B1
Westlands Rd 🔢 SY4 . . . .124 D6
Westleigh Rd 🔢 WV5 . . . .190 F2
WESTLEY 172 C5
West Lullingfield CE Prim
Sch SY4. . . . . .81 A8
West Midland Saf Pk*
DY12 . . . . .211 F2
West Midland
Showground* SY1 . . . . .125 B7
Westminster Cl
🔢 Shrewsbury SY1. . . . .125 C8
Wrexham LL13 . . . . .221 D5
Westminster Dr
🔢 Market Drayton TF9. . .53 A7
Wrexham LL12. . . . . .221 D5
Westminster Way 🔢
TF2 . . . . .133 A1
Westmorland Mews 🔢
SY1. . . . . .125 D8
Westmorland Mews 🔢
TF1. . . . . .131 A5
WESTON
Monkhopton. 186 C4
Oswestry Rural 58 F3
Stowe. 203 F4
Weston-under-Redcastle. .67 F6
Weston Ave SY11 . . . . .58 E6
Weston Bank Cl TF11. . . .135 E2
Weston Cl
🔢 Brewood ST19 . . . . . .148 E8
Oswestry SY10 . . . . .58 D4
WESTONCOMMON. 63 B1
Weston Ct Mews 🔢 SY13. .15 A7
Weston Dr
Shrewsbury SY1. . . . . . . .113 E2
Wellington TF1. . . . . .130 C5
🔢 Wrexham LL11 . . . . . . .221 B6
WESTON HEATH 134 F8
Weston La SY11 . . . . .58 E5
WESTON
LULLINGFIELDS. 81 A6
Weston Rd
Albrighton WV7 . . . . .157 B5
Bucknell SY7 . . . . .204 B4
Oswestry SY10 . . . . .58 D4
WESTON RHYN 23 D4
Weston Rhyn Prim Sch
SY10. . . . . .23 D5
WESTON UNDER
LIZARD 135 F3
WESTONWHARF 81 A8
West Pl SY11. . . . . .41 A8
West Rd
Newcastle on Clun SY7 . .192 D5
🔢 Oakengates/Donnington
TF2 . . . . .131 F1
Wellington TF1. . . . . .130 C3
West St
Knighton LD7 . . . . .203 B3
🔢 Oakengates/Donnington
TF2 . . . . .132 C2
Oswestry SY11 . . . . .58 D7
🔢 Shrewsbury SY1. . . . .125 D7
Wrexham LL11. . . . . .221 B5
Westune SY13 . . . . .14 F6
West View
Butlane Head SY5 . . . . . .169 C4
Chirk Green LL14. . . . . . . .6 E2
West View Terr 🔢 TF7 . . .152 F5
West Way LL13 . . . . .10 E3
Westwood Dr SY3. . . . . . .124 E6
Westwood Pk 🔢 SY21. . . .170 B6
Westwood Rd 🔢 SY21. . . .170 B6
Wetmore La
Bromfield SY8 . . . . .206 A3
Leintwardine SY7. . . . . . .205 F7
WETTLES 183 E2
Weybourne Wlk TF2 . . . . .132 F7
Weybridge TF7 . . . . .152 D6
Weyman Rd
Ludlow SY8 . . . . .217 D6
🔢 Wellington TF1. . . . . .130 D5
Weymore La SY7. . . . . . . .204 E4
Wharage TF8 . . . . .152 B4
Wharf Cl 🔢 TF2 . . . . .132 C3
Wharf Rd SY12 . . . . .27 B2
WHATMORE. 214 E6
Wheatcommon La SY4. . .212 F5
Wheatfield Dr TF11 . . . . .145 F5
WHEATHALL 178 E6
WHEATHILL. 198 E1
Wheathill Ct SY8. . . . . . . .217 E5
Wheatlands SY11 . . . . .78 E7
Wheatlands Rise 🔢
WV16. . . . . .218 D5
Wheatlands The
🔢 Baschurch SY4. . . . . . .99 B8
Bridgnorth WV16. . . . . . .218 D5
Wheatley 🔢 SY1. . . . . . . .113 F2
Wheatley Cres 🔢 TF11. . .131 A6
Wheatsheaf La SY13. . . . . .15 A6
Wheeldale Cl 🔢 TF4. . . . .143 D2
Wheeler Cl SY8. . . . . .217 E5

Wheeler Orch WR15 . . . .220 C3
Wheeler Rd SY6 . . . . .217 E5
WHETTLETON. 195 F5
Whimbrel Cl 🔢 TF1. . . . . .131 B5
Whinchat Cl 🔢 TF1 . . . . .130 F6
Whip La SY10. . . . . .77 D3
Whiston Cl
🔟 Albrighton WV7 . . . . .157 A5
🔢 Shrewsbury SY3 . . . . .124 E3
WHISTON CROSS. 156 C4
Whitbatch Cl SY8. . . . . . .217 C6
Whitbread Rd SY5 . . . . . .217 B5
Whitburn St WV16 . . . . . .218 E5
WHITCHURCH. 15 C8
Whitchurch Bsns Pk SY13 .15 C7
Whitchurch CE Inf Sch
SY13. . . . . .15 B7
Whitchurch CE Jun Sch
SY13. . . . . .15 B7
Whitchurch Com Hospl
SY13. . . . . .15 B8
Whitchurch Dr TF1. . . . . .130 F5
Whitchurch Her Ctr*
SY13. . . . . .15 A8
Whitchurch Rd
Prees SY13 . . . . .32 C1
🔢 Shrewsbury SY1. . . . .113 F3
Wellington TF1. . . . . .130 D7
Wem SY4. . . . . .66 B8
Wem Urban SY4. . . . . .48 B1
Whitchurch Sta SY13 . . . .15 C8
Whitcliffe Rd SY8. . . . . . .217 B3
Whitcomb's Orch 🔢
DY14. . . . . .209 E2
WHITCOT. 182 E6
WHITCOTT KEYSETT. . . .193 A5
White Bank 🔢 SY3 . . . . . .124 B7
Whitebeam Cl 🔢 TF3 . . . .143 F8
Whitebrook Mdw SY13 . . .49 B8
Whitechapel Way TF2. . . .144 D8
Whitecote Dr 🔟 SY3. . . . .124 A7
Whitecroft Rd SY3 . . . . . .125 E3
White Cross DV7. . . . . . . .190 A1
Whitefriars
🔟 Oswestry SY11. . . . . . .41 A1
🔟 Wrexham LL12 . . . . . . .221 E8
White Friars SY8 . . . . . . .217 D5
Whitegate Rd 🔢 LL13. . . .221 E4
WHITE GRIT. 175 E4
Whitehall Gdns TF12 . . . .161 D8
Whitehall St SY2 . . . . . . .125 E6
Whitehall Terr SY2 . . . . . .125 D2
WHITEHAVEN 76 A5
White Heart Cl 🔟 WV12 . .211 C2
White Hill 🔢 TF4 . . . . . . .143 E4
Whitehorse Pas 🔢 SY3 . .125 B6
Whitehouse Ct TF9. . . . . . .73 B6
White House Gdns
Hazler SY6. . . . . .216 E5
🔢 Shrewsbury SY1. . . . .113 E1
Whitehouse La SY4 . . . . .100 E3
White House La DY3 . . . . .190 D1
White House Mus The*
SY7. . . . . .196 F5
White House Sch SY13 . . .15 B5
White Ladies Ct 🔢 WV7. .156 F5
White Lodge Pk SY4 . . . .103 D6
White Mdw Cl 🔢 SY1. . . .113 D1
Whitemeadow Cl 🔢 SY7 .195 E5
Whitemere Rd
Shrewsbury SY1. . . . . . . .113 E2
🔢 Wellington TF1. . . . . .130 C5
White Minst SY1. . . . . .58 C7
Whiteoaks Dr ST19 . . . . .148 E8
White Row SY5. . . . . .190 E5
Whiteway Dr 🔢 TF5. . . . . .130 A8
Whitewayhead La SY8 . . .208 A1
WHITEWELL. 13 D7
Whitewell Rd SY13. . . . . . .13 C8
Whitfield Cl 🔢 SY11 . . . . .59 B8
Whitfley Rd WV7 . . . . . . .156 B7
Whitmore Cl
🔟 Bridgnorth WV16 . . . .218 D6
🔢 Broseley TF12. . . . . . .161 E7
Whitmore La SY4 . . . . .99 A8
Whittal Cl 🔢 WV15. . . . . .201 B3
Whittington Castle
(remains of)* SY11 . . . . .41 E3
WHITTINGSLOW. 183 E3
WHITTINGTON 41 F3
Whittington Bsns Pk SY1 .82 B2
Whittington CE Prim Sch
SY11. . . . . .41 F2
Whittington Cl SY1 . . . . . .114 C2
Whittington Old Rd SY11. .41 A7
Whittington Rd SY11. . . . .41 B6
WHITTON
Leintwardine 205 C4
Tenbury Wells. 214 A7
Whiston Cl 🔢 SY1 . . . . . . .125 F2
WHITTYTREE. 195 F1
Whitwell La SY11 . . . . . . .183 A4
Whitworth Dr TF3. . . . . . .144 C3
WHIXALL. 31 B2
Whixall CE Prim Sch SY13 30 E3
Wicket Cl 🔢 TF2. . . . . . . .132 E8
Widewaters Cl 🔢 TF4. . . .152 F8
Wigeon Gr TF1 . . . . .130 F7
WIGGINTON. 21 E6
WIGMARSH 79 D7
Wigmore La SY5 . . . . .168 C2
Wigmores TF7. . . . . .152 F6
Wilcot Ave SY9 . . . . .97 D2
WILCOTT. 97 D2
WILCOTT MARSH 97 B1
Wilderhope Manor*
TF13. . . . . .185 D3
Wilderley Cres 🔢 SY3. . . .125 B1

Wildings The SY8. . . . . . .217 E5
Wildon Way 🔢 SY3 . . . . .124 E4
Wild Thyme Dr 🔢 TF2. . . .132 E8
Wildwood TF7 . . . . .152 E6
Wildwood Ct 🔢 SY21 . . . .170 B5
Wilfred Owen Ave 🔢
SY11. . . . . .59 A7
Wilfred Owen Cl
🔟 Market Drayton TF9. . .53 A7
🔢 Shrewsbury SY1. . . . . .59 A7
🔢 Shrewsbury SY2. . . . .125 E6
Wilfred Owen Rd SY11. . . .59 A7
Wilfrid Owen Prim Sch The
SY2. . . . . .126 A8
WILKESLEY 17 F7
Wilkins Cl 🔟 WV16 . . . . .200 E3
Wilkinson Ave TF12 . . . . .161 D7
Wilkinson Wlk TF9 . . . . . .36 C1
WILLASTON. 24 F7
Willaston Rd SY13 . . . . . . .33 E4
Willetts Way TF4. . . . . . . .143 E4
WILLEY 161 C3
Willeymoor La SY13. . . . . . .1 D7
William Brookes Sch
TF13. . . . . .159 E6
William Reynolds Jun & Inf
Schools TF7. . . . . .152 E5
Williams Rd TF2 . . . . .120 C3
Willington Cl 🔢 SY1 . . . . .113 E5
Willmoor La TF10 . . . . . . .121 C4
Willow Bank TF4. . . . . . . .153 A8
Willow Cl
Llandysilio SY22. . . . . .94 B1
🔟 Market Drayton TF9. . .52 F8
🔢 St Martin's SY11 . . . . .24 F6
Worfield WV15. . . . . .189 C6
Willow Cres 🔢 SY12 . . . . .27 B2
Willow Ct SY3. . . . . .102 C4
Willowdale Gdns 🔢 SY1 .113 D1
Willow Dr
🔢 Gobowen SY11. . . . . . .41 B8
🔢 Hanwood SY5. . . . . . .173 F8
🔟 Highley WV16. . . . . . .200 E2
Willowfield TF7 . . . . .152 F7
Willow Lea Cl LL11. . . . . .221 A8
Willow Pk 🔢 SY5 . . . . . . .172 E3
Willow Pl
Shawbury SY4 . . . . .103 F7
🔟 Shrewsbury SY1. . . . .125 F2
Willows Cres SY11. . . . . . . .78 D7
Willows Rd TF2 . . . . .132 B3
Willow St
Ellesmere SY12 . . . . .27 B2
Oswestry SY11. . . . . .58 D8
Overton LL13 . . . . .9 C8
Willows The
🔢 Welshpool SY21. . . . .170 B5
🔟🔢 Wombourne WV5 . . .190 F3
🔢 Wrexham LL12. . . . . . .221 D5
WILLSTONE. 184 D6
Wilmore St 🔢 TF13 . . . . .159 E4
Wilmot Dr SY11. . . . . .58 D6
Wilmot Rd SY11 . . . . .58 D6
Wilson Ave LL13 . . . . .221 E4
Wilton Gn 🔢 SY3. . . . . . . .124 E4
Winbrook DY12 . . . . .211 D2
Winchester Dr 🔟 TF2. . . .132 E4
Windermere Dr 🔢 TF2 . . .144 D8
Windermere Rd
🔢 Shrewsbury SY1. . . . .113 F3
🔢 Wrexham LL12. . . . . . .221 E8
Windle Hill SY11 . . . . .216 E5
Windmill Gdns SY13 . . . . .31 C3
Windmill La
Albrighton WV7 . . . . .156 E5
Stockton TF11 . . . . .163 B6
Welshpool SY21. . . . . . . .170 A7
Windmill Prim Sch TF3. . .153 C8
Windrush Cl 🔢 LL13 . . . . .221 E1
Windsor Cl SY11. . . . . .41 A1
Windsor Cres TF12. . . . . .152 C1
Windsor Dr
Market Drayton TF9. . . . . .36 E2
Wrexham LL11. . . . . .221 A4
Windsor Flats TF1 . . . . . .131 A3
Windsor La 🔢 SY4 . . . . . .100 F4
Windsor Pl
Dawley TF4 . . . . .143 E3
🔢 Shrewsbury SY1. . . . .125 C2
Windsor Rd
Albrighton WV7 . . . . .157 A5
Dawley TF4 . . . . .143 E3
Oswestry SY11. . . . . .41 A1
🔢 Pattingham WV6. . . . .166 C2
Windsor St
🔟 Shrewsbury SY1. . . . .113 D1
🔢 Wrexham LL11. . . . . . .221 A4
Windy Arbour TF13 . . . . . .15 A7

Winesbury 🔢 SY3 . . . . . .136 F6
Winfield Cl SY11 . . . . .113 D1
Wingfield Gdns 🔢 LL11 . .113 E1
Winifred Cl 🔢 SY21 . . . . . .21 E1
Winifred's Dr* TF2 . . . . . .132 C7
WINLLAN 92 C8
Winllan La SY22 . . . . .74 A1
Winllan Rd SY22. . . . . .92 B6
WINNINGTON 3 D8
WINNINGTON GREEN . . .167 E2
Winston Dr TF12 . . . . .132 D8
Winston Rd 🔢 SY3. . . . . .190 F1
Winterton Way SY3 . . . . .124 C7
WIRSWALL. 2 A5
Wirswall Rd SY13 . . . . .2 A5
WISTANSTOW 195 D8
Wistanstow CE Prim Sch
SY7. . . . . .195 E8
WISTANSWICK 71 A7
Wisteria Ct LL11 . . . . .221 B4

Witchwell La TF6 . . . . 142 D2
Withering Cl TF1 . . . . 131 A3
Withies Bank DY14 . . . . . 209 D6
WITHINGTON 128 B7
Withington Cl **1** TF2 . . 132 B3
Withy Ave **1** SY21 . . . . 170 D1
Withybrook TF7 . . . . 152 D6
Withy Ct **1** SY21 . . . . . 170 C1
Withywood Dr TF3 . . . . . 144 A5
Witley Gdns **12** WV16. . . 200 E2
Wittering Rd WV7 . . . . . 156 C8
WIXHILL 67 E6
Wodehouse Cl **19** WV5 . . 190 F3
Woden Cl **12** WV5 . . . . . 190 F4
Wold The **4** WV5 . . . . . 189 E4
WOLLASTON 167 F3
WOLLERTON 51 E1
Wolmore La WV5 . . . . . . 190 B5
Wolverhampton Halfpenny
 Gn Airport DY7 . . . . . . 190 B2
Wolverhampton Rd
 Bridgnorth WV15 . . . . . 219 A5
 Pattingham & Patshull
 WV6 . . . . 166 D3
WOLVERLEY 46 E3
Wolverley Ct
 8 Albrighton WV7 . . . . 157 A5
 Madeley TF7 . . . . 152 E6
WOLVERTON 196 B7
WOMBOURNE 190 E2
Wombourne Rd DY3 . . . . 190 F2
WOMBRIDGE 132 A3
Wombridge Prim Sch
 TF2 . . . . 132 A2
Wombridge Rd TF2 . . . . . 131 F3
Wombridge Way TF2 . . . . 131 F4
Wombrook Dale **6** WV5 . 190 E3
Wonderland* TF3 . . . . . . 144 C5
Woodbank Dr **1** SY3 . . . 124 F5
Woodbatch Rd **2** SY9. . . 181 E3
Woodberry Cl
 Bridgnorth WV15 . . . . . 218 D5
 2 Wrexham LL13 . . . . . 221 A2
Woodbine Cl **1** SY5 . . . . 171 F3
Woodbine Dr TF2 . . . . . . 132 E8
Woodbury **2** SY11 . . . . . .24 F7
Wood Cl TF2 . . . . 132 C6
Woodcock Cnr TF11 . . . . 146 E8
Woodcote Edge SY6 . . . . 216 B5
Woodcote Way SY2 . . . . 125 F8
Woodcrest **6** SY3 . . . . . 124 A6
Woodcroft TF7 . . . . 152 F6
Woodfield Ave SY3 . . . . . 124 F5
Woodfield Infants Sch
 SY3 . . . . 124 F6
Woodfield Rd SY3 . . . . . . 124 F5
Woodford Gn **4** TF5 . . . 130 B8
Woodford La WV5 . . . . . . 190 E4
Woodford Way **2** WV5 . . 190 E3
Woodhall Cl SY11 . . . . . . 125 E8
Woodhall Dr SY5 . . . . . . 173 E7
WOODHILL 200 E3
Woodhill Cl **14** WV5 . . . 190 F3
Wood Hill Dr **28** WV5 . . 190 F3
Woodhill Rd WV16 . . . . . 200 E3

Woodhouse Central TF3. .144 B6
Woodhouse Cres TF2 . . . 132 B6
Woodhouse Dr SY11 . . . . .61 A5
Woodhouse La
 Aymestrey SY8. . . . . . . 212 C4
 Boningale WV7 . . . . 157 C3
 Buerton CW3 . . . . .19 D8
 3 Dawley TF2 . . . . 132 E1
 Dawley TF4 . . . . 143 C2
 Knighton LD7 . . . . 203 A1
 Lilleshall & Donnington
 TF10 . . . . 133 B3
Wood La
 Cressage SY5 . . . . 149 C1
 Harley SY5. . . . . 158 C8
 Hinstock TF9 . . . . .72 A4
 Hodnet TF9 . . . . .51 C3
Woodland Cl WV7. . . . . . 157 A6
Woodland Rise **7** DY14 . 209 E3
Woodlands TF8 . . . . 152 D4
Woodlands Ave
 8 Hanwood SY5. . . . . 173 F8
 Wellington TF1 . . . . 130 C4
Woodlands Cl
 Broseley TF12 . . . . 152 C2
 2 Oswestry SY11 . . . . .58 F7
 Withington SY4 . . . . . . 128 B7
Woodlands Gr
 6 Llangollen Rural LL20. . . 6 A7
 Prees Higher Heath SY13 . .32 E5
Woodlands La TF4 . . . . . 143 C1
Woodlands Pk **1** SY2 . . 125 F4
Woodlands Prim Sch
 TF7 . . . . 152 F5
Woodlands Rd
 Broseley TF12 . . . . 152 C2
 Llangollen Rural LL20 . . . .6 A7
 The Gorge TF8 . . . . 152 C4
Woodlands Sch SY4 . . . . . .66 A4
Woodlands The
 Brockton TF10 . . . . 121 C6
 5 Oakengates/Donnington
 TF2 . . . . 132 B4
 Red Lake TF1 . . . . 131 E1
 Wolverley SY4 . . . . .46 F4
Woodland View SY10. . . . .57 E2
WOODLANE 72 A3
WOOD LANE . 44 F6Woodlark Cl
 5 SY1. . . . . 114 C3
Woodlea **5** SY2 . . . . . . 125 F3
Woodpecker Cl
 1 Hadley TF1 . . . . 131 B7
 3 Shrewsbury SY1 . . . . 114 B4
Wood Rd SY4. . . . . 101 F4
Woodridge Cl TF10 . . . . . 109 A4
Woodrows TF7 . . . . 152 F6
Woodrush Heath TF3. . . . 143 F7
WOODSIDE 152 F6
Woodside
 Bicton SY3 . . . . 112 A2
 Ironbridge TF8. . . . . . . 152 B6
 3 Oswestry SY11 . . . . . .40 E1
Woodside Ave TF7 . . . . . 152 D5
Woodside Cl **4** TF1 . . . . 131 D2
Woodside Ct **7** SY11 . . . .40 F1
Woodside Dr SY3 . . . . . . 124 E5

Woodside Prim Sch SY11 .40 E1
Woodside Rd TF1 . . . . . . 131 D2
Woodspring Gr TF2 . . . . . 132 F7
Wood St SY1 . . . . 125 C8
Woodthorpe Dr
 23 Bark Hill DY12 . . . . 211 D2
 1 Bewdley DY12 . . . . . 211 D2
Woodwell **5** TF1 . . . . . . 131 F2
Wood Yd SY8 . . . . 217 C4
WOOFFERTON 213 B3
Woolams The **4** SY3. . . 124 B7
Woollam Rd TF1 . . . . 131 A2
Woolpack Cl **1** TF11 . . . 145 F5
WOOLSTASTON 178 A1
WOOLSTON
 West Felton 77 E5
 Winstanstow 183 D2
Woolston Rd SY10 . . . . . .77 F6
WOORE 5 A2
Woore Prim Sch CW3. . . . .5 A1
Woore Rd CW3 . . . . .4 A2
WOOTTON 201 B8
WOOTTON
 Onibury 60 B4
 Oswestry Rural 206 A5
Worcester Rd
 Dawley TF4 . . . . 143 F4
 Donington WV7 . . . . . . 156 D7
 7 Shrewsbury SY1 . . . . 113 E4
Wordsworth Dr TF9 . . . . .53 A7
Wordsworth Way **8** TF2. 132 D1
Worfe Cl **2** TF3 . . . . . . 144 D4
Worfe Rd TF11. . . . . 145 F6
WORFIELD 189 B6
Worfield CE Prim Sch
 WV15. . . . . 189 B6
Workfield Cl TF7 . . . . 153 C2
Worrow Dr **3** SY3 . . . . . 124 A7
WORTHEN 171 F4
Worthen Prim Sch SY5 . . 171 F3
Worthington Dr
 Albrighton WV7 . . . . . . 156 E6
 9 Shrewsbury SY3 . . . . 124 E4
Worthington St SY13. . . . .15 B8
WOTHERTON 175 B7
WOUNDALE 188 B3
Wrekin Ave TF10 . . . . . . 109 E2
Wrekin Cl **2** TF2 . . . . . . 131 F6
Wrekin Coll TF1 . . . . 130 F4
Wrekin Coll Sports Ctr
 TF1 . . . . 130 F4
Wrekin Course TF6 . . . . . 141 E6
Wrekin Ct SY5. . . . . 138 F3
Wrekin Dr TF2 . . . . 132 C7
Wrekin Rd
 6 Bridgnorth WV16 . . . 218 C6
 Wellington TF1 . . . . 130 D3
Wrekin Ret Pk TF1 . . . . . 131 B1
Wrekin View TF7 . . . . . . 152 E4
Wrekin View Prim Sch
 TF1 . . . . 130 D5
Wrenbury Rd SY13 . . . . . .8 E8
Wren Cl **1** SY1 . . . . 114 C3
Wren's Nest La **5** TF1 . . 131 D2
WRENTNALL 173 D2
Wrexham Central Sta
 LL11 . . . . 221 C3

Wrexham Cty Borough Mus*
 LL11. . . . . 221 C3
Wrexham General Sta
 LL11 . . . . 221 C4
Wrexham Maelor Hospl
 LL13. . . . . 221 A3
Wrexham Rd
 Marchwiel LL13 . . . . . . 221 A1
 Overton LL13 . . . . .9 C8
 4 Whitchurch SY13 . . . .14 E7
WREXHAM (WRECSAM). 221 A8
WRIBBENHALL 211 E2
Wribbenhall Fst Sch
 DY12. . . . . 211 E3
WRICKTON 199 B4
WROCKWARDINE 129 F5
Wrockwardine Rd **1**
 TF1. . . . . 130 C4
WROCKWARDINE
 WOOD 132 C4
Wrockwardine Wood Arts
 Coll TF2. . . . . 132 A4
Wrockwardine Wood CE Jun
 Sch TF2. . . . . 132 B6
Wrockwardine Wood Inf Sch
 TF2. . . . . 132 B5
Wrockwardine Wood Way
 TF2 . . . . 132 B5
WROXETER 139 E5
Wroxeter Roman Site &
 Mus* SY5 . . . . 139 E6
Wroxeter Roman Vineyard*
 SY5. . 139 F4Wroxeter Way TF3
 144 D1
Wych Elm Dr TF5 . . . . . . 130 D8
Wyebourne Rd **10** SY3 . 128 F3
WYKE 151 D1
Wyke La
 Barrow TF12 . . . . 160 F8
 Much Wenlock TF12. . . 151 E1
WYKEN 189 B6
Wyke Rise **7** TF1 . . . . . 130 F5
WYKE THE 145 C2
Wyke Way TF11 . . . . 145 E4
WYKEY 80 A7
Wylcwm St **12** LD7 . . . . 203 B3
WYLDE 212 A3
Wyle Cop SY1 . . . . 125 C5
Wyndham Gr **4** TF2 . . . 132 F2
Wynn Ave LL11 . . . . 221 C6
Wynn Cl **8** DY12. . . . . . 211 E3
Wynnstay Ave LL13. . . . . 221 F4
Wyrebrook Gdns WR15 . . 215 A4
Wyrebrook Orch WR15 . . 215 A4
Wyre Cl **7** WV16 . . . . . . 200 E3
Wyre Forest National Nature
 Reserve* DY12 . . . . . . 211 A3
Wyre Hill DY12 . . . . 211 C1
Wyson Ave SY8 . . . . 213 B3
Wyson La SY8 . . . . 213 A2
Wytheford Rd SY4 . . . . . 103 F6
Wyton Ave WV7 . . . . 156 D8
Wyvern TF7 . . . . 152 D5

Y

Yale Coll (Bersham Rd
 Campus) LL12 . . . . . . 221 B2
Yale Coll (Grove Pk Rd)
 LL12 . . . . 221 C4
Yale Gr LL12 . . . . 221 D5
Yale Pk LL11. . . . . 221 A4
Yale Wlk LL11 . . . . 221 D3
Yardington **5** SY13 . . . . .14 F8
Yarwood Dr **4** LL12 . . . 221 E8
Yates Way TF2 . . . . 144 A8
Y Bwthyn the Cottage **21**
 LD7 . . . . 203 B3
Y Clawdd SY22 . . . . .93 F1
YEATON 99 D3
Yeld Bank SY6 . . . . 216 C8
Yeldside Gdns DY14 . . . . 209 F3
YELD THE 198 A2
Yeld The **2** SY3 . . . . . . 124 A6
Yellowstone Cl **1** TF2 . . 132 D3
Yeomanry Rd SY4 . . . . . . 113 E6
Yeomans The WV16 . . . . 200 D6
Yew Tree Ave SY11 . . . . . .41 E2
Yew Tree Bank SY4 . . . . . 100 E4
Yew Tree Cl
 11 Bewdley DY12 . . . . 211 C2
 Whittington SY11. . . . . .41 E2
Yewtree Dr SY3 . . . . 136 F5
Yew Tree Dr TF10 . . . . . . 121 B2
Yew Tree Gr **4** WV16. . . 200 E3
Yew Tree La
 Bewdley DY12 . . . . 211 C2
 Bridgemere CW5. . . . . . .4 E6
Yew Tree Rd
 Madeley TF7 . . . . 152 F4
 Pattingham WV6 . . . . . 166 C3
YOCKLETON. 169 A1
Yockleton Rd SY5. . . . . . 169 A3
Yorke St LL11 . . . . 221 D3
York Fields SY11. . . . . . . .40 D1
York Rd
 14 Bewdley DY12 . . . . 211 C2
 4 Shrewsbury SY1 . . . . 113 C4
 St Georges & Priorslee
 TF2 . . . . 133 A2
York St SY11. . . . . .40 D1
YORTON 83 E4
YORTON HEATH 83 E1
Yorton Sta SY4 . . . . .83 E4
Young Options Coll
 TF11. . . . . 146 B3
Yr Helfa LL14. . . . . .6 E3
Ysgol Bro Cynllaith SY10. .56 A5
Ysgol Ceiriog Jun Sch
 LL14 . . . . .6 E1
Y Wern LL13. . . . . 221 F2

Addresses

Name and Address	Telephone	Page	Grid reference

Using the Ordnance Survey National Grid

Any feature in this atlas can be given a unique reference to help you find the same feature on other Ordnance Survey maps of the area, or to help someone else locate you if they do not have a Street Atlas.

The grid squares in this atlas match the Ordnance Survey National Grid and are at 500 metre intervals. The small figures at the bottom and sides of every other grid line are the National Grid kilometre values (**00** to **99** km) and are repeated across the country every 100 km (see left).

To give a unique National Grid reference you need to locate where in the country you are. The country is divided into 100 km squares with each square given a unique two-letter reference. Use the administrative map to determine in which 100 km square a particular page of this atlas falls.

The bold letters and numbers between each grid line (**A** to **F**, **1** to **8**) are for use within a specific Street Atlas only, and when used with the page number, are a convenient way of referencing these grid squares.

Example   *The railway bridge over DARLEY GREEN RD in grid square B1*

Step 1: Identify the two-letter reference, in this example the page is in **SP**

Step 2: Identify the 1 km square in which the railway bridge falls. Use the figures in the southwest corner of this square: Eastings **17**, Northings **74**. This gives a unique reference: **SP 17 74**, accurate to 1 km.

Step 3: To give a more precise reference accurate to 100 m you need to estimate how many tenths along and how many tenths up this 1 km square the feature is (to help with this the 1 km square is divided into four 500 m squares). This makes the bridge about **8** tenths along and about **1** tenth up from the southwest corner.

This gives a unique reference: **SP 178 741**, accurate to 100 m.

Eastings (read from left to right along the bottom) come before Northings (read from bottom to top). If you have trouble remembering say to yourself "Along the hall, THEN up the stairs"!

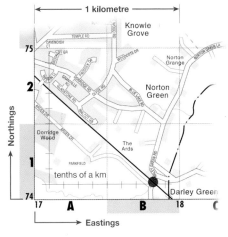

PHILIP'S MAPS
the Gold Standard for drivers

◆ **Philip's street atlases cover every county in England, Wales, Northern Ireland and much of Scotland**

◆ Every named street is shown, including alleys, lanes and walkways

◆ Thousands of additional features marked: stations, public buildings, car parks, places of interest

◆ Route-planning maps to get you close to your destination

◆ Postcodes on the maps and in the index

◆ Widely used by the emergency services, transport companies and local authorities

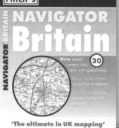

'The ultimate in UK mapping'
The Sunday Times

For national mapping, choose **Philip's Navigator Britain** the most detailed road atlas available of England, Wales and Scotland. Hailed by Auto Express as 'the ultimate road atlas', the atlas shows every road and lane in Britain.

Street atlases currently available

England
Bedfordshire and Luton
Berkshire
Birmingham and West Midlands
Bristol and Bath
Buckinghamshire and Milton Keynes
Cambridgeshire and Peterborough
Cheshire
Cornwall
Cumbria
Derbyshire
Devon
Dorset
County Durham and Teesside
Essex
North Essex
South Essex
Gloucestershire and Bristol
Hampshire
North Hampshire
South Hampshire
Herefordshire Monmouthshire
Hertfordshire
Isle of Wight
Kent
East Kent
West Kent
Lancashire
Leicestershire and Rutland
Lincolnshire
Liverpool and Merseyside
London
Greater Manchester
Norfolk
Northamptonshire
Northumberland
Nottinghamshire
Oxfordshire
Shropshire
Somerset
Staffordshire
Suffolk

Surrey
East Sussex
West Sussex
Tyne and Wear
Warwickshire and Coventry
Wiltshire and Swindon
Worcestershire
East Yorkshire Northern Lincolnshire
North Yorkshire
South Yorkshire
West Yorkshire

Wales
Anglesey, Conwy and Gwynedd
Cardiff, Swansea and The Valleys
Carmarthenshire, Pembrokeshire and Swansea
Ceredigion and South Gwynedd
Denbighshire, Flintshire, Wrexham
Herefordshire Monmouthshire
Powys

Scotland
Aberdeenshire
Ayrshire
Dumfries and Galloway
Edinburgh and East Central Scotland
Fife and Tayside
Glasgow and West Central Scotland
Inverness and Moray
Lanarkshire
Scottish Borders

Northern Ireland
County Antrim and County Londonderry
County Armagh and County Down
Belfast
County Tyrone and County Fermanagh

How to order
Philip's maps and atlases are available from bookshops, motorway services and petrol stations. You can order direct from the publisher by phoning **0207 531 8473** or online at **www.philips-maps.co.uk**
For bulk orders only, e-mail philips@philips-maps.co.uk